The Legal-Economic Nexus

This book examines the legal-economic process in which the body of law is continually evolving. Combining a selection of old and new essays, Warren J. Samuels addresses the role of manufactured belief, power, the nature and sources of rights, the construction of markets by firms and by governments and the problem of continuity and change in the form of the question of the selectively defined status quo and its status.

Samuels questions both the absolutist character of government, rights, markets, and legal principles as well as the accepted ideational structure of law. In examining the processes through which economies and economists work out results, he demonstrates how policy is structured and manipulated by human social construction. The final chapter argues against policy advocacy by professionals qua professionals and for a practice of policy diffidence.

The Legal-Economic Nexus would be of interest to both economists and legal professionals as well as researchers in the history of economic thought and the social construction of law.

Warren J. Samuels is Emeritus Professor of Economics, Michigan State University. Author of a long and prestigious list of books and journal articles, his contributions include the co-editorship of *The History of Economic Thought: A Reader*, also published by Routledge.

The Economics of Legal Relationships
Edited by Nicholas Mercuro and Michael D. Kaplowitz
Michigan State University

* The first three volumes listed above are published by and available from Elsevier.

THE ECONOMICS OF LEGAL RELATIONSHIPS

Sponsored by the Michigan State University College of Law

STATEMENT OF SCOPE

The Economics of Legal Relationships is a book series dedicated to publishing original scholarly contributions that systematically analyze legal-economic issues. Each book can take a variety of forms:

1. It may be comprised of a collection of original articles devoted to a single theme, edited by a guest volume editor.
2. It may be a collection of refereed articles derived from the Series Editors' "call for papers" on a particular legal-economic topic.
3. An individual may wish to (co)author an entire volume.

Each book in the series is published in hardback, approximately 250–300 pages in length and is dedicated to:

- Formulate and/or critique alternative theories of law and economics—including—the new law and economics, the economics of property rights, institutionalist and neoinstitutionalist law and economics, public choice theory, Austrian law and economics, or social norms in law and economics.
- Analyze a variety of public policy issues related to the interface between judicial decisions and/or statutory law and the economy.
- Explore the economic impact of political and legal changes brought on by new technologies and/or environmental and natural resource concerns.
- Examine the broad array of legal/economic issues surrounding the deregulation/re-regulation phenomena.
- Analyze the systematic effects of legal change on incentives and economic performance.

CALL FOR AUTHORS/VOLUME EDITORS/TOPICS

An individual who is interested in either authoring an entire volume, or editing a future volume of *The Economics of Legal Relationships* should submit a 3–5 page prospectus to one of the series editors. Each prospectus must include: (1) the prospective title of the volume; (2) a brief description of the organizing theme of the volume whether single authored or edited; (3) an identification of the line of literature from which the proposed topic emanates; and (4) either a table of contents or, if edited, a list of potential contributors along with tentative titles of their contributions. Send prospectus to either series editor. Please note that the series editors only accepts individual manuscripts for publication consideration in response to a specific "Call for Papers."

Send prospectus directly to either series editor:

Professor Nicholas Mercuro
Michigan State University
College of Law
East Lansing, MI 48824
phone: (517) 432-6897
e-mail mercuro@msu.edu

Professor Michael D. Kaplowitz
Michigan State University
Department of Community Agriculture,
  Recreation, and Resource Studies
East Lansing, MI 48824
phone: (517) 355-0101
e-mail kaplowit@msu.edu

The Legal-Economic Nexus

Warren J. Samuels

**With joint authorship by
James M. Buchanan, Kirk D. Johnson,
Marianne Johnson, A. Allan Schmid, and
James D. Shaffer**

Routledge
Taylor & Francis Group

LONDON AND NEW YORK

First published 2007
by Routledge
2 Park Square, Milton Park, Abingdon, Oxon OX14 4RN

Simultaneously published in the USA and Canada
by Routledge
270 Madison Ave, New York, NY 10016

Routledge is an imprint of the Taylor & Francis Group,
an informa business

Transferred to Digital Printing 2009

© 2007 Warren J. Samuels

Typeset in Baskerville by
Newgen Imaging Systems (P) Ltd, Chennai, India

British Library Cataloguing in Publication Data
A catalogue record for this book is available from the British Library

Library of Congress Cataloging in Publication Data
A catalog record for this book has been requested

ISBN10: 0–415–77179–X (hbk)
ISBN10: 0–415–49360–9 (pbk)
ISBN10: 0–203–96467–5 (ebk)

ISBN13: 978–0–415–77179–5 (hbk)
ISBN13: 978–0–415–49360–4 (pbk)
ISBN13: 978–0–203–96467–5 (ebk)

This collection is dedicated to A. Allan Schmid and Harry M. Trebing, friends and scholars, whose intellectual insights, moral support, and assistance for over thirty-five years have been invaluable

Contents

Notes on contributors

James M. Buchanan was awarded the 1986 Nobel Prize in Economic Science. He is a founder of the field of public choice theory. He has specialized in the study of public finance, the philosophy of economics, and the political aspects of economics.

Kirk D. Johnson is Assistant Professor of Economics at Goldey-Beacom College, Wilmington, Delaware. He specializes in history of economic thought and in economic history.

Marianne Johnson is Assistant Professor of Economics at the University of Wisconsin-Oshkosh. She specializes in history of economic thought and in public economics.

Warren J. Samuels is Professor Emeritus of Economics at Michigan State University. He specializes in history of economic thought, law and economics, and methodology.

A. Allan Schmid is University Distinguished Professor, Emeritus, Department of Agricultural Economics, Michigan State University. He has specialized in public choice theory, law and economics, benefit cost analysis, and institutional and behavioral economics, and is the author of *Conflict and Cooperation: Institutional and Behavioral Economics* and *Property, Power and Public Choice*.

James D. Shaffer is Professor Emeritus of Agricultural Economics in Michigan State University. He specialized in institutional and behavioral economics and in food systems economics, especially practical issues relating to the organization of agricultural production and food distribution, and the relationship of political and economic power.

Preface

Why would anyone expect the domains of law and government and of economics to be different than any other realm of life of man and society, for example, the practice of medicine or the cooking of foods? In every sphere of life there are problems of choice and decision making, multiple perspectives, the quest for status (or as Adam Smith also put it, social recognition and moral approval), selective perspective, wishful thinking, and, *inter alia*, the desire by many people to influence how other people think and do (or not do) things. We often seem to expect differences but are surprised when the differences are not those we anticipated. There is a difference between belief and truth, though we do not agree what the difference is. There is a difference between mentalities: some people require determinacy and closure, others are more or less content with open-endedness and ambiguity, though there is some of each mentality in each of us. There are differences in our beliefs as to what it takes to live together. There are differences in our interest and activity in attempting to change the working rules in each sphere of life in one's own favor, for example, some of us have a law making mentality and others a law taking one.

Two decades ago I made a curious decision which I fortunately did not carry out. For several decades I had worked on the study of the economic role of government and on the history of economic thought, the latter including philosophical methodology and the philosophy of economics. My ostensible, and self-fooling, need to make a choice was predicated upon a sense that although I was deeply interested in both fields, in order to make deeper progress, I should concentrate in the one in which I was, by some unknown metric, "more inter-ested." I should have known better. From a time even before I began graduate school I understood that there were deep connections between the economic role of government and the history of economic thought. As Smith would put it, these connections were often recondite and invisible, and the task of the scholar was to study them together at arm's length. The official makers of law often unwittingly, but often consciously too, put into effect in the law what they thought would make life better for whoever's interest they had in mind; these interests were typically, certainly increasingly, economic. Economics itself had been driven by different positions on the economic role of government and therefore on economic policy, notably insofar as it influenced the distributions of wealth, income, and opportunity.

Much, but by no means all, of my work, therefore, was on the economic role of government in the history of economic thought. In retrospect, there was no way I could, or should, concentrate on one field to the serious disregard of the other. The progress I needed to make was in studying the nexus formed by the two fields, just as the progress I had been making in studying the economic role of government was concentrated in the study of the legal-economic nexus. And thus I continued along the path I had followed since my intellectual beginnings.

The path itself has many sources of and many branches in its development. During the period I was thinking about assembling this book and studying and writing new material, the *Kelo* decision, related to the two Michigan cases principally discussed in Chapter 10, was issued by the United States Supreme Court. The second Michigan decision unanimously held against an economic development exclusion from eminent domain; the *Kelo* decision held, by five to four, the opposite. And while I was completing Chapter 3 on the nature and sources of rights, I read of the efforts of William Empson's father to take advantage of the ancient legal maxim that an owner of surface land owned a conic section starting at the center of the Earth and extending to the end of the universe, a principle entering at various times into legal decision making over subsurface mining rights and airline overflights ("He who owns the ground possesses also to the sky, is the maxim of the law, upwards...and, downwards, whatever is in a direct line between the surface of any land and the center of the earth" (Blackstone, W. (1959) [1765, 1766] *Commentaries on the Laws of England.* J. W. Ehrlich, ed. New York: Capricorn Books: 123)). This arises in Empson's father's will in a situation summarized by a reviewer of the first volume of Empson's biography. Discussing Empson's satiric poem, *Legal Fiction*, which deals with the maxim, John Gross reports that the poem was in part "highly personal,...based on an exceptionally elaborate will left by Empson's father...[who died when Empson, the youngest of four siblings, was nine]... aimed at securing his children and their descendants a share in his estate for the next two hundred years" (John Gross, "The Genius of Ambiguity," *The New York Review of Books*, March 23, 2006: 28). The biographer notes that the father was reacting to the Settled Land Act of 1882, a major consequence of which was removing the presumption that land would be kept in the family (John Haffenden, *William Empson*, Volume 1: *Among the Mandarins*, New York: Oxford University Press, 2005: 44 and *passim*). Gross also compares the views of Empson and I. A. Richards, Empson's supervisor in English at Magdalene College, Cambridge, on a dichotomy which is rampant and in my view central (going back to Adam Smith and beyond) but largely unspecified in modern economics: "Where Richards thought of poetry as a means of attaining harmony,...Empson saw it as an expression of conflict" (Gross 2006: 29).

I want to thank the staff of Routledge and Taylor & Francis for their support, their cooperation, their courtesies, and their professionalism. Alan Jarvis I have known for many years and have admired his capabilities. Rob Langham, an exceedingly capable and decent man, is a pleasure to work with; he is a splendid editor. Taiba Batool is a wonderful and effective facilitator. I have been blessed with many fine and sympathetic publisher's editors; these folks are among the finest.

In the appropriate place in individual chapters in this book I have acknowledged the help, of one kind or another, of many individual scholars. Here I would like to make "lifetime" thank-you acknowledgments to the following people, listed alphabetically: Jeff Biddle, Peter Boettke, Y. S. Brenner, James M. Buchanan, Bob Coats, John Davis, Ross Emmett, Jerry Evensky, Kirk Johnson, Marianne Johnson, Steve Medema, Mark Perlman, Allan Schmid, Jim Shaffer, Harry Trebing, and so many others it is almost unfair to mention these and not more. I value the cost of silence to be greater than the cost of omission.

Acknowledgments

The author appreciates permissions to reprint from publishers, editors, and co-authors for the following: from the *George Washington Law Review*, "The Legal-Economic Nexus," vol. 57 (August 1989), pp. 1556–78; from *Social Research*, "Markets and Their Social Construction," vol. 71, no. 2 (Summer 2004), pp. 357–70, www.socres.org; from Edward Elgar, Brookfield, VT: "Joseph J. Spengler's Concept of the 'Problem of Order': A Reconsideration and Extension," in Philip Arestis, ed., *Employment, Economic Growth and the Tyranny of the Market*, 1996, pp. 185–99, "The Rule of Law and the Capture and Use of Government in a World of Inequality," in Warren J. Samuels, *Economics, Governance and Law*, 2002, pp. 61–79, and "The Duke of Argyll and Henry George: Land Ownership and Governance," co-authored with Kirk D. Johnson and Marianne Johnson, in John Laurent, ed., *Henry George's Legacy in Economic Thought*, 2005, pp. 99–147; from The University of Michigan Press, Ann Arbor, MI, "An Evolutionary Approach to Law and Economics," co-authored with A. Allan Schmid and James D. Shaffer, in Richard W. England, ed., *Evolutionary Concepts in Contemporary Economics*, 1994, pp. 93–110 and "Two Views of Government: A Conversation," co-authored with James M. Buchanan, in David M. Levy and Sandra Peart, eds, *The Street Porter and the Philosopher*; from Elsevier, Amsterdam, "The Status of the Status Quo: The Buchanan Colloquium," *Research in the History of Economic Thought and Methodology*, vol. 22-A, pp. 219–33 and "The Problem of the Status of the Status Quo: Some Comments," *Research in the History of Economic Thought and Methodology*, vol. 22-A, pp. 235–56; from the *Review of Political Economy*, "Some Problems in the Use of Language in Economics," vol. 13, no. 1 (2001), pp. 91–100; from *Storia del Pensiero Economico*, "The Duke of Argyll and Edwin L. Godkin as Precursors to Hayek on the Relation of Ignorance to Policy," co-authored with Marianne Johnson and Kirk Johnson, Part I: vol. 1, no. 1 (2004), pp. 5–32; Part II: vol. 1, no. 2 (2004), pp. 37–67; Part III: vol. 2, no. 1, pp. 35–71, and Part IV: vol. 2, no. 2 (2005), pp. 19–38 ; from M. E. Sharpe, Armonk, NY, "The Pervasive Proposition, 'What Is, Is and Ought to Be': A Critique," in William S. Milberg, ed., *The Megacorp and Macrodynamics: Essays in Memory of Alfred Eichner*, 1992, pp. 273–85.

Chapters 1, 3, 10, 16, and 17 have not hitherto been published.

Part I

Rights, markets, and power

The legal-economic nexus

1 Introduction

Belief and power

Legal-economic discourse

This collection of chapters, some hitherto published and some published here for the first time, manifests a curious irony arising from the juxtaposition of economic theory and law to the history of economic thought and the economic role of government. Our languages, our modes of discourse, especially those of economic theory and law, postulate the economy and the polity (law and government) as two separate domains. In this respect, our language is a function of our ideology or ontology, and our ideology/ontology is a function of our language.

Problems of language in economics, and in law, abound. How we handle them can either help emphasize the inevitable necessity of choice in the two fields or finesse and obfuscate the exercise of choice (see especially Chapters 3 and 10). In this respect, how we handle the problem of choice in our language influences other ideas and the policies through which choices are made.

In actuality, the foregoing is not merely the interaction of the domains of economy and law but their ongoing mutual or recursive reformation, in the sense that through interaction each domain is reconstituted over time. Polity is a function of economy, and economy is a function of polity. Neither need be given ubiquitous and absolute ideological or existential priority.

There are serious issues generated by the separateness of the two domains of polity and economy, the inevitable necessity of choice, and the recursive inter-dependence and over-determination of the two domains. The history of economic thought suggests that how we handle these issues will be a function of the policy proposals we adopt and the policy proposals we adopt will be a function of how we handle those issues.

Consider a simple model in which the world is comprised of A, B, and C domains. Let students of A exclude B and C; similarly with students of B and C. If A, say, is the only domain considered by an analyst, then domains B and C neither enter into anyone's definition of reality nor interact with A or with each other. If A is the economy and B is government/law/politics, then the economy, A, excludes all serious relations with B.

The actual interrelationship(s) of A and B, of economic and legal processes, is the point at issue. Economics scholars tend to omit B and legal scholars tend to exclude A.

The irony is that economic theory and law have strongly been mutually exclusive; economic theorists and legal theorists even though they may discuss them, typically exclude each other's domains. Yet the history of economic thought is heavily laden with discussions of the economic role of government. The economist who considers the law as either given or exogenous to the economy, is motivated to elicit implications from a-institutional economic theory for government policy. The varied treatments of government and law in relation to economics suggest something else is also going on. That something is some combination of two developmental paths. The history of economic thought is driven by efforts to control government policy, and the areas of government policy principally targeted concern the distributions of income, wealth, and opportunity.

The foregoing means that both belief and power are important. Belief, because people act on what they believe, and power, because power determines whose beliefs, or interests, will count, where, and how.

The study of law and economics, or of the economic role of government, does not just happen. Most work on the subject is normative and subjective. It is even very difficult to hold a friendly conversation with someone on a normative topic without at least one party seeking to demand of the other their normative thoughts and to provide likewise their own normative views. When one tries to discuss the matter at issue in a positive, that is, descriptive and/or explanatory, way, the response tends to reflect the perspective of a particular normative position, possibly that of the respondent's favorite politician.

Fundamental conflicts

The chapters comprising this collection together touch on and otherwise exhibit several conflicts. This is because they deal with fundamental aspects of the inter-relations between legal and economic processes or what I have come to call the legal-economic nexus. Two of the conflicts concern the sense in which I intend "fundamental" to be taken.

The first of these two has to do with two types of realism and thereby with social constructionism. Let Realism I connote a subject matter comprised of "the" actual economy in all its complexity and inclusive of individual choice, power structure and comparable factors and forces amounting to social control. Realism I therefore consists of both methodological individualist and method-ological collectivist phenomena rather than a pretense of including only the former while more or less surreptitiously selectively introducing and giving effect to some of the latter. Let Realism I have as its opponent a pure a-institutional conceptual economy relating to no actual economy but driven by a research protocol requiring determinate unique optimal equilibrium solutions to all problems, and expressing itself in supposedly neutral mathematical formalism. Now let Realism II connote a subject matter comprised of a given, transcendent, absolute, and ultimate natural order of things. Suppose further that the conceptual-economy opponent of Realism I is the analytical equivalent of Realism II. One result is to enhance the perceived importance of formal, conceptual analysis insofar as—"really" inasmuch as—it studies the ostensible fundamentals of the economy rather than such actual or so-called epiphenomena as law and custom, power and belief, and so on. The position taken here is that of Realism I. Social constructivism arises inasmuch as the actual economy is created—through deliberative and non-deliberative decision making inextricably combined (Samuels 1999)— and not derived from a given, transcendent, absolute and ultimate natural order of things. Fundamental in this context means important to but not imposed on mankind.

One aspect of the foregoing conflict comprises another fundamental conflict between two mindsets. One way of thinking or mindset, M I, is comfortable with a definition of reality that exhibits ambiguity and open-endedness; let's designate it Realism I, or R I. The other way of thinking, M II, is comfortable only with a definition of reality that projects clarity and closure. Realism I is congruent with the first mindset, M I; most if not all other forms of realism are consonant with the second mindset, M II.

The second conflict has to do with the game of pretense which is part of the legal-economic nexus. On the one hand, I propose to examine with an open mind the fundamental processes of the legal-economic nexus. On the other hand, it is more or less widely felt that social control must not be seen to be social control: the legal-economic nexus, in order to be effective, must be taken as, but not seen to be, part of the mythic, symbolic and linguistic systems of a society. To see those systems as they are, is to render them less absolutist for purposes of social control, and to ask questions, which is to lead to doubt about them. The former means that I must try to penetrate the linguistic self-perceptions that are deployed by the social control forces of society to legitimize their role in society, and so on, in absolutist terms. These self-perceptions have attributed to them an illusory ontological status that is difficult to penetrate. For one thing, they have been drilled into us from early in life. For another, we cannot be certain that what we consider to be the objective fundamentals of the legal-economic nexus are just that and not another version of someone's mythic, symbolic and linguistic systems. Thus many leaders and non-leaders of society privately believe that the social control institutions must resist their examination by someone with an open mind as a danger to the effective functioning of those institutions. They must be seen neither in the nude (as in "the king has no clothes") nor as lacking ontological substance. Some people believe that because they find it convenient, pressure minimizing, and efficient; others, because it offers them and others like them protection in the name of the public interest. I sympathize with but do not concur with the former group; I do not sympathize with the latter group and sometimes find them hypocritical and repugnant. It is sometimes difficult to tell them apart. Fundamental in this sense means congruent with what actually transpires and not with what some economic activists would have us believe. Pervading actual practice is the differences, first, between latent and manifest function and, second, between those with a law-making mentality and those with a law-taking mentality (the law makers seeking to create law takers of the naïve).

The third conflict has to do with one's attitude toward the policy making process. Someone who emphasizes, as I do, the importance of private and public policy in making and remaking the polity and the economy, might be imagined to do so either because they had their own agenda for policy or because, having learned of the importance of policy, they want to be active in its making. I do not castigate those who take an activist stance. I admittedly cast a doubting look at those who are activist on behalf of their own causes but would deny, under color of "laissez faire" (Samuels 2005), the same opportunity to others. Nonetheless, my analysis includes those who undertake the social role of policy activist.

My personal interest, however, is different. I seek to understand what is really (in the sense of Realism I) going on in the legal-economic nexus. I have my own mix of positions—which may appear liberal or conservative to others depending on the ideological interpretation placed on the positions. But I do not feel that as an economist I should use my discipline to advance my positions. In Chapter 17 of this volume, I make the case for policy diffidence rather than policy activism for the economist qua economist. In the contest between objectivity and advocacy I opt for objectivity—with its own array of difficulties.

The reader must decide if in fact I act upon that view. I think I do. But others do not so think. I have published materials in support of the factual basis for believing that the classical economists had an important place for law in providing systemic economic foundations and in serving as an instrument of change and also a place for morals, custom, religion, and education as elements of their theory of economic policy. Some thought that what I said about law could only be written by a statist and what I wrote about moral rules, and so on only by someone who was culturally conservative. Whereas the truth of the matter, as I see it, is that I am only making sense in the form of positive propositions about what the classical economists believed (or what their writings, in my view, reduce to), namely, that the framework of the market had both legal and moral components. I have published on my own behalf, and not as an historian of thought, my views on government being ubiquitous and important, on policy with regard to relative rights not being settled once and for all time, on the ubiquity and importance of power (non-pejoratively defined), and so on. This too has elicited criticism that I am a statist and, apropos of power, perilously close to Marx. Jim Buchanan and I agree that the issues we discuss should be more widely examined among economists. Jim, who I think of, in part, as undertaking the high priest role, thinks of me as subversive for not building into my analyses his or some other propaganda for freedom. Were it only that simple! My only relevant value is a preference for a widespread diffusion of power in order to render power relatively innocuous.

Finally, while some people have remarked about my fondness for calling attention to irony in political and economic affairs, no one, to my knowledge, has remarked about my cynicism (Samuels 1974: 190–2). In the notes for my lectures in my graduate course in law and economics, I pointed out that the "course will aggravate some because it explores the fundamental importance of government for the economy and because it attempts to reach no conclusions as to the proper role of government or as to correct specific policies of government," for example, that "in affirming that government will necessarily promote certain interests rather than others, it affirms nothing as to whose interest will count and be promoted by government—except to affirm that government will promote certain interests rather than others even when it superficially appears that it is not," and that we must "distinguish between language which describes and language which attempts to motivate psychologically for purposes of power." I conclude with the caution that I "will appear greatly cynical in discounting various claims; and admit to great deal of cynicism." Here I point out that, in my view, my legal-economic analyses are not substantively affected by my cynicism; the cynicism enables me to apply high discount factors to language that is ideological, wishful thinking, and adopted to mobilize and motivate.

The legal-economic nexus

The title of this collection needs a brief introductory explanation, particularly for those not familiar with Chapter 2, from which the title is taken, first published in 1989. The concept of a legal-economic nexus was formed in order to overcome conceptually the artificial separation between law and government, on the one hand, and the economy, on the other. It is my conclusion, based on some fifty years of reading and of observation, that the polity and the economy are neither given and transcendental nor separate and self-subsistent. They are matters of continuing human social construction. The process in which this construction and re-construction takes place combines the polity impacting on economy and the economy impacting on polity; to put the matter differently, it combines the so-called private sector impacting the so-called public sector and the public sector impacting the private sector. An investigator cannot know one without also knowing the other, and, far from being only interacting spheres, they mutually determine each other, and can best be studied as emanating from a common nexus.

In most, though not all, of my writings on law and economics I have concentrated on problems of power. Those problems certainly arise in these pages. My concentration here, however, is on the belief system of society, particularly insofar as it relates to the conflict of continuity and change—a conflict ultimately over the structure of power. I am interested in the regnant belief system as the context of meaning for mainstream law and economics. Such work takes place within the dominant belief system of society; it is an extension thereof. I need not assume the accuracy of any particular belief system.

I find that the field of legal-economic theory is an example of Adam Smith's theory of practice in his History of Astronomy (1980). There Smith argued that while truth (correct description or explanation) is the premier desired objective, we very often have to be content merely with propositions that soothe the imagination or, as George Shackle expressed it, put minds at rest (Shackle 1967: 288; Smith 1980). Smith made this point a chief element of his theory of intellectual history, but, with relatively few recent exceptions, it has been largely forgotten in that field. Ironically, Smith's theory itself can be given more than one reading: One is that given here: truth is the desired objective but we very often must settle for propositions that set minds at rest. Another reading is that truth is impossible and we are left with multiple interpretations. Smith's point is that the imagination is soothed, set at rest by providing a satisfying proposition that yields closure.

One tendency of the human mind, reinforced by acculturation, is to treat legal and economic arrangements, typically in terms of rights, as given and transcendent, whereas it is my argument that these are matters of human social construction. While rights structure decision making processes, rights are also a product of decision making processes. I consider the legal-economic nexus to be the domain of society in which all this takes place (Chapter 2). "All this" is an interactive, recursive, over-determined set of relationships. Law, so far from being given by the nature of things, is a matter of policy, not the opposite of policy. The treatment of rights as absolute is part of the process of working things out, things that are relativist and socially constructed. Faith in a given and transcendent natural law and natural rights is either imposed by the socialization of belief, wishful thinking, or a tendency of the human mind consequent to a need for certitude and closure. Two keys to what is going on are, first, the role of belief system in distinguishing the "natural" from the "artificial" and, second, the efforts of political, religious and economic interest groups to manufacture and inculcate the belief system in which policy is made. One characteristic of this process is the recursive dualism in which policy is a function of belief and belief is a function of policy. This is a process of asymmetric mutual manipulation. It is asymmetric because of the various inequalities of power within the legal-economic nexus. Analyzing the legal-economic nexus in static models has the twin effects of reifying the status quo selectively identified and of finessing and casting out of analytical bounds the recursive and evolving nature of the legal-economic nexus.

A preface to rights, their nature, ubiquity, and sources

Rights in general, especially property rights, tend to be treated as absolute whereas in fact they are a matter of social construction and are relative. They are relative to each other, relative in their economic significance, relative to the actions of government and of other economic agents, and relative inasmuch as they may be modeled in different and conflicting ways. Consider two examples.

A common and often publicized occurrence is the announcement that a corporation will restructure its pension program. The term "restructure" is a euphemism for "cut." That a corporation may unilaterally restructure/cut pensions is due to the pension program being neither fully vested in the workers nor fully funded as an operating expense. The pension program is part of the total compensation package constituting payment to labor for its services. The pension program could originate in various ways. It could have been required by legislation. It could have been adopted through collective bargaining. It could have been adopted unilaterally by the corporation. In each case the corporation has retained its right to cut wages in the form of cutting pensions. Under a program that included full vesting in individual workers and full funding, no such "restructuring" would have been possible, at least not without the consent of the workers.

A less conspicuous example concerns changes in university programs enabling individual faculty members to be temporarily relieved of part or all of their teaching load. The dean of the college may have unilaterally instituted the program of research leaves in order to motivate more research and publications. The dean may now seek to either restructure the program or reduce its frequency of award to individual faculty members. In the event, a faculty member says that the program cannot change insofar as it applies to him. The professor bases his claim on the letter sent by the dean offering the faculty member a position in the college and, upon the offer being accepted by the professor, the letter constitutes a contract. The professor claims a right on the basis of his letter of appointment.

The example of corporate restructuring of pensions is significant in several respects. It points to the one-sided construction of contracts, contrary to the imagery of "free contract" and "bargaining." Almost all contracts are drawn up by the economically superior party and the other party can only accept or reject the terms of the contract; no bargaining as to terms can take place. These contracts are standardized contracts of adhesion. Workers can take or reject the total package of contract terms, one of which deals with pensions. The example also points to the power of the economically superior party to change the rights of the other party(ies). At one point in time the employee has stipulated rights to pension income. Subsequently, some part of pension income has been "restructured," that is, cut. Another point concerns the relation of the law of pensions. Pension law can limit the power of corporations to restructure, or cut, pensions, thus establishing certain protections—rights—of value to workers. Such a law, however, tends to favor employers; changes in law tend to be authored by lobbyists, corporate attorneys or the staffs of trade and similar associations.

The research award example has parallels in plans to bring about changes in curricula and correlative changes in staff, changes in health-cost programs, and changes in other insurance programs. The example in general points to the institutionalization of, and conflicts between, several different modes of decision making within colleges and universities. These include, first, the specific terms of personal contracts—representations contained in letters formally offering positions. Were the university to adopt, or be required by law to adopt, a standardized contract, offer letters would have to discuss the limits of the power of the letter's author, given the adopted contract. Second, all colleges and universities have adopted general rules on a variety of subjects, in part giving effect to privacy laws, freedom of information laws, problems of student cheating, sexual or racial harassment laws, administrative discretion, faculty grievances, and so on. These rules are typically presented in a Faculty Handbook. They are adopted and they are changed by one or more decision making processes. One relevant change occurs when a new decision making process is added; examples include student participation and faculty participation. Third, the principal tension in institutions of higher learning is between administrative decision making and faculty decision making. Among the aspects of this tension is administrative determination of budgets and of faculty salaries. Specific allocations of resources between the colleges of a university and between the departments of a college greatly facilitate or constrain the opportunities for decision making by other groups. Many faculty senates and committees are advisory, not policy making. Under propitious conditions, consensus is reached whatever the formal relations between groups. Under unpropitious conditions, acrimony and antagonism dominate.

In all the processes, structures, and interactions identified so far, rights, already a mix of formal and informal, are subtly changed. Another situation occurs when senior faculty have their informal rights, or influence, challenged and limited by newer and younger faculty. Still another situation exists when the legal status of a chairman is that of a head, that is, given by law the power to make all decisions. In practice, some form of "democracy" is achieved informally, for example, an "advisory committee" technically and legally only gives advice but in practice acts as a policy making senate or cabinet. A final example concerns the gray area encompassing the power of the legislature, the legislative committee on financing higher education, the chair of that committee, and the president, and so on of the university, a situation made further complicated, ambiguous, and laden with rights-related subtleties, when a chancellor presides over some or all state institutions of higher learning.

The keys are, first, the locus of the power to change rights and, second, the conflicts between decision making processes. It will be noticed that the technical economic condition enabling pension restructuring is the fact of a future payment. Arguably all other suppliers are immune from efforts to recover past payments to them in whole or in part. They are immune, however, if there is no future relationship between supplier and buyer. There may be no future relationship under the original contract but the supplier may desire future contracts; indeed, if this buyer is their main source of business, the supplier may be willing to sacrifice the present loss of past income in order to have future income. The only other situation negating immunity is if the original contract has a recovery clause—which would be very highly unusual. The political-economic condition pervading these relationships and outcomes is power structure or structure of mutual coercion. The supplier may be a source of subassemblies, marketing and advertising, raw materials, working capital, and long-term financing. Dominant producers like to have numerous suppliers, so that the structure of mutual coercion is skewed in their favor—hence their efforts to structure markets to their advantage—efforts either directly or through government action on their behalf.

The firm seeking pension restructuring will advance in its support the necessity for flexibility. The argument has an obvious basis: flexibility enables management greater options in its policy making. But the argument is selectively applied between capital and labor, within capital, and within labor—depending in large part on relative power. It also depends on whether management is seeking to establish a precedent that might someday be applied to them: golden parachutes and bonuses in the fact of failure.

...And beyond

While Chapter 2 is prelude to much if not all that follows, Chapter 3 addresses the nature and sources of rights. Rights are the key institutions of an economy. They take different forms and arise in different ways. Although they typically are described in absolutist terms, they are probabilistic works in progress (see Chapter 10 and Samuels 1966: appendix; Samuels and Mercuro 1979, 1980, 1999). This chapter first examines the theory of property and the concept of due process of law (see also Chapter 9 of this volume, on the rule of law) both as sources of property in action and of the language in which choices are expressed. I also survey the wide array of ways in which property arises and identify certain problems of legal language relating thereto (see Chapter 10 of this volume, Samuels 2001, and Samuels and Mercuro 1999). Chapter 3 also examines the larger context in which rights are formed. This larger context is comprised of social control in the form of belief and power and their interrelationships, a context that can also be interpreted as populated with power players. People, in this area as in so many other areas, are influenced by their language, their sentiments, their material and ideological interests, and so on. The law of property coupled with the network of constitutional provisions (at state and federal levels) provides the terminology which influences courts and legislatures, and courts and legislatures influence the meaning of the terminology thereafter, in a continuing, perhaps cyclical, reworking of the bundle of elements (sticks, some have called them) that comprises property. Whatever the language, however, the available positions tend to be predictable. Every so often, however, courts and/or legislatures will create new linguistic formulae, new positions on which to hang their decision. The rights of which we speak and over which we argue, emerge from the processes just overviewed. The language is that of the institution of property and of the concept of due process.

I have noted just a few lines before that rights are probabilistic works in progress. By that I intend to be understood as saying that the content and relative interrelations of rights are created in a process of working them out. Rights are neither given nor transcendent nor absolute; they are worked out in the process of governing ourselves. The approach to rights taken here is legal realist, pragmatist and existentialist. Rights are man-made and relative to other rights and to economic conditions. To say that is in aid of accurately comprehending what rights are all about.

Rights are both a condition and a consequence of economic activity. The economic significance of rights arises within markets. Like rights, markets are neither given nor transcendent: markets, too, are socially constructed; the constructing agencies are private corporations and governments. In Chapter 4, markets are examined as a result of human action in the form of the policies of firms and government. This approach indicates the incompleteness of treating "the market" in a purely conceptual a-institutional manner, as the abstract control mechanism of the economy, and as something that willy nilly "works." Through the legal-economic nexus markets are created, comprised of the legal and other institutions that form and operate through them. These institutions and the legal-economic nexus also are what they are because of the policy making activities of firms and governments. A crux of these activities is the competition among firms to control and use government to reconstruct markets to their respective advantage. One potential aspect of markets is indeed "competition." Economists and others do not agree among themselves as to the meaning of competition and the conditions under which it exists. Behavior that is deemed competitive under one definition is non-competitive under another. So if the phrase "the market works" is problematic, so too is the proposition that "markets are inherently competitive." One would have to have an idea as to the meaning of "works" and of "competitive"—and one might disagree. What is much clearer is that firms act not only to produce goods at a profit but also to produce the markets in which they will operate, and do so with or without the aid of government agencies.

Given the ubiquity of government and law, it is not surprising that the juxtaposition of status quo and change of law has become central to the study of law and economics. In a sense, this is what the legal-economic nexus is all about. With the exception of one class of government actions, in changing law government is not intruding into a situation in which it has hitherto been absent but changing the interests to which it is giving legal protection—or the interests to which it is being used to give legal protection. The exception is equally telling: technological change creates the need for a new body of covering law (or the extension of an already existing body of law) in order to establish the rights, duties, immunities, and exposures of the relevant parties. Chapters 5 and 6 deal with James Buchanan's efforts to deploy the concept of the status quo in such a way as to influence government action changing the law and thereby altering the status quo. In effect, these chapters deconstruct the concept of the status quo and suggest the limits of Buchanan's argument. The topics pertinent to the concept of the status quo are vast, and include the complex relations of "is" and "ought" explored in Chapters 13 and 14: the problem of defining the status quo, the curious array of is-ought and continuity-change impacts on different meanings of the status quo, and so on.

The foregoing exhibit elements of the problem of order, that is, the processes of working out more or less temporary solutions to three conflicts: between freedom (or autonomy) and control, between continuity and change, and between hierarchy and equality. Following the lead of Joseph J. Spengler, Chapter 7 reconsiders and extends the content of the concept of order and the processes subsumed therein. One aspect of the conflict between continuity and change is the status of the status quo, dealt with in Chapters 5 and 6. Other aspects include human social construction, selective perception, social control, the ubiquity of politics, the power of language, and radical indeterminacy. If the discussion shows anything, it is how and why decision making in the legal-economic nexus is so complex and frustrating.

Chapter 8 presents a somewhat different overview of the interrelations between nominally economic and legal processes in the legal-economic nexus. The content is much the same, of course, only differently organized. The approach continues to be nonnormative. The chapter first surveys the general characteristics of the authors' evolutionary approach to law and economics. Next, it compares the foregoing approach to that of neoclassicism. Finally, the chapter outlines the principal elements of the developmental analysis at the heart of the evolutionary approach. It is an apt summary to say that in the evolutionary approach, not only is nothing given but no issue is solved once and for all time. Economic life may require settled rights, so that exchange can transfer ownership, but life continues even though new solutions to old and novel issues are worked out. Whenever a major development takes place, say, a decision rendered by a Supreme Court, some of those wedded to the received status quo, at least to the element thereof seemingly being changed by the decision, will cry "foul!" They will aver that this new threat to some rights places all rights in jeopardy, even that the decision threatens capitalism itself. The authors of Chapter 8 merely emphasize that the current decision is only one in a long line of decisions through which the economy has been developed over the centuries. A new status quo augurs to replace the old one, as it were.

A fundamental concept in contemporary economic, political, and legal theory and policy is that of the "rule of law." On the one hand, the meaning of the rule of law varies; one usage would minimize citizen input into government. On the other hand, inasmuch as one meaning of the rule of law is "democracy," it should be noted that another is "no taxation without representation." At the level of fundamental concepts, one finds multiple definitions, multiple uses, and complex and multiple interpretations of history. If a court defines a term—such as due process, rule of law, property, liberty, and so on—one way in its decision, and a later court defines it another way, then the later court has surreptitiously changed the law. Chapter 9 critiques the meaningfulness of the concept of the rule of law in light of actual practice, given the foregoing. It will be seen that identifying the concept as favored by the founding fathers, is a gross misrepresentation of their ideas and, especially, their practice.

John Marshall, the great architect of constitutional interpretation, wrote several statements informative both in and of themselves individually and in their juxtaposition. For our purposes, the following are apposite. In one case, he pleaded that "We must never forget that it is a constitution we are expounding" (*McCulloch v. Maryland*, 4 Wheaton 316, 407 (1819)) —than which no statement affirming judicial social construction can be clearer. In *Cohens v. Virginia*, 6 Wheaton, 19 U.S. 264, 389 (1821), Marshall wrote that "The people made the Constitution, and the people can unmake it. It is the creature of their own will, and lives only by their will"—another affirmation of social construction but now the operative force is declared to be "the people." Third, writing in the context of the conflict of laws, Marshall said that "It is emphatically the province and duty of the judicial department to say what the law is" (*Marbury v. Madison*, 1 Cranch 1317 (1803)).

Referring back to the conflicts outlined earlier in this chapter, it is articulations such as these which challenge the absolutist and obfuscatory argument that courts must be seen to find, not make, the law. Inasmuch as our purpose here is to accurately describe the decision making that is at the heart of the legal-economic nexus—including the role of denials that decision making is in fact going one and that the heart of law is discretion, in its adoption, its wording, its enforcement, and its educational role—it is inevitable that the conflict, itself part of the law-making process, must be both noticed and entered.

Closely related is Chapter 10, a critique of the rhetoric of the Michigan Supreme Court in two of its decisions. At first glance, the argument of this chapter may appear normative. The issue before the Court concerns the use of the power of eminent domain for the purposes of economic development. On this issue, the chapter takes no position. I am not interested in the substance of the holding per se; I am interested in how the justices go about articulating what they are doing. They maintain, *inter alia*, that they are finding the law, that the law is in the constitution as they read it, which is to say, it is in the constitution. From the point of view taken in this book, either they believe that they are finding the law, and not making the law, or that they are pretending to do so for purposes of absolutist legitimization. If the former, given social constructivism, the justices are wrong; if the latter, the argument here is that decision making and articulation can be improved and the use of questionable misleading terminology, in which mere assertions are hidden, can be eliminated or at least greatly reduced. Following Adam Smith's argument in his History of Astronomy, we are not dealing, in these decisions, with Truth, but with propositions that will soothe the mind, whatever the holding. However, laden within soothing the mind is finessing or lulling the power to think, a power surely critical to Marshall's affirmation of popular sovereignty and its effectiveness.

In the most recent (2004) of the two cases centrally figuring in its decision the Michigan Supreme Court not only rejected the economic development rationale, doing so unanimously, but explicitly reversed the earlier decision (1981) which had upheld that rationale. One year after the second Michigan decision, the United States Supreme Court, by a five to four vote, upheld the economic development rationale (*Kelo* et al. *v. City of New London* et al., 125 S. Ct. 2655 (2005)). The juxtaposition could only be more dramatic if the decision in Kelo was as one-sided as the second Michigan decision. The combination of all three decisions yields crucial insight into the role of the courts within the legal-economic nexus and to conflicting conservative principles.

Chapters 11 and 12 summarize and interpret the ideas of the Duke of Argyll, Edwin L. Godkin, Henry George, and Friedrich von Hayek. Chapter 11 shows Argyll and Godkin to be precursors of Hayek's principle of unintended and unforeseen consequences in the context of a much wider-ranging theory of ignorance in relation to policy, particularly the creation of ignorance—the unseen—in the process of manufacturing belief. The arguments herein summarized have at least three facets of significance: the substance of the arguments as such, the context and purposes of the arguments, and how the arguments relate to aspects of the legal-economic nexus. The conflicts over property and other rights are at the heart of their ideas and arguments, and have their parallels in an urban industrial capitalist system, whereas the ideas and arguments of Argyll take place within, and would for Argyll ideally promote, a post-feudal rural agrarian system, and because of the historical and institutional distance involved, enable the reader to more readily analyze the contents of the ideas and arguments. Moreover, as is evident in Chapter 12, the institution of property is by no means exactly as we know it. If property can connote governing power (see Chapter 9), then property in a post-feudal society included quite centrally and specifically the power to rule, and property in a capitalist society elicits the question of its governance status therein. These considerations are examined through an analysis of the controversy between Argyll and Henry George, who would, in the view of some, but not in the view of all, fundamentally change the institution of property. To those defending "property" George's Single Tax appeared to threaten the institution; to those defending George, his policies would further elevate what they considered distribution in accordance with earned productivity while lowering the role of unearned economic rent. At stake, once again, were conflicting nominally "conservative" principles of policy.

Chapter 12 extends the discussion to the governance historically consequent to landownership. We portray Argyll's conception and rationalizations of a particular form of the legal-economic nexus, a form becoming, in the nineteenth century, increasingly passé yet, in its bequest to later generations, critical to an understanding of the dynamics, including the language, or rhetoric, from whence the social and rights structures of modern economies emerged.

Chapters 13 and 14 examine the subtle but pregnant and surprising linguistics of, first, the relation of "ought" and "is" and, second, the ontological and epistemological problem of defining "is." These two chapters extend the discussion of the problem of the status of the status quo presented in Chapters 6 and 7. Chapter 13 deconstructs the use, and affirmation criticism of the proposition, "what is, ought to be," and Chapter 14 does much the same with the proposition, "what is, is what?"

Chapter 15 argues, in light of the foregoing and other ideas, that economists should be more diffident in advocating particular policies. Whereas Chapter 10 argues for more candor on the part of the appellate judiciary, Chapter 15 argues for greater reticence on the part of economists. The difference is due to what I take to be their respective roles in society and the manner in which I see them conducting themselves in the performance of those roles. Appellate justices hear a great variety of types of cases; only an arguably small percentage involves the question of constitutionality. John Marshall is widely given credit for establishing judicial review of constitutionality, though given an active judiciary no less seeking to expand its social role than other branches of government, such likely was inevitable. One could like or dislike judicial review of constitutionality, but factually it exists. (One could say, instead of "like or dislike," "whether it is good or bad," but that linguistic construction would arguably presume absolute categories, whereas "likes" or "dislikes" does not.) In conducting judicial review of constitutionality judges are obviously (to me) making law or participating in the law-making process, something they have always done in Common Law (and even Civil Law) countries. That they indulge in high-priestly absolutist legitimization reflects at least sensitivity to their position (they want to be well thought of) and/or a judgment that their role requires absolutist legitimization in order to better ground social control. Economists, on the other hand, are presumably scholars and scientists, engaging in the serious work of describing and explaining "the economy." For economists to seek determinate unique optimal equilibrium solutions and/or to serve as cheerleaders for the present instantiation of the market, or capitalist, economy, is tantamount to their adoption of a similarly performing high-priest role. So, if judges were more candid and less ontologically pretentious, they might perform their governance functions better; and if economists were less insistent on policy advocacy, they might perform their scholarly investigatory functions better. Greater candor from judges and greater policy diffidence from economists add up to less high-priestly activity. I have made my bases of judgment clear: I assume that judges practice judicial review of constitutionality, whether or not I like for them to do so, and that economists— not quite in the model voiced by John Maynard Keynes in which they would be more like dentists, practice being objective scholars and neither policy prescriptivists nor policy proscriptivists.

This collection might have been subtitled "The Workings of an Open Mind" in order to indicate to the reader that the analyses conducted here are not being driven by elaborate but hidden antecedent normative, or "ought," premises. I acknowledge the tendency for such premises to influence positive, or "is," analysis. My analysis is intended to be motivated by neither selective normative premises nor the research protocol stipulating the production of unique determinate equilibrium optimal solutions, a protocol requiring assumptions that rule out of analytical bounds any consideration threatening the achievement of the protocol. Instead I try to give effect to a desire to know what is going on in working out solutions to problems, and not a desire to design procedures, processes or end results. What I find are the elements of the problem of order, the role of belief system and its manufacture, and the significance of power (on power, see Samuels 1992, 1974).

A final irony: I have lauded Pareto's general social equilibrium work—what I call his model of policy—for its positive, nonnormative importance. He himself thought he was being positive and nonnormative, whereas his normative subjec- tivities are uttered on almost every page of his work. Perhaps I am wrong in urging that positive study is necessary to produce positive results; in his case, normative study seems to have produced positive results—if one works at extracting it. My only escape from this predicament is that my work, as I have said, is driven by the subjective normative preference for objective nonnormative results. And this is an escape only, I think, because of the principle of unintended and unforeseen consequences. But, and this is my final irony, my desired results are neither unintended nor unforeseen!

References

Samuels, W. J. (1966) *The Classical Theory of Economic Policy*, Cleveland, OH: World.
—— (1974) *Pareto on Policy*, New York: Elsevier.

——— (1992) *Essays on the Economic Role of Government*, vol. 1, *Fundamentals*, London: Macmillan.

——— (1999) "Hayek from the Perspective of an Institutionalist Historian of Economic Thought: An Interpretive Essay," *Journal des Economistes et des Etudes Humaines*, IX: 279–90.

——— (2001) "Some Problems in the Use of Language in Economics," *Review of Political Economy*, 13: 91–100.

——— (2005) "Laissez Faire," *Encyclopedia of Economic Sociology*, London: Routledge, 387–9.

Samuels, W. J. and N. Mercuro (1979) "The Role and Resolution of the Compensation Principle in Society: Part One—The Role," *Research in Law and Economics*, 1: 157–94.

——— (1980) "The Role and Resolution of the Compensation Principle in Society: Part Two—The Resolution," *Research in Law and Economics*, 2: 103–28.

——— (eds) (1999) *The Fundamental Interrelationship Between Government and Property*, Stamford, CT: JAI Press.

Shackle, G. L. S. (1967) *The Years of High Theory*, New York: Cambridge University Press.

Smith, A. (1980) "The History of Astronomy," in W. P. D. Wightman and J. C. Bryce (eds) *Essays on Philosophical Subjects*, New York: Oxford University Press, 33–105.

2 The legal-economic nexus

> [I]t is, however, decisive for a realistic understanding of the phenomen [*sic*] of the state to recognize the importance of that group of persons in whom it assumes social form, and of those factors which gain domination over it. This explains the state's real power and the way in which it is used and developed.
>
> (Joseph A. Schumpeter[1])

One of the deepest conceptual structures of the modern mind and discourse, in the sense of Michel Foucault, is the distinction between the "economy" and the "polity." It is a distinction that roughly parallels that between "private" and "public." These distinctions have increasingly predominated thought and discourse since the Enlightenment, since the political theories of Hobbes, Locke, Pufendorf, and Montesquieu, and since the economic theories of Smith and, yes, Marx. Political economic thought of Western civilization is imbued with the concepts, "economy" and "polity," and "private" and "public." Except for "religion" and the "nuclear family," it is difficult if not impossible to identify other such fundamental conceptions that underlie vast reaches of thought. The predominant perception is that the concepts constituting each pair are fundamentally separate and distinct, self-subsistent *vis-à-vis* each other, and in conflict. In ordinary life, we share the fundamental belief that government and the economy are separate and mutually exclusive, a belief reinforced by language and ideology.

The distinction between self-subsistent economy and self-subsistent polity is both reflected in and reinforced by the intellectual division of labor manifest in the coexisting disciplines of economics, political science, and law and jurisprudence. The distinction has actually been exacerbated by efforts (including my own) to trace the "interrelations" between legal-political and economic-market processes, or to examine the "economic foundations" of government-politics and the "legal-political foundations" of the economy. The conventional juxtapositions of "law and economics," "economics and jurisprudence," "government and economics," and "government and business," and the ubiquitous phrase, "the economic role of government," all point to the historically mutual relevance of the two spheres while linguistically continuing to postulate, and thereby reinforce, the sense of deep structural distinction between them. This distinction has also been reinforced by all modern ideologies that are economic and political in orientation.

The distinction between economy and polity both nurtures and is reinforced by our perceptions of the experience of everyday life. The economy is the sphere of production, exchange, distribution, and consumption. The polity is the sphere of elections, political parties, and politics. The economy is the sphere of working and earning a living, receiving and spending income, buying and selling goods, and making the gains from trade. The polity is the sphere of war and peace, pageantry and ceremony, and anxious conflict over controversial issues. The economy is the sphere of business firms, banks and credit unions, stock exchanges, trade unions, contracts and private property, landlords, bosses, department store and bank clerks, and consumers. The polity is the sphere of presidents or prime ministers, legislatures, courts and judges, armies, jails, and the commands or prohibitions of law. In all this terminology there is perceived existential meaning in the difference between going to work, the bank, or the grocery store, and going to the courthouse, the state legislature, or the local IRS office. If behavior is constrained maximization, the economy is perceived to be the sphere of cooperation and opportunity; the polity, the sphere of coercion and constraint. The economy is the sphere of autonomy and freedom; the polity, the sphere of authority and regulation. With this mindset and with these operative notions, the distinction between self-subsistent spheres generates certain "facts"; and the "facts," described in a certain "language" so generated, propagate the distinction between the self-subsistent spheres.

This Essay suggests another view of relevant reality. It argues that the perceived spheres of polity and economy, of law and market, are not self-subsistent, and that it is helpful to understand what transpires by identifying the existence of a legal-economic nexus in which both seemingly distinct spheres commonly originate. The weak form of the argument affirms the legal-economic nexus as a mental construct to help explain certain phenomena. The strong form of the argument affirms as fact that the legal-economic nexus—the sphere of what is really going on at the deepest level of social existence—is the level at which both polity and economy are continuously and simultaneously (re)formed in a manner that negates any conception of their independent self-subsistence. Although not denying the possibility, if not the good sense, of contemplating the legal-economic nexus only as an alternative mode of discourse or analysis, the argument affirms both the actual existence of the legal-economic nexus and the paramount importance of understanding it relative to analyses that postulate separate, self-subsistent, political, and economic spheres.

Given the hold on our minds enjoyed by the reigning distinction between polity and economy, it would be foolhardy to endeavor to persuade. Rather, I shall let the facts, *differently comprehended*, make the case for themselves; I shall let the readers judge for themselves the alternative model's coherence, accuracy, and utility. It will not go unnoticed from the very beginning that if the idea of a legal-economic nexus is correct, our understanding of economy and polity will have to change in fundamental ways. The great problem, however, is to escape from the hold of conventional wisdom and ordinary language, and of the paradigm ensconced therein, a paradigm that posits the separate and self-subsistent existence of the two spheres. A difficult problem of writing as well as reading this essay is that there is no readily available terminology that avoids the use of the terms "polity" and "economy" (or the usual synonyms, such as "law" and "market"). The prevailing political-economic language carries and reinforces the nuance of separate and self-subsistent existence, which, abetted by language, we then perceive in the world around us. Another problem, both substantive and terminological, is the ease with which the idea of "interrelations" between the two self-subsistent spheres also can be used alternatively to explain or encompass the points made in advancing the concept of the legal-economic nexus. This alternative use occurs, in part, because the legal-economic nexus, as conceptualized here, does contain what we conventionally understand as the interrelations between legal and economic processes.

The procedure is as follows: First, certain considerations are raised that suggest the erroneous nature of the belief in separate, independent, self-subsistent spheres of government and economy, revealing the existence of a legal-economic nexus. Second, the nature and scope of the legal-economic nexus are identified. Third, certain implications of contemplating the legal-economic nexus are discussed.

Economy and polity: a false dichotomy

Tax policy as an example of political control of the economy

In Ronald Reagan's first address to Congress as President, he articulated the principle that "[t]he taxing power of government must...not be used to regulate the economy or bring about social change."[2] Shortly thereafter, George Will, the conservative political columnist and personal friend of the President, in his syndicated column of March 1, 1981, after quoting the President's words, wrote:

> [T]he choice of any tax program is a choice from a large universe of alternatives. Any tax program has special social consequences; it raises some revenues rather than others, encourages and discourages particular behavior. And rarely has there been a clearer, bolder, more self-conscious attempt than Reagan's to use the tax system as a lever for moving society in the direction of desired change. But American conservatives are addicted to the pose of hostility to government power, so they systematicaly misdescribe their own attempts to use government energetically.
>
> When, Oh Lord, shall we be delivered from the conservatives' pretense that they, unlike liberals, do not believe in using government to promote their values through social change? If that were true, there would be no point in electing conservatives.[3]

The notice that Will takes of the obscurantist pretense of conservatives that government can be disempowered need not detain us, however instructive it may be to ask how and why such misdescription is functional. Nor need the discussion be limited to taxing policy. The argument applies across the board to everything undertaken by government.

Will's argument is of present significance in several respects. It affirms the inexorable, fundamental importance of government in any status quo. It affirms the importance of determining which and whose agenda is to control the use of government. It acknowledges that the struggle to control and use government is a fundamental social process and couples this acknowledgment with more than a hint that the process includes efforts by established interests (historical elites) to defuse, if not disengage, others' use of government through fostering negative attitudes toward government. It affirms that the determinants of the allocation of resources and the distributions of opportunity, income, and wealth are deeper than market demand-and-supply forces, that they include all manner of uses of government. It implicitly affirms that the economy is an object of legal control and that law—government—is an instrument of securing economic gain or advantage. It raises the questions, first, whether government can be understood independent of its economic consequences and of the forces brought to bear on it selecting and generating those consequences; second, whether the economy can be understood independent of its legal foundations and of the selective performance consequences specific thereto; and third, what is the process of decisionmaking wherein answers or solutions to all questions of the use of government are developed.

Two recently politicized issues relating to reproduction: parental leave and surrogate parenting

In the 1980s two new matters relating to sexual reproduction became matters of public controversy. One has to do with maternity leaves from work for mothers, and possibly paternity leaves for fathers, the core of which is a guaranteed return to the same job. Efforts have been made to secure pregnancy leaves through private contract, including collective bargaining agreements, protective labor legislation, and litigation seeking recognition and protection under the Equal Protection Clause. Although such leaves had not earlier been an issue, they are readily understood as coming within the category of working conditions subject to contract and to protective labor and labor relations legislation and to scrutiny in regard to constitutional protections. The matter of present concern is that the right at issue, the guaranteed return to a job, could in principle be secured through either contract, legislation, or litigation. Whatever the mode of resolution, the result would affect the allocation of labor resources.

The other matter has to do with the legality of surrogate parenting and the respective rights and obligations of parties to surrogate parenting; that is, the recruitment of women, under contract including remuneration for services rendered, to bear the children of husbands of infertile wives, fertilization taking place without copulation. The matter of present concern is whether the practice should be left to private contract or prohibited or otherwise regulated by law. Although policy implications could be drawn from analogies made with the laws governing contract and prostitution, there was no specific, explicit covering body of law. If legal social control means that there is a covering body of law pertaining to all spheres of human action, no body of law unequivocally relates to surrogate parenting, simply because it had not earlier been an issue (which is not to say that some version of the practice, probably involving copulation, as in the case of Abraham and Sarah in the Old Testament, had not taken place earlier). At issue is whether the practice is to be legalized, whether payment for services rendered is to be permitted, and whether the brokerage services of lawyers or physicians are to be legalized. Debate also focuses on the rights of biological parents relative to each other and to their common offspring, and of the child itself. Whatever the result, it will affect the allocation of labor resources.

In both of these cases, problems emanating from ordinary life became issues of law, legal policy, and legal social control. In both instances, law is the process of conflict resolution; it can either facilitate/hinder or strictly determine economic performance. In either case it can govern or channel the allocation of resources and give substance to the social organization of sexual reproduction; certain values, interests, and expectations conflict with other values, interests, and expectations and the conflicts have to be resolved. Government is involved through legislation and judicial decisions, and is influenced by nominally private forces that press for legislation or bring suit. Government decisions influence private circumstances through determination of what private contract can and cannot encompass, thereby determining solutions to such questions as (1) whose interests are to count, (2) whose conception of the morality of the social organization of sexual reproduction is to be realized, and (3) what is to be the relevant allocation of resources.

Conceptualizing property

It is often argued that the function of the law is to protect private property. In response to this argument, it is sometimes pointed out (and more often the case) that determination of the property to be protected is precisely the point at issue. This predicament is a manifestation of the more general situation suggested by the statement that property is not protected because it is property, but is property because it is protected. The predicament in part reflects the juxtaposition of rival claimants of property rights, or of rights some of which are designatable as property and others as the functional equivalent thereof. But it is also in part a matter of such questions as whether property is pre-existent to government; whether property is self-subsistent; whether property is meaningless independent of the government actions that determine its content; and whether government, as a mode of such determination, is self-subsistent and independent of, if not pre-existent to, property. The latter issue raises the further question whether both government and private property are jointly and simultaneously determined in either an original or a continuing manner. That is, what is the process through which *both* property and government are formed?

Public utility regulation

Public utility regulation in the United States proceeds upon the verbal formula, "fair return on fair value." There is a fundamental circularity and incoherence present in this formula: fair return cannot be either comprehended or calculated independent of fair value (the rate base), and the rate base cannot be meaningfully valued independent of consideration of the capitalization of return. Thus all discussion of "confiscation" begs the question that utility regulation helps govern the values involved *ab initio*. Participants in the regulatory process—especially commissioners and judges—are engaged in a process of making reciprocal experiential judgments, of working out some notion of both fair return and fair value. Courts seek guidance from the precedents of other courts, and regulatory commissions seek guidance from the decisions of other commissions, and both look to capital markets to see the consequences of past decisions.[4]

Utility regulation is constrained by the results of market processes, and market processes are constrained by regulation. Valuation is in part a product of regulation, not an exogenous and independent object to be determined and measured. Regulation and valuation are mutually determinative—perhaps more accurately, jointly worked out. The question arises as to the nature of the processes of decision making wherein are worked out answers or solutions to such questions as whose interests are to count in the regulation of public utilities, what will be the relevant allocation of resources, and how the relevant parties at interest are able to participate therein.

The question is further complicated when we consider that, first, the process of regulation is understood to encompass not only the regulated utilities, the regulatory commissioners, the legislature, and the courts, but also consumers and other parties at interest, commonly called "intervenors"; second, decisionmaking both determines the regulatory process itself and defines its participants; and third, operative in both the valuational and regulatory processes are various normative theories as to means and ends. For example, at issue are the meaning of and modes of calculating fair value and fair return; the putative relationships of regulators, the regulated, consumers, and courts; and finally, the theories that various parties seek to have adopted as the operative decisional mode leading to one or another allocative and/or distributional effect. These theories, and the performance results to which they give rise, help condition the expectations of other regulators, courts, consumers, and investors. Further, these expectations (in part as they are operative in capital markets) are in turn later looked to by those in the process of making decisions. In these and other respects, business and government seem to be facets of some larger process; perhaps interacting facets but also perhaps facets of something more fundamental and encompassing, certainly not independent and self-subsistent.

Efficiency *and rights*

Efficiency in the sense of Pareto optimality means the exhaustion of gains from trade of goods. But efficient-optimal allocations are specific to the definition and assignment of rights forming the basis on which trades take place. There is no unique optimal result, only rights-structure-specific optimal results. Moreover, *efficiency* in the Pareto sense cannot dispositively be applied to the definition and assignment of rights themselves, because efficiency requires an antecedent determination of the rights. The dependence of Paretian efficiency on the prior definition and assignment of rights does not preclude, however, the making of antecedent assumptions, implicit or explicit, as to whose interests are to count as rights, thereby determining both the desired efficient result and the interests to be given effect in the definition and assignment of rights. To say, then, that the law is wealth maximizing is not saying anything more than that the law, in determining whose interests will count as rights, determines which non-unique optimal solution will be achieved. In this respect, then, the law is willy-nilly wealth maximizing, whichever or whosever interests it protects as rights. This non-unique choice is accomplished in the arena of the law and the economy, which are not self-subsistent.

Fundamental joint processes operate in this arena. These processes (1) work out optimal, gains-from-trade, wealth-maximizing solutions within existing rights; and (2) work out the interests to which the law will give its protection. The latter includes potential changes of the interests to which the law gives its protection, and resolution of conflicts between claimants of old rights and of old and new rights. The process of redetermining rights and their economic significance is inevitable: the definition and assignment by law of new rights, for example, to the human genome or to new technology, has the inexorable effect of creating or altering the structure of relevant markets and thereby the economic significance and values of hitherto existing rights and the opportunity sets of economic actors. The pretense that these rights existed prior to their definition and assignment is simply that: pretense, a legal fiction, serving a legitimizing function, but devoid of any analytical or descriptive content. Treating certain rights, or certain legal texts, as absolute or as pre-existent, functions to give effect to and render privileged one interpretation over another. In all these respects, there is something going on that transcends and insinuates the seemingly separate spheres of economy and polity.

Rights and externalities

Three concepts can be combined: "the dual nature of rights," the "reciprocal character of externalities," and the "ubiquity of externalities." By the "dual nature of rights" is meant the situation of scarcity in which Alpha and Beta are both in the same field of action, and if a right is assigned to Alpha, then Beta has a non-right and is exposed to the choices made by Alpha. By the "reciprocal character of externalities" is meant the situation that either Alpha or Beta is able to visit injury or benefit on the other. The case of the upstream polluter and the downstream pollutee is apposite: If the upstream polluter has the right to dump toxic waste in the river, then the externality of toxicity is visited upon the downstream pollutee; if the downstream pollutee has the right to clean water, then the externality of having otherwise to dispose of the toxic waste is visited upon the upstream polluter. The questions always are: Who will have what right, and who will be able to visit damage on whom?[5]

Two things will be noted: First, no person is an island; each has scarcity relationships to others, at least in the sense of being a competitor for rights and of visiting impacts upon others or being the recipient of impacts from others. Second, these relationships, centering on the dual nature of rights and the reciprocal character of externalities, are markedly ubiquitous in a large, heavily populated, industrial, urban society. It is essentially selective perception (often guided by ideology and material interest) that prevents our perceiving certain injuries as injuries, and so on. Injuries or benefits that are not perceived as such therefore do not enter into the policy calculus.

In the arena of the economy and the law, processes are necessarily at work through which determinations are made as to who has what right and who can do what to whom. The outputs of this process are the possession of a right by some Alpha and the nonpossession by some Beta; the ability of Alpha to visit injury on Beta; and the exposure of Beta to injury visited by Alpha—and thus the allocation of resources and the distributions of income and wealth *pro tanto* consequent to this structure of rights. The inputs to this legal-economic process are almost infinite: ideology, material interests, lobbying and litigation efforts, trade-offs by legislators, interpretations and applications of common and constitutional law principles by judges (governed by selective perception), market transactions of various types, rights' definition and assignments, and so on. The output of one period, as it were, is the input of the next, in an ongoing process transcending and insinuating both polity and economy.

The legal-economic nexus

The perception of "interrelations" and "interactions" between legal and economic processes is predicated on a conception of these spheres or processes as essentially separate and independent, as they so readily appear at the level of surface phenomena. The view suggested here, however, is that the economy and polity are not essentially self-subsistent and independent spheres or processes. As suggested earlier, one problem is that it is difficult to discuss them in ordinary language without precommitting analysis to the idea of separate spheres. There is a legal-economic nexus in which both originate in an ongoing manner, in which both are manifestations of something more fundamental. The phenomena of interrelations and of interaction may be seen to be manifestations of this nexus.

What can be said of this nexus? The question points to exceedingly broad and complex considerations and can be answered in several steps.

Allocation of resources

The allocation of resources takes place largely through markets which are formed and structured by legal rights which are in turn defined and assigned by government (legislature, executive agencies, courts). The government is the object and conduit of pressures directed to and through it, all of which occurs in the legal-economic nexus. The rules governing how results are worked out are themselves worked out in the legal-economic nexus. The allocative results are worked out through and are the product of complex processes constituting the legal-economic nexus.

The allocative results can be perceived in several ways: as due to market forces or to the rights generated by government, which form and operate through markets; as due to the uses to which government is put in generating rights or to the contest over the use of government. The legal-economic nexus encompasses all the foregoing, and it is misleading to think of the two spheres as separate and self-subsistent.

What goes on in the economy, and especially the legal-economic nexus, as solutions are worked out, is illustrated in the following model: Consider the traditional production possibility curve[6] juxtaposed to a community indifference curve[7] or social welfare function to produce at the point of tangency the socially optimal allocation. Four processes, about which conventional use makes restrictive assumptions in order to reach determinate solutions, underlie this diagram. These assumptions are about factors that in practice are worked out, in part, through the legal-economic nexus. In making these assumptions, economists both limit and channel the results of the four processes, substituting their own preconceptions and preferences for those of actual economic actors. The four processes are those through which are worked out (1) the values on the axes, (2) the shape and location of the production possibility curve, (3) individual preferences, and (4) the power structure. The legal-economic nexus includes, but does not exhaust, these processes.

First, the process through which is determined which values (commodities or goals) are to be represented on the axes, the values between which choice has to be made: When a politician states that "such-and-such is the issue in this election," he or she is in effect endeavoring both to get a particular value on the social agenda and to have it weighted heavily relative to a competing value(s). The values are adopted and worked out through markets, private and group choice, and politics. The legal-economic nexus is the social location wherein, on the basis of ideology or material interest, private individuals and businesses attempt to influence the social agenda, and politicians and courts, through the exercise of government choice, translate pressures and influences into government policy and thereby determine the scope and performance of the market.

Second, the process through which is determined the shape and location of the production possibility curve, which governs the tradeoffs that have to be made: Economists have not studied this process very much, though they understand that both shape and location are influenced by population size, quality of the work force, quantity and quality of natural resources, the bundles of rights accompanying these resources, the level of technology, and so on—factors that change and are themselves in some important respects a matter of policy. Consider the production possibility curve relating price stability and employment levels. Whatever governs the empirical Phillips curve tradeoffs will help govern the slope and location of this production possibility curve. Among the factors are inflationary expectations and whatever governs them, the relationship between employment security and productivity, the relative power of managements and workers in arriving at wage rates, central bank money-supply policy, and the pricing practices of businesses. Economists produce determinate results by making explicit or, more likely, implicit assumptions as to these governing factors, whereas in reality these have to be worked out, in part in the legal-economic nexus. For example, monetary, fiscal, and labor policy is determined in large part in the same manner as are determined the values on the axes.

Third and fourth, inasmuch as the actual social welfare function (in contrast to one assumed by the economic analyst) is the product of individual preferences weighted by power structure, the processes through which individual preferences and power structure are formed.[8] Neither process has been studied very much by economists, but in order to reach determinate solutions, economists make assumptions as to how these processes—and the values ensconced within them—work out. In actuality, individual preferences are formed and reformed on the basis of the subjective perception of experience, encompassing both socialization and individuation. And the power structure is not given once and for all time; it too is formed and reformed, in part through processes endogenous to the economy narrowly defined and in part through broader processes, to wit, the legal-economic nexus and beyond.[9]

In all four regards, implicit presumptions as to who has what preferences and how much they are to be weighted, that is, whose interests are to count, have to be worked out. The legal-economic nexus is the social location wherein this takes place.

Economy and law mutually create each other

In the legal-economic nexus, the law is a function of the economy, and the economy (especially its structure) is a function of law. The economy is a function of law in that law either facilitates or determines what takes place in the economy, for example through government spending or definition and assignment of rights. The law is a function of the economy at least in that the problems confronting law and the materials available to law are economic in origin. Further, it is clear that the fundamental development of law is in some sense derived from the systemic transformation of the economic system. In both regards, the arena of the economy and the law—the economy and the polity—are jointly produced, *not* independently given and *not* merely interacting.

In England when the interests of business gradually and partially succeeded those of the landed aristocracy and gentry as the major source of pressures and demands active upon and through government, the law changed (one example is the use of the fiction of the corporation as a person). And as the law changed, the modern industrial, urban, capitalist system grew and was reinforced. The modern state and the modern economy in the West developed apace. What became "private" did so because of "public" action, and the "public" action was driven by the interaction of "private" interests. The same process subsequently characterized the development of the welfare state. The legal-economic nexus is the social location wherein both the economy as a function of law and law as a function of economy take place. Both are a product of *common* determining forces that are frequently selectively identified with one sphere or the other, whereas in fact they are part of the *common* legal-economic nexus.

The belief or pretense that the law is given independent of the economy, or that the economy pre-exists the state in any practical sense, gives effect to selective perception of government, economy, and their origins and continuing development. James Boyd White, commenting on the falseness of the distinction between the market and government, has stated that to "talk about 'government intervention'" implicitly assumes "that there is a pre-governmental state of nature called the market, into which the government intrudes. But this is obviously silly."[10] The belief treats both law and economy as given, antecedent, and preeminent to man, as existing to be discovered. In fact, law and economy are jointly created through complex human social decision making processes. Both are not discovered, but created simultaneously in the legal-economic nexus. The legal-economic nexus is the key social process in which the social (re)construction of reality takes place.

Power, ideology, and distribution

In the social (re)construction, the fundamental policy question always is whose interests are to count, and it contains inevitable distributional or structural problems. Even if one were to affirm that "individual preferences are to count," the fundamental policy question remains: *whose* interests, or preferences, are to count. The legal-economic nexus is the complex social process in and through which answers to this question are (re)worked out—and in which thereby the social (re)construction of reality is effectuated.

One central concept is "power": power in government, power in the economy, the determination and exercise of power in each, the mutual interaction and especially the mutual definition of economic and political power. Another central concept is "belief system," which provides part of the basis on which policy in the legal-economic nexus is made. Belief system governs the definition of reality that influences policy, and the belief system is itself an object of control and manipulation, as economic and political actors attempt to influence leadership selection and policy through controlling the relevant definition of reality. In the legal-economic nexus, it is true both that beliefs are a function of power, in part that they are weighted by power structure, and that power is in part a function of belief. The legal-economic nexus is the locus of the normative direction given to government, in part channeling the organization and control of the economy.

There is an inexorable necessity of choice as to whose interest will count. No one's interest counts a priori. Interests are *made* to count through law and through control of lawmaking, by power, by ideology (belief system), and by selective perception.

Government, the legal system, and the economy are human artifacts and normative. They accordingly require legal direction. Theories of law, of the economy, and of law and economics are part of the process of creating polity and economy, in part through working out substantive issues of policy. These theories provide selective definitions of reality and of values and thereby channel and (re)create polity and economy.

Noninterventionism, or laissez-faire, is always selectively employed. To the extent that it is employed, it takes largely for granted and gives privileged status to government action already otherwise embedded in the status quo. Theories of laissez-faire almost always have their own specific agendas for government, agendas that constitute the substance of the normative direction given to government, the legal system, and the economy. Ideologies (including those of laissez-faire), selective perceptions (in part driven by ideology), and interests (especially material), *inter alia*, drive the legal-economic nexus.

Theories of government and of the economy function as normative attempts to structure, limit, open, and channel the use of government. They always either protect and/or change but also always selectively interpret the status quo structure of rights. They selectively identify "government," "freedom," "coercion," and other similar concepts. These theories are major inputs to and variables within the legal-economic nexus. They are normative phenomena, though the naturalistic fallacy treats what "is" as if it were real, natural in some absolute sense, thus telescoping "is" and "ought" and obscuring the fact of human (re)construction.

Government and economy are instruments available to whoever can get into a position to control and use them. The legal-economic nexus is the social location of the processes in and through which this system of control and use is (re)worked out. The legal-economic nexus is an arena of power and power play. It is a value clarification and selection process. At any time the polity and the economy are each both independent and dependent variables in a process of cumulative causation. Worked out in the legal-economic nexus are by whom, for whom, and on whose terms the polity and economy will be used; in short, who will use government and economy for what purposes and under what conditions. The legal-economic nexus is in effect a process of collective bargaining, of the formation and mobilization of political psychology, and of the interactions of power, knowledge (belief), and psychology variables.

Economic and state power

In the legal-economic nexus, decisions are a function of power structure, in both the polity and the economy; and power structure is a function of decision, again in either or both the polity and the economy. Power is necessary for the achievement of desired ends and also "for its own sake," that is, for identity reasons. The powerful tend to seek further power, which provides its own rationalization. At any one time, power in the market can be brought to bear on the polity, and vice versa, resulting in a change in both the power structure and the use of power in one or the other or both spheres.

The legal-economic nexus is an arena in which economic power is an important lever for controlling and deploying state power, and the power of government, often because it is subordinate to economic power, is an important lever for controlling and deploying economic power. The legal-economic nexus is the social sphere in which extant economic power and political power are brought to bear on each other, in the process mutually defining and limiting each other.

In the legal-economic nexus, the working rules of law and morals govern the distribution and exercise of power, the distribution and exercise of power govern the development of the working rules of law and morals—with regard to law, as a matter of whose interests and moral conceptions are able to control and be put into effect through government. The legal-economic nexus is that sphere wherein the rules of law and morals are both output and input. In this same dual manner in which power, law, and morals are worked out, so too are the distributions of income and wealth in part a function of law, which law is itself in part a function of the distributions of income and wealth.

In addition, the legal-economic nexus is the social sphere and processes wherein are (re)worked out the mutual definitions of—and modes of interrelation between—economy and polity. Part of that mutual definition includes the determination and assignment of rights, including property rights. Within the legal-economic nexus, efforts are continually being made to obfuscate the use and operation of government in (re)defining—and thereby (re)creating—the economy so as selectively to channel both the (re)definition and the (re)creation of the legal-economic nexus.

The legal-economic nexus is the sphere in which the polity and the economy are (re)worked out, in part through the interactions of power and ideology. If one must understand the state in terms of "that group of persons in whom it assumes social form, and of those factors which gain domination over it," as Schumpeter put it,[11] then one must understand the economy in the same terms. As such, the legal-economic nexus is the sphere in which is worked out how both are "used and developed."

Thus the legal-economic nexus is the social process in which are (re)worked out power structure, law, distribution, and societal values and definitions. In the process, the economy and the polity are continually (re)formed as "one." The so-called interrelations between legal and economic processes are observed. But the phenomena we perceive in our minds—the existence of "interrelations" between independent and self-subsistent spheres—are more fundamentally phenomena of the legal-economic nexus in which both polity and economy are continually (re)formed as one. Though we may retain the perception that both the economy (market) and government (politics, courts) appear to have an "independent" life of their own, they exist only within the larger legal-economic nexus.

Control of the state

The legal-economic nexus is the social sphere wherein is fought out and determined who controls the state and the uses to which the law is to be put. The legal-economic nexus is that sphere of decision making in which decisions are (re)worked out as to whose interests government is to protect, whether as property or other rights or otherwise.

The government's budget forms part of the core of the legal-economic nexus but does not by any means entirely constitute the core. The budget reflects both the legal control of the economy and the economic (nominally private sector) control of government. It is wrought by the bringing to bear on and through government of various efforts to use government as an economic alternative.

The legal-economic nexus is the sphere wherein is determined whose interests are to count, how, and how much. The legal-economic nexus exists in precisely that social space wherein government is controlled, wherein government responds to outside forces and generates solutions to problems with outside impacts; and wherein the economy is controlled, wherein the economic power structure is determined and itself determines which courses of action it will pursue, including the uses to which it will endeavor to put government.

The legal-economic nexus is the sphere in which government operates to (re)define and (re)create the economy, and in which nominally private interests, perhaps especially economic interests, operate to (re)define and (re)channel government, given the dominant belief system, which is itself reformulated and rechannelled through the uses selectively imposed upon or made of it.

The legal-economic nexus is the sphere in which the most proximate critical matter is worked out: the legal change of law, the change by law of the interests to which government is to give its support. The legal-economic nexus exists in that sphere in which problems of legal change of legal rights (and other legal arrangements) are worked out, even when the goal is to maintain the integrity and economic significance of existing rights or arrangements.

The legal-economic nexus is at the center of the process through which, on the basis of the selective legal change of legal rights, trading in economic commodities is undertaken to the point at which, within the existing structure of rights, gains from trade are exhausted (Pareto optimality). The twin processes of pursuing gains from trade and reworking the structure of rights on the basis of which trade takes place are parallelled by the twin processes of (re)working out the economy and the polity—and all this takes place in the legal-economic nexus. Failure to appreciate the legal-economic nexus can only result in partial and attenuated comprehension of what actually goes on at the most fundamental levels of legal-economic life.

Implications of the legal-economic nexus

Transcending professional ideologies

The concept of the legal-economic nexus is advanced here as a nonideological construct to penetrate in an objective manner what arguably may be said actually to be going on in the economy and in law and politics. It is an attempt to transcend particular professional ideologies (particularly those of the law and of economics) and particular political-economic ideologies, with their respective definitions of the world of economy and polity.[12] Each of these ideologies imposes more or less variable but always selective definitions on precisely what is the economy and the polity. The definitions and the language used in those definitions obscure the processes—constituting the legal-economic nexus—through which both polity and economy are (re)determined. There are philosophies of government and of constitutionalism that attempt narrowly to circumscribe the nominally private economic-market sector; and there are philosophies of economics that attempt narrowly to circumscribe the nominally public governmental-political-legal sector. Practitioners of each ideology thereby tend to reify certain specifications of polity and/or economy in the process, treating them as something exogenously or independently given.

Not only ideologues do this. Economic, political, and legal analysts and theorists necessarily do the same, because in order to theorize or analyze, certain legal-economic features, structures, or policies—for example, the set of entitlements—must be taken as given. In taking these legal-economic factors as given, some measure of determinacy is given to their analysis. But inevitably this determinacy must come at the expense of obscuring and foreclosing the processes actually at work in the legal-economic nexus through which those legal-economic factors are (re)worked out in the actual world. By this means analysts tend to inject their own values and preconceptions by substituting their own definitions of reality for those that are achieved as both inputs and outputs in the processes that constitute the legal-economic nexus.

There are those who prefer subtly to participate in the legal-economic nexus, in order to advance their own preconceptions of how the economy and the polity ought to be organized and controlled and of the uses to which both ought to be put. Indeed, such persons may be unhappy with the basic premise of this essay, which is that it is desirable to have the processes constituting the legal-economic nexus *out in the open* rather than obfuscated by selective specifications of economy and polity. It is very tempting to presume that one's own values and definition of reality will be safer if not jeopardized by the opening of certain doors. But, if the analysis given here is correct, both such participation and the giving effect to such temptation are themselves indicative of the operational premise that this essay affirms: that the legal-economic nexus is the sphere in which the contest for the control and use of government and economy is conducted. All this, of course, has been a central argument of Legal Realism since the 1920s.

Let me paraphrase Edward Levi,[13] writing about legal pretense, in this matter of the legal-economic nexus: It is important that the processes of the legal-economic nexus should not be concealed by a certain pretense. The pretense is that the economy and the polity are antecedently given and subject to discovery but not created. The processes of the legal-economic nexus encompass differences of view and ambiguities of words. The legal-economic nexus provides for the participation of the community in the social creation of both polity and economy through the discussion and (re)making of policy.

Discussion of the legal-economic nexus is in the same position as discussion of Bentham's principle of utility. Bentham wrote,

> Nature has placed mankind under the governance of two sovereign masters, *pain* and *pleasure*. It is for them alone to point out what we ought to do, as well as to determine what we shall do. On the one hand the standard of right and wrong, on the other the chain of causes and effects, are fastened to their throne. They govern us in all we do, in all we say, in all we think: every effort we can make to throw off our subjection, will serve but to demonstrate and

confirm it. In words a man may pretend to abjure their empire: but in reality he will remain subject to it all the while.[14]

Whatever one thinks of Benthamite utilitarianism, some of his logic is apposite for the legal-economic nexus: The legal-economic nexus is a human artifact, a result of deliberate and nondeliberative decision making. Whether we like it or not, there is no way to reject it. Every effort we can make to deny it serves both to demonstrate and confirm it; we are always subject to it. We participate in it willy-nilly, as political-economic actors. In one way or another we always participate, even if only by passive acquiescence and effective compliance with structural and other decisions worked out by others. When we vote or otherwise act politically, as Will instructs us, we are inevitably acting to use government to promote certain values through social change, to restructure the economy in one direction or another, no less when we deny that we are doing so than when we acknowledge or laud doing so.

We are aggravated by government partly because it is the place where the hard and divisive issues get attention. We seek to control and use the state because it is important in the social construction of reality, and to reform and redirect reality to our liking. We are aggravated by the economy because our livelihoods and our quality of private and collective life are profoundly affected by it. In part for those reasons we seek to control the economy, to reform and redirect it to our liking, to engage the legal-economic nexus for that purpose. What is "natural"—judging by what is empirically the case—is not "noninterventionism" but our ubiquitous "intervention," which is due to our propensity to try to use government to correct what we perceive as "distortions" or "problems."

Both economy and polity are important in social living; and the legal-economic nexus is the sphere in which both are formed and reformed. Neither is self-subsistent, antecedent to the other, or preeminent. Each is both an open-ended input and output *vis-à-vis* the other in a process in which both are created. The economy is an object of legal control, and the law is an instrument of economic advantage; the legal-economic nexus is the sphere in which the questions of whose control and whose instrument are worked out, and the polity and the economy are created in the process. All that is terribly obscured by the pretense, or the belief, that polity and economy are independent and self-subsistent. It is even more terribly obscured by the pretense of which Will wrote, that government is the enemy, not an instrument of use; a view which is fundamentally ironic and sometimes duplicitous, insofar as it is held by those who have their own agenda for government.

Miller v. Schoene: *a case study*

The actual legal-economic nexus is not what ideology typically makes it out to be. Let me reconsider *Miller v. Schoene*.[15] The Virginia Legislature responded to red cedar rust, a plant disease whose first phase is spent while the fungus resides upon its host, the chiefly ornamental red cedar tree, which is not harmed by the cedar rust.

During a second phase, the rust has a severely adverse effect on apple trees, attacking its leaves and fruit. The legislature passed a statute that permitted the state entomologist, upon study, to declare infected red cedar trees within two miles of an apple orchard a public nuisance and to enforce their destruction.

The state courts uniformly held against the red cedar owners, who claimed that the state was taking or destroying their property to the advantage of the apple orchard owners, that is, not for public use but for the benefit of other private persons. The United States Supreme Court also held for the state against the red cedar tree owners, arguing that

> the state was under the necessity of making a choice between the preservation of one class of property and that of the other wherever both existed in dangerous proximity. It would have been none the less a choice if, instead of enacting the present statute, the state, by doing nothing, had permitted serious injury to the apple orchards within its borders to go on unchecked.[16]

As I have shown,[17] the state, in executing its inexorable necessity of choice, chose, and indeed, had to choose, one interest over the other and thereby structured the system of mutual coercion, which in turn influenced the allocation of resources and the distributions of income and wealth in the market. The allocation and the distributions are power- or rights-structure specific, and the structure is in part a result of legal choice.

When I first wrote about this case, I used in the title the language, "interrelations between legal and economic processes." The premise was that there were two interacting spheres. The result was deeper insight into the economic role of government—another phrase that posits two interacting spheres. But these same relationships and decisions perhaps even more importantly substantiate the idea of the legal-economic nexus. What was present in the red cedar case were the political and economic processes as they existed from the time the rust was discovered and the legislature responded to pressures from apple orchardists, to the decision of the United States Supreme Court, almost a decade and one-half later. The legal-economic nexus comprised the efforts of the red cedar owners and apple orchardists and their representatives before the legislature and courts (lobbyists and lawyers), the legislature, and the state and federal courts, as well as other actors such as the state entomologist. Neither the political nor the economic process was changed in a nonincremental, major respect[18] (though the red cedar and apple orchard owners might have argued over this). But through the process the structure of rights, the pattern of freedom and control, the resolution of the conflict between continuity and change, and the structure of mutual coercion were all materially altered, as was the realization of economic values versus aesthetic interests. Government was not intervening in the economy in the sense in which it had hitherto been absent, but was an instrument available for use by whoever could enlist its support. The apple orchardists, who constituted a major industry in the state and who were organized and powerful, were able to convince the state legislature, the state courts, and the highest federal court. As a result the product of the legislative-judicial system, the structure of nominally private rights, was changed, and with it the performance of the economy.

Both the polity and the economy were incrementally (re)produced in the process. The economy was reconfigured through the change in the structures of rights and of mutual coercion. The polity was used to change the structure of rights, as the apple orchardists utilized other rights (to petition the legislature and to defend their interests in the courts) to use the state to enhance or protect their interests rather than the interests of the red cedar tree owners, which was the consequence of the preexisting law of property given the state of nature with the red cedar rust. As is evident, it is almost impossible to discuss this situation without using the terms "the economy" and "the polity," as if they were independent and self-subsistent. But what they are and what they do are each dependent upon the other, which is to say that they constitute and emanate from the legal-economic nexus.

Contrast the idea of the legal-economic nexus with the views of the parties to the litigation. The red cedar tree owners wanted their rights, which were, given the state of nature with the red cedar rust, effectively protected under the preexisting law of property. These rights did exist and seemed to the red cedar tree owners to exist paramount to government, so that the passage of the control statute seemed to them to take their property for the interests of other private owners. Government was intervening in the pejorative sense; government constituted oppression of their private rights. The apple orchard owners, on the other hand, found that the state of the preexisting law of property in effect enabled the red cedar tree owners, inadvertently to be sure, to visit damage on their apple orchards. The orchardists saw the passage of the control statute (as well as their success in court) as government protection of their interests against private oppression (much more than, if at all, against the oppression of nature, which was the source of the rust). The dominant ideology of our society, which is anti-interventionist, seems to find it difficult to accept the idea of the inexorable necessity of choice by government when private interests conflict. Typically the noninterventionist ideology is on the side of the property right holder the protection of whose interest does not require additional government action, in this case the red cedar tree owners. The interests and ideological perceptions of certain categories of parties are congruent with the dominant ideology[19] and others not. But notice not only that government is willy-nilly involved through its necessarily having to choose between the interests to which it gives its support when they conflict, but also that what government does and how the operation of the economy proceeds are both worked out simultaneously. It is this sphere of continuous simultaneous origin, as it were, that constitutes the legal-economic nexus.

Governance *as a legal-economic process*

This essay affirms the existence of a fundamental legal-economic nexus in which certain behavior is simultaneously legal and economic, in which the two nominally different processes are actually aspects of one fundamental process.

From this perspective, the idea of the self-subsistent existence of economy and polity seems naive and incomplete. The central element of this legal-economic nexus is *governance*, in the sense of a process in which important decisions are made, whether by legislatures, courts, or administrative agencies; by giant manufacturing corporations, cartels, trade associations, pension funds, major banks, and so on; or by alliances of governmental institutions and private organizations.

Economy and polity are not independent and self-subsistent. They can be seen as either mutually defining or jointly arising in the legal-economic nexus. This nexus is a continuing, explorative, and emergent process through which are worked out ongoing solutions to legal-economic problems, such as whose economic and other interests are to count, which economic and other performance results are to be pursued, and who is to make these determinations. Whether or not one accepts the concept of the legal-economic nexus, the emphasis must be on the process by which actors who are simultaneously both economic and political actors themselves work out solutions to problems that are simultaneously both political and economic. Among other things, these solutions simultaneously (re)create both economy and polity. To this process particular ideologies and particular policy analyses and proposals are but particular contributions to the (re)creation of economy and polity.

Recognition of the legal-economic nexus will not privilege certain interests over any other interests. But it will enable independent, objective analysts, if not also the parties themselves, better to understand what is going on in the legal-economic world. It will either prevent presumptuous assumptions from being made as to either or both the polity and the economy, assumptions that channel the results of analysis and substitute the judgments of the analyst for those of the processes of the legal-economic nexus itself, or require that these assumptions, and their tautologous consequences, be brought out into the open. It will prevent the pretense that government is not an object of capture and use, from which Will would deliver us; and it will prevent the pretense that the law is both given and known, rather than something created, from which concealment Levi would also deliver us. The legal-economic nexus is the social location in which meet and are composed the conflicting definitions of reality, values, interests, and expectations held by people within the total social system.

The control and use of the legal-economic nexus in order to control legal-economic change is the critical matter. It is the process through which the economy and the polity are (re)created. Central to this process is the control and use of government by economic (and other) actors—notwithstanding, and indeed because, economic actors have economic standing and significance in part because of the legal-economic nexus and thus government. The legal-economic nexus is important because it *is* the process in which both the economy and, perhaps especially, the government are controlled.

Rights are not produced in a black box called government; and the economy does not operate on its own. A legal-economic nexus is formed by the process in which both are simultaneously (re)determined. At the heart of society and of social (including legal) change is control and use of the legal-economic nexus, and at the heart thereof is the exercise of governance, power, and belief system. The fundamentals of the legal-economic nexus are not as simple and obvious as contemplated by views that maintain that the polity and economy are preexistent, self-subsistent spheres.

Notes

Warren J. Samuels is a Professor of Economics, Michigan State University. I am indebted to Elvin C. Lashbrooke, Steven G. Medema, Nicholas Mercuro, and A. Allan Schmid for helpful comments on a previous draft.

1 Joseph Schumpeter (1954) "The Crisis of the Tax State," *4 International Economic Papers*, 5: 19.
2 Address Before a Joint Session of the Congress on the Program for Economic Recovery, *Public Papers* 1981, pp. 108, 114 (Feb. 18, 1981).
3 George Will (1981) "Reaganism is Not Quite Thatcherism," *Washington Post* (March 1, 1981) at C7, col. 5.
4 This process is not unlike other areas of conflict resolution in which private commercial labor arbitrators observe and seek guidance from the decisions of courts and of each other, and where courts observe and seek guidance from the decisions of each other and private arbitrators.
5 Alternatively, if the waste includes nutrient material enriching the water and thus a desirable input to the downstream producer, and if the upstream producer has the right to dump, then the externality is a benefit rather than an injury to the downstream producer. But these are not typically controversial cases.
6 The production possibility curve comprises the loci of the different possible combinations of outputs of the values (goods or goals) represented on the axes.
7 The social welfare function, or community indifference curve, represents the aggregated preferences of all members of society for the different combinations of the values (goods or goals) represented on the axes. It is consequent to the aggregation of individual preferences for the different combinations, each individual's preferences weighted on the basis of power, for example, income and wealth. Presumably society is indifferent between the various combinations on the highest social welfare function, except insofar as it is tangent to the highest possible production possibility curve. See also *infra* n. 8.
8 Notice that this is not a hypothetical social welfare function designated by an analyst, even one who intends to represent the actual function extant at the time and place. The combination of individuals with preferences for values and a power structure that weights those preferences across individuals (i.e., determines whose preferences count) yields the actual social welfare function. The discussion is not intended to be a mechanistic representation of reality but a tool indicative of what is going on in society.
9 As further indication of the complexity of these (and other) processes, consider the situation in which the power structure arguably does not change but the beliefs of the (hegemonic or decisive) power holders change, thereby changing the decisional outcome. The focus, the object, and the vehicle of these changes is the legal-economic nexus.
10 James Boyd White (1987) "Economics and Law: Two Cultures in Tension," 54 *Tennessee Law Review*, 161: 183.
11 *See supra* n. 1 and accompanying text.
12 In limiting discussion to political and economic belief systems, I do not intend to deny that cultural and moral belief systems are important in precisely the same way as the political and economic. What is called here the legal-economic nexus is obviously much broader than polity and economy. Adam Smith's total system of society, for example, encompassed the formation and operation of moral sentiments and rules, the

economy, and law and jurisprudence as three interacting spheres. I do affirm, however, that in the modern Western world, *the* crucial arena is what is here called the legal-economic nexus.

13 E. H. Levi (1949) *An Introduction to Legal Reasoning 1.*

14 J. Bentham, *An Introduction to the Principles of Morals and Legislation* 1 (J. Burns and H. Hart, ed. 1970) (1780).

15 276 U.S. 272 (1928). *See* Warren Samuels (1971) "Interrelations Between Legal and Economic Processes," *Journal of Law and Economics*, 14: 435–50, reprinted in W. J. Samuels and A. A. Schmid (eds) 1981 *Law and Economics*, 95–110.

16 276 U.S. 279.

17 See Samuels, *supra* n. 15.

18 The typical pattern is that the economy and the polity are each changed more or less slowly by incremental, non-major changes. These incremental changes, each wrought by one piece of legislation, one court decision, one corporate or trade union decision, one transformation of belief system, and so on, accumulate to produce significant changes in the way we live our economic and political lives.

19 Indeed, were the rust situation reversed, and the damage from an apple rust ultimately visited on the red cedar trees, the apple owners would have been voicing the dominant ideological prescriptions.

3 The nature and sources of rights

Introduction

The first two documents, published here for the first time, concern the character of property rights and due process of law. They were written during the early 1960s at the University of Miami, for distribution to undergraduate students in my course in Government and Business, Economics 348. I sought to answer two questions. One had been raised by Pierre Joseph Proudhon (1840), "what is property?" The other was, "what is the meaning of 'due process of law?'" The first concerns the genesis and nature of property, a central institution of society; the second, the nature of a key principle of US constitutional law and, in my view, a discursive means of articulating and declaring "property." They were not written as original research. I had two specific motives in preparing them. One was to enable the student to see the critical issues raised by those questions. The other was to set down my own answers to them. Clearly the questions could not be fully answered in less than thirty typed pages, the combined length of the two original mimeographed documents. Students, however, needed to know where I was coming from in my lectures on a number of topics, and I had to be firmly in grasp of them in order to make sense.

A third document, also published here for the first time, consists of several parts of an article, written in 2005–6, critiquing monetary theory for, among other things, its neglect of the topics presented here. I have combined the notes and the references.

By the early 1960s I had already determined that one of my life-long projects would center on the socio-legal institution of private property. The project would include theories of justification of private property, the psychology of property, the origin and revision of property rights, the nature of rights, the relations between property and democracy, the social functions of property, the legal process relating to property, the context of social theory—including theories of government and of law and economics—in which property had meaning, how the development of property related to the history of the last half-millennium, and so on. I had already studied a vast amount of material on or relevant to the topic. I was accumulating more at a rapid rate. I had studied John R. Commons, Richard T. Ely, Max Weber, Karl Marx, Adam Smith, Roscoe Pound, Robert Lee Hale, Edwin E. Witte, and a wide range of other legal, anthropological, sociological, philosophical, and economic authors. The importance of the two topics guaranteed a continuing expansion of the relevant literature, providing me with additional materials with which to adjust insight but also constituting an increasing workload.

Several themes are taken up which resonate in my later work on law and economics/economic role of government: law as social control, the contest to control government in order to determine the interests it will promote in the exercise of social control, law, especially Constitutional Law, as subject to varying interpretation, the judiciary, as part of government, making, not finding law, the inevitability of some theory of the role of government with regard to freedom versus control, continuity versus change, and equality versus hierarchy, the process of working things out, and so on.

Most topics touched on in the papers were elaborated, first, in my undergraduate Economics 348 lectures at the University of Miami and later in my graduate Economic Role of Government course, Economics 806D/819, at Michigan State University. These topics include the meaning of law, the sources of law, the legal-economic nexus, government *vis-à-vis* governance, the complexities of collective decision making, and so on. In time my interest in property became subsumed in my work on the economic role of government.

The chapters are published in their original form except for minor stylistic changes, the correction of an error and the addition of some citation information. I am uncertain as to which edition of Edwin S. Corwin's *The Constitution and What it Means Today* and of Ronald A. Anderson's textbook was used for the quoted material, in part because of my uncertainty as to the precise dates of writing.

Many of my writings in law and economics and some in the history of economic thought inevitably have had to do with property. Those writings have dealt with the framework function of government, the legal-economic nexus, property in a positive welfare-economics model of power, theories of property, property and philosophy, population density and property, the role of selective perception and sentiment in all aspects of the economic role of government, the principle of the rule of law, the Fifth Amendment takings clause, property under landed aristocracy and middle-class society, the fundamental interrelationships of government and property, and so on. These studies have enriched my understanding of the institution of property, the heuristic use of deconstruction and discourse analyses of language, what the economic role of government in society and in the history of economic thought involve, and other aspects of thought.

The language of political and constitutional theory has its own impact, inasmuch as people tend to understand—selectively perceive—their situation in its terms. People may refer to historical events but the meaning of these events is expressed in terms of the selective political and constitutional theory to which they gave rise. To control language is to control the legal-economic nexus and much else; that is why theories are ensconced in definitions and why definitions are contested ground.

If we discuss something in what seems to be a reasonably and mutually intelligible manner, then it may be said that our discussion presupposes the existence of that object. But does the object exist, and in what sense? The rocks on the moon or on Mars exist even if we do not know enough to discuss them very intelligently. Also, these rocks would exist if mankind did not know of them, and continue to exist even if something wiped out all life on Earth. Not so with the rules of football and not so with principles of the law of property, the law of property, and the jurisprudence of due process of law. The corporation exists only in the contemplation of the law. It would not exist were life eliminated. The sense in which certain things or concepts exist is different from the sense in which other things and concepts exist. Property is not protected because it is property; property is property because it is protected. Not all interests are protected as property; some are protected in different ways and in different terms; some are not protected at all. Moon rocks exist even though we cannot normally hold them in our hands. There is nothing sentimental about their existence, though perhaps there is to some people about their meaning. A right of property does not exist in the same sense as do moon rocks; it is something that exists sentimentally and arguably no more than that, especially if human life is eliminated. Property rights are ontologically subjective and epistemologically objective, at least up to a point—the point defining whether Alpha or Beta has the right and the other party is exposed to it, that is, whether A has the right to harm B or vice versa. There is nothing objectively resident in nature of the problem of whose—Alpha's or Beta's interest or claim of interest—is to count. However, the process of determining whose interest will be protected can be examined in an objective manner. The irony is that because rights tend to be understood in an ontologically objective or absolutist manner, especially in economics, very little effort is made to study the process of determination in an objective manner.[1] The danger is that the relevant language is laden with primitive terms, with everyone who uses them thinking of them in his or her own way but paying little or no attention to the multiple and high variegated usage.

Property is one of the most vibrant, fascinating and productive entry points into what government and society is, in some sense, all about. It is that, however, only if, or to the extent that, one can treat it in an objective, positive, nonnormative (non-ideological) manner, which is exceedingly difficult to do for a number of reasons, such as tautology and circularity in law, the hermeneutic circle, selective perception, general ideology, social control, selective personal identifications with certain of the phenomena with which we live and not others, wishful thinking, and so on. Pervading all of the foregoing are the belief, symbolic, and mythic systems of society.

One curious aspect of the foregoing is how little modern educated people are cognizant of the role of the belief, symbolic, and mythic systems of society—possibly not more than, and probably less than was understood by the educated classes of the ancient Greeks and Romans. The source of this ignorance is the effectiveness of social control. Carl J. Friedrich was only one of numerous scholars who identified a principal characteristic of the eighteenth century in general and of the Enlightenment in particular: policy consciousness, the awareness that institutions are man made, socially constructed, subject to revision by mankind, and not given to mankind by Nature or by Nature's God. This recognition ran counter to the felt needs of those engaged in social control and simultaneously taking advantage of their own position. Accordingly, policy consciousness seems to have been only inadvertently promoted by Church and State.

Consider my use of the phrase, "the socio-legal institution of private property," to describe one of my research interests. If one uses the phrase, as do I, in an empirical and secular manner, such use conflicts with principal themes of the absolutist formulation of property rights as due to nature and God. If by property rights we mean a category of the ultimate nature of things, or of the beneficence of God, without coherent knowledge of the working of nature and/or God, we can have nothing further to say about how nature and God determine new property rights and/or change already existing property rights. We would have to rely upon such formulaic linguistic tropes as, "Everything is for the best," "God has his reasons," "Everything has a reason," and let the matter go with that. What we cannot handle or what we want to render sacred we attribute to God or, more recently, the Market.

I take an empirical and secular view of property rights. My view parallels Adam Smith's treatment of the development of moral rules. In his *Theory of Moral Sentiments*, Smith could have argued that moral rules are due to the actions of God; it is God and not man who is responsible for moral rules. But Smith did not so argue. Smith argues that individuals want for others to think well of them, and, what is more, they want to think well of themselves. This is due in large part to God implanting in mankind two principles, that of approbation and that of disapprobation, of our own behavior and that of others. True enough, but Smith nonetheless does not attribute the moral rules to God; rather he has mankind work out and revise over time the moral rules which will help govern individuals. The moral rules are not rules because they are moral; they are moral (and subject to further checking) either because they are the rules which emerge from the process, or else the generic category of what he is talking about. The same point applies to property. As I have already noted, property is not protected because it is property, it is property because it is protected. In both respects—moral rules and property rights—the linguistics is subtle. But as with Smith on the working out of moral rules, so with us on the working out of property.

Inter alia, however, one must inevitably come to grips with the problem of continuity versus change. The problem of continuity versus change is at the heart of the concept of due process of law. A process that is idiosyncratic and seems to change from case to case is hardly due process. But there must be change. Without change of law, society would still resemble some status quo ante, say, medievalism. The nature of property and of property rights consists in the privileged position given those interests that are protected as property—again, not because they independently exist as property and on that account are protected, but they constitute property because they are protected. This is the problem of continuity versus change, examined in varied detail in later chapters of this volume, especially Chapters 6, 7, 15, and 16. The nature of human affairs renders it necessary that rights, even those privileged as property rights, will change. Joseph Schumpeter provided, inadvertently perhaps, the name for the process, "creative destruction," to him the fundamental characteristic of the market economy's performance.

Capitalism, or the market economy, is said to rest on fully and firmly defined property rights and to do so most effectively when marginal social costs equal marginal private costs, that is, no externalities. An enormous irony inheres in this. The market economy, and the law of property in all its manifestations, may be said to require the protection of established rights of economic significance. But economic agents, through competition and innovation, both directly and by inducing governments to act, create new rights of economic significance and destroy old ones, and no one is in principle protected against such loss.

Clearly, whatever the source of any property right, it must be given legal status, if only to enable the transfer of ownership that is the heart of a purchase and sale. That is to say, everyone with an interest of economic significance must either have that interest protected or else be left exposed to the decisions and actions of those whose interest is protected—except from creative destruction. This means that when the legal process is called upon to establish, at least for now, the respective rights and exposures of the parties in this same field of action, the law limits the economic significance of putatively all other rights by establishing this new right(s).

But let us examine the problem of continuity versus change through the legal concept, *stare decisis*, and in order to do so in an efficient manner let us rely solely on the case holdings used in *Black's Law Dictionary* (hereafter *Black's*) to define the concept. The basic definition given for this Latin legal term is "To abide by, or adhere to, decided cases." The problems, then, would seem to be to determine just which precedent is a precedent for this instant case, when the point at issue therein is already settled, and, moreover, what is meant by "settled." That continuity is a key element is evident from cases quoted in *Black's*. One case held, "Policy of courts to stand by precedent and not to disturb settled point." Another case held, "Doctrine that, when court has once laid down a principle of law as applicable to a certain state of facts, it will adhere to that principle, and apply it to all future cases, where facts are substantially the same." Still another case, however, is quoted to illustrate what I take to be the inevitable necessity of having to consider change:

> Doctrine is one of policy, grounded on theory that security and certainty require that accepted and established legal principle, under which rights may accrue, be recognized and followed, though later found to be not legally sound, but whether previous holding of court shall be adhered to, modified, or overruled is within court's discretion under circumstances of case before it.

A comparable case held that "Under doctrine, when point of law has been settled by decision, it forms precedent which is not afterwards to be departed from, and, while it should ordinarily be strictly adhered to, there are occasions when departure is rendered necessary to vindicate plain, obvious principles of law and remedy continued injustice." *Stare decisis* is beloved of conservatives—except when the previous case holding in question is held now with repugnance. (The matter arose in January 2006 during the Senate Judiciary Committee's hearings on the nomination of Samuel Alito to the Supreme Court *apropos* of *Roe v. Wade*.) The upshot is a position of tautology and/or circularity, hence open-endedness, a situation deeply ironic in being found in the definition of a concept whose gravamen is continuity and indeed continuity based on settled law, but also a concept which, in the nature of the material, must embody change of decisional law: "The doctrine is a salutary one," states one case, "and should not ordinarily be departed from where decision is of long standing and rights have been acquired under it, *unless considerations of public policy demand it*" (Black 1968: 1577–8, italics added; most of the following chapters have reasoning and evidence that bears on the issue of continuity versus change).

Much of the discussion, such as that of *stare decisis*, involves my felt need for objective analysis not to take legal doctrine only at face value but to examine the more or less subordinate components of the doctrine in question, even if one of those components is absolutist formulation.

I have pointed to some ironical aspects of the topics and problems dealt with in these chapters. Perhaps the two greatest ironies of all in this volume are these: First, law is essentially a conservative profession and both the nature of property, the gravamen of *stare decisis* tends to be continuity. Conservatives tend to extol the principle of continuity (unless, as noted, they object to that which exists). And continuity *is* important. The irony is the same as Nicholas Mercuro and I (1979) argued in regard to the use of the takings clause of the Fifth Amendment. The concept of *stare decisis* serves the purpose, unintended to be sure, of providing psychic balm with which to overcome opposition and anxiety over change, to soothe the realization of instrumentalism and pragmatism, and to render change acceptable on the ground that the losing party has had their day in court. Indeed, the takings clause with its requirement of just compensation "quite paradoxically . . . tends to legitimize all legal change . . . whether or not compensated. . . . in having the compensation provision available it induces the acceptance of legal change without compensation" (Samuels and Mercuro 1979: 180, and *passim*; see Samuels 1974a). A corollary irony is that choice between continuity and change is often actually between different modes of change. The second irony relates to the irony examined in the Preface that "criticism of government by those who want to themselves use government is not taken as dangerous but 'telling it how it is' by objective scholars without their own agenda for government is held out to be dangerous." The present irony derives from the appearance of emphasizing change in the Preface and in the first fifteen chapters of the book. After all, I have critiqued, *inter alia*, pro-continuity emphases on the status quo, property itself, due process of law, *stare decisis*, rights, order, and so on. But in Chapter 16, I argue strongly in favor of diffidence on the part of social scientists, economists in particular. I emphasize that economists *qua* economists have no particular, deep and/or conclusive expertise in all matters of economic policy. Mercuro and I have written in favor of an agnostic view of legal-economic analysis. We also have written in favor of direct confrontation with fundamental issues. We said that "the objection that such a view opens the door to deliberative change is not without merit, but it ultimately reduces to the question of whether the power structure operating in the existing world is to be left unexamined" (Samuels and Mercuro 1980: 125). To be candid and fair to those who are unhappy with what is said here about *stare decisis* and elsewhere about the takings clause, we too acknowledge the existence of situations in which diffidence seems the poorer alternative—but each individual and each society will have to work that out for itself (see Chapters 5 and 6).

I want to identify very briefly the empirical, secular sources of rights, particularly but not solely property rights, with two points in mind. One is the multiplicity of sources that historically have been involved. The other is the mundane nature of most if not all of them, given the form of government involved and notwithstanding efforts to legitimize the process and the rights generated by it in absolutist terms. For my purposes I need only call attention to the distinction made between property rights and rights in general, including in the latter those that may be taken to be the functional equivalent of property rights. Property rights receive or are given a more privileged position, so much so that they are often referred to as sacred. The reciprocal character of property rights is indicated by illustrating them as either or both (different cases, different parties) (1) the right to cause problems for, shift costs to, and/or commit a tort against another party and (2) the right to be free from such problems, costs and torts. In slightly different language, the former is being free to and the latter being free from. Non-property rights include turning right on red where permitted, receiving welfare benefits or subsidies, selling commodities to the Department of Defense, holding after an election or appointment a seat in the legislature or a judgeship in court, being paid in lawful money for services rendered, other protective labor legislation, and so on. Property-right functional equivalents are having a right to a job, (possibly) receiving a refund under the existing tax laws, right to be heard or to appeal someone else's decision, and so on. The world of property is very complex and subtle. The freed slave can claim restitution for past loss of freedom and income; the former dispossessed owner can claim compensation for the freeing of his or her slaves and thus the taking of property. Conflicts between property owners can be more dramatic than between propertied and non-propertied interests, because, say, of the reciprocal character of rights. "Rights" is a primitive term whose content is adduced differently by different users, auditors, and readers. It can take the form of being a claim, an adjudicated conflict, and the compensation and/or other protection or satisfaction given to the winner in a court case. One need ask, against whom is a right to be enforced, how, and by whom? Who has an insurable interest in another person? Who can one take to court to secure a claim of violated right to vote, to be safe from discrimination and other forms of violence, to have the meaningful opportunity to have a job or to have stable prices, to be told the truth by politicians, and so on? When is mine safety enforceable and when not, and against whom?

Among the sources of rights have been the following:

- Grants of land to people whom a monarch or representative legislature seeks to reward or on whom to bestow favor.
- Grants of land and/or money to economic interests who have, in effect, purchased the enabling statute by bribery or other corruption, even if not technically illegal under existing law.

- Changes in the rules governing either payment of just compensation under eminent domain or property tax assessment.
- Changing the provisions of regulatory statutes in response to citizen petition of grievances.
- Shifting between taxes and subsidies to internalize the cost of externalities.
- Provisions of mortgages and other instruments of indebtedness issued or controlled by governments.
- Compensation/remuneration paid on the basis of provisions of other government contracts.
- The existence and specific provisions of laws creating or enabling specialized credit institutions, including ownership, membership and other access-to-credit rules.
- Elections and the operative programs of particular political parties.
- The working out of the due process and equal protection clauses, including the operation of selective perception as to what constitutes state action and when is a government action a taking and thereby compensable.
- Competition between bankers and lawyers over social engineering.
- Creating new law and thereby new rights.
- Competition between labor and capital over whose customs and their administration will be incorporated into law.
- Changing corporation law and securities law as to who is exposed to risk generated by others.
- The use of the corporation (possibly of various types) as a mode of economic organization.
- The law governing competition and who can do what to whom.
- The conduct of monetary policy, including the determination and strength of various policy instruments.
- Full employment versus price stability as the goal of macroeconomic policy.
- The rules adopted by administrative commissions governing or applied to public utility rate and other cases.
- The ways various other provisions of the Constitution are used and the ways not used.
- The circumstances likely will differ as between landed property rights and the property rights of capital.
- Rights will vary with how the expenses of government are financed, that is, tax policy, and the activities of government are determined, that is, expenditure policy.
- Private contracting is a source of claims to income, depending upon legal provisions as to conditions.
- Private rights of economic significance will be influenced by their status with respect not only to tort law but to criminal law; some activities now legal were once severely punished.
- Conquest.
- Imperialism.
- "Normal" buying and selling activity in markets.

- Enforcement or non-enforcement of requirement for competitive bidding for government contracts.
- Manipulation of markets by corporate strategies, use of government, and so on.

Some of these sources literally involve *de jure* rights. Others do not but have much the same effect on the distributions of income, opportunity and power. Some phenomena are relatively homogeneous; others are not, that is, courts and legislatures adopt different policies and/or rules. Some phenomena are relatively easily explicable; others need not be. The Supreme Court of Michigan unanimously rejected a claim that eminent domain can be used by local public agencies for economic development purposes, explicitly overruling a case which permitted the purpose and contrasting with a later US Supreme Court decision permitting the use of eminent domain (Chapter 11). Changes in rights can relate to the conditions of their acquisition, their use, and their disposition, and so on.

Rights as we know them are in part a function of the system of government, in part, how the conflicts that comprise property are worked out, and how such provisions as the takings and due process clauses are also worked out.

I reflected to myself at one point on what I have written both so far and later in this chapter, specifically on its seeming focus on the problem of continuity versus change relative to the problems of freedom versus control and on hierarchy versus equality. All three, and more (see Chapter 6), are facets of the problem of order. Given what I have published over the years on these subjects, I sense that readers too will sense and be surprised at a relative neglect of power and power structure. I think that neither my reflection nor the reader's sense is correct, for three reasons. The first reason is that the deepest level on which the conflict of continuity with change operates is that formed by issues of the structure of power, that is, freedom versus control and hierarchy versus equality. The second reason is that, with very few exceptions, issues of power are central to the subjects covered, albeit in different ways. The third reason is what I have to say in the third document about the importance of and interrelationships between belief and power.

None of what is presented in this chapter or in the rest of this volume should be a surprise. Different social, legal and economic systems likely will be taken for granted by those who live in each such system, either because that is how people look upon their society or because they have been induced by social control to believe it is part of the natural order of things. In a society in which land ownership is the dominant institution, it conveys certain *de jure*, and often also *de facto*, rights of governance to landed property owners. In a society in which the ownership and, especially, control of corporate assets is the dominant institution, owners and managers have serious *de facto*, though likely not *de jure*, influence on government. One is a governmental system centering on land, the other is one centering on industrial and financial assets, and both exhibit the principle that government is available for the use of whomever is in a position to control it. If this is no surprise, neither is it *ipso facto* condemnatory. Those who can examine such a system at arm's length and in an agnostic manner will tend to have a different view of polity and economy than that of believers in their respective systems.

One may not like what appears to be corruption in either system and one may elevate one normatively over the other. Each system can also be taken as an object of study. Examining the character and source of property rights (or of different types of rights in general) is critical to the actual evolutionary path of the system. Examining the Constitutional provisions regarding due process of law is in turn critical to how courts in particular approach conflict resolution through the manipulation of jurisprudential language. I now turn, first, to the two documents prepared in the 1960s, whose meaning remains intact for me into the twenty-first century.

The character of property rights

The character of property rights has been the subject of a number of diverse formulations or theories, even aside from the more heterodox views suggested, for example, by the Proudhonian proposition that "Property is robbery" (Proudhon (1840) *First Memoir*, chapter 1, p. 1). Notwithstanding some important subsidiary differences of formulation, however, the great substance of relevant western legal theory may be conveniently reduced to two only somewhat exclusive understandings of the relationship between property and state, and ultimately of the character of property rights. One of these involves a notion of "absolute" private property, property existing independent of the state, the state serving only to protect property; the other involves the idea of a sum or bundle of rights in practice derived through the state, that is, through positive legislation. It would be incorrect to either assert or infer that the two theories are merely one of absolutism and one of relativism. More incisive is the characterization of the first as the theory of individual *dominium* ultimately reducible, at least, to an originally "absolute" and "indivisible" residual quantum of rights independent of the state, and the second as the theory of property as a malleable sum of legally defined rights each and in total presumably serving some ostensible functional or utilitarian purpose in terms of social policy. In the case of the first, the claim of a pre-existent or pre-eminent private *dominium* serves as the sanction for private property; in the case of the second, the ostensible social purpose serves as the criterion of judgment.

As a theory, the former is apparently of earlier vintage, and although it remains strong yet, especially in popular belief (as part of what J. K. Galbraith (1958: Chapter 2) calls the "conventional wisdom"), it would appear to be more of an "organizational fiction,"[2] and has been replaced in more modern times by the latter. It would appear that both are theoretical explanations, but that the first expresses western values to the extent that they have become recognized or incorporated *de jure*, while the second is the one that is descriptively valid *de facto*.

The classic statement of the individual *dominium* theory of property has been provided by William Blackstone. In his *Commentaries on the Laws of England* Blackstone postulated the right of property as

> that sole and despotic dominion which one man claims and exercises over the external things of the world, in total exclusion of the right of any other individual in the universe.
>
> (II, I, 2: 114)

This suggests what Letourneau (1892: xi) called "the ancient formula, 'the right to use and to abuse.'" McIlwain (1932: 265) summarizes the thoughts of John of Paris such that private possessions convey "the only right to such goods, the only power over them, and the sole *dominium* in them, they alone may treat them as their own, no one else has even the power of a *dispensator* over them." More recently Sohn (quoted in Noyes 1936: 297) has also maintained that property is intrinsically unlimited: "Ownership is a right, unlimited in respect of its contents, to exercise control over a thing." Thus did Rousseau, in his *Discourse on Political Economy*, write: "It is certain that the right of property is the most sacred of all rights of citizenship, and even more important in some respects than liberty itself..." (quoted in Schlatter 1951: 207).

There is no question but that this theory has become a central strand of the dominant social ideology of western society, whether it be expressed in terms of naturalist or divine origins.

> What is peculiar to Anglo-American legal thinking, and above all to American legal thinking, is an ultra-individualism, an uncompromising insistence upon individual interest and individual property as the focal point of jurisprudence.
>
> (Pound 1921: 37)

The basic understanding common to most if not all formulations of the *dominium* theory is that private property rights exist, in theory at least, prior to and distinct from the state, and that some medium of substantive rights exist, again in theory at least, even in the absence of the state. As part of the ideology of laissez-faire capitalism the inference is drawn that the state ought to and indeed does exist primarily if not only for the protection of property; and, property conceived as extant independent of the state, for the state to go beyond "protecting" property would infringe upon the rights of property.

The theory of property as the "sole and despotic" *dominium* of an individual may appear at first inspection to be incontrovertibly absolutist in character, but neither Blackstone nor Sohn, for example, failed to recognize or to concede that property "is subject to legal limitations, imposed by the rights of others or by the rules of public law, which subtract from it" (Noyes 1936: 297). Blackstone maintains that one of the "absolute rights"

> inherent in every Englishman, is that of property: which consists in the free use, enjoyment, and disposal of all his acquisitions, *without any control or diminution, save only by the laws of the land.*
>
> (Blackstone 1959: 51, italics added)

Though he holds that "the original of private property is probably founded in nature," he goes on to say that

> but certainly the modifications under which we at present find it, the method of conserving it in the present owner, and of translating it from man to man,

are entirely derived from society; and are some of those civil advantages, in exchange for which every individual has resigned a part of his natural liberty.

(Blackstone 1959: 51, italics added)

The absolutism, "without any control or diminution," is thus transparent; Blackstone recognized that as a matter of fact actual legal rights and relationships are subject to "the laws of the land," that they "are entirely derived from society." Thus does he acknowledge the dependency of property rights upon the actual law pertaining to a given territory at a given time.

But this is not the emphasis of the Blackstonian conception; it is rather a qualification imposed, as it were, by the need to be consonant with reality. The emphasis of the Blackstonian and all other *dominium* theories is upon the private element in *private* property—the emphasis on minimal state activity so congenial to capitalist ideology. Says Blackstone,

> So great moreover is the regard of the law for private property, that it will not authorize the least violation of it; no, not even for the general good of the whole community.... In vain may it be urged, that the good of the individual ought to yield to that of the community; for it would be dangerous to allow any private man, or even any public tribunal, to be the judge of this common good, and to decide whether it be expedient or no. Besides, the public good is in nothing more essentially interested, than in the protection of every individual's private rights, as modeled by the municipal law.
>
> (Blackstone 1959: 52)

Blackstone recognized that the legislature "frequently interposes and compels the individual to acquiesce."

> But how does it interpose and compel? Not by absolutely stripping the subject of his property in an arbitrary manner; but by giving him a full indemnification and equivalent for the injury thereby sustained. The public is now considered as an individual, treating with an individual for an exchange. All that the legislature does is to oblige the owner to alienate his possessions for a reasonable price.
>
> (Blackstone 1959: 52)

The logic of individualism is most explicit with respect to taxation:

> For no subject of England can be constrained to pay any aids or taxes, even for the defense of the realm or the support of government, but such *as are imposed by his own consent*, or that of his representatives in parliament.
>
> (Blackstone 1959: 52, italics added)

Thus does a resolution of the First Continental Congress (1774) read,

> The inhabitants of the English Colonies in North America, by the immutable laws of nature...are entitled to life, liberty, and property and they have ceded to any sovereign power whatever, a right to dispose of either without their consent.
>
> (Quoted in Jones 1941: 7)

Blackstone's example of *eminent domain*—the taking of private property through due process of law with just compensation—is cogent but misleading, for the power to regulate, the *policy power* in the generic and legal sense, is also relevant, and generally at variance with the implications of *eminent domain*. The police power may be taken to mean either (a) the power to regulate in the interests of the public health, safety, welfare and morals, or (b) the power to modify the rights of property and contract through due process of law but without just compensation. In either case the common rights privately enjoyed are constrained by some notion of common rights commonly enjoyed, for example, by remedial legislation. As such it is a manifestation of the continuing interaction between individual rights or drives and collective needs or demands, involving the need to restrict some freedom in order to give substance to another freedom in the course of maximizing freedom. And, what is more, the logic of compensation relevant to eminent domain is irrelevant with respect to the police power, as it is precluded historically by the priority of social considerations.

Furthermore, unless one grants greater weight than appears justified to the phrase "without any control or diminution, save only by the laws of the land," and "as modeled by the municipal law," Blackstone's own descriptive emphasis of private property as "sole and despotic domain" is unrealistic and static even for his own day, regardless of what has transpired since. Even Blackstone was aware that "Almost all the real property of this kingdom is by the policy of our laws, supposed to the granted by, dependent upon and *holden* of some superior lord..." (Blackstone 1959: 145; italics added; see also Noyes 1936: 303). Even more important than the presence of this feudal element, the work of Ely, Dicey, and Pound,[3] for example, suggests that the character and composition of the law of property is in a continual state of flux, even during Blackstone's own time. Such change has been a normal characteristic of the development of Anglo-American law, being a product of changing economic, technological, and institutional conditions, as well as changing ideas as to social values. Even if one prefers to think in terms of an expansion in the law of property rather than a change or a mutation, still the fact remains that important dimensions of property rights have not gone unchanged. Recognition of this has in fact resulted in the substantive modification of the *dominium* theory.

Given all these considerations the theory of property as individual *dominium* has had to be reduced to a notion of a presumably objectively definable residual quantum of rights with respect to which "it might be more appropriate to use the term 'ultimate' than the term 'absolute'" (Noyes 1936: 305). Says Noyes, in developing the notion of a "core right."

It is possible to reduce this so-called "ownership" to the right to vindicate the "ownership" (*nuda proprietas*), so that its only content is the right to claim itself. And this I think accurately portrays the final legal concept of the only property which, in the original feudal sense, can be called absolute. It is that legal relation with respect to objects to which, when every constituent right is removed, something still remains.

Among all these varied assortments of the rights composing complete property we have suggested that one may always be identified because it contains the core right. They are, it is true, parts of a totality; but they are also segments stripped off from a core. And this points to the conclusion that while other fractions may have no relation to each other, all must be related directly or indirectly to the core. The core is, therefore, not a mere disconnected residue. It is the skeleton, however emaciated, upon which the whole complex of complete property depends. Because it is that fraction from which ultimately the titles of all other fractions are derived, it is the apex of the system of derivative and dependent property into which the totality may have been divided. The rights remaining in that fraction may be insignificant. All the practically important rights may have been assigned to other fractions. But the whole complex hinges upon the fraction containing the core right. In it reposes the individuality. For the core right is the only property in the entire complex which complies essentially with the original notion of absolute property (Noyes 1936: 298, 304–5; see also 301–3). Noyes thus differentiates between "absolute" and "complete" property such that after deducting the "social reservations" from complete property there is left the residual quantum of the "core right." It would seem, however, that both concepts, of "absolute property" and of "complete property," "can be reduced to a bare hypothetical residuum" and that each is "a legal artifice—almost a fiction" (Noyes 1936: 299). The notion of a "core right," unless it is reduced to the idea of power, is utterly fictitious and ambiguous with no operational significance; and should it be reduced to power (i.e., ability to make effective decisions), then it begs the ultimate question, namely, wherein rests the locus of ultimate authority concerning effective decision-making? The notion of property involves the "right" to acquire, use and dispose, that is, the "right" to make decisions. The character of property would therefore seem to depend on wherein lies the ultimate ability to determine the character, the scope and the several dimensions of the decision making process. This is what the "bundle-of-rights" theory attempts to meaningfully examine. The reduction of the individual *dominium* theory to the residual quantum formulation serves not to rescue the theory but to involve it in an impossibly unrealistic fiction, a fiction hardly anything more than subjectively definable, a fiction the essence of which is more nearly felt than seen.

The sum- or bundle-of-rights theory of the character of property maintains that property (property rights) is what the law of property has it to be, and that the composition, indeed the very character, of property is subject to revision and reconstitution through a concomitant revision and reconstitution of the law of property. It maintains that the property complex is by no means something given and absolute; rather property is relative and malleable by its very nature.

> Thus, property in any object consists of a "bundle" of rights concerning the object, a bundle that never includes all the possible rights associated with

the object, and that may be broadened or narrowed to include more or less of the possible rights as law or custom may decide.

(Boulding 1958: 30)

Thus another writer has concluded:

> In the light of modern anthropological and legal research, the "bundle of rights" which is usually associated with the notion of *property* appears to be subject to complex processes of social development.
>
> (Suranyi-Unger 1952: 218)

Joseph Schumpeter (1949) and Gunnar Myrdal (1955) have analyzed the substantive role of ideology in the development of economic theory. Commons has expressed essentially the same thoughts in a manner applying equally to economic as well as legal theory.

> [A] mark of the progress that has occurred in economic theory, from the time of Quesnay and Adam Smith, has been the emergence of the concept of good or bad political economy out of mythical entities such as nature's harmony, natural law, natural order, natural rights, divine providence, over-soul, invisible hand, social will, social-labor power, social value, tendency towards equilibrium of forces, and the like, into its proper place as the good or bad, right or wrong, wise or unwise proportioning by man himself of those human faculties and natural resources which are limited in supply and complementary to each other.
>
> (Commons 1924: 2)

The same would seem to be valid with respect to legal theory: while older ideas as to "received" or "discovered" law are still widely held (as is the case with some of the economic concepts noted by Commons), contemporary legal thought is in terms of the, say, wise or unwise, desirable or undesirable, construction of the institutions of society; of the wise or unwise development of the "legal foundations of capitalism." Law thus considered becomes "one of the shaping forces of society" (Frankfurter 1939: 8), one of the organizing techniques of society; thus, an instrument of social control, control necessitating some judgment as to purpose.

> Human beings...have various needs and desires. Many of these relate to external objects with which they are in some way associated.... The law of property may be looked at as an attempt upon the part of the state, acting through its courts and administrative officers, to give a systematized recognition of, and protection to, these attitudes and desires on the part of individuals toward things. These attitudes and desires of various individuals are often in conflict with one another and in resolving conflicts, many elements, including the general interest of the public at large must be taken into account. Obviously ideas of where the line should be drawn as between the conflicting

desires of individuals, what the most advantageous public policy is in a particular situation or in broad questions of general social organization are bound to vary from place to place and from one generation to another and these changes in attitude are sometimes rapidly, sometimes slowly reflected in changes in the law, sometimes in details, sometimes in its broader aspects, and occasionally in its entirety.

(Aigler, Smith and Tefft 1951: 1–2)

Rousseau could not remain an adherent to the notion that property is sacred and absolute, however desirable. In his *Social Contract* Rousseau wrote that "the state, in relation to its members, is master of all their goods by the social contract, which, within the state, is the basis of all rights" (Schlatter 1951: 207). (John Locke also differentiated between the state of nature and the state of civil society, with a similar conclusion.[4])

Law has no divine origin. It is not the establishment of abstract and eternal principles of justice. It does not exist a priori, a system into which social and economic activities are irrevocably fitted. Broadly speaking, social and economic activities come first and determine the course of the development of law. It is true, of course, that law is relied upon to regulate and control certain types of human conduct; but ultimately paradoxical as it may sound, human conduct makes laws. In brief, law is essentially a crystallization of social policy or, to employ a term more commonly used by courts, public policy.

Underlying any social or economic institution is the conviction that in the long run it promotes the best interests of all concerned...

Underlying every rule of law is a judgment of "social good" or "social wisdom."

(Spencer and Gillam 1953: 13; see also the references to Hohfeld and Hearn in Noyes 1936: 301, 303–4)

It is certainly true that there is an interaction pattern between the legal framework and the economic and technological system: "The correct approach is to recognize that the legal framework is important for the shaping of economic systems and that these systems participate in directing the development of property and other legal institutions" (Suranyi-Unger 1952: 218). More important is that *law*, including the law of property, is not given, but is rather, both descriptively and in terms of its origin, a matter of continuously revised social policy, the substance ever-changing and always subject to change.

This being the case, "'Private property' is a shorthand term for a bundle of legal claims and privileges" (Dahl and Lindblom 1953: 512), and the "justification, in terms of the broadening of freedom, for any particular form of institution of property must be argued in terms of whether the losses caused by the restrictions imposed are greater or less than the gains derived from the elimination of costly conflict" (Boulding 1958: 119). Thus, "Private property is a means, and neither its abolition nor its unrestricted right should be an end in itself" (Boulding 1958: 400). The bundle-of-rights theorists thus emphasize the continuing *functional* considerations of "practical expediency, social efficiency, and economic prosperity as the operational criteria for the necessity and current development of property" (Suranyi-Unger 1952: 220–1). What Boulding discusses in terms of the "broadening of freedom" through the restriction of freedom, Dahl and Lindblom describe in terms of "the coordinating function of private property" (Dahl and Lindblom 1953: 513). Given, then, the substantive decision to adopt the institution of private property (itself the "core right?") (Noyes 1936: 305, n. 59), all facets of the sum-or bundle-of-rights theory of property emphasize the malleable character of property rights with no single element of property necessarily exempt from reconstitution.

It would appear, then, even where the *dominium* theory is the theory formally or ideologically incorporated in the law and jurisprudence of the time and place, as in Blackstone's time, that the bundle-of-rights theory is still the more descriptively and logically valid and useful, the *dominium* theory serving essentially only to emphasize individualism, itself important.

One further facet warrants attention, a matter relating to the notion of "fictions" cited earlier. It has come to be recognized that there is a highly important dichotomy necessary to the analysis of any legal system, the *de facto-de jure* dichotomy. Emphasizing that what is recognized in law is not necessarily a matter of factual realism the dichotomy serves to force thought away from the *wording* of prescriptions to the *effectual substance* of practice. Thus, as recognized by Berle and Means (1933), although the American law of property recognizes the stockholder as the *de jure* proprietor, the *de facto* owner is the managerial class having the right to acquire, use, and dispose of the corporate property. A similar development has been paradoxically observed in Soviet society. Thus Milovan Djilas reports that

> Ownership is nothing other than the right of profit and control. If one defines class benefits by this right, the Communist states have seen, in the final analysis, the origin of a new form of ownership or a new ruling and exploiting class.
>
> Property is legally considered social and national property. But, in actuality, a single group manages it in its own interest.
>
> As defined by Roman law, property constitutes the use, enjoyment, and disposition of material goods. The Communist political bureaucracy uses, enjoys, and disposes of nationalized property.
>
> (Djilas 1957: 35, 65, 44)

The dominium theory of property in both its Blackstonian and modern "residual quantum" forms is operationally unrealistic. The bundle-of-rights theory, on the other hand, focuses attention on the continuous reconstitution of the character and dimensions—its very substance—of private property, and to the substantive role of the state in developing *a* law of private property. The Blackstonian individual *dominium* theory has the role of the state protecting property, or, at the most, doing the minimum necessary to institute the system of private property. But in the light of realistic analysis and modern legal theory, such a view is inadequate, for the role of the state, it would seem, cannot be reduced to such a modicum of activity. It would be reasonable to suppose, notwithstanding expressions in terms of the dominium theory that one could discover some more or less substantial considerations in such ostensibly Blackstonian theories that would evidence the bundle-of-rights approach. It would be expected, it should be made clear, because the *dominium* theory has been generally demonstrated to be inadequate. It would thus seem reasonable to infer on a priori grounds that any realistic theory of property has to encompass elements of a non-absolutist bundle-of-rights theory of malleable property rights.

Due Process of Law

Given the premise that government exists as an instrument of social control for the purpose of serving the interests of its citizens, the fundamental problem of the theory of economic policy is: Which theory of what government *should* do is to be adopted to govern the actual functioning of government? Reducing the state to a purely utilitarian instrument, with the interests of the citizens governing the exercise of state power, the proper question is less *which* theory of economic policy, but *whose* theory: in whose interest, on what terms, and for what purpose is economic policy to be conducted? The analysis commences, then, on two points: that social control is exercised over government through the theory of economic policy adopted by government (i.e. by those who exercise the powers of governance, or those who control them), and, that each theory of what government should do reflects the economic and broader interests of those in whose interest the particular theory of economic policy would define the scope of government.

In the American system of government, the fundamental arguments and divisions over what should be the role of government in economic life have taken the form of having to reconcile the Commerce Clause and the Police Power of the national and state governments, respectively, with the respective Due Process of Law Clauses of the Constitution. Beyond this, of course, the Commerce Clause has been opposed by the Police Power under the Reserved Powers Clause, and vice versa, to strengthen or limit the respective powers of the Federal or State levels of government. The genesis of the general problem derives from the fact that the Constitution does not establish, or could not establish, with finality a solution to the problem of the role of government in the economy. A variety of Constitutional interpretation has continued from the beginning of the nation. In a basic sense, this is the burden borne by a pluralist but constitutionalist society.

In addition to the unsettled nature of what the role of government should be, there are the dual problems arising from the fact that there is multiple, arbitrary division of the powers of governance. Power is first split in terms of a federal system of government, and, second, in terms of a division of power within each level. Such a dual division engenders problems peculiar to itself and also ramifies other difficulties, such as the present question of what should be the role of government. In particular the intra-level (but also inter-level) question as to the role of the federal judiciary *vis-á-vis* national and state statutes reflects the basic problem of the locus of decision making authority as to just what theory of policy government (meaning the totality of government) will in tact follow. Since the Court is concerned with the "Constitutionality" of statutes, the question then arises as to what the several phrases of the Constitution mean, which in effect is, which interpretation of what the phrases mean is to be adopted, each interpretation capable of being associated with different theories as to the economic role of government.

The Fifth Amendment of the Constitution provides that "No person shall be deprived of life, liberty or property, without due process of law." The Fourteenth Amendment similarly provides that "nor shall any State deprive any person of life, liberty or property, without due process of law." With respect to liberty and property, since almost all state and national statutes in some manner effectuate a reconstitution of the rights of persons in their economic activities, including the conditions of the use of their property, debate over the desirability of statutes has taken the form of advocating or contesting this or that definition of what constitutes Due Process of Law.

There have been two definitions, or theories, of Due Process of Law; one is Procedural Due Process, the other, Substantive Due Process.

Procedural due process of law relates to regular procedures regularly adhered to in the conduct of legal processes. The emphasis is upon procedures, with each person due his day in court; treated, save for reasonable classification, like other persons; in a word, the rule of law, rather than capricious treatment varying from moment to moment or from person to person.

Where did the procedures constituting Due Process come from, and may they be changed? Basically, the procedures are those "traditional to Anglo-Saxon Law that have emerged from the common and statute law of England and extant at the time of the separation from England. An early interpretation placed stress on the guarantees of Due Process merely extending to the procedure that was customary at or about the time of separation" (*Murray's Lessee v. Hoboken Land & Improvement Co.*, 18 How. 272 (1855)). As one writer has put it, this interpretation

> had the obvious disadvantage of perpetuating for all future ages the procedure as it existed during the era of discovery and colonization. The normal course of judicial history has been for men to change procedure in the endeavor to further the administration of justice.
>
> (Anderson 1950: 26, 1960: 28)

In time the threat of the dead hand was circumvented, "by expanding the concept of due process so that instead of requiring the exact procedure of the colonization era, it was sufficient if the new procedure satisfied the basic standards of the old procedure." In one case the Court so criticized the earlier doctrine: "If that were so the procedure of the first half of the seventeenth century would be fastened upon the American jurisprudence like a straight-jacket, only to be unloosed by constitutional amendment." (*Twining v. N.J.*, 211 U.S. 78 (1908), quoted in Anderson 1960: 28). In *Hurtado v. Calif.* 110 U.S. 516 (1884), quoted in Anderson the Court argued that

> we should expect that the new and various experiences of our own situation and system will mould and shape it into new and not less useful forms. ...It follows that any legal proceeding enforced by public authority, whether sanctioned by age and custom, or newly devised in the discretion of the legislative power, in furtherance of the general public good, which regards and preserves principles of liberty and justice, must be held to be due process of law...
>
> (1950: 26, 1960: 29)

But what are the "basic standards of the old procedure"; what is "in further-ance of the public good"; and when does and when does not a new proceeding "preserve...principles of liberty and justice"? Here is where reasonable men, and men with different economic and other interests, will differ; and, under the American system of government, such differences will take the form of judicial review of legislative enactments as to Due Process of Law—Due Process being variously interpreted. With all of government engaged in exercising the powers of governance, the Court shares with the legislature the resolution of what *should* be done. Chief Justice Marshall wrote, "Courts are the mere instruments of the law, and can will nothing." But he also wrote that the Constitution is "intended to endure for ages to come and, consequently, to be adapted to the various crises of human affairs." So Chief Justice Taney argued,

> It [the Constitution] speaks not only in the same words, but with the same meaning and intent with which it spoke when it came from the hands of its framers, and was voted on and adopted by the people of the United States. Any other rule of construction would abrogate the judicial character of this Court and make it the mere reflex of the popular opinion or passion of the day.

But Chief Justice Hughes contended: "We are under a Constitution, but the Constitution is what the judges say it is" (taken from the list, "Some Judicial Diversities," in various editions of Edward S. Corwin (1947), *The Constitution and What it Means Today*).

It is long settled that Due Process includes *procedure* among its criteria. But does it also include as a criterion of judicial review (i.e., judicial participation in governing) the evaluation of *substance* in terms of whether or not the Constitution allows or disallows this or that statute representative of this or that theory of what government should do by way of economic policy? Historically the Court has in fact so governed; the problem of what government should do has thus been joined to the problem of judicial review "broad or narrow?" On the one hand, the Court may look only to procedure (strictly defined), ignoring (thereby accepting) the theory of policy of the statute; or, on the other hand, the Court could review both procedural facets and substantive questions—whether the social philosophy of the act in question squares with the Constitution—that is with some given interpretation of what the Constitution means.

(It is important to note that division as to the meaning of the Constitution existed immediately after ratification—namely, broad versus strict construction. The fact of the later amendments only complicates the matter. The doctrine of *stare decisis*, that precedents will not be departed from for light and transient cause—being less serious than the matter really requires—is important in two respects: first, that substantive due process as it emerged could claim support in *stare decisis* (in the revival of the doctrine of vested interests), and, second, that there generally are rival precedents to which any given present case can be cited. *Stare decisis* was capable, then, of working on both sides of the street, in support or denial of any approach or social philosophy of economic policy.)

"Accordingly, the guarantee of due process was expanded to guarantee not merely procedural fairness, but also that the substance of the statutes themselves be fair and reasonable." (Anderson 1950: 29, 1960: 32) For purposes of presentation and analysis, the discussion will be divided into, first, that which is "fair" and, second, that which is "reasonable." The former relates to the question of desirability (i.e., fairness according to criteria of fairness; ergo, which criteria?), and the latter to the efficacy of a means (the statute) to its object.

Substantive due process was invoked by those antagonistic to the exercise of new forms of social control by either state or national government. They argued that the doctrine of vested interests, namely, the rights extant at any time had a pre-eminence of authority and government had to maintain these rights rather than abridge them under the guise of promoting the public interest. It was frequently argued that the rights extant at any time were natural rights, transcendent to the state; that government could not arbitrarily alter such rights lest freedom be infringed.

In a long "series" of cases extending over many decades, statutes were upheld or cast down depending upon whether or not substantive due process was invoked; that is, whether or not the Court concurred in the modification of property rights, or the alteration in the pattern of freedom and control, in each particular case. Since the same (or essentially similar) courts, as to membership, both approved and disapproved of regulatory statutes, it is clear that reasonable men may differ as to whether the hurdle of due process is passed or not passed, or that any individual may see infringement violative of the Constitution in one case and not in another. But it may be argued that the dominant social philosophy of the Court, or the majority of the Court (ergo rule by the odd man), also played a role.

Government may (or may not) alter contract rights—by restricting wages, hours, conditions or age of possible employment—or property rights—by instituting regulation over public utilities to preclude charging what the market will bear, or by taxing for the general treasury, or specific funds, to provide welfare and promotional services—but when does such modification of contract or property claims constitute the taking of property without due process? To take a clear example: when government requires a business, at the expense of the business itself, to take precautions against fire, or against unhealthy conditions, such a requirement, by increasing the costs of doing business, clearly reduces the income potential of the business and thereby reduces the value of the business, which means the reduction of the value of the property that is the income claim upon the business by its owner(s). Does such constitute taking property without due process of law? As a restriction upon the Police Power, it might; though in this particular case it would not. But there are a multitude of other cases where, at least, the question is not so simply resolved.

Thus in many cases the court, following substantive due process, held that received practices of contract and property, legitimized as rights, were superior Constitutionally to the claims of the states and national government to regulate business and other private economic activity, and to attempts at social reform by way of welfare programs. Thus child labor, hours of labor in bakeries, public utility rate regulation, antitrust regulation, rail transportation regulation, and a myriad of other statutes were cast down or weakened as taking property without due process of law. Yet close to the year the Court declared unconstitutional a law regulating child labor, it upheld a law regulating narcotics; other similar regulatory statutes upheld covered lotteries, impure or falsely branded foods, white slavery, liquor, and so on.

In his dissent in the Nebbia case (*Nebbia v. New York*, 291 U.S. 502 (1934)), Justice McReynolds epitomized the substantive view as follows:

> This Court has declared that a state may not by legislative fiat convert a private business into a public utility... And if it be now ruled that one dedicates his property to public use whenever he embarks on an enterprise which the legislature may think is desirable to bring under control, this is but to declare that rights guaranteed by the Constitution exist only so long as supposed public interest does not require their extinction. To adopt such a view, of course, would put an end to liberty under the Constitution.
>
> (Anderson 1950: 285–6, 1960: 278)

"That such cases were decided on the basis of economic belief rather than a rule of law is evident..." as is also "The conservative judicial attitude of the Court in regarding itself as the protector of society against the encroachments of radical and evil-minded legislatures..." (Anderson 1950: 30; see also1960: 33). The point is not that their personal social philosophy entered into the picture—for such is always the case; what is important is the recognition that there is a basic and continuing need to reconcile both conflicting individual interests and conflicting individual interests with some definition of the public interest. Said Justice Harlan,

> What is the true ground for the State to take between legitimate protection, by legislation of the public health and liberty of contract is not a question easily solved, nor one in respect of which there is or can be absolute certainty...
>
> (dissent in *Lochner v. New York*, 198 U.S. 45 (1905),
> quoted in Anderson 1950: 31, 1960: 34)

Thus Justice McReynolds also argued in his dissent in Nebbia:

> The legislature cannot lawfully destroy guaranteed rights of one with the prime purpose of enriching another, even if for the moment, this may seem

advantageous to the public. And the adoption of any "concept of jurisprudence" which permits facile disregard of the Constitution as long interpreted and respected will inevitably lead to its destruction. Then, all rights will be subject to the caprice of the hour; government by stable laws will pass.

But, Justice Roberts, in the majority opinion, postulated:

> Under our form of government the use of property and the making of contracts are normally matters of private and not of public concern. The general rule is that both shall be free of governmental interference. But neither property rights nor contract rights are absolute; for government cannot exist if the citizen may at will use his property to the detriment of his fellows, or exercises his freedom of contract to work them harm. Equally fundamental with the private right is that of the public to regulate it in the common interest.
>
> (quoted in Anderson 1950: 280, 1960: 274)

Law, then, represents the balance of conflicting freedoms, and, somehow, the expression of the "social" or "common" interest—both of course depend upon control (or concurrence) of the decision making governmental body.

Substantive due process would seem to have been circumscribed if not outright rejected as inconsistent with the nature of a pluralist society in which government exists to serve the people, or those who control or influence its decisions—subject of course to the problem of reconciling the so-called "majorities" with the so-called "minorities," so that the latter may some day become the former. The emphasis that the constitution must be a constitution of a pluralist society was expressed by Holmes in his dissent in the Lochner case (*Lochner v. New York*, 198 U.S. 45 (1905)):

> This case is decided upon an economic theory which a large part of the country does not entertain. If it were a question whether I agreed with that theory, I should desire to study it further and long before making up my mind. But I do not conceive that to be my duty, because I strongly believe that my agreement or disagreement has nothing to do with the right of a majority to embody their opinions in law. It is settled by various decisions of this court that state constitutions and state laws may regulate life in many ways which we as legislators might think as injudicious or if you like as tyrannical as this, and which equally with this interfere with the liberty contract. Sunday laws and usury laws are ancient examples. A more modern one is the prohibition of lotteries. The liberty of the citizen to do as he likes so long as he does not interfere with the liberty of others to do the same, which has been a shibboleth for some wellknown writers, is interfered with by school laws, by the Post Office, by every state or municipal institution which takes his money for purposes thought desirable, whether he likes it or not.
>
> The Fourteenth Amendment does not enact Mr. Herbert Spencer's Social Statics.... a constitution is not intended to embody a particular economic

theory, whether of paternalism and the organic relation of the citizen to the State or of laissez-faire, it is made for people of fundamentally differing views, and the accident of our finding certain opinions natural and familiar or novel and even shocking ought not to conclude our judgment upon the question whether statutes embodying them conflict with the Constitution of the United States.

General propositions do not decide concrete cases.... Every opinion tends to become a law. I think that the word 'liberty' in the Fourteenth Amendment is perverted when it is held to prevent the natural outcome of a dominant opinion, unless it can be said that a rational and fair man necessarily would admit that the statute proposed would infringe fundamental principles as they have been understood by the traditions of our people and our law. It does not need research to show that no such sweeping condemnation can be passed upon the statute before us.

(Anderson 1950: 31–2, 1960: 35)

In another case (*Moorehead v. New York ex.rel. Tipaldo*, 298 U.S. 587 (1936)), arguing for judicial realism, Justice Stone said as follows:

In the years...since the Adkins case we have had opportunity to learn that a wage is not always the resultant of free bargaining between employers and employees; that it may be one forced upon employees by their economic necessities and upon employers by the most ruthless of their competitors. We have had opportunity to perceive more clearly that a wage insufficient to support the worker does not visit its consequences upon him alone; that it may affect profoundly the entire economic structure of society, and, in any case, that it casts on every taxpayer, and on government itself, the burden of solving the problems of poverty, subsistence, health and morals of large numbers in the community. Because of their nature and extent these are public problems. A generation ago they were for the individual to solve; today they are the burden of the nation. I can perceive no more objection, on constitutional grounds, to their solution by requiring an Industry to bear the subsistence costs of the labor which it employs, than to the imposition upon it of the cost of its industrial accidents.

It is not for the courts to resolve doubts whether [this particular remedy] is as efficacious as many believe, or is better than some other, or is better even than the blind operation of uncontrolled economic forces. The legislature must be free to choose unless government is to be rendered impotent. The Fourteenth Amendment has no more embedded in the Constitution our preference for some particular set of economic beliefs than it has adopted, in the name of liberty, the system of theology which we may happen to approve.

(Anderson 1950: 33, 1960: 35–6)

The minimum wage law (state, re women and children) was upheld in *West Coast Hotel v. Parrish* (300 U.S. 379 (1937)); said Chief Justice Hughes:

The Constitution does not speak of freedom of contract. It speaks of liberty and prohibits the deprivation of liberty without due process of law. In prohibiting that deprivation the Constitution does not recognize an absolute and uncontrollable liberty.... but the liberty safeguarded is liberty in a social organization which requires the protection of law against the evils which menace the health, safety, morals and welfare of the people. Liberty under the Constitution is thus necessarily subject to the restraints of due process, and regulation which is reasonable in relation to its subject and is adopted to the interests of the community is due process.

(Anderson 1950: 35, 1960: 37)

There, then, is the criterion of "reasonableness" in terms of the efficacy of the means to the end. In a more recent decision (*A. F. of L. v. American Sash & Door Co.*, 335 U.S. 538 (1949)), the arguments of Holmes reverberate in Frankfurter's concurring opinion:

[In the 19th century] Adam Smith was treated as though his generalizations had been imparted to him on Sinai and not as a thinker who addressed himself to the elimination of restrictions which had become fetters upon initiative and enterprise in his day. Basic human rights expressed by the constitutional conception of liberty were equated with theories of laissez faire. The result was that economic views of confined validity were treated by lawyers and judges as though the framers had enshrined them in the constitution.

He thus argues that the first interpretation of the constitutional phrase is no more valid or right just because it is first. He continues to say the following:

This misapplication of the notions of the classic economists and resulting disregard of the perduring reach of the constitution led to Mr. Justice Holmes' famous protect in the Lochner case against measuring the fourteenth amendment by Mr. Herbert Spencer's Social Statics.... The attitude... regarded any legislative encroachment upon the existing economic order as infected with unconstitutionality.... But when the tide turned, it was not merely because circumstances had changed and there had arisen a new order with new claims to divine origin [it was because] of increased deference to the legislative judgment...

The question, then, is not just of the significance of due process for reconciling the problems of freedom and order, and of freedom and justice, but of the locus of decision making—that is, how far is judicial review to go, in this artificial division of the powers of governance. Argues Frankfurter,

Even where the social undesirability of a law may be convincingly urged, invalidation of the law by a court debilitates popular democratic government.

(Frankfurter, in *A. F. of L. v. American Sash & Door Co.*, 335 U.S. 538 (1949), quoted in Anderson 1950: 37–8, 1960: 43)

Is there any place for judicial review? If so, is economic legislation excepted?

> Most laws dealing with economic and social problems are matters of trial and error. Examples of legislative experimentation undertaking to meet a recognized need were the bank deposit guarantee laws passed in the wake of the panic of 1907 by Kansas, Nebraska and Oklahoma. Despite serious doubts of their wisdom, the laws were sustained against due process attack. Experience proved the laws to be unworkable...but...it remained possible to profit by past errors and attempt a mature solution of the problem on a national scale.
>
> (Anderson 1950: 38; see also 1960: 39)

But there is reason for judicial restraint in matters of policy deeper than the value of the experiment: it is founded on the recognition of the gulf of difference between sustaining and nullifying legislation...As history amply proves, the judiciary is prone to misconceive the public good by confounding private notions with constitutional requirements, and such misconceptions are not subject to legitimate displacement by the will of the people except at too slow a pace.... Matters of policy...are by definition matters which demand the resolution of conflicts of value, and the elements of conflicting values are largely imponderable. Assessment of their competing worth involves differences of feeling; it is also an exercise in prophecy. Obviously the proper forum for mediating a clash of feelings and rendering a prophetic judgment is the body chosen for those purposes by the people. Its functions can be assumed by this court only in disregard of the historic limits of the Constitution (Frankfurter, concurring opinion, *A. F. of L. v. American Sash & Door Co.*, 335 U.S. 538 (1949); Anderson 1960: 38–9).

In recent years, then, the court has been loath to strike at economic legislation through due process of law, if at all; with respect to protecting civil liberties, on the other hand, the court has given somewhat less freedom of discretion to the democratic majority *vis-à-vis* the minority. The real question—as to decision making—is put thus by Anderson:

> Does this new viewpoint mean that the court is returning to the days when it refused to use the due process clause as a weapon against regulatory legislation? This does not seem to be the case. What is happening seems rather to be that the Court is continuing to decide what is fair and reasonable, a decision that necessarily calls into play the Court's social and economic predilections. The difference lies in the fact that the social and economic philosophy of at least a majority of the justices approves of government regulation and planning, and therefore a regulatory statute is not automatically regarded as capricious and arbitrary because it attempts to regulate free enterprise.
>
> The language of the Court actually goes further than this, for, in stating that the Court will not impose its economic beliefs on the lawmakers, the Court would appear to be stating the doctrine that, even where it was opposed to the economics of a law, it would not declare that law a violation of due process. The real test would arise if a law were based on some radical

economic principle of which a majority of the Justices disapproved. Would the Court hold that the law had no relation to a proper legislative purpose and was therefore arbitrary and unreasonable? Would it merely say that the lawmaker believed in the economic basis of the statute and then hold that this was sufficient to sustain the act even though the Court regarded it as unsound and without merit?

(Anderson 1950: 38–9, 1960: 40)

The two questions most fundamental to the foregoing analysis are the following:

1 What is the proper theory of economic policy, that is, which among alternative proposals should government follow in its relation to the economy?
2 Where is the proper locus of deciding which theory of the role of government in the economy is the proper one in general and in each case?

Given the pluralist nature of American society, which one hopes will continue, in which each and every group in society is "free" to try to have its program or policy be adopted by government, and given the artificial if not arbitrary division of the powers of governance between legislature, judiciary, and executive on the one hand, and the national government and the states on the other, no easy answer can be forthcoming. Both of the two enumerated questions are among the most difficult in all of social philosophy; the pluralism, federalism, and division of powers of American government and American society serve only to further complicate them. To desire the continuation of our form of government is to argue in effect for the continuation of the difficulties involved, difficulties which generate much heat and passion. The alternatives are generally clearly less desirable. We progress somewhat in spite of but more because of our system. The balancing of freedom and order, and of the elements of freedom itself, is not easy. It would seem that when such basic problems as are defined here appear to be firmly settled, they may be soon less settled than ever, and to impose one solution over others is to ignore those disadvantaged under the imposed solution.

The larger context in which rights arise

Rights are made, not found, through legislation, administration, and judicial decisions. Property rights in particular and rights in general are worked out in the manners suggested so far. But more is going on than legal language reveals; indeed, some or much legal language is directed to obfuscation, using, for example, mere assertions (see Chapter 10). Overall, this larger context is comprised of social control in the form of belief and power and their interrelationships.[5]

System of belief

Throughout intellectual history various thinkers have emphasized that what is important is not what people should believe—because true—but what they do believe, because it is the belief, correct or incorrect, even meaningless, on which they act.[6] These thinkers include Adam Smith, John Stuart Mill, Karl Marx, George Herman Mead, Vilfredo Pareto, and Kenneth Boulding. People have a need to believe—to have their minds set at rest. Even people who aver that they have no system of belief hold that view on the basis of a system of belief. Their system of belief may be very different from that of most people but it is nonetheless a system of belief—possibly, but not necessarily, deeper or more "correct" in some sense than others' belief systems (Harris 1971; Kselman 1991).

For present purposes it is useful to contemplate people's mental state as a combination of two positions, one of which is usually dominant. For many people a system of belief is attractive to the extent that it offers a sense of determinacy and closure. Their system of belief defines reality for them. Other people have a dominant system of belief which also provides a definition of reality but these people treat it as more problematic and pragmatic. (I believe that all systems are at bottom pragmatic, but that is another story.) These people are content with open-endedness and ambiguity.

Particularly attractive to those who seek determinacy and closure is the possibility of having only one explanation or a uni-directional line of causation to believe. In such cases, however, there always tend to be significant multiple variations. Multiplicity renders nugatory all claims to determinacy and closure, yet even this is finessed by those who are willing to accept some one variation. It is no surprise, therefore, that constitutional law, theological doctrine, and economic theory exhibit similar problems of interpretation (Samuels 2006b).

Systems of belief are not, or not fully, scientific matters, even within a putative scientific discipline. Systems of belief define reality for people, who thereby are provided with principles of order and/or of authority. A fundamental function of legal-economic theory is to provide, for its field, a definition of reality, with its principles of order and authority. As a system of belief, and so on, mainstream legal-economic theory itself is an institution which defines and structures freedom, power, and opportunity. General economic theory does so likewise, but more broadly and perhaps more deeply.

A system of belief, such as one of those provided by legal-economic theory, provides a filter or sieve through which an individual processes and frames experience, statements of putative fact, and so on. Different systems of belief enable different people to interpret what they read or hear differently. The use of "code words" in political and other discourse, including economic discourse, enables interpretation at the unconscious level. The meaning of terms such as "competition," "freedom," "property," "money," and so on, varies between individuals because of their respective belief systems. Pareto is not the only scholar who combined belief system and noncognitive and rational behavior and choice with the structure and struggle for power (Samuels 1974b; see also, for example, Moessinger (2000) and Parsons (1949), who trace the stability of social structures—their concept of order—to nondeliberative conduct, somewhat in the manner of Friedrich von Hayek, in effect combining psychology and sociology (see Chapters 13 and 14 in this volume).

From the 1620s to the present, Americans have exhibited predominantly two cultural belief systems. One is theological fundamentalism, which would have all people pursue a life of piety; the other is economic fundamentalism, which legitimizes the world of business and trade. Each has its own goals, rules, concept of order, and so on, as well as varied ideational formulations (sects, schools of thought, etc.). The two often co-exist quietly; at other times they clash, reinforcing (and perhaps changing) the distinctiveness of each as well as their contradictions— about God versus Mammon, democracy, work, capitalism, corporate capitalism, wealth, freedom, and so on, including the Money Power, robber barons, and the power elite (see Cottrell and Moggridge 1988; Ellul 1984; Means 2001).[7] In the late nineteenth century the conflict was between Social Darwinism and the Social Gospel. In the half century after the Second World War the conflict was between economic and social conservatism. The assignment of descriptive/interpretive terms is less important than the fact of their opposition (and the genesis of society in their conflict).

In the domain of general culture, an interactive, dialectical or over-determined process seems to exist in which folk etymology and beliefs help form the society's (collective) definition of reality (Rundblad and Kronenfeld 2003, who envision the operation of an invisible-hand process therein) in a process somewhat akin to Thomas Kuhn's notion of scientific revolution. The folk belief system may then become an established, ingrained, and encrusted status-emulative mode of social control, which in turn becomes the object of scorn by new aspirants.

Language

A strong tendency has been observed for people to presume/believe that words correspond with and derive from reality: "the whole point is that if we define the terms precisely and sort out the various possible scenarios, we can learn more about market clearing than if we remain vague" (Gani 2005; see also Kendall 1995 on the selective use of discourse in presidential campaigns). Ludwig Wittgenstein, however, repudiated his earlier holding of this belief on the ground that that was not how language operates. Words—our system of belief—do not derive their meaning from reality; rather, our definition of reality is derived from the words used in our system of belief. To believe that words derive from and correspond with reality is to neglect both the social construction of language and the multiplicity of words/belief systems each of which defines reality for some people. This situation leads to numerous linguistic problems of specification and interpretation in economics and other fields (Chomsky 1988; Jones 1983; Samuels 2001). More generally, in the sense not of less intensively but of greater ubiquity, money, language and thought (perception and definition of monetary reality) critically interact (Shell 1993; see also Binswanger 1994 and Zelizer 1994).

Belief systems as part of the system of social control

Taking social control for granted is tantamount to accepting the felt hegemonic belief system as given. Inasmuch as the substance and objective of social control in any particular case exhibit multiplicity, excluding multiplicity is tantamount to finessing varying antecedent normative and other premises. Nonetheless, such has not kept many people from expressing belief in the omnipotence of words. The psychology of belief (religious (Kselman 1991) or political or economic) has revealed the ubiquitous practice of using words nominally to define reality but especially to control reality (Smith 1980).

Accordingly, belief system is an object of control; society, as spelled out by Pareto (Samuels 1974b), is very much a process of mutual manipulation of belief systems and thereby of power and psychology. Democracy, insofar as it posits individual political judgment, thus becomes a process of mutual manipulation and the manufacture of consent or pseudo-consent. People hold on to belief systems for purposes of psychic balm (having their minds set at rest), and are induced to do so by institutions of social control (having their political propensities promote some meaning of "order" or at least keep quiet). Secularists may debate using some linguistic formulation reducing to "My belief system is truer than yours." Non-secularists use language ultimately reducing to "My invisible friend can beat up your invisible friend." During October 2005, ESPN televised commercials on its own behalf, one line of which ran, "Without sports, what would we hold on to?"

People are induced to adhere to a particular belief system, even when it is undergoing change. Pareto insisted that government social control consisted of force and fraud, the latter involving the manipulation of belief through the use of pseudo-knowledge. In the 1960s, the sports editor of the *Miami Herald* wrote that the principal argument for sports is that sports helps prevent communism. Some observers of high school, college, and professional sports think of them as aphrodisiacal; the Editor seems to widen Karl Marx's thesis of religion as the opiate of the masses (to which Frank Knight added, and the sedative of the classes). The Cold War provided ample opportunity for various interests to promote their cause by investing it with the function of combating communism (or attributing the opposite to their opponents). The stockbroker Charles Merrill "argued that nothing 'would provide a stronger defense against the threat of Communism, than the wide ownership of stocks in the country'" (Wallace 2005: 30; Wallace also quotes Franklin Roosevelt's statement of concern over the money power: "we cannot allow our economic life to be controlled by that small group of men whose chief outlook upon the social welfare is tinctured by the fact that they can make huge profits from the lending of money and the marketing of securities" (Wallace 2005: 30)). The conservative columnist, George Will, has condemned the business, financial and accounting practices that led to the Enron collapse, insisting that "It will remind everyone—some conservatives, painfully—that a mature capitalist economy is a government project. A properly functioning free market system does not spring spontaneously from society's soil as dandelions spring from suburban lawns. Rather, it is a complex creation of laws and mores…" (Will 2002: 3; quoted in Mercuro 2005: 16).

Social control as social construction of reality

Social control is not simply a matter of controlling individual belief and behavior. Social control is surely that, such that actions seen as coercion by some

Alphas are seen as freedom enhancing by some Betas (Samuels 1984, 1995, 1996, 1997). But more is involved than that. A further role of social control is to establish the legal and moral foundations of the economy, not economies in general but the actual economic regime in place. In so doing, social control—the sum of and interactions between agencies and institutions of social control—is engaged in the social construction of reality (Berger and Luckmann 1966; Searle 1995; Sederberg 1984). Social control and the social construction of reality are themselves aspects of the problem of order (Samuels 1996). One aspect thereof is the choice between continuity and change in particular cases but overall encompassing both continuity and change. The adjustment of continuity and change can be posed in terms of property and/or covenants (Taylor 1966) but must encompass both continuity and change.

The legal-economic nexus (Samuels 1989) is the domain in which public and private sectors interact and each is continually being reconstituted through that interaction, that is, over-determination. The economy, for example, business, provides much of the input to and influences the result of the governmental process (legislature and courts) while government simultaneously influences the organization and operation of business. If the legal-economic nexus is narrowly and tightly held, conflict nonetheless exists within and among the ruling class(es). In regimes in which power is more widely diffused, tension still exists among those who seek to capture and control the state for pragmatic (e.g. money making) purposes and among those who seek to dominate the social construction of reality, for example, markets, arguably for non-pragmatic short-term interests, and between the pragmatists and social constructionists. In all cases, the distinction between pragmatic and social control motivations is problematic. In all cases, too, the state will be/must/will tend to be in the hands of some group; the need to provide control or to influence the state is fundamental.

In all the foregoing, a key role is performed by expectations and change of expectations. If manipulation of the system of belief can achieve passive consent if not belief by those putatively objectively negatively affected that their predicament is due to the natural order of things, their predicament will less likely be perceived as a problem to which redress by government is relevant. What people expect and/or do not expect is not only one basis on which conflicting claims of right are worked out by courts, they can serve as a foundation of the basic jural postulates (in the sense of Roscoe Pound and Hans Kelsen). Much legal change ensues from changes in expectations per se or from the expectations which the courts are willing to recognize.

Struggle over power structure and the state

In every type of state/government, the question, "Who decides?," inevitably arises. The state itself is an answer to that question. Thus arises the struggle over control of the institutions of social control, including those of the legal-economic nexus. As Pareto emphasized, much of this struggle takes place through mutual, if asymmetrical, manipulation of the system of belief and of language itself in order to control and mobilize the political psychology which is at the basis of policy (Pareto 1963; Samuels 1974b). This includes the languages of class (Burke and Porter 1987; Corfield 1991; DeGré 1985; Jones 1983; Reddy 1987). Much money is spent on lobbying and litigation to influence government policy—the interests the state will be used to promote and/or inhibit—not because government is unimportant, as some writers would have everyone believe, but because government (collective action) is in fact important.

I increasingly prefer to speak of the entirety of the system of governance, meaning by "governance" the making of decisions which importantly affect other people. Normally there is a more or less ambiguous line of demarcation between public government and private government. The situation is illustrated by the Federal Reserve System which is "privately owned" and an "independent" government agency. It is also found in the Constitution's seemingly exclusive assignment of power to the Congress "To coin Money, regulate the Value thereof, and of foreign coin" (Article I, Section 8) but which has precluded neither paper money, nor state involvements in matters of money and banking, nor the issuance by private banks of perhaps 90 percent of the money supply through credit creation, nor government bonds constituting satisfaction of private banks' required reserves. (James M. Buchanan, A. Allan Schmid and others have proposed that the national debt can be financed through the issue of interest-free bonds. The demand by banks for such bonds would be generated by having them satisfy bank reserve requirements. The present system enables banks to charge government interest on the money it borrows because the government has enabled them to create money and to charge interest. See Buchanan and Flowers (1975: 335); Schmid (1982, 1984, 2004); and Shultz and Harris (1965: 488).) It also resonates in the enforcement of private contracts by the courts, including loan contracts of various types made by banks. Finally, commercial banks and the commercial banking system create, in the process of making loans, the money that they lend and on which they charge interest, and do so in a multiplicable expansionary or contractionary manner.

A millennium ago, the deep interpretive questions were whether the Church was operating in the name of and/or on the behalf of God, or in the interests of churchmen, or as an institution of secular social control (to which a large measure of absolutist legitimization had been added). More recently, the deep interpretive questions were whether government and other institutions, many of the latter operating under color of law, were serving God's will, or the will of their leaders, and/or a ruling elite or the functions of social control. As institutions developed during the transition from feudal and post-feudal to capitalist market economies, comparable questions arose. Money, banking and finance became key parts of the institutions by which a new and still changing ruling class stood astride both government and economy. In time it became increasingly difficult to distinguish whether the monetary and banking system—with its control over both currency and credit, with the latter becoming by far the more important—or, indeed, the economy as a whole, was a socially functional set of institutions or a vehicle of the ruling economic elite. Whether in some sense it was performing in one way or the other, or a bit of both, what came to count was what it was believed to be;

thus, as with government as a whole, enormous efforts were made to manipulate the belief system of the great mass of people. Certainly no independent test was available; it was a matter of what people were induced to believe by the powerful who competed among themselves to control and use government, and who manufactured consent to that end. Thus one interpretation-application of the Constitution would dominate and exclude another not because it was *the law* but it was the law because of whose/which interpretation served the interest of those whose interest counted for more than that of others. The deepest problem may well have become balancing the need for order on almost any terms with the public discussion of the foregoing. Public discussion might mean that the former was threatened; quietude would tend to safeguard the status quo power structure.

One point that is fundamental to the argument presented in this book concerns laissez-faire. For several centuries some people have believed in laissez-faire and governmental nonintervention. Other people have believed, equally sincerely, in government intervention and rejected laissez-faire. These two systems of belief are solely that, systems of belief, and do not accurately describe the economic role of government. Government, like it or not, is important and ubiquitous not solely in the area of money and banking. These are fundamental economic institutions and while some nominally private interests have great influence on, even control over, government, government has great influence on and control over them. Government protection of certain interests *ipso facto* means government nonprotection of other interests in the same field of action. Regulation of Alpha means protection of Beta; deregulation of Alpha means government no longer protecting the conflicting interest of Beta. That some people treat them differently is a function of selective perception of government, a selective perception intimately connected by manufactured and non-manufactured belief systems.

One implication of the foregoing is that laissez-faire, which is not descriptively accurate with regard to the economy and economic policy, nonetheless serves the Paretian function of mobilizing political psychology and manipulating belief systems for many people. What is literally substantively impossible is functionally possible.

Another way of making the point is to say that while the dominant ideology is non-interventionist, the accurate, positivist description of actual legal-economic systems is the ubiquity and importance of government and governance (Samuels 1995) and thereby of politics—meaning by politics having to do with decision making that affects others. The irony here is that arrangements that are political and socially constructed in nature are reified so as to be given the veneer of something given, transcendent, and grandiose. Economic institutions are legal and therefore political in nature, absolutist legitimization to the contrary notwithstanding; laissez-faire is a name for another political agenda. The political meaning of economic institutions is not unique in society. The reach of politics is ubiquitous (Feibleman 1969); meaning is political (Sederberg 1984). Like it or not, identity (Aronowitz 1992), knowledge (Lagemann 1989; Meja and Stehr 1990), including framing paradigms and theories of social change (Janos 1986), information (Anthony Smith 1980), music (Buch 2003), landscape (Turner 1979), and religion

(Tinder 1989) are political in nature. Religion in particular has been deeply involved in the political/legal status of lending, banking, and interest (Jones 1989). The topic of a theology of the corporation is highly suggestive of both the use of religion for economic purposes and the use of economics for religious purposes and thereby the similar nexus between religion and government (Novak and Cooper 1981a,b), suggestive of the absolutist legitimization of business, including banking corporations, paralleling legitimization through absolutist ontological realism. Relevant here is not only what passes for science but also belief without substance (Pareto 1963; Robinson 1921; Samuels 1974b). Knowledge, or what people accept as knowledge and act upon, is often a matter of imagery (Bloor 1991; Boulding 1956) and therefore of illusion (Geuss 2001; Skillen 1978) and myth (Barbour 1974; Bondi 1967; Campbell 1972; Fitzpatrick 1992; Mishan 1986; Samuel and Thompson 1990). Politics is a domain of symbols (Arnold 1935, 1937; Boorstin 1958; Eaton 1925; Edelman 1964) and figures of speech (Lakoff and Johnson 1980; Ortony 1993), a domain populated by entrepreneurs of myth (Nossiter 1964) engaged in the defense and invention of tradition (Hobsbawn 1962; Hobsbawn and Ranger 1983), including demystification (Rex 1974). Each of these topics (for which only a small sample of references is given) has been the subject of diverse, multiple explanations. For present purposes it is the general theme in each case that counts, not the differences of theoretical formulation (consider the variety of theories of value each of which tends to deal with something, *vis-à-vis* price, that is metaphysical), although the matrix analysis of multiplicity is applicable. Further apropos of mystification (and demystification; see Chomsky 1988), giving something a name seems for some or many people tantamount to establishing ontological status.

Silence on the part of a-institutional economic theory/theorists means either that existing institutions are rendered unimportant or that they comport with or exemplify pure abstract theory, neither of which is necessarily true; indeed, it is widely recognized (though not practiced) that the pure theory of economics does not apply to existing institutions. Instead, theory obfuscates the processes of power through which institutions evolve, thereby facilitating the continuity of those processes and the applicability of what an earlier age called "God-given institutions." The world is made safe for economists and the institutions upon which they cast luster. Economists become a member of the ruling elite, occasional criticisms of, for example, governmental and other institutions being miniscule in importance compared with the legitimacy provided by economics and its theory(ies) of the optimality of (money) markets. Considerations such as the foregoing are far more important than the typical ones of economic theory; but on those questions legal-economic monetary theory is relatively silent. Economists tend also to be silent on the question of whether law is policy. Ending this silence would strongly tend to torpedo the laissez-faire and non-interventionist approach to government. If the legal foundations of the entire economy are important and ubiquitous, if legal and law-based institutions are inevitable, if nothing of the foregoing is given by nature but is a matter of the parallelogram of power that is both cause and consequence of the struggle to control and use government, then both conservative and liberal rationalizations of temporarily favored policies are shown to be merely means of marshalling and manipulating political psychology. Politicians can get away with this because much of it is unseen, some has deniability, most non-politicians are emotionally inoculated against the machinations of all politicians and are, besides, more interested in what is closer (they feel, and are induced to feel) to their own lives, and, a sense that, like it or not, this is the nature of collective decision making, that is, politics is the way we govern ourselves, all the alternatives being less fine and more dangerous than "democracy." We did not elude power, after all! Belief and power, as Pareto argued, are inseparable.

One irony of all this is that criticism of government by those who want to use government themselves is not taken as dangerous, but "telling it how it is" by objective scholars without their own agenda for government is held out to be dangerous. The economists and legal scholars who know better but opt to pretend differently thereby comport with regnant social control and appear to be safe. The scholar who knows better and talks about it thereby fails so to comport and appears unsafe. Jeremy Bentham understood that situation. Writing of the Peers, Great Landholders, and Country Gentlemen, Bentham commented sarcastically, "In those men is the chief *property* of the country, and with it—(for in the language of the Aristocratic School, *property* and *virtue* are synonymous terms)—the *virtue* of the country." He then insists that

> it is the greatest happiness of the ruling few, and not that of the greatest number, that is the end pursued on each occasion by the ruling few.... But the interest of the ruling few is, on the greater part of the field of government, in a state of continued opposition to that of the greatest number: accordingly, a principle which, in case of competition, and to the extent of the competition, called for sacrifices to be made of the interests of the class to which he [Alexander Wedderburn, Lord Loughborough] belonged, and which alone was the object of his solicitude, could not but in his eyes be a dangerous one.
>
> (Bentham 1817: xix; Bowring 1962, vol. 2: 463; see also Samuels 1966: 139–40)

Perhaps the objective scholar (which Bentham was not) is dangerous, even subversive, after all. The irony may be, ironically, true. But there is a further irony: the society that has room for those who "tell it how it is" contrary to the dominant system of belief, must have a legal-economic system in which those people can legally do so. Those people have a vested interest in something like the First Amendment of the Constitution of the United States:

> Congress shall make no law respecting an establishment of religion, or prohibiting the free exercise thereof; or abridging the freedom of speech or of the press; or the right of the people peacefully to assemble, and to petition the government for a redress of grievances.

But how can they defend its constitutional status? By treating it as different from other provisions of the Constitution? By treating it as neither a relatively absolute absolute nor an absolutely absolute absolute? The answer is not easy to work out logically or on a priori grounds so as to reach a meaningful result. Doing it pragmatically is about all we can do; in fact, there is no alternative to pragmatism, as all operating social systems are at bottom pragmatic, their absolutist pretensions notwithstanding. This of course gives considerable free rein to various types who would take advantage of their First Amendment freedom. But that, it seems, is part of the essence of pragmatism, to see how things work and react accordingly; and also part of the essence of the First Amendment, to let everyone do their thing (the usual sensible exceptions notwithstanding). They may even be correct.

Notes

1 Perception of the need for including a paragraph such as the foregoing one is most immediately due to correspondence with, and issues and positions raised by, Roger Albin.
2 See Cohen (1937: 226–8), "Fictions," reprinted in Dubin (1951); see also "Organization Fictions," by Dubin (1951: 341–5).
3 See Ely (1914); Dicey (1905); Pound (1921); Pound and T. F. T. Plucknett (1927). See also Commons (1924); Simpson and Stone (1948); Wigmore anad Kocourek (1923); and von Ihering (1913).
4 John Locke, *On Civil Government* (second essay on government; Locke [1690]). Locke qualified his explanation of property in the natural state (paragraphs 26–9, 32–3) by assuming abundance (paragraphs 33, 36) and the use of the qualifying phrase "As much as anyone can make use of" (paragraphs 31, 36). See Larkin (1930: 59–64) and Cairns (1949: 335–61).
5 The following paragraphs have been adopted from Samuels (2007) forthcoming.
6 A colleague once met a former student on the street. The student remarked that something which he had learned in the professor's course was of enormous value to him. The professor asked what that something was. He later told me that the former student's reply made no sense and that if he had taught such a doctrine, it was not only wrong and meaningless, he should have been fired.
7 The most recent account of these conflicts is Fraser (2005). See also, for example, Chesterton (1978); Gatell (1967); Means (2001); Aronson (1977). For money power as economic nationalism, see Hont (2005).

References

Aigler, R. W., A. F. Smith and S. Tefft (1951) *Cases and Materials on the Law of Property*, second edn, St. Paul, MN: West Publishing Co.
Anderson, R. A. (1950) *Government Regulation of Business*, Cincinnati, OH: South-Western Publishing.
——(1960) *Government and Business*, second edn, Cincinnati, OH: South-Western Publishing.
Arnold, T. (1935) *The Symbols of Government*, New Haven, CT: Yale University Press.
——(1937) *The Folklore of Capitalism*, New Haven, CT: Yale University Press.
Aronowitz, S. (1992) *The Politics of Identity*, New York: Routledge.

Aronson, J. D. (1977) *Money and Power: Banks and the World Monetary System*, Beverly Hills, CA: Sage.

Barbour, I. G. (1974) *Myths, Models and Paradigms*, New York: Harper & Row.

Bentham, J. (1817) *Plan of Parliamentary Reform*, London.

Berger, P. L. and T. Luckmann (1966) *The Social Construction of Reality*, Garden City, NY: Doubleday.

Berle, A. A., Jr and G. C. Means (1933) *The Modern Corporation and Private Property*, New York: Macmillan.

Binswanger, H. C. (1994) *Money and Magic: A Critique of the Modern Economy in the Light of Goethe's Faust*, Chicago, IL: University of Chicago Press.

Black, H. C. (ed.) (1968) *Black's Law Dictionary*. Revised fourth edn, St. Paul, MN: West.

Blackstone, W. (1959) [1765, 1766] *Commentaries on the Laws of England*. J. W. Ehrlich (ed.), New York: Capricorn Books.

Bloor, D. (1991) *Knowledge and Social Imagery*, second edn, Chicago, IL: University of Chicago Press.

Bondi, H. (1967) *Assumption and Myth in Physical Theory*, New York: Cambridge University Press.

Boorstin, D. J. (1958) *The Mysterious Science of the Law*, Boston, MA: Beacon.

Boulding, K. E. (1958) *Principles of Economic Policy*, Englewood Cliffs, NJ: Prentice-Hall.

——(1956) *The Image*, Ann Arbor, MI: University of Michigan Press.

Bowring, John. (ed.) (1962) *The Works of Jeremy Bentham*, New York: Russell & Russell.

Buch, E. (2003) *Beethoven's Ninth: A Political History*, Chicago, IL: University of Chicago Press.

Buchanan, J. M. and M. R. Flowers (1975) *The Public Finances*, Homewood, IL: Irwin.

Burke, P. and R. Porter (eds) (1987) *The Social History of Language*, New York: Cambridge University Press.

Cairns, H. (1949) *Legal Philosophy from Plato to Hegel*, Baltimore, MD: The Johns Hopkins Press.

Campbell, J. (1972) *Myths to Live By*, New York: Bantam.

Chesterton, A. K. (1978) *The Menace of the Money-Power: An Analysis of World Government by Finance*, Metairie, LA: Sons of Liberty.

Chomsky, N. (1988) *Language and Politics*, C. P. Otero (ed.), New York: Black Rose Books.

Cohen, M. R. (1937) "Fictions," in E. R. A. Seligman and Alvin Johnson (eds) *Encyclopedia of the Social Sciences*, vol. III, New York: Macmillan, 226–8.

Commons, J. R. (1924) *Legal Foundations of Capitalism*, New York: Macmillan.

Corfield, P. J. (ed.) (1991) *Language, History and Class*, Cambridge, MA: Basil Blackwell.

Corwin, E. S. (1947) *The Constitution and What It Means Today*, ninth edn, Princeton, NJ: Princeton University Press.

Cottrell, P. L. and D. E. Moggridge (eds) (1988) *Money and Power: Essays in Honour of L. S. Pressnell*, Basingstoke: Macmillan.

Dahl, R. A. and C. E. Lindblom (1953) *Politics, Economics and Welfare*, New York: Harpers.

Degré, G. (1985) *The Social Compulsion of Ideas*, New Brunswick, NJ: Transaction Books.

Dicey, A. V. (1905) *Lectures on the Relation Between Law and Public Opinion in England*, London: Macmillan.

Djilas, M. (1957) *The New Class*, New York: Praeger.

Dubin, R. (1951) *Human Relations in Administration*, Englewood Cliffs, NJ: Prentice Hall, Inc.

Eaton, R. M. (1925) *Symbolism and Truth*, Cambridge, MA: Harvard University Press. Reprinted by Dover, New York: 1964.

Edelman, M. (1964) *The Symbolic Uses of Politics*, Urbana, IL: University of Illinois Press.

Ellul, J. (1984) *Money and Power*, Downers Grove, IL: Inter-Varsity Press.

Ely, R. T. (1914) *Property and Contract in their Relations to the Distribution of Wealth*, 2 volumes, New York: Macmillan.

Feibleman, J. K. (1969) *The Reach of Politics: A New Look at Government*, New York: Horizon.

Fitzpatrick, P. (1992) *The Mythology of Modern Law*, New York: Routledge.

Frankfurter, F. (1939) *Mr. Justice Holmes and the Supreme Court*, Cambridge, MA: Harvard University Press.

Fraser, S. (2005) *Every Man a Speculator: A History of Wall Street in American Life*, New York: HarperCollins.

Galbraith, J. K. (1958) *The Affluent Society*, Boston, MA: Houghton Mifflin Co.

Gani, M. (2005) "Why Teach the History of Error?" EH.net, (June 21) 8:19 AM.

Gatell, F. O. (1967) *The Jacksonians and the Money Power, 1829–1840*, Chicago, IL: Rand McNally.

Geuss, R. (2001) *History and Illusion in Politics*, New York: Cambridge University Press.

Harris, N. (1971) *Beliefs in Society*, Baltimore, MD: Penguin.

Hobsbawn, E. J. (1962) *The Age of Revolution, 1789–1848*, Cleveland, OH: World.

Hobsbawn, E. J. and T. Ranger (eds) (1983) *The Invention of Tradition*, New York: Cambridge University Press.

Hont, I. (2005) *Jealousy of Trade: International Competition and the Nation-state in Historical Perspective*, Cambride, MA: Harvard University Press.

Ihering, R. von (1913) *Law as a Means to and End*, Boston, MA: Boston Book Co.

Janos, A. C. (1986) *Politics and Paradigms: Changing Theories of Change in Social Science*, Palo Alto, CA: Stanford University Press.

Jones, A. W. (1941) *Life, Liberty, and Property*, Philadelphia, PA: J.B. Lippincott Co.

Jones, G. S. (1983) *Languages of Class: Studies in English Working Class History, 1832–1982*, New York: Cambridge University Press.

Jones, N. (1989) *God and the Money Lenders*, Boston, MA: Basil Blackwell.

Kendall, K. E. (1995) *Presidential Campaign Discourse: Strategic Communication Problems*, Albany, NY: SUNY Press.

Kselman, Thomas (ed.) (1991) *Belief in History*, Notre Dame, IN: University of Notre Dame Press.

Lagemann, E. C. (1989) *The Politics of Knowledge*, Chicago, IL: University of Chicago Press.

Lakoff, G. and M. Johnson (1980) *Metaphors We Live By*, Chicago, IL: University of Chicago Press.

Larkin, P. (1930) *Property in the Eighteenth Century*, Cork: Cork University Press.

Letourneau, C. (1892) *Property: Its Origin and Development*, New York: Scribner's.

Locke, J. (1690) *Two Treatises of Government*, Cambridge: Cambridge University Press.

McIlwain, C. H. (1932) *The Growth of Political Thought in the West*, New York: Macmillan.

Means, H. B. (2001) *Money and Power: The History of Business*, New York: Wiley.

Meja, V. and N. Stehr (eds) (1990) *Knowledge and Politics: The Sociology of Knowledge Dispute*, New York: Routledge.

Mercuro, N. (2005) "Government's Touch Pervades Technology," *Fedtech*, 2: 16–17.

Mishan, E. J. (1986) *Economic Myths and the Mythology of Economics*, Atlantic Highlands, NJ: Humanities Peress.

Moessinger, P. (2000) *The Paradox of Social Order*, New Brunswick, NJ: Transaction.

Myrdal, G. (1955) *The Political Element in the Development of Economic Theory*, Cambridge, MA: Harvard University Press.

Nossiter, B. D. (1964) *The Mythmakers: An Essay on Power and Wealth*, Boston, MA: Houghton Mifflin.

Novak, M. and J. W. Cooper (eds) (1981a) *The Corporation: A Theological Inquiry*, Washington, DC: American Enterprise Institute for Public Policy Research.
——(1981b) *Toward a Theology of the Corporation*, Washington, DC: American Enterprise Institute for Public Policy Research.
Noyes, C. R. (1936) *The Institution of Property*, New York: Longmans, Green.
Ortony, A. (ed.) (1993) *Metaphor and Thought*, second edn, New York: Cambridge University Press.
Pareto, V. (1963) *The Mind and Society*, New York: Dover.
Parsons, T. (1949) *The Structure of Social Action*, Glencoe, IL: Free Press.
Pound, R. (1921) *The Spirit of the Common Law*, Boston, MA: Marchall Jones Co.
Pound, R. and T. F. T. Pluncknett (eds) (1927) *Readings on the History and System of the Common Law*, third edn, Rochester, NY: Lawyers Co-operative Publishing Co.
Proudhon, P. J. (1840) *What Is Property*, First Memoir, Chapter 1.
Reddy, W. M. (1987) *Money and Liberty in Modern Europe*, New York: Cambridge University Press.
Rex, J. (1974) *Sociology and the Demystification of the Modern World*, Boston, MA: Routledge and Kegan Paul.
Robinson, J. H. (1921) *The Mind in the Making*, New York: Harper.
Rundblad, G. and D. B. Kronenfeld (2003) "The Inevitability of Folk Etymology: A Case of Collective Reality and Invisible Hands," *Journal of Pragmatics*, 35: 119–38.
Samuel, R. and P. Thompson (1990) *The Myths We Live By*, New York: Routledge.
Samuels, W. J. (1966) *The Classical Theory of Economic Policy*, Cleveland, OH: World
——(1974a) "An Economic Perspective on the Compensation Problem," *Wayne Law Review*, 21: 113–34.
——(1974b) *Pareto on Policy*, Cleveland, OH: World.
——(1984) "On the Nature and Existence of Economic Coercion: The Correspondence of Robert Lee Hale and Thomas Nixon Carver," *Journal of Economic Issues*, 18: 1027–48.
——(1989) "The Legal-Economic Nexus," *George Washington Law Review*, 57: 1556–78. Chapter 2 of this volume.
——(1995) "Society is a Process of Mutual Coercion and Governance Selectively Perceived," *Critical Review*, 9: 437–43.
——(1996) "Joseph J. Spengler's Concept of the 'Problem of Order': A Reconsideration and Extension," in P. Arestis (ed.) *Employment, Economic Growth and the Tyranny of the Market*, Brookfield, VT: Edward Elgar, 185–99.
——(1997) "The Concept of 'Coercion' in Economics," in W. J. Samuels, S. G. Medema and A. A. Schmid (eds) *The Economy as a Process of Valuation*, Lyme, NH: Edward Elgar, 129–207.
——(2001) "Some Problems in the Use of Language in Economics," *Review of Political Economy*, 13: 91–100.
——(2006) "Interpreting the Bible, the U.S. Constitution, and the History of Economic Thought," *Research in the History of Economic Thought and Methodology*, vol. 24A: 79–98
——(2007, forthcoming) "Monetary Institutions and Monetary Theory: Reflections on the History of Monetary Economics," in Robert Leeson (ed.) *Archival Insights into the Evolution of Economics, vol. 2, The Anti-Keynesian Tradition*, London: Palgrave Macmillan.
Samuels, W. J. and N. Mercuro (1979) "The Role and Resolution of the Compensation Principle in Society: Part One—The Role," *Research in Law and Economics*, 1: 157–94.
——(1980) "The Role and Resolution of the Compensation Principle in Society: Part Two—The Resolution," *Research in Law and Economics*, 2: 103–28.

Schlatter, R. (1951) *Private Property: The History of an Idea*, New Brunswick, NJ: Rutgers University Press.

Schmid, A. A. (1982) "Symbolic Barriers to Full Employment: The Role of Public Debt," *Journal of Economic Issues*, 35: 281–94.

——(1984) "Broadening Capital Ownership: The Credit System as a Locus of Power," in G. Alperovitz and R. Skurski (eds) *American Economic Perspectives*, Notre Dame, IN: University of Notre Dame Press, 117–37.

——(2004) *Conflict and Cooperation: Institutional and Behavioral Economics*, Malden, MA: Blackwell.

Schumpeter, J. A. (1949) "Science and Ideology," *American Economic Review*, 39: 345–59; reprinted in *Essays*, Cambridge, MA: Addison-Wesley Press, 1951, 267–81.

Searle, J. R. (1995) *The Construction of Social Reality*, New York: Free Press.

Sederberg, P. C. (1984) *The Politics of Meaning: Power and Explanation in the Construction of Social Reality*, Tucson, AZ: University of Arizona Press.

Shell, M. (1993) *Money, Language, and Thought*, Baltimore, MD: Johns Hopkins University Press.

Shultz, W. J. and N. Harris (1965) *American Public Finance*, Englewood Cliffs, NJ: Prentice-Hall.

Simpson, S. P. and J. Stone (1948) *Cases and Readings on Law and Society*, 2 vols, St. Paul, MN: West Publishing Co.

Skillen, A. (1978) *Ruling Illusions: Philosophy and the Social Order*, Atlantic Highlands, NJ: Humanities Press.

Smith, Anthony (1980) *The Geopolitics of Information*, New York: Oxford University Press.

Spencer, W. H. and C. W. Gillam (1953) *A Casebook of Law and Business*, second edn, New York: McGraw-Hill.

Suranyi-Unger, T. (1952) *Comparative Economic Systems*, New York: McGraw-Hill.

Taylor, J. F. A. (1966) *The Masks of Society*, New York: Appleton-Century-Crofts.

Tinder, G. (1989) *The Political Meaning of Christianity: An Interpretation*, Baton Rouge, LA: LSU Press.

Turner, J. (1979) *The Politics of Landscape*, Cambridge, MA: Harvard University Press.

Wallace, M. (2005) "All the World is Green," *The Nation* (April 18): 25–32.

Wigmore, J. H. and A. Kocourek (eds) (1923) *Rational Basis of Legal Institutions*, New York: Macmillan.

Will, G. (2002) "It's time Bush showed anger over Enron," *Jewish World Review* (January 16): 3.

Zelizer, V. A. (1994) *The Social Meaning of Money*, New York: Basic Books.

4 Markets and their social construction

Introduction

My objective is to outline a model of how markets arise and work and are worked. My argument is that markets are neither given nor transcendental but are constructed by the actions of firms and governments. Several qualifications apply.

First, a model is given, not a theory. A model is a set of variables structured in a particular way to explain something. A theory is a hypothesis specified as a particular explanation, the social space to which it is applied, the evidence by which it will be tested, and the decision rule governing acceptance or rejection. Second, no model can answer all questions. To answer other questions, other models are needed. Third, every element of the model can be combined with different theories. Fourth, no particular theory is adopted; the model is suggested in which particular theories have meaning.

Markets

"Market" is typically understood as the price mechanism and analyzed through some definition of "competition." Typical are fix-price and/or flex-price and strategic game-theoretic models, including limit-entry, administered, and mark-up pricing models. Price is not transcendent; it both controls firms and is an instrument of their power and policy. Economic actors are treated as active agents of change.

Markets are socially constructed, neither given and transcendental nor natural but organized to promote some interests rather than others; which interests and how they are chosen and structured, are issues to be determined.

A distinction exists between (a) a pure abstract a-institutional conceptual market, and (b) an actual market that is a function of and gives effect to the institutions and forces that structure and operate through it. One tendency is to theorize in terms of (a) and assume that (b) comports with (a), selectively reinforcing or criticizing existing law.

The market as an institution and a product of other institutions differs from its conceptualization as a mechanism of price formation. The former view of the market—as process, the result of power, and an arena of power—is absent in the latter (Swedberg 2003, chapter five). The belief that markets are necessarily competitive begs the definition of competition.

Markets are not themselves efficient; they can yield efficient results. The "efficient functioning of markets" and "efficient market" lack substantive content. Analyses typically explain and designate an outcome as efficient in the sense of either exhausting gains from trade (Pareto optimality) or output maximization. Efficiency in either sense takes place in markets but is driven by agents' actions, not by "the market" alone. No single efficient result exists. Efficiency is rights-structure dependent; different rights structures yielding different efficient allocations, each specific to and generated by a particular rights structure. Efficiency cannot be used to determine rights without the use of some antecedent normative premise as to whose interests are to count; indeed, the structure of rights is often the point at issue. Resource allocation is driven not by markets alone but by the institutions and forces that form and operate through markets, plus agents' actions.

The evolutionary dynamics of markets—the core of the present model—and the equilibrating adjustment process are more relevant here than the properties of static equilibrium.

One circularity in the concept of "market" relates to the "law of one price": that only one price for a commodity can exist in a market. However, a market is often defined in terms of there being only one price for a commodity.

The "market" is increasingly seen to be a metaphor. But a metaphor for what? A mechanism, an institution, a process, all of the above, or what? If the invisible hand is identified as the market, one metaphor is used to define another metaphor. The "market" is used here as a primitive, undefined term—both begging numerous questions and cautioning the reader not to substitute his or her favored connotation(s).

The model

The social construction of markets combines two models of social control: the market-plus-framework model of the economic role of legal and moral rules and the opportunity-set model of power in which actors' respective opportunity sets are a function, in part, of their legal rights and obligations, the choices made by other actors, and the impact of those choices on a given actor. The combination enables objective analysis of the determination of whose welfare counts through the determination of whose customs and interests count (for details, see Samuels 1989, 1992a,b, 2002; Samuels and Mercuro 1999; Samuels and Schmid 1981; and Samuels, Medema, and Schmid 1997). An alternative formulation is governance, defined as the making of decisions that affect others, including official government and firms whose decisions to expand, contract, relocate, and so on, impact others' opportunity sets.

The analysis premises markets and government as both selection processes and the result of selection processes and as arenas of power, the product of power, the vehicle of power, and a check on power.

Markets exist, are structured by and give effect to a framework of legal and moral rules, each comprised of specific rules and continually contested terrain.

Questions concern the relative reliance upon law and morals, the specific substantive content of the rules, and whose preconceptions and interests enter into the formation and change of the rules. Rules and markets are structured by and give effect to business and other interests seeking to enhance their advantages.

Market participants have opportunity sets, each a function of power and the exercise of choice by all relevant interacting agents. "Power" is participation in decision making and the bases thereof (rights). Externality is the impact on an agent of the decisions made by other agents. The result is a structure of mutual coercion in which economic agents are exposed to decisions made by other agents and government. Government is the process or arena in which rights are formed and reformed, and assigned and reassigned. Rights cover access to and participation in government for the purpose of changing relative rights. Legal rights of economic significance derive from the adoption, interpretation, and application of legal rules.

Some exercise of power is concerned with the manufacturing and marketing of products; some with strategic decisions *vis-à-vis* other firms; some with litigation and lobbying to favorably change the law.

Government

Individual agents operate on both sides of markets but there is no such thing as "the market," only markets partly given effect by the legal construction of markets helping govern who can participate in markets and how.

Governance ultimately has to do with decisions about continuity versus change, freedom versus control, and hierarchy versus equality that are in each respect about the structures of opportunity sets and of mutual coercion, the legal and moral framework of markets and the structure of markets. The law governing who can do what to whom also governs respective opportunity sets.

Economic agents with concentrated, intensive interests tend to have greater impact on the determination of relevant law than agents with limited, diffuse interests. The same applies to small-numbered interests *vis-à-vis* large-numbered interests. Government is an object of control; economic interests seek to use government to enhance their opportunities.

Government and business mutually influence each other within a legal-economic nexus in which opportunities for gain or other advantage accrue to economic actors with political prerogative. Government and businesses are what they are, and do what they do, because of pressures placed upon and uses made of government by business and governmental determination of rights, influencing opportunity sets and relative mutual coercion.

The role of government in the formation and structure of markets is a function of both the strength and weakness of government. The capture of—or long-term successful attack on—a strong government by business enables business to secure its desired market forms. *Governance* is the sum of nominally private and public governing institutions. Noninterventionist sentiments notwithstanding, Western government has been strong enough—and enough under business influence—to produce, ratify, and reinforce certain consolidations of social power of a business society (Brady 1943; Kuttner 1999; Sutton *et al.* 1956).

Firms

Markets do not alone govern outcomes. Desired outcomes are the reasons why firms seek to manipulate markets—and governments. Predatory and other strategic behaviors are important to the formation of markets.

Some understanding of the firm is also important. Firms operate under conditions of radical uncertainty. Different cognitive and different moral communities form firms. Firms must work out substantive goals—defined in terms of profits or otherwise, and what constitutes profit maximization—and therefore internal plans and arrays of productive competencies. All this is a political process and partly path dependent.

Among the causes of change in markets are technological change, firm strategies, firm goals, conditions of supply and demand, and legal and other rules. One author has identified markets as a function of variables commonly treated in theories of the firm, including changes in: productivity leading to changes in relative prices; customary social control, ideology and preferences; the governance structures of firms and thereby in policies; local knowledge due to changes in learning and competence (e.g., changes in technology development and the formation of clusters of competence, in part through improved coordination of expertise); relative ability to use/manipulate government; the formation of alliances in order to minimize transaction costs; coordination through mergers, interlocking boards, and banker policy; the operation of social interpretation and business culture, including the limiting of competition; the relative dominance of finance and marketing *vis-à-vis* production in firm management; the social structure of accumulation, and corporate influence on tax and labor law (Fligstein 2001; Schmid 2003). Each can be traced back, in part, to decisions made by firms.

The impact of firm decision-making on markets is driven by jockeying for position to establish a firm's identity, the deployment of one strategy or another, and the vagaries of the internal organization of firms and of interaction among firms.

Firms help form the markets in which they operate. In Ronald Coase's theory of the firm, firms decide between internal production or external purchase of inputs, thereby helping to form the division between firm and market. Coase says this depends upon transaction costs; others, such as Gardiner Means, stress the quest for power. Mergers between competitors in the same market (producing the same type of good) restructure that market. Mergers between firms in different but related (complementary, substitute goods) markets form and structure a new market. Markets are not independent of and transcendent to firms. Markets are, therefore, a function of firm policies.

Mergers, joint ventures, and acquisitions (vertical and horizontal) restructure markets in favor of dominant firms. Such firms may use strategic pricing, price discrimination, and other means against noncooperating firms. Market share is an indicator of degree of firm dominance, often a target of firm policy.

Comparative advantage is in part a function of the law governing whose interests are a cost to which other agents; rights help govern costs, and costs help govern the economic significance of rights. Law is an instrument of forming advantage. Firms with one set of comparative advantage seek through legislation to have their advantage given a privileged position in restructured markets. The legal treatment of new technology generates new ways of who can do what to whom, and how. Claims of "ruinous competition" channel selective perception and the legal policies governing markets.

Firms are driven in part by the ambitions of leading or would-be leading owners and managers, each with their particular designs on the firm and the market in question. Entrepreneurship may be partly understood as the making of markets *vis-à-vis* their passive acceptance (Casson 2003).

The formation and application of a firm's goals are influenced by transaction costs, principal-agent problems, differences between governance structures, the impact of firms seen as collections of contracts, the operation of the firm as a bureaucracy, an exercise in small-group sociology, as well as a set of power relations (Swedberg 2003, chapter four).

Firms can also be seen as instruments for the control and use of the human labor force in the labor market. The existence and size of a market depends on consumer demand large enough and supply cheap enough to sustain spending on production, advertising, research and development partly financed by government, and lobbying and litigation.

Some firms have greater opportunity than others to form their relevant capital market—for example, through internal financing, arm's length borrowing (though heavy borrowers may have greater mutual coercive power than small borrowers), and participation in capital-market networks.

Some implications

Markets are created, changed, manipulated, and restructured through the actions of government, firms, and groups of firms. The proposition that "institutions matter" can be weak or strong. The weak has analysis touching base with actual institutions. The strong has institutions dominate—organize, structure, and operate through—markets.

> [T]he object of dissent is the conception of the market as the guiding mechanism of the economy or, more broadly, the conception of the economy as organized and guided by the market. It simply is not true that scarce resources are allocated among alternative uses by the market. The real determinant of whatever allocation occurs in any society is the organizational structure of that society—in short, its institutions. At most, the market only gives effect to prevailing institutions. By focusing attention on the market mechanism, economists have ignored the real allocational mechanism.
>
> (Ayres 1957: 26)

As for *how* the institutional structure governs the allocation of resources,

> whatever scope society accords individual choice and valuations is a consequence of the latitude for discretionary action which is built into the

system.... It is through the assured zones of discretion or security of expectations that individual freedom becomes effective and may become power.

(Parsons 1957: 26)

The term "the market works" expresses a laissez-faire ideological sentiment, a matter of selective perception and the manipulation and mobilization of political psychology. "The market" becomes a fig leaf for power, often obfuscating the existence and use of firm power. Arguable predatory activity is made to appear aggressive pursuit of the bottom line. How the market works is a function, in part, of law—often the point at issue, with different states of the law protecting different interests and generating different market performances. Markets are also a function of business strategy and policy that inevitably selectively reinforces, limits, and uses existing law. At stake are the form and structure given capitalism through capitalist control of government, the form taken by their preconceptions, and the selective impact of the dominant ideology (Swedberg 2003: 61). It is out of such factors and forces that markets are in part socially constructed.

The foregoing in relation to Robert Heilbroner

Robert Heilbroner understands important aspects of the deep structures of markets. Heilbroner is sensitive to people's selective perceptions of and reactions to change. First, he comprehends that the present arrangement of markets is a historical product, not something that has existed for all time, and the future to which the present leads will be a part of history, made and not found (Heilbroner 1960). The present is the arena—itself the product of past struggles—in which the future is contested and worked out. Heilbroner is aware that different power structures and weightings of preferences yield different allocations, structures of order, and futures (Heilbroner 1983a); capitalism can run more than one course (Heilbroner 1981).

Second, he locates "the ultimate and irreducible nature of all reality" in the dialectical vision of "motion, not rest, and that to depict things as static or changeless is to disregard or violate the essence of their being." This "idea of imminent change [is] the fundamental nature of reality," but "the very characteristic of changefulness that commends a dialectical viewpoint to our imagination renders it awkward for our cognitive faculties. It is difficult to 'think' about change, even if it is natural to imagine it" (Heilbroner 1980: 25). Change can disturb our cognitive faculties and the creative destruction wrought by existing markets can be deeply emotionally upsetting, so much so that we condemn government even as we seek to use it to solve our problems.

A materialist market economy requires a permissive, not a fundamentalist, religion. Robert Kuttner wrote of Heilbroner's belief that " 'bourgeois' liberties are not a sham, but a triumph, and one that has only thrived in capitalist societies" and that "capitalism is a rationalized and 'desacralized' system, with a complex, indirect ideology rather than a fealty to sacred beliefs" (1985: 45). Such includes the equation of market with capitalism and both with a system of bourgeois = plutocratic power with its own socializing quasi-sacral ideological absolutist ideology. For Heilbroner, "the market" is an ideology protective of and promotive of capital accumulation and the profit motive (Kuttner 1985: 46), and hence promotive of an ideology of the interests of one segment of the ruling class.

For Heilbroner, capitalism is foremost a system of accumulation, one in which "the capitalist, unlike the possessor of aristocratic or feudal or sacred wealth, must constantly place what he has at risk. 'Capital is powerful only insofar as it continuously runs the gauntlet of .... *This continuous dissolution and recapture is the essence of the process of competition*'" (Kuttner 1985: 44, Heilbroner's emphasis). The social construction of markets is partly comprised of the response by business interests to changes seemingly wrought by markets. It can include both desire for security and animosity toward labor (Heilbroner 1987: 101). The quest for security may involve policies akin to those employed for predatory purposes: the policies of monopolistic profits and practices (Heilbroner 1981).

Heilbroner is sympathetic to worker self-management (Heilbroner 1982a) but knows that workers have other things on their mind, may prefer to leave decision making to others—including "the unwillingness of workers' committees to assume responsibility or to take risks"—and that have "difficulties...distinguishing between technical decisions where ordinary people should not intervene and political decisions where they must intervene" (Heilbroner 1982b: 41).

He is aware that economic governance includes but is broader than both firm and market. "Heilbroner counsels," writes Kuttner, "that in analyzing a market political system, with its 'mystifying diffusion of political and economic powers and functions', one should examine the entire 'regime of capital', not just the nominal state: 'There are vital economic functions exercised by the governing branch of capitalism just as there are powerful political ones exercised by its economic branch'" (Kuttner 1985: 46). As Heilbroner (1986: 47) puts it, "one could no longer carry on a conversation that took for granted the absence of political functions in the private sphere and of economic functions in the public sphere."

Using the familiar model of tradition, command, and market (Heilbroner 1989: 8–15), he sees the market as an institution of social control: "the purpose of the market...[is] to subordinate individual enterprise to the collective determination of all enterprises and households" (Heilbroner 1983b: 25). Kuttner correctly states that for Heilbroner "the coercive power of the market is more indirect and elusive than that of the state" (1985: 43).

Markets comprise both freedom and coercion. Private economic interests impact and channel both market and state, and the individual who lauds the putative free market is himself socialized by the market and the state (Heilbroner 1982c). The market is part of a complex structure and process of mutual determination, a "struggle," as Kuttner puts it, "over the terms on which state and market coexist" (1985: 44).

Since "the all-pervasive principle of the expansion of capital...[is] the defining essence of capitalist society, much as the principle of vassalage defined feudal society...nationalization is the manner by which capital is expanded under conditions in which private accumulation, for whatever reason, no longer works" (Heilbroner 1983b: 25). Missing is private corporate accumulation financed, one way or another, by government. Heilbroner does not treat as an absolute the idea that "political or moral intervention will be of no avail because some other ordering principle will assert itself...because 'the market' will invalidate these efforts in one way or another" (Heilbroner 1983a). In view of imperialism, he does not accept that the more capitalist a country the more pacificist it will be and that big business exerts little influence on foreign policy (Heilbroner 1981).

Conclusion

Given how much the market has been studied and how much is known about the social construction of markets, it is remarkable that economists still discuss "the market" as if it were given and transcendent. Undoubtedly this predicament is due to ideological bias, disciplinary shorthand, studied ignorance and trained incapacity, and so on. But if the premise of my analysis is correct—namely, that we are in a position to articulate a meaningful, nonideological model of the market—*some* such model should be near at hand. I offer the one outlined here as a start. It is one that comports with Heilbroner's historically rich political economy.

References

Ayres, Clarence E. (1957) "Institutional Economics: Discussion," *American Economic Review, Papers and Proceedings*, 47(2) (May 1957): 26–7.
Brady, Robert A. (1943) *Business as a System of Power*, New York: Columbia University Press.
Casson, Mark (2003) *The Entrepreneur: An Economic Theory*, second edn, Northampton, MA: Edward Elgar.
Fligstein, Neil (2001) *The Architecture of Markets*, Princeton, NJ: Princeton University Press.
Heilbroner, Robert L. (1960) *The Future as History*, New York: Harper Brothers.
——(1980) "The Dialectical Vision," *The New Republic* (March 1, 1980): 25–31.
——(1981) "Was Schumpeter Right?" *Social Research* 48: 3 (Autumn 1981): 456–71.
——(1982a) "A Pitch for Socialism," *New York Review of Books* (Jun. 10, 1982): 41–3.
——(1982b) "The Way of all Flesh," *New York Review of Books* (Jun. 24, 1982): 44–6.
——(1982c) "The Socialization of the Individual in Adam Smith," *History of Political Economy*, 14: 3 (Fall 1982): 427–39.
——(1983a) "The Problem of Value in the Constitution of Economic Thought," *Social Research*, 50: 2 (Summer 1983): 253–77.
——(1983b)"The Coming Invasion," *The New York Review of Books* (Dec. 8, 1983): 23–5.
——(1986) "The Murky Economists," *New York Review of Books* (Apr. 24, 1986): 46–8.
——(1987) "Hard Times," *The New Yorker* (Sep. 14, 1987): 96–109.
——(1989) *The Making of Economic Society*, eighth edn, Englewood Cliffs, NJ: Prentice-Hall.
Kuttner, Robert (1985) "High Marx," *The New Republic* (Oct. 28, 1985): 43–7.
——(1985) Review of Robert L. Heilbroner, *The Nature and Logic of Capitalism*, New York: Norton.
——(1999) *Everything for Sale: The Virtues and Limits of Markets*, Chicago, IL: University of Chicago Press.
Parsons, Kenneth H. (1957) "Institutional Economics: Discussion," *American Economic Review, Papers and Proceedings* 47: 2 (May 1957): 21–6.

Samuels, Warren J. (ed.) (1989) *Fundamentals of the Economic Role of Government*, Westport, CT: Greenwood Press.

——(1992a) *Essays on the Economic Role of Government, Vol. 1, Fundamentals*, London: Macmillan; New York: New York University Press.

——(1992b) *Essays on the Economic Role of Government, Vol. 2, Applications*, London: Macmillan; New York: New York University Press.

——(2002) *Economics, Governance and Law: Essays on Theory and Policy*, Cheltenham: Edward Elgar.

Samuels, Warren J. and A. Allan Schmid (1981) *Law and Economics: An Institutional Perspective*, Boston, MA: Martinus Nijhoff.

Samuels, Warren J. and Nicholas Mercuro (eds) (1999) *The Fundamental Interrelationship between Government and Property*, Stamford, CN: JAI Press.

Samuels, Warren J., Steven G. Medema, and A. Allan Schmid (1997) *The Economy as a Process of Valuation*, Lyme, NH: Edward Elgar.

Schmid, A. Allan (2003) "Different Heterodox Economic Theories: Different Empirical Results?" Manuscript prepared for a conference on the Future of Heterodox Economics, University of Missouri at Kansas City, June 5–7, 2003.

Sutton, Francis X., Seymour Harris Carl Kaysen, and James Tobin (1956) *The American Business Creed*, Cambridge: Harvard University Press.

Swedberg, Richard (2003) *Principles of Economic Sociology*, Princeton, NJ: Princeton University Press.

Part II
The problem of order

5 Joseph J. Spengler's concept of the "problem of order"

A reconsideration and extension

Economics encompasses several "basic economic problems," commonly, almost conventionally, designated as resource allocation, level of income, and distribution of income. The dichotomy of microeconomics and macroeconomics acquires meaning in this context, as having to do with the scope of economics. As for the methodology of economics, on the one hand, neoclassical economists conventionally seek unique, determinate, optimal equilibrium solutions of conceptual and policy problems; and on the other hand, they strongly tend to work with economic variables in the form of pure abstract concepts, such as "the market." An equally conventional critique of these disciplinary practices stresses several points: they omit consideration of a more fundamental economic problem, namely, the organization and control of the economic system; in order to generate unique, determinate, optimal equilibrium solutions, economics must both make limiting assumptions as to important variables and ignore if not foreclose the process by which the content of these variables is formed and solutions are found; and, *inter alia*, working with pure abstract concepts, such as "the market," ignores the fact that actual markets are a product of and give effect to the institutions/power structure which forms and operates through them. In this view, microeconomic, macroeconomic, and distributional organization, operation, and performance interact with the institutional system as a function of the organization and control of the economy.[1]

One economist who attempted a powerful fundamental conceptual systematization of what is involved was Joseph J. Spengler. He did so by formulating what he called "the problem of order," which he nested within an interactive subsystem approach to social science. He first articulated his schema in "The Problem of Order in Economic Affairs," published in July 1948 and reprinted in Spengler and William Allen's *Essays in Economic Thought* in 1960 (all page references not otherwise identified are to this volume; references to pp. 2–5 are to the editors' introduction). Important aspects of Spengler's argument were added to and amplified in "Hierarchy vs. Equality: Persisting Conflict," published in 1968 in *Kyklos*.

The purpose of this article is to reconsider and extend Spengler's approach by applying it to considerations beyond those directly treated by him. However, the views expressed here are not necessarily to be attributed retroactively to Spengler; and the topics discussed here cannot be adequately treated, not to say exhausted, in the space of one chapter. The next section summarizes Spengler's ideas. The following section reconsiders and extends his ideas.

Spengler's approach is both consistent with and an example of Paul Davidson's emphasis on the economy as a non-ergodic process. Both Spengler and Davidson object to the conception of economic order as a predetermined, preprogrammed or prereconciled reality that can be both described and predicted on the basis of unchanging objective conditional probability functions, whether programmed by natural laws or otherwise. Both insist that whatever economic order exists is largely a product of human action and must be worked out. Order, in other words, is a process and not a condition; it is something made, not found.

Spengler's treatment of the problem of order had three aspects. One was analytical, in which he articulated the nature and elements of the problem. It is this aspect that is of principal concern here. The second was historical and consisted of his survey of how the problem of order was treated in the history of economic thought. The third was personal and consisted of the particular implications which he drew for the American economy (pp. 25–8). The last was a product of his personal ideology and perceptions of problems. For some readers his views may have been too conservative; for others, too liberal. Moreover, his analytical model is precisely that and not a calculus or mechanism by which one can generate unequivocal solutions to problems. This may be unsatisfying to some people, but it is, after all, his point that order is a process of working things out. Finally, the terms in which he identifies the elements of the problem of order are very broad; this open-endedness permits the capture of a complex reality without structural or substantive bias.

Spengler's approach

Spengler approaches the problem of order from three interrelated perspectives. First, he distinguishes the economy from other social sub-processes, or sub-realms, with which it interacts. Second, he distinguishes two realms of being. One is the real, "the earthy, dissonant, bumbled, and seemingly confused (albeit not wholly disorderly) world of affairs" (p. 7). The other is the hypothetical, comprising mental constructs. The economy, as economists (and others) understand it, is a mental construct of a hypothetical sub-realm (p. 7). The hypothetical sub-realm has two components, the irrational ("non-rational" would have been a better term) and the rational. The former involves mythopoeic modes of reasoning; the latter, the manipulation of rational mental constructs (p. 7). Third, he posits a complex model of general interdependence between actual institutions and the belief system associated with them: "Changes in economic–institutional arrangements tend to be accompanied by changes in what is thought of them, and changes in how and what men think of these arrangements tend to be accompanied by changes in the arrangements themselves" (p. 2). The development of economic thought in this context has reflected, first, changes in the manner in which economic life has been organized, and second, the manner in which economists "looked upon the economic sector of a society as distinct from other sectors and hence as essentially self-contained and autonomous" (p. 3). The perennial problem of economic order, accordingly, has received attention from ancient times, though the empirical forms in which the problem is perceived have undergone great change.

Spengler states the problem of economic order in the following words:

> Three somewhat incompatible conditions have combined, at all times and in all economies, to create the problem of order: the *autonomy* of many consuming and factor-organizing and supplying agents; the necessity that these autonomous agents behave in an appropriately cooperative and *coordinate* fashion; and the generally felt need that economic activity be *continuous* and uninterrupted. The problem has been aggravated, moreover, by the force of secular and random change.... In general, it may be said that the problem of economic order is solved in proportion as the three objectives, autonomy, cooperation, and continuity, are achieved and reconciled both with one another and with the force of secular and random change.
>
> (pp. 9–10)

In the context of his 1948 (1960) article, then, the problem of order, stated generically and abstractly, involves the continuing need to work out reconciliations within and between two fundamental tensions: between autonomy (or freedom) and coordination (or control); and between continuity and change. Both his formulation, given here, and this restatement represent a generic problem, one which is independent of particular proposed or perceived solutions to it. In its context "order" is not a condition but a *process*, something to be more or less temporarily achieved and then reconstructed and reformulated.

Most of Spengler's article is a survey of the history of economic thought with regard to the diverse and changing treatment of the problem of order. There is no need to summarize the story he tells in any detail but one major theme is important. He distinguishes between those economists who posit and work with a given, autonomous, abstract, hypothetical realm of economic life, deemed by them to adequately represent what the economy is all about; and those who work with specifications of economic life considered to be more realistic because, *inter alia*, they are institutionally defined. The former envision automaticity and harmony in the context of an economy of abstract entities, such as the market. The latter pay attention to perceived real-world problems, operative structures of power, and the dependence of real-world markets on the institutions which form and operate through them. For the former, legal and non-legal social control is superfluous and problem-causing; for the latter, they are fundamental to real-world economies. It is, in large part, a matter of different selective perceptions and specifications of the economic sub-process generated as the actual economy changed over the ages.[2]

Exactly twenty years after the initial publication of "The Problem of Order in Economic Affairs" Spengler published in 1968 what amounted to a sequel entitled "Hierarchy vs. Equality: Persisting Conflict." Here he surveys the history of economic thought with regard to the "seeming need to reconcile the principle of hierarchy with the principle of equality" (Spengler 1968: 217). The tension is between hierarchical and egalitarian tendencies with regard to power, wealth, opportunity, and income (with due regard to the overlap between these categories). This tension may be considered as either an amplification of the conflict between autonomy and coordination (freedom versus control) or a third component of the problem of order. Whatever the case, it is clear that the matter of autonomy (individual freedom) necessarily involves the question of *whose* autonomy (whose freedom, whose individualism). Apropos of the tension between hierarchy and equality and its treatment in the history of economic thought, Spengler writes that

> This review really yields no conclusion. It merely discloses how economic philosophers have reacted to a persistent social fact—one disagreeable to many—over the past two and one-half millennia. This fact is the persistence of hierarchy in the economy as a whole, or in subsectors of the economy. Since hierarchy, being inherent in all orders, will persist, it follows that its significance for society and the individual in the future will turn largely upon the rate of growth of average output in the future . . . . Conflict persists between those who accept the principle of hierarchy and those who believe the role of hierarchy can be greatly diminished if not abolished.
>
> (Spengler 1968: 235)

Also, that:

> Hierarchy presupposes inequality and thus runs counter to equality which always enjoys sentimental support despite the essentiality of hierarchy to social order. Philosophical and economical writers have therefore sought to reconcile the principle of hierarchy, in particular hierarchy based on other grounds than force, with the principle of equality by isolating sectors in which one or the other principle rules. With the replacement of mythopoeic by rational thought this reconciliation assumed rational form.
>
> (Spengler 1968: 236)

Some of this may be narrow but Spengler clearly establishes the existence of tension between hierarchy and equality both as social forces or tendencies and as values.

The result of both articles is a generic model of the problem of order which posits the ubiquitous and perennial necessity of continuing resolution of the conflicts of autonomy and coordination (freedom and control), continuity and change, and hierarchy and equality. In this model, it is important to note, order is a *process* and not a condition. The next section examines certain implications of and extensions to Spengler's model expressed in the same manner so as to preclude specification of the particular form which the resolution(s) are to take, and with due regard to the impossibility of treating the individual points at all thoroughly.

Spengler's approach reconsidered and extended

I shall proceed through a series of points.

A problem for mankind

If I understand Spengler correctly—though no assumption is made as to whether he would agree in whole or in part with what is written here (I think he would substantially agree)[3]—his analysis attributes a particular perspective to both the operation of the actual economy (society) and the work of the historian of economic thought. The perspective is that the problem of order is relevant to the world of human affairs and policy, that it is not something superimposed on man and society by transcendental forces. If that were not the case; if the solution of the problem of order were a matter of pre-design, of fatalism, then there would be no sense in either analysing it or learning about it for the purposes of improving policy. From Spengler's perspective, the problem is the subject of the history of economic thought and, what is more, of policy analysis (pp. 25–8). Economic observation, analysis and experimentation must be assumed to have some effect, even if some or many of these effects are unforeseen and/or unintended.

The foregoing means that, with the qualifications noted, the economy (society) is an artifact and, at least to some degree, a product of human social construction. Spengler's assumption, and that increasingly of economic and social theory since the Enlightenment, is that resolutions of the problem of order are the product of mankind. Both Spengler and the present author posit a secular, social constructivist meaning to the problem of order.

The foregoing further means that the resolution of the problem of order must continually be worked out; the most fundamental socioeconomic process deals with the problem of order and its constituent conflicts.[4] Human beings in all societies under all circumstances are continually engaged in the exercise of what Adam Smith called the moral sentiments—through the propensities to approve or disapprove, that is, to value, our own and others' behavior—in particular social and economic contexts, and in the construction and reconstruction of moral and legal rules.

Selective perception

Spengler's analysis both implies and predicts the operation of selective perception with regard to both order itself and its constituent conflicts. What "order" means to an individual and what autonomy (freedom), coordination (control), continuity, change, hierarchy, and equality mean to an individual, are a function of position or status, individuated and socialized experience, and straightforward selective perception. Thus people with the same or similar positions and experiences will define and interpret those terms differently.

This means that, given different individuals' different prior definitions of reality and values, the same situation will be interpreted quite differently in terms of order and its constituents by different individuals. What constitutes order will vary between individuals; order is neither given nor self-subsistent. It is one thing to talk about order, or about freedom or continuity; it is quite another to assert that one's selective perceptions actually represent the reality of order in some onto-logical sense. There may be such a sense but man living in society acts upon the premise of social constructivism, and what constitutes order, whatever its basis, is selectively perceived, defined, interpreted, and worked out.

Influences on perception and policy

Two influences bear on perception and policy in the working out of solutions to the problem of order. One is the way in which people give substance to their preconceptions as to the nature and significance of what they take to be the eco-nomic system. Their set of mental constructs of the economic system may center on pure abstract economic concepts, for example, the market, private property, and freedom. Or it may focus on the institutional and other details which consti-tute the market, private property, and freedom in the actual economy. Both sets of constructs are present in the mind of each individual; only their relative weights vary between individuals and over time. In every case, both involve preconcep-tions premised ultimately in terms of autonomy versus coordination, continuity versus change, and hierarchy versus equality.

The second influence is the distribution of opportunity, power, wealth, and income. Debate over issues is always broader and more complicated, but the struggle over distribution is a key, if often masked, influence in policy making. Indeed, considerations of distribution—notably the effort to legitimize or to delegitimize profit—have been a driving force in the history of economics. This means that all three component tensions of the problem of order—freedom versus control, continuity versus change, and hierarchy versus equality—are ubiqui-tously present and given effect by jockeying for position in regard to distribution. Policy issues such as capital gains taxation, and minimum wages are more complicated but they are fundamentally driven by considerations of distribu-tion—which almost always means redistribution.

Diversions

Issues other than distribution are also important, both analytically and for partic-ular people. But attention to these, coupled with deliberate efforts to obfuscate questions of distribution, diverts attention away from the deepest levels of policy making relating to the problem of order. This means that those with a construc-tivist law-making mentality are empowered to participate more actively in policy making in pursuit of their felt interests, whereas those with a passive law-taking mentality are prevented from effectively pursuing their putative interests.

System as solution

Seeing the problem of order as truly fundamental leads to the recognition of economic systems *qua* systems as, to some extent, solutions. Thus, an economy in which the deliberate pursuit of money making and high real incomes predominates is a mode of reconciling the conflicts of freedom with control, continuity with change, and hierarchy with equality in a manner which channels, along systemically approved lines, what otherwise would be more violent predatory activity. The well-recognized civilizing role of a commercial and civil society in the socialization, integration, and coordination of individuals is fundamentally instrumental to the ongoing resolution of the problem of order (though the civilizing takes place within and on the terms of this particular civilization). That people accept the definition of reality and of values of the society into which they have become socialized—to the extent that they reject cultural and other forms of relativism in favor of ethnocentrism—attests to the relatively successful achievement of a solution to the problem of order on the terms of that system.

Collectivist forces

The undoubted utility of methodological individualism should not prevent recognition of the inevitable methodological collectivist forces at work in society. These forces are operative, *inter alia*, with regard to (a) the combined socialization and individuation of individuals within the life styles, and so on both permitted and required by a given society; (b) the working out of solutions which obviously both transcend individuals as explanatory agents and provide the system of meaning in which individuals operate; and (c) the determination of *which* individuals' interests will count.

The private–public interface

Modern society, in direct contrast to medieval society, posits a juxtaposition, if not a conflict, between private and public. But these are not self-subsistent categories. The content of each is a function of selective perception and is itself resolved through the working out of solutions to the problem of order. "Rights," for example, are typically considered private phenomena, yet they are what they are because of what government does and does not do, that is, which interests government protects and which it leaves exposed to the exercise of others' rights (protected interests). Just as there is a difference between the abstract concept of a market relative to actual markets with their particular institutionalized foundations, so too is there a difference between the abstract concept of private rights and the actual rights of the real-world economy and policy that are a product of those very same institutionalized foundations, to wit, law, a decidedly public phenomenon.

Yet even that is not enough. While one can identify law as a public phenomenon, law is what it is, at least in part, because of the interplay and influence of nominally private interests in making it. Both nominally private and nominally public phenomena, such as rights and law, are decided in what may be called the legal–economic nexus; and this working out of rights and of law, and of what is selectively perceived as private and public, is part of the search for resolutions of the problem of order and its component conflicts.

Social control

Society comprises a system of social control, through which are determined both whose interests will count in the sense of whose/which interests will be sacrificed to those of others, and whose freedom will be exposed to and limited by the control of others. Social control is inevitable. It is the process by which the conflicts between autonomy and coordination, continuity and change, and hierarchy and equality are worked out.

Social control is not transcendent. An alternative conceptual formulation of social control is power play, which may take place among individuals or among organizations (e.g., governments, corporations, churches). In every case and at any point in time the individual enjoys an opportunity set which both derives from the working out of the problem of order (the system of social control or power play) and is instrumental in positioning individuals for their future participation in the system. That some facets of social control, power play, freedom, and so on are selectively given absolutist formulation is evidence not of the independent ontological existence thereof but of the "successful" establishment and acceptance of the particular system of social control/power play.

The principle of non-intervention, so-called, is empirically wrong. Collective and social considerations are necessarily imposed through legislation and court decisions in the formation of rights. These considerations are central to whatever constitutes freedom and, for example, private property in the real world.

Pervasive politics

People have a widespread desire, perhaps especially in Western civilization with its emphasis on individualism, for an apolitical economy and society. But politics—understood as the exercise of choice, or power, with impacts on others—is ubiquitous, present even when unperceived, ignored, taken for granted, and/or deliberately obfuscated. Some politics occurs in what is nominally recognized as government. Some takes place in all organizations, such as family, church, corporations, universities, and so on. Medievalism was a system of manorial power; capitalism is a system of bourgeois power. The spheres of both government and production, as well as finance, are arenas of power. Resolving the problem of order involves politics, thus understood, at its deepest level.

Thus one comprehends politics as having to do with the exercise of power with impacts on others, then it is possible to identify the totality of social processes as a domain of governance. Some governance is perceived as public or official government; but some resides in nominally private holders of power, and constitutes private government.

Many questions, therefore, of politics and economics can, perhaps ultimately must, be understood in terms of the problem of order and its constituent elements, rather than, as they typically are, in the terms in which they are experienced, perceived, and/or believed and/or presented for purposes of mobilizing political psychology. Everyday statutes and court decisions ultimately derive their meaning and significance from what they contribute, typically incrementally, to the structuring and exercise of power and thereby the system of governance in the process of working out solutions to the problem of order.

Nowhere do the foregoing become more dramatic than in determinations of the content and reach of what are called property rights. But other determinations—of labor, consumer, investor, environmental interests—produce results which are the analytical or functional equivalent of property rights and also have a bearing on the tensions comprising the problem of order.

A system with a structure

Recognition of the problem of order and of the processes through which it is worked out requires attention to holistic, structural, and evolutionary factors and forces. The system at some point in time is more than the sum of abstract isolated, presumably autonomous individuals. It has a structure which effectively distinguishes different individuals and their social roles. That system is not what it was during some earlier period, for it has evolved in the aggregate, in details, and in structure.

Implications

Recognition of the problem of order in a social constructivist way carries several important implications. First, it will dispel the notion that existing arrangements have some independent ontological existence; second, it will lead to an understanding of the putative limits of philosophical realism and determinism in both philosophy and science and, correlatively, the putative viability and importance of relativism, nihilism, and pragmatism; third, the role of absolutist legitimation will be seen as but part of the solution to the problem of order; fourth, it will be realized that economic science does not discover knowledge about an objectively given, transcendent and unchangeable world but participates in the creative process of the social construction of economic reality, which necessarily involves choice and therefore values. One implication of this is the Heisenbergian recognition of the impact of participant observation and analysis. Finally, it will be understood that order truly is a process rather than a reified condition, to be worked out rather than given or to be reached. This last implication holds even though such a view conflicts with our particular socialized identities, which are themselves dependent and independent variables in the search for solutions to the problem of order.

An all-encompassing theory?

No theory can answer every possible question and no model can encompass every variable. The world is infinitely more complex than any theory or model can handle. Accordingly, different theories and models yield different perceptions of the world. These perceptions are selective in nature and relate differently to different views about the conflict comprising the problem of order, which are themselves subject to selective perception and identification. Economics does not exist apart from the working out of solutions to the problem of order but is part of that process. Moreover, the problem of order applies to the discipline itself.

Contradictions will inevitably exist, between arrangements in terms of autonomy versus coordination (freedom versus control), continuity versus change, and hierarchy versus equality. No society can be constituted through arrangements which represent only one of each pair of terms. Both terms in each case are inevitably present, albeit subject to selective perception, although each has meaning in terms of its relevant tension. Freedom requires control and control permits freedom, albeit differently in each case. Change in some areas requires continuity in others, differently in each. Equality in one area is not inconsistent with hierarchy in another, and vice versa.

Adapt and survive

The difference between systems resides in their respective modes of change. Promotion of continuity (rather than change) of a system does not signify the absence of change but rather the governance of change by the maintained mode of change. Reinforcement of a particular system means reinforcement of its particular mode of change, not blind perpetuation of some fixed arrangements.

Chain of causation

Selective perception applies to both particular policy problems and their solutions, leading to difficulties in the attribution of causation. For example, traditional values and relationships are corroded by market forces and gain-seeking behavior. Solutions to the problems consequent to the corrosion will lead to further problems, enabling some to attribute the problems due to corrosion instead to the solutions, which may or may not be correctly understood to have reinforced or exacerbated the problems due to corrosion.

Freedom and control

Neither freedom nor control is an absolute. The specific meaning of freedom and control resides in the details of the extant system and structure.

Limiting variables

Specific welfare determinations in economics require the attenuation of all that is dynamic in order to reduce the governing variables to a manageable few. This is particularly important in regard to the problem of order. Any optimum welfare designation is specific to some assumed resolution of the problem of order, for example, some specification of rights; whereas the problem of order being an open-ended process, the assumed conditions are problematic at best.

Evaluating institutions

Decision making is both deliberative and non-deliberative, both conscious and rational, and habitual and precognitive. Institutions arise and develop spontaneously and organically, and are subjected to deliberative critique and reform, so that any institution is the product of both modes of decision making. Moreover, even when deliberative collective decision making is not undertaken, deliberative private decision making is part of the organic process. Consequences which are either unintended or unforeseen are subject to both selective perception and selective subjective evaluation. No consequences are normatively self-subsistent. Valuation is a process, not an intrinsic condition, and forms part of the process of working out solutions to the problem of order.

Decision making

All decisions are processes of joint determination. In each case, they must be made (as part of solving the problem of order) about the structure of decision making and within that structure. For example, there is no unique Pareto-optimal resource allocation, only allocations specific to and derivative of particular power (rights) structures. Decisions have to be made about the power structure and the allocation of resources within it.

Changes in power structure (rights) are generally so much subject to selective perception that some changes are not seen as such, but as giving effect to what otherwise should, and perhaps must, be the case.

The power of language

Most questions arise not directly from the problem of order but from the terms in which it is worked out. Most obvious are the symbolic and linguistic expressions which are both the means by which most people usually define their situation and by which the manipulation of political psychology and motivation is conducted. Language must be seen as having two interrelated functions: that of describing and/or explaining, in a more or less neutral, objective, positive manner, its combined ontological and epistemological dimensions; and that of mobilizing and channelling political psychology and behavior—its power dimension.

Conflicting mentalities

Two fundamentally different mentalities conflict in attempting to solve the problem of order. One needs determinacy and closure; the other is comfortable with open-endedness and ambiguity. An individual may exhibit both mentalities. The difference between them resides in both their different combinations and the different institutional identifications associated with each.

Resource allocation

Neoclassical economics has centered on the fundamental conditions of scarcity and interdependence, under the condition that human choice, individual and collective (for example, through the market), matters. For the most part neoclassical economists have endeavoured to generate unique, determinate, optimal equilibrium results. In order to do so, they have generally excluded a wide range of dynamic and structural variables. Scarcity and interdependence imply the necessity of choice and thereby conflict and control. They also imply that choice involves opportunity cost and the problems arising from the choices made; and that the structure of choice (who chooses) governs both the choices made and whose interests will count and whose will not. At the center of the problem of resource allocation, adequately broadly and deeply considered, therefore, is the problem of order, with its constituent elements of autonomy versus coordination (freedom versus control), continuity versus change, and hierarchy versus equality.

Radical indeterminacy

Post Keynesian economics—to which Paul Davidson has made numerous important contributions and in which he has been one of the seminal figures—has focused on structural, expectational, and other variables largely ignored by other schools of macro- and micro-economic thought.

Post Keynesian economists do not entirely dismiss equilibrium methodology but insist that economists must study not only the technical conditions of equilibrium but the several adjustment mechanisms and the factors and forces actually at work in the economy. In doing so they have underscored the process of economic performance, while relatively de-emphasizing determinate mechanical relationships. Such has been eminently consistent with Spengler's approach to the problem of order.

They have emphasized the importance of radical indeterminacy and therefore of uncertainty in real-world decision making. In doing so they here too have been consistent with the open-endedness of the problem.

Post Keynesian economists, in contrast to those from other schools of macroeconomics, have emphasized structural conditions and variables. For example: they have identified and focused on the structural and performance differences between the oligopolistic core and the competitive periphery of the economy. They have stressed the importance of income and wealth distributions as structural variables with macroeconomic consequences. They have centered on the labor market as driven by structural–segmentational factors (for example, a differentiated labor force, differences between oligopoly core and competitive periphery) and so on. In doing so they have given important effect to the conflicts between autonomy and coordination and between hierarchy and equality, with profound implications for that between continuity and change.

In doing all this, and in promoting certain policy considerations largely neglected by monetarist and new classical economists, such as involuntary unemployment and a more complex monetary theory, post Keynesian economists have participated in the processes through which the problem of order in economics has been worked out. And they have done so without any overriding pretence that they were setting aright some natural economic system.

Conclusion

The problem of order is a powerful paradigm in which to consider much of what is important in economics; indeed, in which to consider what is most fundamental in all of economics. The problem of order as specifically constructed by Joseph Spengler is powerful enough to elicit deeply important considerations. I suggest that its expansion to explicitly consider the extensions presented here render it even more powerful.

Notes

1 Many economists, working both within and outside the mainstream of economics have understood and pursued the analysis of these broader considerations. These include Carl Menger, Friedrich von Wieser, Vilfredo Pareto, Thorstein Veblen, John R. Commons, John Maurice Clark, Frank H. Knight, Kenneth E. Boulding, Charles E. Lindblom, Friedrich A. von Hayek, and Robert A. Solo. Adam Smith, Karl Marx, and Max Weber could also be mentioned.

2 Spengler was aware that the abstract model, first produced with regard to individual entrepreneurial capitalism, continued to be used after the emergence of corporate capitalism.

3 This is based in part on my knowledge of his work, not all of which is reported on here, and his approval, expressed in person, of my own past use of his ideas.

4 Spengler chides economists for their failure to appreciate both the problem of order and the process through which it is worked out, generally tending instead to make a priori assumptions about it. Thus, for example, he writes that "Our present incapacity to deal with the problem of economic order arises in large measure from the compounded failure of economists (1) to devise a hypothetical subrealm that adequately represents economic objects in the real subrealm of being, and (2) to take fully into account at the hypothetical level the interdependence of the economic subrealm with other relevant subrealms. In particular, economists have failed sufficiently to recognize that what takes place in the real subrealm of being they are studying is conditioned by the prevailing state of power relations and by the extent to which conduct influencing common values and value attitudes have been integrated" (Spengler 1948: 8–9). Spengler's emphasis on the importance of power relations testifies to his social constructivist approach and belief in the at least partial efficacy of human action.

References

Spengler, J. J. (1948) "The Problem of Order in Economic Affairs," *Southern Economic Journal*, XV(1): 1–29. Reprinted in J. J. Spengler and W. R. Allen (1960): 6–35.

——(1968) "Hierarchy vs. Equality; Persisting Conflict," *Kyklos*, 21, Fasc. 2, 217–38.

Spengler, J. J. and W. R. Allen (eds) (1960) *Essays in Economic Thought: Aristotle to Marshall*, Chicago, IL: Rand McNally.

6 The status of the status quo
The Buchanan colloquium

A conference was held at Virginia Tech, May 29–June 1, 2003, underwritten by James M. Buchanan, on a theme of great significance to him, the status of the status quo. He has held that social change and economic policy must "start from here," meaning from where we are, the status quo. Six papers were presented, by Buchanan, Roger Faith, Hartmut Kliemt, Robert Tollison, Viktor Vanberg, and Geoffrey Brennan, and Alan Hamlin. Other attendees included Noel Reynolds, Nicholas Tideman, Carl Dahlman, Robert Sugden, Deborah Mayo, Djavad Salehi, Aris Spanos, and this author. All were obvious admirers of Buchanan but not all were disciples; only one, this author, has been a critic of some aspects of his work.

The papers were distributed in early May. Shortly thereafter I wrote the comments constituting Chapter 7 below; it was distributed before the conference, thanks to Aris Spanos. This document is an interpretive review of the conference itself. It focuses on the discussion rather than on the papers per se. Many if not all of the papers were labeled "draft." The organizers' intention is to publish final versions in a book.

Each conference paper was presented by an Introducer, who summarized its argument and presented a critique. The author both responded to and participated in discussion of the paper and whatever topics or issues arose in discussion. (In History of Economics Society meetings this format is called the Perlman system.) Members who wished to initiate a topic later raised a full hand; those who wished to join in the discussion of a current topic raised a finger—all run by a chair. Only one paper was considered in each one and one-half hour session.

It was not possible to record manually either all facets of the conversation or always who said what (especially in the case of the Brennan-Hamlin paper, whose session I chaired), though I have recorded what my notes indicate. Different reviewers would undoubtedly focus on different themes, though the identity (if not the entitling) of various topics is relatively unequivocal; in any case, the review is subjective. An effort was made not to duplicate description presented in the second document (written earlier). Apologies are in order if opinions have been misrepresented or wrongly attributed.

In the first document, the review of the conference, the sequence is that of the sessions of the conference. In the second document, the sequence is that which at the time of writing I thought most useful in presenting and criticizing arguments.

The first document is entitled "The language, theory and methodology of 'The status of the status quo,'" because the critical issues and themes have to do with those three topics. These issues and themes are, in part, the use of language to advance certain theories as definitional pictures of the world; the role of expectations *vis-à-vis* other bases of defining the status quo; the status quo as an equilibrium point *vis-à-vis* a process; that, apropos of a world of rules (as in rule of law), two problems were typically neglected: that individual rules could be variously interpreted and applied, and that plural rules are often in conflict, altogether permitting, even engendering, the exercise of deliberative choice it was the purpose of rules to constrain if not prevent; and so on. The conference manifested the use vs. the critique of general condemnations of government; terms without specific content; general models applied to specific institutional arrangements; the concepts of the status quo, productive and unproductive, rule of law, coercion, and voluntary; and rules that promote the "general interest" or constitute the "best solution" to a problem vs. rules giving effect to "special interests"; and so on. It is my view that these topics and issues often are the crux of developments in the history and methodology of economics. Such issues arose, in one way or another, throughout the conference; the circumstances of a conference prohibited intensive and uninterrupted analysis of any one of them. My purpose, in addition to describing and critiquing what was said, is to identify and to establish the importance of these issues.

The language, theory, and methodology of "the status of the status quo": an interpretive review of a conference

Prior to the first session I was asked about my view of rent seeking, mentioned in passing in the document of mine distributed earlier. I replied that my view had three parts. First, I agreed that rent seeking, however defined, was ubiquitous. Second, I argued that rent seeking is not bad per se. Third, I argued that I found particularly disgraceful treatments of the allocation of resources to efforts to change the law as bad rent seeking. Both this person and Jim Buchanan (later in the conference) insisted that rent seeking was objectionable when it involved a transfer without a gain in efficiency, that is the creation of something productive. I responded that this view substituted the analyst's definition of productive for that of the economic agent—who obviously believed that hiring a lawyer, and so on to help bring about a potential change in the law was a desirable, hence productive, use of his or her resources. I further insisted that this definition, especially when it was used in a blanket, indiscriminate way, functioned to privilege existing law and those benefiting from existing law and to deny people access to their government, and that it did so by manipulating the definition of rent seeking to give effect to selective antecedent normative premises hidden within the use of the term "productive" (in at least one discussion the term "artificial" was used). I pointed to this as a problem in the use of language. Further aspects of the terminology of rent seeking will be dealt with later.

The same initial interrogator indicated—in a well-rehearsed litany of complaints—several times then and later in the conference that redistributive welfare-state programs were dysfunctional for the ostensible beneficiaries. I did not ask whether such programs were the price paid for their quietude, and whether positions like his involved attempts to lower the price.

1   James M. Buchanan's "The Status of the Status Quo" was presented and critiqued by Noel Reynolds. *Inter alia*, Reynolds made several points. (1) Economic analysis was a useful tool but can mislead or obscure larger truths. Specifically noted were Pareto optimality, unanimity, mental events (such as expectations), authority, and obligation. (2) Natural law seen as universal values and moral truths, when pursued in practice, leads to great uncertainty. (3) Important problems pervade all relevant discussions, such as those of the public interest, majority rule, and the unanimity principle. He pointed out that the Constitution was only the second contract made by those attending the Philadelphia convention; the first was over the decision to produce and submit to a constitution, and this decision was unanimous. Included were expectations of obeying the rules, making new agreements within the rules, and the maintenance of unanimity, even with both winners and losers, through agreements made within the rule of law. Such reasoning tended to render nugatory Buchanan-like concerns over unanimity, rent seeking, rule of law, and Pareto optimality. Use of Pareto optimality elevated change through markets over change through law (legal change). Rule of law was facilitative as well as constraining.

Nicholas Tideman, taking up the meaning of the status quo, suggested that it is not the way things are. It is shared expectations, based on history; hence it is a forward-looking concept (John R. Commons's notion of futurity is relevant here; as is his concept of forebearance, noted later). Expectations do not capture all aspects of the status quo, for example, its specific set of rules. Argument (over a rule) is a function of dissimilar expectations. The status quo is subjective, and not objective. This means that one does not always know it; that is, there is not a given status quo.

Buchanan commented that the status quo is a laissez-faire, not a conservative position; by laissez-faire he meant change allowing and by conservative he meant continuity over change. It was pointed out that "status quo" is the name given to an amorphous understanding; it has to do with language, not reality.

Reynolds indicated that we had a created reality (the idea of social reality created by human action but not by human design, came up several times during the conference) and produced shared expectations and beliefs as to the true and the good. But not all expectations are shared; disagreement results in the process of working things out. Agreement is a way of coordinating expectations.

Kliemt posed the conflict between the objectivity and the subjectivity of rules. I called attention to both conflicting plural rules and conflicts between different views of each rules. I also indicated that realism shares with idealism a necessity of choice: if everyone were a philosophical realist, they likely would disagree as to the content of reality, and have to choose. Buchanan emphasized agreement on the content of rules (I made written note of our different psychological positions but did not bring it up until later).

Reynolds called attention to two levels of subjectivity: the written law, as the basis of expectations, and subsequent efforts to change the game (this example comes up again, later). Then comes the process of working things out. Most controversies are not contested in the courts; they are resolved on the basis of (relatively objective) facts.

Dahlman commented that the status quo is a Hobbesian jungle; Buchanan and I agree, but he dislikes the fact; for me, that is the way it is (the topic also arises again, when the term "Hobbesian state" is acknowledged to refer to a condition and not a type of political unit).

Tideman said that politics is more than the enabling of mutual advantage; it is also the rectification of injustice, as the status quo has both good and bad. He opposes the idea that a non-positive sum game is necessarily destructive.

Sugden called attention to the necessity of norms in reaching political agreements. Kliemt did likewise to the Kantian position prohibiting one's use of another as only a means.

Buchanan questioned the relevance of my citing the case of guerillas. I said that sometimes revolution is necessary; if it is not possible, people are in a bad way.

Dahlman agreed that there is more to politics than public choice theory covers. I raised the point of out-of-sight manipulation by government and corporation personnel. Discussion turned to the issue of a narrow vs. broad definition of self-interest. I said that it was at least my hope that pluralism of belief has greater survival value than other forms.

2   Faith's "Can We Know the Status Quo?" took up issues raised in the preceding discussion and impacting subsequent discussion (though not as much as they could, or should, have). These issues centered on whether one could define the status quo in terms of rules, beliefs, and so on, objectively, thereby making Buchanan's task easier, or only, or largely, subjectively. Faith's paper went "into some of the conceptual difficulties involved in knowing the status quo, and a fortiori, conceptual difficulties in granting any particular normative status to the status quo." The questions included: "How much time must pass before a given state is deemed the status quo? Does historical precedent have any place in the status quo? Are there temporal or spatial boundaries to the status quo? To whom and to what does the status quo refer?" Faith discusses issues of duration, precedent, and priority, who belongs, and, representation and knowledge. Faith does not oppose "granting status, normative or positive, to the status quo when contemplating policy changes that affect society." He does, however, identify "some sources of ambiguity in the concept of the status quo" and writes that "One somewhat negative conclusion from all this is that one may never truly know the status quo." This is one source of the principle of unintended and unforeseen consequences: "Consequently, when policy changes are proposed or instituted one is never quite certain of where they started or where they will end up."

Nic Tideman, the introducer of Faith's paper, identified the status quo in terms of "becoming" rather than "is." The status quo is dynamic, it is a matter of history (path dependence was stressed by others at various times); it is not a matter of the way things are because they are in a process of change. He, for one, is comfortable with the status quo changing, not merely existing. It is a matter of shared expectations, or probabilities, garnered from history.

At both this point and later points, several speakers introduced if not supported the idea of the status quo as an equilibrium concept. What mattered was its state in equilibrium, not how it got there. Objections to this were expressed. Tideman, for example, argued that the whole story of the status quo is more than the status quo defined as an equilibrium state.

Buchanan introduced the problem of why a new regime would honor the previous regime's debt. An extended discussion centered on legitimacy vs. prudential arguments. (Legitimacy connoted what everyone agrees to. Prudential arguments included maintaining credit with lenders.) Tideman raised the possibility of an international agreement that approved, but established conditions for, repudiation. Buchanan suggested the issue was whether policy would confiscate the property of the bondholders (through repudiation) or of the taxpayers (through having to finance payment).

Dahlman reported upon his experience in the Reagan Administration, namely, being told to "undo something." I pointed out that if the something in place was protecting A's interest from B, undoing that meant protecting B's interest from A, and that analytically the two situations were equivalent; the only difference was in whose interest was being protected, and that is what economic politics is all about. (Of course, the A interests to be undone, on the basis of the Reagan program, were rather distinct: welfare, environmental, and other similar interests.) Dahlman concurred with the logic of my analytical point. Kliemt, however, suggested that to undo violates expectations as to what is, which has prima facie legitimacy. (Again, the question is whose expectations, for example those of people who "expect" their protection to endure indefinitely, or those of people who look forward to changing in their favor protection now advantaging others—two different views of the content of the status quo.)

Tideman returned to an earlier discussion, offering what he considered an alternative to the "we start from here" argument. The alternative centered on one of John Locke's provisos, that we leave unto others the same as we take.

Reynolds suggested that the status quo can be seen as rules plus the preconditions for the change of rules, which become principles of the rule of law. In discussion, someone defined the rule of law as meaning no discrimination between persons. (Where law must choose between conflicting interests, no such definition will do.) Buchanan referred to an exchange between Richard Epstein and Antonin Scalia, with Buchanan siding with Scalia, in which Epstein affirmed (what he took to be) the original right and the others the extant right.

Brennan posed a different question from Faith's "can we know the status quo?," namely, "what can we know of the status quo?" His view was that the status quo is not akin to a stable utility vector, that all members of the status quo in effect hold lottery tickets with uncertain probabilistic values. He wondered whether differences in expectations create problems and not contingencies per se. (All this emphasizes problematicity, and not an objective unique determinate concrete status quo.) Tideman emphasized, in reply, probabilism as a function of attitudes toward risk.

The different positions can be combined, for example, problematicity (and probabilism) generates contingency that leads to differential expectations.

Tideman again stressed that there was more to the definition of the status quo than exchange (and therefore more to public choice than market-like exchange).

Spanos, an econometrician, suggested a definition (from modeling) in terms of initial structure and conditions, dynamics, and stochastic trajectory, that is path dependence.

It was pointed out that (say, technological) change can render traditional rules objectionable and thereby create the necessity to reinvent the rules (e.g. from horse and buggy to the automobile).

Brennan raised the problem of whether it was necessary to know what the status quo is. If the status quo is A, change is change in A; if B, then change in B. For some changes, policy action does not need to know the status quo; for example egalitarian policy and agreements on contract.

At several points in the discussion, Faith's example of a protective tariff came to the foreground. Is the status quo the tariff, partial, or whole repeal of the tariff, or some ideal state without tariffs? This is reminiscent of Plato's emphasis on the ideal derived from the (more or less temporary) actual vs. Aristotle's emphasis on the actual since it does exist (quite aside from defining the actual, or the real).

3   Hartmut Kliemt's paper, "Contractarianism as Liberal Conservatism: Buchanan's (Un-)finished Philosophical Agenda," raised the prospect of different types of conservatism and of contractarianism. His view is that Buchanan's type of contractarianism is a formal type of conservatism that grants normative status to the status quo and possibly blends into classical liberalism, such that a specific form of conservatism, not the idea of contract per se, should be seen as the core of Buchanan-type contractarianism. As Spanos, who introduced Kliemt's paper, suggested, Buchanan's bottom line emphasized unanimous agreement and appeal to some ethical norm or criterion: Agreement alone is not the source of legitimacy; the classical liberal claim is to have a society in which individuals can decide as much as possible themselves; and insofar as maximizing agreement and minimizing coercion are sources of legitimacy, these can be pursued without unanimous agreement. Unmentioned was the facts that no conservative wants to retain everything in the status quo and that the issue may be the retention of the particular dominant mode of change in the status quo, not the substance of the status quo itself.

Among the points made in discussion were the following:

Buchanan's view that hypothetical agreement is useful—as a heuristic, not as a legitimizing principle—in reaching actual agreement.

The problem of the meaning of coercion and its implications. Given an array of meanings, any particular principle may not apply equally and may lead policy astray (Samuels). The avoidance of coercion is an illusion; some coercion cannot be avoided (Kliemt). Utilitarianism has the defect of leading to coercion (e.g. mandatory loss of a kidney for transplant purposes—though perhaps not in a club organized voluntarily for such a purpose).

Pragmatic adjustment is engendered by the need to adapt to a (changed) situation.

Property is a contingent claim to decision-making rights with regard to scarce goods, within social structure, courts, and so on.

A set of rules governing exchange is necessary.

4   Robert Tollison's paper, introduced by Carl Dahlman, was entitled "The Status of the Status Quo." It used the theory of rent seeking combined with Arnold Harberger's model of monopoly as extended to rent seeking by Gordon Tullock. Tollison's argument was "the futility of economic reform of existing deformities in the economic order," that "Genuine reform should ignore the past and possibly look to the future;" it should accept existing deformities and seek to prevent new ones from emerging, and that "the *status quo* has a strong analytical rationale in a world with rent seeking." And again, "there is much to recommend the *status quo* in a general interest world...it is hard to avoid the conclusion that it is best to let the rent seekers prevail (let the big dogs eat)." Dahlman referred to "Bob's simple model." Tollison said it is "not a picture of reality." Vanberg later countered that it does relate to, or is, reality.

I made a number of points critical of Tollison's argument. These had to do with the use of analytical tools to define reality; Ronald Coase's criticism of "black-board economics; and that the legal-economic system included two processes, one centering on production and efficiency, the other on the decision making process, including rights of access to government and for weighting preferences between individuals—the latter involving the use of resources in order to change the law and rights (this point is similar to another, that Tollison's model is used by him and others to deal with matters which go far beyond it. Later I argued against evaluating the allocation of resources to changing the structure or process of decision making by the economic theory of exchange and production. (I used the illustration of using legal services both within and to change the system of land registration and transfer—full well knowing that these systems were instituted and revised by rent-seeking interests.) I also drew a comparison with capital theory. Advocates of different theories of capital strongly tend to assume that only one theory of capital is possible whereas the theories are tools instrumental in and enabling the understanding of different aspects of capital. Different theories of the status quo, of rent seeking, and of other topics need not, therefore be treated in an either-or manner. Salehi contended that Tollison's was an inept one-period policy model.

Tideman returned to his earlier point. One criterion of the status quo could be utility or benefit or GDP maximization. Another could be equitable results. Buying off holders of presently held rights (successful past rent seekers) creates expectations of future buying off. The issue was "do nothing" (Tollison) or "buy off" (others).

Vanberg argued that economic reform is about playing a better game, and has both benefits and costs. The costs here are due to the strategies of the players. Buchanan indicated, first, that he dislikes the term "rent seeking" but has found no suitable alternative; and second, that, yes, the Harberger-Tullock model is simple but Harberger could not understand Tullock's identification of the diagram's area of rent-seeking (as opposed to monopoly) waste.

Tollison argued that representative government allows and engenders rent-seeking waste (see later). In response, Brennan maintained that rent seeking is part of politics, and that to suppress it would be a cure worse than the disease; it amounts to the cost of government.

Vanberg articulated a position that juxtaposed the creation of "the best rules possible" to rules amounting to privileges for rent-seeking "special interests." I argued that the category of "the best rules possible" was a primitive term, that we possessed no conclusive means of distinguishing "the best rules possible" from rules favoring "special interests," that rule making did typically favor one interest over another, and that (following George Stigler) economic agents did pursue their self-interest in their political affairs as they did in their economic affairs. I claimed that having passing in football, smaller or larger strike zones in baseball, or different blocking rules in football, involved favoring one interest over another in each case (that day the newspapers had articles with data on home runs (large strike zone) vs. hit batters (small strike zone); and that owner perceptions and interests in revenue maximization tended strongly to dictate rule changes. I offered hanging on the rim as a candidate of a different type of case.

Buchanan remarked that he found bitching at referees by coaches highly objectionable. I pointed out that, consistent with Vilfredo Pareto's model of mutual psychological manipulation, coaches were trying to manipulate the psychology of referees.

Dahlman suggested that instead of trying to attack rent seekers, policy should seek to limit the producers of rent (see later).

Buchanan characterized his position as the Knightian one of relatively absolute absolutes—thereby acknowledging the force of criticism of his position but maintaining his position intact.

5   Robert Sugden introduced Viktor Vanberg's paper, "The Status Quo in Contractarian Constitutionalist Perspective." The crux of the argument is the search for mutual benefit—understood in the context of exchange and Pareto optimality— and is clearly stated by Vanberg in the following terms: "It is an argument about how we should proceed from here, namely by peaceful, contractual means rather than by coercion and violence, it is not an argument for leaving things as they are. It is an argument not in terms of the merits of the status quo but in terms of the merits of contractual change compared to its alternative, change by coercion and violence." The argument, of course, posits change through market exchange as non-coercive vs. change through government as coercive—ignoring, for example, past and present exercises of coercion in markets.

Vanberg also says that his "exclusive concern in this paper is with the *constitutional status quo* and with the issue of *constitutional reform*. To be sure, calls for constitutional reform, that is for changes in the rules of the game may of course, be motivated by discontent with the pattern of distributional outcomes that result from status quo rules. But it is the concern with changes in the rules themselves, not in outcomes per se, that is of principal interest here. And it is the constitutional status quo, the existing 'structure of legal order' ... that Buchanan defines as the 'here.'" The argument that "we start from here" has the homely appeal of a simple truth: given the problems of identifying or defining the status quo, any change is from it. But Buchanan's formulaic position has another function, namely, to obfuscate and ignore how the status quo came into existence. Taking that into consideration not only raises normative issues but casts positive light on both the status quo and proposals to change it. In a world of giants and pygmies, in which the giants became giants through the capture and use of government, such is relevant to the claims of the giants and their ideological and/or hired spokespeople, that the existing structure of power and how it came to be should be ignored. Such a view reinforces efforts to transfer change to the market and to keep present and future government from having the power of past government—though able and required to protect established giant rights as if they were part of the natural order of things—that is, to reinforce the established system and structure of *governance* (which is the effect of Richard Epstein's view of property rights). Such a view is not a matter of truth but of argument articulated with the intent of manipulating political psychology in favor of established privilege; it is a contribution to politics that denigrates politics—an echo of a public choice theory that denigrates public choice. (At several points Vanberg cites my work on Buchanan; although he does concur with my view a few times, one can interpret his analysis as an effort to shore up Buchanan's position. Thus, one reads, "That for contractual departure from the status quo one must gain the consent of those who are privileged by the status quo does not mean that one cannot employ the 'moral pressure' of public political discourse as a legitimate tool.")

Vanberg distinguishes between "unanimity as a legitimizing principle and unanimity as an in-period decision rule." Only the former requires unanimous approval: "the contractarian postulate of consensual change does not rule out at all changes that do not command unanimous approval, as long as such changes are made according to rules that are legitimized by the consent of the relevant community." The problem, of course, is the ease with which Buchananites go from such a hypothetical situation to the actual historical situation, as if the latter were described by the former.

After summarizing the foregoing, it was Sugden (I believe) who commented that doing politics involves a normative commitment, taking place in a political system in which all parties live together. In this connection, Tideman remarked that the alternatives were only three: fighting, discussion, and contract. Buchanan noted as an aside that British pressure in Northern Ireland might have prolonged the war, which could have been settled earlier by fighting. Later on I noted that government was verbal conflict having replaced physical fighting.

Brennan suggested that conservatism meant that feasibility be taken seriously. Two kinds of constraints, he said, were relevant but very different. One is brute facts, including the content of history, which are hard constraints. Constructed rules are decisional and, in comparison, soft constraints.

Much discussion, at this point and at other times, centered on whether the allocation of resources to determine which decisional contents are to be changed is artificial or unproductive. As given earlier, this gets to the heart of rent seeking.

Vanberg suggested that a lesson of evolutionary psychology is that fighting is part of our genetic, instinctive makeup, and that our becoming civilized takes place in the face of this. He added that ongoing rules are necessary; the potential for revision is also necessary, for legitimacy.

Reynolds maintained that law needed to be taken more seriously. War, he suggested, led to a decision to be ruled by law, which led to politics and to rent seeking within politics. The decision to be ruled by law implied the acceptance of law, a constitutional system of government, authoritative rules, processes for changing the constitution, and norms for assessing the legitimacy of constitutional changes and to maintain the legitimacy of the decision to submit to law. He identified 3 of some 20 norms: (1) the principle of generality, that law apply to all, that is, the rule of law; (2) equality; and (3) prospectivity—no ex post facto changes.

It was clear from the discussion that the issue remained that of privileging the status quo. This implied the further issue, whether we are talking about a process (of working things out, with the Buchananite position being one contribution thereto) or seemingly a priori universal solutions to problems.

Buchanan remarked that much of what was being said leads to a stance of acquiescence, to minimal changes; to which Reynolds replied that such is not the case, otherwise there would be inertia.

I wrote but did not say that some or much involved facilitating recognition of legal change without challenging fundamentals.

Tollison—with a thrust opposite to that of his paper—called attention to political entrepreneurship, to people with vision who try to sell their ideas. This, I said, brought to mind those writers who treated government and politics as a market and found optimizing solutions formed therein. Someone, likely Tollison, referred to Tiebout solutions to problems of disagreement over public-good packages.

Someone suggested a case for actually being privilege free. It is in part a problem of definition, in part one of the test. The speaker argued that agreement with the rules implied the absence of privilege. (One could reply that the absence of revolution meant only that the price thereof was seen to be too high, not that privilege was non-existent.)

I suggested the paradox emanating from the following: to treat equals equally, you need to treat them equally, but to treat unequals equally you need to treat them unequally. Kleimt cited Hayek to the effect that under classical liberalism unequals were treated equally, whereas under modern liberalism, unequals were treated unequally. (If unequals are treated equally, would they now be equals? Was there not then one system of law for the landed and non-landed propertied and another for the non-propertied?)

Deborah Mayo queried as to how much change would transpire if unanimity were required in a contractarian system. Vanberg responded that if privilege existed in the status quo, the privileged can be bought out, they can be made subject to ethical persuasion, contractarian change can take place, or (undesirably) involuntary change can take place. Vanberg stipulated that in his approach no ethical norm could be brought to bear from the outside (a topic raised in his paper in relation to one of my publications). I replied that the definition of "outside" is critical and wondered if every possible norm could be found "inside."

Reynolds queried as to the source of normative individualism. Vanberg replied that normative individualism was not the same thing as laissez-faire and reiterated the conventional distinction between normative individualism and methodological individualism, but did not take up the matter of source.

6   Geoffrey Brennan and Alan Hamlin's "Analytic Conservatism," introduced by Mayo, presented a complex argument. Its elements included: a bias in favor of the status quo is a key component of the conservative disposition; the need to justify such a disposition; distinguishing between the ideal or political end sought and a posture with respect to that ideal; the importance of feasibility considerations and of ignorance of the consequence of policy changes, in the latter case unknowable consequences implying that experimentation is "flying blind" and is a bad bet; that given the antecedents, it is rational to adopt the conservative predisposition to a status quo bias; that the disposition itself requires justificatory argument; and that what motivates conservatives may differ from what justifies conservatism.

The conservative disposition, Brennan and Hamlin wrote, connoted "an intuitive suspicion of all grand schemes, an intrinsic affection for things as they are, an inclination to be reconciled to one's general situation and perhaps strongly self-identified with it, a tendency to evaluate policies and reforms in terms of 'disaster avoidance' rather than utopian aspiration."

The topics of discussion were those of the paper: the conservative disposition or sentiment; multiple types of conservatism; and the strategic reasoning of analytical conservatism, but not the topic of justification *vis-à-vis* motivation (what I consider to be the problem of hypocrisy). Controversies arising in discussion were over: (1) the coherence and sufficiency of the notion of a conservative disposition; and (2) the relation of the disposition to the different types of conservatism. It was pointed out that uncertainty characterized both policy effects and the ideal. Tideman affirmed a partial idealist position—the temperament of the right thing to do.

7   The final session involved open discussion with Buchanan in the chair. He indicated his favorable impression of what he called epistemic defense of the status quo—by people themselves. He voiced his lament that we are losing the status quo ante of Western values—elaborated as the rule of law and adherence to institutions developed in and/or on the basis of eighteenth-century developments. He said that in the contest between explaining by nature and by nurture, the former was winning out—people were fundamentally unequal—but the welfare state was supported by different values. He distinguished between US and European culture with respect to the welfare state: In consensual states, such as the United States and Canada, immigration figured highly; whereas in non-consensual states, such as Europe, personhood was defined by nationality. Very little direct challenge was voiced to this.

Tideman reiterated his displeasure with silence in the face of injustice, to preserve the status quo. Emphasis was made on defining the status quo in terms of its dual modes of change, the market, and moral and legal rules. Reiterated discussion of the Hobbesian state elicited a Buchanan-Samuels definition of "state" in terms of condition, not a political entity.

I juxtaposed two contradictory ideas: (1) that the United States was in a Hobbesian state insofar as people took extreme positions on issues, failed to respect others' different points of view, and so on, including the rise of domestic and foreign-based terrorism, due in part to our support of Israel and becoming a party to conflict with Islam; and (2) that the idea of the US system of government once was something of which Americans were proud and attractive to foreigners. I asked Buchanan, with evident reluctance, whether public choice theory, with its denigration of the concept and practice of democracy and the American system of government, has contributed to what many see as the failure of our belief system. He agreed that that was likely the case. Shortly thereafter Mayo questioned whether conservative, Buchananite ideas were responsible for some of the failures to which they objected.

Someone pointed out the importance of law and government. I noted that Adam Smith defined the stages of his stage theory in terms not of changes in technology or the mode of production but of changes in the system of law and government.

Vanberg presented a discussion that included attention to if not emphasis on people refraining from pursuing the position of their maximum advantage and engaging in negotiation. I called attention to John R. Commons's emphasis on forebearance and negotiational psychology.

Dahlman stressed the rule of law, emphasizing Trent Lott's statement thereon at the time of the impeachment trial of Bill Clinton. I indicated that the concept of the rule of law had a variety of meanings. I juxtaposed to Lott's and Richard Posner's expositions that of Bruce Ackerman and those who were critical of its use as a means of introducing politics into a case of adultery and lying about it. I also cited my article on the rule of law (Chapter 7) in which I criticized its invocation where it did not belong, along with considerable evidence, arguing that there is no rule of law.

Some speakers directly or indirectly supported pluralism. Others explicitly opposed Post-Modernism and relativism, most notably, perhaps, diversity in education. Buchanan reiterated his reliance on relatively absolute absolutes. Largely ignored were the problems posed by Faith, Reynolds, Tideman, Brennan and, *inter alia*, myself as to the coherence of the concept and desirability of the status quo.

This was Buchanan's colloquium. Notwithstanding the use of formulaic expressions and the quest to strengthen his intellectual fortress, it was an interesting, pleasant, and informative discussion. As I said in a toast at dinner, he is a great scholar, a great gentleman, and a good friend.

Still, I came away from the conference agreeing that conservatism is a disposition, a sentiment; that Brennan and Hamlin's description of it is only one but accurate enough for many people; that by their or any other description no one is totally conservative, only selectively so; that the Buchanan project is an effort to wrap his form of conservative argument in scholarly, even scientific garb; that the relation of Buchananite ideas to politics in general and the Republican party in particular is complex; and that among the ironies of the conference were those pointed out in the next document, including the nothing still being said of the enormous Federal deficit, and the Reaganite get-the-government-off-of-our-backs mentality of various domestic terrorists, including Eric Robert Rudolph, who was captured near the start of the conference. Everything is selective, a matter of what once, and in a different field, was called casuistry.

The position I am trying to state was nicely expressed by Overton H. Taylor (*A History of Economic Though*, New York: McGraww-Hill, 1960) who wrote that economics "is in some degree at least a science" (p. xi), but it is also an expression of subjective individual moods and movements, "purely speculative, void of demonstrable or verifiable truth or validity, as largely emotional as intellectual in content or substance, and intent not purely on discovering truth or understanding actualities but largely on inspiring and directing political action toward particular goals and along particular paths. And they are always biased, partisan, fervent, and dogmatic—in short, they are in every way antithetical in spirit and nature to all science" (pp. xi–xii). Taylor's own view was that "Economics . . . is, and long has been, *in some degree* a science, though I emphasize the qualifying phrase . . . But I do not think that economic science, or theoretical work in it, is or has been or can be so perfectly or absolutely scientific—objective, unbiased, neutral . . . —as to make it possible to say . . . that the great contributions . . . have been wholly uninfluenced by . . . political philosophies . . . Nor do I see any point in avoiding recognition and study . . . [of] the influences exerted by the social philosophies . . . Precisely in his effort to achieve objectivity, one should try to make his own social, moral, and political outlook or philosophy as fully explicit, conscious, clear, and self-critically examined as possible . . ." (p. xii). "I do not at all share the inclination toward contemptuous dismissal of [systems of philosophical political thought] as not worth serious, participating study . . . [C]ivilizations, and civilized men, cannot live by or upon scientific knowledge alone . . ." (p. xiii). These views are all the more striking inasmuch as I share Taylor's and Buchanan's "attachment it to . . . classical liberalism—the philosophy or vision of societies of largely free individuals, under limited governments . . . of the liberal-democratic kind, and with economic activities and relations organized mainly in systems of free, private enterprises and competitive markets" (p. xiv).

Perhaps some day someone will write a book on the hypotheses for serious, scientific study contained in Buchanan's ideological, even utopian economics. Such a study would have the structure that Joan Robinson suggested and the content that Buchanan has produced. It would also have a place for Buchanan's high-priest role in his movement, the role verbalized when I have heard him called "Rabbi Buchanan." I expect he would consider that a compliment. Certainly his students understand his role as a conservative economist.

One irony is that Buchanan is a scholar whose work is laden with ideology and the desire to motivate certain reforms yet he has been the most creative scholar in the field of public finance, one who surely merited his Nobel Award. A greater irony is that Buchanan is in principle no different from other reformers who envision problems in contemporary economics and politics and strongly seek to correct them.

7 The problem of the status of the status quo

Some comments

The objective of these notes is that of the Colloquium, namely, to identify certain issues and distinctions that arise when considering the status of the status quo. Because of time pressure and the pressure of other commitments I am unable to present the issues and reasoning as thoroughly as I would prefer.

The status of the status quo (SSQ) is both a positive and a normative problem. I have—unlike apparently most of the other participants in the Colloquium—absolutely no interest in establishing a normative position on SSQ. I would prefer some change and some continuity. I am interested in a positive analysis—as purely positive analysis as can be achieved—of the problem of the SSQ. One positive point is that the status quo manifests some change and some continuity. Others will be identified later.

The first section examines part of a set of notes taken by F. Taylor Ostrander in Frank H. Knight's course, Economics 303, Current Tendencies, during the Winter Semester of 1934 at the University of Chicago. This part of the class notes deals with Knight's treatment of an early version of the problem take up at the Colloquium. The notes in their entirety will be published in Archival Volume 23B (2005) of *Research in the History of Economic Thought and Methodology*. The second part comments on the Colloquium papers distributed in advance in early May 2003. It will surprise no one that I am critical—a sympathetic critic, to a point—of much that is written in those papers. I hope that my bluntness is not taken for hostility. The third parts presents some summary thoughts and random comments.

Knight

One important discussion comes under Knight's heading of "Social Control." To appreciate his argument, one has to understand that Knight's social theory is developed within a tension between: (1) his knowledge that social control is both inevitable and necessary; and (2) his correlative desire for individual autonomy. One *could* add to that a hatred of social control, some of which *is* relevant. But what Knight dislikes is, first, selective elements of existing social control and, second, change of social control, for example change of the law by law, *except for* those changes of the law that remove the selective elements he dislikes; Knight is not opposed to all change of social control. In any event, the problem of social control is also for Knight (as it was for Vilfredo Pareto) the problems of social change and of the status of the status quo as well as of hierarchy.

For the purpose of clarity, one could postulate Knight's alter ego. Let S be the totality of existing social control; K that part that Knight dislikes; R the part that Knight likes but the alter ego dislikes; dK the change in social control that Knight would support; and dR the change that the alter ego would support. The differences between Knight and his alter ego are (1) that which they respectively like and would not change and (2) that which they dislike and would change. Neither is totally for existing social control, neither is for changing everything. Neither can claim the anti-social control high ground. Nor can either claim the anti-legal change high ground—though given existing social control, change of law (or other rules) by law is the point at issue. Some writers, for example Bruno Leone, define coercion as legal change—not the law already in place. If the law in place is L1, the new body of law is L2, and the difference between L1 and L2—legal change—is dL, it is impossible for me to see only dL as coercion. (I surmise that no revolutionary wants to change everything—though it may appear that way to both some of them and some of their opponents; at least that is the record, as I read it, of historical revolutions. This has not prevented conservatives from talking about total as opposed to incremental or marginal changes.) (For exposition of several of the foregoing themes, see Samuels 1973a, 1974, 1997.)

Thus, in the notes, Knight is reported to have repudiated what he called the idea that is "the intellectual element in social enterprise," namely, the "Idea that society is my chariot for me to drive." This, he says, is "Analogous to [the] making of rules for a game—with [the] aim of a *better* game." He has two problems with this. It involves, first, "Making rules for yourself, not for others;" and second, "Aiming at a good game, but... aiming at *winning* the game." It is "childishness," he claims, of those "who want social control, but don't see the elementary fact that what they want is a society that would be *their* plaything; that which would work only if *they* controlled."

Knight goes one step further. He says that "aiming at *winning* the game ... is not analogous to economic theory," that "The step from understanding of economic theory to social policy is a tremendous one," that people "Have enough to understand economic theory—and it *is* essential," and that "talking about social control on a basis of that understanding is overpowering." (Interestingly Knight seems to have a view, close to that of Pareto, of elites competing for control of the masses; here he says, "And the masses love to lie down before the Juggernaught car, if it's done with right technique.")

This additional step raises further questions. Why is economic theory the test? Would economists, or economic theorists, then not become the rule-making authority for others in society? Would not this mean that economists—or some economists—would become the otherwise maligned chariot drivers? On what basis are they to have this exalted position? And which economic theory, and which economists, would control the rule making? (Knight himself would put it, which rules = whose rules.) Further, as given here, inasmuch as there must be rules, the question is not whether or not but which (= whose) rules. And since Knight interposes economic theory, hence economists, against changing the rules, why is his argument not self-referential, or self-reflexive? Or is this but the guise in which one group seeks to become in fact but not in name the chariot drivers of society?

Knight is absolutely descriptively correct when he talks about "Aiming at a good game, but...aiming at *winning* the game." Legislation is not written and enacted neutrally, but by interested parties using law as a political means to their economic and other ends. Objections to legislation sought by others, as class warfare or as violations of non-interventionism or as putting the government on the backs of the citizenry, are not forthcoming from the same objectors when it is *their* legislation on the table. Such is the predicament—call it plutocracy—targeted by John Rawls's notion of a veil of ignorance. Knight may have considered rule making with a view to winning as a violation of economic theory. But George Stigler, a student at Chicago at the same time as Ostrander, much later argued that people pursue their self-interests in politics no less than in economics, or in political no less than economic markets.

Some of the foregoing is echoed in and supported by the following. In an article in the November 27, 2002 issue of *Business Week*, entitled "Biting the Invisible Hand," Martin Fridson, the chief high-yield strategist at Merrill Lynch, is quoted for making a critical distinction apropos of the Enron scandal. His first point was that the Invisible Hand, in his view a metaphor for harnessing individual self-interest to serve the general well-being, is a powerful principle. His second point was that it is a "very convenient cover story for people who are actually trying to stack the deck in their favor"—for people who preach the virtues of competitive capitalism but practice the crony variety.

The same point is made by users of rent-seeking theory who invoke it to condemn all change of law—except those changes they believe necessary to correct existing wrong law. Assuming the ubiquity of rent seeking (= aiming at *winning* the game), such does not render normatively repugnant *all* efforts to change the law; nor do the critics of rent seeking perceive it in their own agendas.

Here we have, rather, arguably empirical support for the general theory of business control of government, of ideology as a system of manipulated (see later, in re Geoffrey Brennan and Alan Hamlin's paper) preconceptions, of capitalism as predatory behavior, and so on.

Predictive power is generally not very powerful in economics, but, absent a desire to predict precisely who will act in a predatory manner and precisely how they will do so, Knight's ideas, like Thorstein Veblen's theories, for example, predict these types of behavior very clearly. The likelihood of business-oriented because business-dominated government, for example, being complicit in arguably numerous ways is successful prediction.

If the problem of social control, therefore, is also the problems of social change and of the status of the status quo, the operative problem is, who decides? The three foregoing examples—the economic theorist, the deck stacker, and the rent-seeking opponent of rent seeking—not only provide answers to that question but demonstrate that normative theorists of the status quo are part of the process of continually remaking the status quo.

Buchanan

The work of James M. Buchanan forms the basis of most if not all of the papers presented at the Colloquium—including, of course, his own, which I consider last.

1   Robert D. Tollison summarizes his "The Status of the Status Quo" as follows:

> This paper employs the theory of rent seeking to show the futility of economic reform of existing deformities in the economic order. Genuine reform should ignore the past and possibly look to the future; it should accept existing deformities and seek to prevent new ones from emerging. Hence, the *status quo* has a strong analytical rationale in a world with rent seeking.

I have criticized the theory of rent seeking earlier and will not repeat the argument here (see Samuels and Mercuro 1984). For present purposes I make the following points, in part in the form of questions.

The conclusion stated in the first sentence is, given the monopoly analysis presented in the paper, only a matter of logic. Given the premises, the conclusion follows. But the conclusion can claim only validity, or logicality; it is not necessarily a true proposition, meaning by "truth" descriptive accuracy and/or correct explanation. Furthermore, the conclusion of the paper is an over-generalization from the monopoly case to all potential change of law and to the totality of the legal-economic system in which that change takes place (see Samuels 1998).

What constitutes an existing "deformity" is a matter of judgment and fundamentally subjective, almost verging on the idiosyncratic in many instances; anything approaching unanimity is highly unlikely. (Party politics, perhaps especially by noted academics, does have the effect of often creating a small number of "official" versions of what constitutes a deformity or not, but that is an artifact of party politics.) To presume substantive content to "deformity" is to omit a fundamental part of the process evaluating SSQ. It renders ostensibly concrete what is actually only a primitive term; doing so is a problem of the use of language in economics (see Samuels 2001).

Do the conclusions as to "the futility of economic reform of existing deformities in the economic order" and ignoring the past apply: (1) fully to our own; and (2) to all economic orders? Has this conclusion, rampant in a certain body of literature, prevented believers from calling for major reforms in this country? Has it prevented them from applauding reforms for transition to a market economy in the former USSR?

As to "futility," this presumes that one knows the actual and not merely the ostensible goals of reforms—a dubious assumption (see later in re hypocrisy).

As for ignoring the past, accepting existing deformities, and possibly looking to preventing new ones from emerging, it is, first, a matter of subjective judgment.

Second, any policy with regard to the new is likely to be tied up with the old. For example, the economic significance or meaning of a right is in part a function of its relation to other rights; and the pecuniary calculus of costs and benefits pertaining to new policy will be a function in part of the price structure generated by the old. Policy toward the new will inevitably influence the old. (Again, all this is rendered almost nugatory by my first point, as to what constitutes a deformity.) Judgments of over- vs. under-investment (in this paper and in others) are a function of which price structure is used by the analyst, one of which (that generated with no deformity) is hypothetical.

The argument is normative but is selectively normative. There is nothing about the larger problem of continuity vs. change other than Tollison's own normative argument. Especially missing is any recognition of other reasons for changing the law, for example to accommodate or inhibit new technology.

The paper (not alone) seriously neglects—or, at best, trivializes—the process of making policy, of working things out.

The conclusion is that "there is much to recommend the *status quo* in a general interest world. Put another way, in a world where trapezoids and not triangles motivate behavior, it is hard to avoid the conclusion that it is best to let the rent seekers prevail (let the big dogs eat)." This conclusion can only lend further credence to the view that the body of theory drawn upon in this chapter is intended to promote the continuation of an oligarchic, plutocratic system of political economy. This applies to the entirety of the legal-economic system. What should be especially important to economists is that markets, in which much of the action takes place, are not given but are in part a function of differential power (in the context of the theories of the firm promulgated by Ronald Coase, Gardiner C. Means, and others).

The "strong analytical rationale" claimed for by the author is anything but strong; it surely is not conclusive.

2   Roger L. Faith's "Can We Know the Status Quo?" raises a number of very important points.

The most important general points are, however, largely implicit: First, the status quo is a social construction in two senses. It is a matter of human construction, through deliberative and non-deliberative decision making (see Samuels 1999). Second, it is also a matter of interpretation.

Although all the papers and these comments speak of *the* status quo, no singular status quo exists; what exists is situational and problematic—a matter of interpretation. Consider, for example, the variety of theories of what the western economic system—even only that of the United States—is all about as brought to mind by such names as Karl Marx, Thorstein Veblen, John Kenneth Galbraith, Paul A. Samuelson, Milton Friedman, Friedrich von Hayek, Charles Lindblom, Mancur Olson, John Maynard Keynes and Max Weber, as well as Jim Buchanan. Which of these is correct, which is the one used in interpreting—and changing— the economic system? Similarly with theories of the nature of mercantilism and the causes of the American revolution, the French Revolution, the US Civil War, the First and Second World Wars, and so on—all matters of interpretation.

Consider, too, the "status quo" of any weapons system, military strategy, physical industrial capital, business strategy, and so on, is a function of the opponent's weapon system and strategy, the competitors' capital and strategy, and so on. The economic significance of one's rights is a function, in part, of others' rights, their respective expectations in case of conflict, and legal doctrine chosen by courts.

The meaning of the status quo is in part a function of what else is taken to be or becomes situationally relevant, of what economic theory is used in constructing its interpretation, and the purpose for which the definition of the status quo is constructed (there may be a different status quo for each different purpose). And, clearly, the design of these papers strongly tends to take place within and give effect to Jim Buchanan's ideational structure; the approach to the status quo forming the premise of the Colloquium is that of his theory of public choice.

While on the subject of rights, several other points should be made (see Samuels and Mercuro 1999). First, property rights are not the only form that rights take, though rights designated as property rights are given a privileged position based on historical developments. All rights constitute the protection of interests. Defining the status quo in terms of property rights typically fails to provide comparable protection to interests not designated property rights yet function as their analytical equivalent, such as rights formalized through environmental legislation, protective labor legislation, and labor relations legislation.

Second, it is impossible to fully define rights. The conventional practice of ostensibly doing so involves a fiction utilizing a primitive term. The pretense that rights can be fully defined is useful, if not necessary, in the legitimation of the process by which legal change is legitimized (see Samuels and Mercuro 1980) but it is still a pretense.

Third, rights are only one part of the total system of legal relations, especially that articulated by Wesley N. Hohfeld and used, for example, by Robert Lee Hale (Samuels 1973b). Other parts include immunities, exposures, and duties. Failure to include these others in definitions of the status quo misapprehends what is going on in the economy and the legal-economic nexus.

Fourth, two ancillary concepts that pervade the papers are "freedom" and "coercion." These are given either no specific definition or stylized ones, engendering their own linguistic problems. In my view, freedom and coercion are many sided and any one specification has meaning only in the context of the parallelograms of freedom and coercion, respectively, that pervade the political economic system (see the essays on these subjects in Samuels 1992 and Samuels *et al.* 1997).

Fifth, another term that is widely used is "voluntary." But as I have shown (following Hale), what actually is being described is "volitional," not "voluntary," action (Samuels 1992; *passim*).

Sixth, the discussion about rights is subject to another limitation. Rights can be seen as independent of government, such that any government action deemed to adversely affect a right constitutes a taking subject to compensation—which enshrines the Court's definition of status quo rights, under the pretense that rights are found and not made; or rights can be seen as a product of an ongoing legal process and not a taking in the constitutional sense (Samuels and

Mercuro 1980). Which of these definitions of rights is used to define the status quo will have profound effects.

One consequence of the foregoing discussion is to underline Faith's identification of some sources of ambiguity in identifying and thus knowing the status quo. As he writes, "just what is the existing state of affairs, and would we know it when we see it," and "one may never truly know the status quo."

There is another respect that may be considered, one akin to the concept of equilibrium. We would not know if the actual economy were in equilibrium if we faced it; and, in fact, we are likely never in equilibrium, in a general equilibrium sense, at least. Likewise, we are never in the status quo (effectively making it a nonsensical, at best a hypothetical concept) because any one element of social reality is contingent on other elements and *some* elements of reality are continually in flux, thereby impacting other elements of reality. This certainly applies to potential legal change. A impacting B, C, D, . . . N or not, but also to external/non-political/non-legal phenomena impacting B, C, and D. For example, technological change can affect the implications of a particular legal rule; therefore the status quo effectively evolves through non-legal/non-political change. Even abstracting from selective perception and other issues, there effectively is no status quo, just as there is no general equilibrium, because things are always changing. Employment of a unanimity rule does not affect this, given that non-political/non-legal change causes changes in the status quo and thus new distributions of gains/winners-losses/losers. The "status quo" is essentially a fiction.

Buchanan argues, for his purpose and in his sense not improperly, all efforts at change start from here, the status quo. But that position finesses the problem of having to identify the status quo and the difficulties encountered in doing so. As Faith argues, conceptual difficulties are involved in knowing the status quo and in granting any particular normative status to the status quo. These difficulties involve duration, precedent and priority, the definition of community, and what (= whose) representation enters into the definition of the status quo. The difficulties also include normative elements—"oughts" in an "is" form.

Faith makes two further points, unfortunately only in footnotes and without either elaboration or application. One of these points I have already made. Faith makes it through summarizing the work of Michel Foucault, saying, "what passes as knowledge is culturally specific. What is known, what is knowable and what is worth knowing varies across time and place. Accordingly, a given set of 'objective' facts could give rise to different conceptions of the status quo." Faith's other point could also have been made using Foucault's work but he cites his own work, saying, "the social institutions governing a set of interacting individuals is determined by the person(s) who occupies the top spot in a hierarchy of strategy-makers. Those institutions comprise the status quo rules. See Earl Thompson and Roger Faith, 'A Pure Theory of Social Interaction,' *American Economic Review* (June, 1984)."

In making this second point, Faith is somewhat heretical for this Colloquium. Consideration of hierarchy, hence of inequality, compromises the imagery of voluntarism, consent, and unanimity. Thus, Viktor Vanberg quotes me in recognizing that the requirement of unanimous consent, allows "the privileged in the status quo to hold out and perpetuate themselves by being able to withhold their consent" (in Samuels and Buchanan 1975: 30).

Vanberg himself treats the problem of hierarchy in different ways. He writes, "What issues should be assigned to the sphere of political-collective choice and what issues should be left to private, market-coordination is itself a matter of constitutional choice, a choice that should be made in light of the relative merits of the working properties of the two arenas." But he does not point out that such "relative merits" are neither inherent in the two arenas nor identically perceived by individuals differently situated in the hierarchy.

Vanberg also writes,

It is perfectly consistent for a contractarian constitutionalist to criticize an existing constitutional regime for its lack of consensual approval and to insist, at the same time, that constitutional reform should be contractual. Neither is such critique of the status quo an invitation to change things in a non-contractual manner, nor does the contractarian argument for contractual change imply that we should ignore deficiencies in the legitimacy of the status quo.

A contractarian critique of the status quo would appear to be called for especially in the case of constitutional regimes that are characterized by *privileges* in the sense of discriminating rules that must be viewed as unjust by those who are discriminated against. Such critique can be based entirely on internal criteria, i.e. the evaluations of the individuals involved in the arrangement, without any need to appeal to external normative standards. There would seem to be no need, therefore, for Buchanan to take issue with W. J. Samuels' (in Buchanan and Samuels 1975, p. 30) talk of "existing systems of privilege," as long as such judgement does not imply recourse to external criteria.[32] We can surely criticize systems of privileges or discriminating regimes without imposing "our private values as criteria for social change" (Buchanan, *ibid.*, p. 33), as regimes that violate the individualist norm that "each man's values are to count as any others" (ibid.) and that do not command agreement of all individuals who are living under them.[33]

This position combines: (1) recognition of privilege due to hierarchy imposed without consent with (2) critique thereof (3) not based on external criteria and (4) critique not based on private values. The strangeness of such a position resides in at least two points: departure from the usual Austrian position emphasizing individual subjective values, and ambiguity as to the nature of internal values or criteria. Once again the footnotes are enlightening. In note 32 Vanberg comments:

In reference to Samuels' talk of "systems of privilege" Buchanan (in Buchanan & Samuels, 1975, p. 35) notes: "This implies that you, somehow, have already introduced some standard, some external criterion, to determine whether or not privilege exists. My approach requires, and allows, no such external criterion to be introduced."—As argued above, I do not find this objection justified. One can speak of privileges in ways that are perfectly consistent with a contractarian constitutionalist perspective, as Buchanan himself has done, of course, on many occasions. See e.g. J. M. Buchanan and R. D. Congleton, 1998.

The criticism of Buchanan is warranted but one can still point out that those situated in upper hierarchical positions are again enabled to veto change. In note 33, one reads,

> To be sure, any classification of constitutional regimes as "systems of privilege" remains subject to the qualification that it "can be appropriately used only to provide inputs in a discussion that might lead to agreement upon change."
>
> (Buchanan 1977b: 145)

This establishes discussion only on terms acceptable to those in upper hierarchical positions. In a world of giants and pygmies, in which the giants became giants in non-consensual ways, it is a further instrument of rule by giants to allow only consensual change. Would one apply this approach to both the United States and the USSR? In the subsequent note 34, Vanberg writes,

> In this sense, to the contractarian constitutionalist position should apply what F. A. Hayek (1972: ixf.) says about the liberal position: "The essence of the liberal position, however, is the denial of all privilege, if privilege is understood in its proper and original meaning of the state granting and protecting rights to some which are not available on equal terms to others."

Four points: Privilege available on equal terms to others, however, is no longer privilege. Where is consent in Hayek's position? Whose selective perception is to determine when a "privilege" exists and when the terms are "equal"? There is a difference between treating equals unequally so as to render them unequal, and treating unequals unequally so as to render them equal; this is so despite the evident fact that people are equal and unequal in different ways, a recognition that both leads to and underscores the process of working things out, a process in which the Buchanan-Hayek-type position is only one consideration.

Vanberg thus further argues,

> W. J. Samuels' (in Buchanan & Samuels, 1975, p. 30) complaint that, "as attractive as the consent (unanimity) rule is, it places too much power in the hands of the already privileged," reflects an ambiguous feeling about the contractarian approach that seems to be shared by many of its critics. While such critics are prepared to acknowledge that the consensus principle may be attractive per se, in and by itself, they object to the idea that it can be

applied to a status quo that is, in their view, normatively unacceptable. They do not quite demand that we start "from someplace else," they demand, however, that we move from "here," the actual status quo, to a different, preferred structure *before* we bind ourselves to contractual procedures for further change.[37] They want to postpone the adoption of consensual procedures until a just starting point has been established, something that, they think, cannot be achieved in a contractual manner.

This may well be the position of others but it is not my position. My position is, first, simply that the Buchanan "consent (unanimity) rule" gives the giants veto power and excludes all other considerations. It is, second, that no formula or rule can be imposed willy nilly; the Buchanan position, like all others, must make its way in the process of working things out. (Wicksell's interest in unanimity was neither efficiency nor to protect the privileged but to help/protect the lowest classes.) Note 37 reads,

> G. Brennan and J. M. Buchanan (1985, p. 141): "This distribution of entitlements may not be acceptable to many persons as the appropriate starting point from which genuine constitutional reform is to be made."

It is both presumptuous and tautological to identify the Buchanan position as the only one comprising "genuine constitutional reform." The Buchanan position seems likely, rather, in the words of *Business Week* already quoted earlier, to be a "very convenient cover story for people who are actually trying to stack the deck in their favor." Even absent hierarchy, the Buchanan position of insisting on the obvious point that "we start from here," namely, the status quo, is deployed to stack the deck in favor of whatever specification of the status quo is made and against those deliberative introductions of legal change of which the deployer disapproves.

3 Turning directly to Vanberg's "The Status Quo in Contractarian Constitutionalist Perspective," he certainly succeeds in "separating two issues the differences between which have not always been sufficiently recognized in the debate, namely, on the one hand, the role of the status quo as the inevitable starting point of any change and, on the other hand, the issue of the normative evaluation of the status quo." This formulation is useful, although it too is rendered ambiguous and inconclusive by the problems of defining the status quo.

In addition to the comments on Vanberg's paper made in regard to Faith's paper, I note the following.

His point that contractarian constitutionalism per se and, by inference, different forms of it, affect "the choice of questions that it seeks to answer" is important. His discussion of "hypothetical imperatives," however, is not helped by his insistence on a

> careful distinction between unanimity as legitimizing principle and unanimity as decision rule. It is certainly true that the agreement among the contracting parties that market transactions enjoy must not be confused with a unanimous

approval by the community at large. In this sense, changes from the status quo that result from market transactions are, indeed, consensual only as far as the contracting parties are concerned, but they may well be imposed on others in the community who would object if they were asked. Yet, again, according to the contractarian norm decisions or transactions qualify as legitimate as long as they are arrived at according to rules that enjoy unanimous approval.

Once again, the problem of veto power arises. Also what are examples of such rules? The only candidate that comes close, in my mind, is the rule against rape (though it, too, has complications, and Richard Posner has written of a market for rape—appropriately condemned by Buchanan). A further problem is that of hypocrisy, considered later. I am especially uncomfortable with the idea of hypothetical imperatives due to rules enjoying unanimous approval. I concur that people do believe they have hypothetical imperatives— though they do not normally stress their hypothetical nature—but this is due to the inculcation of social rules (socialization) and to neither unanimous consent nor the way things are.

Another distinction made by Vanberg is also important:

> My exclusive concern in this paper is with the *constitutional status quo* and with the issue of *constitutional reform*. To be sure, calls for constitutional reform, i.e. for changes in the rules of the game, may, of course, be motivated by discontent with the pattern of distributional outcomes that result from status quo rules. But it is the concern with changes in the rules themselves, not in outcomes per se, that is of principal interest here.

But it, too, is subject to the complications and criticisms made here and in some of the other papers. Vanberg also presents an argument that at first reading seems both obvious and unobjectionable:

> The contractarian argument for peaceful, contractual change is not—and cannot be—derived from the mere fact that we always start from here. Nor does it imply a defense of the status quo. It is an argument about how we should proceed from here, namely by peaceful, contractual means rather than by coercion and violence, it is not an argument for leaving things as they are. It is an argument not in terms of the merits of the status quo but in terms of the merits of contractual change compared to its alternative, change by coercion and violence.

Reminding the reader that I am not considering normative issues, I make two points. First, historically, not everyone agrees with this argument, as is evident from various writings and practice. Second, the term "coercion" has been given a multiplicity of specifications; accordingly, Vanberg's exclusion may apply to little or to much (Samuels 1997).

The remainder of Vanberg's paragraph continues:

> As Buchanan has pointed out, the contractarian project of working out and proposing contractual reforms may be a much more laborious and much less romantic undertaking than the grandiose designs, popular among social reformers, of sweeping changes to be imposed on resisting interests. Yet, in view of the destructive dynamics of coercive change, it offers a more productive approach to constitutional reform than its more impatient counterparts that call for imposing change, raising the question of who is to do the imposing.

This statement raises the problem of self-referentiality and more. Surely, were Buchanan's approach adopted it would constitute the deliberate introduction of a sweeping, revolutionary set of changes. But would not the language of "grandiose designs, popular among social reformers" apply to Buchanan and his disciples? Is not Buchanan a social reformer? What of Geoffrey Brennan and Alan Hamlin's view of "the conservative's attachment to the status quo"? If conservatism does not mean no change, but some change, then: (1) the argument against socialist grand change (= control) is compromised; (2) since the issue is littler changes, what about creeping socialism?; and (3) how do we know that conservatives are preferable to socialists? The upshot of such discussion is that the Buchanan approach is but one strand of conservatism, one contribution to the making, not finding, of conservatism, such that both conservatism and socialism have been in the process of being worked out.

In the next paragraph we read,

> Accordingly, the contractarian postulate of consensual change does not rule out at all changes that do not command unanimous approval, as long as such changes are made according to rules that are legitimized by the consent of the relevant constituency. And this applies to changes in the rules as well, as long as such changes occur in accordance with rules for changing rules that command unanimous approval. It is with regard to changes in the funda-mental, constitutional rules themselves, i.e. for changes that have no established rules to rely on, that the contractarian postulate requires that such changes be made in a contractual, consensual manner.

That such an approach favors existing hierarchical interests, regardless of how their position was attained, should now be obvious, if unwelcome to Buchananites. Additionally, Buchanan has indicated that his hostility toward the Federal government stems from the Civil War. Does this conflict with his "we start from here" position? What if he awoke one day and found a Federal government in the hands of a right-wing militia or a left-wing regime or an Islamic theocracy? Vanberg quotes Buchanan:

> "The status quo defines that which exists. Hence, regardless of its history, it must be evaluated as if it were legitimate contractually." Quite obviously,

there is a contradiction here between the notion that the contractarian perspective "does not amount to a defense of the status quo" and the argument that it requires us to evaluate the status quo "as if it were legitimate contractually." Not both of these views can be simultaneously held, and if a choice is to be made, it would seem that only the first is consistent with the overall thrust of Buchanan's approach.

The quotation is rendered problematic by Faith's identification of problems of precedent and priority. The criticism presented in the remainder of the statement is important and also limiting.

Vanberg argues that "the contractarian's plea is for *consensual* elimination of privileges." I have argued that past and present recipients of privilege will not readily surrender them, as evidenced in history. I also suggest that the psychology of denial will tend to dominate: It is very difficult for one to admit that one has benefited from wrong, from privilege, that one has been among the privileged.
4   Hartmut Kliemt's "Contractarianism as Liberal Conservatism" argues that "Buchanan type contractarianism may be classified as a specific 'formal type' of conservatism that grants normative status to the status quo." Several papers notably Vanberg's and Buchanan's, seek to render saccharine such attribution of normative status.

Apropos of (as it turns out) some of my discussion of Vanberg's paper, Kliemt affirms

the fact that politics is in the end always about coercion. Though politics cannot be based on contract and agreement, good politics is about minimizing coercion. Clearly the latter is at root of the Buchanan enterprise.

Yes, politics is about coercion but so is economics; coercion can be seen in diverse situations. But politics is in part based on contract and agreement—on matters more complex and subtle than exchanging goods and money. It is not clear that coercion can be minimized; in many instances of putative coercion, one system or form of coercion is substituted for another. If minimizing coercion is at the root of the Buchanan enterprise, it is giving effect to selective perception of coercion. If one objects that normative distinctions must be drawn between systems or forms of coercion, I would agree. But I would insist that such must be worked out; for the analyst to impose distinctions is to substitute the analyst's preferences and perceptions for those of economic actors. Kliemt is principally concerned with normative issues, about which I have nothing to say.
5   Brennan and Hamlin's "Analytic Conservatism" presents yet another linguistic alternative formulation of Buchanan's approach. Once again I have nothing to say about their normative argument or, for that matter, their methodological procedures. A central message is the "bias in favour of the *status quo* bias as a key component of the conservative disposition." On the basis of arguments in other Colloquium papers, it is obvious that the concept of a pro-status quo bias is a limited concept; even they emphasize the importance of ignorance. But

their paper does reinforce the sentimental nature of the conservative position at the same time that (though only negligibly in their paper) sentiment attaches to some and not other parts of the putative status quo. Their specific argument, "analytic conservatism," underscores the complexity of the overall conservative argument and, accordingly, the limits of the Buchanan position.

The question of self-referentiality arises when one wonders if the following applies to Buchanan and his disciples:

> In short, the nature of democratic political institutions encourages both activism and rhetorical defences that will rationalise such activism. Further, the content of those defences will often be influenced by the creative exploits of academic scribblers, men of letters, philosophers and other forms of low life, all much in love with and apparently convinced by their own latest theories. And public discussion will be full of confident voices, none of whom are much inclined to confess to their own ignorance, or refrain from grossly simplifying matters that are extremely complex.

I applaud Brennan and Hamlin's candor when I read,

> But there is more to be said here. Even economists are familiar with the thought that there is a distinction between justification and motivation. The market produces the benign outcomes that are claimed for it by "invisible" means. In other words, the properties that serve to *justify* market outcomes are not aspects that necessarily *motivate* any of the agents whose actions produce those outcomes. In the same way here, what works to *motivate* conservatives may not be the same as what justifies conservatism.

and

> In short, the structure of the conservative argument that we have presented here seems entirely hospitable to the idea that one should in most choice circumstances adopt a mode of reasoning and calculation that is distinct from the reasoning that provides the ultimate justification for having that disposition. One can't work things out from first principles all the time. That is too time-consuming and too error prone. And doing it may not ultimately energise sufficiently to induce action: "sicklied o'er with the pale cast of thought" is how Hamlet puts it. In short, the "conservative" element in "analytic conservatism" arises because the conservative disposition operates as a critical piece of the required mental furniture.
>
> Nevertheless, at some level, something beyond the disposition itself is required—something further by way of justificatory argument. The conservative disposition is not *self-evidently* compelling. What we have tried to provide in this paper is one line of such justificatory argument—a line that ought to be intelligible to economists in particular, but also to others in the analytic tradition. We emphasize again that the argument provided here is not the only resource

in rational actor theory that might be called into play in this connection. Nevertheless, the argument we have presented is, we think, an important one— not only in itself, but also for the broader class of arguments that it suggests.

This argument suggests, at least to this writer, what Pareto (among others) deemed hypocrisy: the deployment of an argument intended to motivate, an argument different from the actual justification, an argument appropriate for the intended/expected audience. One thinks recently of the different reasons given for the second war with Iraq and of a tax-cut proposal said to promote economic recovery and jobs (gone is the venerable argument against burdening our grand-children with debt, that is fiscal responsibility, so-called) when the actual intent and ultimate justification is to increase the after-tax incomes of the upper decile (of which I happen to be a member: my own candor). In the present context, the argument suggests that several Colloquium papers ostensibly supporting Buchanan's hard-core position with carefully drawn distinctions and themes, ulti-mately function to support oligarchy/plutocracy. (As to why hypocrisy works, one may consider Knight's recorded statement, quoted earlier, "And the masses love to lie down before the Juggernaught car, if it's done with right technique.") So much irony.

6   Buchanan's "The Status of the Status Quo" continues, as he understands, a long-time quest to limit governmental activism. His Pareto-relevant vs. Pareto-irrelevant distinction, his distinction between constitutional rules and ordinary legislation, his attachment to the theory of rent seeking, and so on, have been attempts to shore up his intellectual fortress against the onslaught of critics, such as myself. I continue in the role of critic.

There is some confusion between positive and normative. The question, "To what extent is the *status quo* privileged?" is a positive and not a normative ques-tion, though it undoubtedly has normative, or subjective, elements to it (e.g. the meaning of "privileged").

When Buchanan considers an example involving the present discounted value of future earnings streams, he remarks,

> These questions bring expectations directly into the exercise, and expecta-tions, in turn, call attention to the rules and institutions that are in being, as vital elements in the *status quo* itself.

Buchanan may or may not want to go so far, but the rules and institutions said to be "vital elements in the *status quo* itself" are themselves matters of (often-conflicting) expectations. On the one hand, this is a matter of infinite regress; on the other, it is a matter—like it or not—of nihilism.

Buchanan uses a narrow goods-and-values model of the status quo. It is, however, an incomplete proxy for the political-economic valuational process in which the changing status quo is formed and reformed.

Buchanan correctly argues that the status quo was not formed or chosen by any single, monolithic decision maker. Three points: First, government itself is no single decision making entity, though it is often treated as if it were. Second, who seriously argues that the status quo is formed or chosen by a single, monolithic decision maker? By seriously I mean by those who write to justify rather than to motivate—though the distinction is subjective in practice. The argument seems intended to discredit deliberative decision making.

Buchanan writes, correctly,

> So long as separate decision makers are in any way interdependent, one with another, the output vector cannot be chosen; it must emerge from the separated but interdependent choices made along the several dimensions of adjustment... That which exists is brought into being by the choices made by many participants along many interdependent dimensions of adjustment. The separated choices, as such, cannot be modified in any particular, step-by-step manner so as to generate a specifically defined comprehensive result. One facet of the fatal conceit of socialism was the failure to understand this point. But it becomes equally naive to presume that because of the multidimensionality and complexity of the interaction process, that which has been brought into being is not subject to explicitly directed change.

Does Buchanan apply this reasoning to himself? Is he self-referential? Using Knight's phraseology, does not Buchanan seek to reform society and thereby make society his plaything? On another topic, Buchanan says,

> we must distinguish between the rules or constraints that restrict or limit the range and exercise of choice and the choices made within such rules.

The distinction is important. But it should not obscure the situation in which "we" find ourselves: all this must be worked out, it cannot be laid out by any Buchananite or Hayekian formula. Indeed, this is one of their fundamental messages. But, again, do they take it self-referentially? A remarkable statement by Buchanan is the following:

> To be meaningful, it seems best to refer to the *status quo* as that set of rules and institutions in being that do serve to constrain choices, but which may be deliberately changed (Buchanan, 1962). There may be, of course, some institutions that have emerged through a slow process of cultural evolution and that cannot be readily modified. Acknowledgment that some such institutions exist does not, however, imply that others that can be deliberately changed are non-existent or unimportant.

Compared to Hayek, or to most people's interpretation of Hayek (but not mine), Buchanan is a constructivist, and this statement, especially the first sentence, illustrates it. But there is only one reason to exclude those described in the second sentence: all institutions are combinations of deliberative and non-deliberative decision making (Samuels 1999).

Buchanan says, "An ongoing firm describes its current situation in terms of a balance sheet." This is correct in regard to the point he is making about the irrelevance of imaginary balance sheets (except insofar as they represent targets). But there is much more to the description of current situations than the picture painted by balance sheets.

Buchanan is to be applauded for recognizing that the proposition "whatever is efficient," in the hands of modern Chicagoans, "becomes almost tautological." He points to the alternative survival argument and its normative implication that "efforts at 'constructivism' are doomed to failure." About both arguments he writes,

> The normative implications of both of these arguments are negative in the sense that they discourage efforts at making improvements in the existing arrangements. These arguments seem to eliminate any role for the political economist as reformer, even if she remains in the ivory tower and removed from hands-on policy discussion.

It is obvious that a tension exists in Buchanan's approach between his constructivism and his pro-status quo position. Both are present in actual political economies, and whereas Hayek strongly tends to reject the former in principle—though both are present when his approach is understood in Mengerian terms—Buchanan accepts, if only grudgingly, both.

Buchanan sees compensation of losers by gainers as a falsification-type test. He does not see (I think) certain welfare-state programs as performing that function. I do not see the corporate plutocracy engaging in this particular game—unless the system was in mortal danger and time had to be bought.

He once again takes up the criticism that his approach privileges the status quo (somehow defined).

> It should be emphasized, however, that this apparent privilege arises not because the *status quo* assumes value because it exists, but rather because there is no means other than agreement of determining whether any proposed move away from the *status quo* is or is not preferred by participants.

If such were the case, no use of hypocrisy would be necessary, and his approach would not elicit such deep criticism. Furthermore, there are other means, and the function of both the use of hypocrisy and his approach is to influence how things work out.

I am reminded of Murray Rothbard's point that liability for compensation at the time of emancipation should lead to payments to the former slaves and not to their former owners. This is a matter of the definition of the rights used in the definition of the status quo. It is one of only a few instances when I agreed with him; after all, he did candidly affirm that his system would (further) empower oligarchism.

I come now to the text that was very helpful to me in understanding Buchanan's position, a position I hitherto have largely seen as an increasingly sophisticated (though perhaps at times convoluted) libertarianism. The text is this:

> Needless to say, I reject this avenue of inquiry, and categorically so. To acknowledge that some claims may conflict in any *status quo*, and further, that general consensus may be attained on few, if any, proposed changes in the set of constraints, does not imply that all claims are up for grabs and that proposed changes may not be evaluated through some appropriate measure of the degree of consensus attained. Empirical evidence may be used to suggest that participants in the sociopolitical-economic nexus go about their ordinary affairs within an acceptance of the legal framework that incorporates the distinctions among separate rights and claims to sources of value.

The difference between us on this point is as follows. Jim seeks determinacy and closure, whereas I am comfortable with ambiguity and open-endedness. In my view but not his, "participants in the sociopolitical-economic nexus [do] go about their ordinary affairs within an acceptance of the legal framework that incorporates the distinctions among separate rights and claims to sources of value." This is because they have been inculcated (socialized) in the belief system of our society, not because such is the way things are in an ontological sense. Over time, "all claims *are* up for grabs," whether we like it or not. Jim illustrates his position with the taking problem:

> Even if, at some conceptualized constitutional level or stage of choice, you might have agreed to authorize democratically organized government to modify your set of rights, it does not at all imply that, at the postconstitutional stage, there is no distinction to be made between an overt "taking" and a compensated "exchange," even if both acts are non-voluntary.
>
> A fully comprehensive definition of the *status quo* would reckon on the formal structure of rights and claims and the expectations that these rights and claims would be protected from confiscation by either private or public predators.

As noted earlier, my view is very different. The distinction between taking and non-taking is not at all hard and fast, nor can it be. This view, however, is anathema to Jim. So must be my relativist if not nihilist treatment of the concept of the rule of law (Samuels 2002b) which here also applies to Jim's notion of constitutionalism.

Interestingly, Jim adopts a high-priest role in prescribing for the world he would like to see:

> In some ultimate sense, politics *must be understood by the members of the public* to be a positive-sum game—a process of exchange for mutual advantage—if society is to remain viable. But any such conceptualization, or model,

requires that the parties to the game, or exchange, acknowledge base positions from which the process commences. (Italics added.)

This goes beyond normativism into design, the kind of design he otherwise rejects. It is a role with which I am uncomfortable. I am uncomfortable with its substance, on positive as well as normative grounds, insofar as it limits change to that due to exchange—which gives effect to and reinforces hierarchy, an important positive and normative consideration.

This difference between us is either that he would prefer to limit change to that due to exchange and I recognize other modes of change to be relevant, or he has a narrow and I a broad definition of what constitutes exchange. I refer to the following passage: "Any change that modifies your ownership rights and that is made without your agreement or consent cannot be modeled as a part of any exchange process."

It is tempting to think of Buchanan as an advocate of laissez-faire—a concept as difficult to work with as that of the status quo. Laissez-faire can be used in three different contexts: minimization of legal change; a particular vision of an economy; and legal change to bring about that particular vision. Some of Jim's thinking is located in each of these. This accounts for part, but only part, of the problem with his approach.

Jim Buchanan is a brilliant and creative thinker. I have learned much from him over the years. But his approach is only one contribution to the process of working things out—even if things are worked out differently than he would prefer.

Summary and random comments

1　Notwithstanding his and other authors' efforts to establish distinctions (themselves otherwise useful) in a quest to defend the core of his approach, Buchanan's approach does constitute protection and preservation of the status quo and its hierarchic structure of power. This is so despite the problems of defining the status quo that are identified by Colloquium authors.

2　So-called voluntary exchange (I prefer volitional exchange) is not wholly analytically equivalent to voting on the rules of social control. Using the exchange model to describe either voting or social control, while it does underscore several important aspects of the conduct of social control, trivializes social control. (The underscored aspects include trade-offs between legislators in voting and one type of legislation as the price of another.)

3　Invocation of voluntarism, unanimity, and rule of law, misrepresents both the actual way things are and what is possible—reflecting reasons for not limiting change to market contracts of exchange.

4　Concern in this Colloquium with the status of the status quo seems driven by a desire for continuity rather than change and/or change only through market contracts of exchange. This orientation is lauded or at least stated by several authors.

5 The theory of voluntary market exchange is only one theory of legal change. It neglects or trivializes the power to control and structure markets enjoyed by institutions of governance both including and extending beyond official government (Samuels 2002a).
6 The otherwise important distinctions drawn by several authors are both narrowly nested and put to questionable use.
7 Some formulations of the economic role of government, especially many in the conservative tradition, are criticized for committing the naturalistic fallacy, that the status quo is the ontological nature of things. Whereas they may perhaps be better understood as absolutist legitimation within the hypocrisy context discussed earlier.

Part of what I have in mind is indicated by Clifford Geertz's review of Tyler Cowen's *Creative Destruction*. Geertz (2003: 27) writes,

> Apologetics—the argumentative defense of how matters play out in the world, the formal and systematic vindication of the received design of things—used to be a theological specialty, most particularly a Christian one. The demonstration that, despite appearances to the contrary on almost every hand, our universe is rationally put together, and is good, and that our place within it, if only we would realize it, is blessed: this was the central task of "the science of things divine"...
>
> With the advent of modernity, and the decline of other-worldly explanations for this-worldly phenomena, the task of reconciling us to the ordained and the inevitable...has fallen into other hands—most notably, this being the age of reckoning, to economics.

8 For several reasons given here, the Buchanan approach is utopian—Platonic idealizations or idealized representations of a much more complex, and messy, reality (Samuels 2003). With regard to the United States, Buchanan's approach is ideology bidding to serve as social control and not an objective picture of what government, governance, property, markets, and so on are actually all about or possibly can be. It is an attempt to frame discussion and policy in a particular way—to motivate, as Brennan and Hamlin put it, a

> conservative disposition—an intuitive suspicion of all grand schemes, an intrinsic affection for things as they are, an inclination to be reconciled to one's general situation and perhaps strongly self-identified with it, a tendency to evaluate policies and reforms in terms of "disaster avoidance" rather than utopian aspiration—...what motivates conservatives, as a matter of descriptive fact.

But Buchanan's approach is also utilitarian, pragmatic and instrumental. Brennan and Hamlin seem to recognize this when they quote Jerry Z. Muller: "Combining the emphases on history and utility, the common denominator of conservative social and political analysis might be termed 'historical utilitarianism'" (Muller 1997: 7).

9   I continue to wonder whether the principles embodied in Buchanan's approach, such as "we start from here," would be applied by him to countries other than the United States, such as the former USSR, North Korea, Saddam's Iraq, and Hitler's Germany.

10   One aspect of the economic role of government not directly brought up in the Colloquium papers is the issue of government in the present having or not having the same power as government in the past.

11   For the historian and methodologist of economic thought the Buchanan phenomenon presents two interesting examples. The first is its accord with Joan Robinson's position that ideological propositions both "express a point of view and formulate feelings which are a guide to conduct and "also provide a quarry from which hypotheses can be drawn" (Robinson 1962: 3). Certainly Jim has demonstrated his brilliance along both lines. To the extent that Jim has contributed to the development of moral and legal rules, surely both the Adam Smith of the *Theory of Moral Sentiments* and the *Lectures on Jurisprudence* and the revolutionary American founding fathers might be surprised with how he has done so.

The second is the externalist nature and origins of his work. His doctrines, in the words of John Kells Ingram (1888: 3) "have owed much of their influence to the fact that they seemed to offer solutions of the urgent problems of the age. Again, every thinker . . . is yet a child of his time." But "this connection of theory with practice" can "be expected to produce exaggerations in doctrine, to lend undue prominence to particular sides of the truth, and to make transitory situations or temporary expedients be regarded as universally normal conditions."

Acknowledgment

The author is indebted to Steven G. Medema for comments on an earlier draft.

References

Geertz, C. (2003) "Off the Menu. Review of Tyler Cowen," *Creative Destruction*, Princeton, NJ: Princeton University Press, 2002, in *The New Republic* (February 17): 27–30.

Ingram, J. K. (1888) *A History of Political Economy*, New York: Macmillan.

Muller, J. Z. (1997) *Conservatism: An Anthology*, Princeton, NJ: Princeton University Press.

Robinson, J. (1962) *Economic philosophy*, Chicago, IL: Aldine.

Samuels, W. J. (1973a) "Review of Gordon Tullock," (ed.) *Explorations in the Theory of Anarchy*, in *Public Choice*, 16 (Fall): 94–7.

Samuels, W. J. (1973b) "The Economy as a System of Power and its Legal Bases: The Legal Economics of Robert Lee Hale," *University of Miami Law Review*, 27 (Spring–Summer): 261–371.

Samuels, W. J. (1974) "Anarchism and the Theory of Power," in G. Tullock (ed.) *Further Explorations in the Theory of Anarchy*, Blacksburg, VA: University Publications, 35–57.

Samuels, W. J. (1992) *Essays on the Economic Role of Government, Vol. 1, Fundamentals*, London and New York: Macmillan and New York University Press.

Samuels, W. J. (1997) "The Concept of 'Coercion' in Economics," in W. J. Samuels, S. G. Medema, and A. A. Schmid (eds) *The Economy as a Process of Valuation*, Lyme, NH: Edward Elgar, 129–207.

Samuels, W. J. (ed.) (1998) *Law and Economics*, 2 vols. London: Pickering & Chatto.

Samuels, W. J. (1999) "Hayek from the Perspective of an Institutionalist Historian of Economic Thought: An Interpretive Essay," *Journal des Economistes et des Etudes Humaines*, IX (Juin–Septembre): 279–90.

Samuels, W. J. (2001) "Some Problems in the Use of Language in Economics," *Review of Political Economy*, 13(1): 91–100.

Samuels, W. J. (2002a) "An Essay on Government and Governance," in Warren J. Samuels (ed.) *Economics, Governance and Law: Essays on Theory and Policy*, Cheltenham: Edward Elgar, 1–37.

Samuels, W. J. (2002b) "The Rule of Law and the Capture and Use of Government in a World of Inequality," in Warren J. Samuels (ed.) *Economics, Governance and Law: Essays on Theory and Policy*, Cheltenham: Edward Elgar, 61–79.

Samuels, W. J. and Buchanan, J. M. (1975) "On Some Fundamental Issues in Political Economy: An Exchange of Correspondence," *Journal of Economic Issues*, 9 (March): 15–38.

Samuels, W. J. and Mercuro, N. (1980) "The Role and Resolution of the Compensation Principle in Society: Part Two—The Resolution," *Research in Law and Economics*, 2: 103–28.

Samuels, W. J. and Mercuro, N. (1984) "A Critique of Rent-Seeking Theory," in D. C. Colander (ed.) *Neoclassical Political Economy*, Cambridge: Ballinger, 55–70.

Samuels, W. J. and Mercuro, N. (eds) (1999) *The Fundamental Interrelationship between Government and Property*, Stamford, CT: JAI Press.

Samuels, W. J., Medema, S. G., and Schmid, A. A. (1997) *The Economy as a Process of Valuation*, Lyme, NH: Edward Elgar.

8 Two views of government

A conversation

With James M. Buchanan

James M. Buchanan—Distinguished Professor Emeritus of Economics, George Mason University and University Distinguished Professor Emeritus of Economics and Philosophy, Virginia Polytechnic and State University

Warren J. Samuels—Professor Emeritus of Economics, Michigan State University
29 July 2004
Summer Institute for the Preservation of the Study of the History of Economics
26–30 July 2004

SP   Sandra Peart
JMB   James M. Buchanan
WJS   Warren J. Samuels
Footnotes added for the reader

SP: We're all in for a real treat this morning.

When we first invited Warren to give some talks at the Summer Institute, he enthusiastically agreed. And then we got the additional idea of asking him to have a conversation with Jim Buchanan, and he, again, enthusiastically agreed.

He did ask me…or remind me…that he thought the Summer Institute was about preserving the history of economic thought and this was rather present. And I responded to him that, "We're gonna make history on preserving economic thought today."

This has been one of the most interesting intellectual debates of this century. And so today, Warren and Jim are going to talk about their differences and perhaps some commonalities.

And I should, before they begin, let you know that we have signed copies of this book of Jim's; we have the *Between Predictive Science and Moral Philosophy*[1] book, and after the discussion today, they're over there. Those of you who don't yet have a copy, or perhaps you do, but want one that's been signed, are welcome after to take a copy. Thanks very much.

WJS: Why don't you go first…

JMB: Well, I was just looking to see whether or not the particular relevant article was in that volume, but it's...it's really not...

The reason I think that...David [Levy] and Sandra [Peart] had the idea of inviting us to have this conversation, after Warren had kindly agreed to participate in the whole session, is based on a dialogue/discussion that Warren and I have had for...going on a long time now, for over thirty years now...which he published a piece...no doubt we'll get into that...he published a piece in the *Journal of Law and Economics*,[2] and then I wrote a piece in response (more or less a criticism of it),[3] and then we had a *long* correspondence about that afterwards...back and forth. And then I give Warren full credit for entrepreneurship here, what he did after a few years, which bottled up that correspondence and put it together and published it as an exchange between Warren Samuels and Jim Buchanan.[4]

Actually as it turns out, now this is sort of my lesson to the rest of you, it turns out that has been a very, very well-received piece, the fact that...that exchange of correspondence where both of us are representing our side, and the idea, that this was in an open way in which we didn't have any idea that it would ultimately be published—this was just back and forth. And the fact that that has appealed to many people, we've had, at least I have, had a lot of comments on that exchange. And that's happened to me another time, and this is the lesson I'm sort of suggesting.

About six years ago or so the people at Munich, Hans-Werner Sinn, had been trying for years to get Richard Musgrave and I to have a debate, and finally we organized one at that center for economic studies group in Munich. And so we had a week-long dialogue/debate/discussion. And at that time we didn't have any idea that they planned to publish the thing, but then they published it. And it's been published in this little book MIT Press printed called *Public Finance and Public Choice*,[5] and that again, like the one with Warren, had been very popular actually, that has sold...that book has sold extremely well.

And so the idea is that people seem to like discussion amongst people who can join issues and approach the issues in a one-on-one way without either talking past each other or, in effect, just simply criticizing each other. It seems to me there is enough commonality of discussion in both those cases—both with Dick Musgrave, on the one hand, and with Warren, on the other—that it makes for an interesting exchange, and people enjoy the sort of dialogue part; they enjoy the dialogic aspects of these discussions. At least in this experience, in both cases it's been very salutary. So any time you have a chance, in a way an opportunity to do this kind of thing, I think I'd suggest that you try it out, because it has...it has certainly worked for me in both of these cases.

Now in some cases it won't work because [in] some cases you have people who really talk past each other. Jim Tobin, who was a friend of mine, was a very ni...was one of the nicest economists I've ever known. On public debt, for example, he and I just talked past [each other]; we could not join, we could never join the argument, just simply talking past each other. We could never have carried out a dialogue comparable to the one that Warren and I had like...like this. So it requires particulars of the two people. But, on the other hand, if you have a chance to organize it, it's worth doing.

And I do think it fits in with the...the Warren...it has already showed up in Warren's comments on my paper the other day...[correcting comment:] my paper, [rather] my presentation the other day.[6] The difference between us *does* lie in this basic fundamental way of how we look at the world and how we can conceive the world of the political economy that we live with. And no doubt we will get into that, and that is...that is central, but I did want to mention at the outset, this usefulness of having this kind of a dialogue, this kind of a discussion, this kind of a conversation. And perhaps I can leave it at that, and we get into the substance of it no doubt as the hour proceeds. Warren, do you want to take over?

WJS: I appreciate the opportunity to be here. If my wife were here, she would say, "Warren doesn't know how to say no,"

[Laughter.]

...but I am learning.

[Laughter.]

I must say, Jim, that your exchange with Musgrave is really great; it's a wonderful volume.

I have to issue a confession, which I had not expected to do. When I was editing the *Journal of Economic Issues*, in which we published our correspondence, my general attitude was not to use the journal to publish my own stuff. And, in fact, I had such a pure conception of that...*extreme* conception of that...that I even had people remove references to my work when I was publishing their articles. And I could elaborate on that, but really...it got to the point where the board of the association felt they had to compel me to contribute to the journal...That's just background.

I did something that Jim doesn't know about; and I don't know what his reaction's gonna be.

In one of the letters that he sent me, he thanked me for the help I was giving him in "erecting his intellectual fortress in a stronger way."

And my confession, sir, is that I excised that...

[Laughter.]

...and didn't tell you about it...

[Laughter.]

...I did not want to publish something that was so nice to me. I appreciate it [the compliment]; and I've felt guilty ever since.

[Laughter.]

That is a black star in my enormously popular record as an editor.

Well, when we talked yesterday about what we were doing here, I...I had interpreted what we were saying was to make a short presentation about where we came from. So let me tell you where I come from.

I may be one of the very few people who got through the 1950s inoculated against extreme "isms." When we were driving over here, it was said that somebody shifted from Marxism to Austrianism. Well, I never had an "ism" of any kind to shift to any other "ism." Why was that?; why was that?

Well, when I was in high school, I learned several things: I learned that there was Euclidean geometry and there was non-Euclidean geometry, and that it wasn't a question of truth or falsity. It was a question of logic... and as long as the logic worked, it was no problem; it was a question of different premises. And that (1) under certain circumstances Euclidean geometry worked and [2] under other circumstances Lobachevskian and Reimannian geometry worked. So there is a kind of relativism here.

I also learned, because of a teacher that I had who gave me a book by James Harvey Robinson, that you could tell different stories of American history, particularly Constitutional history. That opened my mind, and I'm sure that was her intention, to... to be careful about buying into any-thing... whole hog without knowing what you were doing. And if you did that, you probably weren't buying into it whole hog.

Now another thing that happened to me since I became a young adult in the late 1940s and the early 1950s was experience with liberalism vs. conser-vatism. And it struck me, in summary, that liberalism meant different things to different people; conservatism meant different things to different people; that there was an awful lot of potential overlap; that these were not defini-tions of the world in any meaningful sense other than sentiments; and that the sum of all of this was utter confusion; and that one could not rely upon either of these, or any version of these, as a reliable definition of reality.

And then, probably because I was going through adolescence... the period of adolescence where the child or the teenager is driven, on the one hand, to... for the desire to be independent and autonomous, and, the other hand, to have the confidence of knowing you're under the family wing, and that's why you have all the tension between that gives rise to teenage rebellion... I understood that there was this conflict in society that... generated in part by virtue of individuals going through all this and working it out differently, and also because you have the problem of reconciling the individual to society.

My inclination throughout my life has been, contrary to the perceptions of many other people, libertarian to the point of anarchist. But that has been tempered by an enormous, deep, strong recognition that what anybody calls libertarianism or anarchism carries with it its own system of social control, and that without recognition of that, and doing something about it... or doing something with it, it was simply another matter of sentiments.

So, by the time I finished college, I was inoculated against all of this, about things that were bothering other people, and I understood what... why they were being bothered by it—it didn't bother me, because I didn't feel a need to become this or that. What I wanted was essentially a nonideological approach to the economic role of government. And when I was an under-graduate taking a course in government and business, the textbook that was used was not an ordinary textbook (in fact, I don't think it was really a textbook at all); it was Dahl's and Lindblom's *Politics, Economics, and Welfare*,[7] which really hasn't gone very far in influencing the profession, but it had a big influence on me. And the influence was precisely this: it convinced me that you could take a strongly positive, as opposed to normative, approach to the economic role of government—that you didn't have to absorb and give effect to antecedent normative assumptions called liberalism or conservatism or anarchism or what have you. At the same time...you could call this schizophrenia if you like...at the same time, I was aware that there were normative premises...ideology or what Schumpeter called vision or what have you...that w[ere] inevitable and today, of course, I would attribute that to the hermeneutic circle problem.

So I am sensitive to that, so as I wrote in one autobiographical piece, near the end, that I am really...strongly believe in what I've...in what I've had to say about the economic role of government, but I am sensitive to the fact that...it's a subject of the hermeneutic problem.

What I wanted, saying in a little different way, was not just to give effect to some sentimental belief system, but I wanted to understand what really was going on whatever one's beliefs; whatever one's ideological presumptions. And then I eventually came to understand, since I was anarchistically inclined, I was very much a fan of Thomas Jefferson, and yet I...the Jeffersonian ideal (of every man being a property owner, and every...body having a piece of property, and...participating in the government that controlled them), that the reason why that didn't work, unfortunately, was not because somebody had a different ideology, but because we had forces in the country of economic development in which we no longer were gonna have local markets that were isolated; we were going to have national markets, that the logic of what we'll call the merger solution externalities brought about larger and larger systems of social control, if you like, so that the Hamiltonian approach to development was empirically—not normatively— was empirically more correct than Jefferson, *as it turned out*. And that convinced me, since I thought this was a correct analysis, that I *was* right, that one should *not* define the world in terms of how you would prefer it to be, but rather in terms of what is really going on.

So arguments over Constitutional interpretation, I thought were very fascinating—I was a very intense student of Constitutional law—but it made no difference to me which side won; it made no difference to me whether the arguments seemed good to me, or interesting or persuasive—what really impressed me was that however the Court held it was establishing, in Commons words, "the legal foundations of the economic system." And that that was really what was going on—that it was structuring the economic system; it was changing the economic system, that no matter what the ideology of the people were, what happened in the eighteenth, no nine...yeah, eighteenth and nineteenth centuries was the transformation of law, the legal system in this country, from a rural, agrarian, landed property system to an urban, industrial, nonlanded property system. And that ideology was simply the false consciousness, if you like, through which we viewed this.

Well, then, when I was a senior—I got through undergraduate school in three years, so I am not sure what senior was—but in my last year I was exposed to Common's work, and that's why I went to Wisconsin...I wasn't turned off by neoclassicism, but it seemed to me that it was inadequate...in other words, I liked, if I had known it at the time, Abba Lerner's second thing—that politics goes on forever, and economics is not just...exchange once you've solved the political problems. But, as I learned later, I could quote from Paul Samuelson that "politics is economics by other means"— that if you can't maximize within the market, you use the law to change the market, okay? So I was really very much taken with Commons, that's why I went to Wisconsin, and fortunately I had the tail end of the regime of his students, and we were not told to hate neoclassicism, but that neoclassicism had its place, but it was a diff...there were other variables involved.

Q: Where did you go to undergraduate school?

WJS: When I was a graduate student there.

Q: [Unclear.]

WJS: At University of Miami. I was going to go to Princeton and study astro-nomical physics, but I didn't do that for two reasons: I met my wife...or I had met my wife and decided that I didn't want to be a thousand miles away from her, and, second, I was not terribly happy with the kind of jobs theo-retical physicists were going into at that time.

So I...what I've done since then is to try to develop what I will call a positive welfare economics as to whose interests count—not what is the optimal solution, because I don't buy optimality analysis, because you have to constrain everything to reach that, and the work that I've done in...the economic role of government or law and economics or whatever you want to call it—the economics of property rights—is just a continuation of this...attitude that I've had: to try to minimize the impact of ideology; I didn't need ideology in my work; I tried to minimize it. I'm sure it's there, but...the tersest statement I can make of it is that I believe in openness to change. As an empirical fact, and therefore since I agree that...that there's a role for normative and subjective motivations and movements, that there not only is but should be these, but I did not feel myself driven by the need to promote a particular "ism."

Now, having said that, I will also...I will conclude with another schizo-phrenic view...which is very apropos of the present situation in the United States.

On the one hand...the short version of this is that sometimes I see the United States as a narrow plutocracy and, on the other hand...at other times, I see the United States, as several people have called it, man's last great hope for enlightened democracy. The schizophrenia is that the United States...is exactly that—but I can enlarge upon it by saying that there are two strands at least of...America: one is the vision of Jefferson and others of a philosophy of live and let live—a philosophy of democracy and pluralism, of progress; but then, on the other hand, you have the history of a war party, of the United States as any...just like any other country...in trying to extend its influence in the world. So, even more narrowly, I would say it's whether you have American exceptionalism or you don't have American exceptionalism—I am caught on that, and today, with regard to the terrorist threat, it's a very, very different world. But I'll stop; I'll stop there.

JMB: Well...

WJS: ...How have I disturbed you?

[Laughter.]

JMB: I...Well...you haven't disturbed me very much. I...was very interested in that autobiographical sketch, because it's given me an insight into...where you're coming from, that I had never quite appreciated before, and certainly I think this may explain why you and I, although we categorically disagree along several dimensions, can also have a good dialogue, because basically I think we start from, at a very deep foundational level, from very similar roots here in the sense that I, too, like you, am...at the really deepest level, basically I'm a philosophical anarchist, or libertarian, if you want to call it that. So that's where we're ultimately coming from, and, knowing that, I think we share a common starting point in a certain sense.

But the real question is...that we diverge once we go beyond that. Now, I think, if you remember, that I did acknowledge, in that correspondence, that I had falsely accused you at one point in my article of being...belonging to the group of the social-welfare–function maximizers—and you're not that at all; I...it was just a misreading of your whole position, and it was based on my view that anybody who didn't agree with me was a social welfare maximizer...

[Laughter.]

...But the question comes down—the really hard question, and there are lots of hard questions here, but the real question comes down as I've said many times and said the other day, too, that is, the world's out there; it's a complex set of interacting people and institutions and behavior and everything else going on and...social science, generally, or economics, in particular, has a hard time getting a handle on how to look at that world. And I...come back to...and cite Nietzsche all the time on this, and he talked about looking at this world through a...through different windows. Now that's sort of acknowledging, in one sense, that the world is there—we're not getting into this sort of idea that the world is strictly we make it up in our mind—the world is there, there is something there. But the question is how do we look at this world? We're looking almost necessarily, it seems to me...we're looking at that world from a window, a perspective, a predisposition on the way to look at it. And if you look at it differently you get different aspects of that world, you stress different aspects, and you look at it differently, and the question is, and my inclination is to say, that at one level...now this...I think using the word *ideology* is not very proper here in the sense that it's not very...it doesn't carry much meaning here. It seems to me it's a sort of a normative vision that we sort of have—and maybe it's something we *can't* choose, maybe we *can* choose. (And this gets into something I mentioned the other day—whether or not we can choose to look at the world a certain way, or is that just sort of preprogrammed . . . it's a difficult question.) But the point is that we get differing aspects of the way we look at this complex world depending on which window we are looking at it from.

Now where Warren and I think reach our main differences is, I argue that you are necessarily going to look at that world through what I would call a kind of a normative vision, one way or the other, and he seems to think, and he expressed it again today and he has in his other work and this was our basic little . . . our controversy, really, is that somehow or another there is one window that is pure. That is, there's a window out here that doesn't require this sort of precommitted disposition, that somehow or another there is an antiseptic vision that is possible that he has tried to achieve. And we might say, well, you really haven't got there, and it's impossible, and there are implications of your vision and therefore we can read back into what you . . . the way you look at the world, we can read a normative vision into it. Yet he wants to seem somehow to stay with this, what I would call an illusion, that, in fact, he can look at the world as an "antiseptic scientist" in the purer sense, whereas I am much more willing to acknowledge that the way I look at the world is in a sense a precommitment to look at the world that way. And this is not necessarily a conscious *choice* of a way to look at the world—it's not a *chosen* ideology and then moving toward the ideology. It's rather that you're sort of preprogrammed to look at the world that way. I . . . don't really think I could look at the world much differently from the way I do look at the world given my conversion, and it was a conversion as I said the other day; it was akin to a religious-type conversion when I looked at the world . . . started looking at the world as a set of interacting individuals. And that appealed to my fundamental libertarian anarchist roots here, because, until Frank Knight really changed my world, I couldn't see the world that way. And the world seemed chaotic, it seemed confused; and all of a sudden things clicked, and I began to see the world that way. And now that becomes a kind of a normative vision, I must acknowledge, and it's a desirable world. And that's the way I look at the world, and I interpret the world in that framework; and that's the fundamental difference, I think, between us.

Now what I think is another aspect of it that he touched on right at the end that is very interesting, I think, goes back to my Nietzsche metaphor again; I think it's possible, and this came up a little bit yesterday, not quite, but it's possible that we can simultaneously hold views by looking at the world differently through differing windows. We don't necessarily *strictly* stay within one predisposition; we can sort of back off and say, well, I don't like that and that way of looking at the world, but I can see what you're talking about, you see. And I can see Warren's position in this; I can see how he looks at the world as essentially people exercising power over each other through the institutions...legal institutions that exist and carry on or, as he said, as we can see the American structure as a kind of a plutocracy. And we can see that people are exploiting other people; and we can see that people take advantage of other people; and we can examine the unfairness that is proceeded. One thing that has driven me in a normative sense more strongly than anything else is I *can't stand* unfairness; and I *can't stand* people getting ahead of the game unfairly. I hate the rich; everybody knows that. I hated the Kennedy's with a passion—absolute utter and total passion, and I don't like people buying their way through some politics. So I can see an aspect of the world that's very close to Marx in a very differing sort of framework, but, on the other hand, I don't *like* to look at the world that way, I *want* to look at the world differently. And somehow or another, it seems to me that I, personally, have a kind of a moral obligation, if you want to call it that, to look at the world from a window that does, in fact, emphasize the positive features...

And I go back...we were all surprised, I think, with the...a month ago...with the Reagan funeral celebrations. It seemed to me as if the American people were just *longing* for something that would bring them together—that would somehow bring back a kind of a spirit of...of our whole civility, civil order, civic order that Reagan, himself, was able to tap into, and his success was based on that. Now, sure, you can look at Reagan in lots of different ways, but he did convey to the people, generally, a kind of a *spirit* of America, and I surely share the view...that, when you get down to this break that Warren mentions, I think America *is* exceptional. I am a *firm* advocate of American exceptionalism, and I think we are diverging more and more from Europe in...many respects here.

But my point is I have a moral obligation to look at the world through one window, and I think this distinguishes me from Warren here—he wants to shed himself of his moral obligation to look at the world through any particular window. And the main struggle I have with that is the idea that there can be a window in which that's not in there one way or the other. There is no doubt degrees in which we can do that.

But...so that's sort of where we come down and split off here, after having started from common...commonality.

WJS: I agree with much of what Jim says descriptively and even, to some extent, normatively. I, too, don't like unfairness; I don't feel a moral obligation to adopt any particular system of morality or ethics or justice or what not and view the world through that. My feeling is, given the limits to...hermeneutic and otherwise, that my moral obligation,...I don't think in terms of moral obligation...but my preference is for a division of labor. There is no reason why people can't do what Jim does and look through a particular normative pane of glass, but I also think that if you're going to have a grasp on what's really going on in the world (I think this is Hayek's rationale as well, in part), you need to have solid, or as solid knowledge as you can get as to what is really going on. Even though there are going to be normative premises, biases, or ideologies, or whatever you want to call it, that one can extirpate, that one should try as much as one can to develop this body of knowledge without any pretense that it is going to be pure. So...the "pure" version of this I don't like; I can't accept. But I do think the effort should be there, consciously, to find out what is really going on.

I am going to return to that in a minute.

I once published an article in a German journal on three paradigms of distribution. One was the productivity paradigm; the second was the exploitation paradigm; and the third was the Max Weber appropriation paradigm that had no normative assumptions—it's just people jockeying for a position to get at the dinner table to get more or less out of the income stream. Okay? But without any attribution of exploitation, Marxist, or otherwise or you deserve what you got because you're productive. Okay. And I think that approach is...really mutual and enables you to isolate, but not necessarily to exclude, considerations of justice.

Now...how did I get to my present position—I guess there's one thing I should have said earlier. As an undergraduate, I had, in effect, three courses in the history of economics and [in] graduate school I had another three or four courses in the history of economics. Why? Because I had Jim Early's year-long course in it; Martin Bronfenbrenner taught distribution theory for...to a large extent that way; Gene Rotwein taught imperfect competition theory that way. So, if I hadn't been a...even a middling sort of an historian of economic thought, having had it so much, it would have been...almost a miracle. So what I'm getting at is I've had a lot of training in history of economic thought and what came from this...this is egoism, now, and immodesty...what came...and it may be false as well—but what came from this, I think, is the ability to juggle different schools of thought; different bodies of thought; different definitions of reality at the same time. I believe I can think like an Austrian; think like a Marxist; think like an Ayresian; think like a common person; think like a mercantilist—without buying into them, okay? I can hold them at arm's length.

Now, with regard to this business about the dichotomy of Abba Lerner...let me give you a couple examples. Consider maternal benefits, or maternity benefits. I don't care what your view is on that. I would say this: maternity benefits can be accomplished either by individual negotiation with an employer, through collective bargaining, through legislation, or through litigation. Okay. If you want to talk about the rights structure of whose interests count, you should be doing that because that's this power structure within which trade takes place. And that power structure, in part— the part that I'm interested in at any rate—is legal rights, and legal rights come about in different ways. Whether you want that or not, whether you like it or not, that's the way it is. There's going to be something with regard to whose interests count with regard to maternity benefits, okay?

Now, I'll give you another example: surrogate motherhood. Along comes technology that enables us to have surrogate motherhood. You can approach that, as I am sure most of you are aware, in a number of different ways—legally, philosophically, morally. One thing is ubiquitous, and that is the feeling that everyone who's involved in surrogate motherhood should have their rights protected.

Now what are those rights? You're gonna have litigation; you're gonna have legislation... *something will come of this.* The child's rights, the biological parents' rights, the surrogate mother's rights... I personally have no particular feeling on this. I am not an expert on this, except to the extent that I'm telling you about it. What I insist upon, and I think this is *absolutely nonideological,* okay?, is that there is going to be a law governing the respective rights of the parties, who are parties, and what their respective rights are gonna be. Who haven't I mentioned? Grandparents, okay? The courts, and legislation, will ultimately determine who has a piece of this pie, whose interests are exposed to others interests, whose interests are gonna count. This is going to happen. You may not like it, but it's a fact of life, and it's going to be a body of covering law. This is an empirical statement just like the fact that we had bagels, lox, and cream cheese for breakfast. There's no ideology involved. My wife would prefer me not to have so much of the cream cheese...

[Laughter.]

..., but that is a different matter.

I do not believe that this is a conservative view or a liberal view, an anarchical view—it may run against certain people's sentiments, but I would insist that we try to develop a legal/economic analysis of things like that in this way, and I believe that is... not subject to the hermeneutic circle. I may be wrong; I still have the asterisk about that.

Now when I wrote this article that Jim was telling you about in the *Journal of Law and Economics*, about red cedar trees, I knew that some people might get exercised about red cedar trees, others might get exercised about apple orchard... apple trees. And I knew this was Virginia and it was an apple-growing state, etc., but I didn't think it would bother so many people as it bothered Jim.

What can I say? There's going to be a law governing whose interests count. Okay? Whether you like it or not, whether you like one tree or another tree, there's going to be a law. In a broader model there's going to be morals; there's going to be mores; there's going to be custom, but I'm just talking about the law here.

I think I'll stop there.

Oh, one other thing.

[Laughter.]

In that wonderful—I have it here; I forgot to mention it—in that wonderful exchange of lectures and comments with Musgrave, two things came out. Jim was... Jim said that he was motivated to hate the federal government because of what happened in the Civil War, the Civil War period. And this is the same federal government of the United States that attracted Musgrave to North America to escape from Hitler. This is the same America of American exceptionalism that Jim has this reservation about (period).

I can sympathize with both of these guys, because I think that the South should have had the right to secede; I did not ... do not ... did not then and do not now support slavery; and I certainly sympathize as my parents or ... my father came to this country and my mother's parents came to this country to escape the crap of the Old World. So I can sympathize with Buchanan; I can sympathize with Musgrave.

What I'm smiling about is that I think, as much as I can sympathize with both of them, I think that having this reaction or any reaction to the Civil War or having Musgrave's reaction to Hitler or anything like that is a too-thinned slender basis on which to develop a theory, even an ideology, of government. And he [Buchanan] doesn't buy it either, because he thinks about American exceptionalism, and this is the same America that includes the North having beat up on the South.

[Laughter.]

JMB: Well, I acknowledge that I'm split down the middle on a lot of these things...

[Laughter.]

...I don't deny that. But for purposes of clarification, let me ... lots of things I say may be get around to saying, but ... let me just summarize the red cedar case, because then it'll show you where we ... where we did differ in that one context.

This was in 1927 as I remember ... I've got it here, but we'll see, a 1927 case that went up to all the way to the Supreme Court. What had happened was, there was ... there had been a development, a natural event, a development of this kind of fungus that grew on cedar trees, and it didn't harm cedar trees at all. But if the fungus grew on the cedar trees, if there was an apple tree within ... oh, a half a mile of the cedar tree, it would kill or damage, severely damage, the apple tree. So there ... all of a sudden there was an interaction between the apple growers and the cedar tree growers that hadn't happened before. And so this came up ... and so the Virginia state legislature, upon petition by the apple growers, simply passed legislation that allowed the state entomologists to go and look and condemn the cedar trees and force the cedar tree owners to cut down the cedar trees if they were within ... near the apple orchards, without compensation.

Now, Warren's reading of that case—and it went all through the courts, and it was approved, and the courts approved this legislative action— Warren's reading of that case was the courts ... the legislature and the courts ... simply had to make a decision between the values of the damages to the apple growers or ... and the damages to the ... to the cedar tree owners for having to cut their trees down. And they made a decision, now this is more or less arbitrary, that the law, in a sense, is going to decide one or the other ... there's going to be a clarification here, clarify this particular interaction or interdependence that emerged.

The reason I didn't agree with that, and my criticism of Warren's position on that, was that ... the ... what happened was there were in existence a set of property rights—there was a law—and that the apple tree owners did not have any property right in the cedar trees prior to this happening. This happened. It created interdependence, but that also created a potential for gains-from-trade. And the proper way for this to have been resolved would have been for the apple growers to either themselves, voluntarily or through collective action, to have organized in such a way that they would, in fact, either buy off the... or compensate the cedar tree owners, and if it's a gain, if the damage to the apple crop was much more than the damage to the [apple] trees, then there would have been a Coase-type bargain, and they would have bought off the cedar tree owners, and you would have had a voluntaristic Wicksell-Pareto–type solution to the problem. As opposed to coming and bringing politics in when there... anytime that there's a conflict here and saying, "Well, there's got to be a law and, therefore, whoever has the most authority can get the legislature, the majority in the legislature, to pass the law; that, in fact, is the way it should come out." That's the way it comes out, quite arbitrarily in certain situations.

Well, that's the basis for our discussion. I... then... he wrote a piece; then I wrote a piece; and then that correspondence emerged, but it always goes back to that... whether or not there is a kind of a legitimacy in that which is, and we got into this... much discussion about the status quo—we had a conference on this in Blacksburg last year about this... the relevance and the status of the status quo, and I think you circulated your piece, they have... they have copies of that.[8]

So that is the fundamental debate between us—whether or not you look at the world in that sort of different way.

But, I want to switch off that now and go back a little bit to what Warren was saying...

WJS: Can I comment on this...

JMB: Sure.

WJS: ...so we don't lose it?

JMB: Yeah.

WJS: There's gonna be... we agree there's going to be a law—the question is whether we privilege the existing law or the opportunity to change the existing law. The fact of the matter is that, I did not argue in the paper, as Jim will... acknowledges, what was the right thing to do. What I described was what happened and then went on to interpret this. The law changed from L1 to L2, and that meant that under the circumstances of this red cedar rust, the bargaining power in the market changed from the red cedar tree owner to the apple orchard owner. And that... and generalizing that, I suggested that what one thing that law does is structure, what I called in a nonpejorative sense, mutual coercion in the market.

Now, apropos... there's a footnote... the Wicksell-Pareto connection here: One difference between Jim and I is that he buys Wicksell with regard to his use of it—the emphasis on gains-from-trade—but does not buy what Wicksell himself says should be anterior to that, namely, agreement on distribution, which I take to be agreement on the structure of rights. And I insist that in the real world that, too, is an issue; in other words, the political part of Lerner's statement.

Let me allude to a different example between Jim and I. He [and Gordon Tullock] published an article in the *AER* [*American Economic Review*], and I, with Al Schmid, wrote a response to that, and the *AER* turned it down. I sent it to Gordon, who may or may not remember this, and he published it. Our argument was that the Paretian analysis that Jim used was fine, but we wondered why, in setting out the rights within which Pareto optimality was developed through trade, was his...why did he always assign the rights to the producer and not to the consumer?[9]

Now, the point that I am making here is exactly the same point in the...that I made...[was] trying to make in the red cedar tree case—that whoever has the rights is gonna have their interest protected in the structuring of mutual coercion in the market, period. Also...and therefore I could not see why Jim assigned the rights in that...in his article always to the producer. Conceivably there could be justification for this—I personally wasn't interested whether it was one party or the other party that had the rights, but simply in establishing that choosing one party over the other structured mutual coercion in its favor. Therein, too, is this difference between us which goes, I think, beyond the Lerner dichotomy—Jim never responded to that. Maybe he wants to now, I don't know.

JMB: I don't understand it. I don't understand the producer point; I don't understand what you're making there. I don't remember...

WJS: Okay...with regards to externalities...

JMB: Yeah...

WJS: ...you basically said let the affected parties bargain and—the Coase solution—

JMB: Yeah...

WJS: ...but you always gave the right to the...producer of the good and of the pollution. Why not give the protection to the consumer, or the "innocent" third party (innocent in quotes), innocent in the Coasean sense—why not them? Now I have no particular view why they should have it, but why always to the producer?

JMB: What...now my position has never been directional in the sense of saying they ought to have it or not ought to have it, it's just whatever is. You start from...this goes back to the status quo point...you start from whatever is...

WJS: ...I'm not sure that that was the issue in your piece. It may have been...

JMB: ...yeah, yeah...

WJS: ...If it was, then I missed it, but you invariably in that case assume that the right was with the producer. And that may not be the case, that was my point.

JMB: Yeah...[unclear]...

WJS: In fact in the real world, it's not nece...if you start where it is, you now have consumer protection laws—or third-party protection laws. So we do have these innocent differences...

JMB: Yeah (chuckle).

WJS: ...and Gordon was very nice to publish that piece...because *AER* wasn't
interested in doing that.

[Unclear]...[Laughter]...

WJS: On that matter, I agree with you; I'm not sure about everything else.

[Laughter.]

    ...I'm teasing you.

JMB: I want to go back though a little bit further to what you...to one thing you
raised earlier, where you talked about the way that you look at distribution in
terms of the Max Weber thing. You said that there're ways you could look at
it as distribution; you could say as Max Weber...you've cited Max Weber
here...but simply a conflict, people trying to get their share of the pie, just in
a kind of a...with no normative overtones is just the way you put it, or you
could view it as people exerting authority over each other, that is, exploitation
with a kind of Marxist perspective. Or you could think of it in terms of, you
know, productivity, that is, you get out what you put in type of thing.

    Now, I want to change that example a little bit but...the reason why
I don't think you really get much by taking the Max Weber view...Let's take
the way we look at politics—get a little bit away from the distributional
question—but let's just look at politics now...

WJS: I think that politics is distributional...

JMB: ...Okay, fine; that's fine. I have no objection, but let's make it general about
politics.

    Well, it seems to me there are three...at least three ways we can look at
the wo...at politics—and, again, it's a complex matter, and we have to
somehow...be a reductionist and force something on this; I have no objection
to that—they're three ways: basically we can take the position that political
theorists have taken through the centuries since Plato. That is, they say you
can look on politics as the search for the good and the true and the beautiful;
that is the...we're searching for *truth* out there or *beauty* out there, whatever
the *summum bonum*, this sort of...And they model the way people...model the
behavior of politicians as seeking this court of mystical public interest out
there and sort of the collective goal of what I call the "truth/judgment"
politics. And, of course, I reject that categorically—that's what's been *wrong*
with the way people think about politics.

    Or, you can think of politics...this gets back close to the Max Weber
point...as simply conflict—conflict among people...groups forming themselves (individuals *and* groups *and* parties *and* coalitions and various things)
and simply a form of conflict...a war by peaceful means, so to speak, which
includes distributional aspects...It...seems to me that's not a very healthful
way to look at politics, and here it seems to me you're obligated to look at
politics—and, again, this comes back to a kind of moral obligation of having
this vision of politics as a means through which people are...trying to get
together to accomplish purposes...individual purposes...that cannot be
accomplished by their own separate anarchistic developments—legal...you
have to have a legal structure; you have to have a constitutional structure. But

to look at that as basically what I've, in a broader sense, I've said ... that one-half of public choice is politics as exchange, in this ultimate sense—that people are getting together ... to ... try to accomplish shared purposes that they couldn't accomplish on their own. And it seems to me that if you view politics that way, you ... you can offer a meaningful understanding/explanation which *does have* normative implications, as opposed to looking at this as pure conflict or this illusory looking at it as a truth/judgment thing.

Now, and I think you can make a *case* for looking at politics that way, *even though*, if you want to take this scientific antiseptic view, politics is just simply people fighting with each other or pure conflict—I'm taking ... I'm trying to get more of my share. It seems to me this is a categorically different way of looking at politics, and I think that if you stick to your way of looking at it, you have some normative implications here that ... that personally I don't like, and I don't think you like either, really.

WJS: Let me ... let me say this about that. Let me say that I would assume ... let me assume that I agree with you that politics would be healthier if people were trying to work together to achieve goals. I submit ... that ... when they're working together to achieve goals, they're going to differ as to the goals; differ as to the means. And it is conflict in the sense ... I believe this is conflict in the *same* sense that I've been talking about here. I don't believe *conflict by coercion* need be a pejorative term; I find that even in the healthy, to use your phrase (which I like), in a healthy world in which people are trying to work things out together—and I think that's what we *are* doing—they're going to conflict as to ends and means, so you must inevitably come back to what I would call the "Weberian view," if you want to know what is going on. So we have two good guys who love each other, who happen to disagree as to ends and/or means, and somehow, given these conflicts, they have to work it out. I don't see that the fact of conflict is bad; I don't think the fact that there's a structure of mutual coercion is bad; or that law protects *alpha*'s interest rather than *beta*'s interest, or vice versa, is bad—I think this is just the way of the world. I think there is an awful lot of pretense, not by you, that my way is *the right way* and anybody else's is wrong; I think that is kind of like hand-on-the-door bargaining—you either accept my offer or I'm out of here.

So what I'm saying is that if you ac ... I'm prepared to accept your view that healthy-minded people, nobly-motivated people, can still disagree, and in these disagreements, you're going to have a conflict model. Not because I like it or I want it; it's just there, as an empirical fact. Now, it may be that morally I would agree with you it would be better if we all agreed, but then, what-the-hell, life would be dull—but that's another matter.

JMB: Well, let's go back to the ... the ... good example we're talking about here is this red cedar vs. the apple growers case. Now, you see, the way you interpret that—the ... this conflict where one side or the other is gonna win—you don't have conflicts, [which is] not necessarily bad. So they go to the legislature and they both lobby and the apple growers win and so they impose their solution without compensation on the cedar ... red cedar growers. Now, my argument in the critique of that view was, in fact, if you accept *that* view, if you start looking at the world *that* way, you preclude the incentive and the possibilities of these people to get together and work out a bargain. Now there're obviously mutual gains as there is this interdependence, either it is or isn't worthwhile for the apple growers to fully compensate the cedar tree owners...And if you start...if you impose too quickly the *conflict* vision on this, then you encourage these apple growers to go and just...as long as they can get a majority in the legislature...to hell with the...to hell with the cedar tree owners. That's the point—where voluntarism, looking at it from the point of view of working out a compromise, is a quite different thing from starting and say[ing], "Well, it's a conflict, therefore whoever is the strongest wins." You see, it's a quite different way of looking at it, it seems to me.

WJS: I agree that there is that difference; I do not believe that my article's...my position supports...an improper solution. What it does is say this is what happened, and, indeed, I illustrated this by saying, "Consider the reverse case of an apple orchard rust that had adverse effects on red cedar trees"...it's the opposite solution, but to the same effect...I do not...this is a normative subject, now, I do not believe that we should foreclose legal change of law, that...or simply changing the law as an option which Jim's approach does...nor, as a positive matter, do I see in the real world that law is adopted once and for all time. I...I have a friend who's a professor of criminal procedure, and we were talking about some recent Supreme Court cases, and the really funny thing is that every time I talked about law, he interjected, "and legal change." I'm the one who emphasizes legal change in my work or opportunity for it or the fact of it; he felt the need to inject it because I was just saying law, not legal change...Pareto and Knight, as I indicate in the preface to my book on Pareto, both wrote that if this...their work, in which they wrote this, was going to be widely read, they would perhaps not have published it, because it would induce the kind of behavior that...

JMB: (chuckle)

WJS: ...you don't like...I sympathize with that a little bit, but I guess my position is, if I had moral...if I was in your shoes and adopted Moral View 1, I would hope to be smart enough to know that somebody else had Moral View 2— which leads me to the conflict model—and that I would not to so push my Moral View 1 as to foreclose the possibility of Moral View 2, even though I prefer [Moral View] 1. So what I'm saying here is I don't want to foreclose people from...buying each other off under the status quo law, but that's not really my problem. If I thought it was gonna do that, and throw everything into...up, topsy-turvy (everybody could run to court every time we turn around...I mean *real* litigation oriented), I might have the Pareto-Knight sense that, well, if everybody's gonna read this, I wouldn't publish it, but I don't...the sales weren't that big...

[Laughter.]

...I'm trying to describe, if describing something has the effect of influencing people's behavior, I suspect we'll influence people's behavior both ways. I don't know. But, you know there's a...there's a limit to how far one can say "I'm not gonna publish"...But especially, I want a model to accept the fact of legal change...

What are we talking about here? We're talking about a world that you can reduce to a model: X equals the function of A, B, C, D...N. Now, if we each adopt a model on normative grounds because it incorporates certain normative grounds that only has X as a function of A, B, C and drops all the rest, then that model has serious defects; it's not gonna fully explain, and it's gonna prejudice the normative process by only focusing on A, B, and C. I would prefer a wide range of variables—all of them that's manageable—so as not to preclude recognizing what is going on in the world.

Now, let's just go back to traditional, turn-of-the-century neoclassical theory. There was a belief in 19...that century...1900, that there was a governing law for everything. There were...read the textbooks...a law governing rent, law governing wages, interest, property, etc. There was a fellow, whose name escapes me right now [Gustav Kleene], who Taussig published in the *QJE* [*Quarterly Journal of Economics*], who argued the Weberian approach that there was no governing law of anything, but rather the meeting in the marketplace and in the...in politics—politics as exchange, maybe—in which the gathering forces of the one side met the gathering forces of the other, and somehow, something was worked out. Taussig was not entirely...he wrote on this, okay? So I'm not interpreting; I'm telling you what he said...he was not happy with this, but he was not able to rebut it. And now, what do we have?...We don't have governing laws; we have models—models amplified by...by specific theories (so one specific theory might be that of a particular law). But if you...my point is that if you narrow it down to A, B, and C, and forget about D, E, F...N, you bias the view of the world the way it is. And, furthermore, if you want to achieve a certain moral state of the world, okay?...it seems to me you're better off knowing what really is going on so that you can take the right kind of action. Now, it may be, it certainly will be, that there're gonna be unintended and unforeseen consequences. I don't question that. But it seems to me, the more knowledge you have, the more sophisticated the legal change or the moral change you want to bring about will be, and the greater chance you will have *ceteris paribus* to bring about the moral order that you prefer. In other words, the issue is not the end of the moral order, but me...the means appropriate thereto which has operational value; the greater operational value, the more consonant it is with what really is going on. Unless you pull...the people pull the wool over other people['s eyes]—and that's what politics is all about, and that's why I don't like it either.

JMB: Well, I'm under instruction here to open it up for questions, now, for the next fifteen minutes so...

[Laughter.]

WJS: That's a good idea. We've talked to each other.

[Laughter.]

Q&A from here. I will decipher queries at a later date. In the meantime, the responses are below.

JMB: Sam.

Q: [Unclear.]

WJS: It tells me a lot. It does not...many students have said to me, but so what? It doesn't tell me what...whose interest should be protected. Why should I go out on a limb and assume that I know whose interest should be protected?

Q: [Unclear.]

WJS: I couldn't agree more...I agree with Hicks who says, "no theory can answer every question you have." I don't deny other people doing their thing; I'm just doing my thing.

Q: [Unclear.]

WJS: I think my approach has a place for competing moral views or competing interests. I'm not prejudicing it saying it should be under the existing law, and there should be no pressure on people to bargain under the existing law because of the threat of legal change. I am simply asserting that there is in fact legal change.

Now, if I thought, and this would be the infinite [ultimate] ego trip, if I thought that what I wrote was gonna convince people to go to the legislature and litigate, you would...you should have me institutionalized...

[Laughter.]

...In this world, what Warren Samuels writes—describing what's going on—is not going to encourage people to litigate.

[Unclear.]

WJS: You've made your point; I understand.

JMB: Yeah, yeah. Eric.

Q: [Unclear.]

WJS: Well, I haven't given you the full story...

[Laughter.]

...I haven't told anything about...the sources of law; I haven't told you anything about...the question as to what is law; I haven't said anything about a theory—and I do have a theory—of judicial interpretation; I haven't said that I...I haven't told you that I think that at the level of our conversation, the rule of...the concept of the rule of law is vacuous, though I've published a piece on that already. I do have...what you want, and it does provide opportunity to examine the kinds of questions that you are alluding to, and I...in part what...I think Sam was...

Q: [Unclear.]

WJS: It *isn't* a normative enterprise—that's my point. You see...my version of postmodernism does not say that you cannot choose; my point is that what you think is an absolute is really a choice...editorial you...is an absolute is really a choice. That the Supreme Court, for example, doesn't follow precedent, because there are a whole set...there, oh, in every case there're rival sequences of precedent. They reach the decision they want, and then they explicate it in terms of this case ra...and this precedent ra...or sequence rather than the other. So I...I do have that theory...I spell it out and teach it, have taught it in great detail.

JMB: Let me just...I can't refrain from making one comment here. The point that you said the rule of law is vacuous...

[Laughter.]

...That seems to me is a perfect examplar of what we're talking about here, and let me just instance one personal account that I think some of...most of you would agree with had you experienced it.

In 1981, I visited Dennis Mueller in Berlin, and we went over into the East section. We went through Checkpoint Charlie; gave up our passports, everything; went through this East [Berlin]; came back. I have never experienced in my life quite the feeling as when I walked...when I came back from that barrier. It gave a...a sense that you are back where the rule of law would prevail; where people mattered, but when you went back behind that Curtain, you had a sense it was absolutely vanished. You were vulnerable—totally vulnerable. Now, to me the rule of law then is surely not vacuous; it has a *meaning*—it has a *meaning*...

WJS: Jim I said in the...at the level in which we're considering it here...

JMB: [Laughing] Oh, all right...

[Laughter.]

WJS: You forget that...

[Laughter.]

JMB: Okay.

WJS: Let me illustrate...in my book *Economics, Governance and Law*[10] there is a chapter on the rule of law. I commend it to you so you can understand what I'm talking about. Okay?

I obviously agree with Jim, but that phrase, in the sense that we...at the level we're dealing with it here...Let me illustrate this.

In that article I cite several, and summarize the content of several, books that talk about the founding fathers—the Adams, Jefferson, Madison, and what not—and how...they...formulated words in the Constitution that deferred issues to be worked out by the courts; how, in their own careers, they misstated what transpired at the Constitutional Convention; how they used one interpretation of a clause in one context because it was politically efficacious for them, and, in another context, ten years later, they used a different def...interpretation of a clause. Okay? Now if you want to invoke original intent, if you want to invoke rule of law, these are the people who you need to deal with. Okay?

Now let me take up the really interesting case of the Clinton impeachment. The one view is that he committed a "high crime and misdemeanor" by lying to the grand jury about "not having sex with that woman"—or not having sexual relations with that woman—and differing as to what "is" means. But he lied; there's no question about it. Whether that arises...rises to high crimes and misdemeanors is a matter of judgment—which is my point. So one group says that the rule of law requires that the president be impeached if he lies to a grand jury; the other interpretation of the rule of law is that politics, which they believe was the driving force behind the impeachment, should not drive the rule of law.

So you have two different views of the rule of law—I'm not going to sit here and debate with you over this—all I'm trying to establish is that just as at the time of Madison, in the time of Rehnquist, you have different views of what the rule of law means. And that is true of everything. Take, for example, the commerce clause. Is manufacturing...interstate commerce? The original interpretation was that it was, the E. C. Knight case and a whole string of cases; it wasn't—and then it becomes again. What is this? What law is the rule here? It is a matter of interpretation. What we would like— morally, normatively, sentimentally—is a given, strict law that's easily applied. But there is no such thing at this level of discourse, okay? *There is no such thing.* Every clause is subject to interpretation and is going to be interpreted by people who have interests.

Q: [Unclear.]

WJS: At this level of discourse, we didn't go into detail.

Q: [Unclear.]

[Laughter.]

JMB: No, but...this is a very important point; we could spend a lot of time going into this, but, I...let me just see if I can sketch out a little bit of response here.

I think it is...you're right in a certain sense that even children...that's one thing they develop quite early on—a sense of fairness. I mean...Piaget's sum of all his experiments, it's very, very early on—but I do think it does require, and I think it's a very important driving force in the way we think about the world, and so forth and so on, and it is behind all of the Rawlsian enterprise. And the...I'm very sympathetic to the... I have a lot of affinity to John Rawls and what he was trying to accomplish here in this context. But it does require—you say everybody—it's not quite everybody, because you can't have—and this gets directly into the stuff that Sandy [Peart] and David [Levy] are working on—you cannot have a conceptualization of the world in which people are classified hierarchically and have a sense of fairness. You can have justice; you can have, in the sense you define justice there, totally differently. There you define justice in terms of a kind of a compassion, an altruism, benevolence...you can talk about you are just to the man who is poor, but if you classify him totally differently from yourself, you're...you can't apply fairness criteria. Fairness criteria, and the fact that you say everybody honors this, means that you're accepting this idea that basically we're natural equals out there to be considered in the normative sense as natural equals. And so I think that's an important distinction to make; and it does separate these two conceptually.

WJS: I, I agree with what Jim is saying... it really is a vastly difficult topic. We're all professors here—well, most of us are—and others are exposed to our machinations...

JMB: ... at this level of discourse...

[Laughter.]

WJS: Let me give you, let me give you an example. Let me give you an example.

You can argue that the only fair exam is one that goes over the assigned material. Most of you would say, yes. I once had a class in mathematical logic in which the exam did not cover the assigned material, but went to the next step in the development of the mathematical logic—basically asking on each question, "if you understand what we've done thus far, what do you need to do to get to the next step?" (Now, it wasn't quite as blunt as that, but this was an unusually good class, as an undergraduate class; and it was... a lot of scholarship students in it.)

Now, is that fair?... Fairness is a very complex subject, but I agree. I don't believe that my focusing on the importance of a solid, non-normative picture of what actually is going on is inconsistent with having a part of your model... one of the elements in *A, B, C, D*... the normative inputs here. And, as I said to Jim, if you have more than person with a normative input, you're gonna have a conflict, and that's going to have to be worked out. And that is really what I think is going on out there. And that's why I believe that the position that I'm taking here is good old American pragmatism. We all come to it with our own highfalutin sentiments, our highfalutin moral principles, but in reality what is going on is working out solutions to problems... Whether we do it nicely or nastily, that's a different matter.

Now, on this question of fairness. I can remember, when I was a young professor at University of Miami in the early 1990s... early 1960s... The first person who called me a Communist in public...

[Laughter.]

... was a student... (he [Buchanan] called me a Statist)... who was the head of Young Americans for Freedom. And he didn't like my spiel about social control and that, whether you like it or not, government is important... But I was close to him—he eventually went to law school and became a judge. I once ran into him and he said, "You know, you were right on all those issues about law; at Young Americans for Freedom, we were a bunch of nuts."

[Laughter.]

At any rate, I was close to them; I was close to a number of other groups, including the Cuban Student Directorate and... a couple of other Cuban groups, right wing, from the first wave of Castro emigres, and I was also close to students on the left, who were vastly outnumbered, but you had an SDS group there. The people on the right were fearful of a coup d'etat from the left; and the people from the left were afraid of a coup d'etat from the right, okay?. And it was my picture... and I don't think I imagined this... that if there had been one, either one of those coups, the people on the other side would have been "freedom fighters/terrorists." And I could have imagined myself joining them, okay?

Now, what's fair? It depends upon whether it is Moral View 1 or Moral View 2—that has to be worked out in the minds of each individual. Now, if I was a single person, I might have reacted differently under the circumstances...the hypothetical circumstances...than if I had been a father and a husband with two children...as I was, in fact. But if there had been a coup, I'm sure that I would done...joined in. I would have been an enemy of the people to those...in office; I'd have been a wonderful freedom fighter to the other. Now, if you call this moral relativism, fine; I don't care what you call it. I believe the moral absolute here, if you want to call it an absolute, is good old Americanism, pluralism, meaningful civil rights, and markets. But believing that, does not keep me from understanding that law... shapes...markets...and...you...don't...have...markets...given... by...nature, which is the problem of neoclassicism.

SP: Jim, do you want to have the last word?

JMB: No, no.

[Laughter.]

SP: Please join me in thanking Warren and Jim.

[Applause.]

Notes

1 James M. Buchanan (1987) *Economics: Between Predictive Science and Moral Philosophy*, comp. Robert D. Tollison and Viktor J. Vanberg, College Station: Texas A&M University Press.

2 Warren J. Samuels (1971) "Interrelations between Legal and Economic Processes," *Journal of Law and Economics*, 14 (October 1971): 435–50.

3 James M. Buchanan (1972) "Politics, Property, and the Law: An Alternative Interpretation of *Miller et al. V. Schoene*," *Journal of Law and Economics*, 15 (October 1972): 439–52.

4 James M. Buchanan and Warren J. Samuels (1975) "On Some Fundamental Issues in Political Economy: An Exchange of Correspondence," *Journal of Economic Issues*, 9 (March 1975): 15–38.

5 James M. Buchanan and Richard A. Musgrave (1999) *Public Finance and Public Choice: Two Contrasting Visions of the State*, Cambridge: MIT Press. For Warren Samuels's review, see his (2000) "Buchanan and Musgrave on Public Finance and Public Choice: A Review Essay," *Journal of the History of Economic Thought*, 22 (4): 499–507.

6 James M. Buchanan (2004) "Saving the Ideas," Summer Institute for the Preservation of the Study of the History of Economics, 26 July 2004.

7 Robert A. Dahl and Charles E. Lindblom (1953) *Politics, Economics, and Welfare: Planning and Politico-Economic Systems Resolved into Basic Social Processes*, New York: Harper.

8 Reference is to Warren J. Samuels (2004) "The Status of the Status Quo: The Buchanan Colloquium," *Research in the History of Economic Thought and Methodology*, 22A: 219–33; and "The Problem of the Status of the Status Quo: Some Comments," *Research in the history of Economic Thought and Methodology*, 22A: 235–56.

9 James M. Buchanan and Gordon Tullock (1975) "Polluters' Profits and Political Response: Direct Controls versus Taxes," *American Economic Review*, 65 (March 1975): 139–47; Warren J. Samuels and A. Allan Schmid (1976) "Polluters' Profits and Political Response: The Dynamics of Rights Creation," *Public Choice*, 29 (Winter 1976): 99–105.

10 Warren J. Samuels (2002) *Economics, Governance and Law: Essays on Theory and Policy*, Cheltenham: Edward Elgar.

Part III

Language, social choice, and order

9 Some problems in the use of language in economics

The most difficult problem confronting economists is to get a handle on the economy, to know what the economy/political economy is all about. This is, of course, the basic raison d'etre for economists and economics. The second most difficult problem confronting economists is in using ordinary language—verbal and mathematical—to get to know what the economy/political economy is all about. Language may communicate nothing, a little, or much about what the political economy is all about, or it may communicate error or mislead, at either or both the ontological or experiential levels.

In this chapter I propose to examine several ways in which our use of language can get in the way of learning about what the economy is all about. Some of my examples are well known; some are not; most if not all arise daily and are not given the attention and respect they merit. All are at least as significant for political economy as they are for economics.

Obviously I do not propose to do away with the use of language; such would be a poster-ad for absurdity. I do propose alertness over sloppiness and attention to limitations over stylized usages.

For many people, both my argument and my examples may be superfluous, even banal, and I may be preaching, as it were, to the choir. The message may be more important for graduate students but observed deficiencies of professional practice support the view that not every economist is a member of the choir.

Apropos of graduate students, however, during the week in which I began to write this chapter, I found out anew that some of them did not know the difference between a corporation and a partnership regarding liability (this was my biggest shock!)—this *is* an important matter of definition. Some did not understand valuation as the capitalization of actual or expected income at some mathematical interest rate. Some confused the work of knowing what something is all about, the tasks of critiquing it, proposing something better, and making predictions. Some did not appreciate the technical, substantive, and epistemological assumptions of the national-income accounts. In these and other respects, our use of language, including quantification (which, after all, is a form of language), leaves much to be desired in understanding and communicating what the economy is all about.

Candidly, I think that most if not all of us know most if not all of what I am going to say. But I think we too much take it for granted. Above all, we do not regularly and explicitly emphasize the limits of what we do and say as economists. I know that it may be downright boring to continually repeat; but it is also downright misleading if not dangerous to overstep. I also know that the psychodynamics of professional stature—the stature of our discipline and of each of us personally— drives us to make statements more confidently than our epistemology and language warrant. I will address here some of the sources of our quest for unique determinate optimal solutions. An additional source is our anxiety over Harry Truman's displeasure with two-handed economists. It seems to me more sensible, more scientific, if you will, and more honest to admit to limitations, to acknowledge that the economy consists of conflicting forces, with variable and generally unpredictable weights, and with multiple possible outcomes. As Alfred Marshall envisioned it, the economy is an arena of tendencies, and economic laws, or propositions, are statements of tendency more or less specific to particular but variable conditions. The following are some problems in the use of language in economics.

Definitions

Definitions not only define words, when the words are used they define the world for us and that definition may mislead or incompletely define the world.

Example 1. Consider the use of the word "corporation." Unless one knows that corporate stockholders have limited liability, one would not have any idea that the corporate form is a mode of socialized risk not unlike many elements of the welfare state.

Example 2. The use of words to define key terms is inevitable and a necessary part of communication. However, when we use a metaphor to define a metaphor, we have not said much of substance. If "Invisible Hand" is a metaphor and if "market" is a metaphor, then identifying the Invisible Hand—to answer the question, what is the Invisible Hand?—as the market goes only so far. One must then ask the question, what is the market? Doing so leads to a profound difference between pure abstract a-institutional conceptual markets *and* actual markets which are a function of the institutions/power structures that form and operate through them. Then one has to ask, what is an institution? One can go only so far using primitive, undefined terms.

Example 3. Consider the notion of a market as characterized by a single price for a given commodity. Is this a definition, an assumption, or a conclusion? If a conclusion, is it a matter of logical validity or an empirical fact? Is the theory built upon it a tautology, such that finding more than one price does not negate the proposition but implies multiple markets?

Definitions and the use of primitive terms

Very often terms are used in a generic sense. Terms like "private," "public," "voluntary," "freedom," "coercion," "property," "morality," "liberty," and so on, are used as primitive terms with unspecified meaning. They are kaleidoscopic, subject to selective perception, and almost invariably given variable specification.

Their use facilitates the entry into analysis or argument of selective implicit antecedent normative premises. This allows an author to escape questions of both substantive content and the mode of its determination, thereby usually begging a, if not the, important substantive question, leaving it to each reader to provide substantive content. Such terms are often identified with the status quo somehow selectively perceived—often the point at issue.

Perhaps the classic example is the word "natural." It is extraordinarily elastic and problematic. It enables an author to avoid dealing substantively with certain problems. It also permits an author to elicit agreement on a perhaps unjustified basis, as when a reader interprets the author in terms of the reader's own favored attribution. And it permits implicit, if variable, apologia, for example, by selective reification of some status quo.

Consider also such statements as, "If the most is to be made of the new technology, the proper infrastructure must be in place," or that a policy "left things worse, not better," or that a policy "worked," "failed," or "distorted" results. These statements leave unspecified both the substantive meaning of the key terms—proper, worse, better, worked, failed, distorted—and how to determine what they mean. It is left to each reader to provide substantive content. Similarly with statements that say that path dependence does or does not yield the "right path" or that posit "the right institutions." Substantive content must be adduced and it typically will be adduced in conjunction with implicit antecedent normative premises as to whose/which interests are to count as to "right." The situation is manifestly obvious when a statement is made that "every citizen" can "participate" in the economy and/or polity. Participation to be substantive requires some specification of the distributions of wealth and income and of who counts as a "citizen." As such things go it was not too long ago that the frame of reference was the domain of free white propertied males.

It should also be obvious with the term "market." One can discuss markets in the abstract—the idea of a pure a-institutional abstract conceptual market—*vis-à-vis* actual markets that are a function of the institutions and power structure that form and operate through them. One often reads or hears that sometimes one arrangement is most appropriate and sometimes another; for example, one set of laws or another, market or government, and so on. This is logically correct but empty. But how is one to determine when it is one and when the other?

Economic discourse has numerous examples of primitive terms used in such a way as to lead each user to adduce selective, private meanings. The function of these terms may be to give vent to particular ideological sentiments but they are often taken to have substantive content when in fact they do not. Some additional examples include the following:

"Government interference in free markets"—when markets are in part a function of government action, action promoting certain interests and not others, and actions changing the interests to which government gives its support.

Phrases such as "properly designed institutions" and "properly designed institutional change"—with the meaning of "properly," as well as "institution," left unspecified.

Phrases such as "correct solutions," "minimal standards," "deficient versus excessive budgets," "distortion," "good versus bad policy," and that "the function of rules is to restrain harmful behavior"—with the meaning of each critical term left unspecified.

Phrases such as "the optimal set of laws," "the optimal tax and expenditure system," "the optimal balance between private and public sectors," when something is "best served" by each sector, and so on—with the precise substantive meaning and conditions of "optimal" and "best" are left unspecified as well as the precise substantive meaning of "private" and "public."

Consider, too, the phrase, "unduly restrictive over-regulation by government." I am far from saying that such a subjective judgment cannot be substantiated or at least seriously argued. But it is, after all is said and done, a subjective judgment. It logically neglects three things: First, it neglects the problem of whose interests are to be restrained so as to protect and enhance certain rival interests, especially in cases where government must choose, willy nilly. Second, it neglects the background of all regulation by government other than the one in question. Third, it neglects the restrictions and governance imposed by nominally nongovernmental actors, in part enjoying their power as a function of other laws.

The detective-hero in one of J. J. Jance's mystery novels remembers an admonition delivered by his senior English teacher in high school. The lesson was, "You must not use a pronoun unless a noun clearly precedes it. Unless one naturally follows the other, what you write becomes so much babble. People can't make heads or tails of it" (Jance: 197). My point is that babble has many origins.

Definitions and theories

Definitions often assume, embody, and give effect to theories, theories as hypotheses. In post-Second World War courses in Principles of Economics it was common-place to consider the definition of the national income accounts, especially what was and was not included in Gross National, or Domestic, Product. Definitions embody and give effect to conceptions of the world and theories thereof. GNP and GDP do not have an independent existence. They are terms of economic art, and give effect to methodological and substantive judgments. The typical operating assumption is that the definition uniquely and importantly identifies the object or concept being named. But definitions are socially constructed; they do not, or not necessarily, bear any direct relationship to some transcendent, given category. The meaning of a definition derives from the use to which it is put; definitions are instrumental, even when they give effect to preconceptions and theories about the object or concept being defined—in fact, that is one way in which they are instrumental.

During the early decades of the twentieth century, economists engaged in several controversies over definitions. The subjects included: the scope of economics; the nature of economic laws; the nature of production; the identity of the factors of production—land, labor, and capital—and their interrelations; the definitions of capital and of the productivity of capital, and hence of productivity itself; the meaning of value, cost, and utility; the nature—and source and justification—of interest;

and so on. The aggregate of definitions served to identify, and in a way define, the economy as such, for example, the conceptual relations between capital and labor.

The literature of the period was rampant with articles claiming to provide *the* correct definition, and *the* correct ground or theory on which the correct definition rested (typically it was only implicit that a theory was involved). Legendary disputes took place over the meaning (definition) of value, cost, productivity, and capital. Almost no attention was given to the functional or instrumental nature of definitions, or to how it might be possible—if not actually the case (itself, of course, an hypothesis)—to adopt different definitions for different purposes, for example, to concentrate on different facets of the object being defined.

Some of the controversies remain active, though more or less subdued, in contemporary professional literature of economics. Many of these terms, such as capital (and its correlative, investment) are given definitions that, paradoxically, on the one hand, have become standardized, and, on the other, vary both within and between schools of economic thought. A classic case was that definition of inflation that said it was an increase in the supply of money—thereby building into the definition the quantity theory of money.

Necessity of multiple theories

We seem to think that one theory is sufficient to deal with a problem area. But no one theory can answer all the questions we might have. The subject of inquiry may well permit, even require, multiple theories. And for the same reason that we may need multiple theories, we may need multiple definitions, such as of "capital," although in some cases, such as "inflation," neutral definitions that do not presume a theory will suffice. Indeed, multiple definitions arise in physics and the other physical sciences without making them unscientific; for example, light is treated by physicists sometimes as a wave and sometimes as a particle.

Validity and truth

A *valid* argument is one that follows from its premises, given the correct use of the system of logic. The *truth* of a statement is a matter of its descriptive accuracy or correct explanation. A conclusion that is valid may or may not be true. A conclusion may or may not, even if true, say everything that can and/or need be said about the object of inquiry. A conclusion which is necessarily valid may not be true; may, even if true, not deal with important considerations; may be true only with regard to certain social space (data) and not others; and is often taken as true because it follows logically from its premises. No use of language can properly erode the distinction, yet conclusions that are valid are often taken as true and the whole truth.

Is and ought

A *positive*, or "is," proposition is one that describes, explains or states what must be done in order to achieve a particular goal. A *normative* or "ought" proposition is one which affirms either something to be good or the desirability or goodness of seeking something. One can distinguish between positive and normative propositions in principle, but many, perhaps most, statements in economics are blends of "is" and "ought" elements; and one cannot properly move from an "is" proposition to an "ought" proposition without an additional normative, "ought" premise. No use of language can properly erode the distinction, yet arguments are made which try to do so.

Optimality and the role of antecedent normative premises

The term "optimality" as used in economics is fraught with problems of definition, nuance, exclusion, and tautology. The desire for conclusions that can be designated optimal is driven by two motivations: first, the desire to be, at least to be thought of as being, scientific, coupled with the belief that a scientific conclusion must be singularly unique, a state of mind which is reinforced by the notion of equilibrium; and, second, the desire to have something important and persuasive to say about problems policy. The language consequent to these desires typically is misleading in what it excludes from economic analysis and policy.

Reification

Economists generally work with some notion of a pure abstract a-institutional conceptual model of the economy. Economists also tend to identify the status quo with that conceptual model. Primitive terms, for example, are often used as if they were laden with substantive meaning and direct applicability. This can only be done by assuming that the primitive terms of the model are to be understood only in terms of the status quo. One problem is that the so-called status quo is not a given; it is a matter of interpretation. The status quo is selectively perceived and identified. Second, the status quo itself is the ultimate object of inquiry. By identifying it in particular, selective terms and identifying it with the pure conceptual model, economists selectively reify the existing system, rendering it more concrete than it really is. A further problem is that the primitive terms of the model itself—such as "competition"—can be given variable specification.

Specific, definitive texts do not necessarily have definitive meanings. Three examples from U.S. law: First, it has long been understood that the Sherman Antitrust Act of 1890 was a compromise among legislators who had different and often radically conflicting aims. Notwithstanding the mythology which has been built up around the law, for some the law advanced restrictions on matters deemed antisocial, whereas for others it meant forestalling more serious restrictions on business; and for perhaps all, the meaning of its language was left for the courts to work out, as they soon proceeded to do.

Second, the original meaning adduced to "interstate commerce" included manufacturing. Eventually manufacturing was deemed not to be interstate commerce. Still later, the original interpretation was restored. The nature of the original interpretation did not, however, prevent the pretense that the second was the intention of the founders.

Which brings me to my third example, the doctrine of "original intent." A recent book on the subject (Lynch 1999) demonstrates convincingly that the notion of the original intent of the founding fathers—whatever one might think normatively of the matter—has little if any meaning. The author shows, *inter alia*, that during the first six Congresses, the Constitution was interpreted on the basis of immediate policy goals, including state, regional and political interests, and not fidelity to some past position or original intent; that figures such as James Madison not only changed interpretive positions but adopted conflicting ones; that immediate policy goals influenced framers' recollections of the constitutional convention and the ratifying state conventions, the meaning of the *Federalist Papers*, and the interpretation of the Constitution; that elements of the structure of government ensconced within the Constitution were matters of compromise which neither satisfied nor expressed either compromised position; that regional interpretations became reversed, due to changing circumstances and political expectations; that important clauses of the original Constitution and the first ten amendments, the Bill of Rights, comprised compromises of language that deferred to the future the determination of what they might be held to mean; and so on.

Each of these examples illustrates how selective interpretation engenders different reifications of both the past and the status quo. As conditions and therefore interests changed, different readings of the Constitution and of statutes are advanced and adopted. All this is part of the role of language in the continuing social construction of reality, a putative reality that is given selective reification.

Rights

The identification of "rights" in economics is, like other terms, kaleidoscopic, subject to selective perception, given variable specification, often identified with the status quo somehow selectively perceived, and often the point at issue. Rights are relative to other rights and to the legal process through which they emanate and are revised. The concept of "rights" has three levels of meaning: as a claim, as an interest given legal protection, and as the sanction used to enforce that protection. And all rights have their economic significance, including value, limited by the market.

When we speak of property rights in particular, one must recognize that property is a name given to legal protection of certain interests in a way that gives them a privileged status in relation to other rights. Some other rights serve the same function of protecting interests, are the functional equivalent of property rights, but are not given the same status.

Property is also subject to two modes of definition. On the basis of police power reasoning, property is subject to law which seeks to promote the public health, safety, welfare, and morals through the modification of rights of property and contract; in which case property is defined by and a function of law. On the basis of eminent domain reasoning, any regulation is a "taking," compensable "taking," in which property exists independent of law. Analysis that specifies "property rights" or assumes only government protection of property is thus question begging along all the foregoing lines.

Rationality

"Rationality" is another primitive term, like "optimality" and "efficiency," that is both simple and general in a world in which motivation and behavior are very complex and variable. The language of economics that assumes rationality clearly begs important matters, such as the various forms that rationality may take, the formation of preferences, the effect of others' choices on one's own, and so on.

Fallacies

One common fallacy often deployed by economists is the fallacy of composition: what is arguably true of a part is not necessarily true of the whole, and vice versa. Consider the proposition that ours is a voluntary economy. This must be qualified from the start in at least one respect. Individuals exercise volition; they make choices from within their opportunity sets. The content of their opportunity sets is not, or not entirely, a matter of their volition. They do not voluntarily agree so to be constrained. One submits volitionally but not voluntarily to a robber who offers the choice of one's money or one's life. Voluntarism would involve a greater degree of participation by people in the organizations that make decisions that affect them and their opportunity sets in important ways. To use the word "voluntary" obfuscates many important questions.

Let us put that point—the difference between volitional and voluntary—momentarily aside. Clearly it is quite another thing to go from the individual to the group, to the entire economy. To the extent that the individual is socially constructed and to the extent that the group or economy can be structured in different ways, the relevance of both voluntary and volitional is compromised. At the least, again, voluntarism (as distinct from volition) would involve a greater degree of participation by people in the organizations that make decisions that affect them and their opportunity sets in important ways.

Forgetting, therefore, about the distinction between volitional and voluntary, the putative voluntary nature of individual action and choice must confront the problem of the structure, the whole, of which the individual is a part. And the matter is rendered further complex by recognition of inequality. This is because if individuals are unequal in any material respect, treating them equally—for example, by laws that are common, impersonal, abstract, and procedural—is to treat them unequally, whereas to treat them equally may, paradoxically, require that we treat them unequally. The relation of one part to another part and to the whole is, accordingly no simple matter. Our conventional use of language does not do justice to these considerations.

Opportunity cost and the ubiquity and inevitability of problems

It is often deemed sufficient, in both public and professional discourse, when arguing over a controversial policy, to render the policy in question deficient by indicating its cost. But economists also employ the principle of opportunity cost, which states that every choice has as its cost the alternatives foregone. One corollary to the principle of opportunity cost is the principle of the inevitability of problems: No matter which alternative is chosen, we are more or less stuck with both its limitations and the results of not having chosen some alternative. The situation is rendered even more understandable when we recognize that governmental policies typically must choose between conflicting interests. We have done a good job of instructing neither ourselves nor the public in matters of the role of cost.

Criteria of structure versus criteria of results

The interpretation and evaluation of developments can be undertaken on two bases. One involves criteria of structure, such that given an agreed-upon structure, any policy resulting wherefrom is considered a priori acceptable. The other involves criteria of results, such that any structure is evaluated on the basis of how well it achieves the desired policy result(s). Different structures, (e.g. of laws), will tend to generate different results, e.g., different Pareto-optimal outcomes. One fundamental question is, whose criteria of structure and/or of results will become operative as results are worked out? Our typical use of language does not make this distinction clear.

Working things out

One gist of the foregoing is that in every respect results in the real world must be worked out. They cannot be specified in advance without introducing implicit antecedent assumptions as to whose interests are to count, thereby substituting the perceptions and/or preferences of the analyst for those of actual economic actors and foreclosing and/or channeling the operation of actual economic structures and processes.

Another gist of the foregoing is that the same is true of our language. The meaning of primitive terms, for example, must be worked out; they cannot be taken for granted.

Still another is that one of the reasons for the term "political economy" is the nature of the language used in our discipline. It ultimately has to do with the subjective and normative aspects of the definitions we use. If by "political" we mean having to with choice and power, language is political, as is the state. The highest level of political action may well be that taking place in forming the definitions that define our world and channel our policies. It is our language that is so important in determining whose interests are to count.

I worked on this chapter in part during the weekend of February 12–13, 2000. This was the period of both Charles Schultz's death and the last of his

Peanuts cartoons. One of my favorites, as I remember it, was the one in which Charlie Brown tells Lucy that he is going to watch the sun set. Lucy tells him that the sun does not set; the earth turns. After thinking about it, Charlie Brown responds: "I'm going to watch the earth turn."

In conclusion, my admonition is really very simple: Don't jump to conclusions on the basis of language.

References

Jance, J. J. (1996) *Lying in Wait*, New York: Avon.
Lynch, Joseph M. (1999) *Negotiating the Constitution: The Earliest Debates Over Original Intent*, Ithaca, NY: Cornell University Press.

10 *Poletown* and *Hathcock*

An essay on some problems in the language of the law

Introduction

Questions of language, reasoning, and the results and functions of reasoning are present in (i) law and economics and (ii) the history of economic thought. Nowhere is this more evident than in Adam Smith's *History of Astronomy*. Smith, who lectured on moral philosophy, economics, and law and government, says that man is in a state of wonder and awe when confronting his world. Man needs to make sense of this, and it is philosophy that provides

> the science of the connecting principles of nature. ... Philosophy, by representing the invisible chains which bind together all these disjointed objects, endeavours to introduce order into this chaos of jarring and discordant appearances, to allay this tumult of the imagination, and to restore it, when it surveys the great revolutions of the universe, to that tone of tranquility and composure, which is both most agreeable in itself, and most suitable to its nature.[1]

It is, for Smith, the function of "all the different systems of nature" to endeavour "to sooth the imagination, and to render the theatre of nature a more coherent, and therefore a more magnificent spectacle, than otherwise it would have appeared to be";[2] "the repose and tranquility of the imagination is the ultimate end of philosophy...to allay this confusion...and to introduce harmony and order into the mind's conception."[3] Knowledge and belief thus serve as both psychic balm and social control.

Smith suggests that philosophy (science) encompasses those activities that seek knowledge. He also argues that while true knowledge is preferable to mere belief that sets minds at rest, often one has to settle for the latter given the absence of the former. Moreover, Smith understood that his obvious and simple system of natural liberty required, and was itself the product of, three domains of psychic balm and social control: moral rules, the market, and legal rules. One characteristic of his work in all three areas was his attention to language, reasoning, and the results and functioning of reasoning. He seems to have been particularly alert to language in the context of society's mythological, symbolic, and ideological systems, not least in his study of law and government. He was thus alert to the use of language to (1) define reality so as to influence policy and (2) acquire, maintain, and exercise power. This may be especially true for him with regard to those areas of life which lack ontological substance. By lack of ontological substance I mean that which does not exist independent of man but which is created by man, and has nothing in reality with which to correspond as a test of "truth." I refer to the belief or pretense that the fact of law has the same ontological status as geology and the solar system, rather than being a matter of human social construction and, therefore, choice and power. The latter includes, for example, the rules that govern chess, football, and other athletic games, games of chance, and, yes, law, including the law of income taxation, the law comprising the rules of the road, the law of torts, and so on, arguably all of the common law and all of constitutional law.

A law-and-economics scholar of today is aware of the history of jurisprudence and of approaches to, or meta-theories of, law, especially analytical jurisprudence and legal realism. Among the central concerns of these meta-theories are the specific problems identified here: questions of language, reasoning, and the results and functions of reasoning; the legitimization of law as it performs its psychic balm and social control roles.

Deep questions exist as to what law is all about, questions that each scholar, and each member of society, more or less feels the need to understand. The juxtaposition of a recent case, *County of Wayne v. Hathcock*,[4] to the case which it overruled, *Poletown Neighborhood Council v. City of Detroit*,[5] provides the opportunity to raise these questions in a hopefully meaningful way, asking, among other things, what is constitutional law? I suggest the answer that there is no such thing as constitutional law in the ordinary sense and certain linguistic pretenses should be abandoned. At a certain level of abstraction, such is the argument of this chapter.[6]

Law and language

Among the problems encountered in the use of language in law, two in particular are evident in the juxtaposition of *Poletown* and *Hathcock*. One problem is the use of primitive terms. Primitive terms are words that are not—perhaps cannot be— given precise, if any, definition. The user relies on acquiescence to the propositions in which they are used arising from the practice of each reader attributing to the term the meaning he or she holds. Thus readers may concur with the proposition even though each reader understands and/or defines a key term differently. Acquiescence is achieved, in part, through silence as to (a) differences in definition, (b) changes in definition, for example, in government documents, and (c) the operation of selective perception, sentiment, and ideology. This problem applies to the use of "property" and "liberty" in constitutional and other decisions, and the use of the concept of the "rule of law" in such cases and in jurisprudential philosophy generally.[7]

The second problem is the use of declarative descriptive statements having no existential substance yet used for the purposes of social control and psychic balm. Both types of problem include lack of specificity, existential lack of substance, and intentional or unintentional ambiguity for certain purposes. These uses of language give effect to (i) national or societal myths, (ii) selective perception (a cause as well as a means), and (iii) the societal struggle for power over policy.

The two problems can be illustrated by a multifaceted example. In his biography of Herbert Butterfield, one of the leading intellectual historians of the twentieth century, C. T. McIntire discusses a particular theme running through several of Butterfield's books characterized as "patriotic history." The theme is neatly encapsulated in the sentence, "Liberty comes to the world from English traditions, not from French theories."[8] This simple sentence illustrates both problems. The word "liberty" is used without precise if any serious definition. The sentence, and its argument, is declarative, ostensibly intended to provide a description but, as McIntire puts it, without "the usual entanglements of qualifying phrases" often used by Butterfield in such comparisons.[9] The statement is intended to describe and invidiously compare the course of English history relative to that of France. It declares a position on the societal management or balancing of continuity with change. Contrary to the history suggested by the French Revolution, the history of England, as McIntire also quotes Butterfield, has not had "the uprooting of things that have been organic to the development of the country" but has followed "a natural course of development."[10] For some modern readers, the Butterfield position may appear to parallel Frederich A. von Hayek's theory of the superiority of non-deliberative over deliberative social decision making; if so, it has the same defects as Hayek's theory.[11] But Butterfield's position in particular suffers from the defect that it paints a misleading picture of English history. As McIntire writes, "Butterfield depicts a placid scene of steady growth in English history since 1688 where another historian might find instead the struggles of industrializing classes, the triumph of the middle classes, the impoverishment of the underclasses, the suppression of the Irish, and the imperialism of expansion overseas."[12] Here we have primitive terms—"organic," "natural"—conveying a potentially misleading impression, giving effect to national myths, and obfuscating the long struggle (one antedating 1688) for power over policy.[13] It ignores the changes in the meaning of property and of liberty that transpired in England during the preceding four centuries. It is also a descriptive statement useful by those persons endeavoring to influence the present and the future through a particular account of the past.

The utility of simple declarative, ostensibly descriptive historical propositions for the purpose of influencing history also illustrates the distinctions drawn by W. H. Hutt between "rational-thought," "custom-thought," and "power-thought." "Rational-thought" is objective and, especially, disinterested inquiry that can lead to the accumulation of undisputed knowledge in the social sciences (once, as Hutt stipulated, class-driven ideology has been removed). "Custom-thought" signifies modes of thinking that are infused with implicit premises and ideas derived from tradition and customary ways of doing and looking at things. "Power-thought" encompasses modes of thought and expression that are constructed to have intended effects on power, politics, and policy, through their service in psycho-political mobilization.[14] The Italian economist and sociologist, Vilfredo Pareto, had a wide-ranging analysis of social structures and forces that more or less paralleled Hutt's model of language and its use in the political mobilization of psychic states.[15]

In an essay[16] reviewing a book[17] which examines the common problems of Biblical and Constitutional interpretation, I argued that pretty much everything in theology and law, as well as the history of economic thought, is, *as an empirical fact*, a matter of interpretation. An earlier review essay was predicated upon the belief that economics and law are existential disciplines inasmuch as the "future is indeterminate because it is in part created through the very effort to comprehend and control it." It queried, "What, then, does the law-economics scholar do upon ascertaining [that] social awareness—including both economic study and the practice of law in all its ramifications—largely deals with symbols which, while socially functional, lack substance?"[18]

The argument of this chapter is that the two problems encountered in the use of language in law, the difficulties of constitutional interpretation, and the distinctions as to types of thought discussed earlier are evident in the juxtaposition of *Poletown* and *Hathcock*.[19] In these cases, the concepts embodied in words are selectively defined and selectively applied. These concepts are used in the process of defining and (re)making the polity and the economy as if words had independent meaning which judges are trying to achieve. The legal system, the law, and the economy are artifacts, both influencing and influenced by the concepts ensconced in words. On the one hand, texts have multiple possible readings; on the other, there is reification—the rendering absolute of some things and the foreclosing of others in what is in fact a process of being worked out. One cannot avoid the conclusion that legal history is often tautological with the interpreter's preferred policy position, so as to sustain the view supporting that policy; that is, the selective reading and treatment of precedents is a function of the interpreter's policy position.

The paramount issue concerns not the legal-economics scholar but the judge and his or her style of writing, that is, linguistic practice. Law does not deal with some given, absolute, transcendent reality; "the law" refers not to something of substance but to a process of social control that is socially constructed in a complex process of working things out. "The law" is a matter of interpretation of language that projects but masks the underlying, driving sentiment, preconceptions as to policy, and selective perception. The judge engaged in such projection either appreciates that it is the law he or she is helping to make, or feels that the legal substance already exists and is palpable, ready to be applied.

The takings clause: public use

The Fifth Amendment to the Constitution of the United States reads, in its final clause, "nor shall private property be taken for public use, without just compensation." Similar clauses are found in the state constitutions. The constitutional issues arising under this clause include the meaning of "private property," "public use," when government action constitutes a "taking," and what is "just compensation." Underlying the constitutional issues are deep philosophical issues, including the nature and substance of property, the nature of government, the relation of property to government, and who, within government, is to determine the operative answers to these issues. The core issue of many controversies and court decisions often turns on whether the property is to be treated as existing prior to government or as a result of government action. If property exists prior to government, then almost anything government does can be seen as a compensable taking of property. If property exists due to government, then almost anything government does can be seen as part of the process of working out what is property. The issue may well turn on—that is, be expressed as if it turned on— whether the relevant law is held to be that of eminent domain or that of the police power. Neither the law of eminent domain nor the law of the police power, however, is self-subsistent and self-defining. What the law is in any particular case is what the court says it is (or so I have been told by numerous law professors). The law does not impose itself, though the language of the court typically is one of finding and not making the law for the particular case. If law has no independent ontological substance, the law is what people—typically judges—make it out to be. The institutional and substantive diversity of law, both historically and geographically, underscores the foregoing considerations.

The Fifth Amendment of the Constitution, in providing that private property not "be taken for public use, without just compensation," seems to presume that private property can be taken, subject to just compensation, for public use, but only for public use. What about taking private property, even with just compensation, for a private use?

The police power of government is that power which permits its acting in support of the public health, safety, morals, and welfare. Police power actions do not constitute takings, inasmuch as, according to the theory of the police power, no one has a right to endanger the public health, safety, morals, and welfare. Regulation being the means of changing property rights as between parties with conflicting interests, regulation may likely subtract an economically significant opportunity from the opportunity set hitherto putatively held by one property owner in order to protect the opportunity set(s) of another(s); this is a matter of working out, under changing conditions, what are the relative rights of property, that is, working out what property "is." Also, the meanings and substantive content of "health," "safety," "morals," and "welfare" are themselves not given; they are elastic and have to be worked out. Much the same applies to "public," which can be narrowly or broadly defined, or defined according to one putative theory or another. Eminent domain actions enable government, against an unwilling or hold-out owner, to acquire land that the government needs, or says it needs, for roads, bridges, schools, and so on, the more general idea being that the cost of a project should be borne by all owners or taxpayers, not just one or a few. A broad reading of the police power to encompass all regulation would vastly limit eminent domain, and a broad reading of eminent domain would require extensive compensation be paid to owners and vastly limit the police power.[20] (The situation is further complicated when the conflicting parties are themselves property owners—though that is not presently relevant.)

The Fifth Amendment requirement of public use—extended to the States through judicial interpretation of the Fourteenth Amendment (but already contained in state constitutions)—is arguably one aspect of a larger subject, namely, public purpose—though, as we will see later, this latter term also has a narrower use. The typical state constitution requires that government taxing, spending or credit be undertaken only for a public purpose. When choices have to be made between competing interests, for example, in adjusting conflicting claims of property rights, the legislature and the courts presumably base their choices on some notion of public purpose. The relevant legal history of the United States since the period *c.*1820–30 has centered on whether public improvements, so-called, constitute public purpose. Initially often at issue were port and harbor facilities, canals, and similar infrastructure projects. Some cases have adhered to a narrow conception of public purpose; others, to a broad conception. That many of the activities coming under the rubric of public purpose were economic in nature is indicated not only by the just-identified projects but also by tax waivers, subsidies, and gift public investments by government to private firms in order to attract, remain, or expand in the area of the supportive government. Whether such expenditures constitute the public taking of tax money from taxpayers for delivery to a private enterprise(s) and thus not a public use but a private use is a matter of interpretation. Sometimes "use" and "purpose" are used interchangeably; at other times they are distinguished from each other.[21]

The central issue to whose ongoing resolution the courts in the two cases contribute is the nature and relation of property to government. This relation is typically deeply influenced by the mindset of modern Western society in which perceptions of individualism and limited government figure prominently. A famous example is the definition of property given by William Blackstone in his *Commentaries on the Laws of England.* Blackstone postulates the right of property as "that sole and despotic dominion which one man claims and exercises over the external things of the world, in total exclusion of the right of any other individual in the universe." One of the "absolute rights," says Blackstone, "inherent in every Englishman, is that of property: which consists in the free use, enjoyment, and disposal of all his acquisitions, without any control or diminution, save only by the laws of the land."[22] Notice the language: "that sole and despotic dominion," that "absolute right . . . without any control or diminution" but "save only by the laws of the land." The point at issue in every statute law or court decision by government is precisely the control over property, that is, the content and/or conditions of ownership allowed by the laws of the land. (Competition may diminish the economic significance and value of property. This did not just happen; a long history of conflict between claimants to protection of interests has generated the law of competition, a phenomenon largely neglected by economists—as is also the ubiquitous phenomenon of standardized contracts typically written by one party.) When the Opinion of the Court in *Hathcock* begins speaking of "the sacrosanct right of individuals to dominion over their private property,"[23] the objective analyst must appreciate that the content of that right is precisely the point at issue.

Poletown resulted from a project of the Detroit Economic Development Corporation to acquire, by condemnation if necessary, a large tract of land to be conveyed to General Motors Corporation—who first proposed the project—as a site for construction of an assembly plant. The plaintiffs, a neighborhood association and several individual residents, brought suit. The trial court held for the defendants and the plaintiff's claim of appeal, with bypass of the Court of Appeals, went to the Michigan Supreme Court for immediate consideration. The Court affirmed the decision of the trial court. The issue was, "Does the use of eminent domain in this case constitute a taking of private property for private use and, therefore, contravene Const. 19163, Art. 10, § 2?"[24] The section in question followed the construction of the Fifth Amendment by stipulating that the taking of property through eminent domain be for a public use. The Michigan Supreme Court answered the question in the negative, holding that the project was for a public use.

Hathcock involved an effort by Wayne County to acquire parcels of land for a business and technology park just south of a recently expanded Metro airport. The Circuit Court and the Court of Appeals held for the County. The Michigan Supreme Court, upon appeal, reversed the holding, on the ground that the proposed condemnation did not satisfy the constitutional requirement of a public use. The decision in *Hathcock* specifically overruled *Poletown* and did so retroactively. Whereas *Poletown* included two dissenting opinions (the dissenters disagreeing among themselves) *Hathcock* was unanimous, with partial dissents as to the grounds (and retroactivity) of the Court's decision but not to the decision itself.

The purpose of this chapter is to analyze the two decisions with a view to identifying the relevant obvious and not-so-obvious matters of interpretation and arguable misuse of language. Among the possibly not-so-obvious matters are judicial review and the concept of the rule of law.[25] Apropos of the symbolic nature of law, the analysis will turn to the lines of reasoning and the uses of language employed in explicating the decisions in these cases. One might have written "the nature and substance of the lines of reasoning." But at the level of abstraction pursued in this chapter, law and the concept of the rule of law have little substance; their nature is that of language and their substance is a matter largely of selective perception, sentiment, and ideology. As the title suggests, this is an essay on law, interpretation and decision, utilizing the neat juxtaposition of the holdings in these two cases dealing with public/private use under eminent domain. The reader is forewarned that the purpose here is not to take a position on which decision is the "correct" one. The purpose here is to analyze what is going on in these cases as contributions to the making of "law" as a contribution to a democratically and linguistically sounder mode of legal conversation. One view of what is going on was privately expressed to this author by an attorney attending a conference on the cases.[26] The attorney made his point by telling the story of three baseball umpires discussing balls and strikes. One umpire says that he calls pitches what they are, balls or strikes. The second umpire says that he calls pitches as he sees them. The third umpire says that pitches are nothing until he calls them either balls or strikes. A related view is that in the real world independent of man neither pitches nor balls, nor strikes exist.

Constitutional issues: eminent domain and the public use requirement

As expressed in the two decisions of the Michigan Supreme Court and as understood by directly or indirectly interested parties, the principal constitutional issue has to do with the public use requirement of eminent domain law. Here the questions concern, first, the linguistics and law of use versus purpose; and, second, the linguistics and law of public versus private. Also relevant is the constitutional issue of the relative roles of legislature and court in making public policy, the former explicitly and the latter implicitly, though no less effectively, while ostensibly "interpreting" the law of the constitution. In all of these and other respects, we shall find that legal/constitutional language is subject to multiple readings and applications; that no meta-criterion exists to serve as a conclusively dispositive independent test of which interpretation is, in some sense, "correct"; that the majority opinion largely amounts to a declarative assertion that one interpretation is correct; that it is this interpretation which, for the time being at least, constitutes "the law"; that nonetheless even the meaning of "the law" in this interpretation can be further specified in significantly different ways; and that all the foregoing multiplicity is due to selective perception, however driven.

Before considering the doctrinal and linguistic issues at the heart of this chapter, two matters should be briefly explored. The first concerns the legal history alluded to here. One leading textbook in economic history summarizes the relevant story pertaining to the nineteenth century thus:

> the states were active, as they had always been, in legislating to promote and regulate the economy. Every state undertook promotional efforts and granted privileges and immunities that aided special local interests. ... all states had some form of eminent-domain law that gave particular private firms the power to condemn and seize land or other property upon payment of compensation to private owners.[27]

The authors point out that private railroad corporations were commonly aided by granting them the power of eminent domain—going much further than the use of eminent domain in *Poletown* and *Hathcock*.[28] In addition, tax exemptions and other special privileges and subsidy arrangements were extended to a variety of private interests—practices continuing throughout the twentieth century. The authors also note two other modes of promotion: "Not least important were the generous incorporation laws adopted by numerous states" and "particular local interests often received special privileges." All of this was practice. Most of it was at one time or another controversial and subject to litigation, with, as indicated, varying results. When such practices were challenged before the US Supreme Court, the Court's decisions generally validated local practice on the pragmatic grounds of what was locally deemed (as the Court put it) "essential or material for the prosperity of the community."[29]

Harry N. Scheiber, one of the co-authors of the textbook just quoted, was the author of a classic article on the "[e]xpropriation of private property by government"[30] in part for the benefit of other private owners. Clearly, with sufficient frequency, entrepreneurs did not have "to acquire the property they needed for their undertakings through market transactions."[31] The Marxist might well urge that government did not exist merely in the pores of society; it served, then as now, to both abet the primitive accumulation of capital and to channel it in certain directions. Economic and legal historians who are not Marxist could appreciate Scheiber's effort "to identify the directions in which expropriation was purposefully used to allocate resources, to influence the structure of entrepreneurial opportunity, and even to provide effective subsidies for favored types of business enterprise, often at high cost to 'vested rights' in property" (p. 234). Legislatures and courts went their selective ways to protect, or give lip service to protection, of property; but they also went their selective ways to abet economic development as they understood it. Scheiber covers the ins and outs of these efforts. Pertinent to the conflict in *Poletown* and *Hathcock*, he summarized the early situation as follows:

> To validate a set of cost-reducing expediting doctrines, all in the name of great public works, owned and operated by the government, was one thing. But the most important single development in early nineteenth century eminent domain law probably was the wholesale transfer of these doctrines over to the private sector, in aid of incorporated companies on which legislatures devolved the power of eminent domain. That was something else again.[32]

Not only did the legislature facilitate the transfer, ostensibly in support of economic development, the courts did likewise:

> Once a state legislature decided to vest its eminent domain power in a private corporation, the courts would generally rule that this carried with it all the expediting doctrines originally conceived to support the sovereign exercise of governmental power by the state itself.[33]

Such was done for turnpike, bridge, canal, and railroad companies. It was also done for mill dams for millers, including among such privileges "the power to overflow neighboring lands in order to create a mill-pond or reservoir for water power," but also "manufacturing firms in quest of waterpower sites for purposes other than grinding grain."[34] In one case, for example, notwithstanding that the obvious goal of the privately owned firm was private profit, the court said,

> The ever varying condition of society is constantly presenting new objects of public importance and utility; and what shall be considered a public use or benefit, must depend somewhat on the situation and wants of the community for the time being.[35]

Some opponents objected to the use of eminent domain to privilege certain corporations and facilitate monopoly. Opponents also objected to what they perceived as the weakening of property rights. Scheiber reports that when the matter was brought to the US Supreme Court, the Court held that redress rested with the State legislatures and State courts.[36] Scheiber also reports that the expansion of public use that commenced in eminent-domain litigation flowed from there to the law of taxation and of nuisance.

It will not escape the reader that the companies benefiting from the delegation of eminent domain to private interests were arguably as important to economic development in their day as the automobile companies were in the twentieth century.

Scheiber concluded that

> The heyday of expropriation as an instrument of public policy designed to subsidize private enterprise can probably be dated as beginning in the 1870's and lasting until about 1910. ... No longer did judges or framers of state constitutions rely so much upon sophistries about "public use." Instead, they now merely paused to assert prescriptively that one private interest or another—mining, irrigation, lumbering or manufacturing—was so vitally necessary to the common weal as to be a public use by inference.[37]

Scheiber's term is "assert prescriptively." The term used here is "declarative." Courts rarely provide either the reasoning or, where relevant, the evidence underlying their declarative yet also prescriptive assertions and conclusions. The conclusions may rest on an ideology, on identification with and/or the influence of certain powerful interests, and/or some theory of economic development. Whatever the conflicting groups, as Scheiber puts it, "Neither interest group stood for an abstraction that can be termed 'vested rights'; rather, each wanted the upper hand in the rivalry to exploit common resources"; "doctrinal support for such elevation of 'private uses' to an exalted constitutional status" was given by some state constitutions and by court decisions: a "blanket declaration that 'an interest of great public benefit to the community' warranted expropriation for private use."[38] Into the late twentieth century "the interpenetration of private business interests and governmental programs justifying expropriation," wrote Scheiber in 1973, "continues to be a central problem of public policy."[39] Michigan Chief Justice Cooley summed up what Scheiber calls "the most pragmatic sort of validating doctrine," writing that if waterpower development "would largely conduce to the prosperity of the state," then expropriation of land at dam sites was constitutional.[40]

The relevant points are (1) widespread use of the eminent domain power to promote economic development, (2) including use of eminent domain for and, when delegated, by private interests, (3) even though such activism was frequently controversial, and (4) the record of court decisions is not homogeneous for or against. Such, at any rate, are the conclusions of Schieber and the present author. The conclusions, or, rather, arguments of the parties in *Poletown* and *Hathcock* differ significantly from each other and, to some extent, to those just presented.

The second matter can be identified for present purposes more quickly. The question is, what is "law" in discussions such as those found in *Poletown* and *Hathcock*, that is to say, in the typical court case? No singular, unequivocal, common answer is to be found. In the literature of jurisprudence broadly comprehended one finds assertions that the law in court decisions is to be found (1) in the decision itself (the holding), (2) the ratio decidendi of a case (the ground of a decision, the basis of the holding), (3) the operative precedential sequence (somehow interpreted), (4) the overriding principle or rule of which the former are evidence or manifestations, (5) the overarching rule or principle of which the former is a manifestation or evidence, (6) natural law, and (7) divine law. An alternative formulation distinguishes between (1) the law on paper, (2) the law in action, and (3) the exercise of enforcement, prosecutorial, and judicial discretion. In a world in which the question of the sources of law bears on the question of what is law, the sources of law (in part, too, a function of the definition of law) include, in no particular order: (1) custom, (2) morality, (3) equity, (4) public policy, (5) statutes, (6) force (the will of the sovereign, with sovereignty ultimately a matter of force), (7) past judicial decisions (precedents: that is, judicial authority, (8) opinions of experts (academic, and so on authorities), and (9) legal theory. We shall return to both matters in due course.

The constitutional issues center on the public use requirement of Eminent Domain in the Michigan Constitution of 1963, and therefore on the subsidiary issues of use versus purpose and of public versus private. These issues have to do with the meaning of constitutional provisions and past court language. They also have to do with the jurisprudential status of economic development as a goal of policy. All of these issues become focused on the use of eminent domain to substitute for the market insofar as it involves the transfer of property from one private owner(s) to another private owner(s). Eminent domain as a whole, of course, is a substitute for transfer through the market; transfer from one or more private owners to another private owner(s) is but a narrow part thereof.

Two characteristics of *Poletown* and *Hathcock* will be initially considered. The first is the multiplicity of legal meanings and distinctions that can be elicited during litigation and decision making. Such multiplicity is due to the elasticity of legal language. This includes the differential readings of constitutional and other phrases and terminology, of past cases and precedents, as well as of accepted authorities, especially differential understandings of when a case is a precedent and for what or what purpose. The elasticity and its derivative multiplicity are especially manifest in the specific issues of the two cases: (1) use versus purpose, (2) public versus private, (3) economic development as a policy goal, (4) relative benefits as between public and private entities, and (5) the basis on which meaning is to be reckoned. The second characteristic is the declarative nature of the holdings. Other characteristics will be considered in due course.

Use versus purpose

The fundamental general contemporary issue in takings law concerns the scope of the power of eminent domain in relation to the police power, notably if, and if so, when, regulatory action by government is to be treated as a taking subject to compensation, and thence the issue of the ontological status of property in relation to government.[41] In the cases discussed here, the operative twin issues are use versus purpose, and public versus private. Both concern the scope of permitted government action.

Article 10, § 2 of the 1963 Michigan Constitution states that "Private property shall not be taken for public use without just compensation therefore being first made and secured in a manner prescribed by law..." Like the US Constitution the Michigan Constitution assumes the existence of the institution of private property. The two constitutions do not go into detail in identifying the rights, exposures, immunities, and obligations, and so on that comprise the substance of what constitutes property.

They were written on the assumption that these are to be worked out through the legislative and judicial branches of government. What is precisely that substance is the point at issue in all relevant cases. The Michigan language of "not be taken for public use" is universally, or almost universally, taken to mean that government may not take private property for private use, though that is subject to legislatively and judicially created exceptions. But it arguably might be understood, under other circumstances, to be silent as to private use, recognizing that when private property interests clash, the legislature and the courts have an inexorable necessity to choose between them.[42]

Be that as it may, one of the issues in the two cases concerns the relative scope of "use" and "purpose." The courts in *Poletown* and in *Hathcock* disagree as to what the law is with regard to them, that is, their status for the law. Together the two courts provide multiple holdings and interpretations.

The Court in *Poletown* rejected the claim that a distinction must be made between "use" and "purpose." The court stated that

> the terms have been used interchangeably in Michigan statutes and decisions in an effort to describe the protean concept of public benefit. The term "public use" has not received a narrow or inelastic definition by the Court, and indeed changes with changing conditions of society. Indeed, this Court has stated that "[a] public use changes with changing conditions of society" and that "[the] right of the public to receive and enjoy the benefit of the use determines whether the use is public or private."[43]

To the contrary, Justice Ryan argued—afterward quoting from a 1870 decision by Justice Cooley—that

> Well over a century ago, a clear line of demarcation was drawn between the powers of eminent domain and taxation, setting the jurisprudence of the taking clause and, if you will, the "taxing clause" on separate, independent courses. What is "public" for one is not necessarily "public" for the other.[44]

Justice Ryan also argued that

[T]he term "public purposes," as employed to denote the objects for which taxes may be levied, has no relation to the urgency of the public need, or to the extent of the public benefit which is to follow.[45]

Strikingly, however, Justice Ryan wrote that "Justice Cooley construed the concept of public purpose (taxation) more *narrowly* than the concept of public use (eminent domain)."[46] Apropos of Justice Cooley's opinion in the widely quoted but variably interpreted Ryerson case, Justice Ryan wrote,

The language indicates that in 1877 the government was free to employ eminent domain more liberally than the taxing power. That, however, is more indicative of the restrictions upon the taxing power in the last half of the 19th Century than upon the breadth of eminent domain. Since then, however, as noted above, the taxing power has been significantly expanded. Moreover, the private corporations about which the *Ryerson* Court spoke were engaged in the establishment of instrumentalities of commerce. Such corporations, unlike General Motors in this case, fall within a firmly established and carefully defined exception to the general prohibition against the use of eminent domain for the specific benefit of private corporations. Today, therefore, when dealing with eminent domain unrelated to the avenues of commerce, it is reasonable, indeed necessary, to conclude that, for purposes of aiding private corporations, eminent domain is more restrictive than the power of taxation. In fact, the *Ryerson* Court *struck down* a statute authorizing condemnation of property for construction of waterpower mills to be privately owned and operated, calling such action a taking for private use. *Cf. Board of Health of Portage Twp v Van Hoesen*, 87 Mich 533; 49 NW 894 (1891), in which a statute authorizing condemnation by privately controlled corporations to establish and maintain rural cemeteries was held unconstitutional as authorizing a taking for private use.[47]

The present author, to repeat, is not interested here in the question of the desirability of the holdings in *Poletown* and in *Hathcock*. The foregoing is nonetheless extremely suggestive of what is going on. The following comments would not vary should the holdings in the two cases have been the opposite of what they in fact were.

Justice Ryan accepts as given the change in public purpose for taxation law. He affirms a general prohibition against the use of eminent domain for the specific benefit of private corporations. He holds to the instrumentalities-of commerce exception wrought by earlier courts. But he does not accept the majority's opinion in *Poletown*. If he had accepted it, he might have joined what he in fact felt was an expansion of public purpose for eminent domain law (no judgment is herein rendered whether that is ontologically an accurate description). What we have is the finessing of objections against and the construction of an intellectual fortress intended to protect his narrower view of public purpose for eminent domain law. It is an argument of this article, as will be developed more thoroughly later, that nothing transcendental and given, nothing objective and substantive—"the law"—is involved here or in any other decision. What *is* involved here are assertions of declarative/prescriptive holdings that obviously would have different results for "use" versus "purpose" should different assertions be made. In *Poletown* Justice Ryan was in the minority; in *Hathcock*, his alter egos were unanimous (except for dissents on subsidiary points). He (or they) could have made comparable but opposite statements if, for example, he believed differently; changing his wording, "As a general proposition then, in the realm of aid to private corporations, 'public purpose' (taxation) has been construed less restrictively than 'public use' (eminent domain)."[48]

The court in *Hathcock* basically adopted and reviewed Justice Ryan's account of public use from his *Poletown* dissent.[49]

The question of "use" versus "purpose," with one in eminent domain law and the other in tax (and spending) law, suggests the following. The City of Detroit (to whom the legislature, in part through the Economic Development Corporations Act, delegated the power of eminent domain) could have accomplished its goal with regard to the *Poletown* project in two ways; they are arguably economically equivalent. Public tax money was used to buy the land through eminent domain which was then turned over to General Motors. Public tax money could have been used to grant subsidies of one kind or another to General Motors (including the tax expenditure of relieving General Motors from tax obligations). The result is the logical proposition that two alternative policies to accomplish the same end—building the new automotive facility—are analytically economically equivalent, such that it is meaningless to distinguish "use" and "purpose." It need not have no meaning. The government (legislature, city council, and/or courts) could apply different—narrower and broader—tests to each alternative. It is this author's sense that, if such a discussion were held in a situation in which the use-versus-purpose issue was absent, the two terms would have been used interchangeably. But such is not part of the author's argument.

What is suggested is that in a policy-analytic discussion, instead of assertions of a declarative or prescriptive type, the parties could itemize the points for and against each position, without appealing to or invoking insubstantial and elastic terms as if they were given, transcendent, and oracular. Such is hinted at by Justice Ryan. In the case of eminent domain, the burden rests on the forced seller of the land as well as those whose taxes are used to purchase the land, the burden of the latter being more diffused, the burden of the former more concentrated. In the case of taxation the burden is, as just stated, more diffused, or, as Justice Ryan puts it, "manifestly less intrusive." But whether this comparison renders the distinction between use (eminent domain) and purpose (taxation) "fully justified," is quite another matter; policy analysis would have to proceed further.[50]

Anticipating discussion in both the following and a subsequent subsection, Justice Riley, who concurred in part and dissented in part, wrote in *Hathcock*,

> "Public use" is a legal term of art every bit as complex as "just compensation." It has reappeared as a positive limit on the state's power of eminent domain in Michigan's constitutions of 1850, 1908, and 1963, and each invocation of

"public use" has been followed by litigation over the precise contours of this language. Consequently, this Court has weighed in repeatedly on the meaning of this legal term of art. We can uncover the common understanding of Article 10, § 2 only by delving into this body of case law, and thereby determining the "common understanding" among those sophisticated in the law at the time of the Constitution's ratification.[51]

One does not have to be a logician to see the problem: The term in question has repeatedly been argued in the courts. The courts have held contradictory opinions on key issues. Yet one can seek, presumably successfully, the common understanding of those sophisticated in the law at the time of ratification. Without either affirming or rejecting this basis for reckoning meaning, it is highly doubtful whether, with all the multiple views as to what "the law" is, that experts, those sophisticated in the law, would agree; and that is only one historiographic problem.

The court in *Hathcock* agreed that the majority in *Poletown* inconsistently conflated use and purpose in eminent domain and taxation jurisprudence. "This inconsistency aside," the new Court said that "the majority opinion in *Poletown* is most notable for its radical and unabashed departure from the entirety of this Court's pre-1963 eminent domain jurisprudence."[52] The admonition was repeated two pages later, where the majority opinion in the earlier case is said to have had "disregard for constitutional limits on the exercise of the power of eminent domain and the license that opinion appeared to grant to state and local authorities" whereas the opinion in this later decision "simply applies fundamental constitutional principles and enforces the 'public use' requirement as that phrase was used at the time our 1963 Constitution was ratified."[53] As will be seen later, no such study of how the phrase was used was conducted. The Court only affirmed that test; it did not undertake the test. This is the legal equivalent of the economists' "let us assume . . ." It is pure declarative assertion.

Public versus private

Justice Ryan begins the conclusion of his dissent thus:

> The condemnation of land for CIP is not consistent with any of the three significant elements present in the instrumentality of commerce cases, which elements together justify, in a principled manner, the use of eminent domain for private corporations.

Consideration of the general prohibition against the taking of private property for private corporations with the principles justifying exception thereto reveals that a more general principle, consonant with prior decisions of this Court and entirely contrary to the holding of the majority here, is contained in the state taking clause: the right to own and occupy land will not be subordinated to private corporate interests unless the use of the land condemned by or for the corporation is invested with public attributes sufficient to fairly deem the corporate activity governmental. It is a principle consistently honored in the decisions of this Court, until now. In addition to its precedential weight, it reflects a common-sense balance struck in the Constitution for governance of the triangular relationship between government and two competing private parties.[54]

The conflict between use and purpose is one-half, as it were, of the central problem faced by the courts in these cases. The other half is the conflict between "public" and "private." Given the Constitutional language, and given that that language has been interpreted to negate private use, the further questions arise as to the distinction used by the court. The distinction is necessarily forced in any case. When it comes to private property, what is property (or what ownership permits) is a function of law—constitutional law, statute law, common law, and administrative law. Private property is a function of government, a public institution. Private is a function of public. And the reverse is true: Law is mightily influenced by the private sector, before its enactment, through its enactment, and after its enactment, through lobbying and litigation. Public is a function of private. The conflict between private and public in eminent domain matters must be understood within that ambit. Once so understood, the conflict is along relatively narrow lines—lines that, however, given the focus of each case, seem harder and more absolute than they are in total practice.

Thus the issue is whether the power of eminent domain in Michigan can only be used in situations in which either direct governmental use is to be made of the land or in which the private recipient will use it to serve the public. That issue devolves into the meaning of "serve the public." The Court in *Hathcock* speaks of General Motors using the property—acquired by the municipal development corporation through eminent domain—for its own purposes as a private use by a private company interested in maximizing its private profits. This statement has true and semi-true parts but its seeming portrayal of a profit maximizing private company as not serving the public thereby runs counter to part of the modern theory legitimizing business, that is, a company can earn profits only if it serves the public ("consumer sovereignty"). The Opinion in *Hathcock* quotes Justice Cooley to the effect that every lawful business in some manner advances the public interest.[55] Perhaps jurisprudence has come to a dual meaning of serving the public, one involving earning its profits from serving the public and the other serving the public as does a government agency, without regard to profits in the business sense.

One ground therefore of the *Hathcock* court's ruling is that the projects in both cases were rationalized through reasoning that focused on the benefits derived not from the public use basis of the land to which eminent domain was applied but from the benefits derived from the use to which the land was put by the beneficiary private interest. The land in question in both cases was not itself invested with sufficient public attributes for the private corporate activity to be deemed governmental. The land must itself yield benefits to the municipality in a clear and significant way and not in a speculative or marginal way; even if the beneficiary private owner receives benefit, it must be incidental, not the reason for the use of eminent domain. (This view may be juxtaposed to the practice of actually delegating the power of Eminent Domain corporations.) The opinion of the court in *Poletown* states that

> There is no dispute about the law. All agree that condemnation for a public use or purpose is permitted. All agree that condemnation for a private use or purpose is forbidden. Similarly, condemnation for a private use cannot be authorized whatever its incidental public benefit and condemnation for a public purpose cannot be forbidden whatever the incidental private gain. The heart of this dispute is whether the proposed condemnation is for the primary benefit of the public or the private user.[56]

This court found that the taking of the land yielded benefits to the community and that the benefits to General Motors, in comparison, were incidental. Its reasoning turned in part on its view of economic development as a policy goal and the relative benefits as between public and private entities; these considerations cannot be avoided here but will be primarily taken up later. The view of the *Poletown* majority, its main points reiterated several times, was that

> the Legislature has authorized municipalities to acquire property by condemnation in order to provide industrial and commercial sites and the means of transfer from the municipality to private users....

Plaintiffs-appellants do not challenge the declaration of the Legislature that programs to alleviate and prevent conditions of unemployment and to preserve and develop industry and commerce are essential public purposes. Nor do they challenge the proposition that legislation to accomplish this purpose falls within the constitutional grant of general legislative power to the Legislature in Const 1963, art. 4, § 51, which reads as follows:

> "The public health and general welfare of the people of the state are hereby declared to be matters of primary public concern. The legislature shall pass suitable laws for the protection and promotion of the public health."
> What plaintiffs-appellants do challenge is the constitutionality of using the power of eminent domain to condemn one person's property to convey it to another private person in order to bolster the economy. They argue that whatever incidental benefit may accrue to the public, assembling land to General Motors' specifications for conveyance to General Motors for its uncontrolled use in profit making is really a taking for private use and not a public use because General Motors is the primary beneficiary of the condemnation.
> The defendants-appellees contend, on the other hand, that the controlling public purpose in taking this land is to create an industrial site which will be used to alleviate and prevent conditions of unemployment and fiscal distress. The fact that it will be conveyed to and ultimately used by a private manufacturer does not defeat this predominant public purpose.
> . . .
> In the instant case the benefit to be received by the municipality invoking the power of eminent domain is a clear and significant one and is sufficient

to satisfy this Court that such a project was an intended and a legitimate object of the Legislature when it allowed municipalities to exercise condemnation powers even though a private party will also, ultimately, receive a benefit as an incident thereto.

The power of eminent domain is to be used in this instance primarily to accomplish the essential public purposes of alleviating unemployment and revitalizing the economic base of the community. The benefit to a private interest is merely incidental.

Our determination that this project falls within the public purpose, as stated by the Legislature, does not mean that every condemnation proposed by an economic development corporation will meet with similar acceptance simply because it may provide some jobs or add to the industrial or commercial base. If the public benefit was not so clear and significant, we would hesitate to sanction approval of such a project. The power of eminent domain is restricted to furthering public uses and purposes and is not to be exercised without substantial proof that the public is primarily to be benefited. Where, as here, the condemnation power is exercised in a way that benefits specific and identifiable private interests, a court inspects with heightened scrutiny the claim that the public interest is the predominant interest being advanced. Such public benefit cannot be speculative or marginal but must be clear and significant if it is to be within the legitimate purpose as stated by the Legislature. We hold this project is warranted on the basis that its significance for the people of Detroit and the state has been demonstrated.[57]

The Court in *Hathcock*, however, argued and concluded much like Justices Fitzgerald and Ryan in *Poletown*, often citing and applauding their dissents. Some examples of the Court's conclusions follow:

The public benefit arising from the Pinnacle Project is an epiphenomenon of the eventual property owners' collective attempts at profit maximization.[58]

. . .

Wayne County has not directed us to a single case, other than *Poletown*, holding that a vague economic benefit stemming from a private profit-maximizing enterprise is a "public use."[59]

Justice Weaver, in partial dissent, agreed:

This case is indeed a very straightforward example of government taking one person's property for the sole benefit of another.[60]

The instrumentalities-of-commerce exception to the public use requirement, and slum clearance

The Michigan Supreme Court has worked out, over the years, an instrumentalities-of-commerce exception to the requirement that eminent domain should not be used to transfer private property to other private entities. The significance of this having been done by the Court will be taken up later. For now it is important to see that where the Court found the instrumentalities justified by three tests or characteristics, the Court, as Justice Riley put it in *Hathcock*,[61] incorporated them "into the definition of 'public use', given the principles of constitutional interpretation articulated above" (these principles relate to the basis on which the meaning of constitutional provisions is to be reckoned). The three characteristics are (1) public necessity of the extreme sort otherwise impracticable, the necessity referring to private interests "whose very existence depends on the use of land that can be assembled only by the coordination central government alone is capable of achieving"; (2) when the private entity remains accountable to the public in its use of that property; and (3) the selection of the land to be condemned is itself based on public concern, that is, on facts of independent public significance derived from and applying to the underlying purpose of resorting to condemnation, as the basis of satisfying the public use requirement, and not the subsequent use of the condemned land.[62] Such has permitted land condemnation for such private parties as "highways, railroads, canals and other instrumentalities of commerce."[63] Presumably these parties' uses function for the benefit of the public welfare, and so on. The addition of slum clearing for "the benefit of the public health and welfare"[64] amounts to (1) the further introduction of the idea of the public's health, safety, welfare, and morals, at the heart of the police power, into eminent domain and (2) an exception quite different from the instrumentalities-of-commerce exception in regard to both the rationale of government activism and the content of the three tests.

Slum clearing seems a more plausible basis than the instrumentalities exception. The latter involves need, continued public oversight or regulation, or a connection between the condemned land and the condemnation, not the subsequent use of that land. The former does not have the tests and seems to resemble the economic development objective (see the next subsection). But this impressed neither Justice Ryan nor Justice Fitzgerald in their dissents in *Poletown*. Justice Fitzgerald wrote that

> Our approval of the use of eminent domain power in this case takes this state into a new realm of takings of private property; there is simply no precedent for this decision in Michigan cases.
>
> . . .
>
> The city places great reliance on a number of slum clearance cases . . . in which it has been held that the fact that the property taken is eventually transferred to private parties does not defeat a claim that the taking is for a public use. Despite the superficial similarity of these cases to the instant one based on the ultimate disposition of the property, these decisions do not justify the condemnation proposed by the city. The public purpose . . . [in] the slum clearance cases is the benefit to the public health and welfare that arises from the elimination of existing blight, even though the ultimate

disposition of the property will benefit private interests. As we said in *In re Slum Clearance, supra*:

"It seems to us that the public purpose of slum clearance is in any event the one *controlling* purpose of the condemnation. The jury were not asked to decide any necessity to condemn the parcels involved for any purpose of resale, but only for slum clearance.

. . .

[The] resale [abating part of the cost of clearance] is not a primary purpose and is incidental and ancillary to the primary and real purpose of clearance."[65]

However, in the present case the transfer of the property to General Motors after the condemnation cannot be considered incidental to the taking. It is only through the acquisition and use of the property by General Motors that the "public purpose" of promoting employment can be achieved. Thus, it is the economic benefits of the project that are incidental to the private use of the property.[66]

Justice Fitzgerald next argued that the cases that have found the objective of economic development to be a sufficient "public purpose" to support the expenditure of public funds in aid of industry are not applicable here.

The city also points to decisions that have found the objective of economic development to be a sufficient "public purpose" to support the expenditure of public funds in aid of industry. *Advisory Opinion on Constitutionality of 1975 PA 301*, 400 Mich 270, 254 NW2d 528 (1977); *City of Gaylord v Gaylord City Clerk*, 378 Mich 273, 144 NW2d 460 (1966). What constitutes a public purpose in a context of governmental taxing and spending power cannot be equated with the use of that term in connection with eminent domain powers. The potential risk of abuse in the use of eminent domain power is clear. Condemnation places the burden of aiding industry on the few, who are likely to have limited power to protect themselves from the excesses of legislative enthusiasm for the promotion of industry. The burden of taxation is distributed on the great majority of the population, leading to a more effective check on improvident use of public funds.[67]

Justice Ryan agrees, saying that

In fact, the only authorities that even arguably support or justify the use of eminent domain in this case are the "slum clearance" cases. *In re Slum Clearance*, 331 Mich 714; 50 NW2d 340 (1951); *General Development Corp v Detroit*, 322 Mich 495; 33 NW2d 919 (1948); *In re Jeffries Homes Housing Project*, 306 Mich 638; 11 NW2d 272 (1943); *In re Brewster Street Housing Site*, 291 Mich 313; 289 NW 493 (1939). These cases hold that slum clearance is a public use for which eminent domain may be employed. The distinction, however, between those cases and the one at hand is evident. The fact that the private developers in the cited cases, to whom the city sold the cleared land, eventually benefitted from the projects does not lend validity to the condemnation under consideration here. Justice Fitzgerald, in his dissenting opinion, correctly stresses the observation of the *In re Slum Clearance* Court that in those cases the object of eminent domain was found, and the decision to exercise the power was made, entirely apart from considerations relating to private corporations.[68]

Justice Ryan then also quotes from *In re Slum Clearance*:

> It seems to us that the public purpose of slum clearance is in any event the one *controlling* purpose of the condemnation. The jury were not asked to decide any necessity to condemn the parcels involved for any purpose of resale, but only for slum clearance.
>
> . . .
>
> In the instant case, the resale . . . is not a primary purpose and is incidental and ancillary to the primary and real purpose of clearance. Reconstruction was asked for in the petition and resale is necessary for such purpose, but the resale is not for the purpose of enabling the city nor any private owner to make a profit.[69]
>
> . . .
>
> It was not the purpose of this condemnation proceeding to acquire property for resale. It was to remove slums for reasons of the health, morals, safety and welfare of the whole community.[70]

Justice Ryan adds that

> Even if circumstances made redevelopment impossible, slum clearance would be justified on the ground that clearance *in and of itself* is a public use. That is, "[once] the area has been reclaimed and cleared, and is available for development, the public purpose has been fulfilled." *Ellis v Grand Rapids*, 257 F Supp 564, 571 (WD Mich, 1966). Simply put, the object of eminent domain when used in connection with slum clearance is not to convey land to a private corporation as it is in this case, but to erase blight, danger and disease.[71]

The *Hathcock* Court agreed:

> The primary example of a condemnation in this vein is found in *In re Slum Clearance*, a 1951 decision from this Court. In that case, we considered the constitutionality of Detroit's condemnation of blighted housing and its subsequent resale of those properties to private persons. The city's *controlling purpose* in condemning the properties was to remove unfit housing and thereby advance public health and safety; subsequent resale of the land cleared of blight was "incidental" to this goal. We concluded, therefore, that the condemnation was indeed a "public use," despite the fact that the condemned properties would inevitably be put to private use. *In re Slum Clearance* turned on the fact that the act of condemnation *itself*, rather than the use to which the

condemned land eventually would be put, was a public use. Thus, as Justice RYAN observed, the condemnation was a "public use" because the land was selected on the basis of "facts of independent public significance"—namely, the need to remedy urban blight for the sake of public health and safety.[72]

Finally, there is nothing about the *act* of condemning defendants' properties that serves the public good in this case. The only public benefits cited by plaintiff arise after the lands are acquired by the government and put to private use. Thus, the present case is quite unlike *Slum Clearance* because there are no facts of independent public significance (such as the need to promote health and safety) that might justify the condemnation of defendants' lands.[73]

Justice Weaver agreed, even in partial dissent:

> While this Court's evaluation of whether a condemnation is for a "public use" has traditionally involved consideration of the public's use or control over the use of the property condemned, this Court has considered the government purposes to be achieved by the condemnation. For example, this Court held the transportation of oil throughout the state to be a valid legislative purpose and upheld the constitutionality of a statute allowing the condemnation of lands for a pipeline to serve that purpose. There the Court concluded, however, that the pipeline was a "public use benefiting the people of the State of Michigan" and emphasized that the state retained control of the pipeline allowing it to ensure its devotion to public use. The Court has also excused the absence of ultimate public use or control over lands taken and then transferred to a private entity in cases involving the removal of slums and blight that endangered public health, morals, safety, and welfare. In these cases, the Court reasoned that "slum clearance is in any event the one *controlling* purpose of the condemnation."[74]

At the very least it is clear that the conflicting positions are supported by two coherent interpretations. But "coherence" is not enough.

Economic development as a policy goal

The *Poletown* Court said that "There is no dispute about the law"[75] and over the next several pages elaborated its view. The Hathcock Court argued differently.

The rationale of the program at the heart of *Poletown* was the provision of land for manufacturing use by a private corporation; that of *Hathcock* was the transformation of the use of land for a business and technology park. The rationale behind both was dual: economic development, notably jobs, and an enhanced tax base.

The state and its local subdivision were already heavily engaged in the promotion of economic development. The issue here is the use of eminent domain for that purpose. If one supposes that in every case most of the owners of the parcels sought for amalgamation will sell, that leaves the opposition comprised of those who are holding out for a higher price, those who do not want to change residences, and those philosophically opposed to the procedure. The supposition that most will sell is arguable but an empirical matter. In any event there likely will be the four groups, at least the first three. The fourth group is likely to be supported by so-called "libertarian" research and advocacy groups seeking, with a larger agenda, to re-form the law.

Litigation arises in cases of both controversial action and controversial inaction. In the field of the use of the power of eminent domain, most cases seem to involve objections to its use. A line of argument in other cases may be summed up in the statement, "if they want the property so badly, let them propose to acquire it by ordinary purchase or eminent domain." One suspects that another category exists, that of action without objection. In such a case the power of eminent domain is used and no one objects, so no suit is brought, or no one objects so strongly as to warrant bringing suit. In a sense, if government cannot "constitutionally" do X, it *can* continually do X until an objection is raised, litigated, and supported (i.e. found to come within the constitutional prohibition). One suspects that government attorneys would advise against doing X in that circumstance.

Hathcock in effect held that economic development per se—employment, production and tax base—did not constitute an additional exception to the public use requirement of eminent domain. The government could promote economic development in other ways but not through the use of eminent domain. Whereas the mindset of *Poletown* was that the Detroit economy was in such bad shape that it was necessary for the state and its subdivisions to do what it could to promote economic development. General Motors' proposal comported with that mindset. The mindset of *Hathcock* was different. Economic development was a good idea but insufficient grounds to carve out a new exception to the public use requirement and to place such a concentrated burden (even with compensation) on certain property owners. The *Hathcock* Court rejected the idea—and the holding in *Poletown*—that "land can be taken by the government and transferred to a private entity upon the mere showing that the economy will generally benefit from the condemnation"; "even though the park might benefit the region's economy," it violates, the Court held, the "'public use' limitation" of the constitution.[76] The *Hathcock* Court found that the Court in *Poletown* "concluded for the first time in the history of our eminent domain jurisprudence, that a generalized economic benefit was sufficient under art. 10, § 2 to justify the transfer of condemned property to a private entity."[77] Justice Weaver, concurring in part and dissenting in part, agreed with the majority rejecting *"Poletown's* holding that land can be taken by the government and transferred to a private entity upon the economy will generally benefit from the condemnation."[78]

Poletown in effect expanded the reach of the instrumentalities of commerce exception to the public use requirement of eminent domain and went beyond slum clearing as well. The Court held, as we saw earlier, that

> In the instant case the benefit to be received by the municipality invoking the power of eminent domain is a clear and significant one and is sufficient to satisfy this Court that such a project was an intended and a legitimate object

of the Legislature when it allowed municipalities to exercise condemnation powers even though a private party will also, ultimately, receive a benefit as an incident thereto.[79]

The power of eminent domain is to be used in this instance primarily to accomplish the essential public purposes of alleviating unemployment and revitalizing the economic base of the community. The benefit to a private interest is merely incidental.[80]

Our determination that this project falls within the public purpose, as stated by the Legislature, does not mean that every condemnation proposed by an economic development corporation will meet with similar acceptance simply because it may provide some jobs or add to the industrial or commercial base. If the public benefit was not so clear and significant, we would hesitate to sanction approval of such a project. The power of eminent domain is restricted to furthering public uses and purposes and is not to be exercised without substantial proof that the public is primarily to be benefited. Where, as here, the condemnation power is exercised in a way that benefits specific and identifiable private interests, a court inspects with heightened scrutiny the claim that the public interest is the predominant interest being advanced. Such public benefit cannot be speculative or marginal but must be clear and significant if it is to be within the legitimate purpose as stated by the Legislature. We hold this project is warranted on the basis that its significance for the people of Detroit and the state has been demonstrated.[81]

Justice Fitzgerald's dissent in *Poletown* stated a different conclusion:

> Our approval of the use of eminent domain power in this case takes this state into a new realm of takings of private property; there is simply no precedent for this decision in previous Michigan cases. There were several early cases in which there was an attempt to transfer property from one private owner to another through the condemnation power pursuant to express statutory authority. *Board of Health v Van Hoesen*, 87 Mich 533; 49 NW 894 (1891); *Ryerson v Brown*, 35 Mich 333 (1877). In each case, the proposed taking was held impermissible.[82]

Fitzgerald considered that

> in the present case the transfer of the property to General Motors after the condemnation cannot be considered incidental to the taking. It is only through the acquisition and use of the property by General Motors that the "public purpose" of promoting employment can be achieved. Thus, it is the economic benefits of the project that are incidental to the private use of the property.[83]

Not only are the economic benefits of the project incidental to General Motors' private use of the land, the scope of public use represented by economic development through eminent domain is beyond what the courts have hitherto approved. Justice Fitzgerald thus wrote that

> Despite the limited value of decisions in other states, several points can be made. First, while it is difficult and perhaps futile to categorize individual states as utilizing a "broad" or "narrow" interpretation of "public use" for condemnation purposes, Michigan law seems most consistent with that of states that give a more limited construction to the term. While our decisions have sometimes used the phrase "public purpose" (a phrase often associated with a broad interpretation), the result of our decisions has been to limit the eminent domain power to situations in which direct governmental use is to be made of the land or in which the private recipient will use it to serve the public. The slum clearance cases are really the only significant departure from these principles, and, as noted above, those decisions have been sustained only because of the conclusion that the clearing of a blighted area is a public use. In this respect, the scope of "public use" in Michigan is quite similar to that in states that have rejected development projects on the theory that they would improve general economic conditions. *City of Owensboro v McCormick*, 581 SW2d 3 (Ky, 1979); *Karesh v City Council of the City of Charleston*, 271 SC 339; 247 SE2d 342 (1978). Certainly, we have never sustained the use of eminent domain power solely because of the economic benefits of development as have cases that allowed condemnation in similar circumstances. *Prince George's County v Collington Crossroads, Inc*, 275 Md 171, 190–191; 339 A2d 278, 288 (1975); *City of Minneapolis v Wurtele*, 291 NW2d 386, 390 (Minn, 1980).[84]

Three ironies arise from the foregoing. The first irony juxtaposes the overall role of government in our economic system to the *Hathcock* decision. Government at all levels has, for two centuries, pursued economic development and has done so in two respects. Government has facilitated and overseen the general transformation of a rural agrarian economy to an urban industrial economy. Government has promoted specific lines of economic development in numerous ways. Yet *Hathcock* rejects economic development with regard to the use of eminent domain on the foregoing grounds. The facts of government promotion of economic development do not require that every possible use of government power be deployed for that purpose. Nonetheless, it is both striking and ironic that within a governing system in which economic development has been the principal objective of government policy, the court so strongly rejects the objective. One suspects that the motivation of the court is to strengthen the absolutist approach to private property.

The second irony concerns the relation of government to property and is derivative of the first irony. So far from only protecting preexisting property, government must choose between competing interests as to which it will protect as property and which it will not. Property is relative to government in this respect. Property, whose economic significance, including price, is also a function of market forces, is also relative to competition. The function of law here is, in part, to determine which interests will be protected from what other actions by market actors and by government itself. The irony here is that the absolutist language of *Hathcock* tends to obfuscate the utter relativism of property rights.

The third irony arises when one recalls the practice of delegating the power of eminent domain to private companies, pretty much without restriction.

Relative benefits as between public and private entities

The concluding section of Justice Fitzgerald's dissent in *Poletown* begins thus:

> The majority relies on the principle that the concept of public use is an evolving one; however, I cannot believe that this evolution has eroded our historic protection against the taking of private property for private use to the degree sanctioned by this Court's decision today. The decision that the prospect of increased employment, tax revenue, and general economic stimulation makes a taking of private property for transfer to another private party sufficiently "public" to authorize the use of the power of eminent domain means that there is virtually no limit to the use of condemnation to aid private businesses. Any business enterprise produces benefits to society at large. Now that we have authorized local legislative bodies to decide that a different commercial or industrial use of property will produce greater public benefits than its present use, no homeowner's, merchant's or manufacturer's property, however productive or valuable to its owner, is immune from condemnation for the benefit of other private interests that will put it to a "higher" use.[85]

Poletown held that the condemnation of the land so involved must yield the public a clear and significant benefit that is an intended and legitimate objective of the legislature, even though a private party will ultimately receive a benefit that is incidental to the objective. It is the public that is primarily to be benefited; private benefit must be incidental; and the purpose must be to further public uses and purposes.

The dissenters in *Poletown* and the Court in *Hathcock* saw matters differently. The use of the land condemned must be invested with public attributes sufficient for the corporate activity to be deemed governmental; that is, the municipality's benefit must be clear and significant, and neither speculative nor marginal, even though a private party will also ultimately receive a significant benefit as an incident; the public benefit must derive from the land condemned and not the purposes to which the private beneficiary puts the land. The beneficiary, the chief and the intended beneficiary, must be the public. The property that is condemned must be for a governmental purpose rather than that of the private user. The private user should be incidental to the pursuit of a government purpose. The motivation behind the use of eminent domain that results in the transfer of the agglomerated property to a private user(s) should emanate from the government, not from the private beneficiary-user. The selection of the land must be by the government, and not by the private beneficiary; and so on. Their findings were, however, that in *Poletown* the eminent domain process was initiated not by a public agency but by General Motors, who "solicited the city for its aid in locating a site."[86]

Justice Ryan's dissent in *Poletown* devotes considerable space to the relations between the City of Detroit and General Motors. One reads that "in 1980 General Motors made its first overture to the City of Detroit about finding a suitable plant site in the city."[87] ". . . . it was to a city with its economic back to the wall that General Motors presented its highly detailed 'proposal'. . . ."[88] "In a most impressive demonstration of governmental efficiency, the City of Detroit set about its task of meeting General Motors' specifications."[89] "Behind the frenzy of official activity was the unmistakable guiding and sustaining, indeed controlling, hand of the General Motors Corporation."[90] Justice Ryan includes in its entirety a letter from Thomas A. Murphy, Chairman of the Board of Directors of General Motors, to Mayor Coleman A. Young as clearly demonstrating "the control being exercised over the condemnation project by General Motors."[91] On the basis of that letter and a number of other materials, Justice Ryan concludes that, "The evidence then is that what General Motors wanted, General Motors got."[92] Justice Ryan also wrote that "What is reported here is not meant to denigrate either the role or the good faith of General Motors Corporation. ... The point here is not to criticize General Motors, but to relate accurately the facts which attended the city's decision to condemn private property to enable General Motors to build a new plant in Detroit ... General Motors is not the villain of the piece."[93] Even the judiciary was implicated: "The judiciary, cognizant of General Motors' May 1 deadline for the city's taking title to all of the property, moved at flank speed,"[94] referring to the circuit court and to the Supreme court, the latter in regard to its favorable response to an application for leave to appeal prior to the decision of the Court of Appeals. Such description seems to have further induced Justice Ryan's sense that the chief beneficiary was General Motors.

The *Poletown* Court considered General Motors' proposal beneficial to the goals of economic development, namely, jobs and tax base. The *Hathcock* Court considered General Motors' participation in the project indicative of the magnitude of the benefits accruing to it in comparison to the benefits of economic constituting public use. Both factors entered into the position of the dissenters in Poletown and to the *Hathcock* Court: the lower status of economic development as public use and the non-incidental magnitude of benefits accruing to General Motors.

The Court's Opinion in *Hathcock* stated,

> In fact, defendants do not dispute that the proposed condemnations would benefit the public. Instead, ... defendants argue that the benefits that private parties will receive through the Pinnacle Project outweigh any benefits that the general public is likely to receive and, therefore, that plaintiff has failed to establish a "public use or benefit."[95]

The Opinion argued not only the relative magnitudes of the benefits to the public and to private parties; it also quoted Justice Ryan in *Poletown* affirming that the land "will be devoted to the *use* of the public, *independent of the will of the corporation taking it.*"

As a general rule, when the object of eminent domain is to take land for ultimate conveyance to a private corporation to use as it sees fit, the state constitution will forbid it as a taking for private use.

"Land cannot be taken, under the exercise of the power of eminent domain, unless, after it is taken, it will be devoted to the *use* of the public, *independent of the will of the corporation taking it.*" *Berrien Springs Water-Power Co v Berrien Circuit Judge*, 133 Mich 48, 53, 94 NW 379 (1903).

Accordingly, land may not be condemned for private corporations engaged in the business of water-power mills, *Ryerson v Brown*, 35 Mich 333 (1877); cemeteries, *Board of Health v Van Hoesen*, 87 Mich 533, 49 NW 894 (1891); or general retail, *Shizas v Detroit*, 333 Mich 44, 52 NW2d 589 (1952). In this case, land has been condemned solely for a private corporation engaged in the business of manufacturing automobiles.[96]

The Opinion brought to bear slum clearance cases in which "The city's *controlling purpose* was indeed a 'public use', despite the fact that the condemned properties would inevitably be put to private use. *In re Slum Clearance* turned on the fact that the act of condemnation *itself*, rather than the use to which the condemned land eventually would be put, was a public use."[97] Justice Ryan was again quoted: "condemnation was a 'public use' because the land was selected on the basis of 'facts of independent public significance'—namely, the need to remedy urban blight for the sake of public health and safety."[98]

The heart of the dispute was still "whether the proposed condemnation is for the primary benefit of the public or the private user."[99] The crux of the difference between the two courts is that the *Poletown* Court did consider economic development a public purpose with such strength that any consideration likely could not overwhelm it, whereas the *Hathcock* Court did not consider economic such an overwhelming public purpose, especially when the municipal action derived not from its own initiative but from the planning of a private corporation, when the primary benefit (it could be said) accrued to the private beneficiary, and the condemnation related not to the land itself but to the use to which the land was put. General Motors' initiative trumped economic development as a public use making General Motors the chief beneficiary; hence the condemnation transferred property from one private owner(s) to another. "The decision that the prospect of increased employment, tax revenue, and general economic stimulation makes a taking of private property for transfer to another private party sufficiently 'public' to authorize the use of the power of eminent domain means that there is virtually no limit to the use of condemnation to aid private businesses."[100]

The foregoing is clearly and principally a matter of opinion. At stake is the value to the public of the project for which land is being condemned in juxtaposition to its value to the private beneficiary interest. Neither court attempts any study of the relative magnitudes, say, of what must be assumed about each to render one larger than the other. Both courts simply declare one larger than the other based on their selective perception, sentiment, and ideology.

Two considerations further help to place the initiation question in perspective. First, the facts are that municipalities are interested in economic development (community prosperity and contentment, and rising tax base) and that big corporations have an ongoing planning activity. There apparently is no question but that General Motors initiated and ultimately controlled the Poletown project from its beginning. It is likely also true that given the place of General Motors in the Detroit metropolitan economy, the public and private aspects of their relationship involve a continuous and complex process of interaction. It is not necessarily the case that the governmental unit is the more powerful of the two or the more aggressive in its initiative; but the governmental unit is surely the object of control and use by the private corporation; and the two help form a local legal-economic nexus.[101] The second consideration concerns the argument that the condemnation must relate to a public benefit flowing from the land to be taken and independent of the use to which it will be put. This conflicts with land valuation in a market economy. Creation of the internal combustion engine made oil useful and valuable, and the land under which it was found desirable and valuable. Earlier the oil was relatively useless and worthless, and even a detriment to any use of the land. Oil land was part of nature but not a natural *resource* until the demand for gasoline developed due to the automobile. Valuation of land therefore is a function of the use to which the land will be put. Just compensation in the context of eminent domain generally does not permit the past owner to capture the value from the future use of the land by the government or by the private entity to which it is transferred after being taken.

Basis on which meaning is to be reckoned

Another basis of contention derived from the primary objective in interpreting a constitutional provision is to determine the provision's original meaning.[102] But how is such meaning to be reckoned? Several different answers are offered in the *Hathcock* decision, typically in the context of "public use" and among those in agreement on the main issue. The answers include the following.

1   That which was intended by the framers of the Constitution of 1963 (paraphrasing Justice Cooley and Justice Weaver). This basis is the original intent of the framers.[103]
2   That which reasonable minds, the great mass of the people themselves, would give it. Since the Constitution does not derive its force from the convention which framed it, but from the people who ratified it, the intent to be arrived at is that of the people, in the sense most obvious to the common understanding, the Constitution being ratified in the belief that that was the sense designed to be conveyed (paraphrasing Justice Cooley and a 1971 case). This basis is the common understanding at the time of ratification.[104]
3   That where the constitution employs technical or legal terms of art, these words are to be construed in their technical, legal sense, a sense that requires understanding of their history. Some terms of art are so familiar to the people that it is not necessary to employ more popular language to designate it.

The basis or sense is the sense popularly understood, since that is the sense fixed upon the words in legal and constitutional history. This basis is the popularly understood term of art.[105]

4   That where the term of art has a meaning much controlled by necessity and somewhat different from that which it bears generally, and not commonly understood by the people, learned and unlearned, who ratified the constitution, but who understood that it had a technical meaning within the law, the term must be read as a technical term in light of its legal and constitutional history (paraphrasing Justice Cooley and Justice Ryan). The basis is the technical term of art.[106]

5   That which was the common understanding among those sophisticated or versed in the law at the time of the Constitution's ratification. This basis is that of those sophisticated in the law at the 1963 Constitution's ratification,[107] when "no one sophisticated in the law at the 1963 Constitution's ratification would have understood 'public use' to permit condemnation of defendants' properties for the construction of a business and technology park owned by private entities"[108] and the use of eminent domain therefore is unconstitutional. Justice Weaver, however, dissented from Hathcock's majority which held for the common understanding of those " 'sophisticated' or 'versed in the law' at the time of the constitution's ratification." "Until the majority's decision in this case, this Court has never asserted that the term 'public' use is a term of such 'enormous complexity', that the people who ratified the Constitution would be unable to grasp its meaning."[109]

Where does this situation leave us, remembering that the objective of the exercise is intended to ascertain the law of the Constitution, as if it had a transcendental meaning? The situation leaves us with several problems, problems which have answers, but typically plural ones (not examined here to avoid infinite regress).

1   Why be preoccupied with the "original meaning," whatever the basis chosen? Why be tied to either the framers' meaning or any other?

2   What significance arises from the variety of meanings held *among* (1) framers, (2) ratifiers, and (3) those versed and sophisticated in the law?

3   Given the multiplicity of bases, how does one determine whether a particular wording or term comes within the basis chosen?

4   What significance arises from the variety of meanings found in past Michigan Supreme Court and other decisions—as to both eminent domain and areas of law confronted with changing technology and so on?

5   What significance is to be attached to Justice Cooley's opinions and textbook when he can be, and has been, cited in support by more than one side on several key issues?

6   How does one go about determining any of this? Is it possible to research, on every constitutional term, what the relevant reference group had in mind or understood?

Apropos of question 1, it is only by attributing a privileged position to some understanding of original meaning or original intent (see later) that one can hold that "the people's limit on the exercise of eminent domain [through the public use limitation] might be eroded."[110] What happens when the people have changed their opinion? Which basis etc. should be read into the term "public use"?

Apropos of question 3, one finds in *Hathcock* that whereas the majority indicated that it was interpreting "public use" as it would have been understood by those sophisticated or versed in the law at the time of the 1963 Constitution's ratification, Justice Weaver preferred the basis of the common understanding of those who adopted, that is, ratified, the Constitution, which she considered the long-established method of constitutional interpretation.[111] She also complained that a statement by Justice Cooley has been cited "out of context."[112] The issues here are whether a term such as "public use" is a popularly understood or a technical term of art and the significance when they differ. Justice Weaver then announced her view that the majority had earlier "launched its unprecedented rule of constitutional interpretation," namely

> [I]f a constitutional phrase is a technical legal term or a phrase of art in the law, the phrase will be given the meaning that those sophisticated in the law understood at the time of the enactment unless it is clear from the constitutional language that some other meaning was intended.[113]

It may well be that this rule was believed to have been practiced; indeed, it arguably was the rule practiced. Be that as it may, and no answer is offered here, Justice Weaver's position, like all the others, indicates the multiplicity of positions taken and the ambiguity of the relevant "law." Justice Weaver subsequently noted that Justice Cooley[114] concluded that "[n]o satisfactory definition of the term 'public use' has ever been achieved by the courts."[115] She speculates that Justice Cooley preferred the common understanding of the ratifiers, rather than those sophisticated in the law, for the purpose of ensuring restraint by courts in substituting a different meaning of a word to suit its own policy preferences.[116] Be that too as it may, Justice Cooley's conclusion still applies.

Justice Weaver dissents from the majority Opinion's emphasis on the meaning held by those versed and sophisticated in the law. She is most emphatic, calling that view "elitist":

> I dissent from the majority's holding that "public use" must be interpreted as it would have been by those "sophisticated" or "versed in the law" at the time of the 1963 Constitution's ratification and from their application of that holding to the facts of this case. Unlike the majority, I would employ the long-established method of constitutional interpretation that restrains judges by requiring them to ascertain the common understanding of the people who adopted the constitution. The majority's focus on the understanding of those "sophisticated in the law" is elitist; it perverts the primary rule of constitutional interpretation—that constitutions must be interpreted as the people,

learned and unlearned, would commonly understand them. It invites the erosion of constitutional protections intended by the Michigan voters who ratified the 1963 Constitution. The majority's approach ignores the words of Michigan's respected jurist, Justice THOMAS M. COOLEY, who warned against the tendency to force from the Constitution, by "interested subtlety and ingenious refinement," meaning that was never intended by the people who adopted it.[117]

The majority misuses *Peterman* to try to support the majority's elitist holding that art 10, § 2 must be interpreted as it would have been by person's "sophisticated in the law." Read in context above, *Peterman* squarely acknowledged that art 10, § 2 has acquired a well-understood meaning, which the people must be supposed to have had in view. That "public use" might be called a technical term or term of art does not remove it from the understanding of every person. The majority's perversion of the rule of common understanding is more than merely semantic. The majority's approach invites "sophisticated" refinement of the people's "right to govern" themselves through their popular vote. It allows the "sophisticated and learned in the law" to, intentionally or not, strip constitutional provisions of their context and manipulate and distort their meaning. See, e.g., *Peterman, supra* at 185, 521 N.W.2d 499.[118]

I dissent from the majority's reliance on its recently created and elitist rule of constitutional interpretation that gives constitutional terms the meaning that those "versed" and "sophisticated in the law" would have given it at the time of the Constitution's ratification.[119]

Apropos of question 6 (to maintain continuity of discussion), Justice Weaver provides no answer when she defends a 1994 decision for having "acknowledged that art. 10, § 2 has acquired a well-understood meaning." If the conflict between the *Poletown* and *Hathcock* decisions provides any insight, it is that, as Cooley concluded, no "well-understood" meaning of "public use" exists. "That 'public use' might be called a technical term or term of art does not remove it from the understanding of every person," according to Justice Weaver.[120] The problem is that ordinary people are likely no different from those sophisticated in the law (which presumably Supreme Court justices are), and they quite obviously disagree. In any event, any evidence pertaining to any earlier group of any size (e.g. the voters who ratified the 1963 Constitution) will be ad hoc and incomplete. The historiographic problems are enormous. And, as a solution, what "must be supposed" to have been meant is a matter of selective perception as well as wishful thinking. Its role will be taken up shortly.

Justice Weaver again refers to a "legal and constitutional term . . . so embedded in our constitutional law and history and so familiar as to be commonly understood."[121] She rejects any suggestion that "the people's common understanding" is "fictionalized."[122] One wonders how this can be otherwise given the absence of research on the subject, or, in light of all of the preceding, how she can say, that "the majority opinion in *Poletown* is most notable for its radical and unabashed departure from the entirety of this Court's pre-1963 eminent domain jurisprudence."[123]

Moreover, she assumes a continuity in eminent domain jurisprudence from pre-1963 to post-1963. What if a change had taken place? The law, after all, does change; presumably public understanding of the law does also. (There is a potential problem of circular reasoning: determine the meaning of the law by (e.g.) public understanding, and determine public understanding by supposing what they must have meant.) Justice Weaver cites the term "appeal tried de novo" as one "that had no meaning in the common vocabulary." She then says, of a decision in which that matter arose, "The Court noted that scholars disagreed and constitutional convention delegates expressed confusion regarding the term's meaning," words that could readily apply to every major term in the Fifth Amendment and State Constitution's taking clause. She quotes the Court in that case to the effect that one can consult the Constitutional Convention's Address to the people "for its explanation of an ambiguous term" and also "survey contemporaneous judicial decision and legal commentaries for evidence of a consensus within the legal community regarding the meaning of a term."[124] In the present context, two questions arise: First, what if a change in law has taken or is taking place? One would not expect consensus. Second, more generally, such recourse is wishful thinking (used to finesse the problem) because of the elasticity of meaning of all terms and the multiplicity of interpretations found in case decisions and in scholarly writings.

Returning for the moment to the question of *fiction* raised by Justice Weaver in regard to public understanding, she also raises it in connection to the private corporation. As is well understood, the corporation is legally a fictitious person.[125] Apropos of the present issues, she writes, "Whether or not one subscribes to the fiction that, in the instrumentality of commerce cases, the private corporation is merely a public agent...."[126] It is to be noticed that the idea of the corporation, all corporations, performing a public function was originally one of the justifications for incorporation. That justification, and hence its contribution to meaning, has changed; corporations have become willy nilly a major "independent" source of power in society.

"Pain and suffering"

Contemporary debate over tort law reform centers in part on payments to victims for "pain and suffering" that are, according to critics of status quo law, exceedingly high and very harsh in their effects. One effect particularly adverse to potential patients is the reduction in the number of specialists, in response to significant increases in their malpractice insurance.

Vilfredo Pareto, whose ideas were briefly examined earlier, is also the creator of the theory of the circulation of the elite. He argued that society is governed by a ruling class, that the choice between political parties, or otherwise, tends to be between different segments of the ruling class, and that whoever rules, they rule by some combination of force and fraud. By fraud he meant the practice of rulers coming forth with grandiose propositions by which they induce loyalty and quietude. The conflict over tort law reform tends to be between the medical institutions that hire physicians, the insurance companies, the trial lawyers specializing in tort litigation, and the physicians—with potential spillover effects on patients, their families, and their employers. Hence a conflict largely among the elite. The role of fraud is to be found operative in the arguments used to manipulate and mobilize political psychology.

That the economic significance of all private property is subject to, and at the mercy of, the market and is thus problematic, is arguably infinitely more important than the issues raised in *Poletown* and *Hathcock*. While under eminent domain the actual ownership of property is at stake, that is the nature of eminent domain, and afterward at least the owner, however involuntarily, has received just compensation in the form of market price. The threat (and concomitant pain and suffering) of losing one's property only to see it in the hands of another private party on the better-use rationale, is a narrow slice of the probabilistic economic significance of private property. Moreover, the court's solicitude is itself limited. The Court's opinion in *Hathcock* includes the following:

> To justify the exercise of eminent domain solely on the basis of the fact that the use of that property by a private entity seeking its own profit might contribute to the economy's health is to render impotent our constitutional limitations on the government's power of eminent domain. *Poletown*'s "economic benefit" rationale would validate practically *any* exercise of the power of eminent domain on behalf of a private entity. After all, if one's ownership of private property is forever subject to the government's determination that another private party would put one's land to better use, then the ownership of real property is perpetually threatened by the expansion plans of any large discount retailer, "megastore," or the like. Indeed, it is for precisely this reason that this Court has approved the transfer of condemned property to private entities only when certain other conditions—those identified in our pre-1963 eminent domain jurisprudence in Justice RYAN's *Poletown* dissent—are present.[127]

The very nature of eminent domain creates a threat. One can only conclude that, first, the function of eminent domain law is to enable the condemnation while assuring the private owner of land so taken that he or she has had their day in court; and, second, the function of the conservative reconstruction of eminent domain law is to restrict eminent domain while enabling economic development—at least certain modes of development. Both functions seek to minimize pain and suffering.

The problem of the concentration of power

General Motors is at the heart of *Poletown*; while not a party to the case, it is nonetheless omnipresent. In a world of giants and pygmies, General Motors is the giant whose immense presence is manifest in several ways. Justice Ryan says the following of GM:

> Behind the frenzy of official activity was the unmistakable guiding and sustaining, indeed controlling, hand of the General Motors Corporation.[128]
> . . .

The evidence then is that what General Motors wanted, General Motors got. The corporation conceived the project, determined the cost, allocated the financial burdens, selected the site, established the mode of financing, imposed specific deadlines for clearance of the property and taking title, and even demanded 12 years of tax concessions.[129]

In a footnote at this point, Justice Ryan, apparently unwilling to challenge its power or reputation, absolves General Motors from responsibility:

> What is reported here is not meant to denigrate either the role or the good faith of General Motors Corporation. It is a private, profit-making enterprise. Its managers are answerable to a demanding board of directors who, in turn, have a fiduciary obligation to the corporation's shareholders. It is struggling to compete worldwide in a depressed economy. It is a corporation having a history, especially in recent years, of a responsible, even admirable, "social conscience." In fact, this project may well entail compromises of sound business dictates and concomitant financial sacrifices to avoid the worsening unemployment and economic depression which would result if General Motors were to move from the state of Michigan as other major employers have. The point here is not to criticize General Motors, but to relate accurately the facts which attended the city's decision to condemn private property to enable General Motors to build a new plant in Detroit and to "set the scene" in which, as will be seen hereafter, broad-based support for the project was orchestrated in the state, fostering a sense of inevitability and dire consequence if the plan was not approved by all concerned. General Motors is not the villain of the piece.[130]

Shortly thereafter, Justice Ryan notes the exercise of power by all interested parties:

> It is easy to underestimate the overwhelming psychological pressure which was brought to bear upon property owners in the affected area, especially the generally elderly, mostly retired and largely Polish-American residents of the neighborhood which has come to be called Poletown. . . . Labor leaders, bankers, and businessmen, including those for whom a new GM plant would mean new economic life, were joined by radio, television, newspaper and political opinion-makers in extolling the virtues of the bold and innovative fashion in which, almost overnight, a new and modern plant would rise from a little known inner-city neighborhood of minimal tax base significance. . . . It was in such an atmosphere that the plaintiffs sued to enjoin the condemnation of their homes. The judiciary, cognizant of General Motors' May 1 deadline for the city's taking title to all of the property, moved at flank speed.[131]

He nonetheless places the responsibility on the City:

> [I]t could hardly be contended that the existence of the automotive industry or the construction of a New Generaal Motors assembly plant requires the use of eminent domain.
>
> Instead, what defendants are really claiming is that eminent domain is required for the existence of a new General Motors assembly plant within the city limits of Detroit *in order to comply with the specifications of General Motors.* This is an altogether different argument, acceptance of which would vitiate the requirement of "necessity of the extreme sort" and significantly alter the balance between governmental power and private property rights struck by the people and embodied in the taking clause. Just as ominously, it would work a fundamental shift in the relative force between private corporate power and individual property rights having the sanction of the state.[132]
>
> . . .
>
> there are no guarantees from General Motors about employment levels at the new assembly plant. General Motors has made *representations* about the number of employees who will work at the new plant. . . . General Motors will be accountable not to the public, but to its stockholders. . . . Amid these uncertainties, however, one thing is certain. The level of employment at the new GM plant will be determined by private corporate managers primarily with reference, not to the rate of regional unemployment, but to profit.[133]
>
> . . .
>
> Without belaboring the obvious, the location of CIP is, to say the least, solely a result of conditions laid down by General Motors, which were designed to further its private, pecuniary interest. These are facts of private significance.[134]
>
> . . .
>
> when the private corporation to be aided by eminent domain is as large and influential as General Motors, the power of eminent domain, for all practical purposes, is in the hands of the private corporation. The municipality is merely the conduit. In contrast, the broader view of the notion of "public purpose" has not effected a comparable transfer of the power of taxation to the private sector. Government still determines how tax liability is computed and how and under what conditions tax revenues are spent.[135]

Justice Ryan accepts both the profit-maximizing logic and the size of General Motors. The Justice brilliantly notes that "These are facts of private significance." The use of the public's power of eminent domain is another matter:

> Eminent domain is an attribute of sovereignty. When individual citizens are forced to suffer great social dislocation to permit private corporations to construct plants where they deem it most profitable, one is left to wonder who the sovereign is.[136]

Strikingly, Justice Ryan provides both critics and defenders of the existing power structure some ammunition. Justice Ryan positions his argument that a constitutional right of government should not be subordinated to private corporate interests.[137] Unintentionally, one must surmise, in doing so, Justice Ryan points out both that the system is in fact one of power and that property—private decision making—partakes of sovereignty. When Justice Ryan writes of the *Poletown* majority significantly altering "the balance between government power and private property rights struck by the people and embodied in the taking clause" so as to "work a fundamental shift in the relative force between private corporate power and individual property rights having the sanction of the state,"[138] he neglects (1) the shifts in that balance of power made in the past, often in ways not open to the view of "the people," (2) the narrowness of the slice of law represented in these cases, even when writ large; (3) the use of either position as precedent in a variety of legal domains; and (4) the actual balance or structure of power and the narrowness of the slice thereof represented by these cases (the extent to which giants can impact pygmies).

In contrast, the voices heard in the *Hathcock* decision concentrate their attention on the misuse of governmental power and the "erosion of constitutional protections."[139] That, apropos of the use of eminent domain in *Poletown*, government is the instrument of a profit-maximizing private corporate giant pervades the decision but is largely ignored. Of course, in *Hathcock*, there is no General Motors stage-managing the whole affair. In further contrast, when Justice Ryan says that

> The sudden and fundamental change in established law effected by the Court in this case, entailing such a significant diminution of constitutional rights, cannot be justified as a function of judicial construction; the only proper vehicle for change of this dimension is a constitutional amendment.[140]

he is holding out the prospect of adopting a constitutional amendment as unpalatable and thus using the "amendment card" to finesse and negate its possibility. He follows that with these words,

> What has been done in this case can be explained by the overwhelming sense of inevitability that has attended this litigation from the beginning; a sense attributable to the combination and coincidence of the interests of a desperate city administration and a giant corporation willing and able to take advantage of the opportunity that presented itself. The justification for it, like the inevitability of it, has been made to seem more acceptable by the "team spirit" chorus of approval of the project which has been supplied by the voices of labor, business, industry, government, finance, and even the news media. Virtually the only discordant sounds of dissent have come from the minuscule minority of citizens most profoundly affected by this case, the Poletown residents whose neighborhood has been destroyed.[141]

He is thereby, not incorrectly but with possible disingenuous failure of memory (the possibility is that he never has known), neglecting the use of "the law" and other tropisms to sustain "the overwhelming sense of inevitability" with which juridical decision making has been sold to "the people." One wonders what the people "sophisticated and versed in the law" think of all this.

Social control

Rulers are those persons in a position to make decisions that have important impacts on other people. They engage consciously and unconsciously in benefit-cost comparisons, even when these comparisons are subjective rather than objective, or quantitative. This is also a means-ends analysis. The end of social control is the defense and perpetuation of the status quo system and structure, including its processes of change. In the face of potential or incipient rebellion, the rulers can abdicate, fight, or bribe (through making adjustments in the status quo). As Machiavelli and others have advised, the ruler who is to succeed must be sensitive to his or her options and their respective money costs and opportunity costs. Without placing too fine a point on it, Detroit has had a love-hate relationship with much of out-state Michigan. Detroit has had racial unrest and riots. It has had well-above-average unemployment, and so on. The projects at the center of *Poletown* and *Hathcock* need not but can be seen as efforts to neutralize the disaffected. The decision in the two cases can but need not be seen as two different responses: *Poletown* as an effort to respond favorably to pressures to promote economic development, and *Hathcock* as an effort not to so respond; the former Court not wedded to the conservation of the status quo, the latter Court more intransigent in its preservation of the status quo.

A somewhat different alternative interpretation of *Hathcock* would stress the increasingly conservative membership of the Michigan Supreme Court, coupled with support from the Institute for Justice and Mackinac Center for Public Policy, that led to *Poletown* being targeted for reversal. Poletown represented governmental activism on the local level, as would *Hathcock* if the decision had been in line with *Poletown*.

Of course, these are not pure alternatives. One could account for the decision in *Hathcock* by reckoning some justices were motivated in one way and others in another; and of course there are other explanatory factors as well.

Need we assume that the decision in *Hathcock* makes sense or that it has to be explained? Whatever one's answer, in the US system of law and jurisprudence the decision becomes part of the law and jurisprudence of both Michigan law and, by possibility of reference, that of the other states.

Nor is that all. The eminent domain principle in general and the requirement of public use in particular have several roles: (1) They serve in the framework of legal policy-making, in a larger matrix of principles. (2) They serve, in principle, as a check on arbitrary and tyrannical power. Two problems arise, however: (a) when power is used, or is used in an arbitrary and tyrannical way, is a matter of selective perception and (b) the use of power to check perceived abuse of power may itself be seen as abuse of power. This is true in the cases considered here: The Court in *Hathcock* felt that the legislature, the local units, and the Court in *Poletown* were abusing power; the critics of the decision in *Hathcock* felt that the

Court was abusing its power. (3) The very presence of the compensation principle and the public use requirement serve as psychic balm in face of radical indeterminacy, by obscuring the necessity of choice, by affirming the pretense of protected rights, by permitting the absorption of the reality of loss through reference to high principle, and by soothing the realism of instrumentalism and rationality. (4) By legitimizing decisions which determine rights and losses, they paradoxically legitimize all legal change. With regard to compensation in some or many cases, by having the compensation principle available, they induce the acceptance of legal change without compensation; ostensibly as a check on legal social control, albeit itself a mode of social control. Apropos of the public use requirement, by having the requirement available, they induce acceptance of legal change. Each is a means through which the injured are prepared to bear losses or educated to be willing to accept them. (5) The determination of inevitable non-compensated losses through the joint determination of rights, losses, and compensation, and the invocation of the public use requirement, are parts of the determination of rights; again, a means through which the injured are prepared to bear losses or educated to be willing to accept them. (6) The principle of eminent domain in general and the requirement of public use in particular can serve either as a check on the powerful or an instrument by which the powerful can deploy their power. When a situation is of the former or latter nature is a matter of selective perception, and the perception is different for different people.

An example of the foregoing is legislation to either hamper or facilitate the transition of agricultural land into suburban communities, the phenomenon known pejoratively as urban sprawl. The opportunity sets of developers and home buyers will be either enhanced or diminished; and those of farmers and others will be, respectively, either diminished or enhanced. The variety of techniques intended to hamper or facilitate work differently. With respect to eminent domain in general and the public use requirement in particular, in principle all of these techniques will adversely affect some people and benefit other people. But not all of these legal means of achieving change involve either the payment of compensation or the imposition of the public use requirement. The history of zoning, for example, illustrates how major reconstruction of property rights was undertaken without payment of compensation. Of course, those who tend strongly to support an absolutist theory of property, such as Richard Epstein and Justice Scalia, consider such practice unconscionable. But such differences of view are at the heart of social control.

Policy analysis

The court in *Hathcock* held that for an eminent domain action involving the transfer of property from one private owner(s) to another private owner(s) to succeed, the public use must be preeminent to incidental private use. If emphasis on economic development is seen as a public use, akin to the "instrumentalities of commerce" exceptions and to slum clearing/urban renewal, then *Hathcock's* negative conclusion with regard to the public-use clause could be negated. But who is to be doing the "seeing"? Is it the legislature, or the courts? Why that test? And if that is a test, has the court not fashioned in advance another type of exception without saying so? If so, is it closer to the constitution than was *Poletown*? What of the metrics used by future courts?

Language in *Hathcock* makes it clear that the court believes that in the final resort it, and not the legislature, is the decision maker; it is the vision of the court that counts as to what constitutes abuse of power and constitutionality. The court also emphasizes that the law its decision represents, the law from which the holding derives, is found, not made. What the court sees is something it finds, not something it makes—it is declaring, not creating the law. These and other ideas need to be deconstructed. Certain questions need to be posed: Why the courts and not the legislature? What is it that is found, and what is its relation to the language of the decision? The *Hathcock* court considered the decision by the *Poletown* court to be unprecedented and radical; on what grounds did it do so? Since any true legal innovation in a holding will have no precedent—there is never a precedent for the first case with a change, for example, the "instrumentalities-of-commerce" exceptions—what is the significance of "unprecedented"? What is the role of selective perception, ideology, and/or sentiment? How do the exceptions arise from the constitutional phrasing, or where are the exceptions found?, what is the relation of the exceptions to judicial law making (judicial activism), are the exceptions necessarily extant? Is reading into the constitution certain subsidiary and/or elaborative tests a matter of making, not finding, law, and illustrative of inexorable judicial activism—an activism that gives effect to the choices made by the court whatever the numbers in the majority or the minority? Are the first two propositions in this paragraph descriptive propositions or power-language in the sense of Hutt? Descriptive propositions are matters of truth or falsity. Power language is a matter of persuasion, or the political mobilization of psychology and belief. Is the critical function of the courts not so much the "interpretation" of the constitution, though that is obviously undertaken, as the practice of judicial review, and is that not part of governance? And in eminent domain, or taking, cases, is not the court, in upholding eminent domain actions that meets its tests, not, or not only, protecting private property but legitimizing eminent-domain takings? Is it not, by giving support to such actions as pass its tests, itself practicing what the citizen who loses his property would likely say—and the court itself has said—about the legislature and/or local taking body, namely that it is expropriating his property? Is not the penultimate matter the exercise of the powers of governance by courts through judicial review such that the courts partake of the ultimate matter, namely, making choices? Are the appellate courts of today the modern version of the oracles—Apollo and Zeus, respectively—of Delphi and Dodona, of ancient Greece, whose task it was to provide absolutist legitimization to very human decisions? The Court has emphasized that the law they declare is the law they find, not the law they make, but what is that law?

The phenomena of eminent domain, takings, and just compensation inexorably lead one to some of the deepest and recondite problems of society. These problems have to do with the nature of property, government, the relationship between property and government, the social valuational process that includes market and government as well as ideas, the relative decision-making roles of legislature and court, language in regard to all the foregoing and following, constitutional law, and the problem of continuity versus change. In all these respects, the law of eminent domain points to the human belief system with which we interpret social reality, which is itself part of social reality, and which, when serving to legitimize social arrangements, is itself challenged. When one asks, "what is constitutional law?," one is also asking, "what is law?," and "with what degree of illusion, finesse, obfuscation, and candor can legitimization co-exist?"

The objectives of this section are to see what sense can be made of the forego-ing phenomena and how judicial practice can be improved. Several points should be made about that objective. (1) One must always ask, in what sense and on what level of abstraction is a question posed or analysis conducted? (2) The section is entitled "Policy Analysis" to reinforce the idea that all of the foregoing phenom-ena are matters of policy, that is, of power and human social construction. (3) Social co-existence seems to require that certain matters not be discussed, or widely discussed, in public. But in every society before, during, and since the time of Machiavelli there have been people who were law makers rather than law takers; people, that is, who understood the world of power and human social construction, and sought to make it their own. A characteristic of the last 400 years or so, especially the last 250, is the growth in the proportion of the population which was more or less conscious of and could more or less understand the artifact nature of institutions. Correlative with the growth of the policy consciousness has been the continued high proportion of those who seek ontologically absolute metaphysi-cal definitions of social existence. The growth in the number of those who, like Frank H. Knight, could appreciate both the role of only relatively absolute absolutes and society as a conversation has been slow. The domains of absolute absolutes and of relatively absolute absolutes have themselves been affected by the realization by many that all descriptions and explanations of what is going on, say, in law, economy, government, and religion, are essentially matters of pragmatism. Ask, "why?" to every answer to questions about law, economy, government, and religion, and one eventually encounters a pragmatic answer. In any event, the questions of what law is all about and what legal decision making by courts is all about needs to be taken up.

Market versus government determination of best use

Justice Fitzgerald argued in his *Poletown* dissent that

> Any business enterprise produces benefits to society at large. Now that we have authorized local legislative bodies to decide that a different commercial or industrial use of property will produce greater public benefits than its pre-sent use, no homeowner's, merchant's or manufacturer's property, however productive or valuable to its owner, is immune from condemnation for the benefit of other private interests that will put it to a "higher" use.[142]

And Justice Ryan did likewise in his dissent:

> The real controversy which underlies this litigation concerns the propriety of condemning private property for conveyance to another private party because the use of it by the new owner promises greater public "benefit" than the old use. The controversy arises in the context of economic crisis. While unemployment is high throughout the nation, it is of calamitous proportions throughout the state of Michigan, and particularly in the City of Detroit, whose economic lifeblood is the now foundering automobile industry. It is difficult to overstate the magnitude of the crisis.[143]

So too did the Opinion of the Court in *Hathcock*:

> Every business, every productive unit in society, does, as Justice COOLEY noted, contribute in some way to the commonweal. To justify the exercise of eminent domain solely on the basis of the fact that the use of that property by a private entity seeking its own profit might contribute to the economy's health is to render impotent our constitutional limitations on the government's power of eminent domain. *Poletown*'s "economic benefit" rationale would validate practically *any* exercise of the power of eminent domain on behalf of a private entity. After all, if one's ownership of private property is forever subject to the government's determination that another private party would put one's land to better use, then the ownership of real property is perpetually threatened by the expansion plans of any large discount retailer, "megastore," or the like. Indeed, it is for precisely this reason that this Court has approved the transfer of condemned property to private entities only when certain other conditions—those identified in our pre-1963 eminent domain jurisprudence in Justice RYAN's *Poletown* dissent—are present.[144]

Almost all of the reasoning in both cases has to do with the law of eminent domain as part of, or as a restriction on, the law of private property. Here the question is a matter of who is to own the property in question, given the interpretation and application of the relevant constitutional provisions and statutes. The principal economic reasoning in both cases involves the putative contribution their respective projects would make to economic development. The *Hathcock* court did not rebut that contribution; it only said that "economic development" was insufficient to carve out another exception and therefore was unconstitutional for several reasons.

Another economic reasoning, however, enters into both cases, however tacitly or silently. This reasoning has to do with whether the market or the government is the preferable determination of "best use." This is a more complex and a more subtle question than may appear at first glance. The law already enters this determination through (e.g.) the law of torts and the criminal law as well as the law of private property. Such laws say that contrary to what some property owners may prefer, they cannot do what they prefer. The proposition, "the market works, let the market determine best use," is sentimentally attractive but flawed. (1) The market does not always work the way people want it to, in which case they tend to seek corrective action, for example, changing the structure of the market and/or changing the behavior of economic agents in the market. (2) Even where the market could or would work, having it do so contradicts certain ideas or principles of justice and/or morality. Students who have affirmed vigorously that everything should be done through the market in which everyone is free to buy or sell as they see fit, when confronted with the rhetorical offer to establish a market for grades in the class, with payments to the instructor, invariably are stricken with silence. (3) Markets already are what they are in part because of law. Market and law may appear ideologically to be opposites but each market is a function of the law (and other institutions of social control) that helps create and structure, and operate through, the market so created. Indeed, the function of the law of eminent domain, typically understood in terms of the forced devolution of ownership, may be understood in terms of having government operate to determine best use. The law of eminent domain substitutes government for market in regard to establishing best use and does so notwithstanding the narrow exceptions (and their respective tests) to the public use requirement.

It should also be pointed out that "best use" is a function not only of individual preferences but of prices, and the structure of prices is in part a function of law. Let price structure one be a function, in part, of rights structure one; price structure two, a function of rights structure two, et seq.; and let rights structures be in a part a function of law: Law one generates rights structure one, which generates price structure one, which yields best use one, et seq. Government action is never very far away from what happens in the markets government is used to generate. And there is no unique, inflexible "best use," simply because there is none and because, "best use" is a variable, a function of different, and differently structured valuational processes.

The relative roles of legislature and court

The judiciary pretend that their amendatory actions—here the fact of an exception and the tests thereof—is in the constitution or has constitutional status. They speak of what is constitutionally required. They speak as if their amendatory actions are the only ones possible. They affirm that they found the law, not made the law. For all their quibbling over whose original intent is to count—when no unique determinate result can be found, who ratified their amendatory actions? What is going on here?

Let us define "governance" as the making of choices that importantly impact other people. This is akin to "power" understood (analytically and non-pejoratively) as participation in decision making and the (legal) bases thereof. So far as the individual is concerned both terms represent social, or collective, decision making, or "social control."

Governance therefore includes both public government and private government. The former is what we normally think of as government, it is the official government. The latter embraces what we do not normally think of as government, but insofar as, say, the corporate system and its individual entities make decisions that importantly impact other people, they are part of the system of governance. A corporation that opens or closes a plant is an example.

Public government in many countries has a dual tripartite division of power. First, power is divided by level of government: local or municipal, state, and national or federal governments. All are governing, all are part of governance. Second, on each level, power is divided between legislature, executive, and judiciary. The key point is that all three branches are, on their particular level, exercising their part of the division of power; each is governing. The traditional view that the legislature makes the law, the executive enforces the law, and the courts interpret the law, is highly misleading, even wrong. All three branches comprise official government on its level and thereby participate in governance and in making the law by which people must live.

More specifically, when the Supreme Court in its practice of judicial review declares that a statute is unconstitutional, that is participation in governance, it is part of the law-making process. If the equivalent of the Supreme Court were a committee of one of the houses of Congress, or a joint committee, it might be more readily apparent that it was part of the legislative or law-making process. As an "independent branch" of government, it may be less obvious but it is no less part of government. The judiciary as a whole is part of official government in participating in the exercise of governance. It is also part of the system in a less abstract sense, inasmuch as those appointed or elected to the bench are, in one way or another, part of the political process—the political party process—of official government.

One result of the division of power between branches is an *inevitable* tension between them concerning who can do what, which branch can partake of the governance powers either on its level or on another level. This latter is the situation with *Poletown* and *Hathcock*: the Michigan Supreme Court *vis-à-vis* the City of Detroit and County of Wayne, respectively. Our primary concern here is with the inevitable tension between legislature and court; the city and county operate within what constitutional home rule and/or legislation provide. Legislature and court engage in a legal/political *pas de deux*. Each is jockeying for position. It is a contest abstractly pitting John Locke, the political philosopher of legislative government, controlled by the middle class, against Chief Justice John Marshall, the jurisprudential philosophy of judicial review.

There is a disjunction between law as ordinary language and ordinary propositions, on the one hand, and as something found, not made, on the other. It is a disjunction forced by invocation of the high priest function of appellate courts to pass judgment on the "constitutionality" of actions by other branches of government through the exercise of judicial review and by the obvious made-ness of and conflict over law.

The linguistic practice, or trope, represented by the statements that the court is only interpreting the law, that it is determining constitutionality, and that it is finding the law and not making the law, are means of obfuscating, even from the judges themselves, the fact of their participation in governance—the making of decisions that importantly impact others. The practice is akin to the distinction between Emile Durkheim's manifest and latent function. In Durkheim's example, when people enter a church they have a sense of oneness with God; the social function thereof is to enhance their acceptance of status quo institutions as if they were due to God. To the priest, the former is the manifest function; the latter, the latent function. Those who practice this distinction are performing the role of high priest. Judges at the appellate level, especially at the level of the Supreme Court, perform both roles: they decide between plaintiff and defendant, both helping to make the legal rules by which people must live, and legitimizing the system, the law, and their own position. In *Poletown* and *Hathcock*, the city and county, respectively, are making the case for legislative supremacy, and the Michigan Supreme Court, especially in *Hathcock*, is doing likewise for judicial supremacy. The Opinion in *Poletown* thus argued that

> The Legislature has determined that governmental action of the type con-
> templated here meets a public need and serves an essential public purpose.
> The Court's role after such a determination is made is limited.
> "The determination of what constitutes a public purpose is primarily a
> legislative function, subject to review by the courts when abused, and the
> determination of the legislative body of that matter should not be reversed
> except in instances where such determination is palpable and manifestly
> arbitrary and incorrect." *Gregory Marina, Inc v Detroit*, 378 Mich 364, 396;
> 144 NW2d 503 (1966).

The US Supreme Court has held that when a legislature speaks, the public interest has been declared in terms "well-nigh conclusive." *Berman v Parker*, 348 US 26, 32; 75 S Ct 98; 99 L Ed 27 (1954).[145]

On the other hand, Justice Fitzgerald's dissent affirms the distinction between legislative and judicial power differently:

> The city attaches great importance to the explicit legislative findings…It is
> undeniable that such legislative pronouncements are entitled to great defer-
> ence. However, determination whether a taking is for a public or a private use
> is ultimately a judicial question. *E.g., Lakehead Pipe Line Co v Dehn*, 340 Mich
> 25, 39–40; 64 NW2d 903 (1954); *Cleveland v City of Detroit*, 322 Mich 172, 179;
> 33 NW2d 747 (1948). Through the years, this Court has not hesitated to
> declare takings authorized by statute not to be for public use in appropriate
> cases. *E.g., Shizas v City of Detroit*, 333 Mich 44; 52 NW2d 589 (1952); *Berrien
> Springs Water-Power Co v Berrien Circuit Judge*, 133 Mich 48; 94 NW 379 (1903).
> This is as it must be, since if a legislative declaration on the question of
> public use were conclusive, citizens could be subjected to the most outrageous
> confiscation of property for the benefit of other private interests without
> redress. Thus, while mindful of the expression of the legislative view of the

appropriateness of using the eminent domain power in the circumstances of this case, this Court has the responsibility to determine whether the authorization is lawful.

Our role was well stated by Justice Cooley in "A Treatise on the Constitutional Limitations." Writing subsequent to the Court's decision in *People ex rel Detroit and Howell R Co v Salem Twp Board*, 20 Mich 452 (1870), he noted:

> "The question what is a public use is always one of law. Deference will be paid to the legislative judgment, as expressed in enactments providing for an appropriation of property, but it will not be conclusive." 2 Cooley, Constitutional Limitations (8th ed), p 1141.[146]

A telling example is Justice Fitzgerald's statement that "Condemnation places the burden of aiding industry on the few, who are likely to have limited power to protect themselves from the excesses of legislative enthusiasm for the promotion of industry."[147] When one wonders about the putative *excesses of judicial enthusiasm*, the mind is inevitably led to two considerations: that Justice Fitzgerald's position is a function of the division of power between three branches (better stated as three branches sharing power) with nothing approximating a precise statement of the boundaries of power for each of them, and that his position reflects his desire to legitimize judicial review of legislation and other government acts.

Justice Ryan, in his dissent, addresses the foregoing and other points in support of judicial review:

> The distinction is further reflected in the Legislature's proper role, as we have defined it, in describing the ambits of the terms. As this Court has previously said: "[The] determination of what constitutes a public purpose is primarily the responsibility of the Legislature." *Advisory Opinion, supra*, 696. "[The] determination of the legislative body of that matter should not be reversed except in instances where such determination is palpable and manifestly arbitrary and incorrect." *Gregory Marina, Inc v Detroit*, 378 Mich 364, 396; 144 NW2d 503 (1966) (plurality opinion) (quoting 37 Am Jur, Municipal Corporations, § 120). Other decisions of this Court abound with similar statements of deference to legislative determinations respecting the boundaries of "public purpose."
> The eminent domain cases, on the other hand, evince no like commitment to minimal judicial review. Instead, it has always been the case that this Court has accorded little or no weight to legislative determinations of "public use." "Whether the use for which land is sought to be acquired by condemnation is a public one is a *judicial* question." (Emphasis added.) *General Development Corp v Detroit*, 322 Mich 495, 498; 33 NW2d 919 (1948); accord, *Lakehead Pipe Line Co v Dehn*, 340 Mich 25, 39–40; 64 NW2d 903 (1954); *Cleveland v Detroit*, 322 Mich 172, 179; 33 NW2d 747 (1948); *Board of Health of Portage Twp v Van Hoesen*, 87 Mich 533, 539; 49 NW 894 (1891). (*Poletown* at 474).

The majority also relies on *Berman v Parker*, 348 U.S. 26, 32; 75 S Ct 98; 99 L Ed 27 (1954), as did the *Gregory Marina* plurality, where the United States Supreme Court said, "The role of the judiciary in determining whether [the] power [of eminent domain] is being exercised for a public purpose is an extremely narrow one."

The Court's reliance on *Berman* is particularly disingenuous. The case stands for minimal judicial review of acts of *Congress* by *federal* courts with respect to application of the *Fifth Amendment* taking clause, which per se applies only to the the federal government.

It is certainly true that the Fifth Amendment taking clause is incorporated in the Fourteenth Amendment due process clause and applies to the states. *E.g., Penn Central Transportation Co v New York City*, 438 U.S. 104, 122; 98 S Ct 2646; 57 L Ed 2d 631 (1978). It is also true that in construing the Fourteenth Amendment the United States Supreme Court has adopted a deferential standard of review. See *Rindge Co v Los Angeles County*, 262 U.S. 700, 705–706; 43 S Ct 689; 67 L Ed 1186 (1923). But deference is paid *not* to the decisions of state *legislatures* but to the judgments of state *courts* pertaining to the public use question in the context of state law. The distinction is critical and, in this case, makes the whole difference.

"The nature of a use, whether public or private, is ultimately a judicial question. However, the determination of this question is influenced by local conditions; and this Court, while enforcing the Fourteenth Amendment, should keep in view the diversity of such conditions and regard with great respect the judgments of state *courts* upon what should be deemed public uses in any State." *Rindge Co v Los Angeles County, supra*, 705–706, 98 S.Ct. at 692 (emphasis added).

That the United States Supreme Court would defer to the decisions of Congress while interpreting the Fifth Amendment or to this Court while interpreting the Fourteenth Amendment on the issue of public use, is no logical support for the proposition that this Court, in construing the Michigan constitution, should defer to the judgment of the Michigan Legislature.

In point of fact, this Court has *never* employed the minimal standard of review in an eminent domain case which is adopted by the majority in this case. Notwithstanding explicit legislative findings, this Court has always made an *independent* determination of what constitutes a public use for which the power of eminent domain may be utilized.[148]

The Court in *Hathcock* makes the same argument:

In interpreting this statutory language, this Court's primary goal is to give effect to the Legislature's intent. If the Legislature has clearly expressed its intent in the language of a statute, that statute must be enforced as written, free of any "contrary judicial gloss."[149]

After noting constitutional provisions concerning the power of counties, the Court quotes the 1963 Michigan Constitution, art. 7, § 34, that

> The provisions of this constitution and law concerning counties, townships, cities and villages shall be liberally construed in their favor. Powers granted to counties and townships by this constitution and by law shall include those fairly implied and not prohibited by this constitution.[150]

The Court's emphasis is on "liberally construed." Moreover,

> Michigan's courts are bound by a public corporation's determination that a proposed condemnation serves a public necessity unless the party opposing the condemnation demonstrates "fraud, error of law, or abuse of discretion."[151]

Nonetheless there is room for judicial review:

> If the authority to condemn private property conferred by the Legislature lacked any constitutional limits, this Court would be compelled to affirm the decisions of the circuit court and the Court of Appeals. But our state Constitution does, in fact, limit the state's power of eminent domain. Therefore, it must be determined whether the proposed condemnations pass constitutional muster.[152]

And again, first quoting Justice Ryan in *Poletown*,

> In point of fact, this Court has *never* employed the minimal standard of review in an eminent domain case which is adopted by the [*Poletown*] majority.... Notwithstanding explicit legislative findings, this Court has always made an *independent* determination of what constitutes a public use for which the power of eminent domain may be utilized.
> Our eminent domain jurisprudence since Michigan's entry into the union amply supports Justice RYAN's assertion. Questions of public *purpose* aside, whether the proposed condemnations were consistent with the Constitution's "public use" requirement was a constitutional question squarely within the Court's authority.[153]

Justice Weaver weighs in on the side affirming judicial review in such a way as to suggest a preoccupation with judicial power—judicial participation in governance—and its finessing:

> It is true, of course, that this Court must not "lightly overrule precedent." But because *Poletown* itself was such a radical departure from fundamental constitutional principles and over a century of this Court's eminent domain jurisprudence leading up to the 1963 Constitution, we must overrule *Poletown* in order to vindicate our Constitution, protect the people's property rights,

and preserve the legitimacy of the judicial branch as the expositor—not creator—of fundamental law.[154]

. . .

> there is no reason to depart from the usual practice of applying our conclusions of law to the case at hand. Our decision today does not announce a new rule of law, but rather returns our law to that which existed before *Poletown* and which has been mandated by our constitution since it took effect in 1963. Our decision simply applies fundamental constitutional principles and enforces the "public use" requirement as that phrase was used at the time our 1963 Constitution was ratified.[155]

The Court's procedure and objectives should be obvious. The justices' procedure, whatever their position, is to critique and distinguish other cases and other positions. Their objective is to presume, give effect to, and promote their respective views of the meaning of the Michigan Constitution. They perform a linguistic dance as to the respective powers of the legislature and the court, in order similarly to promote their power of judicial review. But critiquing other cases is no substitute for the kind of policy analysis I propose. Critiquing other cases may reflect legal training and custom but it also functions to avoid explicit identification and arguments on issues and positions independent of cases, and does so in such a way as to obfuscate the decision making, the policy making, that is going on. Instead they engage in the fiction of expositing and not creating "the law."

It is true, of course, that this Court must not "lightly overrule precedent." But because *Poletown* itself was such a radical departure from fundamental constitutional principles and over a century of this Court's eminent domain jurisprudence leading up to the 1963 Constitution, we must overrule *Poletown* in order to vindicate our Constitution, protect the people's property rights, and preserve the legitimacy of the judicial branch as the expositor—not creator—of fundamental law.[156]

It should be readily apparent that my argument does not depend solely on interpretation or deconstruction; it also is based on the words of the Court in its opinion and of individual judges in dissent. The Court and its Justices affirm their power of judicial review and that they are finding and not making the law. The present analysis interposes candor between manifest function (defending and articulating the 1963 Constitution) and latent function (defending the governing, law-making role of appellate judges simultaneously with absolving them from interfering with legislative power). At the least, the court is doing more than interpreting the Constitution, it is articulating and defending their view of it. It is also adding to it—that is, making law—through its nominal tasks of interpreting and finding the law.

That the Court is making law and adding to the Constitution is evident—empirically and with minimal interpretation—from the the instrument-of-commerce and slum clearance exceptions it has crafted over the years and from its other distinctions as well, notably that public use must adhere to the land independent of subsequent use by a beneficial owner. The Court refers to these matters as if they were in the Constitution, there for the justices to find. But they are not literally in the constitution; they have been made by the Court.

The justices seem freely to say of the legislature that its actions are "manifestly arbitrary and incorrect"[157] and that it suffers from "legislative enthusiasm."[158] Justice Weaver cautions that the courts must "restrain themselves from substituting a different meaning of a word to suit a court's own policy preferences."[159] But all this is a matter of interpretation, a matter of enforcing a particular perspective.

Several other points are worth making. Two attitudes are evident from the tone with which the justices write about the legislature and its statutes. One attitude is that the court nominally accepts the legislature as a branch of government, perhaps even a co-equal one, but one whose output—statute law—is subject to judicial review as to constitutionality. Another attitude is that the courts seem to rank court law above legislated law—some people have denied that statutes were law either at all or like the common law and constitutional law, unless received and accepted (according to the common law canons of statutory construction or otherwise found not in conflict with common law—when the purpose of the statute was to change "the law") by the courts; whereas arguably both statutes and court decisions are, in this context, law. For example, the majority Opinion in *Hathcock* argues that "public use" is a legal term of art on whose meaning the Court has weighed in repeatedly, saying, "We can uncover the common understanding of art. 10, § 2 only by delving into this body of case law."[160] As noted earlier, this is not analysis of pros and cons; it is reasoning by indirection and obfuscation. Another example is the conflicting treatments of eminent domain. The power of eminent domain is often treated as an attribute or inherent power of sovereignty ("Eminent domain is an inherent power of the sovereign of the same nature as, albeit more severe than, the power to regulate the use of land through zoning or the prohibition of public nuisances.")[161] but not always: Justice Weaver refers to the power as "extraordinary." It is difficult to contemplate something that is inherent in sovereignty as also being extraordinary. But this illustrates the situation-specific use of language, notably in comparing cases from a particular perspective.

Another point concerns the frequently encountered juxtaposition of law and policy: Law is, and has to be, the law; whereas policy is only policy. Such a formulation both elevates law and misrepresents its nature. Law is not something transcendental and given—it is not Justice Holmes' brooding omnipresence in the sky; law, all law, is a human artifact, a function of human social construction.

Moreover, law *is* policy: it embodies judgments as to whose interests will be protected as rights; even if not so baldly stated or acknowledged, the selective normative premises are operative. People tend to refer to law in elevated terms selectively. The law of property in our society is given close to sacred standing. No one refers to the law of personal and federal income taxation or to the laws protecting the environment or safety on the job in such a tone. Moreover, law by its nature is conservative; that is one of its social or human values. The concept of the rule of law, at the present level of abstraction or discourse, is analytically flawed, even non-existent, in the sense of being insubstantial; but it is a very useful concept with which to legitimize whatever law is being supported thereby. Both law and the concept of the rule of law are artifacts of social interaction, if you will, of conflict about the nature and structure of society, of conflict about whose interests should count, of conflict over what should be continued and what changed, and therefore of the processes in which continuity confronts change. Here we have one or more concepts to which conflicting parties can appeal, but these are concepts that are themselves instruments, even if only rhetorical, legitimizing tools, in the conflicts themselves.

Finally, we may note that the position of the justices is akin to that of the philosophical realist. The realist argues that reality exists and that it can be known. They oppose that position to that of the idealist, who argues that reality is made. The problem with the idealist position is that idealists openly disagree as to the content of remaking reality, leading to the need for choice. The realists offer their position as one not requiring choice: reality is given. The problem is that realists disagree as to the content of that given reality, leaving them in the same position as the idealists. Here the problem is that insofar as judges claim to be finding, and not making, the law, if the law were actually there to be found, they should agree; but agreeing that it is so, they nonetheless disagree as to its content. The justices, to state the point directly and briefly, pretend that law is given, not made. They seem, as a general professional characteristic, to almost universally accept that definition of legal reality; but they disagree as to what "the law" of legal reality is contentwise.

The problem of continuity versus change of law

Common and constitutional law have had two unequivocal characteristics, first, the multiplicity of interpretations given to received statements of law, for example, constitutional provisions; and, second, the changes that have taken place in every sphere of law. Law has influenced socioeconomic change and socioeconomic change has influenced law, and law has changed continuously. Such change has been gradual, or incremental, and some innovators who have sought successfully to change the law may have been astonished, a century or so later, at how their efforts did or did not succeed, and/or the effects of their efforts, results unforeseen and unintended. Law is a profoundly conservative phenomenon, so given the context of change, it is inevitable that the factors and forces of change and of continuity will come into conflict, more or less abrasively, more or less inconspicuously. The foregoing is rendered even more complicated because the status quo defined by law can be specified in different ways, because the forces of continuity are multiple and conflict with each other, and likewise with the forces of change. Past developments of law are typically controversial but in time they become part of the status quo, part of the perceived legal nature of things, and their origins in controversy forgotten or never learned. Effort to legitimize law in general tend to legitimize received law more effectively than changed law, yet the law does change, however ignored most of the time by most persons who are not legal professionals.

The *Poletown* and *Hathcock* decisions manifest several phenomena of change in relevant matters of eminent domain law. There is the working out of the instrumentalities-of-commerce exception to the public use requirement, including the identity and specific content of each of the three tests, and much later to permit condemnation for slum clearance. There was the temporarily successful effort by the *Poletown* Court, or its majority, to further extend the public use notion to include general economic development.

Other manifestations of the continuity versus change and selective sentimental character of what the two cases are all about also exist, for example, when it is that a legislative body is deemed abusive and palpably and manifestly arbitrary and incorrect in its efforts.[162] This would most likely (but not only) occur with the first effort of its type, for example, with regard to the *Poletown* project or the Pinnacle project in *Hathcock*. The majority in *Poletown* quoted Justice Cooley, that "the most important consideration in the case of eminent domain is the necessity of accomplishing some public good which is otherwise impracticable, and...the law does not so much regard the means as the need."[163] This certainly looked supportive and/or was relied upon to elicit supportive sentiments by the majority. Justice Fitzgerald surely opposed the majority's line of change:

> Our approval of the use of eminent domain power in this case takes this state into a new realm of takings of private property; there is simply no precedent for this decision in previous Michigan cases. There were several early cases in which there was an attempt to transfer property from one private owner to another through the condemnation power pursuant to express statutory authority. *Board of Health v Van Hoesen*, 87 Mich 533; 49 NW 894 (1891); *Ryerson v Brown*, 35 Mich 333 (1877). In each case, the proposed taking was held impermissible.[164]

In point of fact, *the impermissibility is not due to law; what the court calls law is and is due to its judgment of impermissibility*. Moreover, if the rule was something like, "no precedent, no luck," the common law would never have changed, perhaps never have begun.

The majority relies on the principle that the concept of public use is an evolving one; however, I cannot believe that this evolution has eroded our historic protection against the taking of private property for private use to the degree sanctioned by this Court's decision today. The decision that the prospect of increased employment, tax revenue, and general economic stimulation makes a taking of private property for transfer to another private party sufficiently "public" to authorize the use of the power of eminent domain means that there is virtually no limit to the use of condemnation to aid private businesses. Any business enterprise produces benefits to society at large. Now that we have authorized local legislative bodies to decide that a different commercial or industrial use of property will produce greater public benefits than its present use, no homeowner's, merchant's or manufacturer's property, however productive or valuable to its owner, is immune from condemnation for the benefit of other private interests that will put it to a "higher" use.[165]

The striking aspect of Justice Fitzgerald's dissent, in which Justice Ryan, who authored his own dissent, concurred, is his conclusion:

> The condemnation contemplated in the present action goes beyond the scope of the power of eminent domain in that it takes private property for private use.[166]

As has been seen earlier, this is not the later holding in *Hathcock*. *Hathcock* did not proscribe all takings of private property for private use. It indicated that certain requirements must be satisfied, in which case it allowed such takings. Moreover, the court itself has historically worked out and/or approved exceptions to the taking of private property for private use.

Justice Ryan's separate dissenting opinion began with a dismal specter:

> This is an extraordinary case.
>
> The reverberating clang of its economic, sociological, political, and jurisprudential impact is likely to be heard and felt for generations. By its decision, the Court has altered the law of eminent domain in this state in a most significant way and, in my view, seriously jeopardized the security of all private property ownership.
>
> This case will stand, above all else, despite the sound intentions of the majority, for judicial approval of municipal condemnation of private property for private use. This is more than an example of a hard case making bad law— it is, in the last analysis, good-faith but unwarranted judicial imprimatur upon government action taken under the policy of the end justifying the means.[167]

If Justice Fitzgerald felt that no property should be taken for private use, Justice Ryan considered the instrumentalities-of-commerce exception to have been a considerable modification of common law principles, that is, "historical aberrations justified by 'overriding public necessity'."

> The railroad exception, like those pertaining to other instrumentalities of public transport and commerce such as canals, highways, and bridges, which may in effect permit private companies to exercise the power of eminent domain, are historical aberrations justified by "overriding public necessity."[168]

Someone writes like that only if one is wedded—as a matter of sentiment or material interest—to continuity and is faithful to his feelings. The strong presumption is against changing the received common law, thereby ignoring past change. Any perceived "considerable modification of common law principles" is amenable to being called an "historical aberration." The idea of "overriding public necessity" is not only vague, illusive and potentially elastic, it is also suspect.

The type of difficult position into which such a perspective leads one, is indicated by the following from Justice Ryan's dissent:

> The language indicates that in 1877 the government was free to employ eminent domain more liberally than the taxing power. That, however, is more indicative of the restrictions upon the taxing power in the last half of the 19th Century than upon the breadth of eminent domain. Since then, however, as noted above, the taxing power has been significantly expanded. Moreover, the private corporations about which the *Ryerson* Court spoke were engaged in the establishment of instrumentalities of commerce. Such corporations, unlike General Motors in this case, fall within a firmly established

and carefully defined exception to the general prohibition against the use of eminent domain for the specific benefit of private corporations. Today, therefore, when dealing with eminent domain unrelated to development of the avenues of commerce, it is reasonable, indeed necessary, to conclude that, for purpose of aiding private corporations, eminent domain is more restrictive than the power of taxation. In fact, the *Ryerson* Court *struck down* a statute authorizing condemnation of property for construction of waterpower mills to be privately owned and operated, calling such action a taking for private use. *Cf. Board of Health of Portage Twp v Van Hoesen*, 87 Mich 533; 49 NW 894 (1891), in which a statute authorizing condemnation by privately controlled corporations to establish and maintain rural cemeteries was held unconstitutional as authorizing a taking for private use.[169]

Justice Weaver quoted Justice Cooley to the effect that "the majority invites future judicial distortion of the Constitution."[170]

Four points: First, what Justice Fitzgerald called a "historical aberration," Justice Ryan calls a "firmly established and carefully defined exception." Second, the changing of law in the past—of eminent domain (to permit the instrumentalities of commerce and slum clearance exceptions), of the taxing power—and the historical changing relation between the restrictions on both the eminent domain and the taxing powers, seemingly do not affect Justice Ryan's attitude toward the possibility of still further change. Third, what Justice Weaver, quoting Justice Cooley, cautioned about possible "future judicial distortion of the Constitution," raises the question, how does one know a distortion? Referring to judicial distortion is like referring to legislative enthusiasm: words and only words. Fourth, the foregoing underscores the fact—as if we needed more evidence—that judicial decisions and characterizations are a function of selective perception, ideology, and sentiment. *These decisions elevate selective perception, ideology, and sentiment to the level of constitutional law.* I argue this without denying the inexorable necessity of choices having to be made—indeed emphasizing it. The suggestion is inescapable that invoking "constitutional law" is the modern equivalent of invoking "higher law" or "natural law," and that the two functions served are those of psychic balm and social control, each using absolutist legitimization as a tool.

One thread that runs through both decisions, though taken up more elaborately in *Hathcock*, is that composed of "public use" and "public purpose." It clearly allows one to trace the impact of the conflict between the old and the new through the problem of continuity versus change of what constitutes public use and necessity, including such considerations as economic development and relative benefits as between public and private entities.[171]

A key thread in *Hathcock* has to do with *controlling purpose*. The majority differentiated, for example, slum removal, in which "the act of condemnation *itself*" was the controlling purpose and had public use attached to it, from "the use to which the condemned land eventually would be put" as a very different controlling purpose.[172] The *Hathcock* position on controlling purpose combines easily with its position on relative benefits as between public and private entities.[173]

The *Hathcock* Court found that the projects were not *necessary* (in the sense of "public necessity of the extreme sort otherwise impractical"[174] and the actual land condemned was, for the purposes of their respective cases, not material to public use). The majority in *Poletown* quoted Justice Cooley, that "the most important consideration in the case of eminent domain is the necessity of accomplishing some public good which is otherwise impracticable, and...the law does not so much regard the means as the need."[175] This certainly looked supportive and/or was relied on to that end by the *Poletown* Court. A court more open to change might have looked at matters differently, especially the majority positions in *Hathcock* indicated in the beginning of this paragraph. Instead, the *Hathcock* Court lamented the *Poletown* opinion "for its radical and unabashed departure from the entirety of this Court's pre-1963 eminent domain jurisprudence."[176] The *Hathcock* court preferred instead to deny the conclusions that a generalized or incidental "economic benefit was sufficient under art. 10, § 2 to justify the transfer of condemned property to a private entity" and that a "private entity's pursuit of profit was a 'public use' for constitutional takings purposes simply because one entity's profit maximization contributed to the health of the general economy."[177] The Court also rejected attempts to "force from these instruments [constitutional clauses] a meaning which their framers never held."[178] Of course, the framers of Michigan's original constitution and of its most recent one, respectively, likely had both different and diverse notions, if any at all, of the taking clause beyond its general formulation.

A further thread is the ostensible requirement that a decision have one or more precedents. One problem with this often stated point is that later courts have the same power to innovate as do earlier courts. Another problem is that courts, especially conservative ones, insist on precedent in order to ground both respect for the past (as they interpret it) and the claim that they are finding, not making, the law. The requirement of one or more precedents is simply false. It has not prevented courts from issuing innovating decisions or from reversing past decisions or from engaging in the casuistic game of distinguishing the present case from past cases in order to ground the decision in the present case.[179] Moreover, a court usually has two (or more) precedential sequences which it can invoke to support its decision; the two may not be equally developed but they are typically available for further development. Finally, one could argue, as the United States Supreme Court noted in *Nebbia*,[180] that there is no closed category of governmental actions that could satisfy the public use requirement. There is widespread belief that law and government are not important. But efforts to change the law stimulate much turmoil. Government *is* important, and change in government and in law is also important. Beliefs tend to reflect the sentiments held by people, which motivate change or continuity. Justice Fitzgerald wrote in his dissent that, "The majority relies on the principle that the concept of public use is an evolving one; however, I cannot believe that this evolution has eroded our historic protection against the taking of private property for private use to the degree sanctioned by this Court's decision today."[181] These sentiments associated with continuity tend to reflect a mindset which is comfortable with, values, even requires, closure and determinacy;

those sentiments associated with change tend to reflect comfort with open-endedness and indeterminacy.

Nothing said here is intended to suggest that the decision in *Hathcock* should have been akin to that in *Poletown*; the present author has no position on that matter whatsoever. I suggest that, as a matter of logic, under the present organization of appellate justice, opponents of change cannot, in the face of past change, oppose change per se; and that proponents of change cannot categorically accept any legislative change whatsoever.[182] Further, it raises the question of why such lack of sophistication dominates both sides in both cases. Judges construct and adopt propositions or statements in order to define reality and channel policy debate and decision along certain lines or paths and not others, when everyone knows, whatever their personal predilections, that correlative propositions or statements exist on the "other side." These propositions or statements provide a means of legitimizing policy (though not seen as policy) and setting minds at rest; they manifest a belief in the efficacy of words. And so they should, for the chief functions of law are social control and psychic balm. We come, then, to two key considerations: what is the nature of the statements ostensibly relied upon by the court(s) in order to reach their decisions?, and "what is constitutional "law"?

Declarative nature of holdings

The following statements or propositions are taken from the two cases and may be found in the materials provided so far:

> "Government may not take private property for private use, though that is subject to legislatively and judicially created exceptions."
>
> "For the purposes of aiding private corporations, eminent domain is more restrictive than the power of taxation."
>
> "The power of eminent domain is to be used in this instance primarily to accomplish the essential public purposes of alleviating unemployment and revitalizing the economic base of the community."
>
> "The benefit to a private interest is merely incidental."
>
> "The public benefit arising from the Pinnacle Project is an epiphenomenon of the eventual property owners' collective attempts at profit maximization."
>
> "This case is indeed a very straightforward example of government taking one person's property for the sole benefit of another."
>
> "In the present case the transfer of the property to General Motors after the condemnation cannot be considered incidental to the taking. It is only through the acquisition and use of the property by General Motors that the 'public purpose' of promoting employment can be achieved. Thus, it is the economic benefits of the project that are incidental to the private use of the property."

Plaintiffs-appellants urge us to distinguish between the terms "use" and "purpose," asserting they are not synonymous and have been distinguished in the law of eminent domain. We are persuaded the terms have been used interchangeably in Michigan statutes and decisions in an effort to describe the protean concept of public benefit. The term "public use" has not received a narrow or inelastic definition by this Court in prior cases. Indeed, this Court has stated that " [a] public use changes with changing conditions of society" and that " [the] right of the public to receive and enjoy the benefit of the use determines whether the use is public or private. "

These statements, and others like them, are pure assertions. They are declarative and simultaneously prescriptive and proscriptive. In the first statement the "not" is not an absolute not; it is a relative not. Similarly with "sole" in the fifth statement. No judge favors or opposes all existing law or all proposed changes of law. Close readers will recall that numerous propositions are stated by one side and the opposite statements by the other. The foregoing propositions or statements are not law. They are, at most, articulations of a point of view. They cannot, it seems (if they are to be believed), be acknowledged to be mere articulations of a point of view. Their function as social control and psychic balm require that they be treated as "law."

The declaratory nature of the statements—propositions made on the basis of selective perception, sentiment, and/or ideology and not objective study, indeed, without detailed study of the point at issue of any kind recorded in the decision— is further evident when one considers the following list of matters that are interpretive in nature:

> Economic development as a goal of policy in relation to public use requirement.
> Relative benefits between public and private entities.
> Distinction and relative scope of "use" and "purpose."
>
> That the right to own and occupy land will not be subordinated to private corporate interests unless the use of the land condemned by or for the corporation is invested with public attributes sufficient to fairly deem the corporate activity governmental.
>
> However, in the present case the transfer of the property to General Motors after the condemnation cannot be considered incidental to the taking. It is only through the acquisition and use of the property by General Motors that the "public purpose" of promoting employment can be achieved. Thus, it is the economic benefits of the project that are incidental to the private use of the property. These statements are not law. They are statements of topics on which different positions can be taken, or statements of topics which also indicate a position.

The sentences, and their argument, are declarative, intended to describe and affirm a position on the management or balancing of continuity with change. The sentences often include primitive terms conveying the misleading impression of a transcendent Constitution all the while giving effect to national myths, obfuscating the long struggle over power over policy, and being used to influence that struggle. The argument ignores the changes in the meaning of property and of liberty and of other terms that have transpired and continue to transpire. The sentences are especially susceptible to and functional for certain uses in order to channel present and future change by justices seeking to influence the present and the future through particular accounts of the past as to what the Constitution does and does not allow. The taking clause is every bit as elastic in the multiplicity of its interpretation as any other. The Court is engaged in claiming what Hutt calls "rational-thought," that is, objective and, especially, disinterested inquiry that can lead to the accumulation of undisputed knowledge of "the law," whereas it is practicing some combination of (1) "custom-thought," modes of thinking that are laden with selective implicit premises and ideas derived from tradition and customary ways of doing and looking at things, and (2) "power-thought," modes of thought and expression that are constructed to have intended effects on power, politics, and policy, through their service in psycho-political mobilization, that is, psychic balm and social control.

The concepts used in law are selectively adopted and selectively defined. They are used in the process of defining and (re)making the economy as if words had independent meaning and/or the economy and society had an independent structure which judges are trying to achieve. The legal system, the law, and the economy are artifacts, both influencing and influenced by the concepts ensconced in words. Even a non-ideological court, insofar as it must reach a decision, will, in presenting its decision, hover between what seems to be laissez-faire and protection of property, on the one hand, and manifest pragmatic activism, on the other. Ironically, both laissez-faire and pragmatic activism necessarily involve activism, that is, in each instance, the court protecting some interests and not others, and the court structuring the future in one way and not others.

Law does not deal with some given, absolute, transcendent reality; "the law" refers not to something of substance but to a process of social control that is socially constructed in a complex process of working things out. "The law" is a matter of interpretation of language that projects sentiment, preconceptions as to policy, and selective perception. The judge engaged in such projection either appreciates that it is the law he or she is helping to make, or feels that the legal substance already exists and is palpable, ready to be applied.

The Court is engaged willy nilly in the use of language to (1) define reality so as to (2) influence policy and (3) acquire, maintain and exercise power. This is especially true for those areas of life which lack ontological substance—which is pretty much the entire domain of Constitutional Law. By lack of ontological substance I again mean that which does not exist independent of man, which is created by man, and has nothing in reality with which to correspond as a test of "truth." For the record, my statements in this chapter are intended to be both declarative and empirically correct.

What is constitutional "law"?

The foregoing questions concern what law is all about and what legal decision making by courts is all about. They raise the further question, what is constitutional law? and suggest the answer, there is no such thing as constitutional law. At a certain level of abstraction, such is part of the argument of this chapter.

Consider the following statements, reiterations of propositions made in one or the other of the two cases, and in one instance a summary:

1   In the instant case the benefit to be received by the municipality invoking the power of eminent domain is a clear and significant one and is sufficient to satisfy this Court that such a project was an intended and a legitimate object of the Legislature when it allowed municipalities to exercise condemnation powers even though a private party will also, ultimately, receive a benefit as an incident thereto.

2   The power of eminent domain is to be used in this instance primarily to accomplish the essential public purposes of alleviating unemployment and revitalizing the economic base of the community. The benefit to a private interest is merely incidental.

3   Our determination that this project falls within the public purpose, as stated by the Legislature, does not mean that every condemnation proposed by an economic development corporation will meet with similar acceptance simply because it may provide some jobs or add to the industrial or commercial base. If the public benefit was not so clear and significant, we would hesitate to sanction approval of such a project. The power of eminent domain is restricted to furthering public uses and purposes and is not to be exercised without substantial proof that the public is primarily to be benefited. Where, as here, the condemnation power is exercised in a way that benefits specific and identifiable private interests, a court inspects with heightened scrutiny the claim that the public interest is the predominant interest being advanced. Such public benefit cannot be speculative or marginal but must be clear and significant if it is to be within the legitimate purpose as stated by the Legislature. We hold this project is warranted on the basis that its significance for the people of Detroit and the state has been demonstrated.

4   The right to own and occupy land will not be subordinated to private corporate interests unless the use of the land condemned by or for the corporation is invested with public attributes sufficient to fairly deem the corporate activity governmental.

5   The land must itself yield benefits to the municipality in a clear and significant way and not in a speculative or marginal way; even if the beneficiary private owner receives benefit, it must be incidental, not the reason for the use of eminent domain.

6   However, in the present case the transfer of the property to General Motors after the condemnation cannot be considered incidental to the taking. It is only through the acquisition and use of the property by General Motors that the "public purpose" of promoting employment can be achieved. Thus, it is the economic benefits of the project that are incidental to the private use of the property

7   The resale . . . is not a primary purpose and is incidental and ancillary to the primary and real purpose of clearance. Reconstruction was asked for in the

      petition and resale is necessary for such purpose, but the resale is not for the purpose of enabling the city nor any private owner to make a profit.

8   Even if circumstances made redevelopment impossible, slum clearance would be justified on the ground that clearance *in and of itself* is a public use.

9   The object of eminent domain when used in connection with slum clearance is not to convey land to a private corporation as it is in this case, but to erase blight, danger and disease.

10   In the present case the transfer of the property to General Motors after the condemnation cannot be considered incidental to the taking. It is only through the acquisition and use of the property by General Motors that the "public purpose" of promoting employment can be achieved. Thus, it is the economic benefits of the project that are incidental to the private use of the property.

11   The heart of this dispute is whether the proposed condemnation is for the primary benefit of the public or the private user.

The argument upheld in *Hathcock* is that where a clear beneficiary of the condemnation is a private corporation, where economic development is the rationale, where the motivation for the project stemmed from the company rather than the governmental agency, when the purpose of the confiscation was not the land or conditions associated with the land but with the uses to which the land would supposedly be put bny the new, beneficial private owners, when "no one sophisticated in the law at the 1963 Constitution's ratification would have understood 'public use' to permit condemnation of defendants' properties for the construction of a business and technology park owned by private entities," then the use of eminent domain is unconstitutional.

Is the foregoing law? Is it not a combination of (1) selective perception, ideology and/or sentiment and (2) certain propositions adopted by the Court in past cases and used here through which to give effect to (1)?

Justice Ryan in his dissent in *Poletown* argued that

> The real controversy which underlies this litigation concerns the propriety of condemning private property for conveyance to another private party because the use of it by the new owner promises greater public "benefit" than the old use.[183]

Justice Ryan concluded that "as compelling as" the concerns of the majority were about the need for economic development, jobs and tax base, "they hardly support the constitutionality of the governmental action at issue here."[184] Four pages later, Justice Ryan wrote:

> Stripped of the justifying adornments which have universally attended public description of this controversy, the central jurisprudential issue is the right of government to expropriate property from those who do not wish to sell for

the use and benefit of a strictly private corporation. It is not disputed that this action was authorized by statute. The question is whether such authorization is constitutional.[185]

That is not quite true. The *Hathcock* Opinion does not deny eminent domain to government to "expropriate" property from those who do not wish to sell for the use and benefit of a strictly private corporation. If the government qualifies the action on the basis of the conditions spelled out regarding the instrumentalities of commerce exception or the slum clearance exception (no one seems to glorify it by such a name), or the conditions articulated in the summary found at the end of the list just before this paragraph, then it may convey property from an unwilling seller to a strictly private corporation. The unwilling seller may be unhappy but they receive just compensation; no expropriation takes place.

Justice Ryan also writes that, "Present economic conditions notwithstanding, I can discern no principled ground on which their decision can be reconciled with the body of law interpreting the state taking clause."[186] I submit that this proposition is one which is declarative, a matter of interpretation, and an argument.

The question is what is the "body of law" comprising the public use requirement and its elaboration? Is there a something that comprises a body of *constitutional* law for that subject? What is it that enables the justices to claim that something is or is not "constitutional" or that something has passed or not passed "constitutional requirements"?

Part of the argument of this chapter is that much of what is called constitutional law is not law at all but the articulation and application of selective perception, sentiment and/or ideology, and that the form of the court's decisions, wherein it appears that the conclusion follows from the premises, is but either the selective articulation and/or application of their perceptions, sentiments and/or ideology or simply tautological with their premises. The court makes much of the basis on which judgments are to be made, namely, original intent, disagreeing among themselves as to whether the original intent is to be that of the framers, the ratifiers, or those versed in the law. But I surmise that if the framers or the ratifiers, or those versed in the law had been asked, say in 1793, whether the US Supreme Court could pass judgment on legislation, using judicial review to determine something called constitutionality, they would not have agreed. It was more or less only when Chief Justice John Marshall, in *Marbury v. Madison*,[187] put forth the claim for judicial review of the actions of the other branches that it became part—a very important part—of US jurisprudential theory and practice.

Specifically, the Court in *Hathcock* repeatedly speaks of its role in protecting "our constitutional limitations on the government's power of eminent domain."[188] The question is, what constitutional limitations? Justice Fitzgerald says that

> While our decisions have sometimes used the phrase "public purpose" (a phrase often associated with a broad interpretation), the result of our decisions has been to limit the eminent domain power to situations in which direct governmental use is to be made of the land or in which the private recipient will use it to serve the public.[189]

Were these limitations found, like some brooding omnipresence in the sky, or imported by the court into the constitution they were making? Is it only decisions with which a justice disagrees that "makes" rather than "finds"—as when Justice Ryan implies "making" when he claims that the *Poletown* Court's majority "has altered the law of eminent domain?"[190]

Apropos of the problem of taking private property under eminent domain for transfer to private corporations, is not the concept of an instrumentality-of-commerce exception something read into the Constitution? Are not the "three common elements" used to justify "the use of eminent domain for private corporations" something read into the Constitution? These are, in the summarizing words of Justice Ryan, "(1) *public* necessity of the extreme sort, (2) continuing accountability to the *public*, and (3) selection of land according to facts of independent *public* significance."[191] And similarly with the test of slum clearance. Are these not the invention of the court over time? Are these not made part of the constitution by the court's action? Are not "public use" and "public purpose" capable of different formulation? What about possible alternative tests, not necessarily those which would clearly, perhaps unequivocally, permit both of the projects at stake in *Poletown* and *Hathcock*? Could not alternative tests—perhaps broader, perhaps narrower—be used? Is there not a fiction combined with pretense and coupled with hubris that masks the creative role of the court? Nothing is found here; all is made.

It can be said that the Court is only interpreting the Constitution, and that it is not activist to do so in trying to give effect to what the Constitution says. The problems are that the Constitution does not say very much clearly, that what is given effect is the Court's interpretation of what the Constitution says, that different means to the ostensible end are possible, and that what is going on is a function of selective perception, sentiment, and ideology. That the Court is sometime conservative and at other times liberal—as those terms are each variably interpreted—only identifies different versions of an activist court. For any Court to ask whether something is constitutional is to open the door to the affirmation of their interpretation (e.g. Justice Ryan in *Poletown*: "It is not disputed that this action was authorized by statute. The question is whether such authorization is constitutional.").[192]

The point here, to repeat yet again, is not to pick sides in either these larger questions or the specific issues in *Poletown* and *Hathcock*. It is to use these cases to identify what is going on in the process of Constitutional "interpretation." It may be argued that one should identify neither "the law" nor "the rule of law" as insubstantial, as only so many words, lest the authority of existing institutions, namely the Court, be subverted. My response is that, at the level of the present discussion, such only confirms my claim of the Court serving social control and psychic balm roles, perhaps typically, and admittedly not only, elitist roles; and that such things should be brought out in the open.

The ideas comprising the argument of this chapter are fairly commonplace, if still controversial, today. John Sutton thus can quote both the British philosopher Roger Scruton, "A human loves an explanation, and if a good one is not available, a bad one will be confabulated. We see patterns where there are none, and plan our actions around them," and the economic high-theorist Trygve Haavelmo, who wrote, "it is not to be forgotten that the [explanations we offer] are all our own artificial inventions in search of an understanding of real life; they are not hidden truths to be discovered."[193]

Adam Smith, in his *History of Astronomy*, as we have seen, can be interpreted as claiming to be concerned necessarily more with belief than with truth. But this position engenders several questions. What of the truth of his argument? Is his argument intended to be "soothing" and to set minds to rest? Does he claim to believe the argument or is he describing the views of others? Is his argument self-referential, or reflexive? What, if anything, can be labeled truth? In any event, Smith's position here is a corollary to Hume's argument that we do not perceive external objects directly, only through and as mediated by the mind; the object perceived is in the mind. But Smith is concerned with truth, with ontology and epistemology, with the ontological and epistemological standing of his assertions. Several possibilities as to the meaning of assertions, by no means mutually exclusive, exist:

A proposition or postulate constituting an element in a systematic arrangement of propositions, serving as a conjectural definition of the relevant world, in effect an hypothesis.
A deduced element in a chain of reasoning.
A premise in a logical sequence of reasoning.
An empirical observation.
An empirical generalization.
An element of a model of final versus efficient causes.

Instead of a definition of reality as to human nature, a methodological construct, perhaps an element in a model or paradigm, serving as an analytical, stochastic tool in a larger organon of inquiry. If the analysis centering on psychic balm leaves the ontological and epistemological status of Smith's arguments and explanations hanging, so too does the analysis centering on truth. It may well be, however, that what Smith describes is akin to the usual notion of truth as a matter of what satisfies a community of scholars, or simply a group of people, but also to Peirce's view of the pragmatic production of knowledge: "the action of thought is excited by the irritation of doubt, and ceases when belief is attained, so that the production of belief is the sole function of thought."[194] Substitute "awe and wonder" for "irritation of doubt" (perhaps one needs only to add, not substitute) and consider that attained belief sets minds at rest—allays the tumult of the imagination—and one has Smith. Moreover, these beliefs, once widely enough accepted as justifiably true, become part of the status emulation process of society, and thereby become conventional in the quest for respectability and reputability, that is, social recognition and moral approval. Finally, since the propositions that become truth are likely to be conjectural, and are recognized as such by Smith, it is no surprise that they typically are hedged in his work by the use of such terms as "perhaps" and "seem."[195]

Some of the foregoing reduces to, or includes, something like the adoption of a conjecture as a working assumption with the intention of seeing how far it helps Smith's chain as suggested by its reception by others. Smith possibly would have expected some readers to be disinterested in the matter, others to resist his assumption, and still others to accept his conjecture by virtue of his assertion of it. (It is possible, too, that God is similarly assumed.)

Smith's practice resembles ideas of Freud and Pareto. Freud found that people believe or act as if they believe in the omnipotence of thoughts, or of words, that words alone can have an effect on the world. Paul writes, "The basis of this attitude is the narcissistic overvaluation of one's own psyche and one's power to determine events. In at least part of the mind, the reality principle is rejected as too great a narcissistic blow."[196] That undoubtedly is true of certain people, for example, some of those with deep feelings of inferiority. But prayer, for example, can be simply wishful thinking or psychic balm. Pareto identified certain beliefs as rationalizations[197] or myths that are essentially metaphysical and aprioristic assertions, allegations, and speculations that have no foundation (no possible foundation) in fact; they are imaginary principles.[198] Menand writes (apropos of Chauncey Wright) of the "fetishization of words" and that "concepts...[are] the means, and not the ends, of inquiry."[199] Menand himself writes of the "idolatry of ideas" and the "idolatry of concepts," and "the danger of principle."[200]

One application of the omnipotence of words is the practice of politicians and public-relations specialists of making statements in order to finesse problems or manipulate political psychology by assuaging their auditors' minds even though the statements misrepresent actual policy. Here language is a tool not of truth but of illusion, dissimulation, and obfuscation. One application of the omnipotence of words is the practice of appellate judges of articulating propositions from which they appear to derive conclusions for the cases heard by them, and to call those propositions "law." Whereas they are propositions giving effect to selective perception, sentiment, and/or ideology, and whereas they serve as social control and psychic balm, they also, by virtue of their position in organized society, serve to resolve conflict. It is important that some resolution of conflict be achieved and that their words be instrumental in achieving it. Except that the structure of society, the determination of whose interests are to count, and the allocation of resources, level of income, and distribution of income all are importantly governed by the "law" they articulate, it almost is irrelevant what they hold and how they say it, so long as it does its job.

Law, language, and reality

What are we to make of the linguistic expressions "original intentions," "the constitution," "constitutional law," and "rule of law"? Each is a part of a dualism. Each is a function of historical context. Each is a tool of power players in the reconstruction of context, the changing of history. These and other legal expressions are artifacts whose substance is customary. They have no ontological and epistemological existence. They have no existence independent of man and hence have no transcendental ontological status. Although they may or may not exist as matters of custom, they are not matters of truth and falsity, and therefore have no epistemological status.

They are terms of art, part of the activity of doing law. Having zero ontological and epistemological status, they are, on the one hand, emanations of the processes of working out moral rules and legal social control; and, on the other, the tools of practicing attorneys and the objects of inquiry of scholars engaged in legal, or legal-economic, research. Practicing attorneys use them in "the imaginative pursuit of implications and possibilities"[201] on behalf of clients and causes. Each attorney and legal scholar makes "use of his or her imagination to make something out of the materials of the law, some that [either] responds to or [enables the study of] a problem or conflict in the world."[202]

Two rival mental states confront that situation. One mental state requires determinacy and closure. The other mental state is comfortable with ambiguity and open-endedness. Each tends to make assumptions based on what will set their minds at rest and/or support their positions and goals in the working out of the process of composite choice that is the legal-economic nexus.[203] The systems of belief which most people most of the time take to constitute knowledge are both products of and inputs to that nexus. It is one of the functions of language in general and legal language in particular, typically using primitive terms, to enable and also to structure cooperative and noncooperative activity among those whose have, more or less, their own private systems of meaning. Such structuring is along certain lines and not others. Language is both a mode of social control and a result of the machinations of power players seeking to control social control. Authorship is both concrete and subtle and both deliberative and nondeliberative; authors, legal and otherwise, create and re-create texts with meaning, thereby participating in the process of creating and re-creating the world. Each author, through imaginative use of linguistic and cultural materials, "reconstitutes or remakes his own language and culture, thereby offering us, in a sense, [or contributing to] a remade world (in or through a text)."[204] That is what law is in part about, a means of social control that is itself subject to social control—and "how we necessarily become involved in the constitution and reconstitution of our character (our selves) and our community (our society)."[205]

The view of law just described comports well with those who are comfortable with ambiguity and open-endedness. The opposite view of law is that of traditional analytical jurisprudence, motivated by a felt need for determinacy and closure and/or absolutist legitimization, the former for psychic balm, the latter for social control. As Eisele puts it,

> Traditional jurisprudence treats law as an independently existing object, a physical (or metaphysical) object that exists out there in the world, simply and cleanly unconnected with humans or human efforts and actions, until human being put themselves into relation with it by choice.[206]

The only other activity that commands such a view is religion. That different people have different theologies and different legal solutions to problems of structure and of conflict, that is, the ubiquity of diversity, does not prevent a people from having an absolutist view of its own law and/or theology. Other mass phenomena typically are treated pragmatically, although some individuals have an absolutist view. For example, the rules of football (allowing the forward pass, denying linemen certain blocking modes) and baseball (the size of the strike zone, certain types of pitches) are widely but not universally understood to be driven by profit maximization.

But "this traditional view draws the wrong analogy for law. Law is not a physical object; it is a human art or activity."[207] As such, law depends upon humans for its existence.[208] Not only does the traditional view draw the wrong analogy, it "is misleading and holds dangers for misunderstanding"—to which I would add, dangers for manipulation and autocracy. The traditional "way of relating us to law relies upon the reification of law, and while this process of reification is very natural to us," it must be resisted. "For law ... is not an independent entity, not a system of rules separable from the humans who have made them or from the conditions under which these rules are made, used, and remade or removed."[209] Despite the pretense or belief that rules preexist and are found and not made, rules are more or less like primitive terms, given different meanings by different people. "Rules of law speak not unambiguously or unequivocally, but generally and broadly. They cover a range of possible cases, and thus require that we *work* with them in applying them to any specific case or controversy in order to find or fashion a resolution that is legally acceptable."[210] And determining what is "legally acceptable" typically is the domain of the final appellate court. That is what *Poletown* and *Hathcock* are about: not finding law but making law on the basis of selective perception, sentiment, and ideology. From the standpoint of the *Hathcock* court, *Poletown* represented statism and liberalism run amok; *Hathcock* itself represents the mindset of a court substantially composed of economic conservatives seeking to undo the perceived statism and liberalism of the past. Quite aside from current political and ideational movements, law tends strongly to embody the traditional, so the actions of the *Hathcock* court are not surprising; what they are is misunderstood insofar as the court engages in linguistic games as to "the law," "constitutional law," and the like.

Eisele's article is a solid example of a wide variety of bodies of work that treat language as an artifact. He cites Stanley Cavell, A. W. B. Simpson and James Boyd White in law and Immanuel Kant, Michael Oakeshott, and Ludwig Wittgenstein in philosophy. Other fields manifesting this point of view include sociolinguistics, social studies of science, deconstruction, hermeneutics, and structuralism. With regard to law, Eisele writes, in part summarizing Simpson,

> metaphysically and epistemologically, the common law ... can be thought of as a medium of traditional ideas, concepts, and expressions extending over many years or even centuries, out of which judges and lawyers generate rrules and propositions of law that are, for the time being, accepted (or rejected). ... this activity is a matter of making warranted, acceptable uses of shared legal (and non-legal) materials. ... law takes place as an activity of

meaning and significance within a broader conceptual (and normative) context. This "whole" gives law some of the significance that it has. And, rather than the rationality of the law depending solely upon the logical manipulation of legal rules, Simpson argues that the rationality of legal rules depends upon the whole body of materials that compose the common law. In a sense, then, the common law is a kind of language.[211]

The practice of law—and of economics—is replete with the deployment of arguments used as instruments of persuasion, the choice of which depends upon judgments as to their influence. The same argument may be used in pursuit of comparable or noncomparable purposes; different arguments may be used for the same or similar purposes. When it suited railroad interests in the nineteenth century to combat federal regulatory legislation they claimed regulation was a state matter; when combating state regulation, they claimed it was a federal matter. When public utilities sought rate increases during periods of inflation, they invoked reproduction cost; during periods of deflation, original cost.

It is, as Philip Ryan[212] has argued, one function of the policy sciences, not to take sides in partisan debates, but to point out the partisan manipulation of arguments and words. Ryan identifies an "unmasking turn of mind," which he attributes to hidden motives. The result can also ensue from a sense of the vacuity of the arguments used and/or of their metaphysical, ontological, and epistemic foundations. Where unmasking is the means of strategic and manipulative communication, it has an undermining function, driven by the desire to achieve certain substantive results. Where unmasking has no such intentions, as is the case here, the aim is to elevate the level of argument and make explicit the substance of the issues involved in a conflict. Some of this is wishful thinking, given the apparent willingness of people to use and to respond favorably to empty absolutist arguments resonant with national myths. But the aim is in fact to minimize the manipulative element in policy making, including policies as to decision making structure. To have any chance at such success, discussion must not degenerate into outright political warfare in which those who disagree treat each other as enemies; where such degeneration has taken place, discussion without absolutist arguments and linguistic formulations may be the only means of escape.

The historical record is both mixed and ambiguous but while judicial elitism is present today and has not been absent since judicial review was institutionalized, what Larry D. Kramer[213] calls popular constitutionalism may have been more prevalent earlier and is not absent today. The early conflicts over judicial review seem to parallel those over the notion of rule of law; indeed, one function of "rule of law" is to legitimize judicial review. The context is the conflict over power discussed earlier between legislature and courts. Thus two joint reviewers identify as the "main theme" of Kramer's recent book, that

> Almost from the beginning of the national government the judiciary has been developing an exclusive claim to "say what the law is." To do so it had

to overcome claims of the executive and legislative branches to an equal authority. The court's instrument was judicial review of legislation.[214]

The meaning of "equal authority" is unclear. How are different interpretations resolved? With judicial review, the answer is mixed: judicial review provides a more or less temporary "definitive" result but not a conclusive result. The issue can come up again and the result changed—hence the "more or less temporary." Without judicial review, no short term or temporary result seems possible. But Kramer's interests reside elsewhere. Again in the words of the joint reviewers,

> Before the Civil War, while the courts were creating this system, the other branches of government successfully affirmed their own competence to ascertain what the Constitution meant and were supported by popular constitutionalism embodied in the Whig and Democratic parties. But after the war, the Supreme Court increasingly exercised and stretched judicial review to discover in the Constitution meanings unknown to its authors or to "the people themselves."[215]

And

> during the last half-century the exclusive right of the Supreme Court to settle constitutional issues has won all but universal acceptance.[216]

Nonetheless, Kramer, the Dean of the Stanford Law School, is said to conclude that

> the Supreme Court has arrogated to itself a role that cannot be justified on the basis of our political history and our experience as a people. ... [Kramer seeks to remind] people that the government is their government and that the Constitution is their constitution, subject to their interpretation in their own way. ... [He] challenges conventional constitutional jurisprudence and conventional constitutional history ... [and supports] popular refusal to accept the Supreme Court's usurping title to the people's document.[217]

In the conflict between Locke and Marshall, Kramer sides with Locke: constitutional issues should be decided by either the legislature or directly by the citizens. Such a solution deprives courts of judicial review and potentially pits legislature against people and, in the federal system, legislatures against each other. But it does carry the role of the public, "the people themselves," from approving the constitution to possibly constructing it and certainly interpreting its meaning.

Laurence H. Tribe, in his review of Kramer's book,[218] suggests that Kramer overstates the historical significance of popular constitutionalism. He also interprets judicial review not as the theory that the Court's "power to say what the Constitution means automatically trumps any competing interpretive authority" but as only the presupposition that "the Supreme Court is duty-bound to enforce the Constitution as the supreme law of the land." Tribe accuses Kramer of "pulling the linguistic trick of equating judicial review with a judicial monopoly over constitutional truth" and of supporting "lawless conduct" when he affirms " 'outright defiance' of the court's contentious decisions," withholding of financial support of the court, terminating its jurisdiction over sensitive topics, decreasing its size, packing it with increased members, and/or impeaching justices whose decisions offend.[219]

There is much to be said in favor of both sides of the issue of judicial review. What Kramer considers usurpation, Tribe conventionalizes into a modest pre-supposition. What Kramer considers the uncovering—unmasking—of obfus-cated open-endedness, Tribe considers lawless conduct. Both men appreciate that language is power and that the Supreme Court thrives on its self-promoted powers of judicial review and judicial construction. No less is evident from the conflict between *Poletown* and *Hathcock*.

What, however, is to be said of the pretense and hubris of such language as "intentions of the founders," "constitutional law," "the law," "finding the law," and "rule of law," language which masks selective perception, sentiment, and ideology? Need we do away with judicial review? There is, indeed, much to be said in favor of both sides of the issue of judicial review. Everyone can identify "wrong" decisions by courts.

The proposal here is much less drastic than Kramer's. The proposal is to reform the use of language by the court which uses insubstantial, absolutist terms as if they constituted or referred to transcendent and objective phenomena. The court decides cases ostensibly on the basis of some of its own past decisions which it treats as constitutional law and claims it does so by pursuing the rule of law and only finding the law, whereas in actuality the court is proceding on the basis of (at least) a majority's selective perception, sentiments, and ideology. We would readily see through this if we were outsiders confronting a village shaman. That we are insiders in our own society should not prevent a similar recognition; otherwise we are accomplices.

There is typically no policy analysis explicating why one decision is felt to be better than another. Transforming court language from invocation of insubstan-tial, absolutist terms to analysis of pros and cons, to the grounds on which one policy is preferable to the other, to acknowledgment that it is policy making in which the court is engaged, that the court is making and not finding the law, and so on, would reveal judicial opinions to be what they are, namely, opinions. It would also serve an educational function, training policy analytic minds, helping to minimize the roles of uncontested preconceptions and of jumps from precon-ception to policy. Doing so would not, however, necessarily yield the "correct" policy, but it would both enrich the process of working things out and help mini-mize the practice of intellectual fraud. Among other things it would puncture the illusion that particular cases have unique determinate solutions. Such is illusion in both economics and in law, and is achieved only by assuming out of court/analysis all that would prevent reaching that putative unique solution. Doing so would also disabuse those who fail to see that both legislature and court are part of government and that each can threaten liberty of the individual. But, even more important, it would instruct people that both legislation and court decisions inevitably must include making choices promoting some interests and not others, and that such is the very nature of policy and of social control. The notion of an independent judiciary is partly a fiction. Judges are attractive to those who appoint or elect them because of their political and ideological beliefs and connections. Those judges who on any issue vote against the preferences of those who elect or appoint them may appear traitorous to the latter but their independence is substantive, not fictional.

As Radin has argued, a Wittgensteinian conception of terms such as the rule of law emphasizes both its dependence on social context and on reiterated human activity.[220] Above all, "judges are not functionaries but rather constitute an interpretive community."[221] We are pragmatic even when we least realize it and when we most deny it.[222]

Moreover, the tired old fictional issue of activist versus non-activist judges would be given a decent and much deserved burial under my proposal. All judges are making law; all judges are activist. It is only by selectively identifying certain issues and positions as activist and others as non-activist that the fiction can be deployed.

I have emphasized what is so wrong with the way judges write decisions. Every case has more than one possible resolution. Every court is under an absolute necessity of making a choice. Every decision is to some degree and in some sense arbitrary. Judges seem incapable of imagining that they could write decisions differently, but that is a matter of training and of their adoption of the highpriest mantle, the latter a function of the former. Over the years I have said similar things critical of economic theory and practice. One of the defects of judges' and economists' analyses is their tendency to ground prices on relative costs. But cost is not an independent given; they are a function of human institutions. When the low value of poor lives is used to support dumping toxic waste on less developed countries or spending less on protecting them from natural catastrophe, such only gives effect to the status quo structure of rights or power underlying the prices used to calculate value.[223]

Distinguishing between cases, often on trivial grounds, is not policy analysis. But more is involved than the way judges write decisions. What issues they decide is also important. The Poletown project may or may not have been sensible as public policy, so too the airport business and research park in *Hathcock*, and whether the use of public funds, under the power of eminent domain, to acquire land for a sports stadium to be operated by a professional team is or is not a poor investment for cities using tax receipts diverted from essential needs.[224] But it seems ludicrous to reach such large decisions of policy on such a slight legal basis as the convoluted implied prohibition by the taking clause of using eminent domain for private purposes. It is unlikely that such can be prevented in a blanket manner under current practices. But education in policy analysis, as contemplated here, might lead to a different practice.

Judicial review for many people is an aspect of elitist control of government. The proposal made here would not overturn judicial review but it would tend to make for wider and more open discussion. The proposal would be enhanced by the appointment of non-lawyers to the appellate bench, but such would only work if scholars and other professionals were not appointed because of their politics and ideology. Such, of course, may be visionary.

Conclusion

This chapter questions the probative truth and value of several linguistic formulations and beliefs that are common to cases and decisions of constitutional law. These formulations and beliefs include constitutional law itself, rule of law, the law, judicial non-activism, unconstitutional, and so on. Courts should refrain from certain claims: that past court holdings are part of the constitution or rule of law, that law is found and not made, that denigrate the legislature, that presume and assert that judge-made law is sounder than statute law, that judge-made law becomes part of the constitution, that pursue absolutist legitimization of court-made law, and so on. Despite the seriousness of the legal issues before the courts and the almost-sacerdotal demeanor and behavior of some or many judges and the atmosphere of their courtrooms, these claims and pretenses are almost comical. So too is the claim and pretense that judges follow precedents. Judges can choose from different lines of precedent, which are available to provide seeming logicality to inevitability of any decision the court desires, on balance, to reach. Saying all that does not mean that courts have not made decisions arguably promoting moral sentiments and social policy.

In the place of these terms and the claims and pretenses affected by them, the article calls for the construction of decisions in three parts. The first part would state the history of the litigation and the arguments and so on made by the parties. The second part would first identify the issues in the case. If the judges differ as to their statement of the issues, these differences must be made clear. It would then identify the positions that may be taken on each issue, the pro and con arguments regarding each position on each issue, and the grounds on which the positions and arguments may be ranked. The final part would announce the majority opinion of the court and any dissents, including the reasons for same in light of the foregoing second part. Included in parts two and three might be a comparative analysis of this case and this decision *vis-à-vis* others. Also included in parts two and three must be comparable statements as to the future which the judges seek to promote by their decision. People will know what their law is, the grounds on which the decision rests, and the intentions of the court.

Legal and economic consultants regularly author documents for their principals which seek to identify the alternatives, the grounds on which each alternative may be adopted or rejected, and either abstaining from proposing a solution or propose a choice of alternatives and provide the reasons for their choice. If such can be done by policy analysts for their employers, surely it can be done by the judiciary for the country they serve.

If the proposed reforms presented here are to have a chance to succeed, both status emulation and the quest for power must be defused, in fact and not misrepresented by pretense and pomp. Adam Smith understood and denigrated both, but they are still with us. Their eclipse may be difficult to effectuate. However, in Smith's time the ideas of limited monarchy, democracy, and an "independent" judiciary were given by many little chance of success. Democracy and the conversation that both promotes and derives from it has had enormous, albeit not universal success. Elitism and oligarchical control of government and its use by and to the advantage of those who can control it remain. One element thereof consists of the appellate courts of our governments. Politicians select the judiciary, thus controlling the interpretation as well as the passage of laws. Politics is how we govern ourselves. It can be enriched and further pluralized by making it more open and linguistically meaningful. The appellate courts are a good place to commence our further education.

Acknowledgment

The author is indebted to Richard Dawson and Nicholas Mercuro for comments on an earlier version of this chapter.

Notes

1 Adam Smith (1980) *Essays on Philosophical Subject*, pp. 45–6.
2 Ibid., p. 46.
3 Ibid., p. 61.
4 471 Mich. 445, 684 N.W. 2nd 765 (2004). Hereafter *Hathcock*.
5 410 Mich. 616, 304 N.W. 2nd 455 (1981). Hereafter *Poletown*.
6 My intention is to be straightforward and to engage in a minimum, if any, of pretense and studied obfuscation, that is, with a minimum of lines of reasoning purporting to establish absolutist legitimization when there is no such thing and when the reasoning is fraudulent (in the sense of Vilfredo Pareto; see *infra*), even if well intentioned. These questions concern what decision making by courts is all about.
7 See Warren J. Samuels (2002) "The Rule of Law and the Capture and Use of Government in a World of Inequality," in Warren J. Samuels (ed.) *Economics, Governance and Law: Essays on Theory and Policy*, pp. 61–9.
8 C. T. McIntire (2004) *Herbert Butterfield: Historian as Dissenter*, p. 122.
9 Ibid.
10 Ibid.
11 Warren J. Samuels (1999) "Hayek from the Perspective of an Institutionalist Historian of Economic Thought: An Interpretive Essay," *Journal des Economistes et des Etudes Humaines*, 9: 81–94; and Samuels (2000) "An Essay on the Unmagic of Norms and Rules and of Markets," *Journal des Economistes et des Etudes Humaines*, 10: 95–101.
12 C. T. McIntire, *supra* n. 8, pp. 122–3.
13 For example, are trade unions "organic" or "natural" and are they consonant with "capitalism"?
14 William Harold Hutt (1990) [1936] *Economists and the Public: A Study of Competition and Opinion*, 3 and *passim*.
15 Warren J. Samuels (1974) *Pareto on Policy*.
16 Warren J. Samuels (2006) "Interpreting the Bible, The Constitution, and the History of Economic Thought," 24-A *Research in the History of Economic Thought and Methodology*, 24: 79–98.

17 Jaroslav Pelikan (2004) *Interpreting the Bible and the Constitution.*
18 Warren J. Samuels (1979) "Legal Realism and the Burden of Symbolism: The Correspondence of Thurman Arnold," *Law and Society Review*, 13: 997.
19 For a broader array of problems of language as they arise in economics, see Warren J. Samuels (2001) "Some Problems in the Use of Language in Economics," *Review of Political Economy*, 13(1): 91–100. Chapter 9 in this volume.
20 There is irony present. A century ago it was argued by some that imposing the antitrust or public utility laws kept companies from continuing to realize their monopoly profits, which was their property right and for which they should be compensated. Others denied that such was a property right and argued that compensation should not be paid; paying compensation meant the effective guarantee of monopoly profits. It will be noticed that the common language involves saying something is or is not a property right, whereas the issue is whether the ownership should include that something, that is, an *ought* rather than an *is*. Another pertinent example of irony: When slavery was outlawed and the slaves freed, some felt that this constituted confiscation of their owners' property, and required compensation (i.e. should be compensated); whereas others felt that it was the former slaves who should be compensated, for the past loss of their freedom.
21 If such activist government seems to be anathema to the doctrine of laissez-faire, the explanation is that the doctrine is largely a matter of sentiment and ideology, and not indicative of the actual economic role of government, at all levels, in the history of the United States. Whenever people have encountered problems, they typically have turned to government for solutions.
22 William Blackstone (1765–9) *Commentaries on the Laws of England*, 4 vols, II.I.2.
23 *Hathcock*, p. 769.
24 *Poletown*, p. 457.
25 When the activities leading to the *Poletown* case began, it was obvious to this author that it involved deep issues of policy, equity, and interpretation. After some initial collection of materials, with a view to writing a book, I opted to devote my research to other matters and dropped the project. Several publications have been written, for example, Armond Cohen (1982) *Poletown, Detroit: A Case Study in "Public Use" and Reindustrialization* and Jeanie Wylie (1989) *Poletown: A Community Betrayed*. The present author has published several writings on the takings problem and on the theory of property and government: Warren J. Samuels (1992) *Essays on the Economic Role of Government*, 2 vols; Warren J. Samuels (ed.) (1989) *Fundamentals of the Economic Role of Government*; Warren J. Samuels (1974) "An Economic Perspective on the Compensation Problem," *Wayne L. Rev.*, 21: 113–34; Warren J. Samuels and Nicholas Mercuro (eds) (1999) *The Fundamental Interrelationship Between Government and Property*; Warren J. Samuels and Nicholas Mercuro (1979) "The Role and Resolution of the Compensation Principle in Society: Part One—The Role," *Research in Law and Economics*, 1: 157–94 and Warren J. Samuels and Nicholas Mercuro (1980) "The Role and Resolution of the Compensation Principle in Society: Part Two—The Resolution," *Research in Law and Economics*, 2: 103–28.
26 On November 12, 2004 a half-day symposium was sponsored by the Michigan State University College of Law. The conference was entitled "The Death of *Poletown*: The Future of Eminent Domain and Urban Development After *County of Wayne v. Hathcock*." Substantive presentations on the issues raised by *Hathcock* were delivered by eight speakers and others from the floor. Five of the eight were law professors, two were practicing attorneys whose law firms were involved in both cases, and three were economists, William A. Fischel of Dartmouth College, Nicholas Mercuro and the present author. As will be seen later, the issue in *Hathcock* was economic development, not urban (re)development (as in the symposium title), though one can imagine both glee and fear that the holding on the former might be extended to the latter, though the decision of the court gave nary a hint of that.

27 Harry N. Scheiber, Harold G. Vatter, and Harold Underwood Faulkner (1976) *American Economic History*, p. 300.
28 See text *infra* p.183 n. 30, 31, p.184 n. 40.
29 Ibid., pp. 300–1.
30 Harry N. Scheiber (1973) "Property Law, Expropriation, and Resource Allocation by Government: The United States, 1789–1910," *Journal of Economic History*, 33: 232.
31 Ibid., p. 233.
32 Ibid., p. 237.
33 Ibid.
34 Ibid., p. 239.
35 *Scudder v. Trenton Del. Falls Co.*, 1 N.J. Eq. 694 (1832), quoted in Scheiber, *supra* n. 30, p. 240.
36 Scheiber, *supra* n. 30, p. 241, discussing *Mills v. St. Clair County*, 8 How. 569 (1850), p. 584.
37 Scheiber, *supra* n. 30, p. 243.
38 Ibid., p. 245.
39 Ibid., p. 249.
40 Ibid., p. 240; *Ryerson v. Brown*, 35 Mich. 334, 337 (1877).
41 Samuels and Mercuro (1999), *supra* n. 24.
42 For example, *Miller v. Schoene*, 276 U.S. 272 (1928); see Warren J. Samuels (1971) "Interrelations Between Legal and Economic Processes," *Journal of Law and Economics*, 14: 435–50.
43 *Poletown*, p. 457, quoting from *Hays v. Kalamazoo*, 316 Mich. 443, 453–4, 25 N.W.2d 787, 169 A.L.R. 1218 (1947).
44 *Hathcock*, p. 472.
45 *Poletown*, p. 473, quoting from another decision written by Justice Cooley, in *People ex rel. Detroit & Howell R. Co. v. Salem Twp. Board*, 20 Mich. 452, 485 (1870).
46 Ibid., p. 473.
47 *Poletown*, p. 474; see *Ryerson*, *supra* n. 40.
48 *Poletown*, p. 474.
49 *Hathcock*, pp. 785ff.
50 *Poletown*, p. 474.
51 *Hathcock*, p. 780.
52 Ibid., p. 785.
53 Ibid., p. 787; Justice Weaver's opinion also faults the majority opinion in the earlier case for taking a quote "out of context and twist[ing] its meaning," ibid., p. 790.
54 *Poletown*, pp. 480–1.
55 *Hathcock*, p. 786; the Court itself says that "Every business, every productive unit in society, does, as Justice Cooley noted, contribute in some way to the commonwealth." The Court was not happy with "a vague economic benefit stemming from a private profit-maximizing enterprise [being proposed as] a 'public use'."
56 *Poletown*, p. 458; further presentation of the *Poletown* Court's position, and the *Hathcock* Court's very different position, is found later in the subsections "Economic development as a policy goal" and "Relative benefits as between public and private entities."
57 *Poletown*, pp. 458–9.
58 *Hathcock*, p. 784.
59 Ibid., p. 786.
60 Ibid., p. 796.
61 Ibid., p. 781 n. 56.
62 Quoted and paraphrased from *Hathcock*, pp. 781–3; see also Justice Ryan in *Poletown*.
63 *Hathcock*, p. 781.
64 Justice Fitzgerald, dissenting, in *Poletown*, p. 462.
65 *Poletown*, p. 462, quoting from *In re Slum Clearance*, 331 Mich. 714, p. 720; emphasis in the original.
66 *Poletown*, p. 462.

67 Ibid., p. 463.
68 Ibid., p. 477.
69 Ibid., p. 477.
70 Ibid., p. 477, quoting *In re Slum Clearance*, p. 722 (emphasis in original).
71 *Poletown*, p. 477.
72 *Hathcock*, p. 783.
73 Ibid., p. 784.
74 Ibid., pp. 795–6.
75 *Poletown*, p. 458.
76 *Hathcock*, p. 786.
77 Ibid.
78 Ibid., p. 788.
79 *Poletown*, p. 459.
80 Ibid.
81 Ibid., pp. 459–60.
82 Ibid., p. 462.
83 Ibid., p. 462.
84 Ibid., pp. 463–4.
85 Ibid., p. 464.
86 Ibid.
87 Ibid., p. 466.
88 Ibid., p. 467.
89 Ibid.
90 Ibid., p. 468.
91 Ibid., p. 468 n. 6.
92 Ibid., p. 470.
93 Ibid., p. 470 n. 9.
94 Ibid., p. 471.
95 *Hathcock*, p. 778.
96 *Poletown*, pp. 475–6.
97 *Hathcock*, p. 783.
98 *Hathcock*, p. 783, quoting *Poletown*, p. 478.
99 *Hathcock*, p. 784, quoting *Poletown*, p. 458.
100 Justice Fitzgerald in *Poletown*, p. 464.
101 Warren J. Samuels (1989) "The Legal-Economic Nexus," *George Washington Law Review*, 57 (August 1989): 1556–78.
102 *Hathcock*, p. 779.
103 Ibid., p. 790.
104 Ibid., p. 779.
105 Ibid., p. 779.
106 Ibid., p. 780.
107 Ibid., pp. 780–1, 784.
108 Ibid., p. 784.
109 Ibid., p. 789; Justice Weaver then claimed that the majority both cited Justice Cooley "out of context" and "erroneously equated" terms.
110 Justice Weaver, in *Hathcock*, p. 797.
111 Ibid., pp. 788–9.
112 Ibid., p. 790.
113 Ibid.
114 In 2 Cooley, *Constitutional Limitations* (eighth edn) pp. 1139–40.
115 Agreement seems to exist on that point. The Opinion of the Court presents another quote from Justice Cooley to the same effect: "We find ourselves somewhat at sea, however, when we undertake to define in the light of the judicial decisions, what constitutes a public use." Cooley, *Constitutional Limitations* (1998) (fifth edn, p. 659).

116 *Hathcock*, p. 792.
117 Ibid., pp. 788–9.
118 Ibid., pp. 793–4 n. 23.
119 Ibid., p. 798.
120 Ibid., pp. 793–4 n. 23.
121 Ibid., p. 798.
122 Ibid.
123 Ibid., p. 785.
124 Ibid., p. 792.
125 See Warren J. Samuels and Arthur S. Miller (eds) (1987) *Corporations and Society: Power and Responsibility.*
126 *Hathcock*, p. 479.
127 *Hathcock*, p. 786.
128 *Poletown*, p. 468.
129 Ibid., p. 470.
130 Ibid., p. 470 n.9.
131 Ibid., pp. 470–1.
132 Ibid., p. 478.
133 Ibid., p. 480.
134 Ibid.
135 Ibid., p. 481.
136 Ibid.
137 Ibid., p. 482, paraphrased.
138 Ibid.
139 Justice Weaver in *Hathcock*, p. 789.
140 *Poletown*, p. 481.
141 Ibid.
142 *Poletown*, p. 464.
143 Ibid., p. 465.
144 *Hathcock*, p. 786.
145 *Poletown*, pp. 458–9.
146 Ibid., pp. 461–2.
147 Ibid., p. 463.
148 Ibid., pp. 474–5.
149 *Hathcock*, p. 773.
150 Ibid., p. 775.
151 Ibid., p. 776; in p. 776 n. 32, we read, in re MCL 2113.56(2): "With respect to an acquisition by a public agency, the determination of public necessity by that agency is binding on the court in the absence of a showing of fraud, error of law, or abuse of discretion."
152 Ibid., p. 778.
153 Ibid., p. 785. At this point, p. 785 n. 84 reads: See, for example, *Lakehead Pipe Line Co. v Dehn*, 340 Mich. 25, 39; 64 N.W.2d 903 (1954) ("The question of whether the proposed use is a public use is a judicial one."), quoting *Cleveland v Detroit*, 322 Mich. 172, 179; 33 N.W.2d 747 (1948).
154 *Hathcock*, p. 787.
155 Ibid. In p. 787 n. 97 one reads: "See Baughman, *Justice Moody's lament unanswered: Michigan's unprincipled retroactivity jurisprudence*, 79 Mich. B J 664 (2000), quoting COOLEY, Constitutional Limitations, 91" ("When the Michigan Supreme Court exercises the 'judicial power', it is, as said by Justice Cooley, concerned with a determination of what the existing law is, even in 'changing' a mistaken interpretation, rather than making a 'predetermination of what the law shall be for the regulation of all future cases', which is an act that 'distinguishes a legislative act from a judicial one'.")
156 *Hathcock*, p. 787.

157 *Poletown*, p. 459.
158 Ibid., p. 463.
159 *Hathcock*, p. 792.
160 Ibid., p. 780.
161 *Poletown*, p. 459.
162 Ibid., p. 459.
163 Ibid., quoting *People ex rel Detroit & Howell R Co v Salem Twp Board*, 20 Mich. 452, 480–1 (1870).
164 *Poletown*, p. 462.
165 Ibid., p. 464.
166 Ibid.
167 Ibid., pp. 464–5.
168 Ibid., p. 473 n. 16.
169 Ibid., p. 474.
170 *Hathcock*, p. 791.
171 See, for example, ibid., p. 776 and *passim*.
172 Ibid., p. 783.
173 For example, ibid., p. 778.
174 *Poletown*, p. 478 and *Hathcock*, pp. 781 and 783.
175 *Poletown*, p. 459, quoting *People ex rel Detroit & Howell R Co v Salem Twp Board*, 20 Mich. 452, 480–1 (1870).
176 *Hathcock*, p. 785.
177 Ibid., p. 786.
178 Ibid., p. 791.
179 *Poletown*, p. 464.
180 291 U.S. 502 (1877).
181 *Poletown*, p. 464.
182 Warren J. Samuels (1992) "The Pervasive Proposition, 'What Is, Is and Ought to Be': A Critique," in William S. Millberg (ed.) *The Megacorp and Macrodynamics: Essays in Momory of Alfred Eichner*, pp. 273–85.
183 Ibid., p. 465.
184 Ibid., p. 467 n. 4.
185 Ibid., p. 471.
186 Ibid., p. 481.
187 1 Cranch 137 (1803).
188 Opinion, in *Hathcock*, p. 786.
189 *Poletown*, p. 463.
190 Ibid., p. 464.
191 Ibid., p. 478.
192 *Poletown*, p. 471.
193 John Sutton (2000) *Marshall's Tendencies: What Can Economists Know?*, pp. vii, 16.
194 Charles Sanders Peirce (1957) *Essays in the Philosophy of Science*, p. 36.
195 Willie Henderson (2003) "How Does Smith Achieve a Synthesis in Writing? Evidence from His Analysis of the Propensity to Truck, Barter and Exchange," in Warren J. Samuels, Willie Henderson, Kirk D. Johnson, and Marianne Johnson (eds) *Essays on the history of economics*.
196 Robert A. Paul (1991) "Freud's Anthropology: A Reading of the 'Cultural Books'," in Jerome Neu (ed.) *The Cambridge Companion to Freud*, p. 273.
197 Pareto used the term "derivation"; the comparable term "rationalization" comes from James Harvey Robinson (1921) *The Mind in the Making*, New York: Harper & Brothers.
198 Samuels (1974), *supra* n. 15, p. 34 and *passim*.
199 Louis Menand (2001) *The Metaphysical Club*, p. 212.
200 Ibid., pp. 374, 425.

201 Thomas D. Eisele (1986–7) "The Activity of Being a Lawyer: The Imaginative Pursuit of Implications and Possibilities," *Tennessee. L. Rev.*, 54 (345): 545.
202 Ibid., p. 349.
203 Samuels (1989), *supra* n. 101.
204 Eisele (1987), *supra* n. 201, p. 356.
205 Ibid., p. 357.
206 Ibid., p. 366.
207 Ibid., pp. 366–7.
208 Ibid., p. 367.
209 Ibid., p. 368.
210 Ibid., p. 370.
211 Ibid., p. 374.
212 Philip Ryan (2004) "The Policy Sciences and the Unmasking Turn of Mind," *Review of Policy Research*, 21 (4) (September 2004): 715–28.
213 Larry D. Kramer (2005) *The People Themselves: Popular Constitutionalism and Judicial Review*.
214 Edmund S. Morgan and Marie Morgan (2005) *"Bill of Wrongs,"* *The New York Review of Books* (March 10, 2005): 31, 33 (book review).
215 Ibid., p. 34. By extension, an argument parallel to judicial review would hold that only attorneys could interpret the law, with the effect that social scientists and other trained persons could not publish in law journals. A problem with that argument is that the law assumes that people know the law pertinent to their actions and therefore can be held responsible for their actions.
216 Ibid.
217 Ibid.
218 Laurence H. Tribe (2005) *"The People's Court,"* *New York Times Book Review* (October 24, 2005): 32 (book review).
219 Ibid., p. 33.
220 Margaret Jane Radin (1989) "Reconsidering the Rule of Law," *Boston University L. Rev.*, 69: 781, 797; see also pp. 807, 809, and *passim*.
221 Ibid., p. 813.
222 Ibid., pp. 812ff.
223 Richard Posner's approach to the pragmatic nature of law is sensible but his adoption of the economic metric of comparative costs is unduly analytically narrowing. See Richard A. Posner (2004) *Catastrope: Risk and Response*.
224 Philip Weinberg (2005) "Eminent Domain for Private Sports Stadiums: Fair Ball or Foul?" St. John's Legal Studies Research Paper No. 0 5-04 (January 2005).

11 An evolutionary approach to law and economics

With A. Allan Schmid and James D. Shaffer

The question of the relationships between legal and economic (generally meaning *market*) processes has been a central preoccupation of moral philosophy, political theory, economics, and jurisprudence at least since the time of John Locke and Adam Smith, when the idea of an economy at least conceptually separable from the polity came to the forefront. Within these disciplines, there have been understandings—sometimes explicit, but more typically implicit—of the critical importance of government in economic affairs and of the economy for governmental affairs.

Most attempts to analyze legal and economic processes have been unilineal: either the economy is seen to be a function of law or the law a function of the economy. A few writers have attempted more ambitious models of interrelationships between the two spheres, but most work has dealt with parts of the larger subject in such a way that conclusions on particular topics, or solutions to particular problems, have been driven by the treatments of what is endogenous and what is exogenous. For example, analyses of certain putative or potential rights, or of certain governmental processes, have been conducted in such a way that the results depend on the identification and treatment of the particular rights or processes and on whatever factors and forces are begged by their omission.[1]

Furthermore, most writing on the subject of the economic role of government has been either straightforwardly normative or heavily constrained and channeled by normative, ideological, material, or subjective considerations. Perhaps all social science analysis necessarily is so constrained and channeled, but work on the economic role of government has been particularly normative in character. Arguably all theories of the economic role of government, even those that were presented as minimalist and noninterventionist, constitute agendas for government, giving affect to selective, largely implicit, antecedent normative premises. Ideology in particular has influenced the specification and treatment of endogenous and exogenous variables in economics.

The principal technical approach to law and economics found today in the literatures of economics, political science, and law is that of the neoclassical school. Its genesis can be traced to the work of Coase (1960) on transaction costs, albeit with numerous precursors. Parallel movements include public choice, property rights, rent seeking, and similar versions of neoclassical economic reasoning (e.g. Buchanan and Tullock 1962; Eggertsson 1990; Posner 1973; Williamson 1985). Much of this work involves the normative application of microeconomic reasoning to reach determinate, optimal, and, where feasible, equilibrium solutions to technical problems of theory and policy.

The objective of this chapter is to identify the nature and content of a positive (nonnormative) evolutionary approach to law and economics. At this point it may be stated that the evolutionary approach presented here focuses on, first, a multiplicity of sources of change and adjustment processes;[2] second, the open-endedness of legal-economic processes; and third, the treatment of economic and political agents and variables as both dependent and independent variables in a type of model that can be designated evolutionary, coevolutionary, cumulative causative, or overdeterminist.[3]

It should be understood from the beginning that the evolutionary approach presented here is fundamentally different from the ostensibly deterministic and predictive method conventionally associated with mainstream economics.[4] An evolutionary approach to law and economics is content with a different agenda. It is content with an identification and understanding of what is going on; an understanding specifically of the operative processes, mechanisms, patterns, connections, features, and properties of the interrelationship between legal and economic processes, of the economic role of government, or of the legal-economic nexus. The evolutionary approach is additionally different from the neoclassical approach in that it does not seek optimal solutions, or judgments of fitness (in the sense of rightness, as in social Darwinism). It is content with identifying the sources of change (and of countervailing continuity) and the processes of adjustment during the interaction between legal and economic processes.

The evolutionary approach therefore uses models that do not take positions on questions that in the real world still have to be worked out, and it thereby does not foreclose the operation of process and substitute the ideas (including definitions of reality and preferences) of analysts for those of actual economic actors. The open-ended nature of the evolutionary approach follows from this sort of skeptical practice. Another way of making these same points is to echo Holmes's dictum in *The Common Law* that

> the life of the law has not been logic; it has been experience. The felt necessities of the time, the prevalent moral and political theories, intuitions of public policy, avowed or unconscious, even the prejudices which judges share with their fellows, have a good deal more to do than the syllogism in determining the rules by which men should be governed.
>
> ([1881] 1945: 1)

Considered as a positive statement, this means, in part, that an evolutionary approach must examine the larger questions that more static approaches either take for granted or evade by substituting the premises and preferences of analysts for those of actual legal-economic processes.[5]

In the following pages our purpose is to identify, schematically and programmatically, the principal characteristics of an evolutionary approach to law and economics and to contrast it with the quite different neoclassical approach. Insofar as the two approaches define their respective scope and central problem differently and are not endeavoring to answer the same questions, they are not in those respects competitive. However, they are competitive in the sense that they present different definitions of the legal-economic world and different assertions of what legal-economic theory should do and the way it should be done. While the authors find the questions addressed by an evolutionary approach to law and economics, and the types of answers that such an approach can properly provide, more interesting and less presumptuous and tendentious than those addressed and provided by the neoclassical approach, they do not denigrate either the questions or the approach taken by neoclassicism. Our position is that "there is, there can be, no economic theory which will do for us everything we want all the time" (Hicks 1981: 233), including the evolutionary approach.

General characteristics of an evolutionary approach

What, then, constitutes an evolutionary approach to law and economics?

1   It is conventional to write of the economic role of government and of the interrelations between legal and economic processes as if the two sectors were both substantively separate and normatively different. The evolutionary approach affirms that the economy and the polity are neither given nor independent nor self-subsistent spheres but are continuously reformed in what may be called the legal-economic nexus (Samuels 1989). The economy and the law mutually create each other; what goes on is not just a matter of interaction between the two spheres. Rather, each sphere is itself determined through the process of interaction; the two spheres coevolve:

> The legal-economic nexus is the sphere in which government operates to (re)define and (re)create the economy, and in which nominally private interests, perhaps especially economic interests, operate to (re)define and (re)channel government, given the dominant belief system, which is itself reformulated and rechannelled through the uses selectively imposed upon or made of it.
>
> (Samuels 1989: 1571–2)

Selective perception influences what is taken to be mutable and immutable, what is changeable and what is natural and given. Law is a function of experience, which itself is a function of selective perception (e.g. what constitutes and what exemplifies "fairness"), which is itself influenced by law.

2   The evolutionary approach rejects single-factor and linear explanations in favor of systemic multiple-factor and curvilinear explanations. Each variable is both dependent and independent relative to the other variables. The economy

is a function of law and the law is a function of the economy, but both emerge from a common nexus of activity, activity that is simultaneously both economic and political-legal in character. The spheres that seem so separate emerge from a larger nexus characterized by cumulative causation, coevolution, overdetermination, and evolutionary general interdependence. Neither economy nor polity is self-subsistent; each is reformed through its interactions and, especially, through activities in the common, underlying legal-economic nexus.

Individual agents may be selectively perceived as economic or legal, or as private or public, whereas all units in actuality have both economic and legal aspects to them.

Individual units have variable degrees of autonomy but are also constrained by the system in which they operate and by the aggregation of interactions with other units. But much more than constraint is involved. Institutions constrain, but they also shape what people see and want, as well as liberate and empower individuals to act. Laws help shape preferences, procedures, and habits. Laws help define what is regarded as progress (growth) and productive. Law, in specifying ideals, can sometimes affect behavior toward these ideals and toward other people, even when explicit incentives and sanctions cannot be administered. Experience with collective action can build trust and lessen opportunism, which is useful for future collective action.

3   The key legal-economic questions, the questions that all legal-economic processes operate to resolve, are, first, who is to control government for what purposes; and second, whose interests are to count, how, and how much.

4   The driving forces of legal-economic behavior are: first, ideology and the selective identifications and attributions of ideological patterns and metaphors to policy positions; and second, the continuing contest over the distributions of income and wealth. Each force profoundly influences the other. We cannot stress too much the importance of income and wealth distributions as the key objective of control in capturing and using government.

5   The legal-economic nexus is, in the modern world, the sphere in which resolutions of the problem of order are continually being worked out. The problem of order involves the conflicts between freedom and control, continuity and change, and hierarchy and equality.

6   The legal-economic nexus is not given. Its substance is a matter of the social reconstruction of reality, driven by activity that is, in the present context, simultaneously both legal and economic. The general process through which this social reconstruction of reality takes place is coevolution or over-determination. Central to the social construction of reality is the manufacture of and power play over cultural symbolism and meaning, ultimately governing whose interests are to count.

7   Power, ideology, and institutions are important dependent and independent variables endogenous to the legal-economic nexus.

8   The key adjustment processes[6] are: public opinion, learning and selective perception, expectations and discounting, legitimation, control of government (i.e. of the uses to which government is to be put), administrative agencies,

the legislature, and the courts. These are illustrative of the many and varied processes and transactions through which issues are worked out and conflicts resolved. On the one hand, these processes generate the implicit assumptions underlying operative premises as to rights (entitlements), risk identification and assumption/avoidance, and social goals. On the other hand, these processes are the objects of efforts to capture, channel, or otherwise manipulate them. At the constitutional level the processes are those by which the rules for making rules are generated, these rules being both dependent and independent variables in different circumstances.

9   The principal characteristic of the operation of the legal-economic nexus is *process*. Although it may be useful to use equilibrium models to produce deductively correct and determinate results, in the real legal-economic world all variables and interrelationships are in a continuous process of flux, without either given or actually achieved end points. The legal-economic nexus is a process of working things out, not a matter of the application of technical formulas.

10   In an evolutionary approach to law and economics, the substantive results generated by legal-economic behavior and the operation of the afore-mentioned adjustment processes are treated objectively and nonnormatively. They are neither affirmed in an optimizing/productivity paradigm nor denigrated in an exploitation paradigm, but are treated simply as results, albeit results that can be evaluated differently by economic actors with different perspectives and interests.

11   The substantive results generated by legal-economic behavior and the operation of the adjustment processes manifest the principle of unintended or unforeseen results. That is to say, the results are due, in part, to the interaction between and/or aggregation of behaviors and adjustment processes. This is not to say, however, that various economic agents do not attempt to control or channel behavior or the adjustment processes; nor is it to treat the principle of unintended or unforeseen results as anything but a positive proposition, that is, not as itself a principle of policy.

12   In society—for present purposes, especially regarding the legal-economic nexus—parts are a function of wholes and wholes are a function of parts. Individual units have degrees of autonomy but also are constrained by the system in which they operate and the aggregation of interactions with other units. The evolution of parts is thereby influenced by the evolution of wholes, and vice versa. Evolutionary paths are influenced by enterprise organization, technology, economies of scale, and, *inter alia*, the extent of the market. Private choice in each of these matters (e.g., corporate form) is both influenced by and influences corporate and other (e.g., antitrust) law.

The same is true of different aspects of economic life: for example, production and distribution are in fact intimately interconnected. Their separation for analytical purposes does not negate the situation that production is a function of distribution (e.g., the distributions of income and wealth) and distribution is a function of production (e.g., technology and the relative scarcity of factors of production).

Causal chains in the evolutionary approach to law and economics are long and complex. For example, resource allocation is a function of market demand

and supply, but market demand and supply is in part a function of power structure (including wealth effects) and therefore of legal rights; and legal rights are a function of government, whose actions are a function of who is in a position to control the choices that are made through government determining whose interests are to count.

Conceptual designations in the evolutionary approach to law and economics are problematic, rendering reductionist analysis highly suspect. For example, the distinction between private and public is fundamentally ambiguous, because "public" is ultimately influenced by "private," and "private" is what it is in part because of legal action (see the treatment of the corporation as a legal "person" in Samuels and Miller 1987).

For the foregoing and other reasons it is extraordinarily important in evolutionary analysis to avoid reductionism. This does not mean that the analyst cannot make analysis manageable. It does mean that the analyst must make ample room for multiple, two-way, cumulative, and curvilinear causation.

The neoclassical approach in contrast

The neoclassical approach to law and economics is very different. Preferences are stable and law is modeled as either a constraint or the fulfillment of those preferences. The neoclassical approach seeks determinate optimal equilibrium results to problems of explanation and of policy. It seeks determinate results because it embodies a particular conception of science; equilibrium results because it embodies a unilineal mechanistic conception of the economy; and optimality results because neoclassicism has both a maximizing and a harmonistic conception of the economy and because it embodies a desire to be relevant to questions of policy.

The neoclassical approach is manifestly normative. It is used to purportedly address such questions as who should have what rights; what is the best design of institutions; and why, or by what criteria, the status quo is the best of all possible worlds. The neoclassical approach tends to legitimize, selectively, either some specification of the status quo or some alternative to it. For example, it condemns some legal change as rent-seeking and applauds other legal change as wealth-creating. It tends to promote the conclusion that market or marketlike processes select individual units or performance results that are globally efficient or in some sense superior or comprise a compelling orderliness. It thereby tends to promote the conclusion that surviving arrangements are to be explained in terms of their utility or function, or by their having been selected for their efficiency in serving some purpose. The conclusion is promoted that surviving arrangements represent greater efficiency of, or greater benefits for, the whole, or that there is a single, universal, conclusive indicator or definition of fitness, and so on; that is, that survival connotes something transcendent to survival per se.

Yet such conclusions are highly presumptive and give effect to an assumption that "what is, ought to be" (Samuels 1992). Survival may have no transcendent meaning. Survival, or an optimality result, may only reflect the initial starting point. A local optimality result may conflict with a more inclusive, global one. A particular optimality result may be inconsistent with the maintenance or improvement of the environment. A particular inferior technology may be locked into because of temporary circumstances. And so on.

The microeconomic orientation of the neoclassical approach tends to a focus on simple natural selection and evolution of a unit within an environment, without consideration that the environment itself is subject to selection and evolution. The neoclassical approach, except insofar as it affirms the operation of market process qua market process, is disinterested in the environment-specific character of fitness or optimality; in how changes affect the environment itself; in how the environment of the individual unit is the system of social relations itself, which is subject to change; and in how individual behavior is both the consequence and the cause of environmental change.

Users of the neoclassical approach tend to affirm the existence of a single, universal, conclusive mechanism guaranteeing determinate and optimal results. Yet individual users, while generally affirming the market or price system as the overriding mechanism, tend to further specify quite variably other adjustment processes such as entrepreneurship.

In contrast, therefore, with the evolutionary approach to law and economics, the neoclassical approach has a very different conceptualization of legal-economic reality and a very different agenda as to what its scope and central problem, or analytical and policy objectives, are to be. The neoclassical approach is more apt to seek conclusions as to the optimality or nonoptimality of allocative and other performance results. It also has a narrower range of variables and it tends to treat those variables as given and self-subsistent in a unilinear way. Both the neoclassical and the evolutionary approaches to law and economics are interested in the operation of legal-governmental processes, in the jockeying for position to control government, and, *inter alia*, in the generation of impacts. Each, however, comprehends these subjects quite differently. Both approaches are powerful, but the respects in which they are powerful are quite different.

The principal elements of developmental analysis

A distinction must be made between theories of development and theories of impact, although the line of demarcation ought not to be too strictly held. For our purposes, theories of development focus on the operation and evolution of institutions or systems that produce policy; theories of impact focus on the consequences of policy. The following discussion centers on developmental considerations. But it must be recognized that impacts and consequences are steps or facets of development: from one perspective, development includes both the *ex ante* changes and the adjustment processes that they set in motion; and impact includes the ex-post situation after the adjustment process has run its course, the results.[7] From another perspective, the impact of the developments of one period constitute the foundation or initial condition of the next period. Impacts are part of the developmental process. Among the relevant impact-oriented themes are: performance as a function of structure, behavior as a function of structure and performance, and the importance of unintended and/or unforeseen consequences.

How do these precepts shed light on the legal-economic nexus? What is important when one examines that sphere in the context of the evolutionary paradigm? It would be contrary to the evolutionary approach to say, in answer to those or comparable questions, that a certain outcome inexorably must happen or does happen. The evolutionary process contemplated here is open-ended and contingent, or problematic; it is a matter of working things out. The answers to these questions must be put in terms of processes, patterns, connections, features, properties, and adjustment processes.

Although legal-economic theory qua theory cannot properly say whether one rights-claimant will or should win out over another, this does not mean that nothing important can be said about the evolutionary legal-economic nexus and its adjustment processes:

1   Economies require fundamental institutions that are basically legal in character, though informal cultural institutions are also relevant. Markets are formed by the institutions that operate through them. In order for the Western market economy to have evolved, there simultaneously evolved, and had to evolve, a network of laws—legislative, judicial, and, to a lesser extent, executive— to permit orderly economic activity. These were the laws of property, contract, business organization, negotiable instruments, money and banking, sales, agency, torts, and so on—the very laws that the populations of the former Soviet Union and states of Eastern Europe must somehow have if their hitherto centrally planned economies are to become what are known as "market economies."

These legal institutions did not emerge on their own. They were the result, in part, of governmental agencies, such as courts, deciding conflicts between litigating parties and thereby establishing the rules of the game or the working rules of the market. They were also in part the result of interested parties who wanted, with legal security, to be able to do things in certain ways that they hitherto had been unable to do. In each of these situations, manifest or latent conflicts of interest were resolved and new law and new market arrangements were created, typically incrementally. Yet the Emancipation Proclamation radically changed property law in the United States in one day. Some actors within government saw in the economy an object of legal control, some seeing perhaps that such control was simply necessary, others that control could be exercised to their material or ideological, perhaps political, advantage; other actors, nominally within the economy, saw in government the means to economic gain and/or other advantage.

Much of this activity was, in the United States, at the state and local level (see, for example, Heath 1954; Nelson 1975; and Primm 1954). In the late nineteenth and twentieth centuries, as national markets emerged and as the advantage of national solutions appeared, such activity was increasingly undertaken at the national level.

The transformation of the US economy from a rural, agrarian, and largely precapitalist one to an urban, commercial, industrial, and fully capitalist economy took some two hundred years. It involved the creation of the legal foundations of capitalism and the transformation of law. (We have in mind the work of such writers as Commons (1924), Friedman (1985), Nelson (1975), Horwitz (1977), and various works by James Willard Hurst and Carter Goodwich.) The economic and legal-political changes were two sides of the same coin, both taking place in the legal-economic nexus. The additional critical point is that the transformation of law, the creation of the legal foundations of capitalism, and the rise of a business civilization and culture itself took place gradually, incrementally, evolutionarily, with changes in one area leading to changes in another and then back again ad infinitum, such that each area, the economy and the law, was itself changed in the process: coevolution or overdetermination has been the rule.

The foregoing amounts to a recognition that, with regard to the necessary legal framework within which economic activity can be undertaken, the "planning" inherent in court decisions and statutes in a very fundamental, system sense is inevitable: different configurations of law, including different definitions and assignments of rights, lead to different economic outcomes. Moreover, the specific details ensconced within this legal-framework planning have particular consequences with regard to economic performance. Different systems and structures of rights yield different performance results.

2   According to the dominant ideology of the United States, which is very much a projection of a vibrant individualism, government is exogenous to the system, something that creates rather than solves problems, and therefore should be kept to a minimum. The economy is projected as a natural phenomenon, government as an artifact, something artificial. Contrary to this ideology, the manifestly evident "natural" tendency is for people to resort to government to accomplish their goals, including the therapeutic use of government in the face of perceived problems and untoward developments.

On the plane of ideology, a fundamental breech between economy and polity is posited; whereas on the plane of practical affairs, government is envisioned to be a pragmatic, instrumental, utilitarian tool or vehicle. The resulting cognitive dissonance is overcome by the formula that we resort to government only in emergencies, a model of intervention that can be called "laissez faire with exceptions." But ideology and psychology aside, resort to government has been continual, and the system transformations indicated earlier took effect, without design in the large, by incremental changes in law and in economic practice related to law. To repeat, judging by experience, the natural, or historical, tendency is to use government to accomplish economic purposes.

3   At every point in history there generally has been a body of law relevant to the interdependencies at hand. Not always, however; for example, new laws had to be made as technology opened up new ways of doing things, new social relationships, new ways of benefiting and of injuring others, and it was in the variably intensive interest of the relevant parties to have the law made in their interest. The body of law that is relevant to a new situation is often itself subject to dispute, but there are almost always people who believe that at least some body of law is relevant. (A contemporary example is the technology that permits

surrogate motherhood. Many believe that ordinary contract law is relevant, but others believe that law prohibits anything that amounts to the purchase and sale of a human being.) Conflict proceeds in part by arguing that the new interdependence is similar to a prior one, and thus it is implicitly ordered by existing law *A* rather than law *B*, or it is argued that no precedential sequence is relevant; in both cases, some choice (of analogy and of law, or of interest to be promoted) is made. The critical point is that given the existing network of rights and duties, the legal-economic process continuously involved legal selection and change, direct change in the existing network of rights and duties and indirect change in them through the adoption of complementary new rights and new duties. Most legal and jurisprudential analysis, including court decisions, tends to focus backwards on precedent and origins. But the fundamental significance of law and of legal change is in the future. Law may be made with a view to the past (for guidance as well as for legitimation) but its functioning is in the future; it is future organization and life that is governed by law.

4   As the US economy became increasingly a capitalist, urban, commercial, and industrial economy; as the territory of the nation expanded across the continent; as its population increased; and, *inter alia*, as its technology became ever more sophisticated and roundabout, the economy became increasingly complex and its organizational forms and modes of doing business became increasingly diverse. These changes placed great and increasing pressures on the legal system to accommodate new conditions and various interests. These economic changes also brought about changes in government and law. Historical stages, using the term loosely, have involved both changes in economic and in governmental-legal relations. Each market, each political jurisdiction, became a site in which legal-economic experimentation took place (e.g., state public utility regulation, commencing in the late nineteenth century). And, as we might expect, evolution has meant increasing complexity and diversity.

5   Every society necessarily confronts the problem of order, meaning thereby the continuing need to reconcile conflicts between freedom and control, continuity and change, and hierarchy and equality, with each of the terms of each conflict being subjected to selective perception. If legal change is the most critical, even dramatic, feature of the legal-economic nexus, legal changes, as both dependent and independent variables, are functional with regard to the three subsidiary components of the problem of order. For example, conflicts over the distributions of income and wealth involve all three conflicts and are such that the initial distribution of any period is the basis for the pursuit of those conflicts during the period. The temporary resolutions of those conflicts constitute the resulting distribution for that period, which becomes the initial or *ex ante* distribution for the next period. There is not one single solution to the problem of distribution (or to the three conflicts comprising the problem of order) that can be reached once and for all time, and what transpires in one sphere is both cause and consequence of what happens in other spheres.

The foregoing analytic period analysis is useful in describing other processes and properties of the evolutionary legal-economic process. Agents adapt to the system and agents adapt the system. Agents adapt to their environment but also adapt their environment to their needs, interests, and desires. One mode of adaptation is the law and one source of change necessitating, but not strictly dictating the substance of, adaptation is economic, including technological, change. Both actors and markets change, in part through the process of economic market change and in part through the process of political market change. "Initial" conditions change from analytic period to analytic period, as behavior both changes and is changed by boundary conditions, often those stipulated in law. The initial conditions of any one period are those produced by the adjustment-selection processes of the preceding period(s). Central to the process of changing initial conditions from period to period is the typical, but not necessarily gradual, transformation of rights and other entitlements.

6   Legitimation of the existing status quo is a principal social process. Legitimation tends to be absolutist; even in a pluralistic society, the justification of an institution or other arrangements tends to its affirmation in exclusivist, absolutist terms. Law in particular tends to be treated as an absolute, whereas social evolution indicates the relativity of law to changes in social power—continual change in the status quo, law in general, the interpretation of constitutional and common law doctrines, and judicial choice of precedential alternatives.[8] The practices of absolutist legitimation obscure the artifact and, therefore, the choice character of social control through law. Absolutist legitimation is a technique of both selective social control and social change. On the one hand, it influences the development of social arrangements; on the other, it serves to legitimize whatever arrangements emerge through the social processes.

The ceremonial legitimation of legal-economic arrangements (existing arrangements or some revision thereof) and the formulation of definitions of reality functional with regard to policy, together with the quest for certitude (the former constituting a social control and the latter a psychic balm function), lead to reductionist, unilineal, teleological, and deterministic arguments. The evolutionary process, however, manifests complex, curvilineal, open-ended, and random features. Operating as both cause and consequence of the legitimation cum certitude functions is the law-taker mentality, which induces individuals to accept either existing law or proposed law as either given or transcendent to them; conversely, the evolutionary process manifests law-making as the actual state of society.

7   The social (re)construction of reality, in modern times especially operating through the legal-economic nexus, exhibits dual tendencies. On the one hand, there is considerable openness of evolutionary direction, considerable social discretion as to both the broad outlines and particular details of legal-economic and other arrangements. On the other hand, social evolution, including legal-economic, is path-dependent, heavily constrained by the dominant socioeconomic philosophy of life, that is: (1) economic ideology and/or religious value system— and the particular arrangements selectively rationalized by that value system through identification with its elements; (2) the existing power structure—social, political, and economic, insofar as these may be differentiated; and (3) the social

psychology of peoples, with its selective susceptibility to political mobilization and manipulation. There is frequently a tension between one set of values and another—for example, the emerging legal crisis in the Islamic world (Iran, Algeria, Pakistan) between modern commercial values and traditional values. Modern economics supports some, and conflicts with other, traditional religious values.

Path-dependency and openness are simultaneous properties. Path-dependency constrains current choices and decisions, but current decisions govern path-dependency and the potential traverse (in the sense of Hicks 1969) from one path to another; in both respects future actions and performance results are affected. What is possible is influenced by what institutions came before and the environment of other institutions, as well as by the particular change-oriented decisions that are made (with due regard to the principle of unintended and unforeseen consequences).

This last point underscores the dual aspect of the tension between openendedness and path-dependency: the importance of both choice as to when path-dependency is to be challenged and the personnel who are to exercise authoritative discretion and make those choices. *Authoritative* here does not necessarily mean *official*, for business positions are loci of entrepreneurially generated acts of creative destruction—legal and cultural as well as narrowly technological. The same is true of political entrepreneurs, even in a society in which businesspeople enjoy a privileged position (Lindblom 1977).

Insofar as the social reconstruction of reality is a function of power, knowledge, and psychology, knowledge (or what is accepted as knowledge) is an instrument of power for the manipulation of individual cognition and psychology, ultimately for control of the state and the processes governing legal change. Contests over economic theory, like those over public opinion, contribute to the definition of reality and thereby to the mobilization of political psychology as the basis of policy.

Writers who have analyzed technology have identified such properties as technological innovation, diffusion, and interdependence; technological regimes and trajectories; development paths, path-dependency, and lock-in; and the cumulative nature of technological change (see the works of Dosi, Freeman, Silverberg). Similar points have been made with regard to entrepreneurship. Throughout such studies one finds but openness and constraint, change and continuity. Such dynamic features also appertain to the economic role of government and law. Just as technological change takes place within technological regimes, legal-economic change, including technological change itself, takes place within particular legal-economic-nexus regimes. Neither type of regime is treated in evolutionary analyses as a black box (or as necessarily producing the "right" results). Both types of regime, technological and legal, have both stable and unstable trajectories of development and each can be evaluated differently by different criteria. In both regimes are the processes that govern the direction or substance of economic growth, the distributions of opportunity and sacrifice as well as of income and wealth, and the selective release of entrepreneurial and other energy.

The legal-economic nexus, comprehended in terms of the evolutionary approach, is a system of self-organization, somewhat in the sense of Ilya

Prigogine (Prigogine and Stengers 1984). There is no design external to human beings and society imposed on legal-economic affairs. Human beings organize their own systems, including the legal-economic. All of it is a matter of individual action, some that of individuals acting alone and some, actually very much, that of individuals acting as members of social groups and organizations, including government. One of the reasons why consequences are typically unintended and unforeseen is that such actions are matters of interaction and aggregation, the processes of interaction and aggregation constituting principal elements of self-organization, some of which are deliberative and some nondeliberative.

8   One of the critical features of the legal-economic nexus is the hierarchical nature of the relevant processes. Several points relate to this: First, participation in market choice and public choice in liberal democratic governments tends to be more pluralistic (i.e. to have a wider diffusion of power) than the alternatives, though that is not to say that neither markets nor governments do not have hegemonic powers. Second, the evolution of the modern democratic state has specifically involved governments becoming increasingly responsive to a wider range of interests. Access to government remains heavily asymmetric, but over the last two centuries government in the West has become less the vehicle of rule and opportunity of permanent upper classes, and income has become more equal. Third, both belief in and descriptive accuracy of individualism and democracy should not obfuscate the centrality of the problem: *which* individuals, or *which* individual units, are to have their preferences and interests count.

9   The sources of legal change are numerous and operate on what may be called the demand and supply side. Some interests constitute the demanders of change and other interests constitute the suppliers of change; often the former are self-interested economic actors, sometimes public-spirited reformers of various types; and the latter are those who occupy positions of formal and informal governmental decision making authority, often with their own ideological and material-interest agendas. Use of the metaphor of a demand and supply model, while it can help identify the operative forces of an evolutionary situation, should not, however, lead to a nonevolutionary equilibrium model of social change.

More broadly, economic forces, during the last several centuries, have generally, but by no means completely, replaced or supplemented political forces as the prime mover of historical change. Industrialization, commercialization, and political and economic liberalism (Enlightenment values) have introduced and sustained diversity of mutations or variations and sources of variation, and the consequent necessity to choose. Technology; changing values; power play; war; externalities; selective perception of "problems"; secularization; improved knowledge of the physical and biological world; heightened sense of policy consciousness (that social arrangements are not given but a matter of human construction); mobility; ease of communications; the widened availability of liberal democratic governments; experience and learning; changes in population level, density and interaction; changing relative prices, power relations, and perceptions of opportunity; and so on—these have fueled the dynamics of legal-economic evolution, largely through their interactions.

The evolutionary approach to law and economics identifies both the multiplicity of sources of change and the multiplicity of adjustment and selection processes. It therefore underscores the importance not only of conflict and of the legal resolution, as well as prevention, of conflict but also of legal conflict resolution as an object of control and use by interested parties—in a truly coevolutionary, overdetermined, and/or fundamentally general-equilibrium way.

10   Lending elements of subjectivism, spontaneity, and surprise to legal-economic evolution is selective perception. Selective perceptions of government, rights, legal change, I-thou, freedom, control, continuity, change, hierarchy, equality, progress, growth, decay, and so on, provide inputs to the legal-economic process. In this respect, selective perceptions are independent variables. But selective perceptions, because they are subject to deliberative and nondeliberative political (and religious, etc.) psychological manipulation, are also dependent variables. Institutions selectively provide cognitive frameworks for learning and interpreting sense data and for transforming such data into putatively useful knowledge, such as: what constitutes individualism and what interventionism; what constitutes democracy, the nature and significance of chance, personal character, social relationships, and individual responsibility; and, *inter alia,* the source of selectively perceived policy problems and solutions. Therefore both institutions and the processes of selective perception are the objects of control and use.

11   Several open-ended interactive processes operate in the legal-economic nexus. These may be identified as follows: (A) The dual processes through which (I) efficient-optimal solutions are worked out, given the identification and assignment of rights, and (II) the identification and assignment of rights, including the creation of new rights and duties, that is, the power structure, is changed such that it is through both processes together and interactively that it is determined whose interests and values are to count. (B) The value-clarification process through which values are identified, contrasted, evaluated, and chosen. (C) The interaction between power, knowledge, and psychology, each understood as comprised of multiple variables (e.g., in the Paretian model of power, knowledge, and psychology, and their interactions, going far beyond the limited domain of Pareto optimality; see Samuels 1974). (D) The combination of politics, elections, court appointments, class, material interests, and ideology.

A wide-ranging and suggestive evolutionary model of legal-economic policy can be illustrated using the familiar concepts of a production possibility curve and a social welfare function, with values or goals on the respective axes. This model indicates four fundamental interactive (coevolutionary, over-determined) processes: the process by which the values on the axes are chosen, which is to say the values on the agenda of public choice; the process determining the slope of the production-possibility curve applicable to the values, that is, the necessary trade-offs between the values; and the processes governing both the relative preferences for the values that people have and the power structure governing the weighting of the preferences. Another such evolutionary model posits different economic agents, each with its own respective opportunity sets. Each realizeable opportunity set, over time, is a function of (1) power and the bases of power, for example, legal rights; (2) the choices made at various points in time by individuals (according to their capabilities) from within their respective opportunity sets influencing their opportunity sets in the future; and (3) the impact decisions made by others have on each agent's opportunity set. Putatively included in the opportunity set is the opportunity to seek legal change of the rights of the respective parties and therefore change of their respective opportunity sets (see Samuels 1989).

Conclusion

The foregoing has outlined the principal characteristics and important developmental elements of a nonnormative evolutionary approach to law and economics. Once both escapes from the narrow and misleading thinking that posits determinate optimal equilibrium solutions to problems of law and economics and considers just what a meaningful evolutionary analysis requires, the approach outlined here enables the analyst to identify fundamental processes and problems that are worked out in the legal-economic nexus, processes and problems that the conventional mode of analysis forecloses.

But the important matter is not the critique of the neoclassical approach to law and economics. It tells a story, or set of stories, and these stories are valuable, however limited. Inasmuch as no theory can answer all questions, there must be room for multiple theories in law and economics. The questions raised by and dealt with by an evolutionary approach to law and economics are fundamental and important, and techniques of analysis must be adopted that are suited to deal with them in their enormity and complexity. The important point is that the results of a partial, single-factor, unilinear, and static approach should not be taken for those of a comprehensive, multifactor, curvilinear, and evolutionary approach.[9]

Acknowledgment

The authors are indebted to Jeff Biddle and Richard England for helpful comments on an earlier draft of this chapter.

Notes

1 This situation is very much parallel to the microeconomic static partial-equilibrium analysis of resource allocation using a demand and supply model in which the identification and distribution of existing rights, technology, preferences, institutions, and natural resources are taken as given, that is, treated as exogenous variables. The price mechanism operative in that model can be modeled in various ways, and in each case analysis would both directly reflect the form of modeling and indirectly acknowledge the operation of the exogenous variables in real-world (i.e. non-model) circumstances. Even so-called "general equilibrium theory" is closer in fundamental conceptualization to this static partial-equilibrium theory than to what will be identified later as evolutionary theory.
2 The term *adjustment process* is used instead of *mechanism* because the emphasis is intended to be on the ongoing and choice nature of what is involved, rather than on something transcendental, automatic, and mechanical.

3 The influence of writers such as Max Weber, Karl Marx, Pareto (1963), Schumpeter (1976), Heertje and Perlman (1990), Nelson and Winter (1982), North (1981), Hodgson and Screpanti (1991), and especially the evolutionary institutional economics of Veblen (1919), Commons (1924), and Hodgson (1988) will be obvious. See also Bromley (1989) and the writings collected in Hodgson, Samuels and Tool (1993).

4 We say *ostensibly* deterministic and predictive for specific reasons. First, because in order to reach determinate results, the conventional procedure is to exclude all variables that otherwise would interfere with reaching determinate results—so that the determinate results give effect to and are tautological with the narrowing assumptions. And second, because prediction in economics, when it is not merely a ritualistic epistemological invocation, can properly take place only in the context of a model and not in regard to the real world.

5 It should be understood that—because the actual legal-economic world is complex, multifaceted, and kaleidoscopic, filled with plural theories and models—it should be anticipated that there can be multiple evolutionary approaches. It is for this reason that we have used the word *an* rather than the more presumptuous *the* in the title of our chapter. We are confident, however, that the fundamental characteristics of our approach are reasonably *sui generis* to the class of evolutionary approaches. The approach taken here is generally consistent with the evolutionary treatments of technology and the firm developed by such writers as Nelson and Winter (1982), Dosi (1988), Freeman (1987), Clark and Juma (1987), Elster (1983), and Screpanti (Hodgson and Screpanti 1991). See also Anderson and Sturis (1988), Silverberg (1984, 1987), Lazonick (1991), Hodgson, Samuels, and Tool (1993), and various works by Nathan Rosenberg.

6 Processes in the sense of having to be worked out, thereby including relevant structures.

7 With due regard to the fact that such periodization is an arbitrary model, and that initial changes and adjustments and results comprise ongoing processes.

8 To affirm the "original intent" of the Founding Fathers, the writers of the Constitution, is to assume a particular reading of the document.

9 In addition to authors already cited we want to call attention to the work of such writers as Bromley (1989), Hirschman (1970), and Vanberg (1986).

References

Andersen, D. and J. Sturis (1988) "Chaotic Structures in Generic Management Models: Pedagogical Principles and Examples," *System Dynamics Review*, 4 (Summer): 218–45.

Bromley, D. (1989) *Economic Interests and Institutions: The Conceptual Foundations of Public Policy*, Oxford: Blackwell.

Buchanan, J. and G. Tullock (1962) *Calculus of Consent*, Ann Arbor, MI: University of Michigan Press.

Clark, N. and C. Juma (1987) *Long-run Economics: An Evolutionary Approach to Economic Growth*, London: Pinter.

Coase, R. (1960) "The Problem of Social Cost," *Journal of Law and Economics*, 3 (October): 1–44.

Commons, J. R. (1924) *The Legal Foundations of Capitalism*, New York: Macmillan.

Dosi, G. (1988) "Sources, Procedures and Microeconomic Effects of Innovation," Journal of Economic Literature, 26 (September): 1120–71.

Eggertsson, T. (1990) *Economic Behavior and Institutions*, New York: Cambridge University Press.

Elster, J. (1983) *Explaining Technical Change*, New York: Cambridge University Press.

Freeman, C. (1987) "Technical Progress, Capital Accumulation and Effective Demand: A Self-organisation Model," in D. Batten, J. Casti, and B. Johansson (eds), *Economic Evolution and Structural Adjustment*, Berlin: Springer-Verlag.

Friedman, L. (1985) *A History of American Law*, 2nd edn. New York: Simon and Schuster.

Heath, M. (1954) *The Role of the State in Economic Development in Georgia to 1860*, Cambridge: Harvard University Press.

Heertje, A. and M. Perlman (eds) (1990) *Evolving Technology and Market Structure: Studies in Schumpeterian Economics*, Ann Arbor, MI: University of Michigan Press.

Hicks, J. (1969) *A Theory of Economic History*, New York: Oxford University Press.

——(1981) *Wealth and Welfare*, Cambridge: Harvard University Press.

Hirschman, A. (1970) *Exit, Voice, and Loyalty*, Cambridge: Harvard University Press.

Hodgson, G. (1988) *Economics and Institutions: A Manifesto for a Modern Institutional Economics*, Cambridge and Philadelphia, PA: Polity Press and University of Pennsylvania Press.

Hodgson, G. and E. Screpanti (eds) (1991) *Rethinking Economics: Markets, Technology and Economic Evolution*, Aldershott: Edward Elgar.

Hodgson, G., W. Samuels, and M. Tool (eds) (1993) *Handbook of Institutional and Evolutionary Economics*, Aldershott: Edward Elgar.

Holmes, O. W., Jr [1881] (1945) *The Common Law*, Boston, MA: Little, Brown.

Horwitz, M. (1997) *The Transformation of American Law, 1780–1860*. Cambridge, MA: Harvard University Press.

Lazonick, W. (1991) *Business Organization and the Myth of the Market Economy*, New York: Cambridge University Press.

Lindblom, C. (1977) *Politics and Markets*, New York: Basic Books.

Nelson, W. E. (1975) *Americanization of the Common Law*, Cambridge: Harvard University Press.

Nelson, R. R. and S. Winter (1982) *An Evolutionary Theory of Economic Change*, Cambridge: Harvard University Press.

North, D. (1981) *Structure and Change in Economic History*, New York: W. W. Norton.

Pareto, V. (1963) *The Mind and Society*, 2 vols. New York: Dover.

Posner, R. (1973) *Economic Analysis of Law*, Boston, MA: Little, Brown.

Prigogine, I. and I. Stengers (1984) *Order Out of Chaos: Man's New Dialogue with Nature*, New York: Bantam.

Primm, J. (1954) *Economic Policy in the Development of a Western State: Missouri, 1820–1860*, Cambridge: Harvard University Press.

Samuels, W. (1974) *Pareto on Policy*, New York: Elsevier.

—— (1988) *Institutional Economics*, 3 vols. Aldershott: Edward Elgar.

—— (1989) "The Legal-Economic Nexus," *George Washington Law Review*, 57 (August): 1556–78.

—— (1992) "The Pervasive Proposition, 'What Is, Is and Ought to Be': A Critique" in W. Milberg (ed.), *The Megacorp and Maerodynamics: Essays in Memory of Alfred Eichner*, Armonk, NY: M. E. Sharpe.

Samuels, W. and A. Miller (eds) (1987) *Corporations and Society: Power and Responsibility*, Westport, CT: Greenwood.

Schumpeter, J. A. (1976) *Capitalism, Socialism and Democracy*, 5th edn. London: George Allen and Unwin.

Silverberg, G. (1984) "Embodied Technical Progress in a Dynamic Economic Model: The Self-organization Paradigm," in R. Goodwin, M. Kruger, and A. Vercelli (eds), *Nonlinear Models of Fluctuating Growth*, Berlin: Springer-Verlag.

—— (1987) "Technical Progress, Capital Accumulation and Effective Demand: A Self-organization Model," in D. Batten, J. Casti, and B. Johansson (eds), *Economic Evolution and Structural Adjustment*, Berlin: Springer-Verlag.

Tool, M. (ed) (1988) *Evolutionary Economics*, 2 vols. Armonk, NY: M. E. Sharpe.

Vanberg, V. (1986) "Spontaneous Market Order and Social Rules: A Critique of F. A. Hayek's Theory of Cultural Evolution," *Economics and Philosophy*, 2: 75–100.

—— (1919) *The Place of Science in Modern Civilisation and Other Essays*, New York: Huebsch.

Williamson, O. (1985) *The Economic Institutions of Capitalism*, New York: Free Press.

12 The rule of law and the capture and use of government in a world of inequality*

The rule of law—or, more accurately, the idea of the rule of law—has been prominently before the public in recent years. In the impeachment trial of William Jefferson Clinton the president's prosecutors both accused him of violating the rule of law for perjury and obstruction of justice in his Paula Jones deposition and argued that the rule of law required his removal from office. The president's defenders claimed that the rule of law was jeopardized by the use of constitutional provisions for purely political purposes. In the aftermath of the initial vote in the presidential election of 2000, the supporters of Al Gore defended his legal contest of the Florida certification of electoral delegates as based upon the rule of law, and the supporters of George W. Bush likewise invoked the rule of law in claiming the conclusivity of certification. Paul W. Kahn, a professor of law at Yale Law School and author of *The Reign of Law* (Kahn 1997), characterized the latter situation as one in which "Each campaign...ritualistically claims that it wants nothing more than 'the rule of law', and each side accuses the other of subverting law for the sake of politics" (Kahn 2000). That description is empirically accurate.

Kahn, however, takes the matter several steps further. First, he takes notice that the "rule of law" is a national myth, whereas in fact law is politics. Second, he laments the unveiling or unmasking of the rule of law as myth, and calls for a return of belief.

Kahn begins his argument by noting that, "The grand civics lesson of the past two weeks has introduced the whole nation to the deepest secret of our constitutional life. There is no line between law and politics." Hitherto, only law professors influenced by Legal Realism had "been teaching...that the line between law and politics is illusory. Now, that knowledge has escaped the academy and threatens to subvert our faith in the rule of law."

Kahn does not claim that the rule of law is a matter of truth. Rather it is not truth, it is a myth, a myth justified by its ostensible function of generating harmony:

> The rule of law is our national myth. We must believe the myth if we are to overcome our political disagreements. We need a point of reconciliation beyond our political disputes. That point is our faith in law, and the institutional locus of that faith is the U.S. Supreme Court. To be sure, we can always find

the politician behind the robes of the justice, just as we can always find the man behind the robes of the priest. But faith prevents us from lifting the robe. It limits our vision to a set of symbols.

It is the Supreme Court's role to preserve this national myth. When the court speaks, it speaks in the name of the sovereign people. When it presents to us the Constitution, it purports only to hold up a mirror to the people. Its legitimacy comes neither from its knowledge of legal science nor from the justices' political appointments, but from the capacity to persuade us that the rule of law is the rule of the people. At that moment, we overcome the divide between law and politics.

Kahn's claim that the myth of the rule of law is necessary to generate order may have some truth to it but it is principally an assumption that can be carried too far. The burden must be on advocates of the claim to prove it. Much of life and of public order does not depend on myth.

At least two problems immediately arise: first, whether the defense is of the idea of the rule of law or of the privileged status of lawyers and courts; and second, whether the rule of law is to be understood to be transcendent to man or an expression of the rule of the people (popular sovereignty).

Kahn does not deny that his view is one of jurisprudential metaphysics, even jurisprudential theology. What once was the equation of the rule of law with a sovereign God is now the equation of the rule of law with the rule of the sovereign people; faith in the rule of law replaces faith in God, but to the same end, namely social control.

> This is not fact, but faith—our civic religion. Neither law nor politics defines us as a nation; rather this faith in a popular sovereign who appears only in and through the rule of law. We know that political beliefs are inseparable from legal views. ... No one really believes that law can end our disagreements over these issues [of policy]. Nevertheless, our faith in the rule of law unites us in a common enterprise through all these disputes.

For Kahn, the terminology of the rule of law is a mode of language, not a description of reality; in this respect at least the concept of rule of law resembles those of natural law and natural rights as well as public interest.

> This faith sets the structure of our grand national debates: Each side must claim the support of law, because in and through law it claims the right to speak for the people. Each side must accuse the other of subverting the law and thus subverting the people. Politics in its local and ordinary form is set off from law; ordinary politics can have an air of illegitimacy about it, even in our democracy. Thus, the bizarre accusation that each side is "politicizing" an election. This claim makes sense only when we see that the call to law is a call to a faith in a higher politics.

Kahn takes the conventional high-priest role, notably an affirmation of rejection of wide knowledge of latent function—and their own role:

> Like every faith, our national myth of law's rule can stand only so much public scrutiny. It is vulnerable just because it is a faith. There are no facts by which we can prove it. The popular sovereign is not a subject we can locate, but only a mythical figure through which we understand our history and our identity. Vulnerable as it is, however, we need it; we have no other faith standing in the wings.
>
> So our national civics lesson may be teaching us too much about ourselves. The relentless attack of politics on law may leave us without an institution that can settle our disputes by calling us back to our civic faith. ...
>
> This is the greatest danger of the present moment. The rule of law will lose its foundation as a national faith of the people. Law's rule will be seen as nothing more than another face of ordinary politics.

The foregoing brings to mind Emile Durkheim's theory of manifest and latent function in religion. When a person enters a church, Durkheim argued, he or she feels a sense of awe in the presence of the transcendent; this is the manifest function of religion. Whereas the latent function of religion resides in the re-enforcement of received social structure and social relations— latent, that is, in relation to the laity but not the officials of religion who appreciate the actuality of latent function. Such that one can imagine a situation in which the laity came to know about the latent function, leading the officials to wish for the reestablishment of naïve belief and manifest function in order to restore the latent function. The parallel with the rule of law is not forced.

What are we to make of this predicament, this diagnosis and this prescription? This chapter will take a position quite opposite to that of Kahn. It does so reluctantly, because the *idea* of the rule of law encompasses worthy *ideals*. The rule of law signifies the desideratum that there is one law for all people, not one law for one group and another law for another group, say, one law for the rich and another for the poor, or one law for Protestants and another for Catholics, and so on. The rule of law signifies the desideratum of rational means-end and reasoned decision making. The rule of law signifies the desideratum of independence of legislature from executive and of judiciary from both; it especially signifies the negation of authoritarian caprice by an absolute monarch. It may also signify the desideratum of a tone of civility in political affairs, however laden with controversy. It may also signify democracy—though democracy has often been criticized for its ostensible violation of the rule of law.[1]

The fact of the matter is that the reality of law is nothing like these ideals. Among the problems with thinking otherwise are the following.

The promotion of special interests. Much legislation is enacted on behalf of so-called special interests. Thus, provisions of the Internal Revenue Code were passed to provide favorable tax treatment for specific constituent-clients of particular legislators. The same is true of amendments to the Patent Laws selectively extending the duration of particular patents. And the same is true of such seemingly more general provisions as that enabling the deduction of mortgage interest from income for tax purposes, and so on.

Alpha-Beta conflicts. When Alpha and Beta are in the same field of action, making conflicting claims of interest and of right, case law or statutory law which affirms Alpha's interest as a right *ipso facto* negates Beta's interest as a right. The law cannot equally apply to both. This applies to vast fields of law, perhaps most especially to economists in those fields dealing with interests of economic significance, though this is true of law generally.

The paradox of the equal treatment of unequals. People are unequal in many ways, for example, talents, wealth, and so on; this is a fact of life. A paradox arises because of this inequality. If we treat unequals equally, we may well be treating them unequally; and the only way to treat unequals equally may be to treat them unequally. Among other things, this situation enables the declarers of law to affirm either (1) that although all persons have formal equality of rights, differences in position or circumstance properly operate to modify the rights or (2) that differences in position or circumstance should not operate to modify, even to negate, the rights.

The multiplicity of available law. In any situation it is more than likely, it is almost axiomatic, that more than one simple and straightforward law applies. Thus, each party to a case or other conflict can point to and invoke that law which favors its side. Each side claims that its view, and not that of the other side, comports with the rule of law. This applies to both substantive and procedural law but especially to the former. (A good example is the litigation over the Florida ballot and recount after the November 7, 2000 presidential election.)

New rights. New rights are regularly being created in areas not previously contemplated, such as surrogate motherhood and use of the human genome and other technologies.

Conflicts within a law. Often the various provisions of a law come into conflict in more or less novel fact situations—perhaps because the different provisions were adopted with certain fact situations in mind, fact situations which did not include the novel one.

The division of governmental power. Governmental power in the United States is divided in two ways. Governmental power is divided between state and national governments (also between state and local governments) and among the several branches on each level. The conventional formula—that the legislature makes the law, the executive enforces the law, and the judiciary interprets the law—is severely flawed, actually a fiction. All three branches of government are governing; each rules/makes law in its own way—not least the judiciary. Moreover, there are inevitable tensions and conflicts between state and national governments— for example, between state legislatures and national supreme court—and between each branch on each level—for example, between common, constitutional, statutory, and administrative law.

Conflicting interpretations. The history of constitutional law is replete with conflicting interpretations of particular provisions and of the relationships between provisions. The history of court or common law is also replete with conflicting interpretations of what the law "is." In both domains, as well as, if not especially, in judicial decisions interpreting statutes and/or relating them to constitutional provisions, the case law is replete with conflicting sequences of precedent, such that one can typically, asymptotically to always, find some chain of precedents on which to ground a decision and opinion. Judges disagree as to what is a legal rule, as to their interpretation, and as to the rules of interpretation. The rule of law is therefore instantiated and given substance by the specifics of social power, legal-economic theory, custom, institutional structure, rules and procedures of election and appointment, and so on—all of which is obfuscated by affirmation of a transcendent "rule of law."

The exercise of discretion. The legal system is laden with opportunities, indeed inevitabilities, for the exercise of discretion. These include prosecutorial discretion, choice of precedential sequence, choice of issues with which to frame a decision and opinion, discretion whether to take a case on appeal, and, *inter alia*, the exercise of discretion at the lowest levels of enforcement.

Lawyers' practice. Lawyers specializing in certain areas of the law occasionally represent only plaintiffs or only defendants. Often they represent either side: in one case the plaintiff, and in another the defendant. Their strategy, professed theory of the case, and legal argument in one case will be the opposite of those in the other case. The position of the client is one thing; the strategy, theory, and argument vary with the client's position.

This is all very pragmatic, instrumental, and utilitarian. In the late nineteenth century, railroad attorneys argued that their clients could/should not be subject to state statutes regulating their business because such was the preserve of the national government; when national regulation was before the courts, their argument was that railroad regulation was a state matter. In the early twentieth century, when price levels were rising, in rate cases utility companies proposed use of reproduction cost for the valuation of their rate base and their opponents proposed use of original cost; when price levels were falling, both sides switched positions. In the 2000 post-election imbroglios over hand recounts of votes in the contest between George W. Bush and Al Gore, the arguments were reversed depending on which side was seeking and which side was opposing a recount in different states. At the same time each side deployed situation-specific arguments as to such matters as court versus electoral commission and federal versus state primacy.

Consider, for example, the related doctrine of "original intent." A recent book on the subject (Lynch 1999) demonstrates convincingly that the notion of the original intent of the founding fathers—whatever one might think normatively of the matter—has little if any meaning. The author shows, *inter alia*, that during the first six Congresses, the Constitution was interpreted on the basis of immediate policy goals, including state, regional and political interests, and not fidelity to some past position or original intent; that figures such as James Madison not only changed interpretive positions but adopted conflicting ones; that immediate policy goals influenced framers' recollections of the constitutional convention and the ratifying state conventions, the meaning of the *Federalist Papers*, and the interpretation of the Constitution; that elements of the structure of government ensconced within the Constitution were matters of compromise which neither satisfied nor expressed either compromised position; that regional interpretations became reversed, due to changing circumstances and political expectations; that important clauses of the original Constitution and the first ten amendments, the Bill of Rights, comprised compromises of language that deferred to the future the determination of what they might be held to mean; and so on.

In another recent study (Neely 1999), the author shows how constitutionalism at the time of the American Civil War was interpreted differently by Northerners, by the Southern Confederacy, and by Southern opponents of the Confederacy. Both Abraham Lincoln and Jefferson Davis are shown to have treated law and constitution (all law and all constitutions) as means to their ends, not embodiments of a transcendent "rule of law." In a related study on the question of states' rights during and after the Confederacy (McDonald 2000), the author shows with vast documentation how adherence to a position on an issue or to a cause dominated adherence to a particular constitutional interpretation, even to constitutionalism itself. In an effectively cognate study of civil rights violence in Birmingham in the 1960s (McWhorter 2001), the author shows how far the rule of law in practice departed from the rule of law in theory and ideology, enmeshing the black versus white conflict with those between workers and employers, Roman Catholics and Protestants, Jews and gentiles, and Communism and anti-Communism—evoking memories of the vast US history of the selective use of law and effective denigration of any pretext of an objective rule of law in favor of a reality of law as a weapon. And in a study of the rule of law in Britain, Ewing and Gearty (2001) document how civil liberties were judicially (and otherwise) selectively defined and administered in matters deemed to be subversive, starting well before the inception of the USSR, not least through judgments made by magistrates with direct financial interests in industrial disputes.

Consider, too, a work on constitutionalism, pragmatism, and judicial review (Lipkin 2000). The author demonstrates the thinness, the unreality, of such foundational concepts as neutral principles, objective constitutional interpretation, and constitutional legitimacy. He proposes a theory of constitutional revolutions to explain how certain decisions departed from past precedents and involved terms of legitimation inconsistent with prior jurisprudential interpretation. The idea of a theory of constitutional revolution is presently more important than the content of any particular theory; but still more important is the factual premise of constitutional change.

Perhaps nowhere is the premise more dramatic, and the unrealism of the concept of the rule of law more stark, than in the domain of affirmative action. Whereas once the Constitution was invoked to uphold invidious and discriminatory unequal treatment, it has since been invoked both to uphold remedial affirmative action and to oppose same as reverse discrimination. It is the modern equivalent of sending a high priest to the presumed representative of the gods to determine the wisdom of a policy; both involve processes of legitimation not objective decision making.

The key question to ask is not whether some abstract notion of the "rule of law" has been followed. The key question is, which/whose interests are represented in and protected by the law for the legitimation of which the concept of "rule of law" is invoked.

Yet it has been shown that the "rule of law," as a concept in constitutional discourse, has multiple meanings, meanings involving "mutually incompatible positions." These meanings lack "articulated theories" but have "discernible kernels of meaning." The idealized notion of the rule of law has "multiple strands or elements, which the various ideal types help to illuminate," but, while "Invocations of the Rule of Law are sufficiently meaningful to deserve attention," these invocations "are typically too vague and conclusory to dispel lingering puzzlement" (Fallon 1997: 55–6). Even this view may be too charitable. Legal and constitutional language typically provides the linguistic framework of reference and argument, not the mechanism or process of transcendent unequivocal determination typically evoked by the concept of the "rule of law." Law involves choosing between claimants; the typically use of the concept of the "rule of law" functions to obfuscate the fact of choice.

Reversal or dependence of argument consequent to a change of position seems like hypocrisy to anyone seeking "the law." But anyone familiar with the language theories of Charles Saunders Peirce and Ludwig Wittgenstein knows better. According to those theories, language has meaning as signification, as conveyor of meaning, and not, or not necessarily, as correspondence with reality or a/the true state of things. Such signification may function, and be intended, to steer imagination in certain directions and not others, but at least to convey persuasive meaning. Language, like terms, concepts, and arguments, would thus not correspond to anything ontologically "real," representing instead only conceptual and methodological tools with which to organize and channel thought and exposition and to express and advance arguments. Lawyers believe in the power of people to believe in the constructs of their own imagination, and so practice this themselves, using the linguistic structure of the law for purposes of persuasion, that is, of rhetoric. "The law" and/or "rights" are convenient modes of expression, contest, and persuasion, when the specific content of law and/or of rights is precisely the point at issue. The language of common, statute, and constitutional law provides the linguistic formulations and framework of reference and argument, not mechanism of a transcendent and unequivocal "rule of law."

Not surprisingly, therefore, a recent book (Hutchinson 2000) goes beyond law as politics to law as a game of rhetorical justification. The writing of legal decisions, including the reaching of legal decisions, is not a process of legally reasoning to legal conclusions, fundamentally guided by the "rule of law." It is a rhetorical game in which the players only pretend to articulate or demonstrate "the law"

(= legal "truth"). It is a game of justification of choices and values somehow made. The idea of the rule of law is a stratagem in this justificatory exercise.

Further as to hypocrisy, one readily suspects that knowledge of the falsity of the idea of the rule of law, coupled with understanding of its latent function, engenders both further hypocrisy and contempt for the minds of the electorate.

One is therefore tempted if not compelled to say that there is no more such a thing as "the law" as there is "the market." Yes, one can contemplate and analyze a pure a-institutional abstract conceptual market, but actual markets are a function of the institutions, power structure, and power play/business strategy that form and operate through them. So too one can contemplate and rhapsodize about law in the abstract, but actual law is a function of the institutions, power structure, and power play that form and operate through it.

The law is embodied in and expressed through words, words that are selectively defined and selectively applied. The law as language is used in the process of defining and re-defining, and making and re-making, the economy, polity, and society. The words are used as if they had given, independent, and transcendent meanings that we were trying to achieve or put into practice. But the legal system and the economy are artifacts, and the words used in describing and forming them are also artifacts. The legal and economic systems, and their institutions, and the words influence each other. To think otherwise is to commit the fallacy of misplaced concreteness and/or the naturalistic fallacy (that because something exists it has ontological meaning).

A basic characteristic of law is its futurity. Notwithstanding selective argumentation utilizing past cases and theories, the meaning of a law relates to how it governs relations in the future; the future is in part made through making law. Moreover, much if not all common and constitutional law is expost: one does not "know" "the law" until after the courts decide it.

"The law" has two further dimensions of ambiguity. One has to do with the multiple *sources of law* and therefore the conflicts between them. These sources include (using the terms of art) custom, morality, equity, public policy, statutes, force, past judicial precedents, opinions of experts, legal theory, and so on. The other has to do with the *mode in which law is expressed*. These modes include (again using the terms of art) the holding of a decision, the *ratio decidendi* of a case (the ground of a decision, the basis of the holding), the sequence of precedents somehow interpreted, the overriding principle or rule of which the former are manifestations or evidence, natural law, divine law, and so on. In every case, moreover, conflicting versions are present; for example, the court has to choose between rival claims of custom, even between rival sets of custom, and in the totality of legal decisions different/conflicting sets or chains of precedents may be found and presented.

Kahn is correct: the rule of law is a myth. Law is made, not found, and is done so selectively, in large part as the ongoing product of a process in which competing parties struggle to control government/law thereby to use government/law to advance their interests—interests which are what they are, in part, due to the legal panorama in which the parties operate.

Emphasis on the rule of law serves, first, to establish and legitimize the legal process as instrumental, if not hegemonic, in the ongoing reconstruction of law. The legal process is never hegemonic in isolation, however; it, too, is a function of the inputs made to it, perhaps ultimately, one may say, a function of social structure, power play, and language use. The second function of the concept of the rule of law is to obfuscate government as an object of capture and use, and thereby the operations of social conflict, social control, and choice in the social re-construction of legal-economic reality. This includes but encompasses more than the tendency to identify law in rule-of-law contexts with status quo law; it also includes the process of the selective specification and specific reconstruction of the status quo, all of which are part of the process of law making.

Law itself is a substitute for combat; rather, law substitutes ideational for physical combat. There is much to be said for this. The case can be made, however, for not treating law as a myth and for not pretending both that it is not a myth and that it is an ontological absolute. People have outgrown other myths, such as the divine rule of monarchy, the divine nature of institutions, the innate inferiority of women and of blacks, and so on. People have learned to live with rules as rules and with change of rules as change of rules—even when they are offended. They sense that law is policy; they have policy consciousness as to the nature and operation of institutions. Pretense to the contrary may be given lip service—and believed by some—but human social maturation seems to lead in the opposite direction.

Arguments supporting the concept of the rule of law are almost indistinguishable from claims that stable law is necessary for economic growth. Neither position is entirely false but neither is entirely correct. Claims for the necessary stability of law are generally deployed against particular undesired proposed changes in the law. As a whole, however, the claims are descriptively inaccurate: entrepreneurial activity itself generates the need for new law, or for change of old law, both as an intended means and as an unintended by-product. The economic system called capitalism is characterized by more change of law than any other economic system; such change is part of what Joseph Schumpeter called creative destruction.

So too with language in capitalist economies. There seems to be a powerful association between rhetoric and substantive economic life that has become a feature of capitalistic development. This is presumably true of all economic systems but especially noticeable in capitalism, due in part to the faster and more complex pace of socio-economic change. The development of the economy influences the development of language—not just advertising rhetoric but entire specialist ways of talking that reflect in part the specialization produced by the division of labor and the stylized talk within particular institutions, such as central banks. This may well be a necessary connection given speech.

Perhaps there are two kinds of mentality. One requires—or finds useful— determinacy, certitude, and closure. One is comfortable with ambiguity and open-endedness.

The arguable actual situation is that of the ultimate necessity of choice— choice that is obfuscated by the use of the concept of the rule of law. For the philosophical idealist, the inexorable necessity of choice arises because each idealist likely has a different notion of the ideal, between which choice somehow must be made. For the philosophical realist, even if everyone were a philosophical realist, the necessity of choice arises because of their conflicting definitions of reality, between which choice somehow must be made.

The operative problem is who is to control and use government for what purposes; or, more broadly, who is to control and use the legal-economic nexus for what purposes.

The operative situation is the burden of choice. The operative alternative to its recognition is the selective abdication of choice.

Recognition of the mythic nature of the concept of the rule of law would, hopefully, engender less opportunity for dissimulation and manipulation. If it is recognized that law is policy and that law is being made, perhaps we can gradually adjust from the invocation of absolutes to the discussion of ends and means. As Carl Menger argued, every generation has as its highest calling the deliberative consideration of the possible reform of received institutions, of their possible wisdom and folly. This is thwarted, or selectively channeled, by the absolutist formulation of principles of law and otherwise. This latter is done notwithstanding, actually in pursuit of working out, the multiplicity and conflicts noted earlier.

The alternative to explicit recognition of the non-mythic nature of law is elite control of both the exercise and change of law. Those who treat law as something given and transcendent are law takers. They abdicate their participation in the process of making law. They leave the domain of law = policy to the law makers. These are the people who know that law is something made, an object of control and use, and act to enlist it in the support their interests. They practice, even if they do not preach, a ubiquitous pragmatism, promoting those legal means that suit their ends.

One might tend to think that absolutist formulation in politics leads to the loss of civility and mutual respect and the endangering of polarized, irreconcilable positions, with politics emulating exclusivist and absolutist religion—all under a belief in the rule of law yet with law used as a weapon. One might also think that abnegation of and disbelief in the idea of the rule of law might result in the same disagreeable results. Causation is exceedingly complex; many variables enter the picture. Religion has often engendered but need not engender persecution. A secular, matter-of-fact approach to matters of policy is no guarantee of civility and humanity but the latter seem more likely—wishful thinking?—in the absence of divisive absolutes. If the idea of the rule of law meant working out common, humane solutions under a protocol of placing ourselves in others' positions to see their view of things, then the idea would be unobjectionable. It is when the idea is given ostensibly absolutist substantive content, when in fact there is none, that the trouble begins. Perhaps the key is forebearance, for example, restraining oneself and one's allies from gerrymandering voting districts in such a way as to give your side electoral advantage and from appointing only one's allies to judicial positions while preaching "the law." Doing so marries hypocrisy to the rule of law in such a way as to cast the latter in doubt, indeed, to demonstrate beyond denial the myth of the rule of law and its selective application. The invocation of ideology and myth too readily evades, indeed obfuscates, moral issues and prevents any iota of sympathy and guilt.

The concept of the rule of law is used to promote certain interests over others. It is also true that many of those who seek to unmask the concept are promoting an agenda of their own rather than undertaking the unmasking in the interest of objective scholarship. Both the use and unmasking have unintended consequences, and no meta-criteria or meta-principles exist by which to weigh all the variables in terms of civility, humanity, decency, and justice.

The fact of the matter is that we persist, willy nilly, in a process that can properly be named Benthamite. The question is whether, in seeking through government (law = policy) the greatest good of the greatest number, we do so by promoting the degree of welfare of those most highly benefited or by promoting the number of those benefited. Or in Lockean-Smithian terms, if government is to be used to support property, the question is whether property is to comprise the protected interests of a relative few or those of many. If the rule of law is to have meaning, which/whose law will rule? This needs to be worked out and in this context the idea of the rule of law needs to be seen as being selectively and variably functional in the resolution of the conflicts of freedom with control, hierarchy with equality, and continuity with change.

The foregoing account has no ulterior motive, no hidden agenda, no presumption that certain political consequences or policies will necessarily follow. Recognition of the nonexistence of a transcendent "rule of law" will not necessarily result in any specific political results. Admittedly it is anti-conservative insofar as it foments consciousness of the policy/political nature of law, opens the door to change, and so on. But this is conclusive of nothing necessarily politically specific. As examples, courts deemed "conservative" by one criterion have introduced changes deemed "revolutionary" by another criterion; and the substantive content of being "conservative"—the institutional and power structures defended and reinforced thereby—varies between regimes and over time.

The following was written by Y. S. Brenner in response to the foregoing (numbers in brackets refer to my comments given after the extract):

> I agree with Kahn that the idea of "rule of law" is a myth. However, I believe that it is a myth which not only reflects people's scales of values but influences them. [1]
>
> The rule of God formulated in the Ten Commandments did not only reflect what people thought to be right or wrong and good or bad but influenced their mode of conduct. The myth of God handing down the law to Moses became momentous—a clear standard for correct behavior. It made no difference that there were transgressions because they were always recognized as such. [2]
>
> Democracy postulated the idea of people's equality before the law. Americans were taught to hold it self-evident that all people were created

equal and were entitled to life, liberty etc. This myth gave a particular meaning to two important institutions, namely to elections and to law courts. It made people feel that they have an inalienable right to vote and have their vote acknowledged, and that courts have to determine objectively without resort to considerations of expediency. Whether people are really equal or not and whether the formal rules and procedures of the law courts are really producing equitable just results is immaterial to the myth. It is the myths people believe in which sets their standards of behavior. [3]

Good Christians believed that they must save the heathens' souls and went to the remotest corners of the earth, braving malaria and other dangers, to do what they thought right. Nationalists and honest Communists laid down their lives convinced that it was their duty to show their national uniqueness or to impose on the world economic equality. Americans believing in Democracy, in the right of every person to have a say in determining the political system he chooses to live under and to be free from arbitrary rules, fought in Europe, Korea and Viet-Nam. Myth matters! [1]

It therefore makes little difference whether the rule of law is a myth and human artifact. If people wish to believe in it, it becomes a powerful inspiration for the way they live. They will accept that it is often more seen by transgression than observance but they will still regard it as the guide to right behavior. Even when laws promote special interests which may be in conflict with other socially espoused notions (you mention favorable tax treatment for certain sections of the population, new rights created for surrogate motherhood, etc.), this will not undermine the people's fundamental trust in their rule of law for as long as these things are openly declared (enacted) by a Parliamentary majority or any other formally acknowledged representative assembly. Only when the rule of law is subverted by lawyers or judges machinations people become weary and even disillusioned and the myth begins to crumble. And if this happens people turn to other myths to take its place. [4]

What the Supreme Court did in the case of Bush vs. Gore was to deprive people of the trust that every vote counts, and of the confidence that justice rather than expediency determines its decisions. People use common sense. They know that all the Supreme Court had to say was let them count the votes in Florida because the formalistic setting of time limits to end the count are less important than the preservation of the people's right to have their votes counted—which is the pillar of democracy. Instead the Court took to expediency and hid behind legalistic arguments to avoid further complications. [5]

Taken on its own this is no great matter for concern but in the context of a developing culture in America this is important. It undermines the validity of the trust in the rule of law and in democracy. It undermines the myth that made America great. It reinforces the idea that all that counts is winning and that the entire legacy of moral values is no more than bunk.

As for me, not being an American, it makes little difference if the next president of the US is Bush or Gore (in the end both will have to compromise and the result will be similar) but it is the example set by the Supreme Court which worries me. It confirms my fears that the world is moving toward a period in which expediency overrules truth and the few positive cultural achievements Modernity and of the Post-War era will be replaced by a new Myth, namely that of the survival of the fittest. [6]

(Y. S. Brenner to Warren Samuels, December 14, 2000; slightly corrected)

My comments on Brenner's response are these, coupled with his subsequent replies:

(1) I agree that, as a factual matter, myths both reflect peoples' values and influences them. Myths also are the manipulated means by which actions are rationalized and legitimized in an absolutist manner. Myths are means of social control (a term that I use objectively and non-pejoratively). The issues are always (a) which myths and (b) how are they selectively applied? [See (3).]

(2) The Ten Commandments are not always clear, that is, they have been interpreted differently by different people in different times and places.

(3) This affirms what Vilfredo Pareto (who also said that elites rule by force and fraud) called the social utility of falsity. But social utility has social costs, and both the utility and the costs of falsity are distributed unequally.

In a subsequent email, Brenner wonders why I mention Pareto's "social utility or falsity" in this context. Alas, I mention it because I think that the concept of the rule of law is illusion and myth and not true. (Brenner to Samuels, December 15, 2000)

(4) How does one distinguish between decisions that uphold and those that subvert the rule of law—both if one believes in the idea as such and if the idea is a myth? In this regard public opinion is an object of manipulation. To this Brenner responds as follows:

> To your query, how one was to distinguish between decisions which uphold and which subvert the rule of law, I have no answer. Time usually shows it but this is of little use. One can only feel that the rule of law is subverted, but feeling is subjective and often misleading. If one believes in people's right for their voices to be heard, and this right is denied them, then one cannot help saying that the law has been subverted. Yet, if someone feels that rules of procedure are paramount, then one will think that the rule of law has been upheld, and continue to feel this way even if it later turns out that if votes had been counted the result would have been different. People who arrogate for themselves the position of moralists (as I do) will take one position and lawyers will take another. This is the reason why I never got on well with the legal profession and never in my 74 years went to court about anything.
>
> (Brenner to Samuels, December 15, 2000)

I find that this response helps confirm my emphasis on the role of selective perception, if not also of manipulation.

(5) The interesting things about the Bush vs. Gore case are (a) the equal-protection reasoning was a broad principle applied to a very narrow result and (b) with the implicit qualification that its application here should not be taken to establish a precedent for the application of the principle in other fields, limiting their consideration to the present—narrowly defined—circumstances lest the problem of equal protection introduce complexities to the problem of equal protection in election processes generally, (c) the reasoning, as is usually the case, did not determine the result, it was only the mode of exposition and legitimation, (d) equal protection was "applied" to the recount and not the initial counting, to which, by any objective standard, it also applies, and (e) the court's unwillingness to apply equal protection to differences in funding among school districts within a state (in defense of status quo wealth distribution and it consequences). "The law" did not drive the decision; the desired result helped drive the choice of the language of law to express a rationalization of the choice made. The reasoning by the majority was unusually convoluted and casuistic. The decision rejected certain hand counts of punch-card ballots in Florida but not all such counts. It did so on the ground that different modes of discerning voter intent would deny equal protection but it did not apply the principle to either all hand counts with different modes of discernment or all hand counts or different modes of voting, despite the applicability of the principle to them as well—both within Florida and across the country. Furthermore, the decision was promulgated by a majority that usually seeks to affirm state jurisdiction rather than that of branches of the national government (apropos of the selectivity of "judicial restraint" and "strict construction," see Powe 2000 and Yarbrough 2000).

Although Gore won a narrow majority of citizen votes, Bush won a narrow majority of votes in the electoral college—a device that from the beginning has had as one of its functions (another is to protect small states from large states) the protection of elites from masses (a statement of fact made without either necessarily defining democracy in terms of one person-one vote or affirming that the majority of citizen voters necessarily has the correct position). Before the election, it had been expected by some that Bush would win the majority of citizen votes and Gore the majority of electoral-college votes. It was reported that in such a case, the Republicans would seek a constitutional challenge to the electoral-college result, despite the constitutional status of the procedure. And during the tumultuous period in November 2000, the premise that the equal protection clause of the Fourteenth Amendment would apply to intra-state vote counting was thought so weak and improbably that, it was reported, no case existed for federal jurisdiction. The entire process—on both sides—consisted of exercises in strategic litigation.

While the losing side in the decisive Bush vs. Gore case and in all other related cases—in both state and federal courts—interpreted the relevant court to have usurped some other power (see for example, Ackerman 2001; Bugliosi 2001), either that of the legislature or that of the citizen voters, the situation of fluidity is due in large part to the inexorable open-endedness of the divisions of the powers

of government between the states and the national government and between the
several branches of government on each level (see for example, Barbash 2000).

(6) "Survival of the fittest"—always a system-specific matter—has been around
for a long time, as a myth.

In a second communication via email, Brenner goes on to make the following
points:

> I think that on one point we are fully in agreement, namely that "legal
> decisions in such cases (as the one under discussion) are not about truth but
> about values." You ask: "whose values?" Well, my values! My point is
> that expediency as a function of power rules, and I don't like it. I agree
> that its rule is a function of power but I do not agree that as a result of this
> inevitability one must succumb to it. Power can be removed from one
> holder to another and I want power to move in the direction of truth.
> Copernicus was silenced and Galileo was punished by those in power for
> knowing truth but in the end the powerful were shamed and lost. The
> Soviet bureaucracy was very powerful and lasted for half a century but in
> the end it had to yield. The fact that the rich are more influential in the
> industrialized countries than the poor is a fact but they could not prevent
> the poor (or relatively poor) from creating the Welfare State and a good
> measure of progressive taxation in Europe.
>
> Power has shifted from the rich to the poor and since the 1970s shifted
> back in some measure to the rich, but the myth of fairness (what is fair and
> what is unfair) was kept alive. Tom Paine once wrote that there is no verb "to
> unsee in the English language." One may forget or ignore but one cannot
> "unsee." The American people were taught that all people were created
> equal. They took this myth as a guiding line for their system of government.
> All efforts to tell people that it is the fault of the losers themselves that they
> are what they are has not really eradicated the belief in the desirability of
> equality. Courts of law were thought to make this notion of equality manifest.
> They were expected to determine the truth impartially. The judges of the
> Supreme Court were given life-tenure to make them free to do so. Now it
> turns out that they preferred expediency (not to drag out the process of
> declaring the winner) to finding the truth. This is what worries me. It may
> teach the American public that truth does not really matter.
>
> In the end people learned that Copernicus and Galileo were right and the
> Russians learned that their leaders were deceiving them, but at what price?
> Do the American people deserve to lose their faith in justice—in equality
> before the law—to serve some short-term ends? And what will be the long-
> term consequences of this loss of faith in common sense justice, and the loss
> of faith in that one's voice is registered when one casts one's vote?
>
> Democracy and Justice may well be myths, but they are myths that make
> life more bearable than living without them. Having experienced life without
> these myths (see my Ghana story "life under a dictatorship") I wish better for
> the American people. One can experience personal injustice and lack of say

in matters of state and be disappointed and live with it, but to accept that Justice and the right to have one's say taken notice of is quite a different matter. It destroys the fabric of society and leads into life in a Hobbesian jungle (Brenner to Samuels, December 15, 2000) Brenner's Ghana stories—an interpretive account of economic-development efforts in that country in the 1960s—will appear in a forthcoming volume of *Research in the History of Economic Thought and Methodology*).

I am very much personally sympathetic to Brenner's egalitarian sentiments and what is implicit about scientific, descriptive, and explanatory truth (subject to selective perception and other hermeneutic problems). But truth is one thing; values are another. As for not liking power and the ministrations of psychic balm, I too am not comfortable with them—but I do think they need to be identified, discussed, and analyzed, and not merely given passive effect.

In a third email message, Brenner says the following:

Naturally, no one thinks that there is a final and eternal truth. But it has been one of the few lasting elements in all cultures and an eternal quest of scientists. If truth was not a universal value how could we communicate? We simply take it for granted that most of what people tell us is true. If I tell you that it is raining outside while I am writing this message you believe me. There is no reason for me to tell you that it rains if it isn't true. If I thought you may not believe it, I would not write it to you. So, let me repeat—most of what people say is true and if it were otherwise there could be no social intercourse—there would be no civilization. It is this which makes me shudder when I think of expediency. It may be very expedient for Afro-Americans to claim that Shakespeare, Beethoven, and Abraham Lincoln were black men. It would boost their morale and help them in their struggle for equality. It may be expedient for women's organizations to claim that the works of Shakespeare and Beethoven were written by their wives and that it was the wife of Lincoln who made him place the liberation of the slaves on the political agenda. It may help them in their struggle against "white male chauvinism." It may be expedient to tell the American people that the Supreme Court found that there are no good criteria, and no time to make them, for recounting votes in Florida. But where is this leading to? Sooner or later people find out that Shakespeare and Beethoven were men; and even if the untruths about them had really managed to do some good for blacks and women the price would still be much too high even for them. The "death of truth" would put an end to civilized living and in the end blacks, women and Americans would all slide down the road to anarchy and none be served. If the blacks and the women can say that Shakespeare and Beethoven were black women what would stop the real "white male chauvinists" saying that blacks and women are genetically inferior and must not be given equal rights?

Again all this may be irrelevant in the context of what you were saying, but it may throw some light on why I feel so strongly about what I regard as an expedient which the Supreme Court chose for extricating itself from the mess in Florida.

(Brenner to Samuels, December 16, 2000)

I cannot help but be sympathetic to Brenner's argument. However, I feel that (1) we must distinguish between simple truths (it is raining) and other declarative statements (the constitution has been violated); (2) there is a difference between statements of value (the constitution has been violated), even when they take an "is" form, and statements of fact (this is what the constitution literally says). I also feel that we must distinguish between statements whose function is (intended) to communicate facts or values, and statements whose function is (intended) to manipulate sentiments and motivate action. In all this I accept the basis logic of Vilfredo Pareto's theories of non-logical beliefs and derivations (Samuels 1974). This is in addition to my willingness to use, indeed insist on, the distinction between latent and manifest function.

At bottom, therefore, law *is* politics, politics by other means. Law should be seen as such, rather than continue to be mystified by the idea of the "rule of law," a modern mode of absolutist legitimation that has replaced that of the "divine right of kings" in the strategic, linguistic game of justification.

Notes

* The author is indebted to Y. S. Brenner, Steven G. Medema, A. Allan Schmid, and James D. Shaffer for comments on an earlier draft of this chapter.
1 A. Allan Schmid suggests an important, if minimalist, definition of rule of law: that the judge cannot be directly bought, that decisions are not auctionable; appointment of like-minded judges is only indirect purchase. If minimalist, this definition is nonetheless important. In many countries the judiciary is in fact corrupt. But purchase and sale is one thing; pretense of the possibility and fact of objectivity and of a transcendent law to be found is quite another, and a corruption of its own.

References

Ackerman, Bruce (2001) "Anatomy of a Constitutional Coup," *London Review of Books*, (February 8): 3–6.

Barbash, Fred (2000) "A Brand New Game," *Washington Post* (December 17): B01.

Bugliosi, Vincent (2001) "None Dare Call It Treason," *The Nation* (February 5): 11–19.

Ewing, K. D. and C. A. Gearty (2001) *The Struggle for Civil Liberties: Political Freedom and the Rule of Law in Britain, 1914–1945*, New York: Oxford University Press.

Fallon, Richard H., Jr (1997) " 'The Rule of Law' as a Concept in Constitutional Discourse," *Columbia Law Review*, 97 (January): 1–56.

Hutchinson, Allan C. (2000) *It's All in the Game: A Nonfoundationalist Account of Law and Adjudication*, Durham, NC: Duke University Press.

Kahn, Paul W. (1997) *The Reign of Law*, New Haven, CT: Yale University Press.

Kahn, Paul W. (2000) "The 'Rule of Law' is National Myth," Los Angeles Times-Washington Post News Service. *Lansing State Journal* (November 26, 2000): 13A.

Lipkin, Robert Justin (2000) *Constitutional Revolutions: Pragmatism and the Role of Judicial Review in American Constitutionalism*, Durham, NC: Duke University Press.

Lynch, Joseph M. (1999) *Negotiating the Constitution: The Earliest Debates Over Original Intent*, Ithaca, NY: Cornell University Press.

McDonald, Forrest (2000) *States' Rights and the Union: Imperium in Imperio, 1776–1876*, Lawrence, KS: University Press of Kansas.

McWhorter, Diane (2001) *Carry Me Home: Birmingham, Alabama: The Climactic Battle of the Civil Rights Revolution*, New York: Simon & Schuster.

Neely, Mark, Jr (1999) *Southern Rights: Political Prisoners and the Myth of Confederate Constitutionalism*, Charlottesville, VA: University Press of Virginia.

Powe, Lucas A. (2000) *The Warren Court and American Politics*, Cambridge, MA: Harvard University Press.

Samuels, Warren J. (1974) *Pareto on Policy*, New York: Elsevier.

Yarbrough, Tinsley E. (2000) *The Rehnquist Court and the Constitution*, New York: Oxford University Press.

Part IV

Land and governance

The transformation of order

13 The Duke of Argyll and Edwin L. Godkin as precursors to Hayek on the relation of ignorance to policy

With Kirk D. Johnson and Marianne Johnson

Introduction

The foremost proponent and articulator of the principle of unintended and unforeseen consequences (hereinafter "the principle") in the late twentieth century was Friedrich A. von Hayek. But Hayek is only the most recent author to have articulated the principle, or principle-like reasoning. This chapter explores two nineteenth-century authors, George Douglas Campbell, the eighth Duke of Argyll, and Edwin L. Godkin, one a Scot and the other an American, one a landed and titled aristocrat and the other a journalist, who relied heavily on the principle in formulating their respective arguments. Argyll is primarily addressed in the first part of this chapter; the arguments of Godkin will be discussed in the second part.

Political and economic conservatism is heterogeneous and the complexity and opportunities for internal conflict are increased when varieties of religious and social conservatism are also considered. The divide between economic and social conservatives is well developed and widely known. Another facet of conservatism's heterogeneity is the adoption of principles of continuity *vis-à-vis* change independent of the substance of that which is to be continued or changed *vis-à-vis* the adoption of principles applicable to particular institutions or sets of institutions. With the prospect of the disintegration of the Soviet Union, for example, some conservatives happily supported rapid change, whereas other conservatives, applying their traditional cautionary pro-continuity principles, worried and warned of the dangers of moving too rapidly. Still another facet of conservatism's heterogeneity concerns the treatment of particular institutions as means or as ends. And so on.

One principle widely found throughout conservative thought—a principle now associated with Hayek—proposes that all action has unintended and unforeseen consequences. "All action" can include individual and sub-group action as well as large-scale, governmental action. However, the focus of the conservative deployment of the principle is on government, because of a fundamental antipathy to government or belief that the consequences of government action are likely to be more vast and more difficult to track down and control, but more important to do so, than the others. As for the consequences, although logically the principle encompasses both beneficial and harmful ones, the usual focus of applications of the conservative principle is on the latter.

One supporting ground of the principle is the diffusion of knowledge. Local and tacit knowledge is unavailable to any one person or group, especially central governments. This lack of knowledge constitutes ignorance and because knowledge is neither present nor transparent at the center, for all practical purposes it is unseen, especially by those who make policy or those who analyze the putative consequences of policy. Both the policy maker and policy analyst tend to focus on proximate considerations; deeper cultural and structural considerations are unknown, ignored, and/or neglected and thus remain unseen. In effect, the principle of unintended and unforeseen consequences has as a largely nonspecific but implicit corollary, the principle of unseen causes.

The principal line of reasoning is ubiquitous and can be almost low level in formulation. By the latter we mean that in a debate a readily available line of reasoning is, apropos of local or tacit knowledge, "If you knew what I know, then..." which can translate as, "You don't know, hence are ignorant, and can't see what is going on." The argument also can focus on the unintended and unforeseen consequences of past developments and of ignoring those consequences. The principle of unintended and unforeseen consequences is a more sophisticated version of these lines of reasoning. So also is the corollary principle of unseen causes.

(The concept of the *unseen* is a subcategory of the concept of the *invisible*. Another subcategory is the *hidden*. In a recent article on the "hidden economy" one reads, "The Isa Upanishad[1] tells us that there are two aspects to reality: the manifest and the unmanifest. To know reality is to know these two together" (Dixon 1999: F.335). It is likely that religion is the initial major domain in which the concept of the unseen is used, as in such formulations as, for example, that faith is a matter of accepting the unseen and that entry into heaven is entry into the realm of the unseen. A central foundation concept in economics is the *invisible hand*.)

That ignorance is and should be seen as a limit to action by individuals and by governments (collective action) is a venerable theme. Some, including Aristotle, have seemed to apply the reasoning to both individual and collective action; some conservatives use it in favor of continuity; others, like Hayek, have seemed to apply it only or primarily to collective action, especially state action.

The business corporation seems to have been largely ignored. On the one hand, it is treated legally as a person; on the other hand, it is a creature of law and subject, like all individuals, to legal social control. Large corporations have economic power and influence rivaling that of many nations; and many corporations, trade associations, and wealthy individuals have influence on governments, all in a world of plutocracy in which government is an object of control and use. More important for present purposes, however, if one defines governance as making decisions that affect vital interests of others, then corporations share in the power of governance and generate vast unintended and unforeseen consequences. A frequent issue centers on whether the consequences are in fact unintended or unforeseen, or whether they are derived from decisions to shift costs to others, to enhance the bottom line, or in pursuit of the corporate equivalent of reasons of state. But that owners or users of property create consequences for others is incontrovertible, notwithstanding selectively applied absolutist theories of property or doctrines of laissez-faire, or revisionist approaches to externality and public good theories.

Further apropos whether consequences are in fact unintended or unforeseen, the question of religion inevitably arises. (In fact, as we note later, Argyll cites the Catholic Church in two important regards.) Three points: First, religion is thought to work best as social control if it is not seen as such. Second, the Catholic Church, presumably not alone, has been charged with adopting policies that serve to maintain the humble position and dependence of the laity relative to the priesthood. Third, the distinction between manifest and latent function (developed by Emile Durkheim, Robert K. Merton, and Louis Schneider), pertinent in part to the first point, directly raises the role of the unseen. Manifest function involves those who enter a holy place feeling that they are in the presence of God. Latent function points to the foregoing having the effect of inculcating respect for the status quo, especially high levels of authority. That effect is unseen, as it were, by the lay person but known to, intended, and foreseen by the priesthood.

In any event, ours is a world of ignorance and of the asymmetrical distribution of ignorance. Ignorance in principle is and should be a limit on action. That it often is not a limit is (1) a source of costs borne by second and third, even first, parties, but also (2) a source of material progress by the reckoning of many people. Risk aversion and risk assumption are modes of reaction to ignorance but also a function of ignorance.

If ignorance is and should be seen as a limit to action, what of the spread of information and what of the articulation of the principle? The combination of information and articulation renders the hitherto unseen seen, or more widely seen, thereby tending to render the argument nugatory and emphasizing wider dissemination of both information and structural reform. Such is paradoxical but the paradox may dissolve upon realizing that some authors have written that they would not have published their revelations if they expected their books to have a wide audience.

Still another twist resides in the admonition that it is not what one does not know that can hurt you but what you think you know but is wrong—a different kind of ignorance.

Objective analysis of the principle must confront a number of problems. One problem is that the stated objective of a policy may not be the intended objective; what therefore appears as the unintended and unforeseen consequences are very much intended and foreseen, albeit masked. Another problem is that for some people the consequence is foreseen, leading to the questions, how many, and who, must not foresee for the principle to apply? Still another problem concerns structure: whose local knowledge is to count? Additional problems abound: What is a desirable and what an undesirable consequence is subjective and normative. What is desirable for one person is undesirable for another, raising anew the structural problem. Amplifying perhaps all other problems is making sense of selectivity, namely, applying the pro-continuity principle against government actions one opposes and ignoring it apropos government actions one favors.

Hayek was the foremost proponent and articulator of the principle of unintended and unforeseen consequences in the late twentieth century.[2] Hayek began as an economist concentrating on monetary economics and the theory of business cycles. He transformed into a social theorist and an expositor of classical liberalism (which in the United States is generally called conservatism), in both respects emphasizing the principle. His initial use of the principle, at least its emphasis on local knowledge not available to central planners, was in the socialist calculation debate. His argument was the impossibility of (rational, fully informed) central planning, the reason being the absence of a price system as a mode of bringing local knowledge to bear in plan construction and execution. In several pre-Second World War writings, Hayek extended the basic reasoning to a vaster domain, the entire economy and the entirety of government action even in a market economy.

Hayek combined the principle with another, that of spontaneous order. This principle maintains that collective decision making is of two types. One is deliberative decision making and, for Hayek, is laden with unintended and unforeseen undesirable consequences. The other is non-deliberative decision making, from which arises spontaneous order, which is not so laden. Although it can be shown, or at least argued, that the distinction breaks down and that Hayek's theory is dispositive of neither the positions he takes nor the issues to which his theory is applied (Samuels 1999), such is not directly pertinent here.

Hayek is, however, only the most recent author to have deployed the principle, or principle-like reasoning, in articulating his or her case. George Douglas Campbell, the eighth Duke of Argyll, and Edwin L. Godkin relied heavily on the principle in formulating their respective arguments.

A sensitive problem confronting anyone who seeks to interpret these two writers on the principle is the possibility of creating a structure(s) that is not theirs; we face, in other words, the problem of imposing the present on the past. They did not write with Hayek in mind. But their reasoning is closely akin to principle-like argumentation. In recounting and interpreting what they said, we will stay close to what they said. And, indeed, as suggested by the titles of Argyll's *The Unseen Foundations of Society* and Godkin's *Unforeseen Tendencies of Democracy*, staying close to what they said should be sufficient. No stretching of argument is required, only sensitivity to what they are arguing and how they are going about it.

George Douglas Campbell (1823–1900), the eighth Duke of Argyll and the first in the peerage of the United Kingdom (1892), succeeded his father in 1847. (The first Earl of Argyll dates from 1433; the first Duke of Argyll, 1658, was the tenth Earl of Argyll. At least two Earls were executed in the seventeenth century for treason and rebellion.) Argyll was a cabinet minister almost continuously between 1853 and 1874, the last six as Secretary for India. He also served as

Chancellor of St. Andrews University, President of the Royal Society of Edinburgh, and Postmaster-General. He was an amateur geologist and active religionist and supporter of the Church of Scotland. He acquired the reputation of an effective debater and active controversialist. His daughter, Francis, married the brother of Prime Minister Arthur Balfour; a noted biographer, she campaigned for female emancipation and the reunion of the Church of Scotland with the United Free Church. His son, John (1845–1914), served as a Liberal member of Parliament in the House of Commons, and already had been Governor-General of Canada when he became the nineth Duke of Argyll upon his father's death (Lake Louise is named after his wife). The seat of the Dukes of Argyll is Inveraray Castle, the first house in Scotland to have electricity installed; it has been restored several times after destructive fires.

Argyll's opposition to Charles Darwin's theory of evolution was actually a defense of the orthodox supernaturalist view of the world, or at least one version thereof. In *The Reign of Law* (1867) he argued that if Darwin's theory was a natural law and if natural law governs the world, natural law was but the instrument of God; God acted through these laws. Argyll's concern was that natural law seemed to leave no active role for God and was often treated as an alternative to God, even as evidence of the nonexistence of God. In his view, Darwin's theory had no effect on the orthodox understanding of the world and of God's place in it. Natural laws like Darwin's were the instruments through which God controls the world. Argyll had earlier argued that God controlled the world directly. When Darwin seemed to provide affirmation for control by natural law alone, no role was left for God, a view amounting to atheism. Argyll's approach now argued that God controlled the word through natural law. Thus retrieving a position for God, it was a prominent Victorian solution to the perceived conflict of Christianity with natural law—a conflict, nourished in part by a literalist view of an inerrant Bible, still unresolved in religious circles in the early twenty-first century. Other complications include the problem of an omniscient, benevolent, and omnipotent God, and the related problem of Job; and whether God is active in the world or only set it up by establishing natural laws. Apropos of the latter problem, Argyll's position defended the concept of design. To many believers the design, or watchmaker, argument, the core of Deism, was akin to atheism; but such seemingly was activist enough for Argyll.

The significance of Argyll's work with respect to the problem of ignorance and the principle of unintended and unforeseen consequences resides both in what Argyll says and what he does, that is, how he uses what he says. His overall treatment of ignorance and of the principle is arguably more complex and more suggestive than Hayek's. Both men endeavor to use the problem and the principle for their own purposes, for their own individual intellectual advantage. The same is true of Godkin. The positions taken by the three men and their uses of the principle are interesting and historically important, very much consonant with Vilfredo Pareto's theory of policy (Samuels 1974). But their positions and uses of the principle are more useful here for what they reveal to be deep problems and issues. These latter include the need to reconcile continuity and change, freedom and control, and hierarchy and equality (Samuels 1996). Notwithstanding, therefore, the ease with which it is possible to get emotionally or intellectually attached to the arguments over landownership deployed by Argyll, what is important is not their putative truth or value but their instrumental rhetorical roles apposite to those three needs.

A few words about the Campbell clan are in order (see, for example, MacKinnon 1984, especially: 50–7; 181–3). The Campbells have been one of the four principal clans of Scottish Highlands. For centuries they were engaged in bitter and bloody struggles with the MacDonalds, the Campbells willingly and remuneratively used by Scottish kings to check the power and ambitions of the MacDonalds. Much of Argyll land was ceded to them for services rendered to the Crown. Whereas the MacDonalds opposed the superior power of the Crown, the Campbells did not, preferring in turn to use the Crown for their own purposes. This relationship, and the larger history of which it is a part, is especially interesting in light of Argyll's denigrating description of a similar history in *Irish Nationalism*. Also comparable to Ireland was the combination of straightforward power play and issues of religion and conscience; the writing of history, as Argyll selectively notices in *Irish Nationalism*, thus became selective and partisan.

The picture is amplified by turning to Arthur Herman's *How the Scots Invented the Modern World*. There, one is given a somewhat different picture from that Argyll would have his readers draw by implication, nuance, and suggestion from his, Argyll's, writings. Argyll's position was that of an interested party—a very interested party, one of the great landowners and therefore one of the great landlords. In Herman's book we read, for example: "Men such as the Duke of Argyll of the Campbells . . . routinely demanded a loyalty from their tenants not unlike that of children for a father" (Herman 2001: 122). And again: ". . . the Campbells and their most important chiefs, the Dukes of Argyll, rose to power by serving as the Crown's principal tool in controlling the other western clans" (ibid.: 125; see, for example, 152). The fourth Duke "rose to become the most powerful man in Scotland" (ibid.: 79). Argylls come from a tradition that longed for a "stable and harmonious" community with "the security of a stable, hierarchical social order," and that "extolled the virtues of a rural-based society and the authority of a traditional landowning class." If later Dukes accommodated themselves to and tried to make the best of the industrial capitalist society, many "detested the new rising competitive capitalist society, with its getting and spending, its greedy merchants and vulgar upstarts, its contempt for the old rules, its creative destruction" (ibid.: 136).[3] In the process, "the old Scottish law [that] had been set up to keep tenants under the thumb of their feudal overlords," as Lord Kames pointed out, was replaced. The new law, promoted by Duncan Forbes, helped establish the tenant as a more independent economic agent, "a free individual, who could contract to work his own land and keep the proceeds for himself" (ibid.: 157, not an entirely meaningful legal-economic picture as to details but suggestive of systemic differences in status).

Argyll presents an idyllic picture of tenant-landlord relations. (It should not be necessary to point out that "landlord" comes from "lord of the land," with all that

that implies with regard to status, deference, and governance.) A rather different picture is given by Henry Cockburn (1779–1854), Solicitor General for Scotland and a judge of the Court of Sessions. Writing of the elder Highland Glengarry chieftain of his time, Lord Cockburn wrote that "he was a paltry and odious fellow, with all the vices of the bad chieftain and none of the virtues of the good one; with the selfishness, cruelty, fraud, arrogant pretension and base meanness of the one, without the fidelity to superiors, and the generosity to vassals, the hospitality, or the courage of the other" (quoted in Taylor and Taylor 2002: 425).

Edwin Lawrence Godkin (1831–1902) was born in Ireland. He published a book on the history of Hungary two years after graduating from Queen's College, Belfast, in 1851 (his father, James Godkin, a Presbyterian minister, also became an author, publishing *Religious History of Ireland* (1873)). He was a correspondent to the London *Daily News* on the Crimean War during 1854–6 and the US Civil War, in between studying law in New York City and later practicing law. In 1865 he founded *The Nation*; in 1881, having declined in 1870 the offer of a Harvard professorship in history, he became an editor of the New York *Evening Post*, bringing the magazine with him as a weekly, two years later rising to editor-in-chief, retiring in 1900. An influential and respected editorial writer, a politically independent liberal, he opposed the free coinage of silver, labor unions, and excessive tariffs; he was, in all, an advocate of an economic policy of laissez-faire. Bradley Bateman (2004: 21) has thus written that Godkin "was a staunch advocate of the republican arguments against slavery before the [Civil] war; after the war, he became an apologist for the new inequality and the efficiency of large scale corporations." Thus from M'Cready Sykes's[4] parody we read,

> Godkin the Righteous, known of Old,
> Priest of the Nation's moral health;
> Within whose Post we daily read
> The Gospel of the Rights of Wealth.
>   (Levermore 1907: 170)

And from Godkin himself we read from a letter to Frederic Law Olmsted,[5]

> It seems in America as if a man was made for government, not government for man. These views are all for your private ears; don't give me away. As an editor I am bound to keep cheerful and expect grand things.
>   (Ibid.)

The sentiments and fears expressed by Godkin were still felt over a century later.[6]

Godkin published *Problems of Modern Democracy: Political and Economic Essays* (1898) and *Unforeseen Problems of Modern Democracy* (1898), as well *The Problems of Municipal Government* (1894), among other books.

Historians of economic thought may recall that it was Godkin who campaigned to have Richard T. Ely fired from Johns Hopkins University for suggesting in his book, *The Labor Movement in America* (1886), that future social change and advances in civilization should come from the bottom up (see, for example, Cohen 2002, chapter 7).

Before taking up the substance of our account, it will be useful to consider briefly the methodological or epistemological logic and limitations of an explanation that omits or neglects the unseen, or in the words of Argyll's subtitle to *The Unseen Foundations of Society*, an explanation marred by "the fallacies and failures of economic science due to neglected elements."

Assume that the complete explanation of X resides in A, B, C, D, and E: $X = f(A, B, C, D, E)$. Assume an investigator who limits the explanation to three of the independent variables, A, C, and E, so that $X = f(A, C, E)$. By our assumption, we now have an incomplete explanation. Not only does the explanation exclude B and D, no conclusions drawn from $X = f(A, C, E)$ can properly be applied to B and D. Indeed, not only is the explanation incomplete but the exclusion of B and D is tantamount to rendering them unseen and irrelevant: out of sight, out of mind. Investigators who follow our posited investigator will use $X = f(A, C, E)$ likely without giving a thought to B and D; $X = f(A, C, E)$ will henceforth be the customary, stylized or accepted explanation of X (*vide* the criticisms of mainstream economics by those who complain of its narrow scope of variables or its unduly shortened chains of reasoning; these criticisms apply to and constitute limitations of any *ceteris paribus* using analysis, which are those of all schools). Not only will there be an incomplete explanation of X, policy based on $X = f(A, C, E)$ will be incomplete. Policy discourse and planning will take no cognizance of variables B and D or of the interaction effects of B and D with each other or with A, C, and E. Policies so based will likely have unforeseen and unintended consequences.[7]

Assume now that it is *not* known that $X = f(A, B, C, D, E)$. One implication is that the domain of unintended and unforeseen consequences will be enlarged should, say, analysis and policy be based on variables A and D plus variables M and R that actually do not pertain to the explanation of X but lead to a policy based on A, D, M, and R. The unforeseen and unintended consequences will be a function of a type I error of erroneous exclusion and a type II error of erroneous inclusion and, further, type III and type IV errors due to such consequences being generated by policy encompassing erroneous exclusion and related interaction effects and by policy encompassing erroneous exclusion and related interaction effects, respectively. The reader is assured that any expansion of the sources of unintended and unforeseen consequences beyond erroneous inclusion and erroneous exclusion and their respective accompanying interaction effects will vastly expand our little model—and that the explanatory causes of the principle can readily be so expanded.

George Douglas Campbell, eighth Duke of Argyll, on the unseen

We commence with discussion of the opening chapters of Argyll's *The Unseen Foundations of Society* and his *Essay on . . . Contracts for the Hire of Land* and *Irish*

Nationalism. Subsequently we will take up *Godkin's Unforeseen Tendencies of Democracy* and *Problems of Modern Democracy* and return to Argyll's *Unseen Foundations.* Other materials will also be included.

The Unseen Foundations of Society (1893)

Argyll was very much concerned that the masses, especially the working class, accept that "…the larger natural laws…are the only foundation for any true economic science" (Argyll 1893a: xii). If this were the case, and if Political Economists invoked the correct laws, then policy would be made along lines favorable to the propertied. It almost did not matter if the natural laws stood on their own or were the product or instrument of God. They were selective absolutist formulations serving as a mode of social control, of the masses but also of all classes, so long as they were believed.

> So utterly has the teaching of Political Economy broken down as a controlling, or even as a guiding, power, that its very elements, and not a few of its most certain truths, seem to have lost their hold. … The very idea of Natural Law as a prevailing power in human nature, and in all successful legislation, has almost disappeared in popular discussions. This is a serious condition of things. It must be wrong, and it must be dangerous…. [because of] that impatience of any control over the human will to which we are all continually tempted—a temptation specially powerful over the multitude.
>
> (Argyll 1893a: xiv)

Both the agricultural class, on the one hand, and the manufacturing and trading classes, on the other, had favored Protectionism over the centuries. Now, however, the claims made by the (propertyless) working class for the protection by law of their interests was in conflict with natural law as now understood by the propertied classes.

The lesson important for present purposes is that the masses must be convinced of the soundness of natural economic laws and be kept ignorant of unsafe, unsound misrepresentations of natural law. The problem was not with the masses but with economic science, the old and the (then) new Political Economy. Economists stated the wrong doctrines as economic laws, they often were agnostic if not atheistic about the existence of natural laws, and they made "unjust accusation against the agricultural classes" (ibid.: ix). The only system of Political Economy that Argyll knew was that "of the school of Mill and Ricardo," and it "seemed to be an artificial world, with only a few points of contact with the world of nature and of life" (ibid.: xiii). That school had had "an authority which had been too long and too uncritically admitted" (ibid.: xiv). Its doctrines should be shunned—kept hidden (see also the already quoted passage in ibid.: xiv).

To the historian of economic thought, this view of Classical Political Economy was but one negative or partly negative view. To socialist critics, it was the school of apologists for capitalism or for the interests of property. To the marginalists and subjectivists it had driven the engine down the wrong track of value theory. And so on.

For the authors of this chapter, this view comprises one element in Argyll's treatment of ignorance. That view constitutes, in effect, a dual example of the working of the principle of unintended and unforeseen consequences, namely, on the one hand, how false and unsafe doctrines can have pernicious effects, and, on the other, how certain important ideas, like the idea of natural law itself, have almost "disappeared." Identifying certain doctrines as false and unsafe does not, in Argyll's view, generate ignorance, it counters ignorance, it counters knowing what is false, it permits the reinstatement of truth that has disappeared.

Argyll is, in one respect at least, in a difficult position. He is trying to erect an intellectual fortress, or his own propaganda for economic freedom (the term is Frank Knight's), that serves several functions. He is combating the embourgeois-ment of British society; the reduction in political power of the landed aristocracy and its increase among the middle class; the transformation of law, especially land law, away from landed property and in favor of non-landed property; and so on. He is joining with the owners of other forms of property—non-landed property—to restrain the spread of pluralism and democracy, for example, the extension of the franchise: in part, using the middle class businessmen to check the growth and exercise of power of the propertyless; in part to use the interests of labor and the poor, coupled with threats of legislation disliked by all property owners, to check the exercise and growth power of the non-landed propertied. He is joining with certain segments of the landed aristocracy and other landed interests and with certain agricultural, manufacturing and financial interests to transform agriculture into capitalist enterprise. On some fronts, rear-guard actions against the interests of others; on other fronts, aggressive assertion of his own interests; on still other fronts, the results of compromise and adjustment.

That means that Argyll's readers and interpreters are in a difficult position. On the one hand, we find incongruous policy positions; on the other hand, we are much less, if at all, interested in his positions on substantive policy questions than in his underlying reasoning, that is, on how he uses themes constitutive of the principle to help express and ground his stands.

One of Arygyll's central arguments in the first three chapters of *The Unseen Foundations of Society* (1893a) is the importance of "correct," as in "sound," defin-itions. His principal line of reasoning in presenting this argument is essentially that identified earlier in terms of the logic and limitations of a model with excluded elements. Argyll knows that definitions are important for all thought. Definitions tend to embody theories of that which is being defined. To control the definition is to control not only what is being said but policy pertaining to the object of definition.

One of his strongest complaints against the Classical Political Economists was what he saw as their imprecise and incorrect definitions of different concepts, partly arising due to the economists' lack of practical experience. In Argyll's auto-biography he claims: "The Scottish school of philosophy had the honourable reputation of teaching the philosophy of common-sense, and there is nothing like Nature including, of course, under that great name our own human nature, and a constant living with its mysterious facts, for inspiring us with a wholesome contempt for the verbal fallacies and deceptive formulae which are common in all metaphysical systems" (Argyll 1906: 225).

His critique of Classical economics thus takes the form, in part, of the accusation that they have "omitted...some of the most essential elements in the problems with which they had to deal" (Argyll 1893a: 5). The encountering and engendering of unintended and unforeseen consequences is due to such omissions and the concomitant ignorance. The omitted, or neglected elements include both unknown facts and known facts that are excluded because they are viewed as unimportant or too common to consider ("the omission of facts which may be so well-known and familiar that they are treated as not worthy of notice" (ibid.: 10)). Also, the danger of the omission or neglect of non-quantitative causes—and "nothing can be more certain that many of the most powerful among economic causes cannot be numerically expressed" (ibid.: 11)—can "be positively vicious." Their exclusion "multiplies ten thousand-fold that greatest of all dangers—the danger of neglected elements" (ibid.: 11). The use of mathematical techniques "is a method essentially delusive, because it tends more than any other to multiply the number of neglected elements" (ibid.: 17). Even a verbal formula "pretending to the character of a self-evident or axiomatic truth" requires the making of "an abstraction which rests on nothing but a mere bit or fragment of the facts" (ibid.: 13). The problem of exclusion thus applies to both rationalism and empiricism. Further, "we are in perpetual danger of mistaking the transitory for the permanent, the occasional for the constant" (ibid.: 10). Praising inquiry and technical language which touch "the unseen realities of nature," Argyll laments "the lowering of a large conception down to the level of a small one. It is always easy in this way to eliminate the highest elements of thought which are involved in any science" (ibid.: 21–2). As for economics, "The whole science is infested with this pestilent vocabulary of phrases" (ibid.: 23)—which obscures and thereby renders unseen what is important. He finds that, instead of definitions that register meaning and fact, "...no definition is acceptable to us that does not fit into some favourite theories and pre-conceptions which we wish the new definition to support" (ibid.: 25).

Argyll is interested in definitions (see especially ibid.: 37) not because he is a linguistic theorist who wants to illustrate his analysis with the definition of "wealth" (though he purports to be doing so, warranted by use of the word to express the subject-matter of economic science (ibid.: 36), but because he believes that the definition of "wealth" is important for his purpose. And his purpose is to so describe "wealth" that "possession," its origin, and the role of "religious beliefs and superstitions, moral sentiments and doctrines, legal maxims and traditions" are given effect as "the most powerful of all factors alike in its origin and growth, in its advancement of decay" (ibid.: 42), that is, to promote and safeguard the existing institution of property, to promote its continuity and defend it against ignorant critics who do not appreciate "the unseen foundations of society." It is because of such ignorance that "There is the pressure of discontent, with evils, or with troubles, the causes of which are out of sight. There is the pressure of things visible over things invisible, of things present over things belonging to the past" (ibid.: 93–4).[8]

Interestingly, Argyll affirms as "the great truth, that words are not the result of accident and are not to be treated with caprice. ...the definition of... abstract words... ought to be a pure matter of fact, and not at all a matter of opinion" (ibid.: 65). Thus, Argyll propounds the correspondence theory of truth and transform it into a correspondence theory of definition: definitions should comport with the object being defined—the theory of definition repudiated (eventually) by Ludwig Wittgenstein in favor of a socially constructive theory of definition. But Argyll's affirmation just quoted comes with no independent test and his use of it illustrates the proposition that "... no definition is acceptable to us that does not fit into some favorite theories and pre-conceptions which we wish the new definition to support" (ibid.: 25). Definitions help form the seen and the unseen. Argyll would, by such a definition, transform a problematic socially constructed institution into an ontological given. His use reduces to the defense of the definitions that suit his purposes, defending wealth and capital in such a way that landed property is protected. The defense includes: That the sources and origins of all wealth reside in the sources and origin of all possession, in the causes of relative scarcity, and "those causes which limit, or expand, or shape, or control, the desires of men" (ibid.: 66–7) and that if the distinction between labor and capital "means anything definite at all, it means a fundamental distinction between muscular and mental labor" (ibid.: 76). The older economists, in their discussions of labor and capital,

> forgot that human speech, if powerful to instruct, is also powerful to deceive. They forgot that in the use of words, the visible and material elements of meaning are very apt to engulf the invisible and the immaterial. ...nothing can be more certain than that capital is the embodiment and representative of the very highest kind of labour—namely that in which the mental energy of forethought, expresses itself in the savings and storages of wealth already acquired.
>
> (Ibid.: 77)

> Can there be anything more durable than well-reasoned principles of law, or than well-reasoned applications of those principles to the transactions of men?
> (Ibid.: 86)

Argyll does not recognize the self-referential nature of these last statements, for surely his preferred definitions relate to the position he wishes to support. He does not recognize his own uses of ignorance and of the principle constitute the unseen every bit as much as do the practices of others. He neglects the facts that definitions are unable to embody all the features of the object being defined, that it seems impossible for definitions to include unseen and forgotten elements, that different features and different theories require different definitions, and that just as no theory can answer all of our questions, no definition can embody all of our theories—and conversely no object of definition likely can be dealt with through the use of only one theory. Argyll does not recognize that there are no independent tests of either what should be included in a definition or of the unseen, so that the former is a matter of selective use and the latter a matter of selective interpretation. Or, maybe he does not recognize all that but wants his own definitions for his own purposes rendering unseen its own limits.

Argyll's approach to language was criticized by at least one reviewer, John I. Beare, on grounds consistent with the later work of Ludwig Wittgenstein, rejecting the idea that definitions directly correspond to and indicate reality. Beare criticizes the procedure of describing reality "from the implications of common speech," saying that it does not justify the importance which he [Argyll] attaches to it. "Primitive languages," he writes, "represent primitive modes of looking at things." Even modern science is adversely affected by "the subtlely misleading associations of words. The progress of science is marked by a progressive, but very slow, correction of speech" (Beare 1897: 239). As for Argyll:

> If it were quite true that, as the Duke states, "language is the automatic expression of, and witness to, that which we really do see, all the more to be trusted because of the fact that it is an unconscious witness;" and if "words cannot report anything which does not really shine in upon the self-consciousness of man, or which he does not really see;" the words, "spook" and "fairy," should have objective existence corresponding to them, and from the words "sunset" and "sunrise" we should be justified in inferring the falsity of the heliocentric view of the solar system. The Duke's argument from language proves nothing at all, just because it would prove too much.
>
> (Ibid.: 239–40)

The fact that Argyll devotes so much space to the critique of definitions conflicts with his emphasis on language as an "automatic expression" of reality of which "it is an unconscious witness." If automaticity and unconsciousness (non-deliberativeness) reign, why is so much, if any, criticism necessary?

Some of Argyll's arguments are correct but in practice have only a largely rhetorical role. For matters of theory, what is important is not their putative truth or value but their instrumental rhetorical roles. Once the problem of ignorance is seen, and may or may not be gone, at what may be the highest level of theory, (1) ignorance is both an independent and dependent variable and (2) the formulation and deployment of theories of ignorance and of the principle of intended and unintended consequences are part of the process that they putatively are used to describe.

One way to comprehend Argyll's purpose is as follows. Argyll understood the power of capital in society, especially power over the control and use of the human labor force. He understood the comparable power of landownership. He sought to bring landownership under the rubric of capital in order for landowners to benefit from the increasing hegemony of capital.

Another way to comprehend Argyll's purpose involves a comparison with Hayek. Kenneth Hoover has argued that the analysis supporting Hayek's principle became the epistemological foundation for his attack on socialism (Hoover 1999).

One can make a similar point about Argyll: the analysis supporting his approach to the unseen and to ignorance, as well as his version of the principle, became the epistemological foundation for his defense against those who attacked landownership.

Hoover also makes the point that Hayek did not understand that, or why, societies with highly developed political systems have been successful about economic development. Argyll, however, did, as is clear from his *Irish Nationalism* (1893b)—a lesson being relearned in the early twenty-first century amidst tribal warfare in the Middle East, Africa, and elsewhere.

Argyll employed ignorance, the role of the unseen, and, in his own way, the principle and its constitutive themes in *The Unseen Foundations of Society* (1893a) wherein it is the principal argument. But it is also a, if not the, principal argument of two other works, *Essay on the Commercial Principles Applicable to Contracts for the Hire of Land* (1877) and *Irish Nationalism: An Appeal to History* (also 1893b).

Essay on . . . Contracts for the Hire of Land *(1893)*

In Argyll's *Essay on . . . Contracts for the Hire of Land* the issue is how to provide adequate security for capital invested in the cultivation or improvement of their holding by persons [called occupiers, tenants or farmers] hiring land by contract [from owners of land] for agricultural purposes (Argyll 1877: 21). Argyll presents the landowners' case against giving further protection to tenants for their capital invested through improvements to land they only lease. His first line of argument is:

- That existing law, as defined by the judiciary, should be the starting point of discussion (ibid.: 1–2).
- That how the law developed in the past should be given no weight (ibid.: 2, 6).
- That the question of providing (what he calls) privileged security for the lessee should have no connection with the question of the ownership of land (ibid.: 4, 6); that under present law conditions are adequate to secure an ample supply of tenants (ibid.: 5).
- That individuals, believed to be the best judge of their own pecuniary interests, should be left as free as possible to contract as they see fit (ibid.: 9, 14).
- That legislation to attain moral ends or material results beyond the reach of the individual is more acceptable than the present effort which is to regulate contracts for the hire of land for purely economic results (ibid.: 8–15).
- And that universally prevalent and well-established customs should be accepted (as they are by the courts) as the tacit understanding of the contracting parties (ibid.: 20–1).

It should be apparent that Argyll employs several rhetorical and debating devices and ploys whose purpose, it would appear, is to render unseen and nugatory several arguably important matters whose consequences, favorable to himself, he both foresees and intends. Such would compel application to Argyll himself of one of the elements of his version of the principle. Among the obvious examples are the following:

- Stipulating existing law as defined by the judiciary to be the starting point obfuscates the role of men like Argyll serving in the judiciary and being influenced by their common class interests.
- That stipulation plus the argument that how the law developed in the past obfuscates how the Acts of Enclosure and other legislation and judicial decisions constructed landed property as it then existed, arguably confiscating certain post-feudal rights from those who ended up propertyless and in the role of either hired hand or tenant.
- The argument that under present law conditions are adequate to secure an ample supply of tenants is operative only from the point of view of the owners; it obfuscates the issues of what law is to condition the operation of the land market and of the relative bargaining power of the parties (Argyll rejects arguments emphasizing the inequality of holdings (ibid.: 10–11)).
- To argue that universally prevalent and well-established customs should be accepted (as they are by the courts) as the tacit understanding of the contracting parties, is to obfuscate three things: that legal history is often a matter of conflicting claims as to established custom, or conflicts of competing customs; that the hierarchically and deferentially superior party, the owner, is better positioned to ensconce their interests in custom as well as in law; and that judicial acceptance may only signify approval by men who are economically and classwise similarly situated.

Argyll's second line of argument is predominantly linguistic, showing his appreciation for rhetoric in debate:

- He distinguishes moderate from extreme arguments favoring lessee security (Argyll, 1877: 21ff.; of course, the classification is his).
- He continually uses terms like "compulsory," "forced," and "inquisitorial" (ibid.: 22, 23, 41) in reference to legislation protecting lessee interests as well as statements like "the evils always attending interference in matters purely economic" (ibid.: 35)—begging the questions of the domain of the "economic" and the role of government in establishing his own substantial holdings, and conflicting with an earlier statement that he knows "of no abstract limit to the right of the State to do anything" (ibid.: 6).
- He questions the extent of the problem and the inefficiency and inexpediency of the proposed remedy (ibid.: 22)—neglecting (1) that there is no unique efficient result, (2) that risk distribution and security are in part a function of the law, and (3) assuming existing rights neglects and obscures the fact of calculatory results being a function of the price structure specific to those rights.
- He claims that the extreme argument favoring lessee security would provide that the full future increased return from the investment go to the farmer (ibid.: 23, 25)—an argument contradicting his own arguments

below, and an argument assuming existing ownership rights when those
rights, and the income in part derived from them, are the point at issue
(ibid.: 32).

- He assents to a moderate form of the argument for protecting farmer investments, but only if applied to improvements for which benefits have not yet
arisen (ibid.: 34). His clear desire is to limit the change of legal rights in this
matter (ibid. and *passim*).
- He suggests that arguments and claims made by the farmer against the owner
could be applied by contractors against the farmer (ibid.: 31).

Argyll's third line of argument has to do with aspects of providing security
for farmers making improvements and of the contracts and process of contracting for the hire of land. His objective is to rebut the arguments (1) that the
capital of agricultural tenants is now exposed to widely prevalent, severely felt
special and exceptional risks not likely to be remedied by contracts, and (2) that
it is an easy and simple matter for Parliament to supply a remedy without
involving the evils that always attend interference in matters purely economic
(ibid.: 34–5). His counter-arguments maintain that (1) the claimed insecurity of
farming capital is immensely exaggerated, whereas agricultural tenants' capital
now enjoys greater security than that of almost any other professional class, and
(2) in the long run the proposed legislation cannot give better security (ibid.: 35).
His arguments include:

- That competing tenants are shrewd, sagacious, competent men able to calculate benefits and costs (ibid.); they calculate that they can afford to pay and
on that calculation they make their offer (ibid.: 36); competition is thus keen
and close (ibid.); because of this, for reasons given below, although the average rate of return on farming may not be very high, the capital embarked in
it is exceptionally secure (ibid.); indeed, "this calculation is a safer one than
in almost any other commercial enterprise" (ibid.: 38).
- That farmers under lease cannot have their rent increased during the lease;
that farmers without lease are compensated for theoretical uncertainty
of tenure by a lower scale of rent, and by habits, customs, and traditions of
connection with the owner, so powerful as often to put even undue limits on
the owner (ibid.: 36–7).
- That outlays for improvement by the farmer are usually repaid with profit
(ibid.: 37).
- That farmers who hold under lease benefit from increased returns from their
improvements (ibid.: 38); payment to the farmer by the owner, the object of
proposed legislation, would enable the farmer to recover his capital twice, in
form of profits and in the form of legislated compensation. (ibid.: 38–9); rent
and other payments presumably were adjusted beforehand (ibid.: 40); claims
harmony of relations between owner and farmer-occupier of land, invoking
an "equitable spirit...perhaps more habitually exercised" in their relations
"than in any other business whatever" (ibid.: 41).

- That "whether any particular case" is exceptional "is a question which can be determined only upon data which, speaking generally, can never come into public view. It would be very inquisitorial to make the occupier produce his books," many of whom "probably keep no books at all" (ibid.).
- That another element "which is never taken into consideration" by ignorant critics is "the amount of allowance which the owner may have already given in the form of abated or preferential rent" (ibid.: 41–2); indeed, "the occupier himself may not know, and very often does not know, how large has been the allowance...given to him by the owner," the "owner alone knows" (ibid.: 42), writes of the "influence of favour and of personal feeling" (ibid.); that it is unjust "to attach any prejudice to such feeling by calling it feudalism" (ibid.); also claims that preference given to old tenants is often very large and never subjected to competition at all (ibid.: 43); and claims that preference probably equals more than an average of 10 percent (ibid.).
- That the margin of difference between full rent and actual rent is a margin of security against any risk of loss, an interpretation of the facts likely not seen because of the omission of any mention of it in the specific terms of the contract (ibid.: 44).

The foregoing has principally to do with farmers under written lease. Without passing judgment on putative statements of fact, there is much in Argyll's third line of argument so far which places him subject to his own theory of the unseen and therefore to the principle.

- It is ironical that no evidence is provided for so many claims, and thus they remain unseen.
- If the claimed harmony exists, why has the reform legislation been proposed? This is ironically reminiscent of claims by segregationists in the 1960s that the majority of US blacks were happy with the status quo, and that the only complainants were malcontents and "outsiders."
- The putative inquisitorial nature of having to keep and produce books— which probably are already a contractual requirement—is an example of the unseen being manufactured.
- A central claim, that owners have charged abated or preferential rent unmentioned in the contract of tenancy and unknown in fact and degree to the farmers, seems to make a virtue of the unseen as well as render the claim undecidable.
- The related claim lauding the ostensible traditional generous treatment by superiors of inferiors is derivative of the hierarchical system of deference at the apex of which is the landed aristocracy. Whether it be unjust for ignorant critics (who cannot be anything but ignorant given Argyll's main claim) to call this feudalism, he stressed the fact himself.[9]
- But Argyll is an advocate of capitalist agriculture—which means the replacement of feudal deference by a maximizing mentality and competition (ibid.: 42ff.).

As for farmers under yearly tenancy, Argyll's argument is essentially more of the same:

- " 'Feudal feeling'—the dislike of doing what is disagreeable to friends and neighbours—mere laziness and procrastination—all tend to make many English owners postpone the day of revaluing farms" (ibid.: 45). Add to this lessee consciousness of very easy rents, habit, and dislike of deprivation (through revaluation), and yearly tenants have a degree of farmer security for both continued possession and against even just increments of rent (ibid.). The result is that yearly tenants generally have longer periods of possession than the average of farmers holding under lease (ibid.: 44–5). this depends on the individual character of owners, which character is "nearly as hereditary as the succession to the estate" (ibid.: 45). He reiterates personal and hereditary feelings as the basis of the special and exceptional security to tenants, the extent and prevalence of which is very little known and of farms "let below the full value to an extent of which the public has no conception" (ibid.: 47). He again writes of "a degree of confidence between owners and occupiers" (ibid.: 48), a "sort of traditionary confidence," that can be called feudal but is "an indication of those unbroken and harmonious relations between class and class which have been the basis of our political development, and the historical secret of its success" (ibid.: 49).
- Acknowledges that the foregoing is neither the best nor even a good form of security for agricultural capital, but claims that it "does afford a kind and a degree of security against loss from outlay on improvements which is altogether exceptional" (ibid.: 48).

The reader will notice the several claims made without evidence, including the results of the system of deference. In these and other respects identified earlier, Argyll invokes the role of the unseen, criticizes others for ignorance about what they cannot know, and seeks to take rhetorical advantage thereof, thus further qualifying him as an example of his own theory.

Argyll is a transitional figure, between the old system gradually on the way out and its eventual successor. He seems to relish both the deferential mentality of the old system and the maximizing mentality of the new system. The critics want a fuller system of explicit legal rights for tenants, not a continuation of a system of dependence and reward for deference. Indeed, others may be ignorant about various details but not about the existing system as such.

Such, however, does not prevent Argyll from stating as his conclusion to this point that

> If these facts be so, they certainly tend to show that for the attaining of this security no compulsory legislation is required.
>
> (Ibid.: 49)

Argyll's fourth line of argument is a negative answer to the question of whether any legislation of the kind proposed—compensation payments at expiration of lease—can possibly in the long run add anything to the security already afforded to this investment (ibid.). His first reason for this conclusion is directly akin to the impossibility-of-socialist-calculation argument that a general, central law cannot take advantage of what it cannot do without, namely, local knowledge:

- Such legislation requires an arbitrary scale for certain specified kinds of improvement, with no provision differentiating the worst and best farmers, that is, different degrees of ability and skill, even different qualities of soil and climate (ibid.: 50); that is, "a compulsory law must be rigid and indis-criminating in a matter which . . . requires the greatest possible flexibility" (ibid.: 51).

Argyll's second reason is that

- The owner could not afford to compensate in two separate forms, abated rents and payments at termination of contract (ibid.). Therefore:
- Owners will now accept no rent short of the highest which men of adequate skill and capital could be found to offer (ibid.).[10]
- A law insisting on one form of security against loss will displace all other forms of security. If a legal right be given to occupiers (of which an occupier cannot divest himself) and if the owner is to avoid paying twice, the owner must withdraw an equivalent amount, by eliminating cheap or abated rents (ibid.: 52).
- The owner is posited now to substitute income-maximizing behavior for the traditional generosity of a system of deference. No longer is a system of puta-tive private subsidies reflective of hierarchic power to preclude capitalistic land markets. The change will transpire notwithstanding historical class affin-ity, though with lag:
- "So sound, indeed, and so healthy have the relations hitherto been, both in England and Scotland, between the owners and occupiers of the soil, so habitual and rooted have been the traditional and customary feelings, which are the best foundation for business relations of such endurance as these must always be, that possibly even the most unwise law might not at once put an end to cheap and abated rents" (ibid.).

One rebuttal Argyll is prepared to accept: Since rent is paid out of surplus pro-duce, paying the highest rent signifies the best cultivator and the largest amount of salable produce, both of which are in the public interest (ibid.: 52–3). While such is true, the proposed compulsory law would still destroy—for the foregoing reason—a most widely prevalent form of security, visiting adverse (great and injuriously sudden) results on existing occupiers who enjoy such easy conditions (ibid.: 53). This, he argues, explains the lukewarm support by English tenants for proposed changes (ibid.), though one must ask, if such is the case, why was the new law proposed in first place? But more than that, the proposed law would

> compel owners in self-defence to make the market-price the standard of letting value, [and] moreover, ... tend to make that letting value higher than it was before.
>
> (Ibid.)

Such is an unintended but, after his writing, hardly unforeseen consequence. But Argyll is not through:

> A new element, introduced by the law, will enter into owner's calculation: "Consequently, the whole prospective value of this new privilege would be discounted in the rent market. It would simply enter as a new element in the calculation of rent among those who compete for the hire of farms. ... The very plea ... [of] the severity of competition ... is the proof that legislation is powerless to afford any other or any better security than that which contract gives."
>
> (Ibid.; in recompetition, see also 55–6)

If this last is correct, one must ask, why object? Also, if the legislation encourages a maximizing mindset and behavior, does it not comport with the intentions of those who seek "farming as a pure matter of business"? (ibid.: 56).

The next fifteen pages or so of *Essay on ... Contracts for the Hire of Land* is somewhat repetitious for our purposes but some discussions are worth noting.

Argyll indicates his opinion that the real object of the law is price regulation—"although unconsciously, by many advocates ... But this is not seen by most men; and it is avowed by none" (ibid.). We have some doubts about this but if true it is an example of how the actual and overt intentions of a law may differ, thus somewhat limiting the principle of unintended and unforeseen consequences.

The incidence of a property tax—the difference between rent without and with tax—is discussed and, in a distinctive Argyllian way, becomes another example of the principle (ibid.: 57ff.). He insists on "... another very important conclusion which is not generally perceived," namely the "wide distinction between benefiting the trade of agriculture and benefiting merely" the individual occupiers at time Bill becomes law (ibid.: 61–2), that is, benefits will be captured by present occupiers, with all future occupiers having to pay for them (ibid.: 62). The proposed legislation thus protects the present occupier's interest against the owner of land but not the interest of future occupiers against present occupiers (ibid.: 63ff.). As the owners had been content with rents below the competitive level, so too they had been restrained from exacting "extreme prices" from their successors (ibid.: 64). "Every new right given to the existing tenants will simply be sold by them, when convenient, to the very highest bidder. The whole benefit will be discounted in the market by the fortunate individuals who are occupiers when these new rights are first conferred" (ibid.: 65; see also 66).

As for the old versus the new system, Argyll illustrates the importance of context for using the principle as a tool of inquiry: "But it is true," he says, "that every man has the right to make the best of that which by law and usage is really his own property; and it is a right which will assuredly be used, to the very utmost..." (ibid.: 64). So much for the inherited benevolent treatment by the superior in a relation of deference. Argyll simply reverses his belief system, treating the proposed legislation as the equivalent of Protectionism (ibid.: 65), omitting to mention and thus obfuscating how his holdings involve legal protection of his interests. But he cannot fully let go of the old: each side would now have to be closely and jealously watchful against the other's unjust demands (ibid.: 68). The legislation "sets up on both sides a different class of motives, the operation of which is essentially antagonistic. Liberality of feeling in matters of business must resent the coarse and indiscriminating touch of law" (ibid.: 69).

Contrary to his earlier claim that existing arrangements elicit a sufficient number of lessees, he now reports the opposite: "Some politicians think it a great misfortune that so few persons are interested in the ownership of agricultural land.[11] ... The simple cause is that small ownership does not pay" (ibid.: 69).

He next broaches the sensitive question of the productivity of ownership per se: Writing of "the agitation for extreme claims of Tenant Right..." (ibid.) he disputes the presumed "doctrine that capital when so invested [in land] ... is to have no share in the increase which it affords to labour. ... the doctrine that improvements executed by an occupier upon an owner's land are to belong exclusively to the occupier. This doctrine can only be defended on the ground that the contribution of ownership is no contribution at all..." (ibid.: 70)—apropos of which it will be remembered that the claimed productivity of ownership per se under marginal productivity theory was later criticized as circular.

Argyll's fifth argument takes up the situation of (1) land-use arrangements with no written contract over which (2) as yet no local customs and so on have acquired the force of law (ibid.: 72). "There must be some rule of this nature, either of statute, or of common law, or of sanctioned custom, to regulate all civil obligations where these have not determined by written compact" (ibid.: 71). It is proper to provide by law what the parties have not undertaken in written form themselves, indeed, it is the appropriate province of law. It is improper to claim that this enables parties to "contract out of the law," because law will substitute for parties' intentions. Similar to intestacy, disposition by private will is preferred, but if no will is available, the dispensing of property requires that the state will have to adopt rules (ibid.). He further says, "the great object is not to invade or to confuse, but to simplify and extend the application of the purely commercial principle in the hire of land, leaving to their natural and legitimate operation those personal or hereditary feelings..." (ibid.: 90).

Finally, the proposed legislation, Argyll reiterates, promotes the "habit of considering agriculture as a business, to be prosecuted on business principles" (ibid.: 74). Hitherto, occupiers typically have relied on contracts securing them against removal and against increase in rent during fixed periods of time, thereby enabling other clauses, especially those governing the level of rent, to secure them return on outlay for improvements (ibid.: 75–88, with illustrations). Leases, too, have required cultivation according to rules of "good husbandry." "But the progress of science ... must lead, and is leading, to different conceptions of the things which may be done or may not be done consistently with 'good husbandry'" (ibid.: 88).

This brings Argyll to another claim that compromises "unintended." The real nature of the objections to the system of leases, he argues, is that occupiers, unaccustomed to seeing their business as a commercial one, dislike the prospect of future re-valuation of the farm. On the other hand, some tenants object to being bound by contract for definite periods of time. For their part, "Owners dislike parting with the discretionary power of determining tenancies altogether—even although practically this power is very rarely or even never used" (ibid.: 90).

In his concluding paragraph, Argyll again writes of "those amenities of dealing which arise naturally between men whose relations are founded on agreement" and "a relation which, though it be fundamentally and legally a relation of business, is and ought to be also a relation of personal good feeling and regard" (p. 91).

In some, perhaps many, respects, Argyll presents an idealized, saccharine, conjectural history and portrait of rural practice. The history of European land tenure relationships, while varying as to details from country to country, suggests that Argyll's history and portrait of practice, tactical admissions in practice notwithstanding, is extremely partisan. No one should be surprised by this; Argyll was the major owner of land in Scotland and he wrote on behalf of the landowning class. Such is unseen, as it were, in his writings—even though his stature as an author is due to both the literary and rhetorical qualities of his writings and his position in and affirmation of the social hierarchy. In the case of Friedrich A. von Hayek, the unseen, or ungrasped, is his ennobled origins on both sides of his family (Ebenstein 2001: 11) and an undercurrent in his work of governance by an oligarchic social elite.

Irish Nationalism *(1893)*

Irish Nationalism is a defense against two contradictory criticisms of England. One criticism is that the desperate state of Ireland is due to English imperial policy; the other criticism is that the desperate state of Ireland is due to the neglect of Ireland when England could have acted. Part of Argyll's defense is that for centuries England was powerless to act; another part of his defense is that when England had the power and did act, the actions were in the best interests of the Irish but not recognized as such. Argyll's main defense, however, was that Ireland's predicament was due to natural and cultural conditions, the latter of the Irish's own making.

Much of *Irish Nationalism* is devoted to descriptions of the constant warfare among the tribes or clans, warfare which was cruel, ferocious, and utterly destructive, as well as preclusive of orderly government and modern civilization. The principal forms of property were land and cattle, and these were the objects of war. A principal theme is that such a way of life and premature death is so commonplace that it tends *not to be seen* and is therefore ignored as a cause of the then-present condition of the Irish people. However, the prospect of peaceful pursuits and "a truly national government...found its bitterest enemies among the provincial chiefs who longed to restore anarchy, and were willing to league with the foreigner for that purpose" (Argyll 1893b: 148, quoting an Irish historian). But that is a picture which negates the principle, for the consequences may well be foreseen and intended. Either the chiefs were ignorant of what constant warfare meant as to consequences or they had some understanding of it and cared not, knowing no other way of life and preferring the perversion of governance for "their private purpose" (ibid.: 136).

There is more to Argyll's use of the principle. We pause to note one point. The difference between Ireland and most of the rest of Europe, emerging from the Mediaeval period, was that elsewhere conflicts among local nobility or chiefs, with their private armies, resulted in one of them winning and then establishing their monarchy as the government of what became the modern state. (Subsequent history included wrestling governments away from their monarchical form and control.) In Ireland this did not happen until much later. It is ironic, therefore, that one of the putatively undesirable consequences—unintended and unforeseen, or not—of constant clan warfare was the prevention of modern government, the very governments against which numerous opponents, including Hayek, invoke the principle.

Argyll also deployed the principle in identifying what he considered to be the true causes of Irish misery, all of which are so much a part of what the Irish take to be the nature of things and so early in long chains of cause and effect as to be *unseen*. In the concluding chapter of *Irish Nationalism*, he identifies six such causes.

The first cause is Ireland's isolated geographical position which kept her from the great stream of European history, prolonging her "barbarous customs...even to our own day" (ibid.: 246).

The second cause is Ireland's "Almost wholly wanting in the great mineral resources" (ibid.: 247); in a word, she had nothing like coal.

The point of both of these natural conditions being causes is that it is easier and more presently useful to point one's finger at displeasing government policies than to delve deeply into such remote albeit continually acting causes of adverse consequences.

The third cause is "...the tenacious survival of the mediaeval custom of communal tillage and pasturing...[with] deep-seated effects...in perpetuating poverty" (ibid.: 248). This meant two things: that individuals likely did not farm the same plots from year to year and that multiple plots prevented more productive agriculture and thereby perpetuated poverty.

The fourth cause was the bounties on corn, which contributed to poverty by encouraging production of less productive crops in place of more productive ones. Not only did the bounties violate "doctrines of Free-trade,—as founded on natural laws," they were unseen as a cause of "a very poor and ignorant people" being induced "to spend their labor on a kind of production which would not otherwise be remunerative,...a ruinous policy" (ibid.: 249). The bounty policy produced "a terrible evil which not even Arthur Young foresaw" (ibid.), namely, "stimulating the increase of a population living mainly on potatoes" (ibid.: 250). Ironically, farmers receiving the bounties could see them as relieving their poverty; the role of the bounties in contributing to their poverty would be, however, *unseen.*

Bounties paid to grow corn and tariff protection are, of course, but two examples of ill-advised government policy; examples that illustrate "the inevitable effects of certain political experiments" (ibid.: 265). But, if "inevitable," why and how unseen/unforeseen? If known by Argyll, why not by others?

The fifth cause constituted a further exacerbation of the adverse effects of population growth on poverty. This was the universal custom of sub-letting land, and of sub-sub-letting it over and over again (ibid.: 250), such that "The breeding and the subdivision... acted and reacted upon each other in an inseparable tangle of reciprocal causes and effects," effects that impoverished the land and further impoverished the people (ibid.: 251). To this cause Argyll added a companion, its exacerbation by English and Irish protectionist legislation (ibid.).

The sixth cause involves both an additional but, he believed, unseen or easily neglected effect of population growth and a defense of landowners against the charge of high rents. In Ireland, he wrote, "rents are determined, not by those who let the land, but by those who hire it.... High rents are nothing but an index of the great fact of a population pressing hard on the means of subsistence. They are not the cause of that fact, but its consequences. Of this pressure, high rents, offered and accepted, are simply the external indication" (ibid.: 251–2). And population growth is aggravated by "excessive breeding" (ibid.: 252). "The ignorance on this subject among writers and politicians," he writes, "is profound, but natural" (ibid.).

The seventh and final enumerated cause—education—is unseen both because it largely does not exist and because it is unappreciated: "Through long centuries the Irish had neglected what we now call popular education. ... as regards the mass of the people there had never been anything like a general system of education. The Reformation was too closely and too obviously connected with the revival of secular learning in Europe, to give Catholic priests in general, after that event, any great enthusiasm for education" (ibid.: 253; he compares the deplored Irish situation with the Scottish system of education and thus indicts the Catholic Church with regard to its population and education policies).

As already indicated, the first two causes of untoward consequences are natural conditions. The remaining five causes are comprised of customs, including those pertaining to certain private contractual arrangements, and legal policies, including the promotion of ignorance through failure to educate. They are exacerbated by customary, legal and religious practices that lead to untoward population growth. Altogether the causes reinforce each other, obfuscate what is going on and why, and render invisible, hence unseen, the chain of causes producing certain unintended and unforeseen consequences. In the process of telling that story, Argyll implicitly raises the structural issues (1) of asymmetrical information, say, as between laity and priesthood, and (2) as to precisely whom the consequences are unintended and unforeseen as opposed to intended and foreseen.

THE DUKE OF ARGYLL AS PRECURSOR TO HAYEK ON THE RELATION OF IGNORANCE TO POLICY— (PART TWO)

Argyll on *The Unseen Foundations of Society* (1893)

The first part examined Friedrich Hayek's principles of unintended and unforeseen consequences and of spontaneous order and introduced them as parts of a general theory of ignorance. It also suggested that two precursors of Hayek were George Douglass Campbell, the eighth Duke of Argyll, and Edwin L. Godkin, the nineteenth-century American editor and that a general theory can be found in their work. The presentation of the supporting evidence commenced with discussions of Argyll's *Unseen Foundations of Society* and his essays on contracts for the hire of land and on Irish nationalism. This part examines the remainder of *Unseen Foundations* and material from his other works, including his *Autobiography*. Examining these texts by Argyll we find evidence of a long-evolving and complex theory of unforeseen and/or unintended consequences used as a stratagem to preserve the status quo order and treatment of property. The next part will examine several of Godkin's works. The last part of the chapter will present the theories of both Argyll and Godkin and the general model to which their ideas and those of Hayek lead.

Argyll seeks to render seen, no longer unseen, the importance of exclusive ownership of land and of rent as payment for exclusive use. In the service thereof Argyll confronts any conflicting idea.

Argyll commences chapter IV with the reminders that technical words and phrases can deceive and that their valuable meaning must consist of "its true nature" (Argyll 1893a: 95). His principal concern, however, is with the beginnings of possession. Here he discusses possession as an element in the conception of wealth (ibid.: 96–7 and *passim*); the sources of possession (ibid.: 97ff.); possession as the exclusive right of use (ibid.: 99, 104); the idea of rightful possession (ibid.: 106), which he considers a matter of absolute property, that is, not subject to change (ibid.: 107); the origin of property in conquest and subjugation (ibid.: 110ff.); and possession as a function, therefore, of superiority in war, such that success is a function of fitness in combat (ibid.: 115). One effect of this definition was to effectively eliminate capital as a separate—or special—category.

Included in this discussion is an important tautology, one at the base of some later economic theory but typically unspecified and, ironically, unseen. As Argyll puts it, the explanation for the special "creative evolutionary process" is the "survival of the fittest," meaning thereby "the fittest for a use which was yet to be—the fittest for a future function—the fittest for the service of the Possessor" (ibid.: 103) as part of man's God-given natural inheritance. Fitness is thus property-structure specific, and not an independent test.[12]

Also evident is a particular application of fitness in war: "the very possibility of civilizing Africa depends on the ultimate subjugation of these races, and on the right of exclusive use being taken from them. But it is only because they will be unable to defend it against more civilized men that this can be done" (ibid.: 116).

Wealth and possession are due to the mental and physical superiority of some groups as compared to others (ibid.: 115). Such reasoning was one strand in the complex justification of European, perhaps especially British, imperialism in the nineteenth century. "... the European races, in destroying possession as it existed in Central Africa, and in taking it to themselves, were at least laying the foundations of a better future for the world" (ibid.: 123)—the tautology here used in legitimizing successful imperialism. Many British writers, then and later, say it was blatant hypocrisy.

Some might see in the foregoing not only the justification but the obfuscation—the deliberate rendering as unseen—of such imperialistic or expansionary policies. But Argyll, typically candid, uses this unseen foundation of society for his own purpose. Although its unseen nature is deliberatively constructed, the (unseen) origin of property lends an air of mystery: "We may chafe as we please against this said picture of the origin of all our possessions ... And well we may—because it is full of the mystery which is inseparable from every question touching the origin of man, and of his existing character" (ibid.: 117), and society. What is unseen here has been made so by the deliberate contrivance of language and meaning; and the fact of being unseen is made evidence of a foundation of society—true enough, but a result of policy. The principle of unforeseen and unintended consequences is here the corollary of foreseen and intended consequences coupled with pretence to the contrary. Instead of the principle being one of description and/or explanation, it is now, selectively deployed, a principle of policy.

Chapter V relates the progress of possession. The initial argument is that exclusive use over certain boundaries is a necessity for the highest kind of use (ibid.: 125), including conduct "involving great powers of command over other men" [than the owner] (ibid.: 126). The necessity of possession "implies the universal danger of attacks upon possession, and the consequent need of power and ability to defend it" (ibid.: 127). Rightful possession is a function of might.

The foregoing tautology and its obfuscation arise next in an unspecific tension between two principles. The first principle is that "War ... represents the necessity of getting the exclusive right of use over particular areas of land ... [which has] often involved the expulsion of still earlier possessors" (ibid.: 128). The second principle is the "true natural law ... the great law which makes exclusive and secure possession the one foundation of all human progress" (ibid.: 129). The rub is that it is success in war that determines which party can invoke the first principle against those whom it has displaced and the second principle against those who would displace them. History and affirmation of culture are a function of who wins: it is the former possessors dispossessed by conquest "whose religion was abominably corrupt, and whose superstitions were cruel and destructive" (ibid.: 130).[13]

Further obfuscation derives from the replacement, within each national society, of perpetual fighting against neighbors by "universal acknowledgment of an uncontested right" of individual possession; that is, the "security of acknowledged and uncontested right" (ibid.: 134) within an empire. War, Argyll goes on to say, has its "highest economic use" in "establishing complete internal security for all kinds of individual possession,... the systematised authority of law" leading to "unquestioned and secure" possession (ibid.: 135–6). But this is only in aid of the second principle, now serving the present possessor, they who succeeded in war over possession—and ready to serve a future possessor successful in dispossessing the present successor. The very articulation of the principle is taken to rationalize present possession. The larger situation is obfuscated and unseen, as a matter of policy. When Argyll stresses "the inseparable connection between the security of personal interests and the public welfare" (ibid.: 140), the public welfare, like the price structure in present-day welfare economics, is a function of whose interest is to count by having it protected by government. Invoking the sacredness of property and contract rights (ibid.: 145–6, 157, 193 and *passim*) becomes just another linguistic stratagem, one certainly not used in favor of the first principle, on the basis of which the successful side now invokes the second principle.

When Argyll applauds seeing "all that may remain unnoticed" his is only a selective vision (ibid.: 152). When he applauds "War waged for the legitimate purpose of securing possession" and immediately adds "and thereafter peaceful enjoyment and peaceful work," his is also a selective vision (ibid.: 153). When he applauds "that one great need of life—protection in the exclusive right of use over some bit of the world's surface," he is volunteering neither to acknowledge that he is a leading owner of land in Britain nor to promote its redistribution to extend that protection to the current landless by either legislation or revolution (ibid.: 155).

All of this is in aid of the legitimization and obfuscation of the origins of current landholding: "Possession, which began in arms that can be seen, and touched, and handled, passes into rights which cannot be seen or fingered like swords, or spears, or rifles" (ibid.: 156). Wealth requires the security of rights (ibid.: 157).

Having transferred the origin of rights of possession into the unseen, chapter VI, "The Destruction of Wealth," consists of arguments intended to further defend secure possession. These arguments focus on the insecurity of possession fomented by great monarchies, on rents fixed not by the predatory behavior of landowners but "by the automatic valuations of the market price of possession open to all who had the price to pay" and customs arising not from the disparities of social power but "out of natural adjustments between" sellers and buyers (ibid.: 164–5)—as if all this was due to the natural order of things and not to the evolution of social structure. The argument that "The development of all heathen religions has been, without exception, a development of corruption" (ibid.: 167)—a focus indicative of the role of religion supplementary to that of law in cementing the security of property once acquired by force.

An earlier argument, still treating the two aforementioned principles differently by assuming the sacredness of existing rights, is repeated: "The true function of arms, which is to secure possession and then to hold it in peace" is applauded; the use of arms for purposes of dispossession was denigrated) (ibid.: 168). The regarding of government in those predatory monarchies "not as the great protector, but as the great spoliator and destroyer" (ibid.: 169), does likewise.

Similarly with "the great fundamental truth of economic science, that in the freedom of men to pursue their own individual interests lies the richest fountain of national welfare" (ibid.: 170; see also: 174).

The story is told (not by Argyll) of a man walking down a country road in the United States who meets a farmer working in his field. After some general discussion, the man inquires of the farmer how he acquired his land. The farmer relates that he inherited the land from his father, who had inherited the land from his father, who had fought the Indians for it. The man then says to the farmer, "Let's fight." The farmer would support the second principle; the man would support the first, shifting to the second should he win the fight.

The claims that "bad" ideas "of religion, of government, and of manners" are destructive of individual liberty and incompatible with security of individual possession (ibid.: 181) render what otherwise might have been objective analysis into the high priest role of social control.

The claim that "The natural law—embedded in the very constitution of things—which connects inseparably the growth of wealth with the security of individual possession" (ibid.: 183) will be uttered by a social power only when it has been successful in acquiring possession, not when it is engaged in conquering the possessions of others. This is, again, the selective witnessing of the unseen.

Argyll commences chapter VI with a defense of science in terms of achieving "some intelligible order of cause and of effect" (ibid.: 162). Twenty-five pages into the chapter, he denigrates Bentham for his "scornful question, 'What are those economic laws which are not political?'" (ibid.: 187) "The root-idea of all science," he explains, "is that the reign of law is universal, that there are natural laws in everything, laws which by combination can be made capable of any service, but which cannot be neglected or defied" (ibid.: 187). Like so much else here, this is a winner's interpretation. Thus the "one sole function" of Economic Science is said to consist "in the conviction that man cannot impose his arbitrary will on the constitution and course of things" (ibid.: 192); there are natural laws.

Argyll applauds Cicero to the effect that "Right is not founded on opinion, but in nature," that rights are "the most substantial of all things in the structure of civil society," and that upon the foundation of rights "was reared the most widespread structure of power and opulence..." (ibid.: 188)—also a winner's position.

Interestingly, Argyll would have it both ways in the same sentence. He writes of the fundamental principles of Roman jurisprudence, "They are, at this moment, the rich inheritance of all the great ruling and colonizing nations of the world" (ibid.: 189). There is no reason why one nation's regime and rhetoric could not claim the second principle for itself while applying the first principle to others. (Argyll goes on to attribute the fall of Roman dominion to the combination of absolute political despotism at the top and an industrial system founded upon slavery at the base (ibid.: 190–1). Still, the constant theme is private rights secured for individual possession by government sanctions (ibid.: 193 and *passim*).

It should now be apparent that Argyll is using language in a particular way. W. H. Hutt (1990 [1936]) drew distinctions between "rational thought," "custom thought" and "power thought." By rational thought Hutt means objective and disinterested inquiry leading to the accumulation of undisputed knowledge in the social sciences and which should be the premier basis for understanding both the natural and the social worlds and for policy. By custom thought Hutt means modes of thinking that are infused with implicit premises and ideas derived from traditional and customary ways of doing and looking at things, a tradition sometimes dominated by the interests of upper hierarchic levels and at other times by the wishful-thinking romanticism of the masses, not uninfluenced by the thinking of the upper hierarchic levels. By power thought Hutt means modes of thought and expression that are constructed to have intended effects on power, politics, and policy, and whose significance derives principally from their service in mobilizing political psychology. Even though possibly sincere, power thought is interested in consequences, not in truth (the results of objective and disinterested inquiry) per se. Power thought may serve to reinforce custom thought. Argyll's arguments in *The Unseen Foundations of Society* are a combination of the latter two forms of thought, power thought deployed in the interest of custom thought.

Chapter VI continues the argument that conquest has laid the basis of civilization and enhanced modern society ("all civilization has been built up on conquest" (Argyll 1893a: 206), because it "strengthened and reinforced" the sources of wealth "by the transfer of them into new and stronger hands" (ibid.: 199). This argument is supported by others, including the following, that "equal freedom enjoyed by unequal powers" (ibid.: p. 200) leaves "the inequalities of personal ability or of character...comparatively little room to work" (ibid.: 201); and the dysfunctionality of "perpetually open" reform (legal change), apropos of which Argyll writes, "No words could convey a severed condemnation of any government" (ibid.: 202). Much of this argument is reminiscent of those he made in *Essay on the Commercial Principles Applicable to Contracts for the Hire of* Land (1877), discussed in the first part of this study. Further supporting a hierarchical system is the theme that maxims supporting individual rights function to defend the status quo system of rights, rights that are unequal, against socialist egalitarianism (ibid.: 204–5). Religion is relevant inasmuch, and insofar, as both sword and scepter closely conjoined reinforce the existing system of power and wealth, and also peace (ibid.: 205; see also: 215–16): "Fealty, and the rendering of service to those who have come to wield in our defense the resources of power and of authority, must be not only felt as a necessity, but recognized as an obligation" (ibid.: 213). Morality and law should be "a perpetual reminder that the gradations into which society was divided were nothing but the gradations of history and of nature" (ibid.: 214). Morality and law should be "full of the ideas and doctrines which teach, as an imperative duty, respect" for status quo justice and law (ibid.: 219) and that such is a matter ultimately of the Divinely ordained laws of nature—so that "the possession of property...could be held securely" (ibid.: 220; see also: 253).

This is, again, power thought in support of the second principle—from the viewpoint of the victors. The book provides arguments supporting the rationalization of the existing power structure and system on its own terms, namely, the virtue and utility of secure possession and stable law—that is, the status quo system—especially landed property (ibid.: 221). As for the theme of the unseen foundations of society, Argyll points out that, apropos of "the protection for the safe holding and enjoyment of every kind of property,"

> That which often was and often still is invisible, and therefore forgotten under settled governments and in times of established peace, was then ever forcing its obtrusive presence on the consciousness of all men, and could never be forgotten for a moment.
>
> (Ibid.: 221; see also: 223)

This must be understood in terms of latent and manifest function. Social control works well, indirectly and silently (according to Emile Durkheim and Robert K. Merton) when it is not seen to be social control—for example, when there is no challenge to the existing system. But social control must be seen for what it is, at least at the high-priest level, the target level for which Argyll is writing.

Chapter VIII commences with an identification of the nation with the landowning class: "The universal law is that territorial possession, or the right of exclusive use over some definite portion of the earth's surface, is the essential basis of all national existence" (ibid.: 224). This leads to acclaim for feudalism insofar as it "for the first time linked personal duties and, by consequence, personal rights to the ownership of land" (ibid.: 226). It is feudalism which elevated the language of social control from that "military command and personal fidelity . . . into a great code of order, of subordination, and of law" (ibid.: 228).

Argyll next turns to "economic science." From the perspective of modern positive economics, economics describes and explains; it does not rationalize. The difference is subtle. To say that individual's preferences count on the basis of their respective purchasing power and that optimal output reflects the sovereignty of consumer purchasing power, given costs of production, is to identify (some of) the nature of the market system but, in describing the system in terms of optimal resource allocation, it gives effect to the definition of optimality stated in terms of individual preferences counting through exhausting gains from trade, thereby introducing a rationalizing element. If that is subtle, Argyll's argument is not. To Argyll, economic science must identify that which contributes to secure possession as a means of securing wealth, indeed "the most fundamental of all the conceptions in which the very idea of wealth itself consists" (ibid.: 228). This, he believes, is largely unseen, but must be seen if economic policy is to promote the production of wealth.

The legislator and the judge must articulate rights based on "customary doctrines and the instinctive preconceptions of man's moral and intellectual nature." He goes on to articulate a brilliant exposition of legal rights in their dual nature as social control:

> In its first beginnings, human law does not create rights, but simply recognizes them . . . . But in the very act of recognizing rights, jurisprudence does, of necessity, define them. To make them safe, it must make them clear. But the work of definition is, of necessity, also a work of limitations. Hence the work of the jurist has the double function of so restraining and limiting the

rights which it protects, that they cannot be abused or converted into wrongs.... every rights possessed by one man, or one set of men, has some bearing, direct or indirect, on the competing rights of others.

(Ibid.: 229)

Argyll takes up the topic of Irish chieftains, discussed at length in his *Irish Nationalism*, published the same year (discussed in the first part). The poorer classes, he maintains, became dependent on their military chiefs and suffered the loss of their property through warfare. Their isolated geographical position provided immunity for the Celts from foreign conquest. The principal result was that the "foundations of order and of law had never been laid down there" (ibid.: 236, 238; see also: 240ff.). Inter-clan warfare did not result in one chief having success and becoming the king of Ireland. Conquest was local and more or less temporary; it did not lead to a nation state. The second principle was given no opportunity until very late in history.[14]

The concluding pages of chapter VIII again address economic science, which Argyll calls the "very highest branch" of all the branches of politics (ibid.: 247). One point he makes is that of the principle of unintended and unforeseen consequences. Referring to waging of wars by "the more masterful races of the world for the conquest of the weaker," he writes,

The benefits and the blessings which have resulted from those wars were not consciously sought, or even thought of, by the conquerors, but have arisen by way of natural consequences from a combination of causes which were entirely out of sight to them.

(Ibid.: 249)

In juxtaposition, he cites wars in which the aggressor had the motive of "purest benevolence" and "the soundest appreciation of economic causes" and that these were "consciously entertained and expressed by the statesmen" in those reigns (ibid.: 249). In Argyll's purview, the principle applies sometimes but not always.

Chapter IX addresses the Irish problem and commences with the statement of "the fundamental principle of all economic science." This principle, however, renders the principle of unforeseen and unintended consequences readily seen, removed from the mysterious, shadow world of the unseen—a development that is, of course, the aim of the book.

That principle is, that human habits, customs and institutions have certain determinate effects upon the motives which actuate conduct, and that the actions, so determined, have their own special effects, which follow by way of natural and inevitable consequence.

(Ibid.: 252)

This principle negates the principle of unforeseen and unintended consequences. Interestingly, it does so by articulating a corollary to Hume's principle of the role of institutions in stabilizing conduct. In any event, the laws which govern the production of wealth are natural laws, of which "the human will is the servant and not the master." These laws "govern the will, and the will cannot govern them—except by yoking them to its service through compliance and obedience" (ibid.: 253). Argyll thus presents a subtle view of man's relation to nature in the course of expressing a principle very different from that of Hayek. Still, Hayek's principle is not totally rejected; it is presented with subtlety.

Argyll next takes up several themes which modify, or amplify, the foregoing. First, he notes the "insuperable strength and power" acquired by the "inferior and injurious" Irish system, thus "rendering impossible any successful revolt against it from merely native discontent" (ibid.: 256). The theme of the "insuperable economic effects of certain social institutions, in rendering impossible any reform coming from within" (ibid.: 260) is reiterated. In this connection, while not in the case of the second principle, Argyll stressed the beneficent results of legal change if not change of the system of law. He goes on to reformulate the theme of the unseen. "All the most powerful classes were deeply interested in upholding" the old, dysfunctional law—no unforeseen and unintended consequences here— they benefited from it. "The great mass of the lower classes were too ignorant to understand the causes of their own wretched condition..." (ibid.: 256)—ignorance thus returns. Second, he argues in favor of civilizing conquest: "There must be one central government, and one law protecting all defined rights and enforcing all equally defined obligations" (ibid.: 257).

While discussing possession under the new rules of Irish land tenure, the general topic of chapter IX (see ibid.: 261 for a brief summary; see Argyll 1877, discussed in the first part), Argyll again attacked the predicament of long-time Irish poverty. Argyll evaluates laws on the basis of the outcome of the laws and whether he agrees with the particular outcome, namely the (selective) protection of current property rights. He did so as in effect a corollary to his first principle, opening the door to change—on the basis of a material utilitarianism combined, no less, with moral obligation, concluding with the second principle:

> Had such a condition of things any divine right to immunity from attack, when it not only kept its own people in misery, but endangered also the safety of those higher civilizations which had a right to its allegiance? Economic science must not and cannot be divorced from any of the great leading influences which contribute to that fundamental condition of all wealth— secure possession. And therefore it cannot be divorced from considerations of moral obligation or of political wisdom.
>
> (Ibid.: 262)

Rights under a dysfunctional existing system can be change (within limits) so long as the new system of rights provide secure possession, that is, no further changes (within limits) (ibid.: 262ff.). "Thus the greatest and happiest of all changes came about—that change...which substitutes for the recognition of mere strength and power [of the old system] the universal recognition of legally acknowledged rights. ...What all men longed for was security, not absolute, of course, but under limitations which were known, and subject only to contingencies which could be foreseen and calculated" (ibid.: 272). But what of the arguably more typical contingencies, those which cannot be foreseen and calculated, in which the unseen reign? His principal objection, however, is to the "fatal custom of ever shifting possession" (ibid.: 277). But the problem remains and goes beyond possession. The economic significance of rights is a function not only of possession but of their relation(s) to other rights: Competition, for example, can erase the economic value of property as surely as loss of possession (e.g. exclusive user; see ibid.: 283). And here the principles of ignorance and uncertainty reign.

Chapter X is an attack on the Ricardian theory of rent. It is a doctrine "so erroneous and even absurd that we ought never to have been deceived by" it. "I confess", he writes, "I have been myself among the number of its dupes" (ibid.: 284). He admits to having believed what was seen to be believed by others, yet is wrong. Not only is the Ricardian theory of rent wrong, its fallacies have lent "themselves to the support of political theories which nearly affect the interests and rouse the passions of men..." (ibid.: 285). "...what a load of fallacies can be carried on the back of some little grain of truth" (ibid.: 286).

Argyll's attack is directed at the following: The primary objection is that the Ricardian theory fails to emphasize and thereby weakens the meaning of "rent." This also undermines the prestige or role of the landowner in the economic system. Rent is the term "for the price of hire. ... It is the price for the right of exclusive use over something which is not our own" (ibid.: 288). So too does the theory of rent, not merely its definition. He quibbles not only with Ricardo but with Marshall, being dissatisfied with Marshall's definition which, so far as Argyll can see, confines rent to the "income derived from things of all kinds of which the supply is limited (such as minerals), and cannot be increased by man's action" (ibid.: 290). This he believes to "single out the hire of land as the only kind of hire which ought to get the name of rent" (ibid.: 291). Here he either neglects or implicitly repudiates Marshall's application of the Ricardian theory to other objects of sale under the heading of "quasi-rent." "The limit on land is a visible limit, whereas the limit on other things is generally invisible ... [and] that which is gross and visible is apprehended, whilst that which is invisible is forgotten or neglected" (ibid.: 291). Indeed, "Rights are in their very nature impalpable and invisible" (ibid.: 296). At stake is exclusiveness of use of possession. This use, he argues, "must be exclusive ... this right of exclusive use must have been previously acquired somehow and by somebody ... this acquisition must have been the result of labour of some kind..." (ibid.: 298).

Further objection to the Ricardian theory is directed to its particular way of maintaining that rent is due to demand (ibid.: 308), its use of decreasing returns, its neglect of opportunity cost, its holding that "rent does not enter into the expenses of production" (ibid.: 316), and its holding that rent is a "surplus" (ibid.: 320–1). The Ricardian theory is called "an empty truism" (ibid.: 311), "a barren truth" (ibid.: 302), and "gross sophistry" (ibid.: 315); it is said to be "entirely independent of facts" (ibid.: 309). The Ricardian theory is interpreted and evaluated almost solely on one criterion, namely, whether or not it supports "the natural and universal law that men must pay for the exclusive use of things which are not their own" (ibid.: 324–5) and therefore dependent "on the same laws of supply and demand which regulate the hire of every other thing" (ibid.: 324).

Chapter XI continues the onslaught against Ricardian theory, now his theory of value. Argyll takes umbrage at the language of the theory insofar as it says that the value of all commodities is "regulated by" rather than "calculated by" cost of production; especially "it is a gross fallacy if the words 'regulated by' are understood as 'caused by'" (ibid.: 327–8). He resumes the attack on the proposition that the rent of land is high because the price of produce is high (ibid.: 331ff.) insofar as it leads to the conclusion that "rent, or the price paid for the hire of agricultural land, is no part of the cost of its production" (ibid.: 338). His reasoning is that rent can be both a cause and an effect (ibid.: 338). Further in support of this he seeks to identify as "another dogma of the whole school of orthodox economists, [the proposition] that all price or value depends on the cost of production" (ibid.: 343). Rather, he says, the truth is the reverse, namely, the "universal truth that the cost of production as an element in value is entirely subordinate to that other great element—demand" (ibid.: 344–5). All of the foregoing is chosen because it supports Argyll's chief point, that the theories of rent and value must reflect rent as a payment not for cost of production but for the exclusive use of things, notably land. That payment especially reflects demand. But that payment for the exclusive use of things, he ultimately emphasizes, reflects the distribution of land.

While the first three-quarters of chapter XI is dominated by a running critique of the literature on rent, the final third is a critique of the Ricardian view of the relation of the landed interest to all other interests. This final third commences with the "generalization which identifies the economic position of every man who rises in the least degree above the dead level of those around him, even in respect to the natural gifts of mind and character, with the position of every other man who has any other possession of any kind having the same effect of conferring on him some individual advantage" (ibid.: 354), that is, hierarchy. It then traces the idea to, he says, both its results and its foundations, and finds that "it roots the great economic facts and laws of possession and of property, in the faculties of mind, and in the indelible variety into which nature has distributed those to individual men" (ibid.: 355).

Argyll seeks to render seen, no longer unseen, the importance of exclusive ownership of land and of rent as payment for exclusive use. In the service thereof, Argyll confronts any conflicting idea. In attributing the distribution of possession of landed property to "nature," he is using nature to obfuscate—to render unseen—the role of institutions in distribution. This is one-half of his overall story. The other half of his story is the defense of the institution of landed property and its existing distribution on the basis of the institution's functionality in producing wealth. Appeal to nature provides absolutist formulation for when that is required or will work; when such is insufficient and institutions require defense, different arguments are deployed.

The final third concludes with the point of it all: "Bad analysis" and "ambiguous language" have "much concealed the identity of fundamental principle . . . that fundamentally the hire of land must be classed with the hire or the purchase of every other thing in the whole sphere of human industry" (ibid.: 361–2). Definition and theory which treats land differently is no longer to be seen, is to now be unseen; definition and theory that render land no different is to be seen. To that end he applauds Adam Smith for making evident that "the interests of the agricultural classes must always be [and be seen to be] identical with the true interests of all other classes and of the public as a whole" (ibid.: 356). And to that end he denigrates Ricardo for his "conclusion...that the interest of the landowner is always opposed to that of the consumer and manufacturer, because their profits must always tend to be absorbed by higher wages following on higher prices of corn, and by higher rents always rising in proportion to a more costly and more difficult production" (ibid.: 357). This conclusion and the theory on which it rested was not only "absolutely wrong," it was "a web of absolute non-sense." Ricardo's "argument was essentially a class argument," one intended to raise profits by lowering wages consequent to the repeal of the Corn Laws. "The true argument for free trade in corn" was Cobden's, that "free trade would stimulate production." Ricardo's fallacious reasoning, Argyll argues, is due to his adoption of the "wholly false" labor theory of value (ibid.: 358–9) as well as to his neglect of rent as the price paid for the use of exclusive possession.

Chapter XII further explores what Argyll calls the "speculative fallacies" of Ricardo and others who have contributed "to the most extreme developments of delusion... in the Science of Economics" (ibid.: 367). Practitioners of that science have readily forgotten "some one of [the science's] facts or laws because it belongs to the Unseen" (ibid.: 367). Among these facts and laws (ibid.: 364ff.) are the ubiquity of inequality and of hierarchy, that rent is the price paid for the right of exclusive use (= Possession), and that inequality is due naturally to personal dif-ferences and advantages derived from either natural or acquired possessions and is "inseparable from the condition of humanity" (ibid.: 369). Whether the argu-ment is a labor theory or a conquest explanation of the acquisition of property (Possession), the crux of the argument is that the existing distribution of Possession must be seen as due to "natural facts and laws." Silence "on the ques-tion of the origin of Possession in itself is an index of the assumption that under-lies [i.e., should underlay] all economic science, that we must start from the existence of Possession as an universal fact inseparable from all the other funda-mental facts of our human nature, and of the beginnings of society" (ibid.: 369). This is the view of Possession from the perspective of the devotees of the second principle, the victors in the struggle for possession, and not from the perspective of those promoting the first principle, for whom security of existing property is a target of their attack.

Other "facts and laws" have to do with rent as entering into cost of production (ibid.: 370ff.), the "prior function and larger contribution" of the owner of property (i.e. "wholly neglected, or kept out of view," ibid.: 373), that in civilized societies "Possession rests on Rights which Society has recognized for centuries, which law has enforced..." (ibid.: 375), and so on. Ironically, notwithstanding his criticism of what he calls the "Capital-Letter Fallacy" and of an "economic science [which] has been so infested with it" (ibid.: 373), that is, technical phrases coined and dressed up in capitals but which "represent nothing" (ibid.: 372), he resorts to the practice himself.

The perspective of the second principle is evident in his response to the Ricardian notion of rent as a surplus over cost of production and its root in "the long-continued recognition of Society." He then poses the questions, "whether Society, even by the continuous assent and consent of a thousand years, can establish any obligation [to pay rent] of this kind as against the future? And...whether 'Society' is bound towards its individual members by any honor, or by any duty, or by any continuous obligations of any kind?" (ibid.: 375). He continues by saying, "It is indeed a curious fact that those who seek to elevate that aggregate of individuals called Society into the position of a Supreme Personality, with absolute power over its own units, are the same persons who deny to that Supreme Personality all the highest attributes of character which we admire and respect in individual men. Of course, this denial cuts very deep into the unseen foundations of Society" (ibid.: 375–6). Argyll next attempts to forge an alliance between the owners of landed and of non-landed property, saying that "The right of exclusive use over land is not the only thing possessed by forms of title which are visible and palpable in nothing except the form of recorded statements." Capital in all its forms, money, debt instruments, and so on have a similar character (ibid.: 376). Those who would reform the institution of property would "sap and destroy the unseen foundations of Society." Here Argyll sides with capitalists against reforms, despite his undermining of the concept of capital in the early chapters of *Unseen*. They would dissolve "all the obligations of good faith and of honor, on which all wealth absolutely depends." Ricardo, the author of deep-seated fallacies regarding rent and the rights of possession, did not see the adverse consequences to which the fallacies certainly lead, even though he "was the last man in the world intentionally to sanction such anarchical and immoral doctrines as those which have been founded on a belief in his fallacious theory" (ibid.: 376). "The last man?": The *Unseen Foundations* was published in 1893; in 1884 Argyll had challenged Henry George, who was taking Ricardo far further than he had gone (George 1982).[15]

The degree of Argyll's emotional intensity is suggested by the strength of some of his language. Ricardo preached a doctrine said by Argyll to be almost incredibly rude and crude. The doctrine is "repulsive, hard, harsh, and narrow," its science is pretended, "a frowning presence and a standing menace"; and "some of its foundations have already been proven to be rotten" (Argyll 1893a: 378). Given Argyll's position and premises, it is not surprising that he went so far as to say that "Ricardo's doctrines...have been, and continue to be, the basis of the wildest self-deceptions, and of the most insensate attacks upon the unseen foundations of society." Men, because of "mere ignorance," excessive speculation, or under the "stimulus of suffering" or "the discontents of vice," are said to be "disposed to rebellion against the whole constitution and course of Nature..." all this manifest in "incoherent and subversive theories" (ibid.: 379). Not only that but casual headlines in newspapers which suggest or confirm class antagonism—whereas capital, as in "capital and labor," was nothing but "storages of labour" (ibid.: 379). For all the various reasons, once again summed up, Ricardo is charged with "Possession in all its forms [becoming] an object of hatred" (ibid.: 380). Some of the consequences of his theory of rent "would assuredly have staggered him, and would have scared him, if he had seen them. They would have been fatal to the whole pursuits of his own life as a dealer in capital, and as a large profiteer by the 'differential advantages' which the possession of it secures" (ibid.: 380–1).

Two points seem apposite. First, Karl Marx and his threatening doctrines are nowhere to be seen here—though Henry George is later classed as a Communist (ibid.: 403 and *passim*). Second, no defense of Ricardo and his doctrines is provided, nor perhaps should it have been: Argyll has produced, by intention, a polemic and not an objective, analytical textbook.[16]

Argyll commences chapter XIII with the argument that the doctrine of free trade "is not true as an absolute and universal proposition" and that one has to distinguish between legislative interference that is mischievous and that is absolutely required (ibid.: 383). He generally supports abandoning regulation of purely economic interests while pursuing "regulation of matters in which certain higher interests were concerned" (ibid.: 384). Argyll draws a line between government intervention in economic affairs—restricting individual freedoms—and government protection of individuals through social policies. His example is the Factory Acts. While he holds that "the freedom of the individual will is the fundamental law and condition of all progress," he also is "firmly convinced" of the greater value of "some exceptional laws for the regulation of equally exceptional cases of labor affecting women and children." Without the passage of such Acts, "the social problems which still confront us would have been more difficult and dangerous than they are" (ibid.: 384). One wonders about Argyll's opinion regarding older social legislation such as the parish poor laws that placed the responsibility for poor support on the landowners.

What Argyll does not emphasize—though he might reply that his argument speaks for itself in this regard—is that pragmatism trumps absolutist formulation. For all his emphasis on natural law and so on, legislative policy is a matter of judgment, of compromise and of working things out. What is most readily seen is seemingly watertight, absolutist arguments, perhaps coupled with invective directed at political or philosophical foes. What is left unseen are the ultimate premises of ostensibly absolute propositions and the process of pragmatic compromise. Also unseen is the putative fact that support of the Factory Acts was a political stratagem of the landowning against the commercial and manufacturing classes.

Next comes Argyll's treatment of Henry George, notably the use of absolutist formulation against him. George "directed to prove that almost all the evils of humanity are to be traced to the very existence of landowners, and that by divine right land could only belong to everybody in general and to nobody in particular" (ibid.: 389). (Their exchange of articles is discussed in Samuels, Johnson and Johnson, 2005.) The second-principle character of Argyll's reply to George is indicated by his statement that while "Nobody has any personal interest in believing that the world is flat...many persons have an interest, very personal indeed, in believing that they have a right to appropriate a share in their neighbor's vineyard" (Argyll 1893a: 386).[17]

Among other things he rejects the placing of emphasis on any special facts connected with the process of first settlement and the resulting ownership of land, preferring to look to subsequent speculative purchases for resale at a high profit, due to the rising stream of population, as a perfectly legitimate operation (ibid.: 387, paraphrased) and to landowner outlays for improvement of the land (ibid.: 388). George, he says, has followed the fallacious doctrines of Ricardo (ibid.: 388ff.) as well as the theories of communism which, in their egalitarianism, contradict the true explanation of "the attainment of standards of living and of enjoyment which are never reached except by a very few" (ibid.: 394).

For Argyll, the unseen consists of the principles which his view of society and social structure requires. George therefore also, in Argyll's view, mishandles the difference between Natural Law and Positive Institution (his capitalization).[18] The universality of land ownership, he believes, supports the treatment of human laws of land ownership as having "evolved out of human instincts" that "are among the gifts of nature," that is, "as really natural and as the legitimate expression of fundamental truths" (ibid.: 396). It is the neglect of these too-frequently unseen fundamentals that constitutes the danger to society, "this inherent tendency to corruption [that] has received no check from the democratic constitutions of those many 'new worlds' in which kings were left behind, and aristocracies have not had time to be established" (ibid.: 400). By corruption, of course, Argyll means the policies promoted by George. Invocation of the unseen thus continues to be, in the hands of Argyll, a rhetorical weapon, Hutt's power thought in the service of custom thought and not rational thought. The same is true, *pari passu*, of George.

Selective perception—another aspect of seen versus unseen—pervades much if not all of the foregoing. Emancipation of the slaves during the US Civil War is applauded as a most noble cause, notwithstanding the expropriation it constituted. George's proposal that public debt and private property in land rest "upon the preposterous assumption that one generation may bind another generation" is, however, repudiated at length (ibid.: 406ff.). So too George's "attack on the particular class of capitalists who are owners of land" (ibid.: 411). Whereas Argyll wants to treat land as a species of capital, like any other investment, George wants to distinguish land from capital, because the value (rent) of land derives from the growth of population and not the owners, whereas the value of industrial capital is a function of profits generated by entrepreneurs. Argyll believes he is conservative in promoting the existing institution of landed property, whereas George believes he is conservative in protecting the principle of distribution of income based on productivity from that of mere ownership without productivity.[19]

Here we have two contributions to the matrix formed by all theories of conservatism. Here we have situations in which Argyll and George would render certain principles seen and other principles unseen, or at least rejected—the principle being different in each of their cases. (Argyll understands George very well, for example, "The whole tome [*Progress and Poverty*] is based on the assumption that owners of land are not producers, and that rent does not represent, or represents only in a very minor degree, the interest of capital" (ibid.: 412).) What is involved, of course, is the formulation of arguments by those participating in the continuing process of pragmatically working out the basic institutions of the economy. What is not involved, except selectively, is the use of the categories of seen and unseen to determine, rather than merely to state, which interests government should and should not promote, and how. There are conceptual categories of things seen and unseen, just as in Hayek's principle there are conceptual categories of intended and unintended, and foreseen and unforeseen consequences, and institutions that are spontaneous and others that are deliberative. The two sets of conceptual categories are broadly (rhetorically) descriptive of what, in part, goes on in the domain of policy (that no institution is purely spontaneous or purely deliberative is a quite different matter). They are not capable of determining policy, notwithstanding the efforts of devotees.

The problem also is not what is seen and unseen but that each person sees things differently. Hence there are tautological relations between what is seen and, on the one hand, the hermeneutic base of selective perception and, on the other hand, the policy promoted (or the policy the argument is used to support).

In chapter XIV Argyll attempts to apply criticism of the pre-J. S. Mill wages fund theory to the further defense of landed property. He acknowledges that the wages fund theory "did much harm for many years in the prejudice which it raised [we would say, reinforced] against what was assumed to be the teaching of economic science" on labor (ibid.: 423); not only much harm but "a vicious influence" (ibid.: 427). The objection to the theory is that "Wages are nothing else than one particular form of income, and income of every kind always is, and always must be, derived from some service rendered to others" (ibid.: 427). Furthermore, the wages-fund theory places capital in an important position regarding production. For Argyll "income of every kind" includes rent, and whereas for George (and Ricardo), such income is unearned—accruing to the own but due to the growth of population—for Argyll the services provided by the landowner are the improvement of land and the temporary transfer of exclusive use of Possession, especially the latter:

> ... it is evident that every human being who has anything whatever that other men desire to get, must, so far as that particular thing is concerned, be in a position of "differential advantage" over those who have it not.... the mutual satisfaction produced by the transaction consists in each of them being supplied by the other with something which he desired to get but had not before possessed. Possession ... is one fundamental fact in the whole transaction, and the other fundamental fact is Demand ...
>
> (Ibid.: 429)

This applies to all assets and to the organization of labor,

> yet this seeing of that which is invisible—the full appreciation of these unseen factors in all manual labour, and in all wages earned thereby, is as

difficult often to the most highly educated men, when they enter on abstract speculation, as it is to the manual laborer himself.

(Ibid.: 433)

The problem raised by Georgist and other critics of private ownership of land does not deny that both parties are presumably better off after a transaction. The problem is that of the legitimacy of the institution which assigns ownership of land and receipt of rent from that transaction to the landlord. Argyll makes the same point in his *Essay on Commercial Principles* (1877). And Argyll's response is predicated on, is almost a statement of, the second principle:

> This group of causes on which the value of every man's work both to himself and others absolutely depends, is the group which is connected with the laws that protect all rights, and enforce all contracts, between man and man. It is these alone which create that industrial security without which no venture could possibly be undertaken or even thought of. A system of settled and stable jurisprudence, with an honest and a firm executive—the paramount reign of law in all the relations of men—these are the indispensable, though the too often unseen and unthought of, foundations of every industrial society.
>
> (1893a: 434–5; reiterated on p. 437)

—but a near perfect statement of the argument of the book.

The criticism of the wages fund doctrine is again articulated, now in terms of ignorance, against the theory of unearned increment, that a rise in wages from causes not directly due to workers is nonetheless paid to workers:

> it is none the less true that his right to the higher value is as absolute as was his right to the lower value from which it rose. The fact of that rise in value being due entirely to efforts and causes of which he had no knowledge, and to which he made no contribution, does not in the least degree lower or abate his claim to the whole of it as indeed his own. Possession—the right of exclusive use— of his own faculties is not rendered a less sacred and absolute right because the value of it has risen in the market.... The higher range of wages is given by others only because his labor is worth more to them than it had been before, and in both cases the full equivalent of what is his own, must be his own also.
>
> (Ibid.: 443–4)

The language of the sacred and the absolute comports neatly with the terminology of the unseen. The receipt of income is its own justification. "The same principle evidently applies to every other possession" (ibid.: 444) and should apply to land and landowners. The destruction of the erroneous Ricardian doctrine, that value is derived from labor, should be accompanied by the adoption of the "true theory of wages," that wages are "dependent entirely on Demand" (ibid.: 450).

Chapter XV is, not surprisingly, directed to "the unseen sources of employment." The central argument—now in the context of J. S. Mill's post-refutation amended form of the wages fund theory plus a theory of the entrepreneur, or "Conceiver" (ibid.: 452, 457, 463)—is that the employment of workers depends on "the confident expectation of certain calculated returns" and it "can have no other foundation than the calculable data afforded by the established order of society" (ibid.: 452) and is therefore seen.

Argyll next turns to his version of deliberative versus non-deliberative decision making, deploying it in aid of the second principle:

> The structure of human society in so far as we can, by own conscious work, help to build it up, and shape it to glorious uses, is a structure which must rent on the same unseen foundations [as the conduct of production and employment]. Human laws, if they are to attain their highest aims, must recognize the universal facts of human nature. They must consecrate and enforce all the precepts of natural obligation.
>
> (Ibid.: 458)

One might think that his argument was less against deliberative decision making per se and more for deliberative decision making that followed certain natural facts and precepts and could therefore be successful. But such is not so markedly the case. Argyll's text continues:

> They must be in accordance with a body of accepted doctrine respecting these, which has been taught by the immemorial experience of mankind, and by the spontaneous working of their universal social instincts. They must be founded on the fact that Society is, in very truth, an Organism—with its own natural laws of life and growth, and with its own insuperable conditions for healthy working among a great variety of functional parts or members. Above all, certain demands of ethical obedience must be admitted as of absolute authority over beings who are endowed with a moral nature, but who are also endowed with a speculative intellect, and with a will which is only too free to abuse this as well as all their other gifts.
>
> (Ibid.: 458–9)

The argument is restated in terms of "the secure prevalence and established authority of a system of accepted doctrines," and "a corresponding system of legislation and jurisprudence which recognizes all rights, and enforces all obligations" arising "out of deliberative contracts between man and man" (ibid.: 463). The security is undermined by

> ...speculative reasoning in shaking one of the unseen foundations of society—namely the universal and just assumption that the possessor of anything valuable to other men, has, in the sale of it, an absolute right to the full price, whatever that may be, which the desires of those other men may confer upon it.
>
> (Ibid.: 460)

Again, Argyll places the emphasis on the demand-side of the market. He continues, that violation of this principle would introduce "paralyzing uncertainty" (ibid.: 460) into business decisions. Interference with the "natural laws" is by the "arbitrary—and probably corrupt—action of men who think they acquire a right to any portion of the price of things merely because they wish very much to get them" (ibid.: 460–1).

The key is "Security," said to be "the one indispensable foundation of all wealth" (ibid.: 463). And the conclusion, paralleling Argyll's own, is said to be that of the great utilitarian philosopher, Jeremy Bentham.

Three problems arise with this latter view. First, Bentham wrote in opposition to William Blackstone's grandiose view of English law, such that Bentham's utilitarianism in regard to law, as well as in regard to morals, was considered dangerously revolutionary—a judgment applicable to neither Blackstone nor Argyll. Second, Bentham went through periods in which he stressed security of rights and others in which he stressed the need for change in rights and stressed one or the other, or both, in different publications (as for Argyll, see later). Third, the case can be made that Bentham's utilitarianism is but one form taken by pragmatism and that, as earlier, Argyll was also a pragmatist, notwithstanding his grandiose prose.

In any event, Argyll faults Alfred Marshall for his reformist criticism that Bentham had "an almost superstitious reverence for the existing institutions of private property" that was due to "a kind of scare from the effects of the French Revolution" (ibid.: 464). Again, the key is "security": "the conditions of security on which individual action wholly turns, must be the deepest seated and most abundant of the fountains of economic employment" (ibid.: 464). In retrospect, given the continuous process of legal change of legal rights in the North Atlantic countries, one might think that production and living standards have been endangered; of course, the opposite is the truth. But, as said earlier, all this is in aid of defending the traditional position of landowner possession. This argument is intended to influence policy through the mobilization and manipulation of political and economic psychology and sentiments. It is argument masquerading as definition of reality. As such, it both renders unseen and seen. Highly pregnant but undeveloped, with regard to either what we now attribute to Hayek or a general model of ignorance, are Argyll's following remarks:

> It becomes all the more important to dwell upon this relation between cause and effect, because of what we may call the silence and the secrecy in which it works. It belongs essentially to the Unseen. Its seat of operation lies in the individual mind, and in the power of instinctive motives there. Not only is it generally difficult for other men to trace and to identify its exact effects, but it is not even always consciously known to the individual mind on which that power may be most exerted. ... There are always possible increments, and equally possible decrements in values to be considered—not one of which he can himself influence, and many of which he cannot even foresee. But those

which he may be able in some measure to foresee, can only be so foreseen by calculations and estimates founded on data which are in themselves secure. The slightest suspicion of doubt cast upon any one of these will prevent altogether the very conception of a commercial enterprise. Nor is it merely that any insecurities of this kind will prevent such a conception growing and ripening to the birth, but they will prevent it from ever arising in the mind. The suggestions of opportunity are automatic in their working. They come to us ... out of the action of certain stimuli. ... In the absence of these stimuli the suggestions will not arise at all. But the absence of anything is a mere negation—unfelt, unseen, unknown—except to the highest exercise of reason, and of speculative thought.

(Ibid.: 464–5)

A central problem with Hayek's theory of spontaneous order is that its most complete form requires, not prohibits, deliberative decision making. Hayek follows Carl Menger, who argued that every generation must critique existing institutions and plan and undertake their deliberative reform. Something like this is proposed by Argyll; and though he seems to start out narrowly, the governing principle is broad. Argyll points to the possibility that existing institutions may not provide sufficiently for security or even may tend to weaken the full security required for successful production, and says,

[W]herever this failure in existing laws can be traced and proven, the doctrine, when properly understood, is always a doctrine not opposed, but rather leading, and guiding, to change and to reform. What the doctrine does discourage and condemn is not, necessarily, any change in existing institutions, but only any change which takes a wrong direction. And it specially indicates one direction which must be always wrong.

(Ibid.: 467)

That direction is, of course, any change impairing the motives which are incentives to all human effort by impairing security.

What Argyll does not say—indeed keeps unseen—is, first, that changes of rights may limit the incentives of some while enhancing the incentives of others; and, second, that the Ricardo-George theory of the unearned increment posits that taxing rent will have little if any adverse incentive effect.

Argyll returns to Bentham, saying that "Bentham was himself assuredly no blind admirer of laws existing when he wrote. He was an energetic and, in some respects, an almost revolutionary, reformer" (ibid.: 467). Nonetheless, Argyll's emphasis remains on security; and it does also throughout a lengthy examination of the Physiocrats (ibid.: 468–80) and of the history of Ireland (ibid.: 480–7 and *passim*). The lesson to be remembered, he says, is that the injuries wrought upon production by bad legislation "works for the most part in the dark." He denigrates "any new or arbitrary restraint on the perfect freedom of the market" and the shadow thereby cast on security (ibid.: 487).[20]

Argyll now turns to the subject of unions in light of the Millian wages fund. Workers have the right to combine but should "weigh with great care the indirect and unseen effects of those combinations amongst themselves which are intended to force up higher rates of remuneration." They must connect their actions to their unforeseen and unintended consequences, consequences which occur "without a word said, without any outward or visible sign or warning of any kind," even "almost without any definite consciousness" of those adversely affected. "Nothing is seen, nothing indeed is visible" (ibid.: 488). The adverse consequence is, of course, the drying up of the wages fund, as money is withheld by savers reacting to union demands; the effect, therefore, of economic laws hitherto "unseen, or neglected," even if articulated by a false science (ibid.: 489). Given our better understanding of the order of nature, "the wage-earning classes [should] think most carefully on the influences which do really tell upon the 'Fund' out of which they are paid" (ibid.: 491). One of the "unseen elements in Production," therefore, is this—"that all combinations among wage-earners, which have for their object or their effect, any interference with the management of industrial concerns, is in itself, of necessity, in the highest degree unjust and dangerous to themselves" (ibid.: 495; see also: 499). What you do not see can hurt you.

Once again, Argyll seems to compromise his argument. The same objection, he says, "cannot be made to combinations for the mere purpose of raising, by legitimate and just means, the price of that element which the wage-earner does really himself contribute. It can be successfully done, there is no antecedent objection on the score either of right and wrong, or of any economic truth. But the other question remains, how far it can be really done" (ibid.: 496). Even here certain "unseen elements...are unquestionably involved." These include the effects of "the fear of 'labor troubles'," "want of confidence," and "uncertainty as to the capricious action of trade combinations" (ibid.: 496–7). No independent test exists by which to decide.

Argyll also points to ventures "undertaken by capitalists combined in companies," saying that "There is no reason in the nature of things why the individual capitalists so combined should always be large holders of the storages of wealth." Still, experience shows "very often how dependent all industry is on 'the market'— that is to say, on the desires of other men, and on the 'effective demand' set up by classes on whom [wage-earners] have been inclined before to look with jealousy and suspicion" (ibid.: 501).

On the whole, then, the balance of argument founded on the known, but the unseen, factors in the case, seems to incline largely to recommend at least the greatest possible caution in combined attempts of any class of workers, whether of hand or brain, to enhance artificially the price at which they can readily and ordinarily sell their own contribution to the total of production (ibid.: 498).

The chapter concludes with the admonition that "there are laws higher than those of human legislation.... They are simply the laws of our human nature, of which we are not the authors." They are laws which, when men seek "to traverse, evade, and disobey" them, are "dead...for all purposes of good, and alive only for many purposes of evil" (ibid.: 503). Such are the unseen foundations of society. Ignorance can cause evil.

Chapter XVI continues with the theme articulated in the immediately preceding chapters, namely, the effect of unseen economic laws and their unseen consequences on the sources and prospects of employment. Argyll begins with an account of what he calls "a silent revolution" (ibid.: 507). He has in mind some of the great transformations of the nineteenth century, for example, the growth of cities, of manufacturing, new inventions, the development of new tastes and of distastes for old ways—especially "for old traditional kinds of labor" (ibid.: 507), luxuries becoming necessities, and so on. As for labor, it seeks, he says, not to avoid work but to economize work (ibid.: 512). The chapter ends, as is his wont, on the topic of economic laws and their unseen consequences. "[T]he most certain of all economic laws," he reveals, is "the law which demands security as an absolute condition for enterprise or outlay of any kind" (ibid.: 521). The second principle is again the design base on which everything is built and by which everything must be understood. Another law is also taken up, that enormous imports may preclude or extinguish some domestic industry. "This is a hard doctrine, but it is the Free Trade doctrine; and its consequences must be faced" (ibid.: 525). Similarly, the press cannot extend knowledge of far-away opportunities for more attractive employments and the carrying trade cannot enable their being carried abroad without limiting rural labor at home (ibid.: 526). These are examples of a genre of developments whose consequences were "unforeseen" (ibid.: 528) and whose cost "we have to pay for the want of foresight" because of "ignorance" (ibid.: 529).

On the second page of chapter XVI Argyll instructs his reader that a definition "of any value in science" must indicate "clearly the kind of questions to be asked but also [help] to answer them" (ibid.: 505). On the second page of chapter XVII Argyll takes up the definition of the word "monopoly." Hayek cited language as an illustration of spontaneous, non-deliberative institutional development. That this mistakes the development of language, which is a function of both non-deliberative and deliberative development and their interaction, is suggested by Argyll's effort. That effort is nothing less than a proposal to define "monopoly" in a manner beneficial to the interests of landed property. He argues that when monopoly is "used to designate all individual ownership or possession, and especially in things comparatively scarce" (he says "often used," but this was not so), it is used "loosely and deceptively" as well as erroneously. Whereas "the real meaning is any artificial limitation put on the value of things, whether scarce or abundant, by arbitrary laws." The idea that words have "real meaning" is either pure rhetoric or tantamount to a belief that "correct" definitions correspond to the nature of that to which they refer. That both are presumptuous is illustrated by his effort here. He next admonishes that "Definite words must be kept to definite ideas, or else language becomes worse than useless." The two Greek words which form "monopoly" "do not mean, as is commonly supposed, 'single', sole, or individual, ownership. It does not mean the mere possession of anything, however rare, by one man or by one group of men. The word monopoly means an exclusive right of dealing in any article, which right is given to men to whom the article does not belong. By nature, these two things are inseparable—the ownership of anything, and the free right to dispose of it" (ibid.: 531). Argyll is here concerned with the Protective system in which municipalities assign exclusive rights to buy and to sell certain commodities (ibid.: 530ff.). But while he has some interesting usages to critique (including one by Jevons), his main interest is to prevent the use of the word in regard to landowning, especially through legislation adverse to the interests of landowners (ibid.: 539).

Any effort by municipal bodies to limit personal liberty and the free disposal or everything constituting wealth "must be strictly limited and defined by the national authority" (ibid.: 540). This is one of an infinite number of examples of interests seeking to influence their relative rights and opportunities *vis-à-vis* other interests through influencing government. Such structuring is inevitable in any economic system and is prevalent if not dominant in a market economy.

Using definitions of words to help the cause is relative common, though not generally conspicuous. Argyll places it in the category of the "seen." Once again, Argyll seeks to finesse criticism by noting that "Human affairs are far too complicated to admit of sharp abstract definitions on such practical questions as this.... Only in the most general terms can important principles and distinctions be indicated as needing to be kept in view.... It would be absurd to attempt an abstract definition to guide us in the selection of the powers which can be safely given" (ibid.: 542). The general definition Argyll has in mind provides for "the ordinary powers, duties, and supreme obligations, connected with the protection of property—the maintenance of order and of law," plus "large powers in matters relating to health and morals" (ibid.: 543). It takes no stretch of the imagination to appreciate that this definition is essentially the defense of the status quo, epitomized by the "protection of property" trope.

The chapter concludes with a discussion of corruption, especially involving morals. Here he provides for change of law: "As new forms and opportunities of evil come to be developed, new precautions have had to be, and will have to be, adopted on the same lines" as earlier (ibid.: 548). (See also Argyll's *Property in Land* (1884), in George 1982, on this point.)

Argyll's concluding chapter, XVIII, is entitled "Relation Between Old and New Economic Fallacies. What Economic Science Is: And what It is Not. New Dangers." The chapter, like the book as a whole, is evidence that the principle of unforeseen and unintended consequences, or the principle of ignorance, is a vehicle for introducing the policy analysis preferred by the author. To say that, however, does not necessarily imply that the author's preferred position is wrong; that is quite a different matter.

The bulk of the chapter concerns the nature of an economic science suitable for the author and the relation thereto of old and new economic fallacies, which need not be taken up in detail here.

The chapter commences with a contrary view to the common belief. Namely, government during the Middle Ages did not largely ignore the interests of the wage-earning classes because those classes lacked political influence and power.

To the contrary, Argyll believes much paternalist, even socialist, legislation was directed to helping the poor, including usury laws, price laws, and sumptuary laws (Argyll 1893a: 549–50). This is followed by the claim that in comparatively recent years—the nineteenth century—government interference with personal liberty increased; again, Argyll believes to the contrary, the record is one of "the systematic removal of artificial restrictions," not their extension. Of course, new evils have elicited necessary restrictive legislation (ibid.: 551–2).

The rhetorical nature of at least some of the argument is suggested by Argyll's failure to explore when and how some restrictions are "artificial" and others are not. The same suggestion arises in another way. After arguing against every constraint that is not essential to the equal freedom of all, Argyll next argues that "That qualification or limitation of the principle of individual freedom which demands that it shall not be allowed to interfere with the like freedom in others, is indeed essential. But, properly speaking, it is no limitation at all, because it is involved in the doctrine as part of itself, and belongs to its very definition" (ibid.: 554). In his use, the statement is essentially a tautology. Insofar as it makes a substantive point, however, it conflicts with the second principle. If one defines property exclusive of the police power, the exercise of that power can be seen to be a reduction in, or taking from, property. If, however, one defines property inclusive of the police power, then its exercise does not constitute a reduction or taking. This is because it is "involved in the doctrine as part of itself, and belongs to its very definition." The former definition tends to be hospitable to conservatives; the latter, to liberals. It is the former group who believe that property is protected because it is property, and the latter group who believe it is property because it is protected.

Argyll is principally seeking to promote the anti-egalitarian position: "The just desire that all men should be equal before the law" is confounded by wrong-thinking, even jealous, people who believe "that the law should be employed to establish an artificial level of an unreal equality by suppressing the natural, necessary, and legitimate consequences of individual pre-eminence" (ibid.: 556–7). Here, again the meaning of "artificial" arises as an issue, insofar as distributions of income and wealth are matters of institutions, whose relative artificiality is a matter of selective perception, given that institutions are putatively artificial *vis-à-vis* nature. For Argyll, however, economic science in such matters can be estimable because of its reality (ibid.: 558–60). Nonetheless, Argyll accepts that economic science must not neglect "the duties of benevolence." But while no higher aim can there be than Christian charity, still it is neglectful of the requirements of production to mistakenly pursue "indiscriminate almsgiving." This is "Simply because all [the virtues of charity] cease to exist when they are made compulsory. Rate-paying [government taxation] is not giving. It is not charity" (ibid.: 561–2). Moreover, it is dysfunctional, evoking "a spirit of idleness and of imposture on the one side and of resistance upon the other" (ibid.: 562).

Economic science in such matters, even regarding free trade, may point out its cost, but it "has nothing directly to say on the question whether the cost, however great, ought, or ought not, to be incurred in certain cases" (ibid.: 567). This is a sensible, even brilliant, point, one that applies to every policy proposal. It appears in a modern formulation in the equity-efficiency trade-off. It applies to Argyll's own defense of the interests of landowners. Argyll contemplates restrictions on concentrations of industrial wealth, whose power may adversely affect lesser agencies; or eliminating protective legislation in their interest; but he cautions against "the sacrifice of throwing overboard the deeper underlying laws of individual freedom on which the whole of [economic] science depends" (ibid.: 368). Indeed, "It is the very business of economic science to trace the permanent laws of our human nature under whatever superficial and artificial coverings they may be comparatively hid" (ibid.: 570) and "the doctrines of economic science, in so far as they are really sound and true, are doctrines of universal application" (ibid.: 573). Thus, "To represent economic reasoning as having nothing to say against the wildest follies of legislative interference... is to deny its very existence as a science, or, at least, to deprive it of all value in deciding the most urgent questions now demanding, above all things, its help" (ibid.: 580). Many questions of policy "cannot be absolutely determined one way or another" by the doctrines of economic science (ibid.: 580–1). But economic science can identify the "laws which can indeed be yoked to our service, but which cannot be neglected or defied"; economic science can "cherish and maintain that noble faith in the truthfulness of the Divine government over the whole system of things we live in... that faith which assures us that the laws of nature do really work together for good to all who sincerely seek to know them, who are faithful to them, and who yoke them to their appointed use" (ibid.: 583).

Argyll wants to have it both ways: an economics that cannot definitively determine policy and an economics that can provide the sound and true policy. The result is a mixture of the unseen and the seen, varying from policy to policy.

The position to which Argyll is fundamentally committed is neatly encapsulated in the following statement:

> Inequality of some kind is an universal fact, and inequality in the most imperative forms is so extremely common as to be really the normal condition of affairs.
>
> (Ibid.: 578; see also: 580)

It is surprising neither that such a position would be articulated by a major landowner nor that the doctrine of unseen foundations of society would be enlisted in its defense. His position is precarious. In the larger economy, inequality of, say, purchasing power can be either lamented or tolerated, the latter with the expectation that either oneself or one's progeny will in the future enjoy a higher standard of living. In the economy of landownership, however, the amount of land on the surface of Earth is basically constant. Ownership is limited and readily acquires the aura of monopoly. Argyll recognizes this and, as we have seen (ibid.: 531), to the end of protecting existing institutions of ownership, rejects any definition which points to—renders seen—"all individual ownership or possession, and especially in things comparatively scarce." He favors a definition which establishes that "the real meaning is any artificial limitation put on the value of things, whether scarce or abundant, by arbitrary laws." By shifting the definition of reality from the physically scarce to artificial limitations on value, Argyll changes the mix of the seen and the unseen. Thus, he believes, a postulate that recognizes equal protection by the law of each human unit "in the enjoyment and in the employment of that which is legally its own ... is a postulate which lays deep and broad the foundation for every kind and every degree of inequality which is the natural, necessary, and legitimate result of diverse, various, and unequal gifts" (ibid.: 578). Such a foundation gives effect to the status quo structure of ownership and in doing so obfuscates the fact of inequality and its origins. It deliberatively constructs and deploys a particular mix of the seen and the unseen. Any definition which focuses on the inequality, he both recognizes and insists, "if believed in, and acted upon, ... would be most disastrous. It would fill society with bitter and irreconcilable discontent. ... The idea is indeed anarchic" (ibid.: 579). Any such thing cannot possibly be true, ergo it should not be seen. In aid of this, "True economic science ought to have no neglected elements. It concerns itself with all causes that produce economic effects. ... [so that] in our science the grand conclusion [is that] the real welfare of everybody is bound up with the real welfare of everybody else" (ibid.: 581, 584). The chief cause of prosperity is the integrity of ownership—of Possession and the price it can command.

Autobiography and memoirs (1906)

Argyll's *Autobiography* and the accompanying editorial commentary by the Dowager Duchess of Argyll provide additional or reinforcing insights into Argyll's thoughts, especially to what is here given as his theory of ignorance. Argyll addresses the question of the ground on which people hold beliefs, a question which affects what people see and do not see, that is, what they take as knowledge and how it is influenced by statements in aid of political electioneering. He reports that he was "specially revolted by the spectacle of men sacrificing any truth to electioneering tactics." Eventually he was impressed by "one mitigating fact,"

> That fact is that a large number of our opinions on almost all subjects are held on the insecure tenure of nothing but authority and tradition. We may hold them without doubt, but only because without examination.
>
> (Argyll 1906: 160–1)

Several points may be noted: (1) Our definition of reality and of what is seen and unseen are due to authority and tradition as well as to argument deployed for purposes having no connection, or no necessary connection, with the relevant reality. (2) Hayek seems to have assumed that the local knowledge which central planning cannot access is largely worth taking into consideration. But if such knowledge is opinion due to authority and tradition and political argument, then such may not be the case. Still, democratic theory may require that everyone's social preferences, no matter how false, how meaningless, or how acquired, be counted. But the theory of ignorance must have a place for the manipulation of authority and tradition by political argument, on which Hayek does not say much, focusing more on positivist and socialist misstatements.

Apropos Argyll's negative view of the "narrow and erroneous teaching of Ricardo" asserted in *Unseen Foundations of Society* (and quoted here by the Duchess (ibid.: 553), here he remarks that "It has been a misfortune that none of the professional writers on political economy have had any practical knowledge of the management of landed property" (ibid.: 227; this was not true of Ricardo in the last decade of his life). Argyll seems at least in part to have in mind that familiarity with agrarian affairs would attract economists to the point of view of the landowners, which they would now see in a different light.

Argyll likewise criticizes both political parties for what they do not see, for their ignorance: "The Conservatives had failed to see what was really best worth conserving. Liberals had failed to see what the most sacred of all popular rights demanded of them" (ibid.: 269). Here Argyll posits his vision as conclusively worth having, and neglects both that each party had to make up its own variety of minds and that the overall issues of conservation of the past and of rights. Yet, in a letter to Lord Aberdeen, he recognizes the need to balance continuity and change: "...the ideal of all good government—the uniting of steady progress and a liberal policy with a firm and jealous attachment to all the old institutions and the traditionary [sic] principles of the English people" (ibid.: 372, letter of December 25, 1852). In a world in which the old gives way to and is compromised with the new, what is one to believe? In any event the letter was in response to the offer of the office of Lord Privy Seal, with a seat in the Cabinet, in other words, fluff. The "domestic changes and reforms which," Argyll says, "had altered the whole condition of Parliament and the people," included Roman Catholic Emancipation, abolition of the Sacramental Test in municipal and other offices, and a fuller representative system in the House of Commons (ibid.: 377). (Argyll notes that in the revolutionary year of 1848, "The alarm had been so great that an immense number of the well-do-do classes had offered their services to the Government as special constables, and were drilled in squads in various convenient places" (ibid.: 303–4).)

Of particular interest for our purposes is Argyll's views on a "Bill for the admission of Jews to Parliament, by exempting them from that part of the Parliamentary oath which invoked 'the true faith of a Christian'." The reason for this interest is that almost every important phrase of his exposition—of his own and of others' views—constitutes a definition of reality which, if believed and operated upon, would give effect to particular bundles of seen and unseen. The language of "the true faith of a Christian" is one of them. Here is Argyll's account of his reasoning:

> ...I could not be enthusiastic either way. ...Although a Liberal—almost a Radical—on most questions, [Arnold] had been an eager opponent of this concession. I had never, indeed, accepted Arnold's doctrine of the identity of Church and State. But, on the other hand, I had not submitted to the axiom

that, under no circumstances, had the State a right to make religious faith a condition of the highest rights of citizenship. Neither could I admit Macaulay's dictum that Christianity had no more to do with legislation than with "cobbling." I felt and saw that our noble system of laws was founded on the teachings of Christianity. So far, therefore, I was in favor of Arnold's pleas for exclusion. On the other hand, I felt that, practically, theological arguments had become alien to the work of legislation, and that the banishment of these from debates was due mainly to the divisions of Christians between themselves, so that a small element of Jewish members would practically make no difference in the matter.

> (Ibid.: 302–3; of course, if Christians were relatively equally divided, a close-knit and/or like-minded if small group of Jews might mean the passage or failure of bills)

The other terms include "the identity of Church and State," "the axiom [making] religious faith a condition of the highest rights of citizenship," "noble system of laws…founded on the teachings of Christianity." The phrase "theological arguments had become alien to the work of legislation" indicates not only the role of argument in defining reality but what Argyll takes to be the diminished role of theology in informing both the argument and the definition of reality.

At other points Argyll indicates his wish not "to anticipate the combinations which might arise" (ibid.: 370), presumably to avoid undesirable consequences, and his judgment to rank safety over impulsiveness in temperament (ibid.: 387). Still, the Dowager Duchess illustrates "the main argument" of Argyll's overall philosophy by quoting from St. Paul's introduction to the Epistle to the Romans: "The invisible things of Him from the creation of the world are clearly seen, being understood by the things that are made, even his Eternal Power and Godhead" (ibid.: 546).

Argyll also felt that "in all forms of government in which there is a large democratic element, oratory is, and must be, a great power" (ibid.: 430; and also that while oratory largely has evanescent effects, occasionally "a really fine speech not only decides the fate of a Government, but enlightens the mind of a people, and determines for an indefinite time to come the course of natural legislation" (ibid.: 430); the meaning of "natural legislation" is unclear, though high-sounding; perhaps legislation consonant with the extant hierarchic system).

Argyll not surprisingly feared the spread of democracy and often indicated his "great desire to limit by every possible and plausible device anything like a large enfranchisement" (ibid.: 235). He wrote to Gladstone that he had been "struck with the absolute confidence you always expressed that all fears of danger from the new constituencies were chimerical and absurd, and that the institutions of the country would only be strengthened all round. I never felt the same confidence, but I did feel that we must all just make the best of it." In the same letter he also wrote that "I think it cannot be doubted that many of the doctrines now popular are subversive of society as it has hitherto been organized in all civilized countries" and that "It is very unlucky that the new franchise comes into operation contemporaneously with a universal depression in all industries" (ibid.: 395–6; letter of September 28, 1885). In his next letter to Gladstone, Argyll indicates the role of religion and the Church in maintaining the social order through the definition it imposes on its members: "In theological questions I observe one prominent teaching of yours—namely, that each generation cannot go back on the 'fundamentals' for itself; that the past gains of mankind and of the Church must be accepted, and not re-discussed and re-proved over and over again. Don't you think the same sound Conservative doctrine is applicable in politics? ... Men's minds are being led to consider certain proposals as 'open questions' which ought to be as much 'closed' as the Decalogue" (ibid.: 397–8; letter of October 24, 1885). The Conservative approach to forming what can be seen and what cannot be seen could hardly be more candidly stated. Thus does one's position affect what one sees and does not see, his definition of reality and the consequences he foresees, as well as what he wants the institutions of social control to implant in our minds. No impartial spectator here. (The opposite view was stated in 1594 by Louis Le Roy thusly: "That which is now hidden, with time will come to light; and our successors will wonder that wee [*sic*] were ignorant of them" as quoted in Weisinger 2003, vol. 4: 149.)

(Apropos of Argyll's active and largely conservative religiosity, it is striking that in 1849 the Bishop of Glasgow and Galloway, upon questions provided by a parish priest, decided that Argyll should not present himself for communion within the Episcopal Church of Scotland. The Bishop insisted that there is no public sentence of excommunication, only a request from the Church that Argyll not take communion within the organization. The basis of the exclusion were statements in Argyll's "Essay on the Ecclesiastic History of Scotland." Argyll, feeling that the exclusion was excommunication, responded, "Did I imagine that the body to which you belong is the only one in Scotland entitled to administer the ordinances of the Christian Church, this might be a serious penalty. But I generally communicate with another body, which to others I am apt to call the 'Church of Scotland', but which, I fear you consider better described as the 'Form of Schism' established here. It is only on accidental occasions that I have sometimes communicated with the Episcopal Church in Scotland. I do not anticipate, therefore, any serious inconvenience from your spiritual censures" (Argyll 1906: 6). Charges amounting to indiscipline, and worse, were frequently leveled by fundamentalists at moderates and heretics in the eighteenth and nineteenth centuries.)

Argyll was not the only member of the landowning class who saw himself as the embodiment of culture and assumed both that their interests were in the interest of their society as a whole and that their system of belief should be held by all members of society. The new realities of the hegemony of commerce and of political and social democracy were only slowly recognized by them and were the targets of delaying tactics. Thus one of Argyll's tactics in resisting erosion of the position of landowners was to bring about a definition of reality in which land is seen as belonging to the newly honorific category "capital," referring, for example, to "the particular class of capitalists who are owners of land" (ibid.: 411).

EDWIN L. GODKIN AS PRECURSOR TO HAYEK ON THE RELATION OF IGNORANCE TO POLICY—(PART THREE)

Edwin L. Godkin on ignorance and the unseen: *Unforeseen Tendencies of Democracy* (1898)

The first part of this chapter examined Friedrich Hayek's principles of unintended and unforeseen consequences as parts of a general theory of ignorance. Hayek was not the first to examine these relationships, and we suggest George Douglass Campbell, the eighth Duke of Argyll, and Edwin L. Godkin as precursors. The second part explored Argyll's writings on unintended and unforeseen consequences, including his *Unseen Foundations of Society* and his essays on Irish nationalism. In this part, Godkin as a precursor to Hayek is considered. Finally, the last part will present the theories of Godkin and Argyll and a general model to which their ideas, and those of Hayek, lead.

Godkin's *Unforeseen Tendencies of Democracy* (1898) contains material on other subjects, as do the other works covered here. But it adheres to the theme of the "unforeseen" perhaps more closely and more elaborately than any of the others.

This is already evident in Godkin's *Introduction*. The operation of the principle of unforeseen and unintended consequences surely is affected by expectations, and examples of this appear early in the *Introduction*. Godkin declares as his objective to "describe some of the departures it [democracy] has made from the ways which its earlier promoters expected it to follow.... The growth of democracy... has failed to realize a good many expectations about its conduct of government" (ibid.: iii). One example is that democracies "have not shown that desire to employ leading men in the management of their affairs which they were expected to show" (ibid.: iv). Although it is not obvious that democracies are different, or worse, in this regard than other types of government, he says that any perceived inability to correct mistakes, is actually due to "underestimating the length of time it takes a democratic community to find out that it is going wrong and to acknowledge it" (ibid.: iv). This proposition would appear to be a corollary to Hayek's theme of local knowledge unavailable to the (central) government, thus emphasizing the time element and perhaps the receptiveness of the (central) government.

A theme on which Godkin places considerable weight has to do with the element of ignorance through inexperience—presumably meaning that elected and appointed personnel in a democracy must learn on the job. Democracy is "rarely run [by] men familiar with public affairs, or with human trials in matters of government" (ibid.: v). An aspect of the problem lies in democracy "being called on, almost suddenly to govern the large masses of population called cities, without any experience, either of their special wants or of the means of satisfying them" (ibid.: vi).

Perhaps the most subtle, as well as the most unexpected from him, unforeseen consequence of democracy is the accompanying monetization of life:

> The first danger... is the enormously increased facility for money-making... and the inevitably resulting corruption.... The power of getting

money easily...The demoralization...It is breaking down, not simply the old political, but the old social usages and standards. The aristocratic contempt for money as compared with station and honor, of which we used to hear so much, has completely vanished. The thirst for gold seems to be felt now by all classes equally...

(Ibid.: v–vi)

The first chapter is entitled "Former Democracies" and treats ancient Greece and Rome, plus the states overthrown by Napoleon. Democracy is an old experiment, he says, pursued under widely changed conditions (ibid.: 1). The principal theme of the first third or so of the chapter is that of the genesis and development of states not on the basis of the putative facts of existence but through the dominant belief system of society, including its system of myths. Thus we read that the origin of government is in the natural growth of society, in customs, eventually consolidated through the imposition of superior power. This latter can consist of the conversion by a chief of "influence into positive rule...[thereby becoming] a real political chief, and...[giving] his family a semi-sacred character in the popular eyes, [in this] we have the foundation of a state" (ibid.: 5).

The foregoing means that the foundations of government consist of both non-deliberative and deliberative decision making, primarily or most importantly the former. Godkin writes that "...law begins in custom or religion;...law is the product either of custom or of belief" (ibid.: 4). In part, "The prevalence of the belief among individuals that things must be done in a certain way, and not in others, and that unless things are done in a certain way, and not in others, unpleasant results will follow means organized society" (ibid.: 2–3). The contract theory, that states are founded by discussion and formed by mutual agreement, is erroneous. There is "...no sign in antiquity of the conscious foundation of a state by agreement...no trace of conscious organization. Certain arrangements grow out of existing conditions. They are not made...by discussion...[or] by mutual agreement..." (ibid.: 5 and also 10). The "people" does not exist "in the political sense," as "not simply a collection of individuals...but a body conscious of its own existence as a political organism" (ibid.: 7). There is no democratic state in the sense of Locke and Hooker, characterized by the "majority making laws for the community from time to time, and executing those laws by officers of their own appointment," The "theory that the people had something to do with the management of their own affairs" (ibid.: 9) is only a belief and not how matters actually proceeded. Thus what is seen is a function of the belief system of society and order arises largely through nondeliberative processes—albeit not entirely. Unseen are the actual processes of development, hence the status quo is seen as the natural state of affairs, as the natural order. Ignorance reigns as to what really transpires. Thus religion has functioned as social control such that "the lawgiver always acted with the aid of religion. He was always supposed to have God or his oracles behind him; that is, he had to be in some sense divinely appointed" (ibid.: 12; see the discussion on latent *vis-à-vis* manifest function in the second part).

This situation has continued into modern times. "The ignorance and barbarism of the Middle Ages [has] lingered in the laws and governmental arrangements of every European country" (ibid.: 9).

Godkin and Argyll seem to agree that ignorance, of which the principle of unintended and unforeseen consequences is itself a consequence, is fundamental to the formation of government and law. Both invoke the principle for their own purposes but each has a more complex theory of ignorance and its complexities than does Hayek. His principal's narrower focus is on the inability of central decision makers to be informed of tacit and local knowledge. Whereas for Hayek the principle limits deliberative decision making, for Argyll and Godkin the full panoply of ignorance also affects both the operation of government and law, and their very existence.

Two further points: First, whereas Argyll, Godkin, and Hayek each identifies the system of the unseen, hence the relevance of the principle, it is Argyll and Godkin who create and use for their own purposes a system of the unseen. Or perhaps one should say that, in his relatively narrow formulation of the principle, Hayek creates a system of the unseen for his own purpose; certainly he uses it for his own purpose. Second, as mentioned earlier, all three writers contemplate the system of social control, one aspect of which is the principle. The difference is that Argyll and Godkin envision more elaborately than Hayek the operation of ignorance in general, including the principle, in the history of social control. Hayek seeks to use the principle to limit deliberative social control and resorts to his version of history to justify that limitation. These putative differences may be overly subtle; certainly different readers of their work, and of this work, are likely to perceive differences and similarities among them differently.

Much of the remainder of Godkin's first chapter has to do with structural aspects of governance and property. Pervading the discussion is a sense of why unseen elements in society are left unseen: it is because active power players do not want the masses to see that government comprises a struggle to control and use government. Godkin cites Aristotle's *Politics* for a number of themes with a chief one being that "...every class in a state, if it gets possession of the government, is apt to seek its own advantage exclusively" (ibid.: 14). In doing so it projects the laws providing them with advantage as due, not to any such base struggle, but to the natural order of things. Pseudo-knowledge is thus used to render unseen what is actually going on. Writing about ancient Greece, therefore, Godkin says that

> every little community...was a little democracy, engaged more or less frequently in resisting the attempts of rich men to set up either a monarchy or an aristocracy. ...the rich class were rarely content with the existing state of things, always felt they could do better if they had their way, and were as purely selfish as aristocracies are apt to be. They were convinced that the most important interest of the state was that they, not the many, should be happy and content.

> (Ibid.: 13)

Godkin goes on to say that

> In all ancient democracies...the internal history is generally an account of
> contests between the poor and the rich; meaning by "poor" persons who are
> not rich—not the extremely poor. An oligarchy always consists of rich men;
> a democracy, of what may be called people of moderate means. For the most
> part, the rich seem never to be thoroughly content with the rule of the many,
> and long to rid themselves of it. ...They think themselves entitled to rule,
> and think their contentment the chief object of the state.
>
> (Ibid.: 21)

Godkin could hardly be more explicit. And he restates the argument in such a
manner to indicate the social role of the idea of the sacredness of property, the
government as something to possess and control, either *de jure* or *de facto*; and the
particular role of the legal profession in making law safe for the propertied:

> the idea of the sacredness of property, as we hold it, can hardly be said to have
> existed in the ancient communities. Dispossessions, confiscations, redistribu-
> tions, were not uncommon...making it extremely important for the rich man
> everywhere to get and keep possession of the government. It was only by get-
> ting hold of the administration of the law that he could feel absolutely secure.
>
> (Ibid.: 22)

The rich rule, but are not seen to rule. This is the result of the inculcation in
the masses of the idea of the sacredness of law. This acceptance of law as
"sacred" results from two factors, the law is separately extant and above ordinary
disputes, and the equality of men before the law. What is also not seen is the use
of religion and of law by hierarchical superiors.

The conclusion is inescapable but kept hidden from the masses that arguments
and positions on issues have significance not for their truth value but for the social
control purposes they can fulfill.

The Greek idea of citizenship in a democracy embodied "government by
universal suffrage." What the regnant belief system rendered unseen, however
was that in Greece universal suffrage excluded slaves, that is, the laboring class
(ibid.: 15). Godkin later notes that remembrance of exaggerating demagogues has
led "to the adoption of constitutions changeable only at fixed times or in a prescribed
way. The main object...is to put restrictions on the power of the majority vote"
(ibid.: 19). Given the subjective nature of the identification of an "exaggerating
demagogue" (not unlike freedom fighter *vis-à-vis* terrorist), one wonders if the
driving force is in fact the desire to limit the power of the masses. Thus one could
sense that the ruling elite is rendering the demagogue seen while finessing the real
purpose unseen.

Godkin seems to have anticipated Vilfredo Pareto in his belief that the masses
have been induced to look forward to and accept the substance of any policy that
demonstrates that it has and is willing to use power, to be decisive. In doing so

Godkin, who may or may not have seen this in Smith's *Wealth of Nations*, seem to be giving effect to Smith's doctrine that people respect the opinions of the wealthy and powerful above them. And insofar as this respect and these opinions presume and reinforce the existing system and the mythology providing its legitimization, the security of religion and of law, and of that whose security in turn they legitimize, is promoted. Thus Godkin reports,

> A poor nobility...is never well able to justify itself in the popular eye....the Greek definition of oligarchy or aristocracy as rich men was not far wrong.
>
> (Ibid.: 23)

> the superiority of the government of the few in the matter of continuity of policy...could not have survived the gradual growth of cheap literature. The success of aristocratic policy everywhere is due, in large part, to the possibility of secrecy, and to the possibility of administering through few counselors and without much discussion. The existence and expression of such a thing as "public opinion"...are fatal to it....If the multitude had to be consulted,...boldness would be impossible, owing to uncertainty as to what the final tribunal would think. Consequently, the rise of the newspaper press—furnishing to every man the materials for an opinion of some sort about public affairs...—had naturally a paralyzing effect on aristocratic policy, and would have led to the downfall of aristocratic states even if the French Revolution had never occurred.
>
> (Ibid.: 25)

We have, again, a deliberative policy of the creation of the unseen (including not appreciating some of the seen for what they "really" are), hence of ignorance.

"The states which Napoleon overthrew" were typically, he tells his readers, ones in which "privilege reigned supreme, with harsh, even contemptuous treatment of the poor, and with little or no economy in the administration of the finances, except for military purposes....All its [the government's] political arrangements seem to have been made simply for the purpose of enabling a small class to enjoy themselves, and to indulge in their favorite amusement of commanding armies" (ibid.: 26). Godkin's discussion is even more candid than Argyll's, which is candid enough. Godkin's discussion of matters of structure call attention to how upper hierarchic level control government in order to secure and enhance their position and advantages, and do so in ways which render unseen that they are doing so:

> aristocracy leaves traditions which are strong enough to make the rich desire to inherit them...the desire to belong to a class apart, with other needs than those of the masses, and with claims to consideration not possessed by the non-rich, the tendency to consider themselves in some way superior to the rest of the community, is one of the marks of the wealthy. And this claim on the part of the rich to be the heirs of the old aristocracy, and to possess the

same traditions though perhaps not the same political values, constitutes one of the dangers of the time.

(Ibid.: 27–8)

This last clause should remind the reader that Godkin himself considered his writings to be reasonably objective positivist analysis dealing with the unforeseen tendencies and problems of democracy. In saying the foregoing things (for example), he is describing and interpreting, not lauding these characteristics and developments.

Godwin's first chapter has to do, in effect, with the machinations of the upper hierarchic levels—aristocracy, the rich—and the problems they pose for democracy, including the creation of ignorance rendering unseen those machinations for what they are. The second chapter, "Equality," examines problems for democracy emanating from within democracy and concerning its foremost doctrine.

The doctrine of the equality of men leads to practices which, according to Godkin, render government infirm. And it is belief in the doctrine of equality itself that makes unseen the connection between cause and effect.

Godkin first attends to the varied meanings given the doctrine. In his view, Christianity helped to lead people to think of themselves "as good as anybody" once Christianity had boldly affirmed the "equality of souls after death" (ibid.: 29). Surely that was, before some point, an unintended and unforeseen consequence. Next he finds "not probable" the modern signification "that all men are born equal...and that for public purposes one man's opinion is as good as that of any other man" (ibid.: 30). In the eighteenth century, he believes, equality meant "equality of burdens, the abolition of all exemptions from the common liabilities and of all privileges in running the race of life" (ibid.: 30), "...an equal of rights and burdens..." (ibid.: 31). In the United States starting only in Andrew Jackson's time, he argues, was the "English tradition that a prominent social station entitles a man to some sort of political leadership assailed" (ibid.: 31). The argument from heredity collapsed when it was increasingly recognized that few qualities useful in leadership were passed on from father to son. (Interestingly, Godkin notes that heredity had been successful primarily because property and power, not the ensemble of personal leadership and other qualities, was being passed on (ibid.: 31).) That tradition was further destroyed when "the question of the right of a class to rule in virtue of heredity became a subject of discussion" (ibid.: 33).

Two related points should be noted: First, Frank H. Knight was one of probably numerous people who have remarked that an institution's failure dates not from the time it was challenged but when the question of its position is first raised; as Knight put it, to raise the question is to challenge. It is the function of keeping things unseen—say, by theories of the divine right of institutions—to prevent such question raising. Once policy consciousness arises and the policy character of the institution is on the table, its future is already in doubt. The great transformation of the eighteenth century was policy consciousness, that society and its institutions were socially constructed, as matters of policy; democracy helped foment that consciousness but—in the world of cumulative causation—that consciousness seemingly more so helped make the doctrine of equality more possible and more palpable. Consciousness means here that certain things are being seen. It is one of the functions—largely kept unseen; "some things should not be said in public," a point made by Pareto and Knight—of Hayekian conservatism in its stress on non-deliberative over deliberative decision making is to weaken the sense and effect of policy consciousness.

Second, Godkin is here raising the question of leadership selection. Its classic statement by an economist was given by Joseph A. Schumpeter about Frank William Taussig:

> He was among those few economists who realize that the method by which a society chooses its leaders in what, for its particular structure, is the fundamental social function . . . is one of the most important things about a society, most important for its performance as well as for its fate.
>
> (Schumpeter 1951: 217)

We will see that much of the rest of Godkin's *Unforeseen Tendencies of Democracy* is predicated upon this proposition.

Leadership selection is only one variable; another is the nature of the nation-state system and whether national selection, as it were, was by money-hungry industrial production or the blood-thirsty ambitions of the Napoleons of history or of war parties. The Napoleons of industry may well engender the Napoleons of history; the subject is called imperialism. One implication here is that politics and ideology serve to render unseen many of the questions of national policy likely to arise should the problems of leadership selection and of its environment be discussed.

The problem posed by Godkin is that elections do not elevate men of ability to government and thereby do not promote high quality government. And it is belief in the doctrines of equality and of democracy that again render unseen the connection between cause and effect.

In the English mind, he writes, men of mark are associated with some kind of office-holding and the work of government (Godkin 1898a: 34): "In nothing does modern democracy differ so much from ancient democracy as in this indifference to distinction" (ibid.: 36). "Our democracies . . . are composed of vast bodies of men who have but small acquaintance with the machinery of public affairs, or with the capacity of individuals for managing it" (ibid.: 37). An "amount of knowledge is necessary" for success in business and in government (ibid.: 38), but, after "the exclusion of the old landed class from the work of government" (ibid.: 39), "the really alarming feature . . . of democracy is, that it does not seem to make adequate provision of this new work. Its chief function . . . is to fill offices. It is by the manner in which this is done, more than by the laws which are passed, that the goodness or badness of a government is tested" (ibid.: 41–2); "If the functionaries . . . are ignorant or tyrannical or corrupt, the best constitution is worthless" (ibid.: 42).

In Godkin's view, it is necessary to give "the chief places, at least, to men who had already made a mark in the world by success in some field of activity" (ibid.: 42).

But, "In the popular mind there is...a disposition to believe not only that one man is as good as another, but that he knows as much on any matter of general interest" (ibid.: 44). The popular disposition is to fill elective office on the basis not of competency but of the holding of certain opinions or shades of opinion, rewarding them for their views, independent of their competency to perform their duties (ibid.: 45, paraphrased). "The disregard of special fitness, combined with unwillingness to acknowledge that there can be anything special about any man, which is born of equality, constitutes the great defect of modern democracy" (ibid.: 46). "...in private affairs the penalty of any disregard of this rule comes quickly; in public affairs the operation of all causes is much slower, and their action is obscure" (ibid.: 46). Again, it is belief in the doctrine of equality itself that renders unseen the connection between cause and effect.

In the succeeding three chapters, Godkin traces the consequence of that situation for the nominating system, the legislature, and municipal government. These three of seven chapters contain 135 of 265 pages with some detail, some generalization, and several lines of reasoning in support of his argument.

Godkin starts with the primary, considered "not necessarily a part of the democratic scheme of government," but in which the majority decides both the candidates for office and which of them shall hold office (ibid.: 49; reiterated, pp. 56, 59–60). He reiterates that "previous social distinction," of some kind, "already known to the voters," gave "title to nomination for office" (ibid.: 54–5). Specifically, from the fall of the Roman Empire to almost our time, including the colonies and states, "the world was governed by property, and property was mainly land, and was associated in the popular mind...with political power and prominence" (ibid.: 52–4). Further, population growth meant the inability of most voters to have personal knowledge of the candidates; this was coupled with the situation that people were "too democratic to accept the recommendation of any one claiming superior powers of discrimination" (ibid.: 60). "One result...was to raise the value of [political] party in the popular estimation" (ibid.: 63).

The combination of identification with and loyalty to party, residency requirements to run for public office, and the institution of the nominating convention resulted in the creation of urban political machines, boss control of patronage and nominations, and corruption; and, with those developments, the disappearance of independently distinguished men from public life (ibid.: 64–8, 80–2).

Godkin next exhibits a line of thinking that became increasingly popular among some scholars and journalists a century later. The failure to attend primaries or nominating conventions is due in part to "decreased interest in politics caused by increased individual activity and complexity of private affairs," "a demand for government without trouble, or with very little trouble" government increasingly being "considered as a means to an end, and not an end in itself," and "the great concern of our day [having become] domestic comfort, what is called success in life, or, in other words, pecuniary independence" (ibid.: 70–2). Democracy requires that people value both government and participation in government. Instead they take voting for granted and are disinterested in government (unsavory on the one hand and in competition with personal affairs and goals on the other). They may "know" in some sense that they should do better, but they do not "see" it.

At this point Godkin presents a brilliant statement of ignorance, the unseen, and the principle of unintended and unforeseen consequences:

> It is a dangerous thing to attempt to describe causes in politics; that is, to say exactly to what particular cause any political phenomenon is due. In truth, ... nothing in politics has only one cause. Everything is due to a composition or combination of causes.... the machine could hardly have grown to its present proportions without public apathy; and public apathy, in turn, is due partly to the machine, and partly to the size of the masses which have to be handled and must be persuaded ... So we find ourselves almost in a vicious circle in accounting for any of the leading features of our democracy. Government is, undoubtedly, the product of the national character; but, on the other hand, it does much to mould the national character.
>
> (Ibid.: 74–5)

Godkin may or may not have been accurate for his day or ours but his critique of democratic government surely uses elements of the theory of ignorance to telling effect.

The foregoing analysis of candidate choice also applies to the legislatures, hence the title of his fourth chapter, "The Decline of Legislatures." He commences his diagnosis with an interpretation of the Roman Senate, which, he declares, "saw that everything was done in the Roman or ancient way, and that the unseen forces were likely to favor it" (ibid.: 96–7). In modern legislatures "a great deal of legislation ... [is] intended not so much to benefit the country as to gather up and hold a majority" (ibid.: 104). (More recent debate has centered on majority-minority relations, including unanimity (or fictional unanimity) as a solution; no one has provided an unequivocal method of unequivocally determining the public interest, public purpose, or what benefits the country. The sources of the decline include the party system, the committee system, and the growing power of the Speaker, the "most serious defect" being "the stopper [the committee system] puts on debate" (ibid.: 114). The people do not know better, and for the same reason.)

Godkin's *Unforeseen Tendencies of Democracy* was published in 1898. Only two years earlier Knut Wicksell published his *Finanztheoretische Untersuchungen*, though important parts of which were not published in an English translation until 1958. Among other things, Wicksell argued that one way of achieving rationality and efficiency in government was to combine legislative decision making on spending and on taxing. Godkin uses what much later became the Wicksellian argument as a basis of criticism in this book. His example is the tariff:

> Taxation is avowedly practiced as the art of encouraging domestic industry in some degree. The Committee on Appropriations has no relations with the Ways and Means Committee. It does not concern itself about income.
>
> (Ibid.: 110)

This absence of connection between the levying and the spending authorities would work speedy ruin in any European government. The danger or inconvenience of it here has been concealed by the very rapid growth of the country in wealth and population...

(Ibid.: 111)

...appropriation for purposes not absolutely necessary... [means that] the Committee of Ways and Means is compelled to treat them as if they were legitimate expenses. This separation between the power which lays taxes and the power which spends them... [is a bold and inconvenient experiment].
Its inconveniences are likely to be felt increasingly, as the habits bred by easy circumstances become more fixed.

(Ibid.: 111–12)

The irony of tables having been turned may not have been sensed by Godkin, but he comes close:

All governments are prone to make taxation serve some other purpose than to raise revenue; that is, to foster or maintain some sort of polity. It was used for ages to promote inequality; now it is frequently used to promote certain special interests. In England, the import duties on corn were meant to benefit the landed interest and foster larger estates. In America... to benefit native manufactures indirectly.

(Ibid.: 112)

Unexplained is how promoting inequality is different from promoting certain special interests. The landed interest was, of course, the ruling class and could claim to represent the general interest. Now all interests are special interests and compete to have government promote their particular interests.

Godkin takes up the reasons why this is the case; the reasons are ignorance including the unseen:

protection is the economical creed which the "uninstructed political economist" always lays hold of first. ... [This helps] account for the failure of the free-trade theory to make more way in the world... The arguments by which it is supported are a little too abstract and complex for the popular mind.

(Ibid.: 113)

The remainder of the chapter generally reiterates earlier arguments, for example, "There is nothing... more important... than that the intelligence and character of the nation should find their way into the legislatures..." (ibid.: 115). He add that the "passage of legislative work into less instructed hands" has given a "great stimulus... to legislation itself... The schemes for the regulation of life by law, which are daily submitted to the committees by aspiring reformers, are innumerable" (ibid.: 120).

Returning for a moment to the question of majority-minority relations, Godkin says that, "Democracy really means a profound belief in the wisdom as well as the power of the majority, not on certain occasions, but at whatever time it is consulted" (ibid.: 132) but that the "[electoral] college was the device of those who doubted the wisdom and knowledge of the majority" (ibid.: 135). The matter is a function of relative ignorance and subjective preferences and sentiments masquerading as high principle. Somewhat like Argyll, and Hayek, Godkin seems to believe that the topics forming his critique are matters of truth (even Truth), whereas they are also, and principally matters of judgment as to means and ends.

We come next to a statement by Godkin that initially expresses his displeasure with legislatures but also contributes to the explanation of uncertainty bred by ignorance engineered by the multiplication of laws. Every meeting of a state legislature

> creates undisguised fear of some sort of interference with industry, some sort of legislation for the benefit of one class, or the trial of some hazardous experiment in judicial or administrative procedure, or in public education or taxation.... the law is rendered more and more uncertain by the enormous number of acts passed on all sorts of subjects.

His solution is for much less frequent meetings of the legislature, each of short duration; perhaps two years, even once in five years might be enough (ibid.: 139). (The crux being legal change of law, his solution amounts to retention of status quo law.) Such would attract a higher order of talent and character, like Constitutional conventions. He also supports wider use of the referendum for ordinary legislation (ibid.: 143–4). When making such suggestions Godkin almost always fails to take up the principle of unintended and unforeseen consequences. Another salient example is his suggestion that, in order to attract men of intelligence and character, "the legislatures should be made something more than scenes of obscurity, hard work, and small pay" (ibid.: 115).

Godkin's next chapter explores "Peculiarities of American Municipal Government." The story is the same: the spoils systems, the machine and its boss, the role of Party loyalty. What is unseen or "rarely visible" is the "incompetence or corruption in the work of administration" (ibid.: 159) and the extortion of corporations susceptible to threats of legislative assault (ibid.: 161ff.) The recent reformed machinery of municipal government has about it "an appearance of local representative self-government, but it is only an appearance. The real power...still resides in the legislature at Albany" (ibid.: 171). Agrarian attitudes toward, yet ignorance of, urban life and problems (ibid.: 172ff.) is important because "the farmer is as yet the ruling power in America" (ibid.: 174). Rural members of Congress and the state legislatures, typically located in rural areas, are deprived "of the information and the new ideas" without intercourse with "the most active-minded portion of the population...the portion of the population most immersed in affairs, and...keeping them out of sight..." (ibid.: 177). Isolation of the rural legislator leads to ignorance about world of business and a lessened "sense of the importance of cities" (ibid.: 178). Both the geography and the institutions of government engender ignorance.

Godkin's sixth chapter is entitled "The Growth and Expression of Public Opinion." It begins with the recognition that "Public opinion, like democracy itself, is a new power...since the Middle Ages" (ibid.: 183). "In America public opinion can hardly be said to have existed before the Revolution. The opinions of leading men, of clergymen and large landholders, were very powerful, and settled most of the affairs of state; but the opinion of the majority did not count for much, and the majority, in truth, did not think that it should" (ibid.: 184). Godkin implicitly offers, in that view, a solution to the socialist-calculation problem (which, it will be remembered, was the genesis of Hayek's theories in this area): The knowledge that need count is that of a relatively few people of power, power in part given by large property ownership. In that context Hayek is either laudably or impossibly democratic in seemingly holding that all local knowledge need be brought to bear. Alternatively, Godkin inadvertently identified a socialist-calculation type problem with governments of only "leading men."

Godkin next argues that "there are two kinds of public opinion. One kind is the popular belief in the fitness or rightness of something" and the other is "the public opinion, or consensus of opinion, among large bodies of persons, which acts as a political force, imposing on those certain legislation, or certain lines of policy" (ibid.: 184–5). The aristocratic school believes that public opinion "should emanate only from persons possessing [at least] a moderate amount of property, on the assumption that the possession of property argues some degree of intelligence and interest in public affairs" (ibid.: 185). The democratic school believes public opinion "should emanate from the majority of the adult males, on the assumption that it is only in this way that legislators can be made to consult the greatest good of the greatest number, and that in the long run, the majority of adult males are pretty sure to be right about public questions" (ibid.: 185–6).

Here again we implicitly encounter the problem of the socialist-calculation as to whose interests and knowledge should enter into public policy. Godkin's discussion focuses simultaneously on (1) the requirement of considerable property and then of at least a moderate amount of property and (2) adult males. Subsequently, Godkin offers what in retrospect is another view: "...elections are not often reliable as to particular measures, except through the referendum...[voters] indicate by their votes their confidence in, or distrust of, the party in power, rather than their opinions on any particular measure" (ibid.: 190; see also: 191–2). One implication is that voting conveys information about opinions regarding parties, not information of the type stressed by Hayek. Another implication is, as given here, that power structure is a mode of bringing knowledge together and of evaluating and weighting knowledge.

Godkin stresses the ignorance of and enormous difficulty of discovering public opinion (ibid.: 194) and that "...the difficulty of consulting in a modern democracy...has produced the boss" (ibid.: 194).

This brings Godkin to the role of the newspaper. He is more confident that the opinions newspapers "utter are those of which their readers approve," rather than "that the newspapers make public opinion" (ibid.: 195). The most important figure to the editor is the "advertiser, rather than the subscriber"; the editors do not want to alienate their principal source of revenue. But the advertiser is only a bogey. The advertiser is more interested in a newspaper's circulation than its editorial opinions (ibid.: 195–6).

Apropos of ignorance, the seen and the unseen, and so on, Godkin makes a number of specific points: The reading public has an increasing incapacity for continuous attention, because of "the multiplicity of the objects of attention ... [and] to the opportunities of simple amusement ..." (ibid.: 197). With the enlargement of newspaper coverage, "The sense of proportion about news ... [has been] rapidly destroyed" (ibid.: 199). "[A]ttention ... grows accustomed to short paragraphs ... [which are not remembered] for more than a minute or two" (ibid.: 200).

Godkin is particularly pointed when he turns to newspapers in relation to matters of war and peace:

> [B]usiness prudence prompts an editor, whether he fully understands the matter under discussion or not, to take what seems the patriotic view; and tradition generally makes the selfish, quarrelsome view the patriotic view.
>
> (Ibid.: 204)

> the agitation of the popular mind continues; the press must talk about the matter, and its talk is rarely pacific. It is bound by tradition to take the ground that its own government is right; and that even if it is not, it does not make any difference—the press has to maintain that it is right.
>
> (Ibid.: 205)

> [T]he newspapers have another concern than mere victory in argument. They have to maintain their place in the estimation of their readers, and if possible, to increase the number of these readers. ... the easiest way ... always *seems* to be to influence the public mind against the foreigner. ... It frightens or encourages them [the ministers conducting the negotiations] into taking impossible claims, or in perverting history and law to help their case.
>
> (Ibid.: 206–7)

> In the tumult of a great war, ... the rules of evidence are suspended by passion or anxiety, [and] invention, too, is easy.
>
> (Ibid.: 208)

We find here ignorance that is unintended but hardly unforeseen, and foreseen and intended; asymmetrical information; information that is manufactured; and what is seen and unseen, and what use people are led to put them, is also manufactured. Ignorance etc. is a function of both the deliberative and the non-deliberative.

Whatever else Godkin writes about public opinion, he is interested in the process of its formation. "Of much more importance," he writes, "than the manner in which public opinion finds expression in a democracy is the manner in which it is formed, and this is very much harder to get at. ... There is a whole batch of notions about things public and private, which men of every nation hold because they are national ... —and which are defended or propagated by calling the opposite 'un-English' or 'un-American'. These views come to people by descent. They are inherited rather than formed" (ibid.: 209). Hayek would call this "batch of notions" a nondeliberative domain. Godkin adds, "You can hardly tell what agency is exercising the strongest influence on popular thought on any given occasion. Most localities and classes are subject to some peculiar dominating force, but if you discover what it is, you discover it almost by accident" (ibid.: 210–11).

As for the content of public opinion, Godkin says, "Utilitarianism, however we may feel about it, has fully taken possession of political discussion. ... any writer or speaker on political subjects has to show that his proposition will make people more comfortable or richer" (ibid.: 213); no longer is opinion moulded by religion or morals (ibid.: 212). The sources of public opinion, that is to say, are narrower, with much potentially relevant left unseen.

Godkin is particularly bothered by questions of money, for example, paper versus metal, mono- versus bi-metallism, the functions of money, and so on. He brings to bear on these questions several of his themes in which we are presently interested.

> One would have said, twenty years ago, that the English class of country squires would be the last body in the world, owing to temperament and training, to approve of any change in the English currency. We believe they are to-day largely bimetallists. The reason is that their present liabilities, contracted in good times, have been made increasingly heavy by the fall in agricultural produce.
>
> (Ibid.: 211)

This leads to one of Godkin's more subtle insights: that what people accept (see) as knowledge is derivative, in part, from their economic (and other) inter-est(s). "In the past, the governing class, in part at least, was a reading class. ... Their successors rarely read anything but the newspapers" (ibid.: 213). The implication here is that people themselves—their allocation of time resources—help determine their ignorance.

> The loss of influence or weight by the reading class is therefore of great importance, for to this loss we undoubtedly owe most of the prevalent wild theories about currency. ... the influence of history on politics was never smaller than it is to-day.
>
> (Ibid.: 214)

Three points: (1) What constitutes a "wild theory" about money is subjective; numerous points currently widely accepted were, a century and more ago, deemed wild if not subversive of the economic order. (2) The influence of history on politics is a vast and complicated topic. It can signify the influence of accu-mulated knowledge. It can blindly reinforce the status quo. It is not measurable; judgments of magnitude are subjective. (3) The foregoing points both shape and are shaped by what is seen and unseen.

> The effect of all this is not simply to lead to hasty legislation. It ... [makes] every question seem an 'open' or 'large' question ... [with] a tendency to

seem new to every voter—matters of which each man is as good a judge as
another, and as much entitled to his own opinion. . . . The only obligation he
feels is that of party, and this is imposed to secure victories at the polls, rather
than to insure any particular kind of legislation.

(Ibid.: 215)

This argument continues the preceding one, now on the unequal distribution
of historical knowledge. On the same point and on the distribution of leadership we read:

National policy is something which has to be committed to the custody of a
few men who respect tradition and are familiar with records. . . . the disappearance from the governments . . . of commanding figures, whose authority
or character imposed on minor men . . .

(Ibid.: 216)

Ministers who do not carry personal weight always seek to fortify themselves
by the conciliation of voters, and what will conciliate voters is, under every
democratic régime, a matter of increasing uncertainty, so free is the play of
individual opinion.

(Ibid.: 216–17)

Godkin returns to the subject of money, stressing one criterion over all others,
the difference between private and public views in a world of manufactured
knowledge, and determinacy over floundering:

Nobody is listened to by all as an authority on the subject. . . . The idea that
money should be a standard of value . . . has almost disappeared. Money has
become a means in the hands of governments of alleviating human misery, of
lightening the burdens of unfortunate debtors, and of stimulating industry.

(Ibid.: 218)

Very few who speak on the subject say publicly the things they say in private.
Their public deliverances are modified or toned down . . .

(Ibid.: 219)

. . . a policy about finance—the most important matter in which a nation can
have a policy—is hardly possible. There are too many opinions in the field
for the formation of anything that can be called public opinion. . . . The great
financiers . . . may have been wrong, they may have made mistakes, but they
spoke imperiously and carried their point, whatever it was.

(Ibid.: 219–20)

The final chapter is on democracy in Australia. Godkin twice points out that
he does not know Australia personally, inasmuch as he has not visited it (ibid.:
254, 263). He has acquired what appears an idyllic picture: "The mass of men are

better off each year, mistakes are not serious, mutual helpfulness is the leading note of the community, nobody is looked down on by anybody, and public opinion is all powerful" (ibid.: 264). Somehow he concluded that the "Australians are not tormented by a race question," an issue loaded with manufactured and asymmetrical ignorance; this, the final, sentence ends, thus: "they have not yet come into contact with that greatest difficulty of large democracies, the difficulty of communicating to the mass common ideas and impulses" (ibid.: 264–5). This point is of present interest in at least the following respects. First, his frequent applause given to laissez-faire is here juxtaposed to social control. Second, given the antecedent problem of *whose* version of common ideas and impulses is to be inculcated into individuals, his point involves determination of what is seen and unseen.

He is impressed that the organization of government in Australia greatly enables experimentation (ibid.: 231–2). The new democracy confiscated large landholdings, the result of royal grants, but, he feels, did not prevent "an upper class of the 'English gentleman' type" which, along with the emigration of university graduates from England, helped "preserve the predominance of English conventional ideas" including "the right of men of education and prominence to public offices; that is, men previously raised above the crowd by wealth or rank or education, or by some outward sign of distinction" (ibid.: 233).

The questions of belief system, of what is seen and what unseen, and of whose beliefs govern policy because they are given a privileged position, arise with regard to government per se and religion. With regard to government,

> What one learns … is the difficulty, in a democratic government, of moderation of any description, if it once abandons the policy of laissez faire, and undertakes to be a providence for the masses. There is no limit to the human appetite for unearned or easily earned money. No class is exempt from it. Under the old régime, the aristocrats got all the sinecures, the pensions, and the light jobs of every description. One of the results of the triumph of democracy has been to throw open this source of gratification to the multitude, and every attempt made to satisfy the multitude, in this field, has failed.
> (Ibid.: 251–2; see also: 176)

This is a remarkably important statement. Abandonment of the policy of laissez-faire is equated with democratization in the sense of a wide competition for benefits from the government. But what this wide competition replaces is not a system in which distribution of government largesse is absent; rather under the old régime government-distributed largesse went solely to the aristocrats. Laissez-faire = largesse solely to aristocracy; democracy = largesse thrown open to all. Affirmation of laissez faire does not signify absence of government largesse, only that it is distributed to the aristocrats. The reader will marvel at the manipulation of what is seen and what is not seen by Godkin's statement—or, rather, by a belief system comprising what he has to day. The same is true of the more usual statement that government exists to protect property (ibid.: 255), as if property antedated government. Unintentionally, surely, Godkin's statement throws open the door to reveal the social mythological system at its very core.

Godkin also makes it clear that most of the aforementioned experimentation is "in devices for the protection of labor" (ibid.: 252):

> ...there is as yet no sign of reaction against this minute paternal care of the laborer. The tendency to use the powers of the government chiefly for the promotion of the comfort of the working classes, whether in the matter of land settlement, education, or employment, seems to undergo no diminution.
>
> (Ibid.: 254)

> ...Australia is absolutely free/to democratic experimentation under extremely favorably circumstances. In each colony the state has apparently existed for the benefit of the working classes, who must always constitute the majority of the people in every community, and the masses have been provided with work and protection, in complete disregard of European traditions.
>
> (Ibid.: 257–8)

Returning to the policy of laissez-faire, when Godkin writes that "It is difficult to resist the conclusion that at present we owe a good deal of what remains of laissez-faire in our policy to our constitutions and courts... [for resistance to] the humanitarian feeling which the rise of the democracy has brought with it everywhere" (ibid.: 257), we wonder if implicitly laissez-faire in the United States meant something comparable, that is, our own system of government largesse accruing to hierarchical upper levels. That the picture held by Godkin was mixed but not simplistic is suggested by his statements that

> Down to a very recent period the American was distinguished from the men of all other countries, for looking to the government for nothing but protection to life and property. ... The development of the country by the state...has only recently entered into the heads of our labor and socialist agitators. ... [The past] policy has been pursued so far that, in the opinion of many, the individual has become too powerful, and the government too subservient to private interests. There are in fact few, if any states in the Union which are not said to be dominated by rich men or rich corporations.
>
> (Ibid.: 255–6)

On the one hand, the language of protection of property gives the game away; on the other hand, the picture of government dominated by men of wealth and by corporations also gives the game away, the "game" being the contest over the use of government to promote and protect certain private interests. Laissez-faire is either a misleading name for one system of use of government to capture its largesse or a fiction. Whatever it is taken to be, the economic, or legal-economic, system is seen differently; and, indeed, much is not seen.

With regard to religion, the issue is over having a secular or a religious school system. Whether the school system is run by the state or the Catholic Church, the issue becomes, for our purposes, what is taught, therefore what is seen and what is not seen, or whose or which ignorance. "...the Catholic population...sides with the priests on nearly every public questions...The banishment of the old Irish gentry...deprived the Irish of their natural political leaders" (ibid.: 244–5). "In nearly all countries there is a struggle going on—which ended with us many years ago—to wrest the control of the popular schools...from the hands of the clergy, who have held it for twelve hundred years. No characteristic of the old régime in politics is more prominent than the belief that the priests or ministers only should have charge of the training of youth" (ibid.: 245–6).

Godkin returns to the twin topics, which monetary policy, and who decides it. He finds that "the necessity of making their loans in England, and thus getting the approval of British capitalists for their financial expedients,...has saved the colonies from even worse excesses in currency matters" (ibid.: 242—that is, irredeemable paper currency). Of special interest in this matter is that private banks are presented as part of the system of governance.

Problems of Modern Democracy (1896, 1898)

Copyrighted in 1896 and published in 1898, Godkin's *Problems of Modern Democracy* is a collection of essays. It was reprinted in 1966 by the Belknap Press of Harvard University Press with an Introduction by Morton Keller.

Keller points out that Godkin's criticisms earned him attacks on his Americanism (Godkin 1966: ix). In Keller's view, Godkin demonstrated both "stubborn loyalty to the idea of democracy (after he had condemned nearly all its works and his profound belief in the economics of laissez-faire (after it had passed out of fashion in England itself)" (ibid.: x). Such paradox was accompanied by another: "his staunch commitment to freedom did not preclude a sense of the propriety of a stratified social order" (ibid.: xi). Perhaps neither paradox is apposite: If laissez-faire could mean (see earlier) hierarchical preference in the use of government, so too could freedom have a hierarchical twist, with democracy thereby subject to qualification on all counts. Keller remarks that Godkin "remained faithful to the principle of democracy" but was critical of its specifics in practice (ibid.: xi); and reminds his reader that first pages of the *Nation* "celebrated the 'triumph of American democracy', the resolution of 'the great strife between the few and the many, between privilege and equality, between law and power, between opinion and the sword'" (ibid.: xvii). *Inter alia*, law and power may not, or not only, be a matter of conflict but co-exist in mutually dependent relations; and "opinion and the sword" is reminiscent of Vilfredo Pareto's emphasis that rule is through fraud and force, that is, with the co-existence of both and the content of the former (fraud) being matters of what is, and what is engendered to be, seen and unseen.

Keller suggests that Godkin's thought had two facets. He was an optimist, nationalist, and socio-economic reformer. Both this book and his primary impact and reputation, however, was dominated by "a rigid classical Liberalism that was indifferent to or conservative on social and economic issues; a deep antagonism to the party system and the active State; and an increasingly alienated and despairing view of American society" (ibid.: xix). In other words, it was not unlike its companion volume, *Unforeseen Tendencies of Democracy*. Relevant to the topics of this article, when Keller writes of "how far the American reality of his time had fallen short of the democratic ideal" (ibid.: xxvi) in Godkin's mind, one implication is that social control through idealization always fails to accurately picture reality, another implication is that it is the function of such control to render certain things unseen or in a different light, and still another implication that one could either reject the ideal in preference of something short thereof or accept the actual as on the road to the ideal.

Keller notes that two essays—"Idleness and Immorality" and "The Expenditure of Rich Men"—do not critique wealth per se, but appeal "to the wealthy to take the role of national leadership to which their riches entitle them" and "to the society at large to let these natural leaders play the role that is theirs by right" (ibid.: xxvi). For our purposes we need only note the differences in belief system and thus in what is seen and unseen between that view of wealth accumulation and the view of Matthew 19:24 that "It is easier for a camel to go through the eye of a needle, than for a rich man to enter into the kingdom of God."

Keller also notes that several essays affirm the existence of rigid, overwhelming, certain natural economic laws, laws whose "scientific truth...led inexorably to the immorality of the active State" and to eclipse of sympathy for labor (ibid.: xxvii). In this and all the foregoing respects, what was seen by Godkin was not necessarily seen by others; reality could be defined differently on the basis of selective perception. It was the function of ideational-ideological social control to instill some version of "common ideas and impulses" (*supra*) in people's minds. Keller appropriately suggests that "Politics was for Godkin not so much an instrument for accomplishing the business of society as a stage on which was enacted an unending morality play" (ibid.: xxix). No wonder religion was laden with latent *vis-à-vis* manifest function, with all its implications for what is seen and unseen.

One topic involves Godkin's view of the currency. As Keller neatly puts it, Godkin "did not view the matter as one appropriate for public consideration. That the monetary standard should be 'in politics' at all, and not in the hands of the apolitical experts to whom it belonged, was an intolerable state of affairs" (ibid.: xxxiv–v). Although Keller seems not to say so, Godkin had an unduly narrow view of "politics." If by politics one means, not the machinations of party, but the domain of choice, then monetary issues properly belonged "in politics." Moreover, inasmuch as the monetary "experts" disagreed on every issue, handing these questions over to them did not avoid choice.

Among the possibilities rendered unseen are those significantly different from plutocracy for the upper classes and militarism (the military spirit) for the masses (ibid.: xxxvi). So, too, with his famous line, "It seems in America as if man was made for government, not government for man" (ibid.: xxxvii). Two points seem pertinent. First, it is true both that government is part of the socialization process producing man, and that government is an instrument of man. Second, both this proposition and its opposite represent different sentiments and the spirit of different ages—the opposite being that of John F. Kennedy from his Inaugural Address of January 20, 1961: "And so, my fellow Americans, ask not what your country can do for you; ask what you can do for your country."

If we read Keller correctly, he would concur that Godwin's ideas, even when paradoxical, do not necessarily define reality. They represent sentiments which function to identify the seen and finesse, in one way or another, the unseen.

Numerous topics and themes of this book are also those of its companion. Consequently we can be economical in presenting evidence in support of the topics of interest here.

The first of eleven essays, "Aristocratic Opinions of Democracy" is principally concerned with a critique of opinions of democracy by its supporters and by supporters of oligarchy. The point of such a difference is important: democracy will look differently, and the sums of things seen and unseen and of meaning and interpretation, will vary between the two groups, as well as within. (Even the two volumes of *Democracy in America* present different stories along those lines: In the first volume de Tocqueville is describing and interpreting his subject in its own context; whereas in the second volume he is evaluating the transferability of American institutions, etc. to Europe, an evaluation conducted from an aristocratic perspective. For Godkin's view of de Tocqueville on this, see ibid.: 21.)

Democracy is still the principle of equality somehow defined. Friends of democracy err in ascribing all criticism of democracy only to aristocratic malignity and prejudice (ibid.: 4). Some of that reaction is justified but much is not. Many are apprehensive because they find "that it is fatal in the long run to any high degree of excellence in the arts, sciences, literature, or statesmanship; that it is hostile to every form of distinction, and thus tends to extinguish the nobler kinds of ambition, to create and perpetuate mediocrity... that, by making equality of conditions the highest political good, it makes civil liberty appear valuable only so long or so far as its existence is compatible with equality..." (ibid.: 7). Godkin does not distinguish between equality of fundamental rights of citizenship, equality of opportunity, and equality of results. These are different matters and various complications and ramifications pertain to them differently. One example is John Rawls's theory of justice. But the point relevant here is that different criticisms of equality, complicated by different definitions of equality, yield different stories of what is seen and unseen, etc. Moreover, criticisms can be subtle or gross, nuanced or exaggerated, and so on. Godkin remarks at one point, apropos of one or another body of criticism, "If we asked an American of conservative tastes and opinions to say frankly what he thought" of the picture so presented, "he would probably take exception to a very large portion of it;..." (ibid.: 8). The point is the same.

Among the criticisms Godkin presents are the inability of citizens "to call out anything much better than the philosophy of hotel parlors or the logic of newspaper articles"; and "what is worse...legislation is confessedly more hasty, more reckless, and more ill-digested than formerly" (ibid.: 10). Members of the bar aspire not after forensic distinction but money, and lack learning and preparation for their duties. There "is less respect for authority, not only in the household, but in the state." People are careless in attire, demeanor and even in language (ibid.: 10–12). All of this reflects ignorance of one type or another. (These and other criticisms have been made in the later twentieth century, as if the phenomena being described and criticized were new developments.) Other criticisms include contempt for experience, want of respect for training (ibid.: 41), distrust of formal study and of reliance upon experience (ibid.: 42), and so on, all represent ignorance of various types (see also: 46, 47–8).

Godkin is especially alert to the attribution of any negative development to democracy, "the direct and palpable consequence of universal suffrage" (ibid.: 13). Such opinions, such putative definitions of reality, such variation in things seen and not seen—all are "largely effected by…taste" (ibid.: 13) and subject to exaggeration (ibid.: 16). Especially invidious can be the evaluation of immigrants; says Godkin, "so far from acting as propagators of foreign opinions or manners, the whole energy of the new-comers is spent, for years after their arrival, not in diffusing their own ways of thinking and feeling, but in strenuous and generally successful efforts to get rid of them, and adopt those of their American neighbors" (ibid.: 19). Of course, what comprises the ways of thinking and feeling of being American are matters of selective perception and social control through socialization.

Like de Tocqueville, Godkin emphasizes "the existence of a plurality of causes for all the phenomena of American society" (ibid.: 23). Plural causes imply the possibility of multiple (composite) explanations and therefore confusion and ignorance. The mechanisms by which these explanations are defined and filtered include politics, patriotism, and the like. Each different account presents a different blend of the seen and the unseen. The same applies to what Godkin calls the delusion that the transfer of democratic institutions "to any other country would give rise to precisely the same phenomena" (ibid.: 25).

What are not readily seen, but are nonetheless important causal factors, include enormous increases in population and population density. These, especially the latter, in Godkin's view, have strengthened public opinion, repressed individualism, tightened social relations, and thus given "fixity to old customs and ideas, and stability to authority" (ibid.: 32). Quite aside from the question of accuracy, those initial factors coupled with their results, are not much seen by individuals—individuals who either take the present situation to be both more or less like the past and the natural order of things, or to represent unfortunate departures from some posited edenic, idealized past. Again, what is seen and unseen, and what is foreseen and expected, if not also intended, vary. When religion retains its hold on young and old, its influence can be decisive and severe (ibid.: 33).

Godkin holds that progress is "accelerated by two powerful agencies—the Christian religion and the study of political economy." The argument made in *Unforeseen Tendencies of Democracy* that the Christian doctrine of equality in Heaven has been extended to politics, is repeated (ibid.: 54). The rapid spread of political economy has reinforced the doctrine of equality at least in part because it is "a science which is based on the assumption that men are free and independent" (ibid.: 55).

It is one of the sublime paradoxes of modern Western civilization that the doctrine that men are free and independent, and so on, is both a vehicle of social control and a successful such vehicle, insofar as men are in fact, in comparison with earlier centuries, relatively free and independent. Indeed, "no political system in which [the principle recognizing 'the capacity, as well as...the right, of each human being to seek his own happiness in his own way'] has a place can long avoid conceding to all who live under it equality before the law; and from equality before the law to the possession of an equal share in the making of the laws" (ibid.: 55–6). Still, "the desire of distinction ('the applause and appreciation of his fellows,' or 'fame') is a most powerful incentive to exertion in all civilized countries" (ibid.: 56–7). The result is a deep and widespread tension between equality and hierarchy—and a comparable tension between the bundles of things seen and unseen generated by different situations.

Godkin also writes that de Tocqueville assumed that "the patronage and encouragement of an aristocracy" is the "great encouragement to excellence" whereas "democracy is generally content with mediocrity" (ibid.: 56; no notice is taken that terms like "excellence" and "mediocrity" are subjective and relate to social structure and status emulation). Godkin points out in contrast, however, "the eagerness of everybody to grasp the prizes of which in aristocratic countries only the few have much chance" (ibid.: 58). One could say that this is an example of the Benthamite conflict between maximizing welfare on the intensive or the extensive margins, except that the key terms, like "welfare," are subjective, incapable of objective measurement, and ultimately due to what national ethos enables one to see and not see. Godkin also counters the view of some that excellence in the arts, science or literature requires the leisure provided by the possession of fortune. "This," Godkin says, "men in a democratic society cannot have, because the absence of great hereditary wealth is necessary to the perpetuation of democracy" (ibid.: 62). Godkin also criticizes the absence of contribution to government and political science from men of leisure who also rule, in contrast to the great political reforms forced on the government by the middle and lower classes (ibid.: 65). Of course, different evaluations of policy and reform will emanate from the differences in what is seen and not seen in the respective systems of belief.

The chapter entitled "Popular Government" is not a defense of democracy, though it veers in that direction; rather it is a defense against Sir Henry Maine's arguments "'that the progress of mankind has hitherto been effected by the rise and fall of aristocracies, by the formation of one aristocracy within another', and that 'there have been many so-called democracies which have rendered services beyond price to civilization, but they were only peculiar forms of aristocracy'." Godkin defines Popular Government in "the doctrine that government is the servant of the community, over the doctrine that it is the master of the community" (ibid.: 70; "the belief that the rulers are and ought to be the servants of the ruled" (ibid.: 73)). Immediately it will be obvious, we think, that where these doctrines are held by different groups, respectively, the view each has of the world, their respective networks of meaning and interpretation, what they see and what it means to them, and what they ignore, diminish or exaggerate because of their doctrine, will differ, in significant part because of what their belief system enables them to see and the meaning it attaches thereto.

In history, the aristocratic doctrine preceded the democratic doctrine. Democracy had to overcome aristocracy in order to exist. Consider the following thought experiment. Assume that the democratic doctrine preceded the aristocratic doctrine. In the former, actual case, advocates of the introduction of democracy had to contend with a belief system that, on the one hand, rendered seen and lauded the doings of the aristocracy and, on the other hand, obfuscated the belief system and system of incentives of democracy, and (except when compelled by pressure to do otherwise) rendered unseen and unheralded both those within the masses whose doings were laudatory and those within the aristocracy whose abilities and doings were anything but laudatory. In the hypothetical case, the advocates of replacing democracy with aristocracy would have to contend with an opposite array of the seen and the unseen. The situation in either case is, of course, more complicated; each society will manifest its tendencies toward egalitarianism and toward hierarchy, and each will have different bundles of ways for individuals to rise and to fall.

Godkin is exceptionally perceptive when he declares that:

> How popular Government works can . . . only be known by seeing it in a community in which the doctrine on which it is based is fully and intelligently held by the bulk of the people.
>
> (Ibid.: 73)

Notwithstanding the array of problems of modern democracy identified by him, Godkin says that the United States is

> the one country in the world in which Popular Government, as [Maine] defines it, really exists. They are the one country, that is to say, governed by universal suffrage in which the great mass of the voters have a realizing sense of the fact that the government is their servant and not their master, and that it exists simply to carry out the ideas of the "plain people" who compose the bulk of the community, and not those of a small but more cultivated and more enlightened class; a government, in short, as Lincoln expressed it, "of the people, by the people, for the people."
>
> (Ibid.: 80)

He is even more perceptive when he interprets "Darwin's doctrine expressed in terms of politics," the doctrine being that of the survival of the fittest:

> The progress of civilization under all forms of government has consisted simply in making such changes in the environment of the multitude as will increase the number of the fittest.
>
> (Ibid.: 85)

and when he finds that the reigning belief system will govern what people find convenient, what they see and do not see, and so on, all on the basis of ignorance:

> One sees, I admit [he says], in our own time a good deal to warrant the fear that democratic ignorance will fight unpleasant and inconvenient truths with the pertinacity with which monarchical and aristocratic ignorance has always fought them.
>
> (Ibid.: 87)

The next two chapters, on the tariff and on municipal politics, provide comparatively little evidence useful for our purposes, little but some. A useful discussion concerns the way in which the tariff is constructed. Godwin says it should be submitted to the public "in its true shape, without disguise. This requires a distinct definition both of its object and of its amount" (ibid.: 98). The object is either for protection or for revenue. The amount should include direct payments to the subsidized plus the effect on prices and incomes of duties which keep out foreign goods. Any tariff, he feels, necessarily is "a corruption fund," corrupt in the sense that it encourages laziness, improvidence and/or incompetence in those who know they will be bailed out by the government (ibid.: 101). If the payment is for business loss due to imports, losses from other sources will have to be deducted from any figure of total loss (ibid.: 103). One result of the tariff system is "damage to the moral constitution of those who were benefited by it" (ibid.: 103). Tariff protection, therefore, deals with "votes of money of an indefinite amount, for an ill-defined purpose" (ibid.: 104). This is ignorance manufactured to obfuscate the actual workings of the subsidy system. Godkin's solution is to raise revenues for revenue only (ibid.: 113).

From this, still in the chapter on political aspects of the tariff, Godkin turns to corruption in the legislature, centering on the eliciting of payments from capitalists and corporations to get what they want or to escape a tax on what they already possess (ibid.: 107–8; see also: 111 in re legislators as possible enemies to be bought of or possible benefactors to be rewarded). He feels that "in all past states of society . . . the governing class has been the wealthy class," but in "our day and generation, and in this country, . . . the Government has . . . passed into the hands of the poor, in a rich community" (ibid.: 109). The problem, then, is dual: to control the rapacity of the discontented poor and that of the men of wealth, "the great problem . . . how to keep wealth in subjection to law . . ." Godkin's solution is "to leave [legislators] as little as possible to sell of the things which capitalists are eager to buy" (ibid.: 110). Politics here includes exchange.

Godkin offers a certain expectation as the reason why he firmly believes "that property will always, in every country, be able to take care of itself." One reason is that the "great bulk of the population is, in every country, and above all, in this, composed of those who have property or expect to have it" (ibid.: 114). Expectations help form what is seen and unseen, and are part of the theory of ignorance. (Americans have for generations had the expectation—a belief so palpable they could see if not feel it—that their children's generation would have a higher standard of living than they; and they have been facilitated in having such an expectation by such institutions as the residential mortgage, income tax deduction for mortgage interest, Federal Housing Authority and Veteran's Administration mortgages, and other government institutions promoting home ownership. The result has been a definition of reality, of what is expected, almost as if a matter of right, and of what is, or is believed to be, seen.

The chapter on "criminal politics" illustrates how definitions of words help define reality and thus narrow or enlarge what is seen. The chapter deals with urban politics and its corruption. Godkin covers immigration, the mutual impacts of universal suffrage [*sic*] and urban growth fed by immigration. He distinguishes different nationalities of new voters, emphasizes democracy as a mode of political training (ibid.: 131), and says that the Slav immigrants "do not secure any of the prizes of corruption; and the reason is that they are ignorant of the language and unfamiliar with... [how] a share in the electoral plunder can be obtained" (ibid.: 132). Some of much of the foregoing is a precursor to Public Choice Theory.

The criminal politics that Godkin has in mind is not only the class of burglars, robbers, receivers of stolen goods, or owners of gambling-houses or houses of ill-fame, as he calls them. Also included are "all who associate with them in political work, and who share political spoils with them; who help to shield them from judicial pursuit either by their influence with the district attorney or with the police justices, or with the police; in other words, both the actual perpetrators of crimes and those who are not repelled by them and are willing to profit in politics by their activity" (ibid.: 136).

One's view of government will be influenced by one's narrow or broad definition of "criminal politics." As for the definition of reality—of what is seen and not seen—held by the new poor immigrant, "the idea that the public functionaries are the servants of the people... has as yet not penetrated the popular mind. He is apt to hold on still, in a blind, unreflective way, to the old doctrine that the powers that be are of God, and that what a man in authority says or does is, in some sense the expression of the national morality. He has not as yet learned to criticize public officers or call them to account. He obeys them; he seeks to ingratiate himself with them. He accepts their decisions, if unfavorable, as misfortunes; if favorable, as blessings" (ibid.: 142–3). Godkin may well overstate the passive, authority-accepting mentality; those who migrated to the United States desired to leave such authority behind them, though, of course, such habits of deference were hard to overcome. In any event, Godkin's attention to the "unreflective" indicates a role for non-deliberative decision making.

Here again his analysis is akin to Public Choice Theory. The history of economic thought is laden with those who connect rational economic man with laissez-faire and those who reject both terms comprising the proposition and their connection. Included in the former group is Hayek and his disciples, who would reach laissez-faire on the basis of the principle of unintended and unforeseen consequences and/or the theory of spontaneous order. In his chapter on "The Economic Man," he summarizes the economics thus: "The 'Economic Man' of Ricardo" buys cheap and waits to sell dear, and "he assumes that in so doing he renders the best service in his power to the community. ... His one desire is to make all the money he can by every means not illegal. Laissez-faire, *laissez passer*, comprises the sole and whole duty of the state toward him" (ibid.: 156–7). Such a political economy was erected "on the desires and fears of an entirely mythical personage ... a creature of the economist's imagination" (ibid.: 157). Thus later schools "all agree in repudiating Adam Smith and his economic followers, in denouncing laissez-faire, *laissez passer*, as an economic rule ..." (ibid.: 158). Godkin believes differently, saying, "political economy, no matter how defined, cannot be taught without assuming the existence of an Economic Man who desires above all things, and without reference to ethical considerations, to get as much of the world's good as he can with the least possible expenditure of effort or energy on his own part" (ibid.: 161–2). Moreover, "through our knowledge of the Economic Man we can predict [Gresham's Law's] operation with almost as much certainty as the operation of a law of chemistry or physics" (ibid.: 162).

The foregoing is a definition of reality that many believe to be correct and when that definition of reality is followed it comprises a particular view of what is seen and unseen. Anything else is a challenge not only to economics but to economic efficiency and order. For Godkin, however, "Ethics and religion, in fact, constitute the disturbing forces which make possible the organization and prosperous existence of civilized states" (ibid.: 162–3). This is a paradoxical way of calling ethics and religion "disturbing forces." What is not paradoxical, after Emile Durkheim, Louis Schneider, and Robert K. Merton, is that going to church and believing in Christian religion, for all the talk of rich man and the eye of the needle and of the opposition of God and Mammon, enables economic order.

Godkin approaches the foregoing also in terms of economics as a science, meaning "the law which regulates the succession of phenomena." Scientific investigation means observation and/or experiment as a means to establish such law. "But," he says, "it is only in theology or metaphysics that the scientific investigator creates his own premises, and makes hypotheses which account for nothing." In economic science, "the premises are not furnished by the logician, but by the phenomena of nature" (ibid.: 165). The test of science is prediction of consequences (ibid.: 167). Whereas "the new schools profess to know far more about the will of God, and about duty and the moral sources of happiness, and the ethical foundations of the state, than the older economists." Accordingly he finds the historical school's objection to the policy of laissez-faire to be "an ethical or political, not a scientific, objection" (ibid.: 167). Godkin is thus, like many others, unable to see the ethical or political elements of his own theory. What is seen and unseen varies from school to school (and even within schools).

Godwin, however, shows that the doctrine of laissez-faire is not a bar to the regulation of factory labor; nor is it " 'an exception to the rule of individualism' " (ibid.: 168, quoting Francis A. Walker). He insists that

> it is not an exception in the economic sense. It is a political or social measure, not an economic one. It is a dictate of humanity or physiology or religion.

It is a police regulation, to which the Economic Man is no more opposed than to the restrictions on the use of public water or the municipal prohibition of the storing of gunpowder. It was opposed in the beginning not by economists, but by manufacturers who happened to be at the time strongly combating the kind of government interference with production which had been the rule in Europe ever since the Middle Ages. ... [The] Economic Man has [not] offered any serious impediment to the kind of special interference with distribution for the benefit of the race which is known as socialistic legislation.

(Ibid.: 168–9)

Nor can one expect conclusiveness in economic policy:

There is, unhappily, no absolute test of success in economic legislation. ... no economist can say with certainty that any particular kind of economic legislation is the best possible, or has produced effects which no other kind would or will produce.

(Ibid.: 172)

As Godkin's editor, Morton Keller, seems to imply, there is in Godkin's thinking a multi-faceted contest between Godkin's affirmation of laissez-faire; his understanding of the technical limits of economic doctrines; his belief in the relevance of ethics, religion and politics to economic policy; his love for humanity; his criticisms of actual politics; and so on. This means that variations in each of these facets and in their combination produce different bundles of the seen and the unseen. Such is the bafflement consequent to "the complexity of all sociological problems" (ibid.: 172–3), bafflement amplified because "the state has lost completely, in the eyes of the multitude, the moral and intellectual authority it once possessed" (ibid.: 173).

Godkin seems to have been able, to some degree, to treat separately his personal ideology and his more-or-less personal or more-or-less objective interpretation. Although his writings obviously are intended to influence policy, he seems able to refrain from self-censoring his objective findings in order to protect the plausibility of his personal ideology and policy proposals; in other words, he seems capable of escaping the role of high priest. Stipulating that he is "not now discussing whether this doctrine [discouraging reliance on the state] was or was not pushed too far," he writes, consistent with what has been reported earlier (in re ibid.: 251–2),

I simply say that it was the most natural thing in the world for the working classes of England, for example, which had been so long familiar with legislation for the direct benefit of the middle and upper classes, to receive with anger or suspicion the announcement that the care of any class by the state was a mistake, and that individual independence was the true rule of industrial life. When these classes, therefore, found themselves invested through the

suffrage with political power, it was inevitable that they should seek at once
to improve their condition through legislation.

> (Ibid.: 176; to not do so was to render permanent
> legislation benefiting others)

The next two essays—"Idleness and Immorality" and "The Expenditure of
Rich Men"—do not critique wealth per se, but, as summarized by Keller, the
editor of the 1966 edition, appeal "to the wealthy to take the role of national
leadership to which their riches entitle them" and "to the society at large to let
these natural leaders play the role that is theirs by right" (ibid.: xxvi). The wealthy
until recently "were the owners of the soil. ... the landowners were 'the country' ..."
(ibid.: 181). This was *the seen*, derived from the then-existing order of things: "The
'man of property' was the landed man. He and his followers owned the country,
and it seemed for ages perfectly natural and right that they should govern the
country" (ibid.: 182–3). The country was equated with, or identified by, the land;
unseen "for ages" was the possibility that the country could be defined differently.
"The economical or political revolutions" of the nineteenth century transferred
power "from the owners of the land to people of every kind of occupation,"
the great landowners having been converted into annuitants forming an "idle
class ... no longer render[ing] the state the service which the old feudal tenures
exacted [*sic*] of them" (ibid.: 185). They increasingly "protect themselves by
showing the danger to all property that would probably result from an attack on
their particular kind of property" (ibid.: 185–6). Thus would an argument serve
to define reality, to determine what is seen, even though landed property rights
(like all other rights) have changed throughout time. A parallel argument is
expressed by Godkin pertaining to what the laboring class is encouraged to see
and to not see: "The labor problem" is really the problem of making the manual
laborers of the world content with their lot (ibid.: 193)—a problem aggravated by
conspicuous consumption of the idle class (ibid.: 193–4). His principal concern
here is the loss to society of services performed by the educated men of wealth, a
loss due to both the "alienation of the rich" and their exclusion due to modern
democracy (ibid.: 195–8). The first of these two chapters concludes with the
prediction, "The coming rulers of men are those who mould the thoughts or
sway the passions of the multitude" (ibid.: 198; Vilfredo Pareto argued that
governance consisted of the mutual manipulation of knowledge—largely
pseudo-knowledge—and psychology; see Samuels 1974)—in other words, construct
what is seen and unseen, or the distribution of ignorance in a world of manifest
and latent function.

The second of these two chapters is aptly entitled, "The Duty of Educated
Men in a Democracy." Here Godkin makes some predictions of the results of
confining the suffrage to college graduates (Godkin 1966: 200–2) and generally
laments the exclusion of them from government in a democracy. He points out
that "the hope of better food and clothing, more leisure, and a greater variety of
amusements, has become the religion of the working classes" (ibid.: 206). These
and other descriptions and predictions suggest that Godkin's use of the principle

of unintended and unforeseen consequences was influenced by his classism, his lack of comprehension of the prospects of progress along those lines or of how such a religion was due to social control, to the rationalization of the system. Workers not content with their lot, due not to envy but, say, to the Protestant Ethic, augured social stability, not threat. Oddly, Godkin acclaims both "the growth of knowledge and self-reliance and foresight among the working classes themselves" in Europe (ibid.: 207) and "The great law which Nature seems to have prescribed for the government of the world, . . . that the more intelligent and thoughtful of the race shall inherit the earth and have the best time, and that all others shall find life on the whole dull and unprofitable" (ibid.: 208), but does not see that the former negates the latter.

Godkin's main argument continues to be the loss, and the suffering due to the loss, to the country from the silence and inactivity of educated men of wealth (e.g. ibid.: 211). Among other subordinate topics is that of the optimism of politicians as a road to success: "As a general rule, people like cheerful men and the promise of good times" (ibid.: 213). It is in this connection that Godkin extends his argument to affirm the man "who sees things as they are; and to see things as they are, without glamour or illusion, [is] the first condition of worldly success" (ibid.: 213). Godkin is seemingly unaware that his argument flies in face of much of the rest of his argument, much as Hayek does not apply his principle of unintended and unforeseen consequences to his own prescriptions nor treats his own deliberative activism as he does that of others. But he does go on to say that "A persistent optimist . . . is likely . . . to be just as foolish and unbearable as a persistent pessimist. He is as much out of harmony with the order of nature. The universe is not governed on optimistic any more than on pessimistic principles" (ibid.: 214). Here is a good example of conflicting insights with one likely the most accurate. The principle of unintended and unforeseen results itself is finessed when he says, apropos of the ostensible results of the slavery controversy and of silver purchases, that "yet the experience of mankind afforded abundant reason for anticipating both results" (ibid.: 216).

Godkin quotes (in part here) de Tocqueville's statement that "The European often sees in the public functionaries simply force; the American sees nothing but law." This, however, Godkin argues, "has been greatly modified . . . by two agencies—the 'labor problem,' as it is called, and legislative protection to native industry" (ibid.: 217–18). Both, he says, have modified "the old American conception of the relation of the government to the individual" (ibid.: 218). Of course, the older conception he posited as the government responsive to the higher income. At stake is the definition of reality that is to guide policy, that is, its mix of what is seen and unseen.

This chapter concludes with two points relevant to the theory of ignorance. One is that what is taken to be knowledge—opinions defining reality—may become the absurd: "We see that opinions which at one time everybody held became absurd in the course of half a century—opinions about religion and morals and manners and government" (ibid.: 222). The second penetrates to the heart of what is now seen as the Hayekian process of spontaneous, that is, non-deliberative, order, achieved through interaction producing composite choice:

> No one ever talks freely about anything without contributing something, let it be ever so little, to the unseen forces which carry the race on to its final destiny. Even if he does not make a positive impression, he counteracts or modifies some other impression, or sets in some train of ideas in some one else, which helps to change the face of the world.
>
> (Ibid.: 223–4)

Published shortly before the birth of Hayek in 1899, it would be difficult to find a better expression of Hayek's analysis.

Godkin's next chapter, "Who Will Pay the Bills of Socialism?", attacks what he believes, and would have others believe, is the delusion that welfare-state programs are costless. It is Godkin's objective to render certain things seen that he believes would otherwise be unseen. It is an example of a particular rhetorical strategy. The strategy calls for identifying the cost of something and by implication, at least, to portray the cost as not only something that should not be forgotten (unseen) but as an amount greater than the benefits. It is a version of invoking the principle of opportunity cost, or the injunction, "There is no free lunch."

He proposes that the régimes of feudalism, slavery, and the Manchester School have passed away. The latter is the beginning of the passing of the régime of competition, of the teaching that "the doctrine of *laissez faire* [is] the best rule of living for the community," "individualism", and "that the least possible government was the best." It thus supported the activities of people "whose main desire was to get money with the least possible amount of exertion" and "was willing to let the ablest man get the best things in life, and so on" (ibid.: 226). Such a system of beliefs has these matters very salient but renders other matters quite unseen, for example, that "the least government" is still a great deal of government that the proposition expresses a sentiment and not a meaningful definition of reality, and that the pecuniary system and monetary acquisition was but one game of many and that ability was game-specific, and that nothing was thus being said as to why this game is more laudable than any other.

Nonetheless, Godkin argues that the change from individualism and least possible government to welfare-statism should raise the question, where will the money come from to pay the bill? (ibid.: 230) He then asks, "What is it that makes [the condition of the working class] a 'problem'?" and "Why has it become a question of growing importance ... ?" The answer, he says, is the "the workingman's want of money which makes him the object of so much pity, and dread, and speculation" (ibid.: 233). For Godkin "the labor question is the question why the workingman does not have more money. The answer is that he gets now all there is for him ..." (ibid.: 234). This answer is in effect that of the old Wages Fund Theory, to the effect that the size of the fund limits how much workers can receive, and any growth of the fund must come from an increase of production (with no corresponding increase in population) or from profits or interest on capital or from capital itself—and if the latter sources, with disastrous results.

Once again he does not hesitate from identifying the "capitalistic or saving class" as critical to society (ibid.: 235). He then seeks to combat both "the delusion that there is somewhere a great reservoir of wealth" to be tapped and "the delusion that there is somewhere a reservoir of wisdom still untapped which can be drawn on for the execution of a new law of distribution" (ibid.: 239–40).

His case relies on several rhetorical strategies. He first invokes economic law—the making of them seen. He then minimizes the role of institutions in distribution—the rendering of them relatively unseen. But distribution "will always be the subject of some sort of human arrangement, in which the human will will play a more or less prominent part" (ibid.: 244). Distribution is a result, therefore, of non-deliberative and deliberate decision making, the former a matter of economic law, the latter of "some sort of human arrangement." In passing he notes the disincentive effects of changing distribution and invokes the impression that the costs of disincentives are greater than the benefits of incentives engendered by the change. Insofar as all this is influenced by "government, spiritual or temporal," "some kind of understanding [must exist] as to who or what the deciding authority should be." But, he argues, no government "has ever existed, which had not to keep in subjection a hostile minority by the use of force in some shape" (ibid.: 244). Two implications follow from this which Godkin does not quite make clear. One implication is that government is controlled by the others than that "hostile minority." Here one wonders whether this group is actually the majority. A second implication is that adoption of a suitable belief system as a legitimizing definition of reality serving as social control inoculates all but this "hostile minority" from challenging existing modes of distribution.

He also argues that absent unanimity on such matters, the result will be "the slavery of some portion of the population" (ibid.: 245). No notice is taken that slavery depends on the difference in institutional arrangements concerning distribution and that any such difference can yield the perception of slavery, for example, the idea of "wage slavery."

In "The Political Situation in 1896" Godkin renews and intensifies his criticism of two of what he calls "sequelae of the civil war": the currency and the tariff questions. Apropos of the issue of money becoming a government function—something most people take as given in their definition of economic reality—he indicates his displeasure with the Legal Tender Cases. The Supreme Court upheld as constitutional the power of government to regulate the currency. Godkin argues that this "was really a power to make any kind of money it pleased." The Court's idea, that "every government must have" such power, was derived, says Godkin, from a "definition of sovereignty...obtained by observing the practice of sovereigns," and "not on the justice or honesty of it" (ibid.: 252–3). Thus do definitions of reality inform law, that is, through identifying what is seen and unseen.

Godkin rejects the idea that representative government in a democracy is capable of making sound currency policy—because of its ignorance:

> Moreover, like most other functions of government in times past, the regulation of the currency was always left in the hands of a few experts, that is, of

men who made the currency a matter of scientific observation, and who sought, according to their lights, to make money a measure, as well as a medium, of exchange. For the currency question is not altogether, as many suppose, a question of material or of quantity. It is, essentially or mainly, a question of psychology. ... The merits or demerits of gold or silver or paper as money are to be found not in the things themselves, but in the way in which the people who use them look at them.

(Ibid.: 257–8)

Godkin seems to appreciate neither how much he is giving voice to sentimental understandings about currency nor that experts themselves may be uninformed on monetary fundamentals and may strongly disagree among themselves as to currency policy nor to how much members of a ruling class or section may make currency policy in their own interest. Yet he is extraordinarily insightful and candid about the psychology of belief as it applies to monetary questions—and thus to the psychology underlying definitions of reality. The distrust of the East by the West in the United States, a distrust he finds to be partly social and partly financial, is greatly influenced by "great ignorance about foreigners and foreign relations" and the conditions of foreign exchange (ibid.: 261) as well as "living in its own ideas—the belief that Providence still creates peculiar peoples" (ibid.: 262).

"Much the same things are true, *mutatis mutandis*," he writes, "of the tariff question" (ibid.: 264). The tariff as enacted is not for revenue and is not scientific; it is adopted to make certain industries profitable (ibid.: 264–5). Apropos of Hayek's principles, the effects of such tariff intervention "are always vastly more far-reaching than the promoter ever imagines" (ibid.: 265) and include the misallocation of capital, albeit unseen (ibid.: 266). He says that tariff policy "will be full of excesses and abuses" (ibid.: 266–7), that it has an adverse "effect on public life" (ibid.: 267), especially a changed understanding of government. People "cease to think of it as an instrument for the promotion of the general welfare"; "Their mind gets fixed on it wholly as a means of increasing their own revenues. ... He takes an entirely different view of the State, of the objects of government, of the nature of patriotism, and of the functions of the legislature" (ibid.: 268). Godkin mentions neither that such calculations of profit maximization, in which politics is an extension of economics, can be seen to derive from the nature of the pecuniary mentality in a capitalist market system nor that these calculations entered into the decision making of past monarchical and aristocratic elites who used the state for their own purposes.

The tariff becomes part of reality and its definition; politics becomes business; and opponents of the tariff are seen by its supporters as "assailants of property and order" (ibid.: 269).

In his chapter entitled "The Real Problems of Democracy" Godkin begins with a critique of several authors of works on democracy, for example, W. E. H. Lecky. "The great difficulty" is that

thus far all investigators have been themselves part of the thing to be investigated. Every man, or nearly every man, who takes up a pen to examine the questions what democracy is, and what effect it is likely to have on the race, is himself either an earnest advocate or an earnest opponent of it. He sees in it either the regeneration of mankind or the ruin of our civilization. This is true of nearly every writer of eminence who has touched on it since the French revolution. The most moderate of its enemies seldom admits more on its behalf than his own ignorance of what it promises. Its defenders are, as a rule, too enthusiastic to make their predications of much philosophic value.

(Ibid.: 277)

Clearly, both positions project different mixes of what is seen and unseen, each according to their respective lights. By now we come to expect that phenomenon. What is dramatic is Godkin's assertion that "thus far all investigators have been themselves part of the thing to be investigated." We take this to mean that Godkin recognizes the deliberative nature and creation of the story being told and, through that story, of the phenomenon under study. Each account is a contribution to defining and working out the meaning and historical record of democracy. In economics and the other social sciences, the observer is willy nilly a participant.

Moreover, Godkin suggests something of the process centering on the participant observer. One part is the substance of an author's discussion. Another is the working out of the meaning of patriotism: "In American its [democracy's] success seems so closely connected with the success of the government itself that praise of it and prediction of its complete sufficiency, have become the part of patriotism" (ibid.: 277). Godkin takes up the work and positions of Lecky, de Tocqueville, Montesquieu, and Maine. Sir Henry Maine's work on popular government, for example, Godkin says that "bears the mark of insufficient observation"—surely pertinent to any theory of ignorance—and that, "To crown all, he was essentially an aristocrat, an authority who, rightly or wrongly, felt his position in some sort menaced by the new regime" (ibid.: 278–9)—surely a pointer to bias as an influence on one's definition of reality.

In connection with Lecky, Godkin goes out of his way to illustrate the role of bias, in part by recognizing that one's ideas of "natural justice" derive from and give effect to the principles of the system under which one lives. Referring to the then-recent revision of the Irish land laws, Godkin notes their "dethronement of a great class [but compare Argyll], the apparent sacrifice of the few to the many, on a large scale," and that "this is what democracy calls for, but it is never accomplished without seemingly serious violations of natural justice" (ibid.: 279). Unmentioned are the serious violations of natural justice, a different natural justice, that occurred when the existing system was forged out of battle.

Lecky's work, Godkin points out, "while nominally discussing democracy, it really only points out the apparently bad tendencies of democracy. It errs in this respect somewhat as Burke's *Reflections on the French Revolution* do. One could not get from Burke any idea of the objections to the *ancient régime*" (ibid.: 280–1). By omitting such objections, "The whole outbreak seems gratuitous material, uncaused, and therefore against the order of nature" (ibid.: 281). Here we have the hermeneutic circle at work, connecting a particular status quo with the order of nature, and connecting both with a sense of natural justice. Thus it generated different combinations of the seen and unseen, generated through a process combining deliberative and non-deliberative processes.

Godkin feels, correctly or not, that none of the attacks on democracy have gotten at the truth. The defects of these attacks is the "defect of partial comparison" (ibid.: 283) as well as the related defect of bias. Since he himself is a partial critic of democracy he seems to feel that he can isolate the truth about the nature of democracy independent of praise or criticism.

Godkin again identifies democracy in terms of the principle of equality. Democracy "is simply an experiment in the application of the principle of equality to the management of the common affairs of the community" (ibid.: 285). The reader should note the seen yet unseen element of that proposition. It relates to the final phrase, "the common affairs of the community." Put aside the important problem that, like public interest or general welfare, the phrase is empty and question begging, something to be worked out. Under aristocratic rule, that is, government by owners of landed property, the community either has no such common affairs or they are what the landowners say it is; whereas under democracy, the phrase presumably embraces the interests of all persons, not the elite alone. The notion that under democracy "all men are alike, and are entitled to an equal voice in the management of the common affairs" (ibid.: 286) does not signify that they have the same interests. At any rate rulers are now hired servants, employed as agents, of the mass of the community (ibid.: 285)—though presumably it is these ruler-agents who seek to influence the mindsets of the masses. Ancient democracy was small in scale and number so that the growth of "enormous democracy" was "unforeseen" (ibid.: 288; "the biggest mistake of the theoretic democrats" was that they "never foresaw the big democracies" (ibid.: 290)), the English aristocracy was alert enough to introduce "the merit system, in time to save it from the incoming democracy" (ibid.: 289).

Although Godkin again criticizes the political nominating system, he directs his deepest criticism here to the new phenomenon, the great corporation. "These aggregations of capital in a few hands have created a new power in the State, whose influence on government has been very grave." The managers defend their position and their policies with an argument consisting of a particular definition of reality, that "they are the custodians of large amounts of other people's property, which they are bound to defend, by whomsoever attacked" (ibid.: 293). This is surely not the first instance of the recognition of managerialist ideology introduced when individualist ideology is inadequate (Sutton *et al.* 1956) but Godkin understood both it and its role as social control through defining reality, and the role of social control applied to the corporation and corporate system:

> How to bring these corporations under the law, and at the same time protect them from unjust attacks, is one of the most serious problems of democratic government. ... Corporations are as powerful as individual noblemen or aristocrats were in England in the last century, or in France before the Revolution,

but are far harder to get at or bring to justice, from their habit of making terms with their enemies instead of fighting them.

(Godkin 1966: 294)

Godkin could have noted that corporations are often instrumental in writing the legislation that covers their business.

Godkin includes among the "real problems of democracy" such already-discussed themes as the transfer of the work of government from the rich to the poor, the role of the boss in party politics, the decline in the quality of democratic legislatures, and so on (ibid.: 294ff.). That the party boss and the corporate manager (at least as asserted by managerialist ideology) might serve a coordinating role is not central to his argument—say, in relation to the role(s) attributed to political and economic entrepreneurs a century later.

It is the "transfer of the government to the poor" to which Godkin seems to object the most strenuously. He again reminds his reader that, "except during very short periods in ancient democracies, the world has been governed by rich men; that is, by the great landholders or the great merchants. ... Every government has been a rich man's government." With government transferred to poor men, "through the taxing power rich corporations and rich individuals are at their mercy. They are ... often stimulated by envy or anti-social passions" (ibid.: 300). Once again, this type of admission brings out into the open—into the realm of the seen—what hitherto had been the object of ideology to obfuscate and render unseen. Godkin is candid, to the point, surely, of leading some readers to judge him subversive: such things should not be said in public. Nor is the topic of plutocracy the only one so treated. Patriotism "has been made by the multitude to consist in holding everything [*sic*] that is, to be exactly right, or easily remedied." Any man who would succeed in politics or business "is strongly tempted to proclaim incessantly his great content with the existing order of things, and to treat everything 'American' as sacred" (ibid.: 305). Yet patriotism is the source of much of the definition of reality for a country's people.

Notwithstanding much of the foregoing, Godkin concludes that democracy "is suffering from unforeseen evils, as well as enjoying unforeseen blessings" (ibid.: 308). Hayek's principle is not only present, it is alive and well, even if inconclusive.

The final chapter of *Problems of Modern Democracy* is entitled "The Expenditure of Rich Men." Here Godkin enters the ranks of the tradition stemming from Adam Smith to Thorstein Veblen which maintains that status emulation, and what contributes to it, namely conspicuous consumption, is a key to society. Wealth, Godkin asserts, is desired not only for the sake of power but "also, as a rule, for the sake of display," so that people will "know they were rich" (ibid.: 311). All this, even though the inability of wealth to produce happiness is among the "commonplaces of religion and morality" (ibid.: 312, including Adam Smith). Yet he also writes that "the building of great houses was, down to our own time, a really utilitarian mode of spending wealth. It was intended to maintain and support the influence of the ruling class by means which were sure to impress the popular mind, and which the popular mind called for. The great territorial owners had a recognized place in government and society, which demanded, at first a strong, and later, an extensive, dwelling-place" (ibid.: 318). Social function thus becomes the fig-leaf of the quest for private power in the definition of reality, the seen. Still, the situation is different in the United States than in Europe, giving vent to the belief that public displays of wealth in a democracy should not be immoderate (ibid.: 327). Here we see both great candor and something of how customary and moral attitudes toward wealth are seen to help define (and legitimize) the economic system by making certain things clearly seen and others not, the differences being in what is made seen and unseen.

THE DUKE OF ARGYLL AND EDWIN L. GODKIN AS PRECURSORS TO HAYEK ON THE RELATION OF IGNORANCE TO POLICY—(PART FOUR)

The three positions

The Duke of Argyll writes of the unseen foundations of society. His argument takes the existing system as a given, excepting those elements he would change. These foundations are easily neglected, for they are not readily seen.

Edwin Godkin writes of the unforeseen tendencies and problems of democracy. His argument takes the existing system in which he writes as a given, except those elements he would change. His emphasis is on tendencies and problems that are typically not understood to derive from the nature of democracy, with democracy in a world whose foundations are somewhat at odds with democracy and which produce problems, in the form of unforeseen and unintended consequences. These foundations are often taken for granted, ignored, neglected and whose connections with democracy are not readily seen.

Friedrich Hayek writes of the unintended and unforeseen consequences of human action. His argument takes the existing system in which he writes as a given, except those elements he would change. His emphasis is on the adverse unintended and unforeseen consequences of ignoring the limits of our knowledge, limits easily neglected, limits not readily seen.

All three emphasize the unseen and therefore unknown and/or unappreciated; all three emphasize ignorance as a limit upon effective—intended and foreseeable—action. All three obscure the element of persuasion in their argument or that their theories are not meant to be objective descriptions of reality, insofar as that is possible.

All three tend to downplay any putative adverse consequences of the changes they would bring about—and are, therefore, selective in the use of their analyses. All three obscure the decision process as to why some aspects are subject to or demand change and others do not.

A principal objective of all three is to influence policy, action and the belief system on which policy and action rest; all three wish to influence what is seen and what is not seen.

The principal conclusions

1   The first conclusion is that the principle of unintended and unforeseen consequences is, as far as it goes, a powerful tool of inquiry. We shall return to this.

2   The second conclusion is the deliberative manufacture of belief. Argyll and Godkin make it abundantly clear that the process of political mobilization and manipulation is undertaken by the selective articulation of beliefs that hopefully, in the minds of their progenitors and users, will influence policy. The immediate objective thereof is the manipulation of what is seen and unseen. The manufacture and deployment of belief takes place under conditions of "the silence and the secrecy in which it works" (Argyll 1893: 465).[21] This second conclusion is at least as wide ranging as the first conclusion. For all practical and analytical purposes, each is ubiquitous.

This conclusion is central to the broader work of Vilfredo Pareto (Samuels 1974), who identified the creation and deployment of pseudo-knowledge as means to selectively manipulate political psychology and policy. On the one hand, we suggest that this work of Pareto's, while it has not been suppressed, has been ignored because it would serve to identify political babble as manufactured belief for those purposes. Such is, or would be, itself an example of the practice of this principle of manipulating what is seen and unseen. On the other hand, we suggest the possibility that Hayek adopted his principle of unintended and unforeseen consequences—from Adam Smith, Adam Ferguson, and Carl Menger, among others—in order to manipulate political psychology and policy.

Godkin, Argyll and Hayek were active in the intended manufacture of belief and thereby of what is seen and unseen.[22] Of the three, Hayek undoubtedly has, and will have, the greatest reputation. While important, the principle of unintended and unforeseen consequences, so deeply associated with him, is not more important than the manufacture of belief and thereby of what is seen and unseen.

The manufacture of belief is intended in part to influence policy directly but also, and perhaps in large part, to frame the decision-making process in which policy decision making takes place. Policy then depends on how information, including pseudo-information and the selective provision of information, frames decision making, how decision making is framed relative to citizens' emotions. Certain characteristics of product markets are present in political markets, such as, lying, which directly influences framing and also increases the cost of information, framing per se, leveraging the existence, scope and value of trust, and similarly with deference due to status (the deepest and perhaps most contentious conflicts being those which involve, or are thought to involve, changes in the power and status structures of society) (see, for example, Keep 2003: 349–50; see also: 344, 346).

3   The third conclusion is that the manufacture and deployment of belief is inevitable. For example, there is a tendency—promulgated and deployed by many people who are ostensibly antagonistic to government and law—to affirm something akin to, let the market do it. But no unique market exists, only those formed

and operated through by institutions. Ronald Coase is hardly a radical economist as that term is conventionally used. In his theory of the firm, for example, he argues that while the idea of coordination by the pricing system "has been a towering intellectual achievement and has enduring value,... it is an economics with blinders and has had the unfortunate effect of diverting attention from some very important features of the economic system" (Coase 2004: 205)—one of which is that institutions matter. Ironically, George Stigler's formulation of Coase's theory of social cost, under unrealistic assumptions, argues that the assignment of rights is irrelevant to resource allocation (the so-called Coase Theorem). It has become an example of the selective manufacture and deployment of belief for purposes of influencing policy. Moreover, in Coase's model it is both government and firms that drive the market; to let the market do it, is to give effect to certain uses of government and of firms.

4   The fourth conclusion is that inasmuch as some or much local and/or tacit "knowledge" is manufactured, one cannot a priori, perhaps not even expost, say much conclusively about the operation of the principle of unintended and unforeseen consequences. Much of what people believe is neither accurate, nor complete, nor unmixed with error, nor unaffected by the unseen; much is also a matter of wishful thinking. People will act on pseudo-knowledge; solid knowledge may be acted upon differently by different people. Just what that means may be an open question. It may signify the importance of the principle of unintended and unforeseen consequences. For example, let a political candidate induce voters to believe $z = y$. The candidate wins. The candidate pushes an agenda obfuscated in the campaign. This is unforeseen and perhaps unintended by the voters. It is foreseen and intended by the candidate. Whether or not $z = y$ becomes irrelevant, it has done its job.

5   That which people accept as belief is the fifth principle. What they see is, in part, a function of a variable, lexicographic filtration system, and hence manipulable. Consonance of a belief with some other belief is the condition of surviving the sieve serving the filtration function. Patriotic citizens, for example, typically accept what their military does. But if something done by the military conflicts with another belief, or with a particular desired outcome, the military will be diminished in stature so long as the conflict is salient. Another example: opposition to government deficits, which amount to increases in the national debt, resonates well with notions of fiscal responsibility. It can serve as a means of limiting government spending. Such concern about deficits, however, may not survive the adoption of other political policies, such as tax cuts providing "relief" for favored groups or the pursuit of military action abroad. Such concerns and beliefs are the object of manipulation for purposes of political mobilization.

6   The sixth conclusion is that a general model of *ignorance* can be created on the basis of the work of Argyll, Godkin, and Hayek. We will return to this conclusion below.

Initial commentary

The principle of unintended and unforeseen consequences is, indeed, as far as it goes, a powerful tool of inquiry. The principle, however, has limits. One type of limit is internal to the use of the principle. The consequences may actually have been intended and foreseen by at least some people; the consequences may be interpreted as negative or positive, bad or good, only on the basis of additional normative premises, with different people supplying these additional premises. One aspect thereof is the need to distinguish between the principle as a tool of positive inquiry and as a means of normative policy. Another aspect is that its use as a means of normative policy is always selective. For example, it is deployed against policies and other developments opposed by the user but not against policies and other developments favored by the user. Argyll provides numerous examples of this type of limit.

A second type of limit is external to the principle; it relates to the larger domain of what below will be called the model of ignorance, of which the principle of unintended and unforeseen consequences is but one of many elements. In particular, this larger domain is the structure of things seen and unseen.

A third type of limit pertains to the use of the principle of unintended and unforeseen consequences in combination with an *explanation* of putatively unintended and unforeseen consequences. Phenomena being typically the result of numerous causes, the attribution of (unintended and unforeseen) consequences to one cause begs the relevance of other causes. Each attribution leads to different bundles of things seen and unseen. An explanation omitting certain known variables renders them unseen and irrelevant, and policies based thereon likely to have further unforeseen and unintended consequences. If it is not known that certain variables pertain, decision making will have type I errors of erroneous exclusion, and type II errors of erroneous inclusion, and parallel errors due to policies based thereon. The principle of unintended and unforeseen consequences is one principle in a general model of ignorance, but the principle itself is both a consequence and a cause of ignorance.

In the socialist-calculation debate, Hayek's argument was the impossibility of (rational, fully informed) central planning. The reason for such impossibility was the absence of a price system as a mode of bringing local knowledge to bear in plan construction and execution. In his later work, Hayek extended the basic reasoning to a vaster domain, the entire economy and the entirety of government action even in a market economy and democratic polity.

Three kinds of local knowledge are involved: one consists of the preferences of local persons. These are likely to conflict, entailing the necessity of choice by the central planner or decision maker. The key issue is whose preferences/interests are to count and/or are inevitable, and why. The second consists of manufactured beliefs, the value of which to central planners is uncertain and perhaps, if not likely, dangerous. These beliefs are also likely to conflict, again entailing the necessity of choice by the central planner or decision maker. The third consists of the objective knowledge held by local persons; the knowledge necessary for effective if not also efficient production, and hence rational pricing, that is, especially of costs. The key issue is the extension of this consideration in light of problematicity of all cost calculations in market economy: cost as price-structure specific, hence power-structure specific in a market economy. The major problem in a planned system is the absence of the discipline of the market but that discipline is a function of the definition and assignment of rights, as to whose preferences and other knowledge are to count. Apropos of all three types of local knowledge, each is comprised of what is actually known and of beliefs that are actually false or incomplete, in part due to the allocation of resources to the manufacture of belief.

Apropos of the situation that local and tacit knowledge is not knowable by central decision makers or planners, such that central legal authority cannot take advantage of what it cannot do without, namely, local knowledge: majorities and minorities in power conventionally disregard the preferences of opponents; achieving power has that as its goal. The obfuscation and saccharine treatment of the preferences actually motivating policy tend to generate pseudo-knowledge. There is also what central decision makers or planners do not seek to know. If asked or examined, they might acquire local knowledge, but they choose not to—because of protected interests, ignorance of possible differences across localities, lack of interest in a locality. This type of ignorance is often prevalent in development projects in less developed countries—designed by international groups or organizations or other countries, the projects fail to realize goals because of a lack of local information that was not sought in the initial planning stages. It is also found in developed countries when decision makers select program beneficiaries, either because the information was not sought or it was known, or known of, but disregarded.

Particular emphasis should be placed on the proposition that the principle of unintended and unforeseen consequences itself is a mode of social control. This is especially salient when adverse consequences are emphasized over beneficial ones, and when the principle is otherwise selectively applied to policies not favored by the user but not to policies favored.

Hayek's principles of spontaneous order and of unintended and unforeseen consequences are parts of a general model of ignorance. Insofar as Hayek's work involves a combination of deliberative and non-deliberative decision making, Warren Samuels has shown that they do not apply to different institutions but operate interactively in the development of all institutions, given, hypothetically, their organic, spontaneous, non-deliberative origin—something that is not necessarily the case (Samuels 1999).

Toward a general model of ignorance

A general model of ignorance should structure what we know about, and make sense of, ignorance—its nature, its origins, its consequences, how and why people react to and generate ignorance, the recursive nature of the foregoing, and how the meaning of any proposition or principle regarding ignorance is a function of the entire model of ignorance. A general model of ignorance should, therefore, make sense of, and render seen, that which is seen and unseen in social, political and economic affairs.

The key questions to which a model of ignorance relates include the following:

What determines what we know that is false and what we do not know that is true—truth and falsity having to do with descriptive accuracy and/or correct explanation?

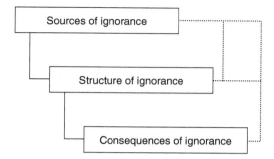

Figure 13.1 Theory of ignorance.

What determines the creation and distribution of ignorance?

If ignorance pertains to what we do not know but is in principle knowable, plus, what we think we know but is unknowable, what is the relation thereof to systems of beliefs?

How can ignorance be reflected in both what we see and what we do not see?

The economy is a world of ignorance. Ignorance is a matter of both not knowing what is knowable and knowing what is not so, that is, what one thinks one knows but does not. Therefore, ignorance is a matter of things seen and unseen: of things seen that are true and that are false or illusory; and of things not seen that are true. Ignorance limits and channels action. How society, subgroups and individuals respond to ignorance constitutes part of the domain of social control. The principle of unintended and unforeseen consequences indicates that ignorance is both a cause and a consequence of ignorance. Ignorance is both an independent variable—a result of forces outside of our control and action—and a dependent variable—a result of our own (or inactivity).

The principle of unintended and unforeseen consequences is, as far as it goes, a powerful tool of inquiry. To accomplish what? Describe "reality" objectively? Manipulate the description of reality? While sources determine structure, which in turn determine the consequences of ignorance, much interdependency exists as the consequences of ignorance may determine the source(s) of ignorance in the next period, as shown in Figure 13.1.

The sources of ignorance

The sources of ignorance found in Argyll and Godkin are listed in Table 13.1.

One source of ignorance is radical indeterminacy: we cannot know the future until we have so acted to produce the future. This may be designated profound ignorance.

Simple ignorance also exists. It is formed when the true history is not known for whatever reason, when only part of the truth is seen, when current practices are unknown, and when "history" is produced by special pleaders or those with a particular agenda.

Table 13.1 Sources of ignorance

---

1. Radical indeterminacy: that the future cannot be known until it has been created.
2. Simple ignorance or ignorance of the knowable, including:
   - True history simply not known, for whatever reason;
   - Seeing only part of the truth;
   - Ignorance of current practice;
   - History produced by special pleaders.
3. Knowing what is not so, but thought so nonetheless; what one thinks one knows, but is wrong.
4. Belief in one interpretation but without conclusive justification *vis-à-vis* other interpretations.
5. Philosophies that enable substitution of *ought* for *is*, thereby obfuscating the policy/socially created nature of institutions.
6. Selective perception, including:
   - Attitudes toward risk aversion *vis-à-vis* risk assumption;
   - Selective use of subsidiary principles, for example, conflicts in applying pro-continuity principles against government actions that one opposes and ignoring them apropos of government action one favors.
7. Selective manufacture of belief, including false and/or incomplete knowledge; manipulation of what is seen and not seen; creation of beliefs masquerading as actual definitions of reality.
8. Obfuscating definitions.
9. Asymmetrical capacity to manufacture belief, that is, generate ignorance.
10. Fads.
11. Unseen causes: policy maker and policy analyst tend to focus on proximate considerations; deeper and structural causes are unknown, ignored and/or neglected, and thus remain unseen.

A corollary source is fads, knowledge of which has transitory significance or is wrong.

Still another, and related, source of ignorance is selective perception of the object of knowledge including attitudes of risk aversion versus risk assumptions, and the selective use of subsidiary principles, for example, conflicts in applying pro-continuity principles against government actions that one opposes and ignoring them apropos of government action that one favors.

Another, and again related, source of ignorance is the selective manufacture of belief, including the creation and/or deployment of false and/or incomplete knowledge—of part, but not all, of what is true, and of what is not true but is pretended to be true. The unseen here is made so by deliberate contrivance of language and meaning. The fact of being unseen may be made evidence of a foundation of society—or the result of policy, that is, of deliberate formulation and manipulation.

The selective manufacturing of beliefs is an activity seeking to define the seen and unseen in a manner to advance agent interests. Such activity renders unseen and nugatory whose interests, favorable to particular agents, are both foreseen and intended.

The structure of ignorance: the form which ignorance takes

Manipulators of systems of belief seek to create particular definitions of reality in order to influence behavior and policy. One mode of defining reality, that is, one mode of engendering the seen and the unseen, is the use of absolutist formulations, including the definitions of words that ostensibly remove the matter in question from any possibility of human policy. These formulations create a sense of false necessity. Such formulations are typically given the cachet of determinism, natural law, and soundness of definition. The deliberative attempt to manipulate definitions conflicts with the assertion that language is not only an automatic expression of reality but develops spontaneously and non-deliberatively. Such an approach would remove the issue from the world of "ought" and locate it in the world of "is" and not a matter of human social construction and policy.

An alternative approach to manipulating definitions of reality in order to influence behavior and policy is to propose, perhaps as a definition of reality, a particular philosophy, such as libertarianism, that both posits a particular "ought" and obfuscates the ubiquity and importance of government policy and the policy nature of law. The claim of this approach subtly mixes both (1) the affirmation of the philosophy as an "is" (part of reality) and (2) the affirmation of the philosophy's "ought." Two problems typically emerge: one is conflict among the heterogeneous formulations of the philosophy, for example, conservatism and liberalism. The other is conflict between principles generally affirming continuity and those affirming the continuity of particular institutions and similarly with regard to principles concerned with change. (Selectivity enters when it is recognized that no one desires either to retain or to change everything in the status quo, and that the status quo can be defined differently.)

The limitations of an explanation that omits certain known variables include rendering them unseen and irrelevant. Policies based on such an explanation are likely to have further unforeseen and unintended consequences. If it is not known that certain, omitted variables pertain, type I errors of erroneous exclusion may result; type II errors of erroneous inclusion may result. Further, parallel errors due to policies based on erroneous exclusion and/or erroneous inclusion may result. The overall consequence is varying bundles of things seen and unseen

The role of government policy relieving distress is likely to be seen; the role of other government policy causing the distress is unlikely to be unseen. If distress is inevitable, why is it unforeseen? If the distress and its cause is known by one person, why is it not known by others? The governmental causes of progress are not likely to be seen by beneficiaries, though likely to have been intended and foreseen by some in government; the progress is more likely to be attributed to personal and ideologically honorific causes. One aspect of the principle of unseen causes has the policy maker and policy analyst tending to focus on proximate and therefore more salient considerations and explanations. Deeper and structural considerations are much less salient and therefore are unknown, ignored, and/or neglected and thus remain unseen.

One principle pertaining to ignorance is that of unintended and unforeseen consequences; that is, one consequence of ignorance is the unintended and unforeseen consequences of action and choosing.

The principle of unintended and unforeseen consequences does not operate in a vacuum, however. It especially operates in the context of the competition over the manufacture of belief, with its type I and type II errors and corresponding errors of policy. The actions generating unintended and unforeseen consequences are themselves a matter of selection in that competition; hence, the specific consequences will be in part selection-specific, that is, what is seen and what is unseen, and in part a function of factors and forces external to the process. Indeed, the entire model of ignorance influences how the principle of unintended and unforeseen consequences plays out. This especially includes selective perception of beneficial and of harmful consequences, the selective and subjective nature of benefits and harm, their weightings, and that for some people the consequences will be foreseen and intended.

Some causes of consequences are unseen and easily neglected. Some causes are unseen and unappreciated. Some causes are natural conditions, others are matters of custom and legal policy. The causes producing consequences are usually multiple and mutually reinforce or counter each other.

The result of the process of competition is varying bundles of things seen and unseen.

To precisely whom the consequences are unintended and unforeseen as opposed to intended and foreseen is a key question, dependent on such variables as whose interests are brought to bear, the asymmetrical distribution of ignorance, the process of competition among manufacturers and purveyors of false and/or partial belief.

Some agents invoke the role of the unseen, then criticize others for what they cannot and/or do not know, and thereby seek to take rhetorical and material advantage thereof.

Selective perception in the form of attitudes of risk aversion versus risk assumption, influences people's definition of reality and therefore what is seen and not seen.

Selection perception arises in and from the selective use of subsidiary principles.

Information, or knowledge, like ignorance, is asymmetrically distributed. The ability to generate, and interest in generating desirable definitions of reality, that is, what is seen and unseen, and by whom, hence the distribution of ignorance, is also asymmetrically distributed. People are asymmetrically situated with regard to their interest in and ability to influence the manufacture of belief, including biased and false knowledge.

Corporations generate vast unintended and unforeseen consequences; however, the issue remains whether the consequences are in fact unintended or unforeseen, for example, decisions that shift costs to others, decisions that inevitably affect others. In general, the stated objectives of a governmental or corporate policy may not be the intended objective; what seems to be unintended and unforeseen consequences are very much intended and foreseen, but masked.

Table 13.2 Structure of ignorance—the form which ignorance takes

1. Limits to knowledge, due to complex phenomena and diffusion of knowledge.
2. Asymmetrical distribution of ignorance.
3. So much for which no evidence is provided, only claimed.
4. Local and tacit knowledge not knowable by central decision makers or planners.
5. Exercise of manifest *vis-à-vis* latent function.
6. Manufacture of belief, including:

   - False knowledge;
   - Competition among manufacturers of belief;
   - Deliberative formulation and manipulation;
   - Pseudo-knowledge, intended to mobilize and manipulate political psychology.

7. Creation of particular definitions of reality to influence behavior and policy.
8. Deliberative approach conflicts with assertion that language is automatic expression of reality, that is, deliberative over non-deliberative decision-making.
9. Conflict among heterogeneous formulations of conservatism and the application of principles of continuity versus change to particular institutions.
10. Philosophies that obfuscate ubiquity and importance of government, policy nature of law; hence different bundles of things seen and unseen.
11. Claims of harmony in the face of evident conflict.
12. The unseen as what is obfuscated by special pleaders' stories and explanation of the past.
13. The unseen as what is obfuscated by the role of opinion in the presentation and interpretation of historical facts.
14. The unseen as due to obfuscation by heat of controversy.
15. The unseen past due to misrepresentation in the service of patriotism, intentional or unintentional.
16. The unseen past due to misrepresentation in the service of religion, intentional or unintentional.

The use of the principle of unintended and unforeseen consequences creates a paradox: the spread of information coupled with the articulation of the principle, renders the hitherto unseen now seen—with unintended and unforeseen consequences.

Obfuscation of what is going on in the chain of causes producing unintended and unforeseen consequences may render some causes invisible, hence unseen. This may be intentional (at least by some people) and foreseen, or may be unintentional and unforeseen.

The foregoing may or may not constitute an evolution argument more or less like that of Argyll. Some people may feel that if something evolved, it neither needs to be nor should be changed. But change is generated by the various processes, hence the principle of unintended and unforeseen consequences and its corollary the principle of intended and foreseen consequences. A summary of the structure of ignorance is found in Table 13.2.

The consequences of ignorance

Consequences result from deliberative and nondeliberative behavior and choice. Behavior and choice may be coupled with pretence to the contrary.

What is unseen here can be made so by deliberative contrivance of language and meaning. The fact of being unseen is made to serve as evidence of a foundation of society—but may actually be a result of policy and choice. The principle of unintended and unforeseen consequences is here a corollary of foreseen and intended consequences, coupled with pretence to the contrary. The principle of unintended and unforeseen consequences is thus a part of the process it is putatively used to describe. Instead of the principle being one of

Table 13.3 Consequences of ignorance

1. Ignorance as a limit to action.
2. Opportunity to manufacture belief and pseudo-knowledge.
3. The role of government in relieving distress is seen, as are also its putatively unintended and unforeseen consequences; but the role of government in causing the initial distress is unseen.
4. The principle of unintended and unforeseen consequences, including the selective applicability of principle to (a) central governments, (b) individuals, (c) corporations and other sub-groups.
5. Issue whether consequences are in fact unintended or unforeseen.
6. Stated objectives of a policy may not be the intended objective; what seems to be unintended and unforeseen consequences are very much intended and foreseen, but masked.
7. Principle is both consequence and cause of ignorance:
   - The principle itself is a mode of social control;
   - The principle itself can be applied to its (selective) use;
   - Applying Hayekian argument only to central government leaves other players in ignorance game/market relatively free to manipulate content and distribution of ignorance; principle is itself a factor.
8. Complexly produced ignorance: causes of unintended and unforeseen consequences operating at a distance or through a long chain of effects.
9. Adoption of ignorant legislation; neglect of natural law.
10. Influence of past policies: comparatively invisible versus comparatively visible results and so on.
11. Surviving old customs operating under new conditions, with effects apt to be confounded with others.
12. Different effects of policy depending on conditions.
13. Isolation due to geographical position and consequent insulation.
14. Resource endowments' consequences.
15. Adoption of dysfunctional customs and practices.
16. Use of limited models with their "comparatively contracted circuit of ideas"—an artificial world.
17. Principle of unintended and unforeseen consequences.
18. Selective applicability to beneficial and to harmful results: Subjective nature of benefits and harm, and of comparison, weights.
19. Paradox of spread of information coupled with articulation of principle of unintended and unforeseen consequences, rendering hitherto unseen now seen.
20. What is unseen here is made so by deliberate contrivance of language and meaning; fact of being unseen is made evidence of a foundation of society—but a result of policy.
21. Principle of unintended and unforeseen consequences is corollary of foreseen and intended consequences, coupled with pretence to the contrary.
22. Instead of principle being one of description and/or explanation and/or admonition, it is selectively deployed as a principle of policy.

description and/or explanation (and/or admonition), it is selectively deployed as a principle of policy. The principle of unintended consequences is thus a consequence but also a cause of ignorance. The consequences of ignorance are listed in Table 13.3.

We have shown three things: (1) that the ideas of the eighth Duke of Argyll and of Edwin L. Godkin are both relevant and precursors to the foregoing principles of Hayek, especially the latter; (2) that in their writings additional themes pertaining to ignorance are present which go beyond Hayek; and (3) that a general model of ignorance can be formed utilizing the contributions of all three men.

Argyll and Godkin, of course, did not write with Hayek in mind. Their arguments, however, contain themes readily comprising elements of a general model of ignorance. We need only stay close to what they said. No stretching of argument is required, only sensitivity to what they argued and how they went about it. One result is that their overall treatment of ignorance—the theory of ignorance we can discern in and construct from what they wrote—is arguably more complex and more suggestive than Hayek's. That is not necessarily to judge that theory of ignorance more highly than Hayek's deployment of the principles of unintended and unforeseen consequences and of spontaneous order: his times were different from theirs. It does suggest that there is arguably more going on in the larger domain in which the two principles operate than may appear at first, or even second, glance in connection with Hayek's use of them. In particular, if ignorance is contrived, locally and at the center, then Hayek's arguments have constrained meaning and applicability. Such is not intended here to be a rebuttal to his socialist calculation argument, though it is relevant thereto; the purpose here, however, is to establish that the domain and processes of ignorance are deeper and wider than those dealt with by Hayek in his two principles.

The tendency of anyone reading either a polemical exposition of arguments or a deconstruction or interpretation of those arguments is to reach a judgment as to the truth value of the arguments. Which arguments do we accept and which do we reject? We suggest here that for present purposes the truth value of an argument must be distinguished from two other values. One value is the instrumental rhetorical role intended by their promulgator(s) in order to achieve certain purposes with regard to policy. The other value is the ability to distill from the array of arguments a general model of the subject to which they relate, here a general model of ignorance. It is with regard to ignorance that the arguments are made, willy nilly; the authors are issuing statements implicitly constituting positions on subjects comprising a model of ignorance. Whether the arguments represent truth or are only proffered statements of putative belief, the subjects to which they pertain have to do with, or have meaning for, a general model of ignorance.

As an aside for some readers and as an important point for other readers, the present interpretations of Argyll and Godkin are consistent with the argument formulated by Vilfredo Pareto in his sociological analysis. A very brief summary of his much more complex analysis, expressed in modern terms, runs like this: Policy is a function of what people consider to be knowledge, even if some, perhaps much, is pseudo-knowledge. The influence of putative knowledge on them is a function of their psychic states. These psychic states are the object of mutual manipulation by power players. The manipulation typically takes the form of bringing into play certain beliefs, which may be knowledge or pseudo-knowledge, and which function to support or weaken one or another policy position. Overall, policy is a function of three sets of variables: knowledge, psychology and power, each of which influences the others; especially, action is manipulated by power players who attempt to mobilize and motivate political psychology through deploying and manipulating beliefs (Samuels 1974). These ideas are uncomfortable because they conflict with several modern preconceptions and lines of wishful thinking, such as belief in the importance of truth and the denigration of manipulation of belief in a putatively free society. Be that as it may, it is somewhat common today to distinguish the intended or achieved rhetorical role from the truth value of statements and both from the use of statements to intuit a general model of the subject on which the statements take positions and have meaning. As for the concept of a free society, some people understand it in terms of freedom from manipulation while other see it in terms of freedom to manipulate.

Hayek's relevant analyses, considered as positive propositions, are three: the principle of unintended and unforeseen consequences, the principle of spontaneous order, and the importance of the rule of law. These three propositions are very important. However, they neither exhaust the theory of ignorance nor do they constitute conclusive solutions to the problems to which they are usually applied.

The principle of unintended and unforeseen consequences has several limitations. First, whether the consequences are deemed negative or positive is subjective. Second, the distinction between and roles of manifest and latent function is an example of privately intended and foreseen. (Argyll seems to recognize that this is a possibility, but provides no solution. See his discussion on Protectionism, Argyll 1877: 65–6.)

The principle of spontaneous order has two relevant limitations. One is the subjective nature of "order." It is essentially a primitive, undefined term, in which case the meaning is that supplied by readers or auditors, and is subject to selective perception and also bias. When defined, it is likely to be incompletely or narrowly defined. The second limitation concerns its emphasis on non-deliberative over deliberative decision making. Applied, as it usually is, to institutions, every institution manifests both types of decision making, and not two different types of institutions. Key to this view is Carl Menger's recognition that even institutions which arise non-deliberately must be and are subjected each generation to critique in order to revise when deemed desirably or necessary.

The principle of the rule of law is often deemed Hayek's solution to the inconclusiveness of the foregoing two principles. The concept of the rule of law is usually deployed in opposition to politics and some notion of arbitrariness. The limitations to the rule of law are several: first, while the rule of law is elevated over politics, politics influences, even dictates, the meaning and application of the rule of law. (For example, some envisioned President Bill Clinton's impeachment as mandated by his perjury in a deposition whereas others interpreted the impeachment as itself an exercise of politics.) The rule of law is largely a myth; law involves choice and therefore is politics. Second, the idea of the rule of law forms a civic religion (metaphysics) and is a mode of discourse, in both respects serving as social control. (See Samuels 2002.)

All three principles are part of the larger model of ignorance, including its creation and distribution. Hayek has another pair of solutions, each of which accepts its inconclusive application. These solutions are, first, composite choice, decision making and results; and second, pattern models.

Argyll and Godkin

Argyll and Godkin intended to express a point of view. Both, perhaps especially Argyll, favored a hierarchic society. This they expressed in no uncertain terms, though in terms they hoped made their position saccharine and thereby palatable. Argyll went more out of his way to obfuscate the hierarchic premises of his views. Godkin was more sympathetic to democracy, at least the male-franchise version of it, but was also more explicitly critical of the forms through which it had come to operate.

Both men were consciously and actively engaged in manufacturing what they hoped their readers would see and not see. Each was selective.

Both men also engaged in ontological construction. When they write of the protection of life and property and of natural political leaders, they are, with the exception of life, reifying the systems of property and of political leadership (which may be the same) so as to give them an independent ontological status; whereas in fact they are socially constructed and continually reconstructed. The seen and the unseen are not givens; they too are constructed, deliberatively and nondeliberatively.

Adam Smith treated each of his stages of history as predicated upon its own system of government and law; and while he saw tensions as one stage morphed into the next stage, he felt no need to justify both; his task was almost purely descriptive (almost purely: he did laud the commercial stage, though without denigrating the previous ones). Argyll treats both the situation of aggression and the situation after one aggressor succeeds in achieving hegemony each on their own terms but is motivated by a need to justify each. This is, one surmises, because aggression was the source of his social position and political and economic power as a landlord and because settled hegemony was now in his interest. It is as if the morality of giants thrashing the pygmies is succeeded by the morality of the reign of giants, to induce acquiescence by later pygmies, with no evident sense of contradiction. Morality is thus the servant of power, although, as Frank Knight put it, religion may be the opiate of the masses but it is also the sedative of the (upper) classes. Our point is different: Both systems of morality, and of patriotism, too, engender their respective definitions of reality and thereby of what is seen and unseen.

Further commentary

The materials covered in this study suggest and help identify certain confluent topics which form the axial framework of relevant ideas and policy positions. Among these topics are: (1) People have different general psychological postures toward the world, each person's individual psychological posture being some combination of two seemingly incongruent elements: (a) need for determinacy and closure and (b) tolerance of ambiguity and open-endedness. (2) Individuals confront, willy nilly, the problem of order, each person having some combination of general positions and specific attachments with regard to the components of the problem of order: (a) freedom versus control, (b) continuity versus change, (c) hierarchy versus egalitarianism, and (d) the relation of idealized formulation of the status quo to the actual status quo. (3) Individuals may or may not meaningfully identify the core systems of belief which distinguish different particular socio-economic systems. (4) Individuals, willy nilly, make sense of the mixture of deliberative and nondeliberative decision making found in either actual or idealized status quo systems, assuming, for example, that all institutions (however defined) and all systems (ditto) are combinations of both, rather than examples of one or the other. *Inter alia*, the individual also can distinguish positions on the basis of the individual's (5) views on the nature and source of social progress and of social problems, and (6) views on the distribution of benefits and sacrifice in society. All that is in addition to (7) different views on the nature and significance of ignorance in society.

In the kaleidoscopic and selectively perceived world formed by these topics, the meaning of such terms as conservative, liberal, culture, human nature, individualism, social control and so on, is diverse and reminiscent of the story of the Tower of Babel. One approach to making sense of all that is to differentiate individual positions on the combined topics in terms of (a) absolutely required fundamentals and (b) elements that are flexible and discretionary, say, so long as they do not compromise fundamentals.

One characteristic of most if not all attempts to identify particular systems is a focus on the key core structural component presumed to operate at the most fundamental level. (1) In the systems of feudal and post-feudal agriculture, the key structural component is the landed aristocracy and gentry who somehow together manage the system and control and manipulate the human labor force. (2) In the systems of technologically advanced capital-using manufacture, the key structural component is the saving-investment elite whose decisions somehow together drive and operate the system and control and manipulate the human labor force. Both (a) conventional Western capitalism and (b) the central planning system of the former Soviet Union belong in the second category, however otherwise differentiable. The saving-investment elite includes, in capitalism, households in the upper income brackets who provide society's net saving and managers of firms who invest funds both internally saved and acquired, in various ways, from outsiders who have saving. In both (1) and (2) and in both (a) and (b), the importance of the key structural component is central to the self-perception of the individuals involved, whether the individual is a lord of the land, a manager of a firm, or a director of central planning.

A characteristic of most if not all positions or theories of collective decision making (deliberative *vis-à-vis* nondeliberative) is their varied formulation. Two examples will suffice: Hayek lauds nondeliberative decision making and is wary of intellectuals who have plans to save the world by changing it through their proposed government policies. Yet Hayek has his own agenda for what government should and should not do in order to save the world. Milton Friedman has a differently oriented but effectively similar approach to the economic role of government. He supports cutting taxes (seemingly under any circumstances and for any excuse, for any reason, whenever it's possible) and constitutional limits on raising taxes, in order to hold down government spending; privatizing social security; a flat income tax; decriminalization of recreational drugs; school vouchers; and so on. He minimizes short run individual (working class) sacrifices in favor of long run gains in output. He opposes special legislation for labor standards and environmental protection, labor unions and government-sponsored cartels. He opposes progressive taxation in general and high levels of taxation on the rich because they "provide the funds, the capital, and the entrepreneurship for the new industries" (Friedman 2004).

Both Hayek and Friedman, in the face of their deliberative policy activism, cannot be distinguished from their opposite numbers, called liberals in the US. So much for Hayek's cautionary tale of spontaneous order being preferable to deliberative decision making subject to the negative results of the principle of unintended and unforeseen consequences and for his not-so-often voiced but nonetheless held hierarchism. Similarly with Friedman.

That feudalism and post-feudalism with their landed-property elite have been replaced by sundry forms of capitalism with their non-landed and landed property elites is evidence of the continued hold of hierarchy in society. The modern economy, accordingly, has variants of its ideology and belief system as well as its more-or-less objective reality. Individualism derives from the basic self-perception of modern society—facilitated by political democracy, institutional pluralism, and, possibly, somewhat greater economic equality. Managerialism derives from the concentration of decision-making power in the hands of corporate managers. The first part of this chapter commenced with attention to the heterogeneity of conservatism. Perhaps its newest branch is managerialism, though forms of managerialist thinking have been around for over a century.

The reader, in considering the preceding six paragraphs, is invited to consider the implications thereof for what is seen and not seen, and the origins and uses thereof; the principle of unintended and unforeseen consequences, and the origins and uses thereof; the principle of spontaneous order, and the origins and uses thereof; and, *inter alia*, the role of latent and manifest function, and the origins and uses thereof;—all in a hierarchical world. We suggest that

Argyll and Godkin's ideas and implicit theoretical system predicated on ignorance, considered as positive analysis, remain important and, because they are broader, are likely more informative than Hayek's. Their respective normative analyses we leave to the reader. We do urge that one distinction be kept in mind, that between (1) the positive identification and analysis of (a) a belief system and (b) a system of the unseen, and (2) the normative acceptance or rejection of (a) and/or (b).[23]

The foregoing implies that applying Hayekian argument only to the central government leaves other players in the ignorance game/market relatively free to manipulate content and distribution of ignorance.

One final dimension of seen and unseen remains. A recent study of the rhetoric of Winston Churchill's military histories includes the statement, "The signal feature of Churchill's histories is the way they maintain an aristocratic perspective in democratic times without losing their democratic sympathies" (Valiunas 2002: 2; quoted in Teagarden 2004). How can our present subjects be characterized along these lines? Argyll maintains an aristocratic perspective in a period of transformation from aristocratic to democratic structures and does so with evident relish but without either the evident harshness or antagonism found in other defenders of hierarchy or strong democratic sympathies. Godkin is rather like Churchill, or Valiunas's view of him, in maintaining an aristocratic perspective in democratic times without losing his democratic sympathies. Hayek seems to have done likewise. Godkin, Argyll, and Hayek want to change the structure of society, system of governance, path of societal development, and set of dominant policies, though not along the same lines. The doctrines of each of them render certain beliefs not only seen but salient and other beliefs not only unseen but obfuscated. The elements of only two of the three are dealt with extensively here but each of them provided, in effect, a wide-ranging theory of ignorance in society.

Notes

1 The Isa Upanishad is the last of forty chapters of the Vajasaneyi Saamhita, a holy book of the Vajasaneyi school of Hinduism. It teaches the essential unity·of God and the world, that God is all-pervasive and controls all.
2 Hayek is not the only major author to develop the principle either normatively or analytically; he himself claims to follow Adam Smith, Adam Ferguson and, *inter alia*, Carl Menger. See also the writings of Edmund Burke, Joseph de Maistre, Michael Oakeshott, and others. For a variety of recent approaches, see Boudon (1982), Dahrendorf (2000), Gillon (2000), Gutzman (2002), and Tenner (1996). A treatment of the principle in the form of a novel is Ross (1996).
3 Argyll writes that he has "never been, in anything like complete sympathy with what has been called the 'Manchester school'." He singles out "the narrow and erroneous teaching of Ricardo" and the "curious delusion that protectionism was the special and the evil device of land-owners," forgetting "that the trading and manufacturing classes had been the earliest, and...most vehement, supporters of protection and monopolies" (Argyll 1893a: xi).
4 M'Cready Sykes was an attorney, journalist, poet, and author.

5 Frederick Law Olmsted was a famous landscape architect, writer on slaveholding society, and advocate of state and national parks and city planning.

6 Compare John F. Kennedy's admonition in his inaugural address, "Ask not what your country can do for you. Ask what you can do for your country."

7 This is akin to the issue of omitted variable bias in econometrics: if there are variables in the error term that are related to the independent variables (x's) but not explicitly included, they can cause the estimated coefficients of the regression to be biased.

8 Another way to think about his claims might be by looking at the not-very-practical length necessary to simply define wealth—all of Chapter 3 in *His Unseen Foundations of Society*.

9 Warren Samuels knew a Southern corporate lawyer in the 1960s who provided free legal service to an African American man he employed at home; the lawyer, undoubtedly like Argyll's landowner, would be so generous only given some requisite level of deference.

10 That is, maximizing now though not hitherto.

11 Argyll seems to use this as foil to introduce that in which he does not necessarily believe.

12 While Argyll adopts the survival of the fittest mentality here, Argyll has problems with Darwin—objecting to his natural survival of the fittest theory (at least in the form presented by Darwin) because it lacks room for Divine intervention.

13 This was a predominant pre-World War attitude.

14 Instability or unsettledness—meaning decentralized, constant warfare, undeveloped—of the political system explains why feudal laws can be considered non-binding or changeable, compared to the laws of the current legal system. This is, however, a very complex matter. The "official" ideal of the feudal period was that of the continuity of social institutions, whereas they were typically up for grabs in the manner discussed by Argyll. But law in current legal systems is very much subject to change, inasmuch as people recognized the artifact nature of human institutions and are motivated to seek legal change as a means to their economic and other ends.

15 See Argyll's *Property in Land* (1884) in George 1884.

16 Argyll states, "Never, perhaps, have communistic theories assumed a form more curious or lent themselves to more fruitful processes of analysis than in the writings of Mr. Henry George" (*Property in Land*, 1884: 12; see also: 14).

17 The identical passages appear in *Property in Land* (1884: 10–11).

18 See also the highly similar discussion in *Property in Land* (1884: 10).

19 Perhaps this is directed at Ricardo, who earned his fortune as a financier and capitalist before settling down to landownership.

20 Argyll discusses Turgot and Turgot's unseen (ibid.: 477).

21 A relatively recent editorial in the *International Review of Financial Analysis*, entitled "Axioms—What is Seen and What is Not Seen" (Frankfurter 1994: v–vii) argues that "most of the axioms that we take for granted are self-serving," that most disturbing "are those axioms that are never stated explicitly," that these latter, the "not seen," are "the more perilous," this "because the refutation of the dogma is contingent on the validity of the unseen axioms. Since they are 'not seen', they are cloaked in taboo and, thus, not open to questioning." Argyll, in seeking to manufacture belief, clearly seeks to identify the unseen which he believes to be neglected in policy. Those which he desires to establish as important, and thereby seen, are accompanied by others which he leaves unseen.

22 The (selective) identification of the seen and the unseen is a leit motiv in the history of policy analysis and criticism. Caplan and Cowen (2004: 405) maintain that "The distinction between the seen and the unseen is one of the most important truths of economics." Manufacture of the dichotomy takes place selectively and, in part, converts the identifications into normative categories—true even when we agree with them.

A review of a book on collateral damage due to the use of Agent Orange in Vietnam is entitled "Evidence of Things Not Seen" (Hedges 2004).

23 Warren Samuels had a colleague in marketing who invited him to hear a presentation by a representative of Southern Bell. The gentleman first outlined the procedure by which they marketed/preached the company's point of view or belief system—what, in effect, they wanted the public to see—and then segued into a presentation of that belief system. The gentleman evidently believed that the first part of his presentation provided cachet for the second part. (Candor requires that Samuels acknowledge that he was for some seven or eight years the principal beneficiary of a continuing research grant, to the University of Miami School of Business, used by him for copying archival research material.)

References

Argyll, 8th Duke of (Campbell, George Douglas) (1877) *Essay on the Commercial Principles Applicable to Contracts for the Hire of Land*, London: Cassell, Petter and Galpin.
——(1893a) *The Unseen Foundations of Society*, London: John Murray.
——(1893b) *Irish Nationalism: An Appeal to History*, London: John Murray.
——(1906a) *Autobiography and Memoirs*, Dowager Duchess of Argyll (ed.) 2 vols, London: John Murray.
——(1906b) *Autobiography and Memoirs*, Dowager Duchess of Argyll (ed.) 2 vols, New York: E. P. Dutton.
Bateman, Bradley W. (2004) *Bringing in the State? The Life and Times of Laissez-Faire in the 19th Century United States*. Manuscript.
Beare, John I. (1897) "Review of Duke of Argyll The Philosophy of Belief; or, Law in Christian Theology," *International Journal of Ethics*, 7 (2) (January): 238–42.
Boudon, Raymond (1982) *The Unintended Consequences of Social Action*, London: Macmillan.
Caplan, Bryan and Tyler Cowen (2004) "Do we Underestimate the Benefits of Culture Competition?" *American Economic Review, Papers and Proceedings*, 94 (May): 402–7.
Coase, Ronald H. (2004) "Ronald H. Coase," in William Breit and Barry T. Hirsch (eds) *Lives of the Laureates*. Fourth edn, Cambridge, MA: MIT Press.
Cohen, Nancy (2002) *The Reconstruction of American Liberalism, 1865–1914*, Chapel Hill, NC: University of North Carolina Press.
Dahrendorf, Ralf (2000) *The Paradoxes of Unintended Consequences*, Budapest and New York: Central European University Press.
Dixon, Huw (1999) "Controversy: On the Use of the 'Hidden Economy' Estimates," *Economic Journal*, 109 (June): F335–7.
Ebenstein, Alan (2001) *Friedrich Hayek: A Biography*, New York: Palgrave.
Ely, Richard T. (1886) *The Labor Movement in America*, New York: T. Y. Crowell.
Frankfurter, George (1994) "Axioms—What Is Seen and What Is Not Seen," *International Review of Financial Analysis*, 3 (1): v–vii.
Friedman, Milton (2004) "An Interview with Milton Friedman," John Hawkins, interviewer, at http://www.rightwingnews.com/interviews/friedman.php, via CONSERVATIVENET @LISTSERV.UIC.EDU, received July 16.
George, Henry (1982) [1884] *The Land Question*, New York: Robert Schalkenbach Foundation.
Gillon, Steven M. (2000) *That's Not What We Meant To Do: Reform and Its Unintended Consequences*, New York: W. W. Norton.

Godkin E. L. (1898) *Unforeseen Tendencies of Democracy*, Boston, MA: Houghton, Mifflin, and Cambridge, MA: Riverside Press. Republished by Books for Libraries Press, Freeport, NY, 1971.

——(1966 [1896, 1898]) *Problems of Modern Democracy: Political and Economic Essays*, C. Scribner's Sons, New York: Republished by M. Keller (ed.) Cambridge, MA: Harvard University Press, 1966.

Gutzman, Alexis D. (2002) *Unforeseen Circumstances*, New York and London: AMACOM.

Hedges, Chris (2004) "Evidence of Things Not Seen," *The Nation* (May 24): 31–4.

Herman, Arthur (2001) *How the Scots Invented the Modern World*, New York: Three Rivers Press.

Hoover, Kenneth R. (1999) "Ideologizing Institutions: Laski, Hayek, Keynes and the Creation of Contemporary Politics," *Journal of Political Ideologies*, 4 (1): 87–115. http://www.ac.wwu.edu/~khoover/khl.html

Hutt, William Harold (1990) [1936] *Economics and the Public: A Study of Competition and Opinion*, New Brunswick, NJ: Transaction.

Keep, William (2003) "Adam Smith's Imperfect Invisible Hand: Motivations to Mislead," *Business Ethics: A European Review*, vol. 12 (October): 343–3.

Levermore, Charles H. (1907) "Life and Letters of Edwin Lawrence Godkin," in Rollo Ogden (ed.) *American Historical Review*, 13 (1) (October): 168–71, New York: Macmillan.

MacKinnon, Charles, of Dunakin (1984) *The Scottish Highlanders: A Personal View*, New York: Barnes & Noble Books.

Ross, John (1996) *Unintended Consequences*, St. Louis, MO: Accurate Press.

Samuels, Warren J. (1974) *Pareto on Policy*, Cleveland, OH: World, Amsterdam: Elsevier.

——(1996) "Joseph J. Spengler's Concept of the 'Problem of Order': A Reconsideration and Extension," in Philip Arestis (ed.) *Employment, Economic Growth and the Tyranny of the Market*, Brookfield, VT: Edward Elgar, 185–99.

——(1999) "Hayek from the Perspective of an Institutionalist Historian of Economic Thought: An Interpretive Essay," *Journal des Economistes et des Etudes Humaines*, IX (Juin–Septembre): 279–90; reprinted in Warren J. Samuels, *Economics, Governance and Law*, Northampton, MA: Edward Elgar: 81–94.

—— (2002) "The Rule of Law and the Capture and Use of Government in a World Inequality," in Warren J. Samuels, *Economics, Governance and Law*, Northampton MA: Edward Elagar: 61–79

Samuels, Warren, J., Kirk D. Johnson, and Marianne Johnson (2005) "The Duke of Argyll and Henry George: Land Ownership and Governance: An Essay in Interpretation," in John Laurent (ed.) *Henry George's Legacy in Economic Thought*, Northampton, MA: Edward Elgar, 99–147.

Schumpeter J. A. (1951) *Ten Great Economists*, New York: Oxford University Press.

Sutton F. X., Harris S., Kaysen C., and Tobin J. (1956) *The American Business Creed*, Cambridge, MA: Harvard University Press.

Taylor, Irene and Alan Taylor (eds) (2002) *The Assassin's Cloak*, Edinburgh: Canongate Books. Excerpt from Lord Henry Cockburn (1889) *Circuit Journeys*, Edinburgh: David Douglas.

Teagarden, Ernest (2004) "Review of Algis Valiunas, Churchill's Military Histories: A Rhetorical Study," Lanham, MD: Roman and Littlefield, 2002. Reviewed for H-Albion and H-Net, received August 19, 2004 from CONSERVATIVENET@LISTSERV. UIC.EDU

Tenner, Edward (1996) *Why Things Bite Back: Technology and the Revenge of Unintended Consequences*, New York: Vintage Books.

Valiunas, Algis (2002) *Churchill's Military Histories: A Rhetorical Study*, Lanham, MD: Roman and Littlefield.

Weisinger, Herbert (2003) "Renaissance Literature and Historiography," in *Dictionary of the History of Ideas*, 4: 147–52. Charlottesville, VA: Electronic Text Center, University of Virginia. WWW:CB 5.D52.2003 or http://etext.lib.virginia.edu/cgi-local/DHI/dhiana.cgi?id=dv4-21

14 The Duke of Argyll and Henry George

Land ownership and governance

With Kirk D. Johnson and Marianne Johnson

The objective of this essay is to consider, place in context, and otherwise interpret one aspect of the social and legal-economic theory of rent developed by David Ricardo and Henry George. The aspect is the crucial relationship between land ownership and the system of governance. Ricardo and George opposed in different ways and to different extents the system of land ownership and the system of governance by a landed aristocracy. The abstract issues are whose customs and whose interests will be protected, in part as private property, as the basis of both the distribution of rent and the system of governance. The issues are more than abstract. At stake is the role of a landed aristocracy, in fact if not in name, and later, the role of a propertied—landed and non-landed—aristocracy in fact if not in name. Also at stake is whether the political-economic system is a democracy *and* whether democracy is only some combination of legitimizing the status quo and/or a safety valve for a plutocracy *or* whether democracy is only the form in which Vilfredo Pareto's circulation of the elite takes place.

One means of pursuing that interpretation will be a comparison with Henry George of some of the ideas of George Douglas Campbell, the eighth Duke of Argyll. Argyll and George actively debated the nature and role of land ownership, both as they apply to the production process and as they apply to the organization of society. Their most direct and revealing exchange came in *Property in Land: A Passage-At-Arms between the Duke of Argyll and Henry George*—see George (1982) [1884].

The best-known aspect of George's theory is the Single Tax. The tax involves differential rates on unimproved and improved land. An example of serious critique is Pullen (2005). Perhaps the least-known aspects are George's moral-philosophical approach to justice in which he adhered to a belief in natural law, and his acceptance of free trade and other doctrines of the Classical economists. His radicalism in advocating the capture of socially produced rent was justified by him on conservative grounds; his other ideas were largely consonant with nineteenth-century economic conservatism (see later). Much of George's economic analysis turns on the concept of the unearned increment. The doctrine is simultaneously conservative and radical. It is radical to someone like Argyll, who emphasizes possession and that the rental income received by possessors testifies to their productivity. It is radical to someone like George, who emphasizes that land is inelastic in supply and yields increasing rent because of the growth of population and the shift of the demand for land to the right, hence unearned by the possessors, whoever they are institutionalized to be.

The economic and social theory of rent

David Ricardo—among others, including Thomas Robert Malthus and Richard Jones—developed a theory of rent in the early nineteenth century. The theory embodied the principle of diminishing returns and concluded that rent was the sum of the supra-marginal returns, its level driven by population growth *vis-à-vis* the supply of land. As population increased, resort would be made to land on the extensive and intensive margins of decreasing productivity, or at increasingly costly levels of production. Rent was equal to the sum of the differences between market price and unit cost throughout the supra-marginal levels of production. Such rent was called pure or economic rent, and eventually designated Ricardian rent. Pure rent is not what the ordinary person thinks of as rent, which typically includes a return to capital (profit) and always is a matter of the institutions governing the distribution of rent; that is, not all economic rent goes to the nominal owner of the land (Samuels 1992a).

The theory of rent stood on its own. However, its application depended on the systemic assumption with which it was combined. Malthus and others assumed a society governed by a land-owning aristocracy; their receipt of rent helped support that aristocracy. Ricardo and others assumed a commercial and industrial society governed, in substantial part, by the middle class; rent had the effect of lowering the profits, which helped support the middle class.

Several issues comprise the context within which the foregoing has meaning. The constitutional issue was the distribution of governing power between the landed aristocracy and other owners of land, on the one side, and the middle-class owners of non-landed property consisting of plant and equipment and of financial instruments such as stocks, bonds, and commercial paper, on the other side. The legislative issue was the Corn Laws, whose intended functions were, first, to maintain the level of domestic grain prices, and therefore rent, by limiting the import of grain, and, second, thereby to maintain the rental incomes of landowners. Pervading both issues was the ownership—especially in England and Scotland—of an extremely high percentage of the land by an extremely low percentage of families. Such concentration led some people to think of rent as a monopoly return.

The theory of rent postulated a given supply of land, that the return to investments in improvements of land was profit (and irrelevant to discussions of pure rent), and that the level of pure rent was driven by the demand for food, itself driven by population growth, against the supply of food grown on land—a function of the supply of land, the rate of decreasing returns, and the level of technology. In short, the theory involved a rightward moving demand-for-land function and a relatively given and inelastic supply-of-land function. One implication of the theory was that the level of rent is independent of the ownership of land.

The landowner did nothing to earn his or her rent; rent is unearned, increases in rent are unearned increments. The level of rent is a function of the growth of society, specifically a function of the growth of population. Even the cost-lowering results of improved technology would accrue to the owner of land.

A further implication was that no ontologically given or fundamental connection existed between land ownership, receipt of rent, and governance by landowners. That England and Scotland were then principally governed by rent-receiving landowners was a matter not of the economics of pure rent but of the institutions controlling the distribution of pure rent and the institutions controlling the distribution of the powers of governance.

The Whigs sought not only repeal of the Corn Laws but change in the distribution of governing power. They used the theory of rent to disparage both increases in rent levels and the unnecessary need for the rental income of landowners to finance an unnecessary and undesirable governing class. The owners of land, on the other hand, sought to maintain the status of landed property on three grounds: that landed property was their ownership protected by law, that among the interests so protected was that of receiving rent, and that another was the role of the landowners, in the unwritten constitution, to comprise, as they then were in the early nineteenth century, a vast majority in Parliament, or as they became in the late nineteenth century, still a majority therein. At issue then, were, in ascending order, the receipt of rent, the ownership of land (full rights, in the minds of owners), and the control of government and thereby of government policy.

A further significance of the theory of rent has had to do with taxation. That part of the theory, which portrays rent as an unearned increment, implies that it was a fit subject of taxation. This conclusion shares some similarities with that of the Physiocrats, as will be discussed later in this chapter. The theory portrays rent as a residual, after the payment of wages and profits, and implies that taxing rent will have no adverse incentive effects. In a world in which government expenditures in peacetime were around 3 percent or so of gross national product, the idea that taxing rent could likely finance much if not all of those expenditures was a logical possibility. The idea did not readily come to mind for most people, but it did for Henry George.

George accepted the Ricardian theory of rent and used it to develop his proposal of a Single Tax, his diagnosis of social ills, and his social philosophy. The proposal for a tax on rent which would at least substantially finance the cost of government is clear enough. George's diagnosis of social ills centered on the idea of poverty amidst plenty, some or much if not all of the poverty being caused by inequality in the distributions of wealth, especially private property in land, and of income, especially through private receipt of rent. That no one factor is the cause of social problems does not render inequality à la George irrelevant. His social philosophy proceeded from the values of equality amongst hard-working, employed people. The values of George's social philosophy were largely those of the Protestant Ethic, centring on hard, honest work as the basis of income and the ownership of property. This view has long roots in American economic thought, deriving originally from the Puritan mindset of New England and evident in the work of

Francis Wayland. In this and other respects, George was both a Classical economist and a conservative. What distinguished George from many other conservatives was that he wanted all individuals, not merely a favored few, to benefit from the system. His key point was that the existing institution of private ownership of land, inclusive of the private receipt of land, prevented that result.

George's argument—at the very least that private property in land was questionable and especially morally dubious in a world in which a relative handful owned land—called for the taxation of economic rent. In practice, this came to mean taxing unimproved land and the land portion of improved land at higher rates than the improvements, for example, buildings. Landowners who learned of the Ricardo–George theory of rent and especially of George's proposals to extract from land ownership the right to receive and fully retain rent, saw such as an attack on their property, a confiscation if ever there was one, as tantamount to the loss of their property and as a threat to all other property. Even worse, George, in challenging the origins, the fact, and the social consequences of private ownership of land, as diagnosed by him, sometimes appeared to be calling not merely for the taxing away of one right of land ownership—receipt of rent—but for ending the institution of land ownership as a whole.

George could readily be seen as radical, as a socialist, or a communist. He portrayed land and other natural resources as economic assets whose benefits in terms of rent should be shared by all, in the form of paying for the cost of government. He justified the tax on rent on the grounds that land was originally the property of all people. These views seemed aptly to describe his views as being socialist or communist. This is the position taken by Argyll, who accuses George of being a communist in a vituperative attack in *Property in Land* (1982) [1884].

George was anathema to the owners of landed property, to those who envisioned their children, if not themselves, as owners of landed property, and, as it seemed, to economists (Gaffney 1994; Lissner and Lissner 1991). There are speculative reasons why Georgist ideas did not widely take hold. Interestingly, for all the invective hurled by economists at George, a surprising diversity of conservative and liberal economists have believed in taxing land rent. So long as George could be lumped together with Karl Marx, however, economists sensitive to the reputation and safety of economics as a professional discipline refused to accept his ideas—what could be more unsafe than association with someone deemed a threat to the institution of private property? But that is only one hypothesis (Samuels 2003). The same sort of views are held today by taxpayers: that while they might not currently be in the top tax bracket or subject to the estate tax, they either hope they will or that their children will, and therefore support lowering these tax rates. This seems to be a particularly American point of view.

But George believed precisely the opposite of those who sensed socialism. Taxation of rent did in effect nationalize rent. But it did not constitute confiscation because land rent was not produced by the owners, land ownership actually should not have been theirs to begin with, especially if it included the right to receive rent, moreover, taxing rent would have no disincentive effects, for the reason given earlier. The taxation of rent would actually promote the values usually affirmed for the market or capitalist system, those of hard work and therefore productivity; this in contrast to rent as an unearned income.

Two conflicting theories of productivity were involved in the debate over the taxation of rent. According to one theory, income was and of right ought to be a function of productivity and receipt of income was understood, in the light of this theory, to connote productivity. That circular reasoning was involved—one identifies income as due to productivity and the test of productivity being that income was received—did not much diminish the rhetorical force of a line of reasoning seemingly so consonant with both the Protestant Ethic and the urging of self-importance. The theory applied, however, not only to labor but to the ownership of property; it assumed that property—all property, including land—was productive in the same sense and that the productivity was due to the owner. The two theories of productivity have one characteristic in common. The term "productivity" having honorific status, each theory is used to rationalize certain institutional arrangements, the difference being that one equates productivity with the institution of ownership and the other with earned income.

Of course, to George, land was not productive of rent, and the landowners did not earn their rent; income from land did not constitute evidence of productivity. Land ownership was a matter of past conquest coupled with inheritance and purchase and sale. Rent was not a matter of productivity. George believed that the capitalist system did work on the basis of productivity—except in the matter of land and its rent. Land and its rent, instead of being an example, like much other property,[1] was inconsistent with distribution according to capitalism's principles and, moreover, a threat to those principles. Earned income was the key to productivity; unearned income was both its negation and a transfer of income from producers to non-producers.

The fact of the matter is that at the level of pure economic theory both theories of distribution in terms of productivity are incomplete if not wrong—though our point does not disturb the putative difference between the two theories. The theories are at least misleading on the following reasoning. Let marginal income be equal to the marginal revenue product. Marginal revenue product is a function of marginal physical product multiplied by product price. Marginal physical product is a function of technology and of the process which yields technology. Product price is a function of demand and supply under a variety of market types and structures. What is normally thought of as productivity—George had a labour theory of value, which is also not meaningful—is almost entirely misleading. Agricultural technology is now only slightly private-farm developed; product price is a function of many variables, one of which is consumer demand. So a comprehensive account would include the circularity of productivity producer and consumers as producer. Moreover, while one theory identifies productivity with earned income, the other identifies productivity with ownership, and ownership is a matter of institutions. Improvements in technology, for example, can come from many different sources and thus have many different claimants; the actual distribution depends on institutions, including those institutions which both help form and operate through markets. The distribution of rent is a function of custom and law, that is, of power and institutions (see Ezekiel 1957; Samuels 1992a).

George's doctrine of the unearned increment is simultaneously both conservative and radical. It is radical in its attack on the major form of property for untold generations. It is conservative in its affirmation of certain basic values—saccharine but not fully descriptive—of the last several hundred years. The two theories of productivity help us to understand four alternative emphases of conservatism—also saccharine, but neither fully accurate nor meaningful. One emphasis is on maintaining the continuity of received institutions, whatever they are, and thereby of the distribution of income based on them. The second emphasis is on the distribution of income believed to *ipso facto* reward the productivity of ownership. The third emphasis is on productivity defined as earned income. The fourth emphasis is on widespread ownership of land, widespread receipt of pure rent, and widespread control of government.

The foregoing account of the theory of economic rent and its implications is over-whelmingly conventional in works on rent theory and on the history of economic thought. One recent example, authored by a distinguished historian of economic thought, comments on "the passage from classical to neo-classical economics":

> In the classical view things had value because of their direct and indirect labour costs at the margin. Land qua land (rural and urban) has no labour cost of production—it is a free gift of Nature. But it commands a price. The difference is Ricardian rent; a pure surplus arising from its fixity and scarcity relative to demand. Unlike commodities, a rise in the price of land has no tendency to be reversed by a rise in supply (though land-saving innovations might shift down the demand). As a pure surplus, there is an economic and ethical case for collecting these community-created rents for state revenues: the impot unique, anybody? Then along came the neo-classicals. There is no surplus. Intra-marginal land might attract high rents, but you could use it for either corn or potatoes, or for an office or a cinema. Look to the opportunity cost, and the surplus largely disappears. A much more comfortable theory for the property-owning classes.
>
> (Sandilands 2004)

Before concluding this section, we should point out that Argyll's complaint about taxing land applied not only to Ricardo and George but to Adam Smith. In his *Wealth of Nations*, Smith proposed that rents on land (ground rents) were a suitable object of taxation, the entire burden of which falls on the landowner, "who acts always as a monopolist" (Smith 1976a, Vol. II: 843). It was Smith's view that such rents, "so far as they exceed the ordinary rent of land, are altogether owing to the good government of the sovereign..." (Vol. II: 844). It is good government that "by giving both the most perfect security...and by procuring...the most extensive market" (Vol. II: 833), enables the receipt and enjoyment of rent: "Nothing can be more reasonable than that a fund which owes its existence to the good government of the state should be taxed peculiarly, or should contribute something more than the greater part of other funds, towards the support of that government" (Vol. II: 844). Further, contrary to Argyll's positive view, Smith had a negative view of the landlords' efforts to improve the land, saying, "It seldom happens, however, that a great proprietor is a great improver" (Vol. II: 385; see also Smith 1977: 32, and Young 1997: 174–5).

Twin nineteenth-century reactions to the middle-class transformation of economy and society

After several hundred years during which the foundations of modern commercial and industrial capitalism were laid in Great Britain and the United States, by the time of Adam Smith and then Ricardo, the new economic system was well under way. The system was for all practical purposes new but it was more than an economic system, it was an economic and political system, a new legal-economic nexus. The then-recent centuries comprised a period of both nation building and national-economy building. The economy was transformed, organized religion was transformed, the law was transformed, the system of social belief was transformed, and the nation-state was transformed. One fundamental characteristic of all these transformations was the blossoming of individualism. Another was the development of policy consciousness; probably more the spread of policy consciousness than its initial development. For centuries, even millennia, rulers knew that social arrangements were a matter of social construction, of choice, of policy; indeed, their activities as rulers were largely devoted to reconstruction of social arrangements to their felt advantage.

At any rate, by the time of Ricardo and his friend James Mill, in the early nineteenth century, the transformations were well under way in England and Scotland, products of several centuries of conflict, centring on control of the monarchy, control of Parliament, and reformation of law, religion, and belief systems. By the time of the Reform Act in England in 1832 it was reasonably clear that the landowning class, titled and untitled, but a very small slice of the population, was going to have to share the powers of government, have its body of landed property law further expanded to include non-landed property, and face an expanded suffrage. (One historian points out that although the American colonists did not accept "Britain's hereditary class structure," they did have "the belief that the ownership of land, or the possession of enough other property to ensure an independent livelihood, was a prerequisite to the full rights and duties of citizenship" (McDonald 2004: 169; see also Williamson 1960).) All that basically took another century; in fact, it is still going on, as membership in and the power of the House of Lords faces further restrictions. Arguments of claimed right have become increasingly transformed into arguments of claimed utility on pragmatic grounds.

Eventually, in the twentieth century, the responses to these and other developments came to include the regulatory state, so-called, and the welfare state. In the nineteenth century, however, the pertinent responses included: (1) German and

English romanticism, a return to a fancied golden era, which need not concern us here (Argyll does not fit in with this view); (2) socialism of various types; (3) the trade union movement, which also need not concern us here; and (4) land reform. Our present interest concerns the fourth but it must be seen as an alternative to the second. By the third decade of the nineteenth century, a further historic change was taking place. When the inferior nobility, for several centuries, competed with the monarch for power, they were in effect continuing the struggle for power among local rulers, one of whom had defeated his rivals and become king. When the middle class grew in number and in economic power, in their contest with the landed aristocracy and monarchy, they emulated the rhetoric of the earlier struggle. That rhetoric proceeded as if they spoke for all the disadvantaged members of society. In the language of the French Revolution, they sought liberty, equality, and fraternity. The rhetoric succeeded in mobilizing the incipient political psychology of the masses. The masses believed that they, too, would participate in a relatively free and open society, and no longer suffer the pains inflicted by the *Ancien Régime.*

In time, however, it became clear to increasing numbers of members of the working class and peasantry that the middle class had intended no such thing. The middle class was now intent on establishing concentrations of economic and political power in its hands, no longer, if possible, in the hands of the landed aristocracy, and certainly not sharing power with the masses. Instead of the rhetoric-marketed free society, the middle class sought to substitute its hegemony for that of the landed aristocracy, or at least join with the latter in a system of governance dominated by property, landed and non-landed. Republican government already compromised the promise of democracy. Economic concentration would further erode the promise of a free society. What had been, or was becoming, the victory of commercial and industrial capitalism over a post-feudal agrarian regime and of middle-class over aristocratic control of government was also coming to be seen as the consolidation of the rule of capital in both economic and political matters. The new rulers were no better than the ones they were displacing.

In the second quarter of the nineteenth century, two movements in particular formed in reaction to the foregoing. One focused on landed property. As seen earlier, the Classical economists, representing one part of the middle-class Whig movement, focused on the repeal of the Corn Laws in order to enhance the profits of non-landed property and to reduce the social and political power of the landed interest. The attack on land did not begin with them but their chapter in the history of economic thought became an important part of that history. Eventually a series of underground chapters, as it were, was written. The two principal figures were the Italian, Achille Loria, and the American, Henry George. (American land views at this point in time differed significantly from those of Europe as the Western Expansion continued unabated, aided by Land and Homestead Acts and a universal American belief in Manifest Destiny.) In sum, both traced the social problems of their respective continents to the history of the institutionalization of land. In Europe, the history either ran through or started with feudalism and ended with the then-present stratified society ultimately driven by private property in land and its grossly unequal distribution. In the United States, though lacking feudalism, land-based stratification was clearly visible. The ability to use Ricardo's theory of rent reinforced lines of reasoning whose genesis resided in other considerations. In both continents the masses were repressed by having to submit to extortion as the price of the use of land owned by others.

The land-oriented movement had numerous adherents, but it did not come to dominate social reform. Among the likely reasons was the increasing opportunity for people of modest means to purchase land; the institution of land banks and mortgage instruments to finance purchase and improvement had much to do with the increasing opportunity. In the United States institutions to help finance home ownership gave many people the opportunity to generate equity for themselves rather than for landlords; and if this did not significantly affect the percentile distribution of wealth by income class, and one or another index of concentration, it did give people a sense of being owners of property. The intent of some institutional innovators was to create a more conservative working class, and, as it turned out, they correctly foresaw that coming to pass. Nonetheless, it is this movement, and certain of its aspects, that are the focus of this chapter.

The other movement, socialism, is so well known, because it was so central to nineteenth- and twentieth-century history, that not much need be said about it in order to appreciate its juxtaposition with the land-oriented movement. Whereas the center of gravity of the Loria and George movements was the conflict between the masses and the owners of land, that of socialism was the conflict between the masses and the owners of capital. Common to both movements is a determination that the privileges of a few become the rights of all. The differences turn on the framework of thought through which each movement expresses, philosophically and technically, its point of view. Each framework rested on a particular foundational determination. The Georgist framework of thought was based on the notion of rent as an unearned income to which land ownership provided access. The Marxist framework of thought was more complex. It rested on the notion that the profits of capital, and rent, derived from the creation of surplus value consequent to the power of capital to compel workers to work each day more hours than was necessary to repay the capitalist for the value of the labor power they advanced; profit too was unearned by those to whom ownership of capital provided access.

Also common to both positions was the belief that mainstream economics, though not necessarily all mainstream economists, provided the legitimizing rationalization of the regnant, exploitative economic system, and the institution of property on which it rested. Not surprisingly, many mainstream economists said foul things about the two theories of unearned income, provoking the "heretics" claim that the economists were the "hired guns" of the capitalists. What also happened during the second quarter of the nineteenth century was the marriage of accommodation and convenience between the owners of landed property and of non-landed property. They would continue to struggle over the control and use of government to promote their respective interests. But they would unite to confront the third major group in society, the masses, the working class, the class of those without property.

Land ownership

One major characteristic of data on landownership is how little is available. The second major characteristic concerns the difficulties imposed on assembling and publishing data on landownership. The third major characteristic is that data on landownership must be compiled but before it can be compiled—as is usually the case with data construction—significant decisions must be made concerning a multiplicity of definitional and recording issues. The fourth major characteristic is the concentration of landownership in many areas of the world.

Among the crucial decisions are: the definition of owning unit, limits on land registration and reporting, the treatment of varieties of common land, and so on. Also important are the widely different views toward land acquisition, ownership, and availability in Great Britain and the United States in the nineteenth century. Because so much discussion pertinent to this chapter relates to Britain, especially to England and Scotland, we provide a rough summary of conclusions for this area. Because the state of Hawaii has such a dramatically high level of concentration, and for other reasons, it has been intensively studied, and a summary of conclusions for it is also provided. For reasons already noted, the data are indicative rather than accurate, notwithstanding the greater or lesser precise comparability of some numbers.[2]

Britain

The content, limits, mode of presentation, and summary of the data depend on the manner of its collection:[3]

- Some 6,000 landowners—mostly landed aristocrats but also large institutions, including the Crown—own about 40 million acres, about two-thirds of the 60 million acres of land of the country.
- Of the 59 million people who live on those 60 million acres, some 99.9 percent live on less than 10 percent of the land, possibly on as little as 4.4 million acres.
- An additional 14.6 million acres are designated as woodland, mountain, waste, roads, and so on.
- The remaining 40 million or so acres are owned by 189,000 individuals or families. The 59 million people, minus the members of those families, live on land at an average density of 12–13 persons per acre. The land of the group owning two-thirds of the land has an average density of one person per 90 acres.
- In 1875—in the midst of the period in which Argyll and George were writing—the English journal *The Spectator* used a four-volume report, "The Return of Owners of Land, in England, Scotland, Ireland and Wales," to calculate that 710 persons possessed one-quarter of the land in England and Wales.

- Currently almost 26 million acres of land in England and Wales are occupied by almost 160 thousand individuals or families. This 0.28 percent of the population owns 64 percent of the land.
- The Duke of Buccleuch and Queensberry owns some 270,700 acres; the Duke of Westminster owns 129,300 acres, including parts of Belgravia and Mayfair in central London; the Queen owns 73,000 acres and Prince Charles, 141,000 acres; the Duke of Northumberland owns 132,200 acres.

The policies and programs that led to such concentration included various episodes of land assignment, such as the division of land by William the Conqueror among himself, the Church and the lesser nobility; Henry VIII's distribution of expropriated land held by Catholic monasteries to some 1,500 favored families; and the Acts of Enclosure. The policies that accompany such concentration attest to the legislative and judicial influence of the beneficiaries. The benefits of policies appear to include the following: Many wealthy landowners pay no taxes on their land holdings. Many receive grants and subsidies on the basis of their land ownership. The subsidies to the 189,000 individuals or families amount to about £4 billion, or £12,000 or so per year. They pay some £103 million annually in council (property) tax, whereas the 59 million people who live on perhaps 4.4 million acres pay somewhat over £10 billion or an average of £550 such tax per household per year.

The Blair government continued the reform of the House of Lords, excluding hereditary peers, thereby severing some 785 of the wealthiest families, owning perhaps one-third of the land, from these positions of government power.

Hawaii

Recent statistics (Government of Hawaii 1987) indicate the following:

Federal land	280,000 acres	7.1%
State land	1,122,000 acres	28.5%
County land	14,000 acres	0.4%
Private land	2,515,000 acres	64.0%
	3,931,000 acres	

In 1986, the six largest private owners held title to 938,000 acres, or 23.9 percent of all land and 37.3 percent of all private land. The largest single owner, the Bishop estate, held 341,000 acres.

The facts on Great Britain are very interesting and telling, but parallel structure ideally demands similar facts for the United States, which are not available. Hawaii is interesting, but is not representative of the United States.

Land ownership and governance

That those in control of government will seek to use government to advance what they consider to be their interests is an aspect of a general principle: that government is an instrument of use and therefore an object of control by those who would use it as an instrument for their own gain or advantage (Samuels 1992b). This is not necessarily nefarious, though it may involve conflict of interest and corruption. People will tend to promote—vote for—their own interests. When membership in state government legislatures disproportionately favored rural and agricultural interests, legislation tended strongly to promote those interests; reapportionment tended to change the profiles of membership and of the interests promoted.

One curious feature of the property tax in some states of the United States is that only landed property owners may vote on the level of the property tax used to finance public education, police and fire protection, and other government services. Those without ownership of landed property cannot vote. This feature of the property tax is curious for two reasons. The first reason is a matter of the shifting and incidence of taxation. Owners of landed property both remit the tax and bear its burden; there is no further transaction through which they can shift the tax to others. People who lease landed property—apartments, houses—do not remit any tax; the tax is literally paid by the owners of the leased property. But since there is a further transaction, the monthly "rental" payment, the owner is able to shift the tax to the lessee. Some states recognize the shifting process and that, therefore, the lease payment includes rent, and takes that into account in other provisions of the tax code. In any event, insofar as the final resting place of the property tax is generally concerned, there is no difference between the owner who cannot shift and the lessee to whom the tax is shifted and who cannot further shift it; both bear the tax. But only one can vote on the tax.

The property tax in such jurisdictions is curious for a second reason. In giving the right to vote on the tax only to the owner of the landed property, it is giving only to the owner the power to determine spending on various government programs. The owner of landed property has power that one would think belongs to all citizens. Most state constitutions provide for the latter, in effect rejecting the former as unjust. The presently interesting aspect of this unusual tax arrangement is that it presents a microcosm of the way things were when the suffrage, the right to vote, was limited to those who owned landed property. It was these people, and basically only these people, who controlled what the government did and for whom it did it. It was a government of, by, and for the landed property owners.

An example at the federal level comparable for present purposes involved cotton and other farmers having the power to determine the levels of both crop subsidy payments and supply-control measures (i.e. reduction of planted acreage). Farmers wanted subsidies but bristled at controls over supply, necessary if the level of payments was not to become exorbitant. Two relevant features of various pieces of legislation may be identified. First, only the landlords voted on the two levels; no other citizen could vote. Second, an early (1934–5) Act left in the hands of the landlords the division of payments between landowners and sharecroppers and the division of the burden of the reduced demand for sharecropper labor that resulted from the reduction in planted acreage (Schweikhardt 2004: 6–7). Again, landownership conveyed powers of governance. A final example is from Europe. From at least the fourteenth century onward, the governing class of towns and cities was recruited from those who owned land. Considered Patrician, they included traders and artisans—so long as they were landowners.

Let us turn to the first school of economic thought, the French Physiocrats, who wrote in the middle of the eighteenth century (for Argyll's treatment of the Physiocrats, see Argyll 1893b: 468ff.). They tended to write of the natural order to which government policy should adhere, of a minimal level of government (specifically legislative) activity, and of a philosophy of non-intervention or laissez-faire. Their *bête noire* were the several French versions of Mercantilism and Protectionism. They sought to establish in their place an agricultural system, one populated by rich farmers, in order to enable them to adopt capitalist methods of operation. In this system, they wrote, the government has only three principal duties. One is to uphold and put into effect the natural order, and with it the right of possession, that is, a system of secure private property. The second is to provide for the education of the people, especially instruction in the natural order. The third is the provision of public works, as a form of foundational investment (Gide and Rist 1948 [1915]).

It has since been shown that this articulation of the economic role of government in the Physiocratic system is extremely misleading. To say that government policy should adhere to the natural order and establish the agricultural system called for by the natural order is to say that government is a top-down instrument of social reconstruction, hardly the minimalist institution one might think from reading their writings. Actually, the functions of government put forth in their practical as distinct from their esoteric grandiose statements, were: government as an instrument of social change, including the construction of an agricultural kingdom, the reorganization and redirection of the state itself; and government having an agenda of both economic development and economic stability (Samuels 1962). Naturalist language does not preclude governmental activism; naturalist language facilitates the making of governmental activism seem non-political, that is, derived from the nature of things—something rebutted by a sense of policy consciousness.

Several aspects of the foregoing situation warrant our attention. First, it is clear that the Physiocrats considered themselves the teachers of all citizens and especially the Crown as to what the natural order required on every issue. They were to be the power behind the throne. Second, while the power of the legislature was to be constrained—in language seemingly laden with non-interventionism (laissez-faire, *laissez-passer*)—no such constraint was to apply to the sovereign, the Crown. That the Crown was to act on the basis of the natural order, as specified by the Physiocrats, may have sounded saccharine but it did not negate the absolute authority of the Crown. They seemingly had no idea that the French Revolution, a few years later, would attack—though by no means precisely eliminate—the principle of monarchical absolutism.

Let us turn to Gide and Rist, whose famous textbook, *A History of Economic Doctrines*, identified the Physiocrats as the first founders of the discipline (and also gives an extended account of Henry George's doctrines and of different lines of criticism (pp. 562–70)). Their way of raising our problem is to ask, "How can we explain this apparent contradiction and such love of despotism among the apostles of *laissez-faire?*" (p. 35). Gide and Rist develop the problem to that point in the following manner. First, they identify the nature of their natural order:

> ...the "natural order" was that order which seemed obviously the best, not to any individual whomsoever, but to rational, cultured, liberal-minded men like the Physiocrats. It was not the product of the observation of external facts; it was the revelation of a principle within. And this is one reason why the Physiocrats showed such respect for property and authority. It seemed to them that these formed the very basis of the "natural order."
>
> (p. 9)

Such a system, they claimed, was endowed with the "double attributes of universality and immutability" (p. 10). Of course, this system as yet existed nowhere, and it had to be brought into existence by properly instructed rulers. By calling their system of privilege the "natural order" they were utilizing a venerable, if question-begging, mode of rhetorical absolutist legitimization and obfuscation, in part to promote "faith in a pre-established order" (p. 11). Second, Gide and Rist note that the Physiocrats claimed that within such a system particular private interests will be harmonious with the common interest of all, thus facilitating spontaneous activity by all citizens (p. 11). "This is," they write, "*laissez-faire* pure and simple" (p. 11). Third, this is not a philosophy of non-interventionism:

> Laissez-faire does not of necessity mean that nothing will be done. It is not a doctrine of passivity or fatalism. ...It is true that there will not be much work for the Government, but the task of that body will by no means be a light one, especially if it intends carrying out the Physiocratic programme. This included upholding the rights of private property and individual liberty by removing all artificial barriers, and punishing all those who threatened the existence of any of these rights; while, most important of all, there was the duty of giving instruction in the laws of the "natural order."
>
> (pp. 11–12)

What these rights were and what was artificial depended on the substance of the Physiocrats' conception of the natural order. Fourth, the Physiocrats' natural order, Gide and Rist remind their readers, was comprised of three classes: (1) the productive class of farmers, fishermen, and miners, especially the first, who create the net product; (2) the proprietary class; and (3) the sterile class of merchants, manufacturers, domestic servants, and members of the professions (p. 19). For the Physiocrats, and therefore for us, the proprietary class includes:

> ...not only landed proprietors, but also any who have the slightest title to sovereignty of any kind—a survival of feudalism, where the two ideas of sovereignty and property are always linked together.
>
> (p. 19; see also p. 38)

The property that counted in the Physiocrats *royaume agricole* was that of land, not of capital. This is evident in the Physiocrats' *Tableau économique* in which, as described and critiqued by Gide and Rist:

> the class which enjoys two-fifths of the national revenue does nothing in return for it. We should not have been surprised if such glaring parasitism had given to the work of the Physiocrats a distinctly socialistic tone. But they were impervious to all such ideas. They never appreciated the weakness of the landowners' position, and they always treated them with the greatest reverence. The epithet "sterile" is applied, not to them, but to manufacturers and artisans! Property is the foundation-stone of the "natural order." The proprietors have been entrusted with the task of supplying the staff of life, and are endued with a kind of priestly sacredness. It is from their hands that all of us receive the elements of nutrition. It is a "divine" institution—the word is there. Such idolatry needs some explanation.
>
> One might have expected—even from their own point of view—that the premier position would have been given to the class which they termed productive, *i.e.* to the cultivators of the soil, who were mostly farmers and *métayers*. The land was not of their making, it is true. They had simply received it from the proprietors. This latter class takes precedence because God has willed that it should be the first dispenser of all wealth.
>
> (pp. 21–2)

The landowners are held in reverence for their organization and management of production. They *do* do *something*.

But the landowners are also legitimized for their second role. They do something else as well, they rule: The nobility, together with the throne, constituted the upper levels of the social hierarchy—the "sovereign authority in the guise of a hereditary monarchy" (p. 35) and class of lesser nobility—and it was these levels of the hierarchy that governed—even if to the myopic Physiocrats this meant inculcating and ruling in accordance with their principles and not some other set. The landowners received payments in the Physiocratic system because their rights of property were simultaneously rights of ownership and rights of sovereignty, rights of economic governance and rights of political governance.

> Knowing only feudal society, *with its economic and political activities governed and directed by idle proprietors,*[4] they suffered from an illusion as to the necessity for landed property similar to that which led Aristotle to defend the institution of slavery.
>
> (p. 22, emphasis added)

Fifth, Gide and Rist identify the subtle nature of the legislative role. When the Physiocrats argued for reducing "legislative activity to a minimum" one must read into this not the ordinary, literal meaning of words but their meaning in the Physiocratic system. Legislation is to put into place that which is required—according to the Physiocrats—by the natural order, that is, "copies of the unwritten laws of Nature." Legislatures are to "abolish useless laws," that is, useless in terms of the Physiocratic system (p. 33). It is in this system-specific sense, therefore, that one must read Gide and Rist's further summarizing point: "Neither men nor Government can make laws, for they have not the necessary ability. Every law should be an expression of that Divine wisdom which rules the universe. Hence the true title of lawgiver, not law-maker" (pp. 33–4).

What does this mean in practice? The philosophical realist argues that mankind does not choose between different idealist versions of social reality. Social reality exists independent of mankind. But in a world in which everyone was a philosophical realist, people would still disagree as to what constituted social reality. Thus, in a Physiocratic state, legislators would still disagree as to what constituted the Physiocratic system, for example, when Physiocratic principles conflicted. (Gide and Rist illustrate this situation in comparing A. R. J. Turgot's positions on issues with the positions of other Physiocrats (pp. 47ff.).) Governance would still involve choice in a context of conflict. Even absent conflict about the details of the Physiocratic program, conflict would occur between it and all other programs and proposals. Which brings us, finally, to the problem of "apparent contradiction and such love of despotism among the apostles of *laissez-faire*." Gide and Rist's explanation runs in two parts, as follows. First, a prelude to despotism and the basis for the contradiction:

> What they wanted to see was the minimum of legislation with a maximum of authority. The two things are by no means incompatible. The liberal policy of limitation and control would have found scant favour with them. Their ideal was neither democratic self-government, as . . . in the Greek republics, nor a parliamentary *régime* such as we find in England. Both were detested.
>
> On the other hand, great respect was shown for the social hierarchy, and they were strong in their condemnation of every doctrine that aimed at attacking either the throne or the nobility. What they desired was to have sovereign authority in the guise of a hereditary monarchy. In short, what they really wanted—and they were not frightened by the name—was despotism.
>
> (pp. 34–5)

For example:

> There is no mention of representation as a corollary of taxation. This form of guarantee, which marks the beginnings of parliamentary government, could have no real significance for the Physiocrats. Taxation was just a right inherent in the conception of proprietary sovereignty, a territorial revenue [i.e., based on land ownership], which was in no way dependent upon the people's will.
>
> (p. 35)

Second, the nature of despotism and of freedom:

> Despotism, in the eyes of the Physiocrats, had a peculiar significance of its own. It was the work of freedom, not of bondage. It did not signify the rule of the benevolent despot, prepared to make men happy, even against their own will. It was just the sovereignty of the "natural order"—nothing more.
>
> ...At bottom the system affords a barrier against the autocracy of the sovereign—a barrier that is much more effective than a parliamentary vote.
>
> (pp. 35, 44)

One is free to do what the natural order requires, as articulated in the principles enunciated by the Physiocrats and legislated, as it were, through a society governed in its economic and political activities by a government in which property and sovereignty were indistinguishable. George Douglas Campbell, the eighth Duke of Argyll, was no Physiocrat but he did represent, and defend, the agrarian way of life and as much economic and political governance by landowners as could be secured in the modern world. Henry George, on the other hand, would have been influenced by the Physiocratic tradition in America, handed down in the writings of Benjamin Franklin, Thomas Jefferson, and the agrarians of the late eighteenth century.

Argyll wanted so to define landownership as to render it productive. One way was to portray the landowner as a factor in/of production. Another was to emphasize the role of landowners in government/governance, going beyond the admonition that wealth carries responsibilities. Still another was to denigrate the ideas of unearned income and the associated life-style of a leisure class of conspicuous consumption then being identified by Thorstein Veblen. Surely Argyll would have resisted the economics of leisure in which leisure is treated as a normal good in the sense that people work less if their unearned income rises (Mirrlees 1974: 258)?

The Duke of Argyll and land ownership and governance

This section considers a number of Argyll's positions pertinent to the topic of landownership and governance. We take up Argyll's major writings in chronological order.

Essay on... Contracts for the Hire of Land *(1877)*

Argyll wrote a great deal on a wide range of issues. He was recognized as a formidable debater, a rhetorician of considerable skill. One of his tactics was to concede a point in order to render more palatable another point or position specific to the issue at hand. For example, in his *Essay on... Contracts for the Hire of Land* (1877), he wants to have the rights of tenants and of owners "taken as they are" (p. 2), because he wants to minimize the impact of two bodies of fact; one concerning how the landowners became landowners, and the other, the evolution of the relative rights of tenants and owners. Insofar as the latter is inexorably present, by "taken as they are" he means, and says, "they are what they are defined to be, not by the antiquarians, but by the judge" (p. 2). The "antiquarians" are those who would look to history. But Argyll would have discussion focus on the judge—because the judiciary then largely came from the landowning class. No wonder he is willing to insist—concede, as it were—that, as for "the right of the State to restrict individual freedom.... I know of no abstract limit to the right of the State to do anything" (p. 6). Insofar as this means political choice as between conflicting claimants of rights and also surrenders all invocation of abstract natural law, the result is one meaning of arbitrary, one meaning of coercion, and/or despotism as discussed by Gide and Rist—and acceptable to Argyll because of the safe class position of the judges. (This does not prevent Argyll from distinguishing between the economic and moral ends of legislation as a constraint upon the State (pp. 8ff.). For the irrelevance of matters relating to the vesting of ownership and of the identity of landowners, see p. 4.)

In *Essay on...Contracts for the Hire of Land* the issue is how to provide adequate security for capital invested in the cultivation or improvement of their holding by persons [called occupiers, tenants or farmers] hiring land by contract [from owners of land] for agricultural purposes (Argyll 1877: 21). Argyll presents the landowners' case against giving further protection to tenants for their capital invested through improvements to land they only lease. One of his lines of argument ultimately presumes the inherited benevolent treatment by the superior in a relation of deference and thus the situation of harmony in the relation of owner and tenant. It is a favorite line of argument, evidenced by its frequent articulation and invocation. We thus read of:

> That equitable spirit which is essential to the conduct of life in every calling, and which is perhaps more habitually exercised in the relations between owner and occupier of land than in any other business whatever.
>
> (p. 41)

Argyll emphasizes that "under the influence of favour and of personal feeling" owners give an allowance "in the form of abated rent" (p. 42). Of this practice he insists, "Nor is it just to attach any prejudice to such feeling by calling it feudalism" (p. 42); that it would be "a dangerous presumption" to think "that abated rents...far below the fair letting value are comparatively rare. ... on the contrary, such cases are very common...the preference given to old tenants is often very large" and "probably equals more than an average of 10 per cent" (p. 43). We also read of:

> those personal and hereditary feelings on which I have now been dwelling as a special and exceptional security to tenants, the extent and prevalence of which is little known.
>
> (p. 47)

And again:

> So sound, indeed, and so healthy have the relations hitherto been, both in England and Scotland, between the owners and occupiers of the soil, so habitual and rooted have been the traditional and customary feelings, which are the best foundation for business relations of such endurance as these must always be, that possibly even the most unwise law might not at once put an end to cheap and abated rents.
>
> (p. 52)

Several considerations immediately arise in the modern mind. One consideration in question form is, if the claimed harmony and benevolent treatment exists, why has the reform legislation been proposed? Another consideration is precisely the matter of feudal relations: the lessees are treated more like feudal subjects than independent economic actors with rights in competitive markets. Still another consideration is reminiscent of claims made by segregationists in the 1960s that the majority of American blacks were happy with the status quo, and that the only complainants were a relatively few "malcontents" and "outsiders."

Actually, Argyll wants the best of both worlds, that of a set of contented and deferential tenants and rent-maximizing behavior (pp. 42ff., 51, 54ff., 59, 63ff.). He also notes that some tenants "have never been accustomed to look upon their business as a commercial one at all" and that owners "dislike parting with the discretionary power of determining tenancies altogether—even although practically this power is very rarely or even never exercised" (p. 90). Both dislikes reflect the situation of superior and inferior in a structure of hierarchical relations.

The Physiocrats' postulate of a landowning class with a claim to income grounded in their ownership per se and further legitimized by reference to their economic, as well as political, function, is echoed in the following position articulated by Argyll:

> It is quite true that . . . the farmer or hirer of land can say with justice to the owner, "It is my labour that has given to your soil this largely increased return." But it is equally true that the owner can reply with justice to the farmer, "It is the quality and situation of my land which has yielded to your labour this rich and unusual reward."
>
> (pp. 30–1)

No clearer affirmation of rent distribution as a function of ownership could be stated. The Ricardian position, also that of George, is that rent is driven by population growth. Ownership has nothing to do with the genesis of rent, only with its distribution. With this position Argyll will have nothing to do; he must, by the nature of his position, affirm rent as a matter of the yield on his land—"my land," Thus, apropos of "the doctrine that improvements executed by an occupier upon an owner's land are to belong exclusively to the occupier," Argyll argues, "This doctrine can only be defended on the ground that the contribution of ownership is no contribution at all" and that landed property does not have "the character or the incidents which belong to capital in every other form" (p. 70; the issue is whether the increased productivity due to farmer-hirer investment is a joint result of other, owner investments).

The Land Question *(1884)*

Argyll felt compelled to defend property in land against the assault levelled on it by Henry George, and George, in his turn, prepared a reply.[5] Both men were at the peak of their rhetorical powers and were amply motivated. Although both men appealed to natural law and both were conservative, their conceptions of what constituted natural law and of what conservatism meant differed widely. Thus, Argyll is able to say, first, of George's *Progress and Poverty* that it "was directed to prove that almost all the evils of humanity are to be traced to the very existence of landowners, and that by divine right land could only belong to everybody in general and to nobody in particular" (Argyll, in George 1982 [1884]: 10); if true, these evils traced to landownership would constitute a hitherto unseen foundation of society. Argyll's second revelation is that George is one of those who "have an interest, very personal indeed, in believing that they have a right to appropriate a share in their neighbor's vineyard" (p. 10). The irony here is that Argyll elsewhere acknowledges that titles of ownership in land ultimately trace to conquest; but here as elsewhere Argyll wants for discussion to start with landownership as it is in the present; in other words, he prefers to keep the origins of the distribution of land unseen. More than that, he finds George's analysis to be communist in nature (pp. 11–12). Argyll composed mighty rhetorical blasts in George's direction but received from George as good as he gave.

The Prophet of San Francisco, *by the Duke of Argyll*

One charge brought by Argyll is that George neglects the fact that the institution of property pervades, however unseen, relations between people and between people and government:

> It is one thing for any given political society to refuse to divide its vacant territory among individual owners. It is quite another thing for a political society, which for ages has recognized such ownership and encouraged it, to break faith with those who have acquired such ownership and have lived and labored, and bought and sold, and willed upon the faith of it.
>
> (1884: 17–18)

This is a rationalistic and legitimizing view of the history of an institution early and still laden with conquest and coercion; the late-nineteenth-century development of the institution in the American West was in territory hardly previously unoccupied (as he puts it (p. 18)). That, too, remains unsaid and unseen. Every history has been given multiple interpretations, each yielding its own combination of the seen and unseen. Curiously or not, Argyll, having given such a saccharine view of government and government policy, then disparages both:

> In the disposal and application of wealth, as well as in the acquisition of it, are men more pure and honest when they act in public capacities as members of a Government or of a Legislature, than when they act in private capacities toward their fellow-men? Is it not notoriously the reverse? Is it not obvious that men will do, and are constantly seen doing, as politicians, what they would be ashamed to do in private life?
>
> (p. 19)

Argyll wants to accomplish two things: to render honorific the institution of property as achieved through government, and to denigrate the process of government and the people in government; the former to reify property and the latter to disable government's power to change it in a major way. This has been a strategy of Establishment parties and politicians in Britain and the United States for centuries—disparaging the government they otherwise refer to as duly constituted authority and for whose offices they are campaigning, in order to limit its use as an instrument of change in bringing about a different consolidation of social interests. Argyll is, however, more interested in promoting property than disparaging government; after all, he is a part of the governance structure. He thus reiterates the first argument, saying that George:

> is not content with urging that no more bits of unoccupied land should be ever sold, but he insists upon it that the ownership of every bit already sold shall be resumed without compensation to the settler who has bought it, who has spent upon it years of labor, and who from first to last has relied on the security of the State and on the honor of its Government.
>
> (p. 22)

Nor does he stop with land ownership; he moves on, first, to tenancy and then to all property:

> Nay, more, is there any reason why the doctrine of repudiation should be confined to pledges respecting either the tenancy or the ownership of land?
>
> (p. 23)

According to George:

> All National Debts are as unjust as property in land.
>
> (p. 24)

Saying that "The world has never seen such a Preacher of Unrighteousness as Mr. Henry George" (p. 25), Argyll quotes George's repudiation of the dead hand of the past:

> The institution of public debts, like the institution of private property in land, rests upon the preposterous assumption that one generation may bind another generation.
>
> (p. 25)

> Yet upon this assumption that ascendants may bind descendants, that one generation may legislate for another generation, rests the assumed validity of our land titles and public debts.
>
> (p. 26)

(One wonders what Argyll and George would say when confronted by the proposal, by economists across the political spectrum, of an interest-free national debt coupled with the requirement that some part of bank reserves be comprised of such debt—a proposal in part predicated upon the idea that the banking system need not receive a rent for generating the money supply.) And still more, cautions Argyll:

> All the other accumulations of industry must be as rightfully liable to confiscation.
>
> (p. 26)

One position taken by Argyll here is in support of the Northern States in opposing slavery. He calls it "as noble a cause as any which has ever called men to arms" (p. 27) and lauds the "patient and willing submission of the masses, as of one man, not only to the desolating sacrifice of life which it entailed, but to the heavy and lasting burden of taxation which was inseparable from it" (p. 27). He berates George for lamenting the failure to impose a capital levy ("an act of stealing") on those who held government bonds: "he speaks with absolute bitterness of the folly which led the Government to 'shrink' from at once seizing the whole, or all but a mere fraction, of the property of the few individual citizens who had the reputation of being exceptionally rich" (p. 28).

Argyll's position is particularly interesting because he is silent on the issue that has bedevilled so many others, namely, whether the former slaveholders should have been compensated for the emancipation of their property, the slaves, or whether the slaves should have been compensated for their former loss of liberty. (We shall see later that George is similarly restrained.)[6]

When Argyll returns to his defence of landownership, he is at his rhetorical best. Notwithstanding his later call, in the early chapters of *The Unseen Foundations of Society*, for the careful construction of definitions, Argyll wants to wrap landownership in the historically growing affirmative status of capitalist, using the phrase:

> the particular class of capitalists who are owners of land.
>
> (p. 31)

Other relevant examples of his argument include:

> The whole tone [of George's argument] is based on the assumption that owners of land are not producers, and that rent does not represent, or represents only in a very minor degree, the interest of capital [again: "a book assuming that landowners are not producers"].
>
> In every county the great landowners, and very often the smaller, were the great pioneers in a process which has transformed the whole face of the country. To such outlays [on improvements] landowners are incited very often, and to a great extent, by the mere love of seeing a happier landscape and a more prosperous people. From much of the capital so invested they often seek no return at all, and from very little of it indeed do they ever get a high rate of interest. ... When a man tells me ... that in all this I and others have been serving no interests but our own ... he is talking the most arrant nonsense.
>
> There was to be [in Bengal] no confiscation by the State of the increased value of any land, any more than of the increased value of other kinds of property, on the pretext that this increase was unearned.

(pp. 32–4, 37)

It seems that Argyll perceived no need to take up further or more directly the governance aspects of landownership. His reference to them is somewhat oblique:

> the functions and duties which in more civilized countries are discharged by the institution of private ownership in land.

(p. 36)

The Reduction of Iniquity, *by Henry George*

George takes his title from an accusatory flight of language in Argyll's final paragraph. He accuses Argyll of misrepresentation on a number of issues, achieved by exaggerating or distorting George's argument (e.g. 1885: 43). He might have criticized Argyll for claiming distrust of the institution to which he is appealing, namely, the State (see *supra*); instead, he derides him for expressing distrust of the moral faculties, "the very tribunal to which he appeals" (p. 43). But he, too, appeals to the work of the Creator, albeit invoking different moral lights and a different moral compass (p. 45). George agrees "that robbery is a violation of the moral law, and is therefore, without further inquiry, to be condemned," and that robbery is "the taking or withholding from another of what which rightfully belongs to him." Then comes the disagreement with Argyll: "That which *rightfully* belongs to him, be it observed, not that which legally belongs to him." In an argument distinguishing between making one's case by appeal to human or to moral law, he writes:

> Landholders must elect to try their case either by human law or by moral law. If ... by human law, they cannot charge those who would change that law

with advocating robbery. But if they charge that such change in human law would be robbery, then they must show that land is rightfully property irrespective of human law.

(p. 46)

George states his conclusion:

For land is not of that species of things to which the presumption of rightful property attaches ... [which are] things ... that are the produce of labor ... the moral basis of property, which makes certain things rightfully property totally irrespective of human law.

(p. 46)

—some things, but not land. "[P]roperty in land rests only on human enactment, which may, at any time, be changed without violation of moral law." As for property being derived from appropriation, "Appropriation can give no right." Right "is derived from labor, not from appropriation." More than that, the division of land, private landownership, has been effectuated by " 'right of strength', ... evidently ... what they really mean who talk of the right given by appropriation" (p. 47). George then cites Argyll on conquest:

This "right of conquest," this power of the strong, is the only basis of property in land to which the Duke ventures to refer.
... [T]he titles to the ownership of land ... rest historically upon the forcible spoliation of the masses.

(pp. 47–9)

George concurs with Argyll that "how ownership was acquired in the past can have no bearing upon the question of how we should treat land now; yet," he adds, "the inquiry is interesting, as showing the nature of the institution"— which is:

that the exclusive ownership of land has everywhere had its beginnings in force and fraud, in selfish greed and unscrupulous cunning.

(p. 49)

It is at this point where George makes the first of several references to slavery, deriding the Duke for not following the logic of his argument to support chattel slavery (p. 49). Another reference is to those who declared "the slave-trade piracy [but] still legalized the enslavement of those already enslaved" (p. 54). Still another reference makes the initial comparison much more poignantly:

In fact, the plea of the landlords that they, as landlords, assist in production, is very much like the plea of the slaveholders that they gave a living to the slaves...the gross inconsistency between the views he [the Duke] expresses as to negro slavery and the position he assumes as to property in land.

(pp. 66–7)

These allusions to slavery, but not to the compensation question, come amidst a continuation of the argument; first, from natural moral law, one expression of which is:

Is there not, therefore, a violation of the intent of Nature in human laws which give to one more land than he can possibly use, and deny any land to the other?

(p. 52, referring, in order, to duke and peasant)

and, second, from more secular reasoning:

...property in land means...a continuous confiscation of labor and the results of labor. ...to make so many other Scotsmen, in whole or in part, his serfs—to compel them to labor for him without pay, or to enable him to take from them their earnings without return.

(p. 54)

Further, George would differentiate what Argyll would combine:

In assuming that denial of the justice of property in land is the prelude to an attack upon all rights of property, the Duke ignores the essential distinction between land and things rightfully property. ... things...produced by human exertion.

(p. 55)

Indeed,

to treat it [land] as individual property is to weaken and endanger the true rights of property.

(p. 58)

George challenges Argyll's principal assumption underlying both his defence of landownership and his critique of George. "The Duke," he writes, "will justify his complaint if he will show how the owning of land can produce anything" (p. 64). The policy logic of the Georgist movement turned in part from nationalization of land to nationalization of land rent (the Single Tax) because it seemed to be more palatable to have government spend the proceeds of the tax than manage land and natural resources. The logic of Argyll's assumption was that ownership per se is productive in such a way that warrants others to have to labor for the owner, through the payment of economic rent. This policy logic succeeded because it was attractive in two ways. First, it seemed to be defended by productivity theory, notwithstanding the circularity of the argument. Second, it seemed to be negated in practice by the hope and anticipation that in the future one's children, if not also oneself, would own property. George treats the problem of governance in much the same way as he treats the land question, combining naturalistic and secular reasoning, for example:

> ...political corruption...springs...not from excess but from deficiency of democracy, and mainly from our failure to recognize the equality of natural rights as well as of political rights.
>
> (pp. 58–9)

All the foregoing leads to the question of land ownership and governance, George writes personally of the Duke and not abstractly. Comparing slavery and property in land, he finds them "essentially the same" as "two systems of appropriating the labor of other men" and explicates the situation in terms of landownership comprising economic and political authority in the hands of a few over the lives of many:

> ...a human being is as completely enslaved when the land on which he must live is made the property of another as when his own flesh and blood are made the property of that other. ...And...the effects of the two systems are substantially the same. He is, for instance, an hereditary legislator, with power in making laws which other Scotsmen, who have little or no voice in making laws, must obey under penalty of being fined, imprisoned, or hanged. He has this power, which is essentially that of the master to compel the slave, not because any one thinks that Nature gives wisdom and patriotism to eldest sons more than to younger sons, or to some families more than to other families, but because as the legal owner of a considerable part of Scotland, he is deemed to have greater rights in making laws than other Scotsmen, who can live in their native land only by paying some of the legal owners of Scotland for the privilege.

The situation would have as its contemporary analogy an official, that is, constitutionally explicit, plutocracy in which only billionaires (perhaps adjusted for changes in the price level) may sit in Congress and for whom only billionaires may vote. Prior to the Reform Act of 1832 (which did not by any interpretation greatly reverse matters) the right to vote and the ability to control membership in Parliament were in the hands of the less than ten per cent of the English population who satisfied what amounted to property requirements.

Irish Nationalism *(1893)*

In Argyll's *Irish Nationalism* (1893a), he acknowledges two major themes. One theme is that nation-states were formed as a result of victories by eventual kings over other nobles and would-be kings. The consolidation of central monarchy is the means of or road to union (p. 51). He contrasts the ravaging, destructive wars of the Irish chief-led tribes with the equally ferocious but constructive wars of the English:

> They [the Irish] were tribes...hereditary castes animated with all the passions which raged throughout the land; and actually taking part in the cruel and ferocious wars to which these passions led.
>
> (p. 27)

These wars had "not one single aim or object which could be dignified by the name 'political',...they were wars of mere plunder, slaughter, and devastation" (p. 27). The Irish wars were savage but also utterly useless and purely destructive, failing to generate a nation and a national government (pp. 30–1). The English people fought ferocious and barbaric wars, "but they fought for things worth fighting for. They were re-constructive, not purely destructive" (p. 31). The English "contended for true conquest—dominion–settlement—not for mere plunder, devastation, and ravage" (p. 31). Whereas the Anglo-Saxons had within 150 years founded kingdoms—"political communities with well-established principles of government, of industry, and of law"—and within another 350 years "had consolidated these kingdoms into one central monarchy, highly civilized, Christian, and to some degree even Imperial" (p. 32), the Celtic tribes had not made a single step forward, their interminable wars being mere savage raids, "destructive alike of peaceful industry and of the very beginnings of political organization" (p. 43). In feudal and post-feudal Europe, the conquering of land as an economic and political base meant that ownership and sovereignty went together; land ownership and governance grew up simultaneously. The other theme is that the history of Europe is a history of conquest or attempted conquest. Conquest and imperialism have both economic and political dimensions, that is, economic and political governance are inextricably intertwined. Argyll writes of the "process which had effected the civilization of all the rest of Europe—namely, conquest by a fresh race, and a higher and an older civilisation" (p. 147). "The thrones of kings have never been first established on abstract theories of duty; nor has the dominion of great nations ever been founded on mere philanthropy" (p. 150). Religion, in the age of the Reformation, is part of the story:

> Religion and politics were inseparably interwoven. That Christ's kingdom is "not of this world" was a doctrine neither accepted nor even understood by anybody....Catholicism did not represent religion—pure and unmixed. It represented, in a preeminent degree, politics in its most fundamental principles. It represented ambitions of domination...[t]he English Government and people...the spirit of a proud nationality.
>
> (pp. 186–7)

Argyll adds, "....t is quite idle to blame either party," but the English were the cause "best representing the lasting interests of mankind" (p. 187). The "seventeenth century...was everywhere an epoch of civil and of foreign wars and of political troubles—all...animated with, and some...entirely dominated by, the fiercest religious passions" (p. 189). "It was a century mainly occupied by the completion of the necessary work of conquest [of Ireland]" (p. 195).

The Unseen Foundations of Society *(1893)*

As John W. Mason noted, *The Unseen Foundations of Society* "was written partly as a riposte to Henry George's *Progress* and *Poverty*" of 1879 and "revealed the embattled mind of a large property owner in the 1890s" (Mason 1980: 578–9).[7] Argyll is overwhelmingly concerned with the defence of the institution of property as it then existed and of which he was a signal beneficiary. The chief form of wealth was landed property and the first of six heads making up the definition of wealth was Possession. Possession is not appropriation, he insists. "Appropriation is an act. Possession is a state or a condition" (Argyll 1893b: 40). "Possession means, in all ordinary use, lawful and legitimate possession. ... [N]o things, however valuable, can become wealth until they are gotten or possessed. ... [N]one of them will be wealth to us until we hold them as our own" (p. 41). He goes on to say, "It makes an immense difference in economic science if, in seeking the origin of wealth, we are compelled to begin with, and to think of, the origin of possession" (p. 42). Argyll concedes the danger arising from considering the origins of wealth, from "the throwing down of all containing walls." But he finds even more important the role of the social belief system in protecting the institution of property:

> If wealth does certainly include Possession, and if the mental attitude which constitutes the desire of acquisition be also included in it, then we must recognize as an indisputable fact, that religious beliefs and superstitions, moral sentiments and doctrines, legal maxims and traditions, have been the most powerful of all factors alike in its origin and growth, in its advancement or decay.
>
> (p. 42)

The social belief system, including religious and legal doctrines, is the protective belt surrounding and insulating that which has come to be designated property. Against the erosion of landed property by the forces and mindset of non-landed property, Argyll seeks to restore as much as he can of the protection once given landed property and now enjoyed by the owners of capital. This means the elevation of the principles of continuity over those of change. He inquires:

> Can there be anything more durable than well-reasoned principles of law, or than well-reasoned applications of those principles to the transactions of men?
>
> (p. 86)

Thus he quotes from Adam Smith's *Wealth of Nations*:

> That security which the laws in Great Britain give to every man that he shall enjoy the fruits of his own labour, is alone sufficient to make any country flourish.

(1893b: 86)

Argyll thereby combines continuity and security in such a way (as we have seen earlier) as to equate income with productivity, the fruits of one's own income, with the hope that the income of land will come under the same rubric. Thus does the doctrine of productivity find its usefulness in the belt protecting property.

Argyll's *The Unseen Foundations of Society* is essentially an extended brief that assumes a landowner-dominated society, polity, and economy and proceeds to argue that landownership is a, if not the, foundation of society, including governance. In such an economy, economists and ordinary people will formulate understandings of what is going on. These stories will derive from the experiences of people under the economic systems. The situation is comparable to the ruling elite contemplated by the Physiocrats. The ruling elite, essentially landlords, will dominate both the economy, including the saving-investment function, and the polity (ruling), all by virtue of their ownership of land in a legal-economic system in which rulership is vested in landownership. A story will be told of the essential services the landowning class provides to the rest of society: *their* prosperity will facilitate saving and investment and their ability to serve as rulers. What is seen is taken to be true: governance and saving investment are provided by them. What is not seen is not taken to be true: that governance and saving-investment can be undertaken in other ways. Inasmuch as one function of social control is to promote belief in the existing order, economic ideology, and religion will promote a story that reinforces the position of the landowning and ruling class, thereby further validating the story thus told. Ignorance is in this manner dissipated, created, and distributed. What is seen is a function of experience under particularly organized economic systems and of ideological training of perception. Neither experience nor trained perception picks up what remains unseen. In a variation on the foregoing, beneficiaries of the various systems can complain that critics of their system do not see what is fundamental to the existing system. Such is the gravamen of Argyll's *Unseen Foundations of Society*. What is obfuscated is the selective socially constructed nature of the existing system, that is, that the hierarchic positions being legitimized by the story are system-specific. A system of belief substitutes for an ontological absolute. That system of belief interprets and legitimizes the system and the system validates the system of belief. Argyll thus presents defences against criticism of inequality per se, the origins of inequality in coercion and conquest, class and hierarchy, and of land ownership-based governance. We now turn to the arguments for his position that are deployed in *Unseen Foundations*.

One argument is that "Possession means, in all ordinary use, lawful and legitimate possession" and in this sense "enters as an essential constituent into the concept of wealth" (Argyll 1893b: 41; see also pp. 42 and 281 ("the vivifying influence of possession")). Argyll wants to legitimize land ownership, in part obfuscating or diminishing the origin of ownership in conquest (which he acknowledges; see pp. 128–9, 199, 205–6, 236, 249, 369, and *passim*), and in part, as the victors in conquest, emphasizing the value of stable laws governing property and permitting the landowners to perform their function (the tension between expulsion of earlier possessors and secure possession for their successors is strikingly evident on pp. 128–9; see also 236). It is after conquest that the victors seek the "first foundations of wealth, which consist in a general desire for the legal definition of all rights and obligations" (p. 241), thereby affirming that policy should start from the status quo. Government is used, in "protecting property," to validate and legitimize as well as to put into economic effect the results of conquest. A corollary is that land should be seen as part of capital (*vide* "the particular class of capitalists who are owners of land" (p. 411), and therefore in terms of the functions of ownership:

> ...nothing can be more certain that capital is the embodiment and representative of the very highest kind of labour—namely that in which the mental energy if forethought, expresses itself in the savings and storages of wealth already acquired.
>
> Can there be anything more durable than well-reasoned principles of law, or than well-reasoned applications of these principles to the transactions of men?
>
> (pp. 72, 86)

The defence of inequality and hierarchical relations under existing institutions is a further argument (the qualification "under existing institutions" is important, because the same laudatory statements could be made about the new landlord class if class positions were reversed):

> For it is an inevitable law that equal freedom enjoyed by unequal powers is incompatible with a dead level of individual conditions.... the inequalities of personal ability or of character... [must have] room to work.
> (pp. 200–1; reiterated on pp. 578–9)
>
> ...the gradations into which society was divided were nothing but the gradations of history and of nature—the ranks into which men have been sifted and sorted in the streams and currents of actual life, according to corresponding disparities of mind and character.
> (p. 214; see also pp. 576–7 and *passim*)

Still another argument involves the denigration of the Ricardian theory of rent, which he calls "one of the most extraordinary delusions which has ever been accepted by reasoning men" (p. 305; see pp. 358ff. and *passim*; see earlier). When he declares against "such anarchical and immoral doctrines as those which have been founded on a belief in his [Ricardo's] theory" (p. 376; he also calls them "subversive deductions" (p. 381)) it is clear that Argyll has Henry George in mind (see pp. 387–420).

Notwithstanding his effort to render landed property safe through the perpetuation of stable law favoring landownership, Argyll also seeks to divorce property from government, treating property as a natural phenomenon and government as something separate if not exogenous. This position is evident in his statement that "it is [not] quite certain that any Governments, even the best, spend wealth on the whole better for the public interests than those to whom it belongs by the natural processes of acquisition" (p. 417). When Argyll takes up governance he defends those governments which were the instruments of the landed aristocracy and similarly situated folk against the charge that they sought only their own interests:

> There can be no broader mistake made in respect to historical fact than that which is now often repeated, that Parliaments and Government were careless of the interests of the wage-earning classes during the ages when these classes were not in the possession of political power.
>
> (p. 550)

Adam Smith, Edwin L. Godkin, and Rosa Luxemburg

That quite a different story could be told is evident from Adam Smith's *Wealth of Nations*, from Arygll's contemporary, Edwin L. Godkin, the American journalist (also a lawyer) who founded *The Nation*, and the Polish revolutionary Marxist, Rosa Luxemburg. These writers address very complex topics, with quite divergent themes, so it is not surprising that they can be interpreted in different ways. But on the topic of concern here, they are clear and in agreement. Property is the interests protected as property (it is property because it is protected, not protected because it is property) and those in control of government use it to protect their interests either as property per se or rights that are the functional equivalent of property. Smith's and Godkin's stories, in Argyll's view, are both mistaken and subversively uttered. But all three men agree on the class nature of property, the ostensible role of government with regard to property, and the powers of governance inhering in property.

Adam Smith

Smith wrote the following:

> Men may live together in society with some tolerable degree of security, though there is no civil magistrate to protect them from the injustice of those passions. But avarice and ambition in the rich, in the poor the hatred of labour and the love of present ease and enjoyment, are the passions which prompt to invade property, passions much more steady in their operation,

and much more universal in their influence. Wherever there is great property there is great inequality. For one very rich man there must be at least five hundred poor, and the affluence of the few supposes the indigence of the many. The affluence of the rich excites the indignation of the poor, who are often both driven by want, and prompted by envy, to invade his possessions. It is only under the shelter of the civil magistrate that the owner of that valuable property, which is acquired by the labour of many years, or perhaps of many successive generations, can sleep a single night in security. He is at all times surrounded by unknown enemies, whom, though he never provoked, he can never appease, and from whose injustice he can be protected only by the powerful arm of the civil magistrate continually held up to chastise it. The acquisition of valuable and extensive property, therefore, necessarily requires the establishment of civil government. Where there is no property, or at least none that exceeds the value of two or three days' labour, civil government is not so necessary.

Civil government supposes a certain subordination. But as the necessity of civil government gradually grows up with the acquisition of valuable property, so the principal causes which naturally introduce subordination gradually grow up with the growth of that valuable property. The causes or circumstances which naturally introduce subordination, or which naturally, and antecedent to any civil institution, give some men some superiority over the greater part of their brethren, seem to be four in number.

(Smith 1976a, Vol. I: 709–10)

It is in the age of shepherds, in the second period of society, that the inequality of fortune first begins to take place, and introduces among men a degree of authority and subordination which could not possibly exist before. It thereby introduces some degree of that civil government which is indispensably necessary for its own preservation: and it seems to do this naturally, and even independent of the consideration of that necessity. The consideration of that necessity comes no doubt afterwards to contribute very much to maintain and secure that authority and subordination. The rich, in particular, are necessarily interested to support that order of things which can alone secure them in the possession of their own advantages. Men of inferior wealth combine to defend those of superior wealth in the possession of their property, in order that men of superior wealth may combine to defend them in the possession of theirs. All the inferior shepherds and herdsmen feel that the security of their own herds and flocks depends upon the security of those of the great shepherd or herdsman; that the maintenance of their lesser authority depends upon that of his greater authority, and that upon their subordination to him depends his power of keeping their inferiors in subordination to them. They constitute a sort of little nobility, who feel themselves interested to defend the property and to support the authority of their own little sovereign in order that he may be able to defend their property and to support their authority. Civil government, so far as it is instituted for the security of property, is in reality instituted for the defence of the rich against the poor, or of those who have some property against those who have none at all.

(Smith 1976a, Vol. I: 715)

For Smith, government itself is not exogenous to the system; government is due to and to a large extent the instrument of the propertied, of those, that is, who use government to cement and institutionalize their systemic social power. As Smith says, "Till there be property there can be no government, the very end of which is to secure wealth and to defend the rich from the poor" (Smith 1977: 404). Social control through law must be understood to be a function of social structure.

Edwin L. Godkin

Smith published his great work in 1776, well before the two nineteenth-century reactions to the middle-class transformation of economy and society discussed earlier. Smith may have favored free markets (within the law) but he deals neither with the transformations of economy and society that transpired in the nineteenth century. Godkin, on the other hand, not only lived during that period but was intellectually a part of it, and there is much more than in Smith's time to be candid about.

In his *Unforeseen Tendencies of Democracy* (1898) Godkin says of the ancient democracies of Greece and Rome that they faced the problem of "more or less frequently...resisting the attempts of rich men to set up either a monarchy or an aristocracy. ...[T]he rich class were rarely content with the existing state of things, always felt they could do better if they had their way, and were as purely selfish as aristocracies are apt to be. They were convinced that the most important interest of the state was that they, not the many, should be happy and content" (p. 13). The point is very important to Godkin:

In all ancient democracies...the internal history is generally an account of contests between the poor and the rich; meaning by "poor" persons who are not rich,—not the extremely poor. An oligarchy always consists of rich men; a democracy, of what may be called people of moderate means. For the most part, the rich seem never to be thoroughly content with the rule of the many, and long to rid themselves of it. ...They think themselves entitled to rule, and think their contentment the chief object of the state.

(p. 21)

As with Smith, for the rich (whose rights were derived from their past use of government) to advance their interests, they needed, they felt, the control of government. Godkin also says of the Middle Ages that:

The citizens or burgesses owned the state or city as property, and transmitted it to their children. They gave nothing to non-citizens but permission to reside and protection. The idea that mere birth and residence ought to give citizenship gained ground only after the French Revolution, and was not really received in England until the reform of the municipalities in 1832. The old confinement of the citizenship to a small body of property-holders, or descendants of property-holders, undoubtedly gave the property qualification to such of the modern European states as set up an elected legislature or council. Down to the passage of the Reform Bill in England, the exclusion of all but freeholders from the franchise seemed a perfectly natural arrangement. It was very difficult for most Englishmen, and the same thing is true of the earlier Americans, to suppose that any one could take a genuine interest in the welfare of the country, or be willing to make sacrifices for its sake, who did not own land in it. The central idea of the ancient city was in this way made to cover the larger area of a modern kingdom.

(p. 17)

As for the treatment of the non-propertied masses, Godkin, in contrast to the last quotation here from Argyll, argues that:

in nearly every country on the Continent, outside Switzerland, privilege reigned supreme, with harsh, even contemptuous treatment of the poor.... All its political arrangements seem to have been made simply for the purpose of enabling a small class to enjoy themselves, and to indulge in their favorite amusement of commanding armies.

(p. 26)

Godkin then discusses various meanings of the principle of equality, but the historical focus and foundation of much of his writing are the consequences which he felt flowed from the adoption of political democracy. He thus writes of "the exclusion of the old landed class from the work of government, a process which began soon after the French Revolution..." (p. 39). But even in America, "In all the colonies, and for some years in all the states, offices were reserved naturally for men of local mark, generally created by property and social position" (p. 53)—many of whom, George would argue, achieved and maintained that position through the receipt of rent. Godkin accepts as given the close historical connection between property and government, in which control of government derives from property and property derives from control of government; in short, the world whose passing is lamented by Argyll. Says Godkin:

In fact, from the fall of the Roman Empire almost to our time, the world was governed by property, and property was mainly land, and was associated in the popular mind, to a degree which we now find it difficult to understand, with political power and prominence. A landless man was held to have no "stake in the country," and therefore to have no right to manage public affairs. ...Probably nothing did as much to democratize America as the abundance of land and the ease of its acquisition. People began to perceive that a large landowner was not necessarily a great man, and the idea of government by landholders, which had held possession of the world for a thousand years, was killed by the perception.

> (pp. 53–4, emphasis added; see also
> Godkin 1966 [1896]: 181)

Earlier, public opinion in the colonies existed largely as follows:

> The opinions of leading men, of clergymen and large landholders, were very powerful, and settled most of the affairs of state; but the opinion of the majority did not count for much, and the majority, in truth, did not think that it should.
>
> (p. 184)

Instead of public opinion emanating "from the majority of adult males":

> According to the aristocratic school, it should emanate only from persons possessing [at least] a moderate amount of property, on the assumption that the possession of property argues some degree of intelligence and interest in public affairs.
>
> (p. 185)

At one point Godkin seemingly acknowledges the power of governance residing in the hands of bankers and other capitalists whose approval for loans is required (p. 242). In a market economy, that is, fundamental decisions that impact others are made by those in command of property.

Godkin writes of a Georgist tax policy adopted in New South Wales, in Australia. For our purposes it is instructive that he interprets that policy as rendering "the state ... a landlord on an extensive scale" because it receives a share of economic rent, a situation, he laments, which led to the question of rents growing "into a great political question" (p. 247). Finally, in *Unforeseen Tendencies*, Godkin says that "Down to a very recent period," Americans looked "to the government for nothing but protection of life and property" (p. 255). That property was property because it received the protection of government, and not vice versa, is an important point. But in his second relevant book there is an extremely important sequel.

In his *Problems of Modern Democracy* (1966 [1896]) Godkin in part expands, in part reiterates, and in part updates the foregoing themes. One major theme is that the wealthy should not abstain from politics/governance; they should, as natural leaders, assume the role of leadership "to which their riches entitle them" (p. xxvi, Morton Keller's Introduction; see also pp. xxx–xxxi, regarding the "prime constituency" of the Republican Party being that "portion of the population 'which possesses the larger share of the intelligence, public spirit, thrift, industry, foresight, and accumulated property of the country', " quoting Godkin). Some policy issues, he believed, like the monetary standard, should be in the hands of apolitical experts (pp. xxxiv–xxxv), as if experts are not political and agree. This devotee of laissez-faire could not be comfortable with his prediction, in 1898 (the year of the war with Spain), that "the government will shortly undergo great changes which will be presided over, not by men of light and learning, but by capitalists and adroit politicians... the military spirit has taken possession of the masses, to whom power has passed" (p. xxxvi, letter to Charles Eliot Norton, November 29, 1898). The United States did not have a landed aristocracy, but he felt that no change in its transformation "has been so marked as the transfer to wealth of the political and social influence which was formerly shared, if not absorbed, by literary, oratorical, or professional distinction" (p. xxxviii).

His principal argument, for our purposes, is expressed in various ways. The principle of equality is said to result in conceding to all persons equality before the law, from which it is a very short step "to the possession of an equal share in the making of the laws" (p. 56; see also pp. 285–6). This represents a shift from ideal to ideal; he himself, however, emphasizes among the problems of modern democracy considerable inequality in law-making power. In the late nineteenth century, he found "as in France, Germany, and England, the poorer classes were just becoming aware of the extent of the power over the government which universal suffrage had put into their hands" (p. 175). He states his principal argument to include more than the landowning elite:

> I simply say that it was the most natural thing in the world for the working classes of England, for example, which had been so long familiar with legislation for the direct benefit of the middle and upper classes, to receive with anger or suspicion the announcement that the care of any class by the state was a mistake, and that individual independence was the true rule of industrial life. When these classes, therefore, found themselves invested through the suffrage with political power, it was inevitable that they should seek at once to improve their condition through legislation.
>
> (p. 176; to not do so was to render permanent legislation benefiting others)

> What one learns... is the difficulty, in a democratic government, of moderation of any description, if it once abandons the policy of *laissez faire*, and undertakes to be a providence for the masses. There is no limit to the human appetite for unearned or easily earned money. No class is exempt from it. Under the old régime, the aristocrats got all the sinecures, the pensions, and the light jobs of every description. One of the results of the triumph of democracy has been to throw open this source of gratification to the multitude, and every attempt made to satisfy the multitude, in this field, has failed.
>
> (Godkin 1898: 251–2)

These are remarkably important statements. Abandonment of the policy of laissez-faire is equated with democratization in the sense of a wide competition for benefits from the government. This wide competition replaces not a system in which the distribution of government largesse is absent; rather, under the old régime government-distributed largesse went solely to the aristocrats. Laissez-faire = largesse solely to aristocracy; democracy = largesse thrown open to all.

Affirmation of laissez-faire does not signify absence of government largesse, only that it is distributed to the aristocrats.

But the principal argument connecting landownership with governance is reiterated time and again:

> Now, the governing class...was...the wealthy class; and the wealthy class until the present century were the owners of the soil...on the theory that the landowners were the country.
>
> (pp. 180–1)

The theory, of course, did not lead to the institution. That was a matter of conquest. The theory came later, to provide justification.

> The "man of property" was the landed man. He and his followers owned the country, and it seemed for ages perfectly natural and right that they should govern the country.
>
> (pp. 182–3)

Godkin also presents his argument about landownership and governing power in a manner that seems to validate George's position. "The economical or political revolutions" of the nineteenth century transferred power "from the owners of the land to people of every kind of occupation," the great landowners having been converted into annuitants forming an "idle class...no longer render[ing] the state the service which the old feudal tenures exacted of them, and their enjoyment of large incomes...becomes increasingly difficult to defend in the forum of abstract justice" (p. 185; on status emulation and conspicuous consumption, see p. 318). They increasingly "protect themselves by showing the danger to all property that would probably result from an attack on their particular kind of property" (pp. 185–6). He points out that while "The labour problem" is really the problem of making the manual laborers of the world content with their lot—clearly the view of social control from the top down—"the existing discontent is, and not unreasonably, aggravated by the spectacle of the...idle class" (pp. 193–4). George, if he had read Godkin, might have been pleased in learning that "The taxes paid by the annuitant or *rentier* class are but a trifling return, in reality, for the security they possess for person and property" (p. 194; see also p. 203). On land and governance reform, Godkin wrote, "The recent Irish land laws are the dethronement of a great class, the apparent sacrifice of the few to the many, on a large scale; this is what democracy calls for, but it is never accomplished without seemingly serious violations of natural justice" (p. 279). There are several points to note here: "Natural justice" is ambiguous but likely composed in terms favorable to the status quo prior to the reforms. No implication is intended here regarding the reforms. The main point is that a beneficiary of an old, received power structure and set of customs will inevitably have such views when confronted with a new structure and set—and our saying so privileges neither the old nor the new. Godkin also notes that the English aristocracy was alert enough to introduce "the merit system, in time to save it from the incoming democracy" (p. 289).

Land ownership is but one form of property and wealth; governance derived from land ownership is also derived, often enough, from other forms of property and wealth. In this connection, Godkin criticizes the new phenomenon, the great corporation. "These aggregations of capital in a few hands have created a new power in the State, whose influence on government has been very grave." The managers defend their position and their policies with an argument consisting of a particular definition of reality, that "they are the custodians of large amounts of other people's property, which they are bound to defend, by whomsoever attacked" (p. 293). Godkin understood the role of corporate management as social control through their influence on, if not control of, government.

> How to bring these corporations under the law, and at the same time protect them from unjust attacks, is one of the most serious problems of democratic government. ...Corporations are as powerful as individual noblemen or aristocrats were in England in the last century, or in France before the Revolution, but are far harder to get at or bring to justice, from their habit of making terms with their enemies instead of fighting them.
>
> (p. 294)

Godkin could have added that corporations are often instrumental in writing the legislation that covers their business. Godkin seems to object the most strenuously to the "transfer of the government to the poor." He again reminds his reader that, "except during very short periods in ancient democracies, the world has been governed by rich men; that is, by the great landholders or the great merchants. ... Every government has been a rich man's government." With government transferred to poor men, "through the taxing power rich corporations and rich individuals are at their mercy. They are ... often stimulated by envy or antisocial passions" (p. 300). This type of admission brings out into the open what hitherto had been the object of ideology to obfuscate and render unseen. Godkin is candid, to the point, surely, of leading some readers to judge him subversive: such things should not be said in public. Nor is the topic of plutocracy the only one so treated. Patriotism "has been made by the multitude to consist in holding everything [*sic*] that is, to be exactly right, or easily remedied." Any man who would succeed in politics or business "is strongly tempted to proclaim incessantly his great content with the existing order of things, and to treat everything 'American' as sacred" (p. 305). It is views such as these that George confronted, even though he felt that his views were more consonant with American ideals than those of these other people.

Rosa Luxemburg

Rosa Luxemburg articulated a point of view similar to the others presented here. Not only does she, too, find that governance derived from land ownership, she identifies the governance founded on land ownership to include all three branches of what is now seen as the division of power, and, further, interprets land ownership and governance with regard to the control of the human labor force. Only two brief quotations need be given:

> ...each great noble lord of the middle ages, especially at the time of Charlemagne, was a similar emperor on a smaller scale—because his free noble ownership of the land made him lawmaker, tax-collector, and judge over all the inhabitants of his manors.
>
>   ...it happened that in all of Europe the formerly free peasant lands had been transformed into noble domains from which tributes and rents were exacted, how the formerly free peasantry had been transformed into an oppressed class constrained to perform labor services, to be bound to the land, even, during the later stages.
>
> (Waters 1970: 229–31)

Such unanimity should occasion no surprise. Otto von Gierke established that governance was an attribute of land ownership: "Rulership and Ownership were blent" (Gierke 1958: 88).

Conclusion

In his *Theory of Moral Sentiments*, Adam Smith uses the term "invisible hand" to explain how spending by the rich gives employment to the poor and thereby makes the distribution of consumption more equal than the distributions of income or wealth:

> It is to no purpose, that the proud and unfeeling landlord views his extensive fields, and without a thought for the wants of his brethren, in imagination consumes himself the whole harvest that grows upon them. The homely and vulgar proverb, that the eye is larger than the belly, never was more fully verified than with regard to him. The capacity of his stomach bears no proportion to the immensity of his desires, and will receive no more than that of the meanest peasant. The rest he is obliged to distribute among those, who prepare, in the nicest manner, that little which he himself makes use of, among those who fit up the palace in which this little is to be consumed, among those who provide and keep in order all the different baubles and trinkets, which are employed in the economy of greatness; all of whom thus derive from his luxury and caprice, that share of the necessaries of life, which they would in vain have expected from his humanity or his justice. The produce of the soil maintains at all times nearly that number of inhabitants which it is capable of maintaining. The rich only select from the heap what is most precious and agreeable. They consume little more than the poor, and in spite of their natural selfishness and rapacity, though they mean only their own conveniency, though the sole end which they propose from the labours of all the thousands whom they employ, be the gratification of their own vain and insatiable desires, they divide with the poor the produce of all their

improvements. They are led by an invisible hand to make nearly the same distribution of the necessaries of life, which would have been made, had the earth been divided into equal portions among all its inhabitants, and thus without intending it, without knowing it, advance the interest of the society, and afford means to the multiplication of the species. When Providence divided the earth among a few lordly masters, it neither forgot nor abandoned those who seemed to have been left out in the partition. These last too enjoy their share of all that it produces. In what constitutes the real happiness of human life, they are in no respect inferior to those who would seem so much above them. In ease of body and peace of mind, all the different ranks of life are nearly upon a level, and the beggar, who suns himself by the side of the highway, possesses that security which kings are fighting for.

(Smith 1976b: 184–5)

We suspect that the eighth Duke of Argyll would have strongly objected to the first sentence of this quotation. He surely did not consider himself a "proud and unfeeling landlord [who] views his extensive fields, and without a thought for the wants of his brethren, in imagination consumes himself the whole harvest that grows upon them." But equally surely he understood that consumption is not the issue; the issue is the distribution of wealth, in part the accumulation of capital and in part the division of landed property. John Locke had shown, or at least argued, that the introduction of money permitted unequal acquisition of assets, whereas in the state of nature each individual could appropriate from the common pool only that which he and his family could consume and then only if as much and as good remained for others. Now Smith presents a "trickle down" picture in which spending by the rich gives employment to the poor and thereby makes the distribution of consumption more equal than the distributions of income or wealth.

The use of money permits unlimited acquisition—of consumer goods, of capital goods, of financial instruments, and of land. But land became unequally owned, historically, through conquest and favoritism by rulers; and this unequal ownership had as one of its potential features an accompanying "monopoly" of sovereignty, that is, of governance, by landowners. Even in Smith's story, we read of "Providence divid[ing] the earth among a few lordly masters." Smith understood that land ownership brought economic and political power; owning land made one the master. George Douglas Campbell, the eighth Duke of Argyll, understood that, too. He may have been uncomfortable with the public attribution of power but he certainly understood that he had economic and political power (in a non-pejorative sense). And his claim of providing living accommodations for others, for poorer other people, is akin in intended meaning to what Smith wrote. Moreover, Argyll wrote with the purpose of maintaining the system in which he enjoyed such power. And so did Henry George understand, except that he condemned that system.

What, then, is the difference between Argyll and George? Extreme and absolutist claims and other statements can be put aside as so much rhetoric and/or bargaining positions; so too with flowery language. These were two motivated, indeed, ardent supporters of their positions. The Duke and the writer from the working class came from two very different worlds. One is reminded of Lord and Lady Chatterley looking upon what is supposedly Manchester and the husband wondering aloud how he would have turned out had he been raised in Manchester (Lawrence 1928). The difference between Argyll and George seems in part to be in the language that they respectively use in describing the social world of ownership. At bottom, however, the picture is the same. The difference is almost wholly in their normative positions. Argyll is at least prepared to accept his lot in life and the system from which it emanates. Likely he more than accepts it; he relishes it. It is a system with problems, like any system. But it works, it is basically sound, it is moral, it is beneficent, it is the work of centuries of unseen forces, and, above all, it *is*, and has to be reckoned with, not lightly dismissed.

George is not prepared to passively accept his lot in life and the system that permits and gives rise to it. He detests the system. It is not merely a system with problems, it is a system which, from its origins, has condemned the majority of people to inferiority, to suffering, and, even worse, to premature death. It is a system run by and for the ruling class(es). However, the system, when not perverted, could abide by true morality, that of honest labor, hard work, and reward based thereon. The existing system is different. Its inequality derives from (1) the acquisition of the lion's share of land and its unearned income by a relative handful of households and families, (2) the majority's unequal ability to accumulate capital because others, benefiting in part from unequal ownership of land, had gotten a head start, and (3) perhaps the largest part, the landowners' historical control of government, increasingly in partnership with the owners of non-landed property.

What Argyll sees as an advantage and as the object of his program of retention, George sees as a predicament, a major obstacle, and the object of his program of reform. Both men identify and accept the reality of the power of governance derived from—and reinforced by—the ownership of land. Governance included private governance authority running with land ownership and public government position running likewise, with positions as local magistrates or sheriffs spanning both. Within their respective normative positions they also differ on their positive analyses of how arrangements work especially on the genesis of rent and the relation of landownership to human wellbeing.

Argyll considers George's program to be socialist, because it would nationalize and transfer economic rent from its hitherto private recipients into the government's treasury. George believes, however, that rent has been an unearned income for the landowners and that so far from taking from the landowners what is theirs, his Single Tax will not only prevent private receipt of unearned income but promote the values that lead to earned income. How, therefore, George believes, could such a program be socialist? It protects true earned income-based property and ends spoliation by those who took over the land and turned it over to their heirs and assigns. In response to these claims, Argyll claims that land ownership is productive and that the proof and measure of its productivity is the income that it receives. To which, in turn, George responds: landownership per se is not productive.

George believes that the capture by government of economic rent will avoid the adverse effects of progress, the poverty that has accompanied the production of greater wealth. The Single Tax will also avoid the conditions that many associate from population increase but in reality are due to the capture of land rent by private owners. George believes in the reform of governance. Government should not be in the hands of landowners; it should not be in the hands of the propertied, period. Property owners should have no greater share in making the laws than a comparable number of non-owners. In the mid-nineteenth century some appointed government office holders, intending both to take advantage of their positions and to foreclose the idea of a professional civil service, argued that their appointments constituted legal property rights to their positions. If they had succeeded, government itself would have been made into private property, like land.

George's position largely turns on the unearned nature of rent. The notion of unearned income can be seen in several ways. The idea of something being unearned seems to be normative to some people. To others the distinction between earned and unearned income rests on an objective, positivist basis, that is, the growth of society. To still others, following David Hume's injunction that one cannot go from an "is" to an "ought" without an additional normative premise, the matter is more complicated. But more is involved in George's position than the unearned increment. Also relevant are the normative matters of whether land should be within the institution of private property and whether land ownership should convey powers of governance. Another arguable matter is whether property *is* sovereignty.

Frank H. Knight was no disciple of Henry George (see Tideman and Plassmann 2004) but neither did he agree with Argyll that ownership per se was sufficient warrant. In his *Ethics of Competition* (1936: 56), Knight wrote, "... income does not go to factors but to their owners, and can in no case have more ethical justification than has the fact of ownership. The ownership of personal or material productive capacity is based on a complex mixture of inheritance, luck and effort.... What is the ideal distribution from the standpoint of... ethics may be disputed but of the three considerations named above certainly none but the effort can have ethical validity." He also wrote, "It [the market] distributes the produce of industry on the basis of power which is ethical only insofar as right and might are one. It [the market] is a confessed failure in the field of promoting social progress, and its functions in this regard are being progressively taken over by other social agencies" (1936: 58). In *Freedom and Reform* (1947: 67) Knight noted that the savings and dissavings determined through time in a market characterized by unequal initial endowments of income-earning rights and privileges can be expected to lead to "cumulative increase in inequality of... power." And for Knight, power connoted governance.

The power that is governance is obviously political. It is also, perhaps not so obviously, economic. In the case of both landowners and capital owners, economic power resides in their constituting a saving-investment elite, the providers of income to the working class (including hired hands and tenants), and the combination of their organization for production and of production.

Social functions—productivity—are latent therein. Ownership per se is a matter of who performs those functions, and is derived from historic processes and patterns of inequality.

The immediately foregoing paragraph is further revealing once unpacked or deconstructed. One element concerns Argyll's identification of the mental role of entrepreneurship in the creation of wealth. The history of economic thought on the entrepreneur turns in large part on the positions taken on two questions. One question concerns the precise nature of the role of the entrepreneur. Suffice it to say that a multiplicity of specifications of that role have been made, some possibly in conflict with others. In the preceding paragraph I have generalized (and begged) them by stipulating activities leading to the organization for production and the organization of production. Argyll makes no original contribution here. His principal lasting point, also recognized by Alfred Marshall, who made it another factor of production, is that management, entrepreneurship or whatever it is called, must be recognized as performing an important organizing function.[8]

The second question concerns the entrepreneurial function and whether it is performed by a specific group of people or is an aspect of the activity of all economic agents. For example, if by role is meant, alternatively, the discovery or the creation of niches—opportunities for gain—this may be undertaken by all agents or only by a select group of agents. Argyll advances an elite theory: the entrepreneur is the capitalist and landowner and their entrepreneurial role is combined with that of a savings-investment elite. The elite theory of the entrepreneur is part, a large part, of his defence of possession of private property, the second element. He wants to argue, though perhaps not so baldly, that property ownership is what enables a person to be in a position to perform that role. Again a circular argument: the role is performed by the propertied, and owning property enables them to perform the role. The inconclusiveness of the argument turns in part on whether the existing distribution of property can be shown to empower those with the most ability to organize production. (The parallel question in politics was raised with regard to lines of hereditary monarchs and their progeny's ability to govern.) Some of this was recognized by John W. Mason a quarter-century ago. Mason noted that Argyll "became self-appointed spokesman for the landed classes in a period when they were under a great threat" (Mason 1980: 579), concluded that he combined free exchange and elite theories (p. 587), and judged "much less convincing... [Argyll's] attempt to prove that the existing distribution of wealth, both landed and non-landed, accurately reflected the distribution of potential wealth-creating talent" (p. 580). (Some, perhaps much, of this is similar to Vilfredo Pareto's theory of the circulation of the elite.)

That conclusion is reinforced by two further considerations. One is that there is no unique wealth-creating distribution of entitlements/property ownership. Each different set of entitlements, or each different distribution of property, yields a different and non-comparable result (i.e. different and non-comparable Pareto-optimal results), the non-comparability due to the absence of a metric common to all results (i.e. a non-comparable price structure specific to each result). The other is that some African colonies of European nations prevented the native population from owning land but required them to pay taxes in the ruling white man's money, thus forcing them into the white man's labor market in which free exchange could be claimed to exist.

Argyll did his argument little good by recognizing, as he must, that land owner-ship has been a matter of both conquest and purchase and sale. That the "very possession of land was evidence of the successful outcome of a fierce struggle—military and economic" (Mason 1980: 579) did not conduce to a belief—unless one started with it—that the talents useful in such struggle were also useful in the organization for and of production, say, in a hierarchical landowning aristocracy.

The ideas and political developments of at least the last two centuries can be seen as turning on the conflict between elitist and democratic republicanism. The former means the control of government by a more or less loosely ruling ruling class; the latter, control of the government by all people, including, and especially, the ordinary, common people—whom Abraham Lincoln meant when he spoke of "government of the people, by the people, and for the people." The former lauds either the special qualities of the elite or the relative ease of upward mobility; the latter condemns enormous inequalities of income and wealth, and the political power of the wealthy that conduces to further inequality through their control and use of government.

All of what is described in this article is thus played out against, or within, the working out of the pair of twin tendencies in society, hierarchy and equality, and continuity and change. Such was the stage, and Argyll and George were players in this continuing drama. Each believed he had Truth on his side, but truth or Truth has very little to do with it. Propositions, such as the inviolability of private property (Mason 1980: 578), have meaning not in terms of their substantive claims but in the role to which they are put. As Ritchie (1893: 522) put it, "legal security and political stability are essential to social welfare; but the greatest enemies of security and stability are those who resist every change in institutions, while such changes can still be made by legal and constitutional means." The Duke of Argyll, for all his use of absolutist formulation in making the case for continuity of property arrangements against proposals for change he disliked, was a leader in the movement to consolidate holdings—the elimination of the runrig system of dispersed strips.[9] It was more than a superficial rearrangement of holdings. It "deeply affected" the "circumstances of the broad mass of the cultivating population." It "betokened more drastic social experiment," because it was "entangled with conscious attempts on the part of the landlords to alter the underlying relation of land and people: to re-align tenants in new social groups: and to force industrial experiments on traditionally agricultural groups" (Gray 1952: 46).[10] Argyll was thus a major player in processes which confirm de Jouvenel's dictum that history "is in essence a battle of dominant wills, fighting in every way they can for the material which is common to everything they construct: the human labor force" (de Jouvenel 1962: 177). Henry George understood that that was what ownership of land was all about, namely, property as gover-nance: the organization of production, the control of the human labor force, and the control of the state and its use for those purposes.

One final dimension of seen and unseen remains. A recent study of the rhetoric in Winston Churchill's military histories includes the statement, "The signal feature of Churchill's histories is the way they maintain an aristocratic perspective in democratic times without losing their democratic sympathies" (Valiunas 2002: 2; quoted in Teagarden 2004). How can our subjects be characterized along these lines? Argyll maintains an aristocratic perspective in a period of transformation from aristocratic to democratic structures and does so with evident relish but without the harshness or antagonism found in other defenders of hierarchy. Godkin is rather like Churchill, or Valiunas's view of him, in maintaining an aristocratic perspective in democratic times without losing his democratic sympathies. Hayek seems to have done likewise. Henry George has very different ideas. George maintains a democratic perspective in a society that continues to have strong aristocratic perspectives and structural elements. He would change society in ways that would limit certain *rentier* and other hierarchic forces of the past but is in other respects as conservative as David Ricardo. All four want to change the structure of society, system of governance, path of societal development, and set of dominant policies. The doctrines of each of them render certain beliefs not only seen but salient and other beliefs not only unseen but obfuscated.

At bottom, debates over ownership and governance are part of the process of working out the legal-economic nexus (Samuels 1989). Simultaneously worked out in this nexus are the features of the political system (or what is conventionally perceived as such) that impact the economic system (or what is conventionally perceived as such) and of the features of the economic system (or what is conventionally perceived as such) that impact the political system (or what is conventionally perceived as such). The parenthetic language is reiterated in order to emphasize selective perception and the manipulation of perception. Argyll and George were not alone in operating upon such an understanding of the recursive relations within the legal-economic nexus. For example, it has recently been written of Robert Lowe (1811–92), the English economist and politician, that he conducted a "campaign against the extension of the franchise. Political economy was prominent in his argument, Lowe alleging that working-class voters would be protectionist, stateist and use their power to plunder the property of the rich via punitive taxation" (Rutherford 2004, Vol. II: 698). At the core of the matter is power, and political and economic power are but twin aspects of the working out of the power structure governing whose interests count. And in the larger sphere of things, it is not only the rights of landed property that are involved but the rights of non-landed property and rights not designated property rights at all, as well as the legal-economic nexus itself.

Notes

1 Property derived from financial manipulation was also anathema of George.
2 The reader should search using Google for "land ownership in Britain" and "land ownership in Hawaii."
3 Data is taken from Cahill 2001; Cramb 2000; Wightman 1999. See www.canongate. net/list/glp.taf?_p = 5431 and www.red-star-research.org.uk/rap/rap6.html

4 Gide and Rist's use of the term "idle" is specialized. The landowners are idle in comparison with the productive class, the cultivators, in the Physiocrats' system; they still have the two roles to perform.

5 Argyll's "The Prophet of San Francisco" was published in the *Nineteenth Century* for April 1884 and George's reply, "Reduction of Iniquity," was published in the July 1884 number. The two essays were published as *Property in Land* by Funk & Wagnalls (New York, 1884). The latter is reproduced in the collection, Henry George, *The Land Question* (1982 [1884]).

6 An early reviewer of *The Unseen Foundations of Society* questioned the coherence of Argyll's notions of the laws of nature and of the role of legitimacy in the definition of wealth ("legitimate possession"), asking,

> If, then, slavery be an institution contrary to the "law of nature," are we bound to deny that slaves could ever be or have been a form of wealth? And if slaves were not wealth, why did the British government give compensation to the West Indian planters? If any one sincerely believes that the possession of large estates, or of vast sums of capital, is not a morally legitimate object of desire, would he, in the Duke of Argyll's opinion, be justified in treating the great land-owner or capitalist as not really owning what he seems to own?
>
> (Ritchie 1893: 517)

7 E. A. Ross's review likewise wrote that the book is "a defense of reactionary economic individualism" and has "the intellectual ear-marks of the Liberty and Property Defense League...the outcome of the practical instinct of self-preservation. Throughout the book is the note of alarm at the menacing attitude that later reform movements assume toward property and vested interests...the anxious special pleading of the great landowner and capitalist" (Ross 1893: 723).

8 See Alfred Marshall, *Principles of Economics*, eighth edit. (London: Macmillan, 1920), Book VI, Chapters vi–viii. —Ed.

9 The crofting system of land use and township organization grew up in the eighteenth and nineteenth centuries. Previously the land was held by clans and distributed to clansmen in the "runrig" system of widely dispersed holdings. This system was also to a large extent communal, but the focus was upon the clan. With the decline of the clan system, the community became more geographically oriented. The primary difference between crofting and the runrig system was that in crofting, individual holdings were consolidated. With the Crofters Holdings Act of 1886, crofting areas were defined, and assurance was given of security of tenure, hereditary succession, and fair rent. See Ducey (1956).—Ed.

10 Paralleling the enclosure movement in England, which in effect expropriated peasant rights, was the granting and enforcing of plenary mining rights to noblemen in France, effectively confiscating peasant rights. From one point of view, such enabled larger, more efficient production; but such does not negate the confiscation. More broadly, in England and elsewhere, the period *c.*1600–1900 witnessed the transformation of the legal foundations of the economy from that of an agrarian, landed-property society to that of an urban, non-landed property society. Even the adoption and assignment of new rights of economic significance had a confiscatory effect. In none of this was compensation paid. What confiscation yieldeth, confiscation taketh away.

References

Argyll, 8th Duke of (George Douglas Campbell) (1877) *Essay on the Commercial Principles Applicable to Contracts for the Hire of Land*, London: Cassell, Petter and Galpin.

—— (1884) *The Prophet of San Francisco: A Criticism of the Attack on Private Ownership of Land in Henry George's* Progress and Poverty *and* Social Problems, reprinted from *The Nineteenth Century*, London: Kegan Paul & Co.

—— (1893a) *The Unseen Foundations of Society*, London: John Murray.

—— (1893b) *Irish Nationalism: An Appeal to History*, London: John Murray.

Cahill, Kevin (2001) *Who Owns Britain?* Edinburgh: Canongate Books.

Cramb, Auslan (2000) *Who Owns Scotland Now?* Edinburgh: Mainstream.

Ducey, P. R. (1956) *Cultural Continuity and Population Change on the Isle of Skye*, Ann Arbor, MI: University Microfilms (no. 00–17, 051).

Ezekiel, Mordechai (1957) "Distribution of Gains from Rising Technical Efficiency in Progressing Countries," *American Economic Review/Supplement*, 47: 361–75.

Gaffney, Mason (1994) *The Corruption of Economics*, London: Shepheard-Walwyn.

George, Henry (1982) [1884] *The Land Question*, New York: Robert Schalkenbach Foundation.

George, H. (1885) "The Reduction of Iniquity," in G. D. Campbell (ed.) *The Peer and the Prophet: Being the Duke of Argyll's article on* The Prophet of San Francisco *and the Reply of Henry George*, reprinted from *The Nineteenth Century*, London: William Reeves.

Gide, Charles and Charles Rist (1948) [1915] *A History of Economic Doctrines*, Boston, MA: D.C. Heath.

Gierke, Otto von (1958) *Political Theories of the Middle Age*, F. W. Maitland (trans.) Boston, MA: Beacon Press.

Godkin, Edwin L. (1966) [1896] *Problems of Modern Democracy: Political and Economic Essays*, Cambridge, MA: Harvard University Press.

—— (1898) *Unforeseen Tendencies of Democracy*, Boston, MA: Houghton, Mifflin.

Gray, Malcolm (1952) "The Abolition of Runrig in the Highlands of Scotland," *Economic History Review*, 5: 46–57.

Hawaii, Department of Business, Economic Development and Tourism (1987) *Land Ownership in Hawaii*, www.hawaii.gov/dbedt/srs/sr208.pdf

de Jouvenel, Bertrand (1962) *On Power*, Boston, MA: Beacon Press.

Knight, Frank H. (1936) *The Ethics of Competition*, New York: Harper.

—— (1947) *Freedom and Reform*, New York: Harper.

Lawrence, D. H. (1928) *Lady Chatterley's Lover*, Florence: privately printed.

Lissner, Will and Dorothy Burnham Lissner (eds) (1991) *George and the Scholars*, New York: Robert Schalkenbach Foundation.

McDonald, Forrest (2004) *Recovering the Past: A Historian's Memoir*, Lawrence, KA: University Press of Kansas.

Mason, John W. (1980) "Political Economy and the Response to Socialism in Britain, 1870–1914," *Historical Journal*, 23: 565–87.

Mirrlees, J. A. (1974) "Notes on Welfare Economics, Information, and Uncertainty," in M. S. Balch, D. McFadden, and W. Y. Wu (eds) *Essays on Equilibrium Behavior under Uncertainity*, Amsterdam: North-Holland, 243–58.

Pullen, John (2005), "The Philosophy and Feasibility of Henry George's Land-Value Tax: Criticisms and Defences, with Particular References to the Problem of the Land-Rich-and-Income-Poor," in John Lauret (ed.) *Henry George's Legacy in Economic thought*, Northampton, MA: Elgar, 99–147

Ritchie, David G. (1893) Book Review, *International Journal of Ethics*, 3: 514–22.

Ross, Edward A. (1893) "The Unseen Foundations of Society," *Political Science Quarterly*, 8: 722–32.

Rutherford, Donald (ed.) (2004) *The Biographical Dictionary of British Economists*, 2 vols, Bristol: Thoemmes Continuum.

Samuels, Warren J. (1962) "The Physiocratic Theory of Economic Policy," *Quarterly Journal of Economics*, 76: 145–62. Reprinted in *Essays in the History of Mainstream Political Economy*, London: Macmillan, 1992, 28–46.

Samuels, Warren J. (1989) "The Legal-Economic Nexus," *George Washington Law Review*, 57: 1556–78.

—— (1992a) "Institutions and Distribution: Ownership and the Identification of Rent," *Journal of Income Distribution*, 2: 125–40.

—— (1992b) *Essays on the Economic Role of Government, Vol. 1, Principles*. London: Macmillan.

—— (2003) "Why the Georgist Movement has not Succeeded: A Speculative Memorandum," *American Journal of Economics and Sociology*, 62: 583–92.

Sandilands, Roger (2004) "What is Something Worth?" Received 20 February 2004 from hes@eh.net

Schweikhardt, David (2004) "An Examination of the Shifting Balance of Individual and Collective Legal Rights: The Case of U.S. Agricultural Commodity Programs," Michigan State University, Department of Agricultural Economics, manuscript.

Smith, Adam (1976a) *An Inquiry into the Nature and Causes of the Wealth of Nations*, 2 vols, New York: Oxford University Press.

Smith, Adam (1976b) *The Theory of Moral Sentiments*, Oxford, UK: Oxford University Press.

Smith, Adam (1977) *The Correspondence of Adam Smith*, E. C. Mossner and I. S. Ross (eds) Oxford: Clarendon Press.

Teagarden, Ernest (2004) Review of Algis Valiunas, *Churchill's Military Histories: A Rhetorical Study*, Lanham, MD: Roman and Littlefield. Reviewed for H-Albion and H-Net, received 19 August 2004 from conservativenet@listserv.uic.ed

Tideman, Nicolaus and Florenz Plassman (2004) "Knight: Nemesis from the Chicago School," in Robert V. Andelson (ed.) *Critics of Henry George*, second edn, revised and enlarged, Oxford: Blackwell, 541–69.

Valiunas, Algis (2002) *Churchill's Military Histories: A Rhetorical Study*, Lanham, MD: Roman and Littlefield.

Waters, Mary-Alice (ed.) (1970) *Rosa Luxemburg Speaks*, New York: Pathfinder Press.

Wightman, Andy (1999) *Scotland: Land and Power*, Edinburgh: Luath Press.

Williamson, Chilton (1960) *American Suffrage: From Property to Democracy, 1760–1860*, Princeton, NJ: Princeton University Press.

Young, Jeffrey T. (1997) *Economics as a Moral Science: The Political Economy of Adam Smith*, Cheltenham, UK and Lyme, USA: Edward Elgar.

Part V

The subtleties of policy making

15 The pervasive proposition, "what is, is and ought to be"

A critique

Alas! How dreary would be the world if there were...only a belief that what is is probably Pareto optimal, and if it were not it would eventually be.

(Leonard Silk 1989: 8)

The distinction between positive and normative, between what is and what ought to be, has been of great importance in economics. The epistemological justifications of induction, empiricism, positivism, and science *qua* science have been erected in part on the belief that the distinction is meaningful in both theory and practice. Yet the probative value of the distinction has been in serious doubt. The *conceptual* distinction between what is and what ought to be has not been in question. What has been controversial is whether analysis, even straightforward statements, can in practice be value- and ideology-free. Even many who accept the conceptual distinction find that because of the practical exercise of normative choice in the selection of topics for research, the formulation of problems for analysis, the role of preconceptions, the use of theory-laden data infused with valuational or ideological assumptions, the exercise of selective subjective perception, and so on, it is difficult, if not impossible, to conduct purely nonnormative inquiry and to make value- and ideology-free statements. The most convincing solution to this problem seems no longer to be the further development and use of presumably objective techniques, but the explicit identification of all value premises. Thus, John C. Harsanyi, in his *New Palgrave* entry on "Value Judgements," concludes by affirming that:

> Of course, value judgements often play an important role in economics even when they are not the main subjects of investigation. They influence the policy recommendations made by economists and their judgements about the merits of alternative systems of economic organization. But this need not impair the social utility of the work done by economists as long as it is work of high intellectual quality and as long as the economists concerned know what they are doing, know the qualifications their conclusions are subject to, and tell their readers what these qualifications are. In particular, intellectual honesty requires economists to state their political and moral value

judgements and to make clear how their conclusions differ from those that economists of different points of view would tend to reach on the problems under discussion.

(Harsanyi 1987: 793)

Controversy will remain as to just what precise value judgments are in fact being made. But following Harsanyi, in the tradition of Gunnar Myrdal, would make for a richer and deeper comprehension of the content of both economic theorizing and the economic policy recommendations so typically drawn therefrom.

One subtle mode of entry of normative premises is reasoning that reduces to the proposition, "what is, is and ought to be." It may be that literally no one affirms, a propos of everything that exists, that "what is, is and ought to be" (hereafter "the proposition"). No one accepts everything that exists. This itself makes the proposition inconclusive. It is argued here, however, that the proposition very subtly enters into economic analysis and the generation of conclusions applicable to policy—and a normatively privileged position is given to whatever is identified as the status quo or to whatever is identified as the putative result of a model or process.

The purposes of this article are, first, to critique the proposition, "what is, is and ought to be," in order to show in what precise ways it is in fact inconclusive, and, second, to identify two cases—the theory of employment-unemployment of Say's Law and New Classical Economics; and the reasoning of a strict interpretation of the Coase theorem, and the notion of Pareto optimality on which it rests—in which the proposition is in fact subtly operative in economics. The exercise is an example of how to go about identifying and thus both knowing and telling (to use Harsanyi's terms) the implicit value judgments that drive certain theoretical exercises.

The inconclusive proposition

1   Consider the claims that the following are good: war, abortion, the USSR, toxic waste dumping, murder, pornography, rape, racism, liberalism, course examinations, fur coats, the English monarchy, the Chinese crackdown on dissidents (revolutionary hooligans) in Tiananmen Square, liquor consumption, crack cocaine consumption, right-(left-)wing death squads, inflation, Marxian economics, labor unions, and so on. Two things can be said about this list, assuming that the definitions of each term can be agreed upon: first, that all exist or have existed; and second, that it is highly unlikely that one person will consider all of them good. People do not in practice simply apply a normative rule such as "Whatever is, is and ought to be." The rule is too all-encompassing to use in all cases; therefore, if for no other reason, the proposition is intrinsically inconclusive. In practice people apply other, supplementary normative premises to distinguish between those existing phenomena of which they approve and disapprove. The status quo is subjectively and selectively both perceived and evaluated. It seems that no one is prepared to accept everything

around him or her. This does not prevent the subtle attribution of privileged status to "what already is" in certain analyses, but whether cognitively or non-cognitively, people do discriminate among phenomena of the status quo, for reasons to which others may or may not assent.[1] The proposition is, therefore, ineluctably inconclusive in practice.

2   There are two historic critiques of the proposition. The first is David Hume's argument that one cannot derive an "ought" from an "is" alone, that one requires an additional normative premise(s). Given the putative identification of "what is," to reach the conclusion that "what is, is *and ought to be*" requires more than a statement of "what is," it requires additional normative input. Moreover, different people would adopt different normative premises.

From the Humean point of view, therefore, the existence of something, for example, an institution, does not conclusively demonstrate its own legitimacy. Premises, normative in character, in addition to the fact of existence are necessary. That these additional normative premises may be derived from the system in which the institution exists, and to which it may be specific, serves to indicate the relevance of the Humean argument to the system itself.

The second critique is the claim that the proposition involves the naturalistic fallacy, treating "what is" as real, natural, self-subsistent, and/or transcendently independent or autonomous in some ontologically absolute sense. This both telescopes "is" and "ought" and obfuscates any possible distinction between "natural" (given to man) and "artifact" (due to man) and, thereby, the possible element of choice. For the social sciences, the fact is that there is considerable diversity and change both among social, political, and economic systems and arrangements and within a given system or society. Little or nothing seems to be gained by affirming that each is "natural," except for purposes of social control. The naturalistic fallacy points to the exercise of piety toward "what is" but, through an equation of "what is" with "natural," affirms what is "natural" as a matter of selective perception—especially with regard to "policy," which is presumably a matter of human decision making.

A variation of the second critique is that of "presentism," the claim that the argument that "what is" is superior to and indeed the basis for evaluating "what was" and "what will be," and gives an unduly privileged status to "what is."

The implication of these critiques is that the proposition is either logically incorrect and/or inconclusive.

3   The status quo is always necessarily selectively identified or specified, raising the question of the coherence of "what is" considered as the "status quo." Five points need to be made. First, the status quo is comprised of heterogeneous elements that can be variously identified or specified. This means that it can be specified differently by different people.

Second, different people interpret the status quo from different standpoints or perspectives. This means that it is in fact identified or specified differently by different people.

Third, among what is distinctive about any status quo, and what one chooses when one supports that status quo, is its specific mechanism(s) of change.

Choice of a status quo constitutes choice not of complete continuity but of its distinctive mechanism of change and of the changes consequent thereto, for example, the market, industrialization, politics.

Fourth, every status quo is a point on an ongoing path and is time period dependent. Choice of "the status quo" is the choice of one status quo point on a path comprising a series of status quos. Change of the status quo arises in part from within (e.g. through its mechanism of change) and in part from without (shocks of one sort or another). When one speaks of the "status quo," one addresses both its mechanism of change and a process of change, perhaps change distinctive to it but change nonetheless.

The foregoing means that the "status quo," "what is," is fundamentally ambiguous, possessed of whatever substantive content is selectively adduced to it. Without a coherent and putatively conclusive identification of what is meant by the status quo, which is well nigh impossible, statements of "what is" are essentially incoherent and inconclusive.

4   The status quo is necessarily selectively evaluated. Application of the proposition is a normative exercise in the selective acceptance-rejection of elements of the status quo.

5   Affirmation of the proposition seems to be premised on three lines of reasoning. The first affirms that what exists has survived a complex selection process, indicative that what exists should continue to exist, if only because survival per se is a compelling quality. The second affirms that existing arrangements or phenomena contain both accumulated instrumental wisdom and social utility. The first combined with the second comprise an Aristotelian injunction not to treat what exists lightly; after all, it does in fact exist. The third affirms that a moral duty exists to maintain the status quo because it does in fact exist.

The three lines of argument are subject to questions of perspective that are themselves both substantive (subject to positive analysis) and normative. With regard to the selection process: what is it, what governs it? With regard to received wisdom: what wisdom, whose selective perception of it; what about received folly; what about arrangements or solutions arguably dysfunctional for present problems; and who determines what is wisdom and what is folly, and what is functional and what is dysfunctional? The same types of questions apply to the moral duty argument, which also begs questions of both the moral duty of change and the moral status of the status quo.

All three arguments presume the propriety of both the selection process and the power structure that both forms and operates through it, and which together produce the specific substantive content of the status quo with regard to wisdom and morality. Argument would then regress to, first, whether selection mechanism, received wisdom, and moral duty, as well as the substantive content of folly and dysfunctionality, are in fact matters of power structure, and if so, what is the status of the three arguments with regard to received power structure; and second, the status of the selection process itself, whether what it is "ought to be"?

The survival or natural-selection argument is also laden with paradox: it must encompass or provide for current and future change, and thus both begs the issues of the status of the present status quo and provides blanket approval for any future changes, even those presently opposed because they do not yet exist and something else does.

All three arguments seem to foreclose consideration of the processes that (1) resolve the problem of the status of the presently operative mechanism(s) of change; (2) operate within the existing mechanism(s) of change; and (3) constitute the power structure that affects both matters.

6 The proposition is subject to diverse interpretations concerning the role of human choice. It was stated earlier that the proposition seems to foreclose consideration of choice processes governing both the selection of the existing mechanism(s) of change and their operation. In these respects the proposition seems to postulate a separation of subject and object and thereby to obviate what is evidently, or at least arguably, the process through which, in the social sphere, "what is" is determined and redetermined. The proposition seems to reify "what is," considering the object to be independent and transcendental to human choice processes. Yet it was also asserted that acceptance of the proposition literally requires exercise of supplemental normative judgment because no one would accept every existing arrangement or phenomenon. Normative decision making in the application or use of the proposition seems necessary and is necessarily selective. The proposition is ambivalent and therefore ambiguous and inconclusive with regard to the roles of human choice and reification contemplated by it.

This conflict arises in part because, in the proposition "what is, is and ought to be," the concept "ought" has two meanings in ordinary usage. In one, choice is possible (say, within the existing opportunity set of choices), and the concept affirms making a particular choice. In the other, no choice is possible; rather, there is only the "natural" or otherwise determined, and determinate, path to take. In one, one ought to make the desirable choice; in the other, one ought to do that to which one is driven by necessity. The "ought" element of the proposition is additionally inconclusive in this respect.

If, or to the extent that, the past has comprised the process(es) of choice from within ongoing opportunity sets, then the present is *pro tanto* the result of the effective choices made in the past. One formulation of the belief that the past has been a process of choice is the surviving wisdom presumably contained within the status quo. But unless the process of choice is deemed to have reached its climax, then the proposition is not dispositive of the issue to which it has been applied, which is the revision of the status quo. The proposition is therefore inconclusive with regard to its putatively differential treatment of present and future in relation to past choice.

On the other hand, inasmuch as not all persons believe that the past has been a process of choice, believing instead that everything that has happened was preordained or happened because conditions were such that nothing else could have happened, for these persons the proposition is fundamentally irrelevant. The proposition is ostensibly directed to the question of the revision of the status quo, but, given the irrelevance of choice, that question is vacuous and the proposition, with its ostensible presumption of continuity over change, is superfluous. Of course, if no choice is possible, the question arises of what the argument is all about.

7   The proposition constitutes a legitimizing argument, a mode of persuasion; it performs a social control function. On this, four points: First, the proposition assumes the propriety of the status quo and of arguing in favor of the status quo. It assumes the propriety of the very thing whose propriety it affirms. It privileges the status quo by virtue of its being the status quo. The search for absolute and invariant values, which is itself equivocal, is equated or identified with the status quo.

Second, yet the proposition is always used selectively, with regard to the selective specification of the status quo, its identification with the natural, and the selective acceptance/rejection of elements of the status quo. It is seemingly never used in an all-encompassing manner.

Third, the proposition is an aspect of the generation of tradition, through which tradition itself undergoes change, such that the proposition is itself formally empty, devoid of any content other than that which change—ostensibly negated by the proposition itself—and selective usage provides. Indeed, the instrumental function of the proposition in the generation of tradition, the selective generation of the status quo itself, may be the most fundamental thing that can be said about the proposition.

Fourth, use of the proposition as social control can represent strategic absolutist formulation functional against affirmations of change deemed drastic or incongruous with the status quo, and not against all change. Of course, it also can represent simple failure to think analysis through to its deepest premises.

8   The proposition manifests a psychic balm function. It accords with and reinforces the "natural" human tendency to identify with or hold to whatever is, or whatever is happening, which is deemed to be, or to be consistent with, the accustomed existing mores of life. (That not all happenings are so evaluated is evidence of the selective use of the proposition.)

9   The proposition is, contrary to its evident logic, not necessarily conservative. Insofar as it affirms whatever change is generated by the received mechanism(s) of change, and inasmuch as, for example, what is happening may be inconsistent with arrangements subjectively deemed to be customary—which are, of course, also a matter of selective perception—the proposition is only selectively conservative. Some people would apply the proposition only to change deemed consonant with perceived tradition; some, only to change due to reasoned and deliberative change; and some, not to deliberative change, preferring change through nondeliberative, presumably spontaneous order, processes. Both the substance and the mode of change can be critical topics, though perhaps not always to the same persons.

The proposition may appeal to those conservatives who emphasize tradition (or authority) and not, or not so much, to those who emphasize freedom, although both tradition (which itself generally connotes some mechanism of change and some notion of freedom) and change are subject to selective perception. Controversy can exist about whether a particular change is a change due to the operation of the already existing mode of change or to a change of the mode of change; about whether particular perceived exercises of freedom are consonant with perceived tradition; and so on.

The concept of "reactionary" has three meanings in common usage. According to one, no change is either possible or desirable; the second is that change constituting return to the status quo that existed before the rejected current status quo is both possible and desirable; and the third is that evaluation is affirmatively elitist or antidemocratic, identifying the status quo with the presumed status quo hierarchical structure and especially its hegemonic upper level(s).

10   The proposition seems to render absolute that which arguably has been and may continue to be relativist, while either actually or seemingly denying relativism. Yet the argument advanced by the proposition is fundamentally relativist: "what is" changes through existing processes of change. Moreover, "what is" is not necessarily accepted on its own merits but on the premise that the existing mechanism of change is a priori normatively acceptable. In the event of change of the mechanism of change, the premise of normative acceptability would be transferred to the new mechanism. As with the natural selection or survival argument, the proposition must make provision for change and thereby begs the question of the status of the present status quo and provides blanket approval for any future change. Because of its evident relativism and open-endedness, the proposition is inconclusive.

11   The foregoing raises problems of the hermeneutic circle and of infinite regress. Selection of an argument supporting the proposition raises the question of the basis of the selection, which itself can be subjected to the proposition itself. All of this is further compromised or at least complicated by the fact that elements of the status quo are treated selectively by each individual and selectively differently by different individuals.

12   The conclusion seems inexorable, albeit not surprising, that the proposition, "what is, is and ought to be," is not and cannot be conclusively dispositive of the issues to which it is usually addressed, issues that focus on the origin, content, and status of the status quo. The proposition is always combined in practice with supplementary principles or is simply practiced selectively, thereby enabling or embodying the possibility of not accepting "what is" because it "is and therefore ought to be." Furthermore, the fact of selective use readily engenders the charge that all use is disingenuous and casuistic.

The proposition encompasses an argument that is formally empty with regard to the status quo until substantive content is selectively adduced to it by various users, and can be invoked by advocates of quite different, indeed contradictory, regimes.

The proposition in practice often involves an identification with some sacred symbol (constitution, market, religious or ideological code or rule), however selectively applied and however much in conflict with other symbols.

The proposition, although typically understood to comprise an argument, itself constitutes an assumption, one that is typically buried in analysis or ideology and that, again, is both used selectively and subject to the hermeneutic circle.

Subtle presence in economics

There is a strong tendency in economics to seek and to give privileged status to a determinate solution reached within a model. This gives effect to selectivity in choosing the model, defining the terms of the model, and working with the model. In order to reach determinate results, not to say results desired on ideological grounds, assumptions are made that foreclose the operation of actual economic processes and that substitute the preferences of the analyst for those of the aggregate of economic actors (see Samuels 1978, 1989a,b). This applies also to the attainment of presumptively optimal results. There also is a tendency to finesse criticism of a theory by casuistically making assumptions that rule out of consideration the factors and forces that compromise and limit the result sought by using the theory. This has been done by advocates of Say's Law and the Coase theorem. In both cases, the proposition "what is, is and ought to be" is subtly given effect by giving a privileged status to a result permitted by ruling out of analytical and policy bounds all other conflicting results.

Let us consider two introductory matters, the presumptiveness of Pareto optimality and the concept of the natural rate of unemployment. Pareto optimality signifies a condition in which all mutual gains from trade have been exhausted such that one party can now gain only at a cost to the other party(ies). Notice that there is no unique Pareto optimal solution or result, only a set of Pareto optimal results, each specific to initial entitlements and rules governing assignment and use of entitlements. Notice also that when the Pareto principle is used in conjunction with the status quo distribution of entitlements and rules, it both gives effect to, reinforces, and casts luster on that set of entitlements and rules. Notice further that Pareto optimality gives effect to a particular notion of optimality (including justice, or fairness), which interprets optimality in terms of individual self-choice and adjustment within market trade—a view that finesses such questions as the distribution of entitlements ("which individuals?"), the social formation of entitlements and rules, and other processes of collective decision making.[2] Notice too that the principle of Pareto optimality is in one sense all-encompassing: it affirms the optimality of both whatever trade takes place and of no trade taking place (in which case there are no mutual gains from trade perceived by the would-be traders). Whatever is, is and ought to be. We shall see that the Coase theorem follows the logic of Pareto optimality and exhibits the proposition with which this essay deals.

The term "natural rate of unemployment" has been given quite different definitions, including that rate of unemployment at which the inflation rate is zero and that rate of unemployment at which the inflation rate does not change. Economists use the concept in such a manner as to give a privileged status to whatever way the term is defined. Through building in specific definitions, use of the concept gives effect to the proposition "what is, is and ought to be" by post-ulating what "naturally is." The same would be the case if one were to reverse the discursive structure and define the "natural rate of inflation" as, for example, zero unemployment or 3.3 percent or some other rate of unemployment (perhaps deemed frictional unemployment).[3] All this follows from the use of the term "natural" and involves the naturalistic fallacy in the form given by assuming what is the "natural" unemployment or inflation rate and then using that assumption as the basis of both analysis and policy recommendation.

Let us now consider Say's Law and the Coase theorem. The argument is simple and straightforward: in each case, (1) the result is reached through the casuistic exclusion, by assumption, of factors that would otherwise prevent the desired result; and (2) whatever is the realized level of unemployment in one case and the realized level of externality in the other, is deemed what ought to be the result.

Say's Law is generally taken to mean that the economy is operating at a stable level of full employment output without inflation. This conclusion can be reached only on certain assumptions. Historically, the assumptions were largely introduced in response to objections to the conclusion because of the claimed interference of whatever came to be ruled out of bounds by assumption. Thus, four assumptions can be specified: (1) that money is only a medium of exchange; (2) that the interest rate equates saving and investment; (3) that all prices are sufficiently flexible that all markets clear; and (4) that all wants are insatiable. The first assumption excludes the operation of money as a store of value, and thereby the operation of liquidity preference (i.e. holding money as an argument in utility functions) and the role of money in deferring decisions to spend, therefore no monetary leakage from the spending stream. The second assumption means that consumption plus saving for year one will equal consumption plus investment for year two, therefore no change in spending and income. The third assumption prevents, among other things, both the net unintended accumulation of inventories and motivation for adjusting production, therefore no reason for changes in the expected rate of profit to lead to changes in spending and income. The fourth assumption means that consumers will in fact be motivated to spend on consumption and that saving will be taken up by investors who are in fact motivated to invest. This means that under all circumstances consumers have an infinite capacity to derive utility and businessmen an infinite capacity to accumulate capital, therefore no diminution in consumption due to anxiety over future job holding or price levels and no diminution in investment due to a partial failure of expectations underlying the marginal efficiency of capital. Given the operation of these assumptions, supply *ipso facto* constitutes its own demand, the presence of suppliers in the market *ipso facto* connotes the presence of demanders, all output is taken, and all income is spent; therefore the level of income, output, and employment is at the full-employment level.

What is meant by "full employment"? The meaning that is conventional (which does not make it correct) is the labor force minus frictional unemployment. Defining the labor force is no easy matter because of discouraged workers and elasticity of supply for some potential workers, but that problem aside, the only question is the estimation (for that is what it must be) of the level of frictional unemployment, including exploration of why that level may rise or fall. This definition of full employment imposes an independently given, and subjective, specification of what constitutes full employment. In accordance with this usage, there *can* be unemployment, and there can be involuntary unemployment. The actual level of unemployment need not be the desired level.

In the case of Say's Law, and in the roughly equivalent though superficially more sophisticated case of New Classical Economics, the economy is engaged in continuous, spontaneous, automatic market clearing. The level of employment is determined by the presence of suppliers (of labor) in the market; the labor market will clear given the level of labor supply; and any unemployment is voluntary, inasmuch as willingness to work (provision of oneself as supply) will lead to employment as the market clears. That is to say, the realized level of employment is the full employment level, quite independent of the full-employment level arrived at by subtracting frictional unemployment from labor force. The Say's Law-New Classical Economics full-employment level is independent of whether the supply of capital or the level of effective demand or the level of liquidity preference are sufficient to provide jobs—all ruled out of analytical and policy bounds by the assumptions. The actual level of employment is and should be the level of employment.

The Coase theorem is generally taken to mean either or both of two things: First, that a market (and therefore a solution) for externalities can be generated through the full definition of rights, thereby permitting the nonowner of a right to pollute to purchase the right to pollute, thereby eliminating such pollution as the two parties can agree to through trade. Second, that the final allocation of resources is invariant with the initial assignment of rights, that is, the allocative neutrality of rights assignment, because the most valued use will receive the resources, through either the owner of a right not selling it or the former non-owner buying it. In both respects, the theorem reduces to the argument that the realized externality is and ought to be the result.

The logic of the first meaning of the Coase theorem is that there either will or will not be a market for an externality; if there is a market, it will reach a solution; if there is no market, that *ipso facto* constitutes a solution because it signifies that the parties do not find it in their interest to form a market and exchange rights. In either case, the realized externality, or realized level of externality, will be the optimal externality (what is, is and ought to be). It can reach this conclusion only by assuming that the realized level of externality achieved through interindividual exchange of rights in markets is the correct level and that such trade is the accepted mode of collective decision making, thereby assuming away other specifications of the correct level and mode of determining the correct level. The further complexities and subsidiary assumptions on which the first meaning of the Coase theorem rests can be ascertained by examining the second meaning.

The logic of the second meaning is that whoever is the assignee of the legally determined and assigned right will either sell or not sell the right to the other party. If there is a sale, that signifies that the right is going to the most highly valued use; if there is no sale, that likewise signifies that the right is going to the most highly valued use; and if the other party were the assignee, the same result would be generated. This reasoning, which of course embodies the logic of the first meaning, that there will be a market for externalities through the market for fully defined rights, must be based on certain assumptions in order for the allocative neutrality of rights assignment to be concluded—that is, everything that would otherwise interfere with allocative neutrality must be ruled out of analytical bounds.

The most widely acknowledged assumption has to do with transaction costs: unless transaction costs are zero, different transaction cost systems can be expected to result in different externality solutions and thereby different resource allocations, such that the initial assignment of rights will not be allocatively neutral.

But other assumptions also govern whether there will be markets for such rights and thereby for externalities, and the realized levels of externalities and the consequent allocations of resources. These other assumptions include but are not necessarily limited to the following: (1) indifference to the existing distributions of income and wealth, which affect the ability to make offers for rights held by others or the willingness to receive offers for rights held by oneself; (2) indifference to the fact that typically an individual's buying and selling prices are not the same; (3) indifference to the resulting distributions of income and wealth consequent to the assignment and possible purchase/sale of rights; (4) indifference to the existing social power structure and its control of government in the matter of the determination of the definition and assignment of rights; (5) indifference to existing technology, resources, and tastes, and their formation; (6) a bounded consumption set, that is, that each and all parties survive the externality—which may be the logical equivalent to assuming that all parties have an independent source of income, for example, that each party is a farmer working only part-time in an outside job, or through the welfare state; (7) indifference to asymmetry of information and of the capacity to acquire information; and (8) indifference to consequences following from large versus small number cases; and, *inter alia*, (9) unequivocal acceptance of a local optimum as a proxy for the global optimum, which seems to be the logical equivalent of assuming that system optimality means only individual adjustment through trade. Because of these assumptions, which casuistically would remove all circumstances leading to contrary results in the case of both forms of the theorem, the theorem reduces to the argument that the realized externality is and ought to be the result.

In the case, then, of both the level of full employment contemplated by Say's Law and New Classical Economics and the level of optimal externality contemplated by the Coase theorem, reality is defined in such a way as to lead to conclusions about results such that whatever is, is and ought to be the case. The models are constructed in such a way that factors inconsistent with the desired result are finessed and ruled out of analytical bounds. In both cases, what is and what ought to be are both equated and defined in terms of how markets are ideally understood to behave and thereby in terms of individual adjustment within markets, quite independent of circumstances that render such definitions of reality irrelevant to actual practice. That changes in liquidity preference or declines in effective demand or profit expectations can lead to a decreasing supply of jobs (decreasing demand for labor) and thereby to involuntary unemployment, or that the level of realized externality achieved by interindividual trade of rights can lead to adverse effects upon others as well as upon the prospects for planetary life as a whole, are rendered irrelevant and inoperative.

Both sets of conclusions about the level of involuntary unemployment and the level of optimum externality, are inconclusive. Inasmuch as both Say's Law and the Coase theorem reduce to the proposition that what is, is and ought to be, the foregoing critique of the proposition applies to them. Economic affairs are, arguably, not quite so simple. Until economics can do better, economics will not be a discipline worth being called a science (Eichner 1983). Moreover, until such time as economics does better, it will tend to have a pernicious, subtle effect in casting the luster of science on tools and analyses that are at best selectively deployed. This occurs in part when Say's Law and the Coase theorem are seen as ideal situations to the realization of which policy should adjust the actual working of the economy—which it can do only selectively and presumptively. Such analysis starts with a purported scientific description and turns into an idealist prescription, quite in violation of Hume's argument, that is, only through the addition of selective implicit normative premises as to what ought to be. This is driven either by the unthinking use of conventional tools and concepts or by ideology, as well as by dubious and always debatable notions of optimality and voluntarism. What is not (yet) is taken for what should be.

There is a more reasonable alternative by which we can avoid the pretense that Say's Law and the Coase theorem represent how things actually work out in the economy. This is to state them so as to represent modes of identifying the factors and forces actually at work in the economy that yield results different from what the law and the theorem postulate as happening in the absence of such factors and forces: that is, to identify what is necessary for Say's Law and the Coase theorem to work out and yet is not happening. In such a way, no privileged status and no luster is cast either on the actual result achieved in the economy or on some idealized result, such that what is, is and ought to be; that is, no privileged status and no luster is cast on results somehow deemed optimal because all the factors that would prevent those results have been assumed away. In the real world there is (involuntary) unemployment and there are externality problems, theory to the contrary notwithstanding, theory that at bottom suggests that "what is, is and ought to be."

Notes

The author is indebted to Todd Gustafson for research assistance and comments, and to members of the History of Economic Thought and Methodology Workshop of Michigan State University, including Jeff Biddle, Allan Schmid, Thomas Schuster, James Shaffer, and Hyun-Ho Song, for further comments and suggestions.

1 The converse situation is that in which opponents to something that exists denigrate efforts to study the matter for fear that the implicit premise that the object is worth studying will cast luster of the object itself. A noteworthy example of this was trade unions and "socialism" in the decades before the First World War. Moreover, it may well have been true that most, though by no means all, students of unions have been pro-union.

2 Individuals can be institutions, such as corporations. The logic of Pareto optimality applies to both domestic and international trade.
3 Interestingly, Gustav Cassel's definition of "natural equilibrium" included a specification of full employment, namely, "that ideal economy where every factor of production is fully employed" (quoted in Englund 1943: 468).

References

Eichner, Alfred S. (ed.) (1983) *Why Economics is not yet a Science*, Armonk, NY: M.E. Sharpe.
Englund, Eric (1943) "Gustav Cassel's Autobiography," *Quarterly Journal of Economics*, 57 (May): 468.
Harsanyi, John C. (1987) "Value Judgements," in John Eatwell, Murray Milgate, and Peter Newman (eds), *The New Palgrave*, vol. 4, New York: Stockton Press.
Samuels, Warren J. (1978) "Normative Premises in Regulatory Theory," *Journal of Post Keynesian Economics*, 1 (Fall): 100–14.
—— (1989a) "Determinate Solutions and Valuational Processes: Overcoming the Foreclosure of Process," *Journal of Post Keynesian Economics*, 11 (Summer): 531–46.
—— (1989b) "The Methodology of Economics and the Case for Policy Diffidence and Restraint," *Review of Social Economy*, 47 (Summer): 113–33.
Silk, Leonard (1989) "Yes, Virginia, Institutionalists do Exist," *Journal of Post Keynesian Economics*, 12 (Fall): 3–9.

16 What is, is what?

The New England transcendentalist Margaret Fuller finally formulated her philosophy rather succinctly: "I accept the universe." When Thomas Carlyle heard of this, his remark was: "Gad! She'd better!"

(Ramsey 1964: 46)

A decade ago I published an article, "The Pervasive Proposition, 'What Is, Is and Ought to Be': A Critique" (Samuels 1992; Chapter 15 of this volume). The article was misnamed. The article was a critique and interpretation of lines of reasoning pertaining to the meaning and social significance of propositions relating "is" and "ought." The article should have been titled "The Pervasive Proposition, 'What Is, Ought to Be': A Critique." Nothing in it pertained to the phrase "What Is, Is" in the title, which was, accordingly, a partial misrepresentation. The objective of this chapter is to remedy the omission by conducting a critique and interpretation of lines of reasoning pertaining to the meaning and social significance of propositions affirming, in one way or another, "What Is, Is."

It will be useful in what follows to summarize the main themes of my original article, at least in part to identify what I mean by a critique and interpretation of lines of reasoning pertaining to the meaning and social significance of propositions.

Two historic critiques exist of the proposition "what is ought to be." The first is David Hume's argument that an "ought" cannot be derived from an "is" alone, that an additional normative premise is required. The second is the claim that the proposition involves the naturalistic fallacy, treating "what is" as real, natural, self-subsistent, given, and/or transcendently independent or autonomous in some ontologically absolute sense,[1] thereby telescoping "is" and "ought" and obfuscating any possible distinction between "natural" and "artifact" and thereby the possible element of choice. As we shall see, the second critique also applies to the present proposition, "what is, is."

Among the further themes are these: (1) Because the status quo is selectively perceived and because each status quo is a point on an ongoing path and is time-period dependent, the "status quo"—"what is"—is fundamentally ambiguous. (2) The principal affirmations of the proposition have serious infirmities and limitations; moreover the affirmations foreclose consideration of the processes that (a) determine the presently operative mechanisms of change, (b) operate within the existing mechanisms of change, and (c) constitute the power structure that affects both (a) and (b). (3) The proposition is open to diverse interpretations as to the role of human choice. (4) The proposition is a legitimizing matter— social control and psychic balm achieved through absolutist legitimization. As such it is always used selectively. The proposition is a variable aspect of the generation of tradition but is itself formally empty. (5) The proposition affirms whatever change (e.g. Joseph Schumpeter's creative destruction) is generated by received institutions and mechanisms of change. (6) The proposition seems to render absolute that which arguably has been relativist. (7) The proposition encounters problems of the hermeneutic circle and of infinite regress.

The conclusion is that the proposition, or equivalent terminology, is not and cannot be conclusively dispositive of the issues to which it is usually addressed.

The problem of "What Is, Is"

Propositions having to do with "What Is, Is" have two interrelated domains of significance: (1) ontology and (2) the theory of knowledge in relation to social action. Ontology has to do with our beliefs concerning the ultimate nature and content of reality. The theory of knowledge in relation to social action has to do with our attitudes toward our ontological beliefs as a basis for policy, choice and action.[2] Pertinent to both domains are two dichotomies.

The first dichotomy is realism versus idealism.[3] As articulated by Plato and Aristotle, respectively, and by philosophers ever since, both idealists and realists agree that knowledge (of reality, the object of inquiry) is the product of experience, which is itself a matter of perception and reasoning; that careful observation and careful reasoning are important; that knowledge requires the supremacy of mind over body, that is, of ordered experience over sensation; and, inter alia, that the principles of epistemology are important for both observation and reasoning. At this point idealism and realism diverge and conflict.

Idealism holds that on the basis of our knowledge (thus determined) we derive a conception of the ideal. The ideal is derived from reality, or rather from our perception of reality. The actuality that is extant reality is imperfect; the ideal derived from our perceived experience of that reality is the good and our task is to so act as to secure its actualization. The emphasis is not on extant reality per se but on the idea thereof, thence the ideal derived from extant reality, the ideal serving as a basis and objective of action. The presently extant reality is not good enough; idealism is a philosophy of reform or of potential reform. Reality does not command itself; what commands is the ideal derived from reality. The relevant ontology pertains less to extant reality and more to the ideal derived from it.

Idealism has certain characteristics: (1) Idealism has realist facets to it, namely, the reality to which it is applied (say, the status quo) and which is the basis of the ideal derived from it. (2) Idealism encompasses, indeed is the result of, an act of creative imagination. Reality does itself not generate its own ideal; that requires creative imagination. Ideals are products of extant reality plus the normative premises ensconced within and given effect by creative imagination. (3) Idealism is an analytical abstraction: the idea of reality and the derived ideal are treated normatively and imperatively; *is* knowledge is transformed into and treated as an *ought*. (4) Idealism generates a multiplicity of ideals, as creative imagination is applied, to either the same reality or different perceived realities, from different standpoints or perspectives, thereby engendering a necessity of choice between proffered ideals. As we shall see, this burden of an ineluctable necessity of choice is critical.

Realism emphasizes the object of inquiry itself, that is, reality. It is real in itself, it has a separate existence quite apart from our perception(s) of it. The important thing is not the ideal(s) derivable from the reality but the reality itself; reality, since it is presumed to exist, must be accepted as such, inasmuch as, after all, it *is*.[4] Realism affirms necessarily neither a denial of reform nor a fatalistic acceptance of the status quo; it affirms, rather, a caution that that which is has to be reckoned with and not changed for light and transient reasons. The caution is due to the existence in nature of the real thing itself, of which the mind has only an uncertain image.

Realism has certain characteristics. (1) Realism has idealist facets to it, namely, the idea of reality produced by the mind. Any inference deduced from reality is produced by the mind, through perception and/or reasoning. (2) Realism is the result of acts of creative imagination. Reality does not itself generate its own identity; that requires creative imagination. (3) Realism is inevitably an analytical abstraction insofar as reality is not known directly and conclusively. (4) Realism generates a multiplicity of identifications of the real, as creative imagination is applied from different standpoints or perspectives, thereby engendering a necessity of choice as between proffered definitions of reality. Realism thus has its own burden of an ineluctable necessity of choice.

The idealist is less concerned with the extent to which the absence of perfect knowledge of reality is or should be treated as a constraint on action and more eager to institute improvements in reality. Inasmuch as it is extremely unlikely that all ideals derived from an extant reality will be identical, the result is an ineluctable necessity of choice.

The realist is less prone to abandon the status quo and more cautious about the untried, both because the status quo exists and the untried does not yet exist. Inasmuch as it is extremely unlikely that all definitions of reality derived from an extant reality will be identical, the result is an ineluctable necessity of choice.

Just as idealism has a realist element, namely, the status quo reality from which ideals are derived through creative imagination, so too does realism have three idealist elements, namely, the role of mind in perceiving reality, the role of creative imagination in forming definitions of reality and the role of mind in choosing from among multiple definitions of reality. Realism is not independent of idealism; realism willy nilly gives effect to idealism in generating multiple definitions of reality. Realist definitions of reality are, ironically, the result of applications of idealism; realist claims are a matter of idealism formulation.

If realism is attractive because it seems to augur or promise choice-free specification of reality, such is illusory. If idealism is attractive because it seems to augur or promise opportunity for choice and reform, then it too rests upon a particular definition of reality, a particular ontology.

This brings me to the second dichotomy, one involving the conflict of two mentalities or mindsets. One mentality requires determinacy and closure. The other mentality is more or less comfortable with indeterminacy and open-endedness. The former mindset has a predisposed, noncognitive antagonism to anything smacking of relativism and/or nihilism. The latter mindset may or may not prefer something other than relativism and nihilism. Those who may not prefer something other than relativism and nihilism, are comfortable with and may even laud indeterminacy and open-endedness. Those who may prefer something other than relativism and nihilism, are at least comfortable with indeterminacy and open-endedness.

Possessors of the latter mentality tend to believe that indeterminacy and open-endedness are conclusively evidenced by social constructivism, the exercise of choice, and diversity of social arrangements. Possessors of the former mentality are convinced that all that is illusory, or applies only to relatively insignificant details (what those are, is, of course, a matter of judgment and choice).

If social constructivism and open-endedness are ultimately matters of interpretation, diversity of social arrangements is not. If, for example, the written constitutions of different countries vary in important regards, it seems impossible to hold that one and not the other derives from the ultimate nature of things. Yet possessors of the former mentality tend strongly to include their constitution in the definition of reality and to resist any formulation that either derives from or supports a relativist view of things. For example, possessors of the former mentality tend strongly to believe in a higher law, a divinely inspired constitution, and a uniquely deterministic analytical jurisprudence; whereas possessors of the latter mentality tend strongly to believe in social constructivism, human choice, and legal realism in which the social constructivism and human choice figure prominently.

On the basis of what has already been said, the proposition, "What is, is," is seen to be unclear as to meaning, as to substantive content, and as to the context in which it is to be understood. It is essentially a tautology subject to different readings as to meaning and content, and is, accordingly, inconclusive. These different readings take place along different pairs of axes: (1) Definition of a given reality versus specification of ideals. (2) Definition of general reality versus specification of particulars. (3) Definition of reality versus absolutist legitimation of status quo arrangements. (4) Definitions of reality versus definitions of the status quo, including the relation of status quo to reality. These readings also involve matters of (5) multiplicity, (6) diversity, (7) development, evolution and change, (8) selectivity, and (9) choice.

Definition of a given reality versus specification of ideals

Much of what has been said so far gives substance to this problem. When one speaks of "what is," one could be referring to either a/the given reality or the reality transformable/transformed by ideals. That is, "what is" can refer to a/the given reality or the process of specification and/or transformation through acting upon certain ideals, in which case reality encompasses ideals.

Notice the several senses of "reality" present here: First, R1, a postulated *initial given reality*. Second, R2, the *process of forming ideals*. Third, R3, the process of *selecting and acting upon ideals*. Fourth, R4, the *reality newly produced thereby*.

R1, an *initial given reality*, may have been produced in the same way as R4 but in the past. R1 can be given transcendent, given status by assuming it to be part of the natural order of things. Or R1 can be given privileged status because it is in place, it *is* the status quo, notwithstanding the putative fact that it was produced in the past. History can be seen/defined in terms of a string of R1s, each of which is treated in its time in a privileged manner. The problem arises, therefore, whether the relevant reality is some R1 or the string of R1s. The string of R1s might be understood to be R1 in general and each R1 might be seen as a particular manifestation thereof (see also the following section). "What Is" can be defined as some R1—the R1 in place at the time, though possibly some other R1—or as the string of R1s.

R2, the *process of forming ideals*, is itself arguably part of reality. Many such processes can exist and each can change over time. The comparable problem arises, therefore, whether the relevant reality is a particular R2 or a particular set of R2s or the string of R2s over time, with the same implication regarding R2 in general and particular manifestations thereof.

The same is true of R3, the process of *selecting and acting upon ideals* and R4, the *reality newly produced thereby*. All the foregoing—and more—can constitute answers to or positions on "What is." That is the case whether reality be further specified in terms of "nature" or some "natural" system or whether it be contemplated in the physical or social domains. "Natural" itself has multiple meanings and the same problems arise. Moreover, what is taken to be "nature" or "natural" is in part a product of past human action, even though typically such results are minuscule in comparison with the results of physical forces, such as plate tectonics, erosion, weather and so on. And what is taken to be "society" or "social" is in part, perhaps in large part, a matter of past social control. In both cases—natural and social—the same problem arises whether reality constitutes particular manifestations, some underlying transcendent order, or the string of manifestations.

A further central problem has to do with the relevance of the correspondence theory of truth. This theory, in affirming that truth involves language corresponding to reality, postulates that a reality exists to which language can refer (subject of course to epistemological considerations and criteria). Ludwig Wittgenstein has raised fundamental objections to the correspondence theory. There is no simple answer to the "What" in "What Is."

Definition of a given reality versus specification of particulars

Important aspects of the problem of general reality and particular manifestations have been dealt with in the preceding section.

One key issue that is often begged or somehow finessed is whether reality inevitably imposes itself or whether it requires human action in order for it to be instantiated. "What" would mean very different things as between the two positions. Many schools of economic thought—most notably the Phyiocrats—believed that they had put their finger on the pulse of the natural order of things. But this natural order of things does not automatically exist. It must be institutionalized through policies congenial to their beliefs. What is reality—What Is? Is it the order of things that might not exist, or a particular blueprint, or the particular system instituted through the adoption of certain legal foundations and not others? Notice, too, (1) that many such schools exist, exemplifying the idealist necessity of choice in a realist context and (2) that differences of opinion as to theory and policy exist within each school, further exemplifying the idealist necessity of choice in a realist context.

Consideration of generals and particulars need not be esoteric; it can involve the mundane: chickens and prices. What exists, chicken as a category—chickenness, if you will? Notice that this necessarily involves ideas and ideals, hence idealism. For some people, chickens are food; for others, pets; for others, religious objects (consider if my example had been cows and cowness); and so on. Or do only actual chickens exist? And which chickens? Chickens can be bred for racing (consider if my example had been horses and horseness); do we mean chickens as early humans found them, as present-day humans found them, or as recent humans have changed them? Since the Second World War, chickens have been bred to increase the ratios of meat to bone and of white to dark meat; very recently, Japanese scientists have bred featherless chickens. What does one mean when one posits "What Is" about chickens?

Economists deal with prices. What is the meaning of a price? For centuries, economists distinguished between *price*—the actual rate of exchange in the market—and *value*—the absolute and invariant basis of price. The assumption was that prices were so important they had to have such a transcendental basis. Even though substantially all economists believed in value over against price, they did not agree as to what constituted that basis. The chief conflicts were between the labor theory of value, cost of production, utility, and demand and supply theories. (Earlier Just Price theorists also contemplated intrinsic value, value in regard to social structure, and so on.) Largely only relatively late in the twentieth century did economists treat value and price as synonymous and defined in terms of price. They then concentrated on the price mechanism, sometimes in purely abstract a-institutional conceptual terms, sometimes with regards to actual markets and the institutions that form and operate through them.

Price also became a highly relativist matter, though economists were reluctant to discuss it in such terms. Price was, in Joseph Schumpeter's felicitous term, a coefficient of scarcity, each price relative to all other prices; in other words, prices were temporary resting points in a dance of demand and supply—and nothing more fundamental than that. What, then, does one mean when posits "What Is" about prices?

Another matter involving generals and particulars is the proposition raised by both Thomas Aquinas and Oliver Wendell Holmes, Jr, that general principles do not decide concrete cases, only particular principles. Given our belief in the *existence* of both general and particular principles, what is the meaning and status for "What Is" of these principles, and do the two types of principle have the same meaning and status? Furthermore, what of the process of working out applications of both general and particular principles? What of the premise that both types of principles exist in the plural, so that one must choose among them? And what of the applications, such as they may be?

Definition of reality versus absolutist legitimization of status quo arrangements

Most of the foregoing discussion has to do with "What Is" in matters pertaining to the definition of reality. But "What Is" also has to do with the definition of reality *in relation to social action*, with our attitudes toward our ontological and other beliefs as a basis for policy, choice, and action.

Policy has to be legitimized. One mode of legitimization is to affirm that a policy is congruent with the ultimate nature of reality (as done, for example, by the Physiocrats and many others). If a monarch can convince his or her subjects that they rule by divine grace, or by some past social contract, or that their policies are called for by the ultimate nature of reality, they have tried and succeeded in establishing an absolutist legitimization of their policies. The same is true of economic policy makers. They may not invoke the more esoteric legitimizations but the putative grounding of policy in theory amounts to absolutist legitimization.

Absolutist legitimization serves both social control and psychic balm functions. The immediate foregoing is part of the social control function. The psychic balm function is performed by assuring those who seek determinacy and closure that such exists.

I wrote, two paragraphs earlier, "putative grounding of policy in theory." Often, belief in a theory leads to affirmation of a policy derived from the theory. Four problems arise. The first two problems have to do with the status of a policy implication derived from a theory.

The first problem concerns theory X yielding policy implication XX. But this implication XX is due to the addition to X of a particular antecedent normative premise, N1. Another devotee of X can add a different particular antecedent normative premise N2, so that now we have XX1 and XX2.

The second problem is this: Because a theory gives rise to a policy implication, that in itself does not conclusively command the theory to us. The policy implication is tautological with the theory from which it has been derived. The process is only a matter of logic; nothing of substance or normative status is conclusively involved. The theory and its policy implication must be compared with other theories and their policy implications.

The third problem has to do with the further definition of reality to which a policy is directed. Consider the variety of macroeconomic, monetary, and business cycle theories and the policies to which they lead. These policies must be tempered to actual economic conditions, for example, to the stage of the business cycle—or, rather, to the stage which one's theory (and predictions based thereon) leads you to expect (is inflation or unemployment just around the corner?).

The fourth problem is that policy is often, likely more often adopted, for the purposes of political manipulation and mobilization, and theory (in some form) is deployed, if not created, for purposes of (absolutist) legitimization. What is the status of all these views in regard to the definition of reality in identifying "What Is?" Is this instrumental, political use of theory part of our definition of "What Is" or is it cynicism? When is a theory a matter of defining reality, when is it matter of manipulating people (and, arguably, reality), and when do these processes help constitute our substantive identification of "What Is"?[5] What is the status of all these views in regard to the definition of reality in identifying "What Is"?

Definitions of reality in relation to the status quo

Several problems arise in considering the relation of the status quo to definitions of reality. One has already been seen: the invocation of "reality," actually some selective perception or specification of reality, in pursuit of absolutist legitimization of the "status quo," actually some selective perception or specification of the status quo. The selectively identified status quo is thus given transcendental and universal credentials.

Even more basic is the problem of whether the status quo itself is to be identified as reality. This problem inevitably engenders certain questions: Is there a transcendent reality different ontologically from the status quo? If reality is transcendent to the status quo, how is it possible to have different status quos? If the status quo is reality, how is it possible to have different status quos? Given the diversity of status quos, can *any* status quo be equated with reality? Clearly, different answers to these questions, ultimately different positions on the relation of the status quo to reality, will generate different, and conflicting, positions on the meaning of "What Is."

It is often and not entirely erroneously stated that considerations of reform "start from here." Two problems arise: First, such an approach obfuscates the nature, content, and history of past reform, giving the status quo a privileged position as if it were a matter of the ultimate nature of reality, thereby finessing the social constructivist character of the status quo. Second, to say that we start "from here" logically raises the question, "What is 'here?' " Different definitions of "here" will profoundly influence the object and means of reform. The definition of "here"—the status quo—is often the central issue in controversies about reform.

It is critical to an understanding of social, political, and economic affairs that recognition be given to the *constructivist nature of actions within the status quo*. The Fifth Amendment of the US Constitution contains the provisions that "No person shall be...deprived of life, liberty or property, without due process of law; nor shall private property be taken for public use without just compensation" (the Fifth Amendment applies to the Federal government; the Fourteenth Amendment, applying to the States, also has a due process clause). The terms used therein are neither defined therein nor self-defining; "life," "liberty," "property," "due process of law," and "taken" are elastic terms, their interpretation and application subject to several different theories; historically their definitions have changed. The principal presently relevant point is that they are (re)defined through legislation and court decisions. "What is" property, for example, is ultimately a function of the definition and scope given "taken" by the courts; judicial review is thus a process through which property is made and remade. Property is not protected because it is property; property is property because it is protected. The taking clause seems on the surface to protect property. But it is a means of determining what property "really" is, which/whose interests are protected as property and which/whose are not. It is also a means of administering psychic balm, assuring losers—and in all such cases there are inevitable losers—that they have had their day in court. That such abets absolutist legitimization of the new status quo thereby worked out, will not be missed by the reader (see Samuels 1974 and Samuels and Mercuro 1979, 1980).

It can therefore further be said that the heart of the status quo is its decision making process, its power structure, for example, who determines what "property" will be and thereby "what is."

Power structure is both cause and consequence. Power structure is, therefore, a critical object of reform. Who can vote, who can run for office, the powers of officeholders, the recourse of all others, and so on, have been the issues motivating reform, for example, in England from the Reform Act of 1832 down to the present. Accordingly, the definition of "What Is" can center on the ordinary phenomena and artifacts of daily life or on the structure and operation of decision making— and not only of government but all of governance (Samuels 2002)—or both.

One can imagine a group of people, perhaps economists, from different countries sitting around a table and discussing topics of mutual interest. They may use the same language but it is more than likely that they will mean different things by those words (2001). Another scenario has two "property owners" with conflicting claims each being told, differently, by their respective lawyers, what "the law" is as pertains to their respective interests. In both instances, the differences will turn on the problems raised earlier.

Multiplicity

One characteristic running through the foregoing is *multiplicity*: multiplicity of definitions of reality, of the status quo, and of a host of subsidiary terms and relationships. "What Is" is rendered determinate, singular, and unique only by ignoring or somehow finessing multiplicity, typically by begging the operative question.

Diversity

The same is true of *diversity*. One reason for multiplicity and for taking multiplicity seriously is the fact of diversity. Different countries have different cultures, different constitutions and laws, different power structures, and so on. If citizens of each country identify their respective status quo arrangements with reality, reality itself would seem to be heterogeneous. In this light, defining reality seems less important than promulgating absolutist legitimization and psychic balm.

Development, evolution, and change

As we have seen, the fact that a society changes over time raises serious questions pertaining to the meaning of the assertion "What Is, Is." Is the reality constituting "what is" the status quo, somehow selectively defined? Or is it the string of successive status quos? Or is it the idea thereof—and/or the ideal derived from it? Or that society's power structure—which itself undergoes alteration?

The fact of evolution, or change, compounds multiplicity and diversity and renders inconclusive perhaps all positions on "What Is, Is." The conclusion initially suggested earlier is thereby strengthened: The proposition, "What is, is," is seen to be unclear as to meaning, as to substantive content, and as to the context in which it is to be understood. It is essentially a tautology subject to different readings as to meaning and content, and is, accordingly, inconclusive.

Ostensibly pro-laissez-faire ideologies pertaining to the economic role of government have their own agendas for governmental activism, the activism obfuscated by the implicit if not explicit identification of its content with the natural order of things—a natural order which does not impose itself but must be instituted. Similarly, selective positions on "What is" function to help channel development, evolution, and change.

Selectivity

The proposition "what is, ought to be" is never applied to everything in a society. Some phenomena are given approbation and others, disapprobation. The proposition is not applied to the latter. (Economists who opposed gradual reform in capitalist countries were avid supporters of rapid transition in the countries of the former Soviet Union.) Selectivity is involved. The same is true of the proposition "what is, is." (Economists who lauded capitalism and denigrated communism would not treat capitalist and communist countries equally in ontological terms. Only "the market" is given ontological status—though questions arise as to whether positions on "what is" are to rest on pure a-institutional conceptual markets or on actual markets that are formed and operated through by institutions/power structure.) The selectivity may be a function of material interest, ideology, national culture, and so on. Just as the economic role of government is conducted or worked out pragmatically, through the legal-economic nexus, so too are positions on "what is." Selective perception both supports and is combined with selective valuation to help form policy, and thereby "what is."

Conclusion: choice

As we have seen, the fundamental problem of philosophical realism is that it does not avoid the ineluctable necessity of choice. The same is true of the seemingly realist proposition "what is, is." The case can therefore be made that the proposition "what is, is" masks processes that are engaged willy nilly in making choices.

The dread of relativism and nihilism by people with a mentality requiring determinacy and closure is, in a sense, very "real." But it is arguably misdirected and illusory. If the analysis of this article is correct, it is illusion, social control in aid of certain powers and interests and not others, and psychic crutch in aid of psychic balm, to accept as determinate and closed the position one believes, or is induced to believe, as to "what is, is."[6] This too is a matter of choice: choosing social control and psychological comfort over putative truth. And this too is a position on "what is." The analysis of this article is self-consciously self-referential.

The conclusion is, nonetheless, that the proposition "What Is" is not and cannot be conclusively dispositive of the issues to which it, or equivalent terminology, is usually addressed.

Notes

1 The meaning of each of these terms varies among users and uses.
2 Epistemology—having to do with the credentials of what we accept as knowledge—is pertinent to everything said here but is not dealt with here.
3 The following is by no means intended to be a comprehensive, not to say complete analysis of philosophical realism and idealism.
4 The possibility that perceived reality within realism (and idealism, for that matter) is, for example, false, illusory, and/or a product of wishful thinking is a serious limitation on realism.
5 Democracy—which can be defined in a number of ways—is usually debated on instrumentalist/utilitarian and moral/justice grounds. Apropos of absolutist legitimization, one writer argues that "The problem with the realist style is twofold: (1) It is disingenuous in denying its own 'rhetoricity.' ... (2) By disparaging political discourse, the realist undermines the persuasive norms that govern a healthy democratic culture" (Aune 2001: 42; quoted in Ziliak 2003: 334).
6 Relatedly, *politicization* can be defined in two ways: as activities or beliefs that ostensibly thrust into politics what was not hitherto already in politics, and as activities or beliefs that ostensibly recognized an original and continuing political element hitherto ignored and now surfaced. This distinction has obvious basic implications for the content assigned to "what is" (Samuels 1980).

References

Aune, J. A. (2001) *Selling the Free Market: The Rhetoric of Economic Correctness*, New York: Guilford Press.

Ramsey, B. J. (1964) *The Little Book of Famous Insults*, Mount Vernon, NY: Peter Pauper Press.

Samuels, W. J. (1974) "An Economic Perspective on the Compensation Problem," *Wayne Law Review*, 21 (November): 113–34.

——— (1980) "Two Concepts of 'Politicization'," *Social Science*, 55: 67–70. Reprinted in *Essays on the Methodology and Discourse of Economics*, London: Macmillan, 11–14.

——— (1992) "The Pervasive Proposition, 'What Is, Is and Ought to Be': A Critique," in W. S. Millberg (ed.) *The Megacorp and Macrodynamics: Essays in Memory of Alfred Eichner*, Armonk, NY: M. E. Sharpe, 273–85. Reprinted in *Essays on the Methodology and Discourse of Economics*, London: Macmillan, 315–29. Chapter 15 in this volume.

—— (2001) "Some Problems in the Use of Language in Economics," *Review of Political Economy*, 13: 91–100.

—— (2002) *Economics, Governance and Law: Essays on Theory and Policy*, Cheltenham: Edward Elgar.

Samuels, W. J. and N. Mercuro (1979) "The Role and Resolution of the Compensation Principle in Society: Part One—The Role," *Research in Law and Economics*, 1: 157–94.

—— (1980) "The Role and Resolution of the Compensation Principle in Society: Part Two—The Resolution," *Research in Law and Economics*, 2: 103–28.

Ziliak, S. T. (2003) "Freedom to Exchange and the Rhetoric of Economic Correctness," *Research in the History of Economic Thought and Methodology*, 21A: 194–207.

17 Professional policy advocacy or policy diffidence?

A point of view

This chapter has two arguments. The first is that economists should participate in the process of making policy like any other citizen. They can propose ends and the means to those ends; they can interpret and apply the means-ends continuum to problems of policy. They can help understand when and in what respect or sense, and for whom, a problem is a problem. They may well be more informed factually—however much fact is a function of theory—than the typical non-economist and therefore in some respects may be more reliable. Their other advantage may reside in their ability as technical experts to indicate the assumptions and likely consequences of alternative ends and of alternative means.

The second, and much more controversial, argument is that economists *qua* economists should not claim *special* competence over ends and means. They should not seek to speak *professionally* as to what policy should be, nor should they be expected to do so. The problem is the difficulty in pursuing both parts of the argument simultaneously; pursuit of the first inevitably tends to devolve into violating the second. The only solution is diligence in emphatically distinguishing between the two—the problem then becomes the situation that one person's diligent differentiation is another's advocacy.

The *bête noire*, therefore, of this chapter is the universal practice of policy advocacy driven by professional hubris and given substance by ideological position, to which sometimes is added the pragmatic needs of manipulating and/or mobilizing political psychology.

The argument is considered in several steps, the initial ones centering on advocacy per se and the subsequent ones dealing with the role of theory in regard to policy and the policy process. Every point in the argument, the reader will readily be aware, has a history of controversy; inasmuch as this article argues a position, the author feels no compunction in largely avoiding historical accounts thereof, which would unduly lengthen the text if done correctly and get in the way of the argument itself.

Advocacy

Economists, by virtue of their field of training and expertise, desire to have something to say about matters of policy. Many economists have been and perhaps still are initially drawn to their study of economics because it bears on improving the world. Also, non-economists often look to economists for advice on matters of policy, in part because of their presumed expertise and in part because they tend to exude a confidence that they know what should, indeed must, be done. Many economists act upon the view that not only do they know what the domains of policy and of policy-making are all about but they know precisely *the* correct policy to adopt. This is surely presumptuous and pretentious, driven more by professional and political ideology than objective science.

In having and giving effect to that desire to make recommendations on matters of policy, economists pursue the social role of the person of knowledge; they pursue a form of status—personal and/or disciplinary status. In doing so, even—perhaps especially—when responding to non-economists, economists act as normal persons in a manner known to such diverse intellects as Adam Smith and Thorstein Veblen: the pursuit of status emulation. The pursuit, however, is wedded to ideologically driven policies. The situation is illustrated by a late member of the Chicago School, a friend of the author's, whose every public appearance was clearly dedicated to promoting economics, the Chicago School, and Chicago-School policies, simultaneously.

Admittedly it is sometimes difficult to determine when an action is in pursuit of status emulation, when political ideology, and when something else. Some people do sometimes care more about good policy than the status gains from policy advocacy and other participation. However, very little relevant activity, it would seem, is undertaken anonymously.

Several consequences flow from the pursuit of status channeled by ideology. One consequence is the historic desire of many economists that professional economists propose the *same* policy. It is felt that the confidence that others have in the pronouncements of economists, and thus the status with which economics and economists are held, would be enhanced if economists spoke with one voice, with one policy view. The problem is that economists have never proposed the same policy, have never spoken with one voice. Economists have always professed multiple views on every question. And even when economists have agreed, they have done so in the terms of the disparate contexts of their respective paradigms and ideologies.

Another consequence is the tension, if not conflict, between advocacy and objectivity. The status that economists seek for themselves and their discipline in the role of the person of knowledge is that of the objective scientist. For well over a century, "science" and "scientist" have been honorific designations one presumed characteristic of which is "objectivity." The pursuit of policy activism, of having something to say about policy, is a matter of advocacy. Advocacy and objectivity clearly conflict.

They conflict, that is to say, unless one can say that one's policy is either congruent with or derived from the nature of economic reality itself. This situation is one source of the attractiveness of a variety of philosophical realist interpretations of the economy itself—and hence of economic policy. This solution falters in part because philosophical realists disagree among themselves as to the substance of reality and therefore as to the policy presumably dictated by reality. Neither realists nor others have spoken with one voice.

Still another consequence pertains to the relation between economic specialty and policy advocacy. It is widely recognized that medical doctors tend to diagnose illness and prescribe therapy largely on the basis of their own specialties. Radiologists, surgeons, neurologists, and so on, see the world of medicine through the lens of their particular training and practice. Much the same tendency characterizes monetary and non-monetary economists, different types of monetary and/or macroeconomists and of development economists, members of different schools of thought, and so on. Each practices and pursues status on the basis of his or her particular specialty. The completely specialty-agnostic economist is as rare as their medical counterparts.

That is not to deny that in both fields some or many things are relatively cut and dry, relatively routine and mundane. But many things are not, and reliance on one's specialist is to give effect to their specialty and its antecedent assumptions, and so on.

One implication of the foregoing is that economic advice/consultation should be delivered by teams of specialists. Even teaching in some fields could/should be team-taught by specialists with different perspectives; in which case the students would be exposed not to the Truth as delivered by one true-believer but to the issues involved and the array of possible standpoints from which they may be approached. (Politicians and other clients desire that only their point of view be presented; but such should not drive disciplinary practice.) Economists are not, as yet, of course, widely experienced in teaming.

If, and to the extent that, economics has replaced or supplemented religion as social control (a positive, not a normative, statement), it is not surprising that economic preaching is so prevalent. Neither professor nor minister-mullah-priest-rabbi is typically satisfied with identifying issues and the various positions on issues; they typically seek to impart their unequivocal, even seemingly sacred position.

Paul Samuelson once alluded to a student taking at one hour a course on the economics of full employment and the next hour a course on the economics of less-than-full employment. Alternatively, a course covering both subjects could be taught by one professor in an agnostic manner or jointly by two professors who agreed to present both sides and to examine the issues with respect to which each side took positions and even defined terms and manipulated models differently. Similar staffing in another department could be made for a course on different theories of religion or on the array of world religions. But most such instructors seem inclined to promote only the view that they have—and the policy implications thereof. It is a rare professor like Frank Knight who can teach a course on institutional economics while he was a committed neoclassicist. Knight appreciated that institutional economists raised issues not adequately if at all typically covered by neoclassicism, issues with respect to which a matrix of definitions, issues, and positions existed, a matrix that formed the framework of meaning for all theoretical and policy views. And he so taught the course, it would appear, that the student also learned of Knight's own position—and likely his own psyche as well. Most professors present their own point of view as if a matter of high religion. At a meeting I once heard a future Nobel laureate referred to as "Rabbi..." because of his dogmatic adherence to and application of his form of economic theory.

Claimed expertise, wrapped in specialized language, can readily constitute a monopolizing or privileging strategy, or at least have that effect, making the student or the general public dependent upon the ostensible expertise of the expert—when that is, to some degree at least, a matter of mastering a certain language, a certain view of the world, and surviving a certain socialization. Part of the socialization process emphasizes the achievement of "expert" status.

Mathematical formalism is a case in point, whatever else can be said about it. Both Philip Mirowski, in his *More Heat than Light* (1989), and Bruna Ingrao and Giorgio Israel, in their *The Invisible Hand* (1990), trace the origin of modern economics to status emulation, to economists emulating and copying both physics and mathematics. Whereas Mirowski focuses on nineteenth-century mathematics of energy physics, Ingrao and Israel relate developments in economics since the 1930s to parallel developments in mathematics. They, too, produced a status-emulation explanation of formalism, arguing that mathematization is not a secondary feature of general equilibrium theory but rather a basic reason for its creation and development.

The question arises as to whether economists *qua* economists should dominate the process of determining policy ends and means—something that is at least implicit in the view that economists know *the* correct policy. I have observed the hubristic practice performed by members of all schools of economic thought. But would one expect academic or other professional specialists on the Middle East or on Islam or on Arabic culture to determine policy—US or any country's policy— toward that part of the world, for example, oil, the Israeli-Palestinian conflict, and so on? Would one expect academic engineers or environmentalists to determine environmental policies? Why should academic economists govern, or have a disproportionate influence on, such trade-offs as inflation versus unemployment, environmental and labor rules versus trade promotion, externality solutions in general, whose interest is a cost to others, and so on?

To some extent, engineering and other specialists, in their determinations of technical information—such as why a bridge or building collapses, why fish die in a lake, and so on—do help make policy. In the view formulated here, this is akin to economists serving as means-ends specialists. It is analytically different from the recommendation to act or not act, one way or another, based on political and/or ideological considerations.

I have proposed to state legislators the following model of their behavior when faced with someone else's bill. They follow a lexicographic model in which they first ask themselves of their ideological commitments and/or political obligations require them to take one or another position. Second, when the first yields no unequivocal position, they immerse themselves (or their staff members) in the materials pertaining to the proposed legislation, to see if some position seems most sensible and defensible to them. When the second, too, yields no unequivocal position, they turn to vote trading. The legislators responded that such was how they performed, though perhaps not so neatly.

Those whom economists (and others) advise are often confronted with conflicting advice. Achieved status—sometimes approaching the projection of hubris—can influence the weights assigned to these different advisements. It is not clear, however, that the quality of advice corresponds to the level of status.

The forte of economists is as means-ends technicians, including the role of ends as means to further ends in a complex and ongoing means-end continuum. This includes indicating the likely economic consequences of proposed legislation and of current developments. Economists, being human and interested, do have a tendency to impose their individual mind-sets—their own wishful thinking and ideology—on their work as means-ends technicians and drawers of likely consequences.

Economists have no monopoly on such skills but clearly tend to have them. Economists can indicate the premises and likely consequences—the opportunity cost—of choosing one or another means, one or another ends, or one or another institutional arrangement. Economists, however, have neither special expertise nor any monopoly on determining which means, which ends, and which set of trade-offs should be chosen—though they often speak and write as if they do. Economists have no special expertise as to the socially desirable realization and distribution of benefits and costs, of welfare contribution and sacrifice—though they often speak and write as if the costs and sacrifices of their proposed policies inexorably are less than the benefits and welfare contribution.

Economists are quick to juxtapose market and government, as if the two were mutually contradictory and exclusive categories. Economists are prone, by virtue of widespread (but not universal) disciplinary convention to deal with pure abstract a-institutional conceptual markets and then to apply them to selectively specified actual markets as if the latter were the only or best way of realizing the former. But pure abstract a-institutional conceptual markets exist only in the minds of economists. Actual markets are a function of and give effect to the institutions—power structure, rules and rights—that are largely legal/governmental in character and, especially important, of which considerable variation can exist. Economists have no special expertise by which to determine the institutions and legal rules that will form and operate through markets. Government is present willy nilly, and different legal rules will help protect different interests and help form different markets; economists can only choose between them on the basis of antecedent normative assumptions as to whose interests are to count, and so on. Economists have no special expertise with which to do so.

Neither of the usual connotations of "efficiency" can help without the introduction of antecedent normative assumptions. Pareto optimality—exhausting gains from trade—does not stipulate the institutional or power structure of markets or rules of trading; different sets of initial entitlements, differently structured markets, and different trading rules will yield different optimal results. Maximizing output—in any sense—cannot be accomplished by recourse to any unequivocal transcendental metric by which different output combinations—not to mention their corresponding combinations of opportunity costs and sacrifices—can be measured and judged.

In the real world, the world of policy, decisions must be reached as to whose interests are to count. Some power structure, some decision-making structure, must exist. Which one exists will determine whose interests will count. Contributions to the formation of the power structure will be influenced by past or existing power structure and by operative systems of belief. The former governs whose interests count. The latter include economists' antecedent normative premises and, more generally, their definitions of reality. Economists' professional expertise may or may not enrich those premises and those definitions of reality relative to non-economists'. Surely, economists have no unequivocal claim to dominate any aspect of these processes, especially those governing directly the choice of means, ends, power structure, and whose interests count.

None of the foregoing is intended to deny that our choices are influenced by both our ideas and economic circumstances and that over long periods it is true both that belief system governs practice and practice governs belief system. People, including professional economists, bring to the world of policy their own antecedent normative premises and their own definitions of reality, or systems of belief. These are both the product and source of selective perceptions. These selective perceptions are of benefits and costs, of interests, of power structure, of class, of the meaning of a "market" economy or "capitalist" system, and so on. Economists have no special professional expertise with which to dictate what these selective perceptions should be. This applies to a wide range of issues, from whether labor unions are consonant with a market or capitalist system, to whether growth should be subsidized by permissive environmental policies, to whether commercial and investment banking should be commingled, to whether insider trading should or should not be permitted, and so on.

It is well known that professional economists—most conspicuously, of course, John Maynard Keynes—were involved in the formation of the Bretton Woods institutions that governed international finance for decades after the Second World War. Economists were active also in the later formation of the European Monetary Union. Unquestionably, economists contributed much as means-ends technicians. Unquestionably, too, economists differed in their preconceptions of what the system of international monetary organization and control was all about, including the grand governance purposes of the new organizations and the relation of the organizations' practices to the international balance of power and to traditional monetary theory and precepts of "sound money." Unquestionably also, however, economists had no monopoly on, and perhaps very little expertise about, organization making.

Many if not most economists have strong feelings about antitrust law and its enforcement. But economists vary very differently in their conceptions of "competition," of "relevant market," of what constitutes a violation, and the relative costs and benefits of enforcement and non-enforcement. These conceptions become the elements of another conception held by economists and others, namely, the "public interest."

Some notion of the "public interest" necessarily arises. It is sometimes portrayed that recourse to some notion of the "public interest" is anathema. This portrait is wrongheaded. Some notion of public interest or public purpose will be followed. Most legislation and most court decisions—most if not asymptotic to all—directly or indirectly involve conflicts of interest between some Alpha(s) and some Beta(s). Enactments and decisions ultimately turn on, or are at least rationalized in terms of some notion of public interest or public purpose. The question is, which notion?

The economy is not given to us. It is a matter of social construction—actually continuous social-re-construction. Some basis or target of construction must be chosen and made operative. Following such divergent thinkers as Aristotle and Jeremy Bentham, the frameworks of relevance and of decision may be the interests of one, of a few, or of the many, each with its putative benevolent and malevolent forms. The category of "public interest" involves the process of articulating and selecting values. Insofar as government must act, indeed, insofar as government acts willy nilly no matter what it does, the notion of public interest is the normative, linguistic, and analytical framework through which different notions of the public interest are articulated and compete.

The category of "public purpose" is also relevant; it can be considered a synonym for "public interest." For present purposes, the notion of public purpose applies to any situation in which a choice must be made between competing interests—not between good and bad, or between benefit and cost, but between some Alpha's legitimate interest and some Beta's legitimate interest, where Alpha and Beta are in the same field of action. The interests can be between inflation and unemployment, between development and environmental protection, and so on.

A comparable, conventional economics concept is the "social welfare function," not any one theorist's stipulation thereof but the actual social welfare function extant at any place and time. Four interrelated ongoing processes are involved in its formation and its relation to the relevant production-possibility curve: the determination of (1) the values on the axes, between which choice is to be made; (2) the slope of the production-possibility curve, governing the trade-offs that must be made between values; and (3) the formation of preferences, pertaining to those values, and (4) the power structure by which those preferences are weighted to form the actual social welfare function.

(I am no enthusiast of the mechanistic use of the concept of a social welfare function, in part because it readily permits the surreptitious introduction of antecedent normative and positive premises and in part because there are sets of choices that may not necessarily be represented in terms of the maximization of some social welfare function, for example, the values not on the axes. But the non-presumptive, schematic type of use just made has minimal defects.)

The gravamen of the foregoing is, first, that some notion of public interest, public purpose, and social welfare is inexorable and, second, that the specialized training and expertise of professional economists does not render them, individually or collectively, the possessor of ultimate wisdom in these matters. Economists may know more than the typical layman about the genesis of inflation and unemployment and what might be done about them. But economists vary in their preconceptions about inflation and unemployment. They differ in their proclivities to forecast one or the other, in the policy instruments that they would bring to bear, and in their general definitions of reality that generate both of the foregoing. This multiplicity is a fact of life; it also underscores the diffidence with which any pronouncement by any economist must be greeted.

All matters of policy—definitions of reality, whose interest is to count, ends, means, public purpose, public interest, and so on—must be worked out. They will be worked out through one decision making structure or another, and that structure itself is a matter of policy. With all due respect, I do not see that professional economists *qua* economists have any unequivocal special competence in such matters such as to warrant a dominant position in policy making, except along the lines of means-ends technicians and so on.

Quite aside from the epistemological limits of the concept of "truth," policy is not a matter of truth. It is a matter of felt exigency, belief, preferences, interests, and the process—recognized by Adam Smith and Vilfredo Pareto, among others—through which the substance of public needs, public purpose, and public interest are worked out. The process is one of manipulating public opinion—taking part in the process of forming public opinion—that enables particular outcomes desired by certain parties to become identified as matters of public importance, that is, of public interest or purpose. Two lines of rebuttal are typically made to such reasoning.

According to one rebuttal, such a position as is outlined here would lessen the demand for economists, the esteem and status in which economists are held, and the market value of economists. Several replies can be made. This rebuttal gives effect to a line of reasoning that most economists seem reluctant to make in regard to any other market, namely, that economists seek and could effectively deploy the power to manipulate their own market. (This rebuttal reminds me of an argument made by a Soviet planner. The planner advocated higher salaries for planners in the Soviet Union because they were so important. Yet in both a centrally planned economy and a market economy (I, too, can deploy broad abstract concepts!) prices, including the prices of different types of labor, are algorithms performing certain social functions, such as market clearing, incentives, and so on.)

According to the other rebuttal, if the alternative to professional economists in the determination of policy is, say, journalists or theologians, why not prefer economists? The reply is simple and straightforward: in various ways, professional economists who seek to dominate policy making themselves strongly tend to behave as journalists and/or theologians.

Economists should participate in the making of policy but without the hubris and the arrogance so typically found in practice as they wave the flag of their professional status. The point of view argued here is neatly expressed by Y. S. Brenner (email to author, May 15, 2002):

> I do not see economists as persons who have a special position as economists in the determination of social policy. I see them as citizens who may have

opinions on how society should be governed and have the right, even the obligation, to voice their opinions on social matters and to vote according to them in political elections, but I do not grant them any special position in the determination of the policies which ought to be pursued. The selection of these preferences I hold them no better equipped than members of any other profession. The way I see them is as people better equipped than others to throw light on the economic feasibility of proposed policies, and I see their duty to inform the public of the consequences of political choices. In other words, I see the social task of economists in separating wishful thinking or dreams from what can actually be achieved and in informing the various groups and classes of what a given or proposed policy may mean for them.

Naturally, I am writing this regarding Macro-economists. Micro-economists have a different agenda. Their duty is to keep the business by which they are employed solvent. But this is a completely different ball-game.

Theory

The previous section dealt with the limits of advocacy. This section deals with the limits of theory in a world of working things out.

Theory and the processes through which theory is articulated and tested and critiqued are among mankind's most precious possessions. Almost all thought is erected upon theory; substantially all fact is theory laden. Notwithstanding such encomia, theory is limited (Samuels 2001) it is and can be only part of the epistemics and epistemology by which we produce and reckon knowledge. Theory is both inevitable and limited. Especially is it the case that theory does not necessarily yield truth.

Theory has a number of meanings and exists, therefore, in a varying relationship with other, cognate terms, such as model, paradigm, and concept (Samuels 1994: 23–8). Theory also has a number of different, often interrelated, roles: explanation, description, prediction, hypothesis, confirmed hypothesis, definition of reality, providing a sense of economic order, understanding (verstehen), heuristic, tool of analysis, facilitating manageability, an element in a logical/epistemological structure, prescription, the basis of social construction of reality, the basis of legitimization and of criticism, a means of projection, social control, psychic balm, tell a story, give economics the status of a science, and serve as a vehicle of ideology, wishful thinking, and paradigm. It also has several discursive or rhetorical roles, such as systematizing ideas, providing a framework of discussion, an organizing principle, and mode of concentrating attention (Samuels 1994: 29–40).

The problem with theory considered here is due to the combination of ostensible comprehensiveness and determinacy, hence conclusivity, with which many theories are treated. A person has a theory and the world is examined and policy is made on the basis of that theory, as if that theory is all that one needs to know and make policy.

One problem with theory is the conventional confusion of the two principal characteristics that may attach to a theory: validity and truth. Validity has to do with the proper use of a system of logic in drawing conclusions from premises. Truth has to do with correct description or explanation. That a theory has been validly drawn does not necessarily make, it true. Moreover, validity may be a necessary basis for policy but it is certainly not sufficient. The same applies to truth: many truths exist between which choice must be made, and norms—and choice of norms—must also come into play.

Another problem with theory is that no theory can include every relevant variable. Doing so would mean the nonfalsifiability of the theory, as nothing could fall beyond its compass. Nonfalsifiability is a matter of epistemology or philosophy of science; some other reason may be more important in practice. Theories tend to be distinct through their emphasis on one definition of reality and not another(s), likely through emphasis on one critical variable. Inclusion of every relevant variable would destroy the psychodynamic and ideological power of a theory. It would also confuse the policy relevance of a theory.

A further problem with theory is that no theory can answer every question we can address to it. John R. Hicks has expressed this point very well: "There is, there can be, no economic theory which will do for us everything we want all the time" (Hicks 1981: 4–5). Economists have developed no tests or procedures with which to determine which theory applies when—other than common sense, ideology, wishful thinking, personal insight, and so on, none of which comport well with the dominant conception of economics as a science or give a sense of solidity to policy.

A still further problem concerns the conventional practice whereby a theory—or some particular specification of it, plus a definition of social space and a stipulation of the decision rule by which the theory is accepted or rejected—is tested. That a theory passes the empirical test does not render it either correct in all cases or in some cases or in this case. Pertinent to this point are the strengths of Popperian falsifiability, the inconclusivity of empirical tests—the possibility of future falsification—and so on. Because an object of inquiry may be caused by different causes, confident explanation requires that the theory be proven correct (impossible because of possible future falsification) and be proven correct for this case. Thus, if T can be due to R or S, and we have T, we do not know whether the instant T is due to R or to S. If the policy implications of R and S are significantly different, then the blind choice of R or S can misapply policy and erroneously reconstruct the world. One basic problem is that social scientists, economists in particular, generally do not test theories against other theories, or one theory against another theory. If a theory somehow "makes sense," then it is deemed true and applicable to policy.

The fact of different types of theory also renders dangerous the application of a theory to policy. In one type of theory, the theory is inevitably supplemented with different supporting principles or ancilliary assumptions. In a second, the theory has multiple possibilities built into it. And in a third, the theory presumes that its singular explanation is sufficient. In the first case, policy is driven not by the theory—which becomes at least in part if not largely a matter of rhetoric, a mode of expression—but by the particular supporting principle or ancilliary assumption added to it. In the second case, the theory will have no metaprinciple by which to determine which possibility is called for by the theory. And in the third case, to assume a particular singular explanation is sufficient is to beg the question. Let us consider some examples of theory.

Friedrich von Hayek's theory of spontaneous order has room for both deliberative and nondeliberative decision making, even though the Hayekian approach emphasizes the latter (see Samuels 1999)—a second-type theory. Hayek does not elaborate in operational terms the criteria governing when decision making is to be deliberative and when nondeliberative; indeed, he does not—and actually cannot—meaningfully and unequivocally distinguish when action is spontaneous and when not.

Adam Smith's simple and obvious system of natural liberty, or classical liberalist equivalents, is a first-type theory. The theory is made applicable to policy only by the addition of further assumptions as to whose interests are to count or by some other normative antecedent premise.

Karl Marx's theory of revolution, driven by historical or dialectical materialism is also a second-type theory. Marx does not advocate revolution at every instant, only when conditions are propitious. He does not fully elaborate in operational terms the criteria governing when conditions are propitious. Nor does he unequivocally indicate when reform is and is not congruent with future revolution.

Economists, notably mainstream neoclassical economists, especially those in the field of law and economics, typically affirm that rights be efficient, as if some single independent test of an efficient right existed. But there is no such test; efficiency is a function of rights, not the other way around; and rights can be selectively deemed efficient only by assuming whose interest is to count. This is another example of a first-type theory.

The quantity theory of money is a theory that presumes a certain definition of inflation, argues for a particular explanation of inflation, affirms inflation as the transcendent macroeconomic problem, and directs policy along the foregoing lines. It is a third-type theory inasmuch as it constitutes a particular assertion and excludes any possibility of an alternative position. Policy is biased and myopic if not blind.

Clarence Ayres's neo-institutionalism affirms the technology-institutions dichotomy. The former encourages change and presumably generates progress and the latter generates stability and inhibits progress. The problem is that the two terms cannot be defined in a mutually exclusive manner, hence it is not clear when a phenomenon is one or the other, and how relevant policy should be formulated. It is a second-type theory. Suffice it to say, therefore, that theory is not an unequivocal and conclusive basis of policy.

The predicament is exacerbated when one considers that facts, which are often theory based, cannot alone support a policy. This latter is the Humean proposition that an *ought* cannot be derived from an *is* alone.

Conclusion

The Smith-Hayek tradition, nursed along by Hayek and his disciples, points to the principle of unintended and unexpected consequences. This may or may not be the single most important principle in the social sciences, as some of its devotees argue, and it surely applies to their efforts as well. But it does help identify the nature of policy and policy making. One reason why the principle is operative is that socioeconomic phenomena are a function of the interaction and aggregation of many variables, factors and forces. Just as no one theory can meaningfully cover all variables and answer every question we have, no one set of decision makers, no one set of decisions, no one policy can produce these phenomena. Adherents to a theory mislead themselves if they believe that there is a one to one relation between their theory, together with policy ostensibly based on it, and the phenomena of the actual economy.

The fact of the matter is that adherents of a theory provide only one set of inputs into a process of working things out—often a heterogeneous set. No one theory can capture the complexity and open-endedness of that process. Nor can any one ideology or political program represent all the interests that, in the modern world, compete in the process of working things out one way and not some other. Indeed, the purpose of ideologies and programs is to skew how both the process and the results are worked out.

Such open-endedness and pluralism are anathema to those whose mentality requires closure and determinacy, and those whose interests and ideology—or conception of science—mean more to them than democracy and pluralism. They are more congenial to those who can cope with openness and indeterminacy. Charles Lindblom's notion of "muddling through" is not satisficing for everyone; but it is an apt description of government, its processes, and its discontents (see Smith and Polsby 1981 and Holden's 1981 review, entitled "Muddling Through").

In short, the situation, I believe warrants policy diffidence by professional economists, not policy advocacy. Such does not preclude; rather it emphasizes the role of economists as means-ends technicians.

Acknowledgment

I am indebted to Roger Backhouse, Y. S. Brenner, John Davis, and Kirk D. Johnson for comments on an early version of this chapter. This chapter is a sequel to Samuels (1966, 1978, 1989, 1992, 1994, 1996, 2001).

References

Hicks, J. R. (1981) *Wealth and Welfare. Collected Essays on Economic Theory*, vol. 1, Cambridge, MA: Harvard University Press.

Holden, A. (1981) "Muddling Through," *The New Republic* (January 24): 30–4.

Ingrao, B. and G. Israel (1990) *The Invisible Hand: Economic Equilibrium in the History of Science*, Cambridge, MA: MIT Press.

Lindblom, C. E. (1958) "Policy Analysis," *American Economic Review*, 48: 298–312.

Mirowski, P. (1989) *More Heat than Light*, New York: Cambridge University Press.

Samuels, W. J. (1966) "The Nature and Scope of Economic Policy," in W. J. Samuels (ed.), *The Classical Theory of Economic Policy*, Cleveland, OH: World, 237–309.

Samuels, W. J. (1978) "Normative Premises in Regulatory Theory," *Journal of Post-Keynesian Economics*, 1: 100–14.

—— (1989) "The Methodology of Economics and the Case for Policy Diffidence and Restraint," *Review of Social Economy*, 47: 113–33. Reprinted in D. L. Prychitko (ed.) (1998) *Why Economists Disagree*, Albany: SUNY Press, 345–66.

—— (1992) "The Pervasive Proposition, 'What Is, Is and Ought to Be': A Critique," in W. S. Millberg (ed.), *The Megacorp and Macrodynamics: Essays in Memory of Alfred Eichner*, Armonk, NY: M. E. Sharpe, 273–85. Chapter 15 in this volume.

—— (1994) "The Roles of Theory in Economics," in P. A. Klein (ed.), *The Role of Economic Theory*, Boston, MA: Kluwer, 21–45.

—— (1996) "Joseph J. Spengler's Concept of the 'Problem of Order': A Reconsideration and Extension," in P. Arestis (ed.), *Employment, Economic Growth and the Tyranny of the Market*, Brookfield, VT: Edward Elgar, 185–99. Chapter 5 in this volume.

—— (1999) "Hayek from the Perspective of an Institutionalist Historian of Economic Thought: An Interpretive Essay," *Journal des Economistes et des Etudes Humaines*, IX: 279–90.

—— (2001) "Deduction and the Practice of Economics: The Necessity of a Sense of Limits," *Journal of Economic Methodology*, 8: 99–104.

Smith, G. and N. W. Polsby (1981) *British Government and Its Discontents*, New York: Basic Books.

Name index

Subject index

For Product Safety Concerns and Information please contact our EU
representative GPSR@taylorandfrancis.com
Taylor & Francis Verlag GmbH, Kaufingerstraße 24, 80331 München, Germany

www.ingramcontent.com/pod-product-compliance
Ingram Content Group UK Ltd.
Pitfield, Milton Keynes, MK11 3LW, UK
UKHW021624240425
457818UK00018B/725